ACCLAIM FOR BARBARA WALTERS'

Audition

"*Audition* contains some fascinating stories (Walters censoring her interview with a sloshed Betty Ford), a good deal of frankness (defending her friendship with GOP power broker Roy Cohn), and grand old war stories from her groundbreaking stints with *Today* and ABC News."
—*Entertainment Weekly*

"She doesn't shy from the tough stuff. . . . Nor does Walters, an entertainer as much as a groundbreaking journalist, skimp on the fun bits."
—*People*

"The crowning glory of a remarkable career."   —*New York Post*

"A smart, funny, fascinating book in which Walters captures possibly her most elusive subject: herself."   —*Booklist* (starred)

BARBARA WALTERS

Audition

Barbara Walters is an award-winning journalist and the first woman to ever cohost a network news program. She is the recipient of a Lifetime Achievement Award from the National Academy of Television Arts and Sciences. She is an ABC News correspondent, host of *The Barbara Walters Specials* and the creator, cohost, and executive producer of ABC Daytime's *The View*. She resides in New York City.

ALSO BY BARBARA WALTERS

How to Talk with Practically Anybody
about Practically Anything

Audition

BARBARA WALTERS

Audition

A MEMOIR

VINTAGE BOOKS

A DIVISION OF RANDOM HOUSE, INC.

NEW YORK

FIRST VINTAGE BOOKS EDITION, MAY 2009

The Library of Congress has cataloged the Knopf edition as follows:
Walters, Barbara, [date]
Audition: a memoir / by Barbara Walters.—1st ed.
p. cm.
Includes index.
1. Walters, Barbara, [date]. 2. Journalists—United States—
Biography. I. Title.
PN4874.W285A3 2008
070.92—dc22
[B] 2008005843

Vintage ISBN: 978-0-307-27996-5

Book design by Virginia Tan

www.vintagebooks.com

Printed in the United States of America
10 9 8 7 6 5 4 3 2 1

To the memory of my sister, Jacqueline Walters,
and to my amazing daughter, Jacqueline Walters Danforth,
both of whom changed my life

Contents

Audition

Prologue

SISTER.
I thought for a while that is what the title of this memoir should be because it was my older and only sister, Jacqueline, who was unwittingly the strongest influence in my life. Jackie was three years older than I, but all our lives she appeared younger. My sister was mentally retarded, as the condition was called then, though only mildly so. Just enough to prevent her from attending regular school, from having friends, from getting a job, from marrying. Just enough to stop her from having a real life.

Her condition also altered my life. I think I knew from a very early age that at some point Jackie would become my responsibility. That awareness was one of the main reasons I was driven to work so hard. But my feelings went beyond financial responsibility.

For so many years I was embarrassed by her, ashamed of her, guilty that I had so much and she had so little. Very little was understood about retardation almost eighty years ago when Jackie was born. There were few schools that dealt with what we now call the "intellectually impaired," few workshops where they could go and learn a trade, few employers who could figure out how to use their talents and their loyalty.

Today Jackie could probably get a job, something simple but productive. She might even have met and married a nice man. But back then Jackie's life was essentially one of isolation, except for the relationships she had with me and my mother and father.

My parents protected her. They never discussed her outside the family or explained her condition to anyone. People wouldn't understand, they felt, and Jackie would be shunned and humiliated.

Jackie's isolation also contributed to my own sense of isolation. As a child I didn't have birthday parties because Jackie didn't. I didn't join the Girl Scouts because Jackie couldn't join. I rarely had friends over to the house because they didn't know what to make of my sister and I would hear the whispers—real or imagined.

When I was older, my mother, heartsick at Jackie's loneliness, would often ask me, when I was going out with a girlfriend or on a date with a boy, to take her along. I loved my sister. She was sweet and affectionate and she was, after all, my sister. But there were times I hated her, too. For being different. For making *me* feel different. For the restraints she put on my life. I didn't like that hatred, but there's no denying that I felt it. Perhaps you'll be horrified at my admission. Or perhaps you're guilty of some of the same emotions and will feel relief that you are not alone. I imagine, as I write this, that almost anyone who has a sibling who is chronically ill or mentally or physically impaired will understand what I mean.

I recently came across a book that helped explain a lot about the impact Jackie had on my life. It's called *The Normal One: Life with a Difficult or Damaged Sibling*, written by Jeanne Safer, a psychotherapist who grew up with a very difficult brother. I recognized myself on almost every page: "the prematurely mature child; the looming responsibility for a sibling's care and well-being; the compulsion to be an over-achiever; the fear of failure." I wish I had read the book earlier in my life, but I'm not sure it would really have made a difference. Jackie would still have been Jackie. And the same set of circumstances would have driven my life.

Much of the need I had to prove myself, to achieve, to provide, to protect, can be traced to my feelings about Jackie. But there must be something more, the "something" that makes one need to excel. Some may call it ambition. I can live with that. Some may call it insecurity, although that is such a boring, common label, like being called shy, that means little. But as I look back, it feels to me that my life has been one long audition—an attempt to make a difference and to be accepted.

My sister was a very pretty child. Her mental condition had nothing to do with her physical appearance. She was fair haired, fair skinned, with a sweet smile, shorter than I, curvier than I. I had dark hair, a sallow complexion, I was often told, and was skinny. "Skinnymalinkydink" was what my parents lovingly called me. (Yes, it was meant lovingly.) You wouldn't have known by looking at Jackie that there was anything different about her, until she opened her mouth to talk. Jackie was the worst stutterer I have ever known. She stuttered so badly that sometimes when she was trying to get a word out, her tongue protruded from her mouth. My parents tried almost every technique available to help her as she was growing up, but nothing seemed to make a difference. At one point they even took her to see the man who supposedly helped Britain's King George VI get over his speech impediment. He couldn't do anything for my sister. It was frustrating to listen to her. It was hard to be patient and easy to mock her. My first memory of my sister is when I was about three and Jackie six; the boys in the neighborhood were pulling at her skirt and making fun of her because they'd heard her talk. We both ran crying into the house.

Until Jackie died from ovarian cancer in 1988, I worried about her, supported her, made decisions for her that my parents couldn't make, and agonized over the fact that although I couldn't always love her, she always loved me. She taught me compassion and understanding. (In later years these feelings would be important to me in interviewing.) Often frustrated herself, often cranky and prone to tantrums, she never expressed resentment or jealousy of me.

When my daughter was born, I named her Jacqueline—Jackie. I wanted the grown Jackie to feel that she, too, had a child, because I knew by this time she never would. So yes, though I had mixed feelings about my sister, I do believe the love was stronger than the resentment, and the sympathy for her was overwhelming.

I tell you all this because young people starting out in television sometimes say to me: "I want to be you." My stock reply is always: "Then you have to take the whole package." They laugh politely, not knowing what I'm talking about, and I don't elaborate. I've guarded my sister's privacy for years. And though she was the central force in my life, she was part of the package that I'm about to unwrap on these pages.

That package also includes my brilliant and mercurial impresario of a father, my loving but frustrated and conflicted mother, the amazing and celebrated people I met from childhood on, and my professional career in television. Oh, that! But mostly this memoir is a personal story of how and why I got from there to here.

Before I end this prologue, let me tell you a story. Back in the sixties, when I was appearing daily on NBC's *Today* show, I was living on Seventh Avenue and Fifty-seventh Street. My apartment was across from Carnegie Hall and on the corner of a very busy street. It was also near several large hotels that catered to businessmen. Perhaps because of this, the corner was the gathering place for some of the most attractive "ladies of the evening." Each morning at five o'clock I would emerge from my building wearing dark glasses, as I hadn't yet had my makeup done, and I was usually carrying a garment bag. It seemed obvious to the "ladies" that there was some big "number" I had just left. Now, bear in mind that, even then, I wasn't exactly a spring chicken. But I would emerge and look at the young ladies, some of whom were still teenagers. "Good morning," I would say. "Good morning," they would answer. And then I would get into this long black limousine with its uniformed driver, and we would glide off into the early morning light. And you know what effect all this had on the ladies?

I gave them hope.

Perhaps this book may do that for you.

So here it is, the whole package, from the beginning.

Lou, Dena, and My Princess Grandmother

M Y MOTHER, Dena Seletsky, met my father, Lou Walters, at a charity dance in Boston in 1919. They were introduced by a friend of my father, who would later marry my mother's sister. My mother was twenty-two and quite striking, with long, black hair, high cheekbones, a big bosom (too big, she always thought), great legs, and lovely brown eyes through which she could barely see. She was dreadfully nearsighted and always wore thick glasses, the bane of her existence. Whenever she posed for pictures she took them off.

My father, then twenty-four, was not especially good-looking. He was short, about five seven, slight of build, and had light brown hair and a prominent nose that he would later have surgically reshaped. He, too, wore glasses, but had a different problem with his sight. He had a glass eye, having lost one of his eyes from the shards of a shattered milk bottle in a childhood accident. But he was always impeccably dressed and had a certain elegance, probably because he had grown up in England. He had an English accent, very appealing then as now.

He was also well on his way to making his first fortune. My father was in the business many people envied but rarely dared enter—show business. He opened his own booking company, the Lou Walters Agency, in Boston around the same time that he met my mother.

Vaudeville was king in the prosperous post–World War I giddiness known as the Roaring Twenties, and my father owned the keys to the kingdom, at least in New England. Vaudeville halls were packed with people who never stopped partying. And my father kept the party going. You wanted flappers? The Lou Walters Agency had them. You wanted a Charleston band? No problem. Magicians, dancers, comics, big stars, little stars—my father had them all. The money was pouring in. He was only in his twenties.

My mother, on the other hand, was working in a men's neckwear store, wrapping packages. Not much of a career, but her father, who was in the shoe business, had heart trouble, and she was helping her parents support the six younger kids. My mother, I am told, always seemed above her job. She, too, had a certain elegance that set her apart from most of her friends. She spoke beautifully and had a good, if slightly caustic, sense of humor.

My parents married a year after they met. May 30, 1920, is the date that officially began their often tortuous relationship, one that somehow lasted for nearly sixty years and survived personal tragedy, the heights of success, and the depths of financial ruin.

On paper they seemed ideally suited for each other. Each was a member of what seems now to be a huge family—seven children. Each was a child of immigrant parents whose journey from persecution in the "old country" could be the history of thousands of Jewish refugees transforming their lives in America.

Both sets of my grandparents came from what was then part of the Russian empire and is now eastern Europe, my mother's family from a village in Lithuania and my father's family from Łodz, Poland. (This discovery would have startled some members of the family who firmly believed my father's "superior" side of the family came from the scholarly and highly religious city of Vilnius, known as the Jerusalem of Lithuania.) I'm no genealogist—my cousin Shirley was the self-appointed historian of the Walters family until her death in 1997, and she always claimed their superior Vilnius connection—but the old records I found, while researching this memoir, show the 1868 birth of my paternal grandfather, Isaac Abrahams, in Łodz, and the birth of my maternal grandfather, Jacob Seletsky, at about the same time, in Russia.

Both the Seletskys and the Abrahamses are thought to have joined the flood of Jews fleeing anti-Semitism in imperial Russia. By the 1890s, my mother's side of the family seems to have immigrated directly to America, where they settled in Boston. My father's side of the family went to London.

My cousin Shirley loved to tell the fairy tale of how my paternal grandfather met, and subsequently married, my grandmother. In Shirley's version, Isaac Abrahams, then around twenty-two, arrived in London orphaned, uneducated, and penniless. He somehow met a well-off family named Schwartz who had left eastern Europe some years before and by then owned several highly profitable knitting mills in

England. Mr. and Mrs. Schwartz, impressed by Isaac's intelligence, manners, and good looks, more or less adopted him, giving him a job as an apprentice in one of the knitting mills and educating him as well, starting with teaching him English.

Enter their daughter, Lillian.

Every fairy tale has to have a princess, and Lillian, their only daughter, more than filled the role. On holidays her parents sent her to the knitting mills with baskets of food—turkeys, geese, ducklings, bread and cakes—for all the apprentices. On the fateful day the princess first laid eyes on the handsome orphan, according to Shirley, Lillian was wearing a pale blue coat and a little white ermine muff and hat. It was love at first sight. Forbidden love. The best kind. The plucky princess followed her heart and, ignoring her family's orders to give up this penniless suitor, eloped with Isaac.

The Schwartzes weren't thrilled with this marriage, but they had trained Isaac well in the mills, and he became a prosperous custom tailor in London. And the princess became a mother—seven times: first Rose, my cousin Shirley's mother; then my father, Lou; followed by Harry, Barnet, Rebecca, Belle, and Florence. (Don't worry, there won't be a quiz.)

While Lillian and my grandfather Isaac were begetting my father's side of the family in London, my maternal grandparents were busy with their own begetting in Boston. My maternal grandfather, Jacob Seletsky, who started his life in the new country as a peddler, had gone into the shoe business with his brother, Joseph, when he met and married my grandmother Celia Sakowitz, in 1895. They, too, produced seven children: my mother, Dena; her sister, Lena (not much imagination in this family); and then a whole slew of sons—Edward, Samuel, Max, and twins, Daniel and Herman.

I never did know my maternal grandfather, but I remember my grandmother Celia very well. She was short and stout with thick glasses, like my mother. Everybody listened to her; she was evidently strong and tough. She spoke English with a heavy Yiddish accent, and the few Yiddish words I remember I learned from Grandma . . . like *nebbish*, meaning sweet but pathetic . . . or *mishugas*, meaning a whole lot of stuff going on . . . or *mishuga*, meaning crazy person . . . or *farbissener*, a sourpuss. There must be better spellings of these words, but you get the drift. Unfortunately my mother's side of the family did not have a historian like Shirley, so if there are any colorful Seletsky stories, I don't know them.

The Schwartzes had educated my grandfather well, and Isaac

became an avid reader and writer. He passed that passion for reading on to my father, whom I picture always with a book. Isaac also passed his talent for writing on to his eldest son. As a schoolboy in London my father received a silver medal for academic excellence for an essay he'd written. Needless to say my father was declared brilliant by his family.

But Grandfather Isaac must have been having a difficult time in London. The clothing trade in the East End was notorious at the time for its abuse of immigrant Jewish laborers. The working conditions were beyond terrible, with low-paid employees, many of them children, jammed into hot, airless rooms with little or no sanitation, seven days a week. Such "sweated labour," as it was referred to then, gave rise to the term "sweatshop"—and inevitably to social unrest and riots.

I don't know if Isaac owned a sweatshop or worked in one, but it is believed that the bitterness and unrest in the clothing business, which spawned a strike in 1906, led him to pick up his family and relocate to Belfast, in Northern Ireland. Though there was a sizable and growing number of Jewish immigrants there, the family didn't stay long. They immigrated to America in 1909. My grandfather Isaac and his three sons—my father, Harry, and Barnet—arrived in New York from Liverpool aboard the SS *Cedric* on August 28. According to the passenger manifest, they were detained overnight on Ellis Island because my father's loss of an eye required a doctor to certify his ability to enter the country. When they were released they stayed with relatives, eventually moving to Rivington Street, in a community of Jewish immigrants on Manhattan's Lower East Side. They were joined there seven months later by my grandmother and the four girls, who arrived on the SS *Columbia*. They, too, were detained overnight on Ellis Island until my grandfather came and picked them up. And my family's American odyssey began.

It is not clear when—or why—the Abrahams family dropped Abrahams and renamed themselves Walters. But many immigrants at the time adopted English-sounding names to blend into the American melting pot. Two of my mother's brothers in Boston, for example, had already exchanged Seletsky for Selette. So my grandfather Isaac Abrahams became Abraham Walters, his princess wife became Lillian Walters, and their oldest son became Louis Edward Walters.

Cousin Shirley, who, along with her divorced mother, lived for a while with my grandparents, would regale me later with stories about my very grand grandmother. Lillian took a nap every day after lunch, slathered her face with Pond's Dry Skin cream, and put cold cucumber slices on her eyes. (When I was older I remember Shirley telling me, before a date, to lie down and put cucumber slices on my eyes. They dripped on the pillow.) Lillian also took milk baths and erased any rough skin on her elbows with lemons.

Although they were happily in the "new world," my paternal grandparents remained British to the core. Sunday breakfast consisted of kippers and eggs and onions, and every afternoon my grandmother presided over a high tea with crustless watercress and cucumber sandwiches. So rooted were they in their British backgrounds that years later, the 1936 abdication of King Edward VIII to marry the twice-divorced American, Wallis Simpson, sent the whole family into paroxysms of grief. According to Shirley, my grandparents sobbed while listening to Edward's famous speech on the radio giving up his throne for the woman he loved. (Many years later, in some sort of divine family justice, my father would present a command performance of one of his shows to the Duke and Duchess of Windsor in the Bahamas and he and my mother would join them for dinner.)

I never knew my father's parents. I was born around the time my grandfather Abraham died of a heart attack in 1931, at the age of fifty-six. Lillian followed five years later. On the morning of the day she died, my princess grandmother asked Shirley to do her nails. "A lady should never live like this," she said to Shirley. "How could she die like this?" Then she proclaimed herself a virgin, to which Shirley naturally responded, "How could you be, Grandma? You have seven children." But my grandmother had the last word. "I know," she said. "But I never participated."

MY FATHER WAS FIFTEEN when he arrived on these shores and almost immediately started looking for a job. He wrote about that search much later, when he was seventy, in his unpublished treasure of a memoir, "It's a Long Walk." He makes no mention of going to school in New York, which is sad, but then again, there was a newly arrived family of nine to help support, and there were many more boys his age seeking jobs than there were openings.

Every morning around 8:00 a.m., he wrote, he would begin that long three-mile walk from Rivington Street in Lower Manhattan to Times Square. The want ads of the day, which he read "every morning for months," were posted in the windows of a building at the corner of Broadway and Forty-second Street. My father would rush over to the nearest address on the list, but he never seemed to get there first. Often there were twenty or thirty boys ahead of him, and soon another twenty or thirty behind him. When it was announced that the position was filled, he'd race over to the next nearest address, where by then there would be forty boys ahead of him. "It was hopeless," he wrote.

It took him seven months to land a job—and inadvertently start his life's work. "Office boy wanted. Independent Booking Offices. 1440 Broadway. Apply after 2:00 p.m.," one of the want ads in the window read on the morning of April 5, 1910. My father had no idea what a booking office did, but a job was a job, and after standing fruitlessly in line for several other openings, he wandered over to the office in the Knickerbocker Theater Building on the corner of Thirty-eighth Street and Broadway. It was only noon. He knew he was early, but the months of frustration led him to inform the desk clerk that he had come to apply for the job. To his amazement he was ushered in to see the boss, a Mr. Stermdorf. It paid only six dollars a week. Had he worked anywhere before? No. Could he type? No. And hadn't he read the "after 2:00 p.m." for job applicants? That was at least a yes, with my father's explanation that he was afraid of once again finding a long line and the job being filled before he got the chance for an interview. Mr. Stermdorf sent him packing and told him to come back at the designated time.

My father was back at five minutes to two. The reception room was jammed with people, all of whom he assumed were looking for the office job but actually were entertainers looking for work. And then the ax fell. "Sorry, the job's been filled," the desk clerk informed him. My discouraged father was halfway down the stairs when he realized the job couldn't have been filled before two, so he went back. "Oh, you're Lou Walters, the one who came early," the desk clerk said. "Come in."

Why did he get the job? Mr. Stermdorf, it turned out, was also British, and my father attributed his good fortune to their shared English accents. Personally I think it was because my father showed such gumption, applying for the job not once but twice and making sure he was the first boy in line.

He evidently learned the trade very quickly, submitting daily lists of the agency's clients to the bookers for chains of theaters and vaudeville halls. And so, for better or worse, he began his lifelong career in show business.

It started off "for better." One of the owners of the agency he worked for opened a branch office in Boston and my father went along, as did his parents and all his younger siblings. It was in Boston that the Seletskys, my mother's side of the family, and the Walters, my father's side, began to converge. The Seletskys owned two shoe stores and were well established, and my paternal grandfather, Abraham, seems to have done okay there as a custom tailor. But for some reason he decided Boston wasn't for him and, leaving my father behind, he moved the rest of the family to New Jersey, where some of the Walters family live to this day.

My father did very well in Boston, and before too long left to open his own booking agency, aptly named Lou Walters Booking Agency. He traveled to vaudeville halls in the smallest of towns—all towns had vaudeville halls in those pre-TV, silent-movie days—and found new acts, made contacts, traveled some more, found more acts.

He discovered the comedian Fred Allen, then a juggler, who went on to have his own hugely successful radio and television shows. He also discovered Jack Haley, another comedian, who later starred as the Tin Man in the classic film *The Wizard of Oz*. By the time my father met my mother, he had become the definition of a "good catch."

My father bought my mother a mink stole, and they moved into a fourteen-room mansion in Newton, a prosperous Boston suburb. My sister was born while they lived there. Two years after my parents married, my mother's father died of heart failure, leaving my grandmother Celia with five children still at home to raise. My father immediately invited the entire family, including my mother's sister, Lena, to live with them. When Lena married, she moved her new husband, Sidney, into the house. The house was large enough for everyone to live in comfortably, and they were able to get around in style. My father owned four luxury cars—two Cadillacs, a Pierce-Arrow, and a Packard.

I never saw any of it.

My Childhood

B Y THE TIME I was born in Boston (I am now in my seventies and that is as specific as I will get), my father had lost his first fortune. The financial roller coaster of his business life would have an enormous impact on me.

Throughout my life my father made and lost several fortunes in show business. When I was growing up most of the kids I knew had fathers who were in rather prosaic, safer businesses. My uncles sold shoes. My mother's brother-in-law sold cheap dresses. A big deal was to be a dentist, and the height of it all was to be able to brag about "my husband, the doctor." Not a lot of people could brag about "my husband, the booking agent." Certainly my mother didn't, especially after their lives were turned upside down.

It wasn't his fault. First of all there was the stock market crash of 1929, which brought the Roaring Twenties, with all its luxury and indulgences, to an abrupt end. This was followed by the decade-long Great Depression. But what really doomed my father's business was an actor named Al Jolson.

The Jazz Singer, starring Jolson, was released in 1927 and was a show business miracle. The pioneer "talkie" revolutionized the motion picture business. Not only did the era of silent films end almost overnight, but also, more gradually, did the market for live shows. As more and more vaudeville halls were converted into movie theaters, my father's once-flourishing business sputtered. Therefore I didn't go home from the hospital in Boston wrapped in my mother's fur stole, which by then had been sold, nor did I travel in one of the four cars, all of which were gone, nor was I ensconced in a crib in the big house in Newton. Instead I was brought to a modest two-family house in Brookline, also a suburb of Boston, but not nearly as grand as Newton.

Still, it wasn't a bad place in which to grow up. Brookline, when I was a child, still had some fields where you could even see a horse or two. It had a small shopping center called, then and now, Coolidge Corner, with a bakery, I remember still, named Dorothy Muriel's, where you could buy yummy cupcakes. It also had one movie theater and, when I was older, I could walk there. The first time I went to the movies alone, I saw Daphne du Maurier's classic, *Rebecca*, in which the formidable housekeeper Mrs. Danvers burned down the ancestral home known as Manderley. I was scared to death and loved it.

My father, meanwhile, had to close his agency in Boston because he couldn't pay the rent. He was reduced to selling acts or small shows to out-of-town theaters which hadn't yet switched over full-time to movies. He also began to book banal industrial shows put on by organizations like the Massachusetts Shoe Manufacturing Association. Not very glamorous, but it helped pay the bills.

When I was five or six my father had another miniroll of financial success. Though vaudeville was dead, the era of nightclubs had risen from the ashes, and he became an instant and talented nightclub producer. His first show, staged for a Boston club called the Lido Venice, featured a female impersonator from New York and what my father promoted as "a Chorus of Lovely Debutantes." Actually they were young girls he'd recruited from local dancing schools. The first two-week run was a smash. The second was over the top.

My father persuaded Evelyn Nesbit to appear at the Lido. She was the ravishing young woman whose affair some years before with the famous architect Stanford White had led her millionaire husband, Harry Thaw, to shoot White dead on the roof of Madison Square Garden. Nesbit had only two accomplishments going for her, my father wrote later in his memoir. One was that her picture had been on the front page of the *Police Gazette* as well as every newspaper in the country. The other was an ability to draw crowds. And draw them she did, reciting "The Persian Kitten," a popular parody of the time, onstage to virtually every Bostonian, including the mayor and the chief of police.

When my father was producing and directing these shows, he would often take Jackie and me to the rehearsals, where the performers would make a big fuss over us. The dancers would sometimes twirl me around until I got dizzy with pleasure. Then my father would take us for hot dogs on buns, which he loved and so did we.

But the good times didn't last. The Lido was sold, and though my father went on to produce a show at the Cascades Room in the Bradford Hotel, the ripple effect of the Great Depression caught up with him.

The hotel chain that owned the Bradford went out of business. So, once again, did my father.

He soon began, as they say, to "take to the road." In search of business, he toured all over the eastern seaboard, with a traveling road company of some twenty performers and musicians jammed into four cars. On the main car there was a big sign that read "Stop. Look. And Listen." At one point he went hundreds of miles north with this moving caravan to Toronto, and then to Nova Scotia, to try to find a paying audience. Sometimes we wouldn't see him for weeks. As a result, when I was a child I barely knew my father. I have a vague memory of him coming back from one of these northern trips carrying matching white coats with hoods for Jackie and me. They didn't fit, and my mother scolded him for wasting the money.

My parents were by now an oddly matched couple. My mother was practical and somewhat depressed. She had a lot to be depressed about. Not only were there financial worries, but she had a child who was already being diagnosed as backward. Furthermore, four years before my sister's birth, my parents had lost a son. His name was Burton, and I was evidently named after him as both of our names started with a "B." He died from pneumonia at the age of fourteen months. I never heard my parents talk about him, but I remember when my grandmother died, I went with my mother to visit her grave. Next to it was a tiny gravestone that read "Burton Walters." My mother knelt and cried.

So there were my mother and father, married with two young daughters. My mother, greatly loving to her daughters, but a practical woman without time for a lot of fantasy in her life. My father, just the opposite—a kind of poet who read all the time, seemed to live in his own head, and had a hard time showing affection. I don't remember ever trying to hug him, even after he came home from a long trip.

My father's only escape, throughout his life, was playing cards. Mostly he played pinochle and gin rummy. He played for money and usually lost, in part because a lot of his cardplaying friends were in on the secret of his half blindness and, it was said, would often discard to his fake eye to confuse him. But he was compulsive about playing cards. To keep him home at least one night a week, my mother agreed to have his cardplaying sessions at the apartment, usually on Friday nights. His friends would come over, and the house would smell of cigar smoke for days.

My mother, who never liked to play games, would nag him about his gambling and complain that he was risking much-needed money. I understood her insecurity and apprehension. I, myself, never liked to gamble. But it would take me years to appreciate my sensitive and gifted father and the extraordinary effort he made, in spite of the gambling, to support us during those hard times, only to be met at home with criticism.

I do have some sporadic memories of my father taking my sister and me out and giving my mother some well-earned time off. Besides those wonderful rehearsals at the Lido Venice, he sometimes took us into Boston to ride on the Swan Boats in the Public Garden. And to Boston's Chinatown for chicken chow mein. But those are rare recollections. I was very much my mother's daughter. She was so soft and loving to me. I used to tell her that when I grew up, I would buy her a beautiful house right next to mine. I never did. I can't tell you how much I wish I had.

How did my mother truly feel about my father? I just don't know. She took good care of him and cooked all his favorite foods when he came home—steak, french fried potatoes, made, of course, in those days from scratch, frankfurters and baked beans. She always gave my father the tenderest part of the steak. She brewed the tea he drank. She never used a tea bag.

I know my father admired my mother's dignity and elegance. He often said so. She must have realized that his admiration meant he was sensitive and intelligent. He had not even graduated from high school, but he had read many of the classics, could quote from Shakespeare, and when he was home, read me to sleep with stories about Greek gods. To this day I have a library of my father's books. They are almost all first or limited editions.

But did they love each other? I can't remember my parents ever kissing in front of us, or hugging or even having a laugh. Would they have stayed married today? I don't know. I only know they stayed married for nearly sixty years, until death parted them.

If my mother was judgmental about my father (he often said she saw the seams and not the satin), to Jackie and me she was unfailingly kind and patient. If she and my father went out with friends, which was rare, she made sure we had the same sitter—an elderly, wiry woman, nicknamed "Dotey," who brought us soggy cookies she had made and herself smelled of cookie dough. Other than with Dotey, my mother never left us. She dressed both of us beautifully, sometimes alike (which I hated), put big taffeta bows, the fashion of the time, on our carefully brushed hair, cooked every meal herself, washed and ironed every day. In her spare time she made wonderful hats for herself. I remember her sewing bright red cherries on a big black straw hat. She modeled it for us. I tried it on, too, and it came down over my eyes. I was delighted.

To be with my mother was my greatest pleasure, even though I was the recipient of her complaints, usually about my father. She didn't have many friends, mostly because she didn't play cards or the later rage, mah-jongg, and she was afraid to drive. Her closest companion was her sister, Lena, but Lena lived in another suburb, Dorchester, and had two young sons. She couldn't come to Brookline very often, although some Sundays she would drive over and pick us up to visit with her and my grandmother, who lived with her.

But most nights after she had cooked dinner my mother, Jackie, and I sat at the kitchen table. My sister would sit silently, lost in her own thoughts, as I talked about my day at school. My mother, after listening and kissing me, would then often discuss my father, the lack of money, and his absence when she needed him. It did not seem odd to me that I was her confidante, but looking back now, I realize I was never young.

We moved a lot in those days, usually down. At one point we lived next to a funeral home. Another move took us to an apartment where, because my father was usually not there to help, my mother had to stoke the furnace in the basement. This hurt her back. My mother was sure things were going to get worse, and for a long time they did.

In those days I thought that everybody had a sister who was mentally retarded, that all fathers gambled and were rarely at home. I knew that I had my mother's love, and I remember her often saying that she wished she had six of me, I was such an obedient and easy child. But in my mind then, it didn't seem like enough.

Was I jealous of the extra time my mother spent on my sister, whose tears and tantrums she had to control, whom she often had to dress, whose hair she brushed and combed all of my sister's life? Did I want to be treated like a child and not another adult? I must have, because I remember often coming into my mother's bedroom when I was about seven or eight, and whining about having a pain in my stomach. Since I was such a good child and rarely caused any trouble, she took these complaints very seriously. She would then leave my sister with Dotey and take me on rounds of visits to doctors who would examine me, take the needed tests, and find nothing wrong.

But I continued to insist that I was in pain. After the doctor visits, mother and I would stop off at a restaurant where I could order my favorite, spaghetti. Bliss. Obviously the stomach pains weren't affecting my appetite. Finally one bewildered doctor said I should have my appendix taken out. It seemed the only choice. So I did, happily. More attention.

When I got home from the hospital I was even happier because I was moved from my small bedroom in the back of the apartment, which was originally built to be a maid's room, into my parents' big bedroom overlooking a gas station. From their bedroom window I could sneak peeks at the gas attendant. Every night after work he closed the gas station and took off his overalls and stood in his underwear pulling on his pants. Exciting view for an eight-year-old!

My incision became infected, causing my mother to lavish even more attention on me. How sweetly sad these memories are. One stands out. When I was in the hospital recovering from the operation, which in those days kept you in bed for almost a week, my mother would take the streetcar back and forth from Brookline to Boston every day to see me. She had to then walk a good ten blocks to the hospital. One night I heard someone entering my room and, thinking it was the nurse, whom I didn't want to see, I kept my eyes closed. When the person left the room, I finally opened my eyes and saw at the foot of my bed my favorite doll. My mother, worried that I would feel alone, had taken the streetcar at night to visit me one more time. The memory has stayed with me all these years. I can barely write about it even today. It makes me so sad for her.

Another view of my mother and me has also stayed so clear, a memory that goes back more than sixty years. One Christmas I remember saving money to buy my mother a cut-glass perfume bottle, which many women then kept on their dressing tables. My mother had a considerable collection, and I was sure she would want to keep adding to it. I carefully chose what I thought was the perfect one, chiseled in the shape of a half-moon. I wanted my mother to love it and not want to return it, as she did so many of my father's gifts. She returned his presents so often that he stopped buying anything for her. I have kept this lesson in mind all my life. No matter what anybody gives me as a gift, I say, "Terrific," and wear it at least twice (before trying to return it).

The day before Christmas, unable to keep my secret totally to myself, I asked my mother if she would like another bottle for her collection. "Not really," she said. "I have too many already." I could barely keep back my tears, but it was too late. The next morning I gave her my shiny wrapped present. She opened it, took me in her arms, and exclaimed, "Of all my perfume bottles, this is the most beautiful. It makes all the others look dreadful. I am going to give them all away and only keep this one." And she did.

By the way, none of these traumas, large or small, seem to have affected my schoolwork. I was an overly serious student. I did my homework on time and got good grades. Someone once interviewed a few of my teachers at the Lawrence School, the small public school in Brookline that I attended. According to my fifth-grade teacher, Miss (Mildred) Gillis, I was "a very serious pupil." She had given me an A, though she said she was usually "stingy" with her As. She also said that I was "delightful" and a "good writer." (Where are you now that I need you, Miss Gillis?)

More revealing, perhaps, was her observation that she couldn't recall my having any playmates. "I don't remember Barbara as being social," Miss Gillis said. "School was a place of business for her."

I disagree with that last pronouncement. I desperately wanted playmates, to have friends over to my house, to belong instead of always feeling like an outsider. When I was about seven years old, the school put on a little performance for adoring parents. It featured a robin redbreast as the lead and a chorus of little brown-costumed chirpers. I was assigned the leading role of the robin. But here's the thing: I didn't want to be the star. I wanted to be in the chorus, to be like all the other kids. So to this day I recall going home and watching my mother, who sewed very well, cheerfully making my robin costume. I tried it on, with its big, gorgeous red belly, spread my wings, and burst into tears. When I told my mother why, she came to school with me the next day and explained the situation to the bewildered teacher. My mother and I went home, tore up the costume, and I became a chirper in the chorus like everyone else.

My sister also went to the Lawrence School, but only briefly. And she didn't get to chirp at all. According to another interview, this with Elizabeth McGuire, the school nurse, Jackie was placed in the "ungraded group," a euphemism for children with developmental disabilities. Jackie evidently had to repeat first grade at least once, and there is no record of her achieving second. My poor parents. My poor Jackie.

Also interesting to me was Miss McGuire's diagnosis of Jackie's condition as something usually caused by a birth injury. Years later, when my mother and I did talk about Jackie's condition, my mother thought that Jackie had been delivered by forceps, so Miss McGuire may have been right. Miss McGuire cited Jackie's lack of coordination, her "unsteady gait," and her stuttering. "Perhaps," she offered, "Jackie suffered from a mild form of cerebral palsy." Later Jackie was tested for this, but it didn't seem to be the case. We never did know what caused her condition.

Now I wonder if it wasn't genetic. Would Jackie today be diagnosed as "autistic"? Two of my cousin's children have some form of "developmental disabilities," but live relatively normal lives. They are considered to be autistic. The word "autism" didn't exist when Jackie was young. Today there are special treatments, diagnosticians, workshops, support groups. Most of all there is understanding. But then there was no place for my sister or my parents to go. Seeking guidance, my mother was often told to "just send her away to an institution." That was never a consideration.

For a short time Jackie was enrolled in another public school called Devotion, which also had a program for the "ungraded," but she didn't last long there either. She then stayed at home and had tutors who taught her to read and write, although I'm not sure at what level, as I never remember her being tested. (I would guess third- or fourth-grade level.) Nor do I know her IQ. She was home, always.

My mother did her best not to make Jackie feel different. It usually didn't work. Once there was a neighborhood talent show. Jackie and I were taking tap-dancing lessons, and my mother allowed us to enter the contest. She made us matching costumes, and off we went to perform. Well, Jackie got panic-stricken and forgot the few steps she had learned. She just couldn't follow the music, and finally she simply stood there on the stage watching me. The audience booed. I was embarrassed and frightened. I took Jackie's hand and we walked home to our mother.

But was it a terrible childhood? A friend once said, when another pal was complaining about her childhood, "You didn't have a terrible childhood. Helen Keller had a terrible childhood." I had love. I never lacked for food or clothes. I had cousins with whom I happily played, especially in the summers. I had uncles who taught me to swim and took us to amusement parks. I had a mother and a grandmother who doted on me. I had a father who, although often absent, was never unkind or abusive.

I did have a friend here and there. (I remember one when I was about ten, with whom I smoked cigarettes stolen from her mother.) So if I was a sad and serious little girl, I can't say that my early childhood package was wrapped in plain brown paper. It had some shiny paper, too, provided by occasional excursions into my father's unusual life. And it also had some pretty bows, tied carefully by my mother.

"Skinnymalinkydink"

OVER THE YEARS as I was growing up, Mother, Dad, Jackie, and I would from time to time visit the Walters family in New Jersey. My uncle Harry Walters was a leading citizen in Asbury Park, New Jersey, just over an hour from Manhattan. He and his wife, my aunt Minna, owned a big dry goods store in Asbury Park. They sold sheets, towels, and even children's clothes. They did very well. When we visited, Uncle Harry would give us presents from the store.

Uncle Harry and Aunt Minna had three daughters around my age (sadly all have died, but I do still see their children). My cousins had a governess, an honest-to-god governess. The sisters loved one another and played together.

I never remember either of my parents setting foot in a temple. My father used to say he was an atheist. But Uncle Harry was very involved in the synagogue. He and Aunt Minna celebrated the Jewish holidays; they fasted on Yom Kippur and celebrated Passover with big feasts for the family. We never did. The closest we ever got was when my mother would light Sabbath candles on Friday night. Friday was the only night my father would make a special effort to be home. We certainly knew full well that we were Jewish. But practicing the religion just never seemed important. As a result I have no Jewish education or any religious education and don't observe the holidays.

One more thing about Uncle Harry and Aunt Minna. They seemed to have a very good marriage. Everyone in the Walters family came to them for advice, comfort, and, oh yes, money. Uncle Harry headed the family. He was handsome, easygoing, sweet, and, I guess, predictable. His older brother, Lou, my father, was adventurous, a gambler, an artist in his way, and definitely not a family man. I envied my three happy cousins (talk about belonging), and yet, when we grew up—forgive me for saying this—my life was so much more interesting than theirs. Not necessarily better, but much more interesting. And for better or worse I came to value "interesting" far more than "normal."

The Walters side of the family always looked down on the more common Seletsky side. And, no surprise, my father never fitted in with the Seletskys. But we spent much more time with my mother's relatives.

Every summer for about five years, when I was a little girl, my mother, father, Jackie, and I shared a house with my mother's sister, Aunt Lena Alkon; her husband, Sidney; and their two sons, Selig and Alvin, in Nantasket. Nantasket, now a Boston suburban community called Hull, was, and is, a skinny peninsula twenty miles or so from Boston with Massachusetts Bay on one side and Hingham Bay on the other. It wasn't a swank summer resort like Hyannis Port on Cape Cod, site of the home compound for the Kennedys. But I loved it, partly because I was with Selig, my hero, who was five years older than I, and Alvin, who was two years older and my best friend.

Our house was smack on the main street of the tiny town, so all cars going in and out of Nantasket had to pass us. It was not a location most people would want, and it had just a small front yard and a porch facing the street. But all life passed by, and we felt very much in the swing of things. In addition, because it was such an unprivate and crammed piece of property, it was cheap to rent.

In contrast to our quiet life in Brookline, the summers were busy and boisterous. Also sharing the house with us were my grandmother Celia and, at one time or another, at least two or three of my uncles, all of whom had nicknames ending in *y* or *ie*—uncles Sammy, Maxie, Eddie, Danny, and Hermie. There was only one bathroom, which we all used. Perhaps that is where I developed the bladder of a camel, something that would prove to be a huge asset in the countless hours I would spend live on camera. I cannot, however, attribute my other invaluable career asset to the Nantasket summers. I don't perspire. No matter how hot the television lights or how broiling the setting is, like the inferno of shooting for hours in the Saudi desert, for me it is "no sweat."

The Nantasket beach was long and beautiful. The ocean was cold, with big waves. We would get up each morning praying for a "beach day," and while my mother or Aunt Lena was cooking or cleaning up after all of us, usually one or more of my uncles would walk with us the six very long blocks to the beach and help to teach us how to swim. There was no such thing as a swimming pool. It was straight into the waves.

Some days my mother would come to the beach. I remember her in a one-piece black knitted bathing suit that came down almost to her knees. She had those beautiful legs and that ample bosom. My mother wore her dark hair in a bun, but sometimes, coming out of the ocean, she would let down her hair, and it spilled to her waist. I thought she was just gorgeous. My sister, usually holding on to my mother's hand, also had a lovely round little body. Only I was all angles and bones, like a little dark spider. My nickname, as I've told you, was "Skinnymalinkydink." (If only someone would call me that name today—and mean it!)

Meals were cooked by my mother, the better cook, or Aunt Lena, the quicker cook, who was described by her son Selig as "an Olympic-quality bad cook." But cooking anything in that kitchen was no mean accomplishment. It had an old coal stove you lit with a match and had to stoke constantly. The word "icebox" was also current in Nantasket. Though by then there were millions of Freon gas–fueled refrigerators in the United States, our house gave meaning to "the iceman cometh." And "cometh" he did, every day or so, lugging a new block of ice with giant tongs and putting it in the top of the icebox, where it kept the milk and eggs cool and dripped into a waiting basin. You could also chip off pieces of ice to dissolve on your tongue on sweltering days. Divine. Forget air-conditioning. Never heard of it back then. Just open the windows. And listen in at night as the adults tuned in to their favorite radio programs, like *Major Bowes' Amateur Hour* or ventriloquist Edgar Bergen (Candice's father) and his irreverent wooden companion, Charlie McCarthy.

And of course you could always hear my aunt Lena. Aunt Lena didn't talk. She yelled. She used to terrify me when I was a child, but I later loved her almost as much as I loved my mother. The two sisters could not have been more different. My mother cared about clothes. Lena couldn't have cared less. My reserved mother had only one or two close friends. She didn't play cards. Lena belonged to four bridge clubs and seemed to know every woman within ten blocks of any neighborhood she lived in. My mother couldn't or wouldn't learn to drive. (Neither, unfortunately, would I.)

Lena did the shopping for the whole house and anyone else who needed something. She would travel miles to save three cents on a roll of toilet paper. It would drive my mother crazy. Yet, as much as they were oil and water, they were very close. Close and so different that they bickered all the time and argued over virtually everything. We were all used to it. We didn't even hear them.

Still, years later, when our family left Boston and moved around to other cities, it was Lena who would come with my mother on every move, helping her sister pack and unpack, hang up and put away at each new house. Lena was the salt of the earth, the noisy, loving center of the Seletsky family. My grandmother until she died lived with Lena. My bachelor uncles also lived with her. Lena is real and visible to me in my mind to this day.

WHEN MY FATHER was due to arrive home from his travels, Mother would arrange Jackie's and my hair in braids like coronets over our heads and dress us up in our best clothes. When home on Sundays, Daddy would take us to the local baseball game to watch Nantasket play a neighboring team. I am sure my father would rather have gone alone or with one of my uncles, but Sunday was our day, and my dad patiently taught Jackie and me all about the game. To this day, thanks to him, I love baseball. I am a Yankees fan now, but then I rooted for the Boston Red Sox.

It all sounds very ordinary, doesn't it? Well, it was. The summers were a welcome respite from the quieter, darker days of our winters. And it probably wouldn't have changed drastically through the years. Dad would have continued to eke out a living doing shows wherever he could. I would have gone from public grammar school in Brookline to Brookline High and then maybe on a scholarship to the state university. I might still be living in Boston.

But the cancan girls changed our lives forever.

Sixty-three Cents

*Y*OU KNOW THAT EXPRESSION "My life turned on a dime"?
Well, ours turned on sixty-three cents. That's all my father
had left in his pocket in 1937 when he took over the lease on
what had been an old Greek Orthodox church in Boston and turned it
into a nightclub. The club was called the Latin Quarter. It made my
father successful, rich, and famous.

At the beginning, however, it was a huge gamble. The deconsecrated
church at 46 Winchester Street had been the setting for a series of failed
ventures like an expensive club with an Egyptian theme named the Kar-
nak, and a Chinese restaurant, but my father had a vision.

Boston had its share of nightclubs already. What Boston did not have
was an inexpensive nightclub that served a full dinner for under ten dollars and was naughty enough for grownups but tame enough for families. My father toyed at first with using the Congo as a theme, with lions
and tigers painted on the walls and a chorus line of pretend native dancing girls. His next idea was to re-create a more bohemian club, like
those in New York's artsy Greenwich Village. But after seeing the new
movie *Gold Diggers in Paris*, starring Rudy Vallee as a nightclub owner
with a chorus line of American girls transported to Paris, he decided to
do the same thing in reverse: He would bring Paris to Boston.

What to name his vision? Of course. The perfect name was right
there in one of the songs in the film. He would call his nightclub the
"Latin Quarter."

Getting the money together to turn the church into Left Bank
Parisian exotica was a scramble. "What if it fails?" my mother worried.
"What then? With two young children to support?"

The bad thing about my father was that he was, by nature, a gambler.

The good thing about my father was that he was, by nature, a gambler. He took whatever small amount of money he had saved and put it toward transforming the old church. But that money wasn't nearly enough. No bank would give him a loan for a nightclub, so my father borrowed from everyone he knew, a little here, a little there. Perhaps these friends thought that backing a club would inject a little excitement into their own lives.

My mother's family had no spare money to offer and besides, they were, like my mother, too cautious to be excited by the prospects of a club where my father would be responsible for everything. They passed. But that didn't slow down my father. When the money he'd borrowed from his friends wasn't enough, he bartered and promised and begged for credit.

For $250, and a promise of $500 more, he sweet-talked some local artists into painting wall murals of Parisian café scenes and "girls with watching eyes," as my father described them—"black haired, slit-skirted, French prostitute looking." He bought discarded tables and chairs from the Salvation Army, had tablecloths made of cheap red-and-white gingham, and weeks before the opening began melting candles around the necks of empty wine bottles to give the club the feel of a French café.

My father knew everyone in town by that time. He was well liked, and after calling his old patron and friend Joe Timilty, Boston's police commissioner, who in turn called his close friend Governor James Michael Curley, my father got a liquor license. He also managed to hire a headwaiter who had a following, and a club manager, a very bright young man with red hair named Eddie Risman, who would stay with my father for the next twenty-five years. And so it came to pass that on October 1, 1937, Lou Walters Latin Quarter opened.

My mother put on one of her few dressy dresses, had her hair done, called for Dotey to come and stay with Jackie and me, and with fear in her eyes but hope in her heart, she joined my father for the opening night of the brand-new, but old-looking nightclub. Just before the doors opened, the story goes, my father reached into his pocket, took out all the money he then had, sixty-three cents, and turning to a nearby waiter, handed him the change. "Here," my father said. "Now I start from scratch."

He needn't have worried about his next sixty-three cents. Boston had never seen anything like it. The Latin Quarter was a smash from day one.

There were two shows a night, and even as little girls, Jackie and I went often on weekends. We would sit way in the back of the room at my father's small table.

The acts—singers, acrobats, a comedian here and there—changed each week, but the big and constant attraction was what my father billed as "petite mamzelles." This was a chorus line of fresh-faced young girls, recruited as in the old days, from local dance schools.

These shows were the forerunner of the big girly production numbers in Las Vegas decades later. The girls were all good dancers, and every show ended with their doing my father's version of what he considered a French cancan. With whoops of "Ooh-la-la!" they danced and pranced around the stage, kicking in unison as they raised their multicolored ruffled skirts with their many petticoats. For the finale they would shout even louder, and drop, one by one, into a deep split, raising their skirts over their heads and showing their ruffled panties.

Cancan, indeed! If it wasn't authentic, the Bostonians sure didn't know the difference, and the dance became the trademark ending for almost all of my father's future shows. Give me a glass or two of wine now and I'll sing the theme song that opened every show. It began:

> So this is gay Pa-ree! Come on along with me.
> We're stepping out to see—the Latin Quarter.
> Put on your old beret. Let's sing the Marseillaise
> And put our wine away like water.

We were soon able to move to a much bigger apartment on a much more fashionable street. We even had a maid named Katherine, a funny young Irish girl who had a favorite saying when things got too much for her. "Someday," she would say to my mother, "I'm going to wake up and find myself dead." "Not today though, Katherine," my mother would always reply.

These were much happier days for my parents. There was money to be spent, probably for the first time since I was born. My father's success spilled over to other members of her family. My uncle Max was on the payroll full-time. He was a confirmed bachelor but now a successful much-desired confirmed bachelor. My father was definitely on another roll. The Latin Quarter grossed three-quarters of a million dollars in its first season, and he began looking for new venues.

The first, and to me now the most incomprehensible, was at a small resort in Falmouth, Massachusetts, called Old Silver Beach. Air-conditioning was a relatively new luxury in the late thirties, causing the Latin Quarter in Boston to close for the months of July and August. So my father followed the summer audience to this resort town on Cape Cod, where on Sunday afternoons and evenings he staged shows in a Howard Johnson's–type restaurant right on the beach. One part of the building was the nightclub and the other a fast-food restaurant with a counter serving hamburgers, hot dogs, and ice-cream cones. My memories of those shows seem surreal: people in bathing suits eating hot dogs and watching the cancan dancers.

I missed Nantasket and the family summers there, but our cottage in Falmouth was right across the street from the club, so I had more time with my mother and I could hang out a bit with the chorus girls. My sister in particular loved being with the girls, who were very kind to her.

I also got to see more of my father during this weird period of the Latin Quarter by the sea. He still stayed out late dealing with the details of the club and planning the September reopening of the Latin Quarter in Boston, but I would see him midday when I was having lunch and he was having breakfast. His nocturnal rhythms became a family joke. My cousin Selig came to visit us and had been there several days when he chanced upon my father having breakfast at noon. "How nice to see you," my father said to him. "When are you coming to stay with us?"

But staying anywhere for any length of time became an increasingly elusive quality for my family. My father's vision for the Latin Quarter was not confined to Boston or to Falmouth. He had thoughts of Latin Quarters all over the country. I realize now that he was a true impresario, brimming with talent and creativity. But I certainly didn't feel appreciative of his talents when, some months after we returned to Brookline and I was once more settled into the Lawrence School, my father announced that we were moving again. And not to yet another apartment or house or anywhere in Brookline. This time, in the middle of my fifth-grade year, we were heading to Miami.

The Pistachio Green House

O N A C O L D November day we said good-bye to Brookline. We left my small public school and my teachers, who had known me since kindergarten. We left our pretty, cozy apartment. We hugged and kissed Grandma, Aunt Lena, Uncle Sidney, and my cousins Selig and Alvin, and off we went to Miami Beach to live in the hugest mansion I had ever seen in all of my young years. What's more, the mansion was green. Pistachio green, just like the ice cream.

This humongous house was on five beautiful acres of hibiscus, bougainvillea, and palm trees. Fifteen rooms. Right on the water, with an honest-to-god swimming pool. I not only had my own bedroom, I had my own *playroom*. It was fantastic in the true sense of the word. The only thing was, it was in the middle of nowhere.

The pistachio house, you see, was on a tiny artificially made strip of land called Palm Island. It was guarded by a security gate and reachable only by a causeway that connected the two cities of Miami and Miami Beach. There were few other houses on Palm Island then, though now it's jammed. One house was owned by Al Capone, the notorious gangster, who lived just down the street. There seemed to be no other kids on the island. At first I was very lonely. I missed Brookline. Who needed this huge, ice-cream-colored house?

The reason we were there was the even bigger, white shiny building across the street—the Palm Island Club. The building, which has since been demolished and the grounds turned into a public park, had housed a famous nightclub and casino until the late thirties, when gambling was outlawed and the casino/club went bankrupt.

Enter my father.

It was love at first sight. Not only did the dozen steps leading to the

Palm Island Club's marble entrance make it look like a nightclub movie set, the building came fully equipped with a state-of-the-art kitchen, cutlery, china, tables, chairs, everything except linens. There was seating for six hundred, three times the capacity of the Boston Latin Quarter, dormitories for the dancers, a ten-room house for the management staff, and, across the street, the pistachio mansion. "I was in love with the big, beautiful Palm Island Club," my dad wrote later in his memoir. "I was in love with the adjoining 15-room mansion."

In short order my father leased the club for $7,500 a year for ten years from a mortgage company in Baltimore. Even better, the mortgage company told him, he could lease the house across the street for just $2,500 more. It was a steal. Then came the hitch.

The hitch was named Bill Dwyer. My childhood memories are of a big, distinguished-looking man with rimless glasses, whom I called Mr. Dwyer, and who inexplicably lived with us in the pistachio house. As did his chauffeur or bodyguard, I never quite knew which he was. And then there was Mrs. Speiler, middle aged, also distinguished looking, who, we were told, was the housekeeper. She, too, came with the house.

It was not until I read my father's memoir years later that I learned the story of Bill Dwyer. His arrival in the house one December morning in 1939 had simply been announced by Mrs. Speiler. "Mr. Dwyer is here," she said. And there he stood, in front of a pile of suitcases, with his bodyguard/chauffeur. My father had heard of Bill Dwyer. He had owned the Palm Island Club and Casino and was known locally as the "Fixer." During Prohibition it was Mr. Dwyer who could arrange to have a shipload of rum land without trouble from the police, and who was the payoff man between the Mob and the law. "You took care of Bill, Bill took care of you," my father wrote. And there was the "Fixer" in our living room, prepared to move in.

There was a rational explanation. Mr. Dwyer had mortgaged and lost the club across the street to the mortgage company in Baltimore and had no claim on that. My father owned it now. But Mr. Dwyer still thought he had a claim on the house, which he had been renting for years. His lease had run out the year before, but it was his understanding that the Baltimore company would not rerent it without informing him. He hadn't heard from the company, so he had simply come home for the winter months.

"They say your life passes in front of you in a flash when you are drowning, that a drowning man clutches at straws," my father wrote about this first encounter with Bill Dwyer. On the one hand, my father had an airtight lease on the house and the nightclub across the street, which was due to open in two days. He could have thrown him out. On the other hand, he did not know what Bill Dwyer was thinking behind his big smile or what role his henchman might play.

It seemed inconceivable to my father that he would allow a gangster to live in the house alongside his wife and two daughters. But then again, he knew that Mr. Dwyer was president of Tropical Park, a popular racetrack in Miami. He couldn't be all bad. Nor, to the best of my father's knowledge, had Mr. Dwyer murdered anyone or spent time in jail. The house had seven bedrooms, after all, of which we occupied only three. The prudent choice, my father decided, was to invite Mr. Dwyer to be his guest in the house until he had sorted it out with the mortgage company (which apparently took until April 1940, because that's when Dwyer, the bodyguard, and Mrs. Speiler disappeared).

Welcoming Mr. Dwyer into the house was not the only gamble my father took. There was a risk in opening a Latin Quarter on an island that was accessible only via causeway by car while so many flashy nightclubs and hotels in Miami Beach were within walking distance of one another. But my father was never one to listen to naysayers, which, in this case, was wise. "Lou Walters Miami Beach Latin Quarter" opened on December 23, 1940, and even more sunshine entered our lives. The Latin Quarter was filled to capacity from the night it opened.

Later my father would hire stars like Milton Berle, Martha Raye, Joe E. Lewis, and Sophie Tucker. But in the beginning the attraction at the Latin Quarter was the show itself. It was big and lavish, lasting almost two hours, performed twice a night, and starring my father's famous cancan girls and showgirls as well as acrobats, singers, and novelty acts never seen before in Miami. His popular "Apaches" (a French act correctly pronounced a-*pa*-shay) mimicked a brawl between a tough lower-class man and his women. At the end of the act one of the women shot the man. (In private life they were a happily married couple.)

The show was bright, happy, sexy, and glamorous. My father's club quickly became the "in spot" for vacationers in what was rapidly becoming paradise by the sea. During the thirties a whole bunch of art deco hotels had sprung up like palm trees in Miami Beach. (Many of them, refurbished and repainted, exist today in what is now called South Beach.) Tourism was booming, fueled by the Depression-weary "snowbirds" from northern cities like Chicago, Boston, and New York—the winter population had grown from an estimated 60,000 in 1935 to around 75,000 in 1940.

The chauffeured cars pulling up to the marble Latin Quarter entrance disgorged such well-known people as Howard Hughes, the superrich oilman, movie producer, and aviation tycoon, and Joseph Kennedy, the patriarch of the Kennedy family. In fact Joe Kennedy became a frequent visitor to the club, driving down from his large home in Palm Beach. He knew my dad from the days of the Latin Quarter in Falmouth, which was a short distance from the Kennedy compound in Hyannis. Mr. Kennedy also used to go to the Latin Quarter in Boston with his political cronies Governor Curley and Commissioner Timilty, so it was not surprising that his patronage of the Latin Quarter continued in Florida. He became such a regular that years later, when I went to see him after he'd had a stroke (I was interviewing Rose Kennedy for the *Today* show), I introduced myself not as Barbara Walters from the *Today* show, but as Barbara Walters, Lou Walters's daughter. Only then did I get a glimmer of recognition.

Once I adapted to the big green house and Mr. Dwyer and Mrs. Speiler, that first winter in Miami Beach turned out to be one of the happier times of my young life. I am still pained to remember that much of it had to do with the absence of Jackie. My parents had been trying for years to find a place where my sister could be with children who were more or less like her. If I was a somewhat lonely child, you can imagine how lonely life was for Jackie. My parents also hoped that she could get some kind of an education, have some kind of a life. So, after much investigation, they sent her to a boarding school for special-needs children in Pennsylvania. This meant that I had my parents all to myself, which was wonderful for me but agonizing for Jackie. It turned out that she was not retarded enough for the school. She also missed my mother desperately. Jackie came home six months after she'd left, and my parents never sent her away again.

Even with my sister's return, those were happy days for me. Because the Latin Quarter was right across the street from the house, just as our cottage had been in Falmouth, when I got home from school my mother and often my father were around. I remember my parents dressing to go to the Latin Quarter for dinner and the shows, both of them looking so spiffy. I have memories, too, of leaving for school early in the morning and meeting my parents just coming home. They would kiss me hello or good-bye or both and then go off to bed. None of this seemed unusual to me.

If there is one thing that distinguishes that early time in Florida, it is my parents' joy. Especially my mother's. I had never seen her so happy, and that, of course, made me happy. My father gave her a beautiful lynx coat to wear on chilly evenings, and she treasured it. I can still picture her in that fluffy coat, looking radiant.

It was extremely hard for my mother to live on Palm Island and not be able to drive. She had to be chauffeured everywhere. Just as I was driven to elementary school in Miami Beach every morning by the gardener and then picked up every day after school, my mother, if she wanted to buy even a pair of stockings or go to the market, had to be dropped off and picked up again. So, without telling my father, my mother tried to overcome her fears and took driving lessons.

I wore braces on my teeth in those days, the ones with elastic bands on each end (I hated them, of course), and my orthodontist was located in Miami, so my mother practiced her driving by taking me to and from the dentist. He had a parking lot, so she didn't have to worry too much about parallel parking, which was not her strength. Then came the big day when my father was returning from a trip to Boston. My mother and I surprised him at the airport, and my mother drove us home. My father was thrilled.

My mother drove for a short time after that, but she never really lost her fear; when the city became more crowded she gave it up. In case you don't believe in parental influence, to this day I don't drive. It's a real pain in the neck. I did drive shortly after graduating from college. My father even bought me an Oldsmobile convertible, but my mother's fear was deep in me and I stopped, never to start again. I was always afraid of hitting another car and am still a nervous backseat passenger.

Now remember, when I talk about this driving business, that my little friends from school also couldn't drive and their parents thought it a nuisance to drive them to and from Palm Island, so the girlfriends I made at school rarely came home to play with me. Guess who became my "new best friend"? Mr. Dwyer.

What can I say? He took a shine to me. He went to his racetrack every day and often took me with him on weekends. I wasn't allowed inside the track because I was too young, but we parked where I could see the horses. I would give Mr. Dwyer the few dollars my father had given me, and Mr. Dwyer would make bets for me. Magically I always won.

One of the things I hope happens as a result of this book is that I somehow get answers to questions that have puzzled me for years. Like what became of Mr. Dwyer after he left our house? And who was the chauffeur/bodyguard who shared his bedroom? Is it possible that Mr.

Dwyer was gay? In those days the only reference to "gay" I'd ever heard was in the Latin Quarter's theme song, "So This Is Gay Paree." But in retrospect it seems somewhat logical. I don't remember my parents ever talking about him again after that year, and I haven't really thought about Mr. Dwyer until now. But I'd love to know the truth about him.

I did have one friend from school, Phyllis Fine, whose show business father, Larry Fine, was one of the now-legendary Three Stooges. They lived in a hotel in Miami Beach. Phyllis was pretty and blond, and like me, was alone a lot. She would sometimes come to visit me on Palm Island, and occasionally I would sleep over at the hotel with her, but those visits were rare. Again, we had to be picked up, waited for, and driven home.

School was a whole new challenge. I entered three months into the school year. The curriculum was entirely foreign to me. I had teachers who didn't know me from Adam, let alone Eve. They not only had to cope with me and what I knew or didn't know, but with a whole bunch of other kids whose parents had come to Miami Beach just for the winter months.

It was a public school, not too big, and coed, but I was a shy, introverted child and I felt I had to audition for a new role I didn't know how to play. I coped by doing more homework than was probably necessary and hoping that this would be a day when Phyllis and I could play together.

The dress code also bothered me. It was, after all, Florida, sunny and warm, and many of the girls in my class wore shorts. (We were in the dark ages before the universal wearing of jeans.) But I thought my legs were too skinny to be displayed, so shorts were not for me. I wore blouses and skirts. My mother and I went to Lincoln Road, the chic shopping street in Miami Beach, and we bought a whole new wardrobe. We packed away the heavy sweaters and mostly plaid wool skirts I had worn in Brookline, but we didn't buy one pair of shorts.

I don't remember any sporting activities. You would think we would go to the beach and swim now and then, but we never did. It was okay with me not to have sports. I have never been particularly athletic. Overall the school was an all-right experience for me. Not great, not bad, not memorable.

I adjusted pretty well. After doing my homework when I got home from school, I played with my dolls. I absolutely loved my doll's house and could play for hours in happy solitude. I was also, then as now, a voracious reader and could easily get lost for hours in a book. Then, too, the island was one of the attractions on the sightseeing boat tours around Biscayne Bay, and I would often wander down to the dock and sit there, alone, waving at the passing tourists.

A bigger adventure was to ride my bike past Al Capone's house, hoping to catch a glimpse of the infamous Public Enemy Number One, though I never did. Having spent the last eight years in jail for tax evasion, Capone had arrived back at his house on Palm Island in 1939 at about the same time we did. He was much more of a gangster than Mr. Dwyer. Al Capone had been a massive bootlegger, alleged murderer, and the Chicago gang leader who is thought to have masterminded the 1929 St. Valentine's Day massacre, in which seven rival gang members were gunned down. By the time he returned to Palm Island, he was sick with late-stage syphilis and suffering from dementia, but I didn't know anything about that. Nor, apparently, did my father, who wrote that Al Capone was an occasional visitor to the Latin Quarter, where he sat at the bar, sipped a club soda, and paid with a twenty-dollar bill out of the wad of new bills in his pocket. "He never interfered with anyone and believe me, no one wanted to interfere with him," my father wrote. When Al Capone died in 1947 as peacefully as if he were "a buttonhole maker," my father recalled, there was "just a bartender to mourn his passing."

As I write about my young life on Palm Island, it sounds rather like Eloise at the Plaza, except that Palm Island was no chic hotel. Nor did Eloise spend days at a racetrack and weekend evenings in a nightclub lighting booth.

Unlike the Latin Quarter in Boston and later in New York, the club in Florida was not a place for family celebrations. The shows were sophisticated and not for children, so I hid away in the small lighting booth high above the dance floor, where the main electrician controlled the onstage lights. Crouched next to the technician, I watched the shows weekend after weekend until I could do practically all the numbers. My sister's escape, when she finally came home, was to go backstage and sit in the dressing room with the chorus girls, who were very kind to her. I was uncomfortable doing that and preferred the lighting booth.

As I said, in the first year of the Latin Quarter, my dad didn't hire big stars. He wasn't sure he could afford them. But the second year Jimmy Durante played the club. So did Sophie Tucker, known as the "Last of the Red Hot Mamas," belting out her theme song, "You're Gonna Miss Your Red Hot Mama Some of These Days." Milton Berle played there, too. I saw his act so many times I can still do it practically in my sleep. Want to hear the opening lines? He would walk up to the standing microphone, touch it, then jump back as if in shock and say, "I've just been goosed by Westinghouse."

By the way, this early education has never come in particularly handy. And I never did learn how to maneuver those huge white feather fans that the scantily clad Sally Rand, a very well-known exotic dancer, swished back and forth in her famous peekaboo fan dance.

One of my other favorite acts was not well known. His name was Emil Boreo. He spoke with a heavy accent and did an act that seems quite odd to me today. He wore a soft felt hat with a big brim and by changing the brim, said he could be anyone. Here, as I remember it more than sixty years later, is the opening of his act: "It's not what I do, it's not what I say, it's the way I wear my hat. I can be most anyone with a twist of my brim like that." Then he would turn that hat into a Frenchman's beret or an Englishman's bowler. (How come no one wants me to do his act today?)

Then there was the brilliant Spanish ventriloquist who years later many readers will remember from the *Ed Sullivan Show*, Señor Wences. I can do his routine, too. He would make a fist and, with his thumb around his fingers, color his closed finger with lipstick for a mouth, make two "eyes" with black chalk, and create his so-called little friend named Johnny, or, as Señor Wences pronounced the name, "Yonnie." Yonnie was fresh and funny, and he tormented the kind, dignified Señor Wences, who also had another talking companion, a head in a wooden box. Every time Señor Wences opened the box, Yonnie would say, "Close the box," and the head would say, "Open the box." I am not making this up. I guess I should also tell you that I managed to learn all this and still pass all my tests at school.

But the real crowd-pleaser, as usual, was my father's parade of gorgeous showgirls, who would walk around the stage wearing huge multicolored headdresses, and little else. Complete nudity was as illegal as gambling in Miami Beach, and these gorgeous Amazons wore tiny sequined "pasties" to hide their nipples and used feathers, sequins, and sometimes little fur muffs to cover their G-strings. One of the sensations at an early Palm Island Latin Quarter show was a Chinese girl who carried a real little black kitten in a fur-lined muff over her private parts. In my innocence I fixated on the kitten and wanted to take it home.

I also loved the dancers or "ponies," who would strut their stuff on the stage, whirling, high-kicking, doing my father's version of the cancan before dropping to the floor in a split. I tried that routine at home once and practically dismembered myself.

My father had three "golden rules" for his girls: (1) Do your best show even if it is only a rehearsal. (2) Don't get tan (a rule inspired by Twinnie, one of the showgirls, who loved to sun herself on the roof of the Palm Island Club, which set her apart from her pale twin sister, Winnie, in the show's "Parade of the Wooden Soldiers." "Your father didn't want to have a Chocolate Soldier and a Vanilla Soldier," Twinnie told me years later). Rule number three? Don't get fat.

I saw all this through the prism of a child's eyes. It took me years to recognize that my father was a sorcerer of magic and fantasy, although the audiences got it from the beginning. What I did learn, at this young age, was that behind these fantasy figures were real people. They may have been glamorous onstage, but I saw them offstage without their costumes and makeup, and they had problems, just like everyone else. I knew that Sophie Tucker had a son she rarely saw, that Sally Rand was sick of her fan dance even though it had made her famous, that many of the chorus girls had families they were supporting. This gave me an understanding of celebrities that I never would have had. As a result I was not in awe, years and years later, when I began doing interviews with big-name stars.

Those early years at the Latin Quarter also affected the way I later asked questions and listened to answers. I knew that the childhood years of most celebrities were their most poignant and could often explain their future choices as, of course, it has mine. I learned when to be quiet and just listen. And I knew what could bring tears. (Now, I have been so often accused of making celebrities cry that I go out of my way *not* to bring on the tears. "You cry on this program and I won't run any of it!" I once warned Robin Williams as he pretended to weep.)

You may think it odd that I am writing so much about my father and the Latin Quarter when this is *my* memoir, but that nightclub controlled our lives. Everything we did revolved around it. Everything we owned, every meal we ate, the shirts on our backs, so to speak, stemmed from the Latin Quarter. The Walters and the Latin Quarter were inseparable. The rest of the family, too, gravitated toward Palm Island. Aunt Lena often came to visit us. Uncle Max, my mother's brother, was already working for my father so he was there, too. So, for six months, was another of her brothers, Uncle Dan Seletsky. He had had an operation just before the Latin Quarter's second season, and my father not only gave him an apartment on the property to recuperate in, but gave his wife, Aunt Ann, a job: She became my father's office manager.

The success of the Palm Island Latin Quarter continued to grow, and with it my father's reputation as a brilliant showman. He became such a darling of the local papers that nationally syndicated columnists started mentioning the Latin Quarter in their columns. One such all-important columnist and radio broadcaster was Walter Winchell, who practically invented the gossip column. The more my father appeared in print, the greater his reputation grew. The combination of the two led to a new offer.

The way my father tells the story in his memoir, he was sitting alone in the Palm Island Latin Quarter on New Year's Day 1941, when a press agent named Irving Zussman approached him. "How'd you like to run a nightclub on Broadway? In Times Square. The best location in the world. And you won't have to put up a cent." The space was available for a ten-year lease, Zussman told him. And there was a backer who wanted to get into the nightclub business, a millionaire named E. M. Loew, who owned a circuit of movie houses. My father had known Loew for twenty-five years. (He had booked vaudeville acts into some of Loew's theaters.) Loew would put up all the money; my father would produce the shows. They would be partners.

My mother was skeptical—another risk. Why not let well enough alone? But my father's eyes were dancing. He had seen the building which had been a fancy Chinese restaurant called the Palais d'Or, then the post-Harlem Cotton Club, then the Gay White Way. None of those nightclubs succeeded, but it could seat between six and seven hundred people, and my optimistic father felt he had the magic touch. So, without further thought, my father made a deal with the tightfisted E. M. Loew, whom he would later deem "as fine a gentleman as ever hated to pay a bill."

So, for better or worse, we were on the move again. It was time to audition in a new city, at a new school, for new friends. This time we were off to New York.

New York, New York

I THINK THE PROBLEM was my "Cuban heels." My entrée into New York did not go well as I started the eighth grade at Fieldston, my third school in as many years. Cuban heels had nothing to do with Havana or Miami. Mine were open-toed shoes with one-inch-high square heels that were the rage for young girls and were meant to be worn on dress-up evenings, with silk stockings with seams down the back. The shoes were usually brown or black. During the day one wore either brown loafers or laced-up saddle shoes. Saddle shoes were white with brown sides and with them, you wore ankle socks.

Now, this digression about footwear is to tell you that I had the whole deal messed up. I guess I had heard about the Cuban heels, but coming from Miami, my mother and I bought the shoes in white. The Miami stores didn't carry them in black. To make matters worse, I wore the open-toed shoes not with the prescribed silk stockings but with white ankle socks. So I arrived that first day particularly dressed up, not knowing a soul in the school and looking like some hick, which of course I was. I also, in those days, had a strong Boston accent. It was long before the Kennedys made the accent fashionable, and to the New Yorkers I sounded affected saying "cahn't" and "auhnt" instead of "can't" and "aunt."

Fieldston was then, and is now, a highly respected and difficult-to-get-into private school. I am amazed that my mother even knew about it and sent in an application. The main school is located in Riverdale, on the outskirts of the city. It also has an elementary school in Manhattan, and most of the kids had been going to the school since kindergarten or first grade. It was coed and full of cliques. This girl was best friends with that girl. This was the girl all the boys liked. This was the A group. This group didn't matter. I was most definitely in the latter group.

In the beginning the toughest part of the day was lunch in the school cafeteria. I would take my tray and slowly walk around the room hoping that one of the A group would look up and ask me to sit down. Whomever you sat with for lunch defined your social standing. But even after I dumped the white Cuban heels for saddle shoes, I never really made the A group. I was more or less a B or C-plus. But we social underlings could occasionally ask one of the A girls for a "date" on a Saturday afternoon. We actually made dates, real dates. You would ask a girl if she wanted to spend Saturday with you, and then, if she said yes, you would have lunch and usually go to the movies. In those days, New York had dozens of movie theaters all around Broadway with great big stage shows. Broadway was very safe. And there were so many other places a teenager could go.

There was Radio City Music Hall, with its famed chorus line of high-kicking Rockettes. There were all the theaters hosting the big bands: Tommy Dorsey, Glenn Miller, Benny Goodman. Singing with Dorsey's band was a skinny, hollow-cheeked, bow-tied fellow named Frank Sinatra, who looked as if a strong wind would blow him away, but he sang love songs like no one else and the young girls went wild. Sinatra's adolescent fans, including me, were dubbed "bobby-sockers," from obviously our short socks. When Sinatra appeared solo at the Paramount Theater in 1942, my mother, Jackie, and I stood in line to get tickets to see him. His appearance created such hysteria among young girls, including fits of swooning, that newspapers turned to psychiatrists for explanations. I didn't swoon, but I loved his voice then and always.

Two years later his return to the Paramount caused what became known as the "Columbus Day Riot." On his opening day in October 1944, ten thousand bobby-sockers, jammed the ticket line and an estimated twenty thousand others piled into Times Square, breaking windows in the crush. Sinatra burst into the nation's awareness in a way that would not be matched until the arrival of Elvis Presley in the fifties and then the Beatles in the sixties. By the way, several years later, when Sinatra had lost his popularity and before his legendary comeback, he played the Latin Quarter.

But the point of all this is that a person, young or old, could go to a movie and watch the stage show and spend the whole day being entertained. And what a treat if you were going with one of the popular girls. To this day I remember the sort of adoring court that formed around those girls. One A-group member was tiny and graceful with little hands and feet. Another, the class beauty, had long, blond hair to her waist and a perfect pompadour—the look back then—hair swept high off the face in a big roll. The really older boys—the fifteen-year-olds—thought she was divine. Years and years later I met her again. She didn't look as great, and I was already on the *Today* show. Okay, so I'm bragging, but after all those years of pushing so hard, I'm entitled.

It isn't that I was a dog in those days, but I saw myself as too thin, and my pompadour never looked quite right. Slowly, though, I did make good friends and the B-list had some good kids. Also, slowly, I began to like my life in New York.

My family started off living in a residential hotel called the Buckingham, located at Fifty-seventh Street and Sixth Avenue (since renamed the Avenue of the Americas, although I've never heard a New Yorker refer to it that way). It was in the heart of the city, one block from one of my favorite places, the Automat. The legendary brainchild of Horn & Hardart, the Automat had branches all over New York and was like a big cafeteria, only a lot of the food—the sandwiches, the salads, the pieces of pie—were behind little glass doors. You put your nickels into a slot and the door opened to present you with the dish of your choice. The Automat had a memorable slogan—Less Work for Mother—and was not only great fun but a brilliant forerunner of today's fast-food chains.

Some of the Automat's patrons stayed all day, especially those with little money. They would eat the free saltines and ketchup that were on the tables, get a tea bag and some hot water, and hang around for hours. After a while we recognized these regulars. We would smile at them, and they would smile at us. The Automat was such a part of the New York scene that when Horn & Hardart finally closed its doors (the last one, on Forty-second Street and Third Avenue, closed in 1991) editorials were written and the old-timers actually grieved.

My problem, as ever, was Jackie. First of all Jackie and I had to share a bedroom, but a larger problem was that she had nothing to do. During the week I went to school, and whatever my mother did or wherever my mother went, Jackie went, too. By now she was a teenager. My mother, her heart aching at the loneliness of my sister, would often look at me pleadingly when I had one of my coveted Saturday afternoon "dates" and ask me to take Jackie along. I can still hear my mother's voice: "Can't you take your sister? It would mean so much to her." My mother probably shouldn't have done it, but she loved both of her daughters and one of them was so alone.

Me, I was just ashamed. Intolerant and ashamed. When Jackie stuttered, trying to get a word out, or didn't seem able to join in the conversation, my friends would look uncomfortable. "What school does she go to?" they would question me. The next day they would ask me, shyly, if Jackie could dress herself. What did it mean to be "slow" or "retarded"? Did that mean she was crazy?

Today it's hard to understand how much ignorance there was, but subjects like this were not discussed. If you had a child like my sister, you did what my parents did: protect her and hope no one would notice.

It must have been so difficult for my sister. She would have great spells of crying, tantrums of frustration, and, especially in later years, scream at my mother, but she never turned her anger on me.

I can't say the same for myself. I could be short or angry with her, and to this day I regret every harsh word I said to her. Why *didn't* I take my sister to the movies on a Saturday afternoon? There I was, her younger sister, with everything. And there was Jackie—with so little. The phone rang for me, but never for her. Friends came to see me, but not her. I even got her clothes. As Jackie and I grew older, she grew plumper, and if the new clothes my mother bought for her didn't fit, I got them. Why didn't she hate me? I don't know. But she never did.

If conditions at home were difficult, conditions on Broadway and Forty-eighth street were not. The New York Latin Quarter opened on April 22, 1942, four months after the Japanese attacked Pearl Harbor and we entered World War II. The government started rationing gas, and we were issued ration cards for food. We even had blackout nights when we pulled down our shades and turned down the lights in case an enemy plane flew over the city. That would seem to have been an inauspicious time to launch a nightclub, but the reality was quite the opposite. The opulent fantasy world my father had created—red-velvet-lined walls, a thickly quilted pink ceiling, fountains spouting colored water, mirrors on the staircase, and indirect lighting seeping through ostrich feathers—turned out to be the perfect antidote to the harsh, wartime world outside the club's mauve double doors. In its first year, the standing-room-only club grossed $1.6 million, a huge number in those days.

The *Saturday Evening Post* noted the phenomenon a year after the Latin Quarter opened: "It became one of the most amazing operations in Broadway history and no one could figure out how Walters had done it." My father knew, of course. And he didn't hesitate to share his formula in one magazine article after another.

"Everything in a nightclub should be a little bit better than you can afford," he said, describing the club's opulent decor. As for the customers: "Fill them full of food and take their breath away. Don't let them relax and feel normal for a minute. The man who goes to a night-club goes in the spirit of splurging, and you've got to splurge right along with him."

What made the Latin Quarter's success a true phenomenon was its success in the face of great competition. In this pre-TV era of night-clubs, the Latin Quarter was just one of many famous clubs in New York. There was, first and foremost, the Copacabana, owned, it was said, by the Mob. (The Mafia had nothing to do with the Latin Quarter. The Mob was very active in Las Vegas, but my father, remember, had come from Boston and started as a small-time booking agent. Their paths had not crossed. He had no dealings with these men and barely knew them when he opened his nightclubs. I used to joke, sometimes, that I wish he *had* known them because we would have been a lot richer.) The Copa was in the basement of a hotel just off Fifth Avenue and always hazy from cigarette smoke. But it had the most beautiful line of girls, the cel-ebrated "Copa girls." They could barely dance, but they didn't have to. They just smiled and walked slowly and looked gorgeous. The Copa would later be the nightclub where a hilarious young comedy team, Jerry Lewis and Dean Martin, played season after season to packed houses.

Then there was the ever-so-chic Stork Club—no dancing girls, but nearly impossible to get into. The much-feared gossip columnist who had first noticed and written about my father, Walter Winchell, had his own table there every night. There was also the exclusive, high-society El Morocco, with its signature zebra-patterned banquettes and its pow-erful maître d' who kept customers waiting for hours behind a velvet rope while he let in celebrities like Errol Flynn and Humphrey Bogart. El Morocco had dancing but no show; the famous patrons were the show. Billy Rose's famous Diamond Horseshoe was my father's main competition because it, too, had a big show and chorus girls.

What set the Latin Quarter apart was the modest price—a two-dollar minimum and an average dinner tab of eight dollars a person, which could include shrimp cocktail, salad, steak, and dessert. And while most of the other clubs were definitely for adults only, the New York Latin Quarter (unlike the Palm Island Latin Quarter) welcomed fami-lies. It became the club of choice for high school seniors after their proms and for their grandmothers' birthdays. Servicemen on leave, many of whom over the years have sent me their old Latin Quarter pho-tos, also flocked to the club. My father didn't charge them.

The Latin Quarter was such an important fixture in the cultural history of New York that more than sixty years later, Mayor Michael Bloomberg—after a vote by the city council—changed the name of Forty-eighth Street and Broadway, where the Latin Quarter reigned for two decades, to "Lou Walters Way." I went to the unveiling ceremony, presided over by the mayor, on a beautiful spring morning in April 2006.

When my father died, we never had a memorial. In a way this was it. I found out who among my father's chorus girls was still alive (they were in their seventies and eighties) and I invited them. Twelve of them came, including the still beautiful movie actress Arlene Dahl (who had been in the chorus when she was eighteen), and the irrepressible former cancan dancers, the identical twins Twinnie and Winnie, now octogenarians, who stood on either side of the mayor and, in front of the photographers, kicked a leg straight up over their heads, revealing their lacy underwear. The mayor turned red and burst out laughing, as did we all on that happy occasion. Two of the showgirls wore their old costumes, at least parts of them, and showed up in their headdresses and feather boas. They brought treasures, like old photographs of themselves as much younger showgirls at the Latin Quarter, and had many fond memories of my father. I took them to lunch after the ceremony, and one after another told me that my father was the kindest and gentlest of bosses. They adored him, which is why, even now, six decades and counting after the Latin Quarter closed, the chorus girls still have annual reunions and reminisce about what they describe as the best years of their lives. When I can, I join them.

When I was a kid, however, I didn't feel the pride for my father that I would later with Mayor Bloomberg. The Latin Quarter may have been a special treat for everybody and his uncle, but not for me. I was old enough to recognize how other families lived, and they were not like mine. The fathers came home every night to have dinner with the stay-at-home mothers and the children. Cousins, aunts, and uncles gathered in their dining rooms for Thanksgiving and Christmas. Other kids had birthday parties at home and invited all their friends. We did none of that. We celebrated every Thanksgiving, Christmas, New Year's, and all our birthdays at the Latin Quarter. My father coming home for dinner once a week, on Fridays, was almost the only time I saw him. Other nights he came home long after I was asleep and he himself slept late into the morning.

My father, I realize now, did try to include us in his life. Although the featured acts might change every two weeks, the big, elaborate productions usually changed just twice a year. When that happened my mother, Jackie, and I went with him on opening night. We sat at his table nearest the door, and he would spend most of the show talking over an intercom on the table to the lighting technicians or to Madame Kamerova, his longtime production director and choreographer. For the most part I just sat there quietly, and only roused myself, with my mother, to critique each new show. We usually forgot to tell my father how great it was and, God knows, I myself know today how much one wants to hear praise after a performance. Instead, more often than not, we told him only what was wrong.

On some level I guess I was punishing him for not being the father-next-door. I even refused to pay much attention to the influential Broadway columnists who stopped by our table—Ed Sullivan, Leonard Lyons, Earl Wilson, Louis Sobol, sometimes even Walter Winchell. My silence must have hurt my father, who, in turn, hurt me. "Your problem is that you have an inferiority complex," he told me on one of those evenings. "That's why you never want to talk to anybody."

Jackie, on the other hand, loved the Latin Quarter. It became her home away from home, and she would spend whatever time she was allowed to backstage with the chorus girls. They were wonderfully kind to her as, in years to come, were many of the big stars my father hired, particularly Frank Sinatra, Carol Channing, and the singer Johnnie Ray. Johnnie Ray was famous for his song "The Little White Cloud That Cried," and Jackie developed a serious crush on him. He, in turn, reciprocated by calling her "Jackie darling" and sending her birthday cards and autographed pictures from wherever he was on tour.

Perhaps it was because he, too, had a childhood disability—he was partially deaf and wore a hearing aid. Jackie felt that Johnnie Ray was as in love with her as she was with him. Years after her death I read her diary. Jackie could write, not well, but certainly legibly. The diary was laced with references to him, such as: "Johnnie is working in Chicago. Hope he calls me." "Johnnie is in Dallas. Someday I will marry him." So touching was that diary that I could barely look through it. Even today reading it for this book brought me to tears.

When Jackie wasn't at the Latin Quarter, she was at the movies with my mother. Any movie. Night after night. Just the two of them. The empty days and nights must have seemed endless to both of them. Around this time my parents tried hiring companions for Jackie, but they disagreed about what kind of companion to hire. My father wanted someone more like Jackie, perhaps a bit slow herself. My mother wanted someone who would be more responsible and teach Jackie to read or write better. Neither type worked out.

If the companion was bright, as several were, the "friend-for-hire" had nothing in common with Jackie, leaving my sister just as isolated. But the few borderline companions were also failures. They were apt to forget about Jackie for their own pleasures. I remember one time Jackie and a companion went to the skating rink at Rockefeller Center. They skated around a bit and then the companion picked up some guy skating alone and left Jackie for hours on her own. When Jackie finally came home, she told my parents, and that was that. So, after a while, my parents gave up this experiment and again kept Jackie to themselves. Only once do I remember my parents ever having a holiday without her. They left Jackie with a chorus girl named Baby Lake, an adorable person whom we all liked, and went off to the Bahamas. But my parents telephoned home three times a day.

All this naturally put a great strain on their marriage. In Florida the close proximity of the Palm Island Club to our pistachio house afforded them time to be together, but that was not the case in New York.

After our first few months at the Buckingham, we moved into a magnificent penthouse on Central Park West. We would live in a series of penthouses over the years, but my mother rarely saw my father. He spent his nights at the Latin Quarter, his mornings asleep in the apartment, and his afternoons playing cards at the Friars Club, the renowned hangout for men in show business.

Money became an issue again between my parents. For all that the New York Latin Quarter was a runaway success, the productions were very expensive—each cost $75,000 to $80,000, a huge amount in those days—and the profit margin slim. My father was very generous—he never put my mother on an allowance as some husbands did—but she was always afraid that something would happen to the club or that my father would lose too heavily at cards, and they'd wind up broke again.

This fear was communicated to me from an early age. I became consumed with the same worry. What would we do when the money ran out? I can remember my parents arguing about putting some money into savings, about buying insurance, about making secure investments. My father's response? He went off and produced a series of very expensive musical revues on Broadway. He wanted to be an even bigger success.

His first Broadway extravaganza at the Winter Garden Theater was the *Ziegfeld Follies of 1943*, a revival of the hugely successful musical revues that the great showman Florenz Ziegfeld had produced annually from 1907 to 1931. My father's version was very similar to the show at the Latin Quarter, except even more extravagant. I went with my parents on opening night, and the next morning we held our breath, hoping the reviews would be good. They weren't, but the wartime audiences loved it and kept it running for an impressive 523 performances.

That experience convinced my father to go after more projects on the Great White Way. In short order he wrote, produced, and directed *Artists and Models*, an updated vaudeville revue from the 1920s. The show opened at the Broadway Theater on November 5, 1943, and starred a then-famous singer named Jane Froman, who had lost the use of her legs in a plane accident. She was wheeled onto the stage in a specially built wheelchair. *Artists and Models* also starred a young comedian named Jackie Gleason. But despite the best efforts of its stars, and a very funny Gleason, it closed three weeks later. My father lost a lot of money, but that didn't deter him. Less than three months later he revived and produced another early revue, *Take a Bow*. Even its star, Chico Marx of the famed Marx Brothers, couldn't save it. The show closed after fourteen performances. Thousands more dollars of my father's money were lost.

So here is how we were: my father, a gambler and a dreamer. My mother, a realist whom my father considered a pessimist. Me? I was a worrier whom both parents considered to be too serious for a very young girl.

It all came to a head one afternoon when I returned from school to find my mother in tears. "Daddy has left us," she told me. "You go talk to him. Tell him to come back." Being their go-between was not an unfamiliar role for me. My mother often used me to convey whatever grievance she had. "You talk to Daddy," she would say, and I would try to get to him on those Friday nights when he was home. Most often everything turned out all right, but this seemed far more serious than usual. My mother asked me to take my sister, perhaps to create more sympathy. So I took Jackie's hand and off we went to the Latin Quarter.

I remember very clearly sitting with my father at his table in that darkened, empty nightclub, crying and begging him not to leave us. Jackie, too, was crying, although she was not completely sure what was going on. I learned many years later that my father was said to be having an affair with one of his showgirls. If true, I certainly can't judge him too harshly. Let's face it, it would have made sense. Most people in show business were, and are, romantically involved with other people in show business. My father was surrounded by the most beautiful young women, and he was married to an ordinary, middle-aged woman. For her part my mother would probably have been happier married to a man who worked in the dress business, who brought home a paycheck every week and lived a stable life. But we didn't know anything about a show-girl then.

My father didn't say anything during my plea. He kissed Jackie and me and simply said he had to go back to work. I didn't know what to do. I definitely didn't know what to tell my mother. So I took Jackie to a movie with a stage show playing nearby. I dreaded returning home, and we sat in the theater for hours. But when we did go home, my mother was smiling. She told me my father had changed his mind and decided not to leave. My anguish was over.

I didn't understand then what had made the difference, but I do today. For all his gambling and extravagance, my father was a principled and decent man. He also loved his introverted, shy younger daughter and his touching and sweet older daughter. How could he just walk out and leave us? It is also possible that in his own way he loved his wife. He certainly respected her. The crisis passed.

I FINISHED THAT FIRST YEAR at Fieldston in pretty good shape. I got As and Bs in most of my subjects, but I was lousy at gym. I envied the girls with their hockey sticks running across the field madly chasing after the ball. They were a breed apart. (I always thought, not especially kindly, of this particular kind of girl, confident and athletic, as a "hockey player.") I wished then that I, too, were an athlete. It would have given me some sort of positive identity as a newcomer to the school. But there it was and is. I have never been good at any sport, be it basketball, volleyball, soccer, you name it. I never learned to play tennis. I was bored when I tried golf. I won't drown in the water, but don't ask me to do a backflip into the pool.

That lack of athletic expertise followed me to sleepaway camp. The summer of my first year in New York, I went off to the Poconos with my New Jersey cousin, Helen. She was a terrific girl and I liked her a lot. So, obviously, did everyone else. At the end of the six weeks we were away, Helen was voted not only "Best Athlete" but "Best All-Around Camper." This was the kind of camp that felt every child should go home with some award to show her parents. Therefore, I was voted "Most Improved Athlete." Need I say more?

Although I did well at Fieldston, the school, it turned out, was having a problem with me. It had to do with my father's shows. Every time a new show opened at the Latin Quarter or on Broadway, my mother, Jackie, and I attended. Often after the show we would go with my father to Lindy's, a famous late-night delicatessen. All the show folks in town seemed to end up there, especially the comedians. They all knew my father and made a fuss over Jackie and me. This meant that we got home very late and my mother then would keep me home the next day so I could sleep. Even though I was a good student, the school disapproved of the days I missed. They told my parents that if I wanted to return to Fieldston the next year, I would not be allowed to skip so much school. As it happened it wasn't something we had to consider.

At the end of the school year, my father told us we would again be pulling up stakes and leaving what I'd come to think of as home. I was furious. I had finally made friends. I had a life. Once again I was having to leave it all behind. As the song goes, "Another opening of another show." For me another audition. For my father a new challenge. The Latin Quarter was doing so well in New York that it didn't need his constant attention, and he had another project in mind. Would you believe it? We were going back to Miami Beach.

Miami at War

THE LAST TIME I had gone to school in Miami Beach, the only noises I heard outside the classroom were the shouts and laughter from the older kids who had recess an hour after we did. This time the sounds that resonated were loud masculine voices repeating in unison, "Sound off, one two, sound off, three four."

It was 1944, America's third year in World War II. While I was in high school, the army was ensconced in virtually every hotel in Miami Beach. They had commandeered almost four hundred of them to house the thousands of servicemen being trained under the palm trees and along the pristine beaches to go to war. The U.S. military had taken over paradise, and there was no room anymore for tourists.

The army was in Miami Beach. Across the causeways the navy was headquartered in Miami. I even remember seeing open trucks carrying German soldiers who were prisoners of war. The Germans weren't marching or counting off. Dressed in jeans and shirts with *PW* stenciled on the backs, they were being taken to clean the streets in Miami Beach. There must have been prisoner-of-war camps nearby. But was Miami Beach a paradise for the German prisoners of war? I doubt it. Then again, I didn't give it much thought. As I look back, I didn't give anything much thought other than my own personal life.

Strangely enough I wasn't sure then, and still don't know, why my father wanted to return to Miami Beach. The Latin Quarter on Palm Island had been requisitioned by the army as one of its many commissaries to feed the trainees. The pistachio green house had also been militarized. It was now living quarters for some lucky officers. Our family, however, continued to live on an island, a different one, off the same causeway. Just a short bike ride away from Palm Island, over a little bridge, was Hibiscus Island. Here my father and mother rented a beautiful white house with a lovely lawn and a swimming pool.

So without the Latin Quarter, what were we doing there? I guess my father felt that there was still business to be done, for he rented another club called the Colonial Inn on the outskirts of Miami.

It is not clear to me how long Dad ran the Colonial Inn. There were very few visitors to Miami or Miami Beach because it was almost impossible to get hotel rooms. Perhaps my father felt that he could attract the Palm Beach crowd, just an hour and a half away. There was far less of a military presence there, although how he expected people to drive to his club with such strict wartime gas rationing puzzles me. But I wasn't thinking too much about my father's problems that year. I was in a new school, and this time the auditioning wasn't too tough.

I still knew some kids from our last stint in Florida, and my classmates were nowhere near as snobbish as those in my first year at Fieldston. (I probably still had my white Cuban heels.) Not that there weren't also cliques. Here the cliques were called sororities and fraternities. They had Greek names, and the deal was this: At the start of each school year the older girls and boys of a particular sorority or fraternity invited some of the new kids to join. Ever since this experience, I have always felt that sororities and fraternities are exclusionary, discriminating, and hurtful. But remember that robin who wanted so badly to belong back in second grade? Nothing had really changed.

The more exclusive of the girls' sororities was called Kappa Pi. The lesser sorority was called Lambda Pi. I started off at the beginning of the school year and was told that Lambda chose its members first, but if I waited I would certainly be asked to join Kappa Pi. I was afraid, though, that if I waited I might not be chosen by either, and that was something I couldn't face. So as soon as I was asked to pledge Lambda Pi, I said yes.

Pledging meant giving your total commitment to the group and rejecting friendship with any of the girls in Kappa Pi. Ridiculous? Not at the time. I belonged. I was part of the chorus. I had friends. And I had a good time that year. In case you're wondering if any black ("colored" was the term in those days) girls or boys were asked to pledge, remember that in the 1940s there were strict segregation laws in the South. Miami Beach was definitely the South. So the answer is a resounding no. But we weren't thinking of social issues then, only our own small social lives, which were busy and active. We had after-school dances where I learned to do the jitterbug or, as it was also called, the Lindy. Once in a while now when I go to a wedding and the band strikes up the music of the forties, I watch the sixty- or seventy-year-old men take to the floor with glee, twirl their wives around, and all but throw them over their shoulders. Once you learn the Lindy, you never forget how to do it.

I still wouldn't wear shorts to school, as many of the other girls did, although, believe me, my legs were probably my best feature. (Even today I think of Marlene Dietrich, who supposedly said, "The legs are the last to go.") I had a few boyfriends. One I remember was named Ed Klein. We didn't go steady, as the term for exclusivity was then, but we saw a lot of each other. He was in the class above me. When Ed grew up he became a judge in Miami, and a few years ago he wrote and asked if he and his wife could come to watch my daytime television show *The View*. I introduced him from the audience, and he still seemed like a real nice guy.

Jackie was, by then, a very pretty girl in her late teens, still always by my mother's side. Now and then friends of the family would tell us about a soldier or sailor they knew from Boston or New York and suggest we call him. I saw a bit of one sweet guy, still in his teens, who was in the army. With my mother still asking, "Can't you take your sister?" a double date was arranged with a friend of my new friend.

We went to one of the hotels where servicemen could go to relax. Jackie was quiet, and although I was never very comfortable with her, being the technically younger but ever watchful and emotionally "older" sister, things seemed to be going pretty well. Until, that is, I heard her date asking Jackie to leave us and go off with him alone for a drink. Jackie didn't know what to say or do. I did. I said, "We're going home." I was so afraid that Jackie, in her inexperience and innocence, would be taken advantage of. Did I spoil things for her? She never said a word so I just don't know, but I didn't want to take the chance.

There was another man who was interested in Jackie, and when we got to know him well and trusted him, my parents let him take her to a few movies. His name was Bert something. He was older, in his late twenties, and I don't remember how he came into our lives. He was a perfectly pleasant man, not good-looking, a bit short and plump, but he had a very cheery disposition, and my mother in particular liked him a lot. He seemed to be very attracted to Jackie. He talked patiently to her and something might have come of it, but Jackie showed no interest.

Bert continued to visit for a while, then gradually went out of our lives. I don't remember any other man ever coming around to see her, and although I feel that I am intruding into her very personal being as I write this, I am sure my sister lived her whole life as a virgin.

What I remember most about that period in Florida is not Jackie being with Bert but Jackie again being alone while I was not. This is, of course, a recurring theme in my life. I had a big pool party once at the Hibiscus Island house for my sorority pals and their dates. There was food, music, dancing—a big deal. We were playing Benny Goodman and Tommy Dorsey records and Lindying away when, at one point, I had to go into the house. There, sitting quietly, were my mother and Jackie. My mother was holding Jackie's hand as they listened silently to the music drifting in from my party. My mother, knowing how I felt and wanting me to have a good time, did not, this time, ask me to include my sister, nor did I offer to. It's difficult for me to admit all this, and it makes me feel wretched just thinking about my selfishness. But in general I have to say that year was a happy one for me. We girls of Lambda Pi had get-togethers at one another's houses and planned events with the boys from the fraternities. We went to the beach and to movies. We experimented with makeup. Tangee Natural was the lipstick of choice. You could really smear it on heavily and it still looked like your own lips.

Now and then we had dances at school. I still had to be picked up and dropped off, and with gas rationing this was no easy thing, so sometimes I stayed over at a friend's house. That was a real treat. I should mention that my grades were excellent. I was even chosen "Miss French Club," whatever that meant. It was certainly better than "Most Improved Athlete." Things were definitely okay.

Then, on May 8, 1945, Miami erupted into a giant celebration when the Allies officially declared victory over the Germans in Europe. The defeat of the Japanese in the Pacific was still three months away, but for the thousands of servicemen in Miami, VE Day was the beginning of life returning to normal. My father, who remained British to the core, took us all to the movies to see the newsreel of the nonstop celebrations in London.

The end of the war in Europe was frosting on the cake for my tenth-grade year in Florida. I was looking forward to the years ahead in sunny Florida. But it didn't happen. Shortly after school let out for the summer, we moved back to New York. This time for good.

"A very normal girl"

B Y N OW you know the drill. The new school, on the Upper West Side, was called Birch Wathen, founded by two proper ladies named—surprise!—Miss Birch and Miss Wathen. There were new friends (much easier this time) and a new penthouse to live in (the biggest and grandest so far).

In the postwar euphoria the Latin Quarter was the hottest nightclub in New York. Returning servicemen and tourists flocked to my father's lavish shows, making the club second only to Radio City Music Hall as a tourist destination. In the city that never sleeps, neither did the Latin Quarter. It was open 365 days a year, closing for just two days in 1945 to honor the death of President Franklin Roosevelt. All the biggest stars were now playing there. Milton Berle now started his routine: "I knew Lou Walters before he could speak Latin and didn't have a quarter."

The Palm Island Latin Quarter also reopened after the war to capacity audiences. America was in the mood to celebrate and Miami Beach was booming. More and more hotels were springing up all over Miami Beach, filled not only with war-starved sun worshippers from the North, but with former servicemen who had trained there. Dressed in Hawaiian shirts now instead of khaki, they were returning by the thousands to celebrate with their families, and they all went to the Latin Quarter.

No reason, then, not to have one of the best possible apartments in all of New York. It was a penthouse in the Sixties on Central Park West. The only apartment on the floor, it was surrounded on all four sides by huge terraces planted with flowers and small trees. My parents' bedroom overlooked the park, as did Jackie's. Mine did not, but it had another little room attached to it where other families' nannies had probably slept. So essentially I had my own suite.

The rest of the apartment was vast. There was an enormous wood-paneled living room, a music room with a piano nobody played, a library, a dining room, a huge kitchen with a butler's pantry, four bedrooms, and up a short flight of stairs, a playroom with a bar and its own kitchen and bath, which we never used. One of our butlers did, though. He turned out to be an alcoholic and we found all his bottles stashed up there.

The apartment may have belonged previously to the Hearsts, the billionaire publishing family. When, later, my cousin Selig visited the Hearst Castle in San Simeon, California, he was struck by the familiar paneling and was told by a guard that it had come from the Hearsts' penthouse in New York. In any case there we were in our own castle in New York, with our own treasures. My father filled the library shelves with his growing collection of first editions, the same books that are now in my own library.

My mother, who had decorated all our previous homes herself, really went to town on this one. She bought red leather couches and chairs for the library, but the pièce de résistance was the living room. Here my mother chose a combination of pale yellow and lavender brocade for the couches and chairs. Lots of pillows and tassels. The whole thing looked like a huge Easter egg.

Mother hired a couple to cook and care for all our needs, but she still worried about our financial future. She'd gone from rags to riches to rags before with my father. Well, maybe not rags. More like going to cloth coats from fur. So I'm not sure she really trusted or enjoyed this newfound good fortune. I shared her unease.

We both recognized my father's extravagant lifestyle and his equally extravagant approach to the shows he was producing. The costumes alone cost a small fortune. Many were designed by Erté, the famous Russian-born Paris designer and art deco painter who also designed the costumes for the Folies-Bergère in Paris. The fabrics my father insisted on were top quality—silk, satin, velvet—no rayon for him and his girls. The sequins had to be sewn on by hand because they looked better than machine-stitched sequins. The underskirts of the cancan costumes had to have layers of individual ruffles, not cheaper, all-in-one ruffles. Erté kept designing one more lavishly unique costume after another.

His watercolor sketches for the costumes and the sets turned out to be works of art in themselves. I have collected many over the years. One reads, on the back, "For the finale of the first act." Another reads: "This is for the girl with the red hair." The sketches now cover a whole wall in my apartment.

The sheer volume of custom-made costumes from the Latin Quarters in New York and Palm Island led my father to open his own costume company in a warehouse in Manhattan. He made a sizable profit by renting the costumes to other shows and productions. He also used the expensive costumes to outfit the Latin Quarter touring companies he now began to launch.

There were more and more showgirls to deck out in Erté's unique costumes. There were thirty-six young women in the chorus line, more than any Broadway musical today. Once or twice a year my father went to Europe and came back with new chorus girls and dancers, sometimes more than a dozen at a time. The girls' pay in postwar Europe was a pittance compared to the seventy-five dollars a week my father was willing to pay them. The most prized were the cancan dancers he brought back from the Lido nightclub in Paris. The Parisiennes not only did splits, but defied gravity and anatomy by jumping high in the air and landing *in* the splits. My father's American cancan dancers were somewhat intimidated by the French, but the Latin Quarter audiences loved them.

The only thorn in my father's side, besides my anxious mother, was his partner in both the New York and Florida clubs, E. M. Loew. Perhaps because the one in New York was known as "Lou Walters Latin Quarter," and my father was well-known, the celebrity, E.M., as he was always called, felt compelled to throw his weight around. He had a lot of weight.

He was a large man, loud and vulgar, and he tried his best to make my father seem small, and not just in physical size. He was heavy-handed, the kind of man who would whack you on the back to make a point. He spoke with a thick Russian accent. Well, so did my beloved grandmother, but when Loew spoke it was guttural, and he often spit as he talked. He always called my father "Louie." My father hated being called "Louie." Still, I think my father could probably have lived with that. The real problem was that Loew was a bottom-line bean counter, the dark counterforce to my father's dazzle. He fought every production penny my father spent, every hand-sewn sequin, everything that made the Latin Quarter so singular and special. "Louie," Loew would say. "Vy do you have to get new costumes for the finale? Keep last year's. Who vill know the difference?"

E.M.'s wife, Sonja, was also hard to take. She was noisy and proprietary at the Latin Quarter, demanding special service, ordering everyone around. "I am Mrs. E. M. Loew," she would proclaim. "I own this place." While we always sat with my father in the back of the club, Sonja insisted on being seated at a table in the front row, though those prime, ringside tables should have gone to paying customers. She always had half a dozen hangers-on at her table who drank too much, as did Sonja. Perhaps you have picked up on the fact that the Loews were not my favorite couple.

In retrospect, however, I have to admit that Loew's iron hand on the Latin Quarter's purse strings probably accounted for my father's spectacular fifteen-year run in New York. By reining him in Loew boosted the club's profit margin, but I couldn't forgive him for diminishing my father. Even though I had my own problems with Lou Walters, I recognized his dignity. And after all, he was my father.

Mercifully Loew lived in Boston and was not always on the scene in New York. When he did come, it was as if darkness descended. I had murderous dreams about Loew. They were sometimes so real to me that, in my fantasies, I tried to figure out how I could get away with his murder. Of course I didn't kill E. M. Loew, and he would outlive my father by seven years, dying in 1984. I did not go to his funeral.

During my last two years of high school I was having smooth sailing. I was unhappy at first that Fieldston had refused to readmit me, thanks to my erratic attendance record, but I soon made new friends at Birch Wathen. Again, I studied hard and got good grades. I began to date. Mostly we went to the movies or to another friend's house. Sex was not even a remote consideration. We were years away from the birth control pill. All my girlfriends were virgins. Me, too.

It was a special time to be in New York. On Broadway a whole new kind of musical was gathering steam, shows with songs and lyrics that sprang from and were integrated into the plot. My father took us to many opening nights, and those evenings were as glamorous as you could get. Women dressed in long gowns, often with pearls around their necks and sometimes white ermine coats over their shoulders. Men wore tuxedos. I marvel today when I go to the theater and see much of the audience in jeans and T-shirts.

My father took us to the opening of *Oklahoma!*, which made show business history, thanks to its glorious score by Rodgers and Hammerstein, and ushered in what became known as the golden age of musicals. We saw them all. We went to the opening of the revival of the 1927 epic *Show Boat*, to the romantic *Carousel*, also by Rodgers and Hammerstein, at the Majestic Theater, to Irving Berlin's *Annie Get Your Gun*, which starred Ethel Merman. I'll never forget the opening night of *South Pacific* in 1949, with another exquisite score by Rodgers and Hammerstein and opera bass Ezio Pinza singing "Some Enchanted Evening" to Mary Martin. During this period my whole life felt enchanted.

Our summers were as busy as our winters. At this time there were quite a few big, rambling resort hotels that were open only in the summer—the Lido in Long Island; another, the Griswold, in Connecticut; still another, the Sagamore in upstate New York's Adirondack Mountains. We went to all of them. They were full of kids my age and were very popular.

On weekends the women got dressed up and decked themselves out with all their jewelry. The men, who came from the city only for the weekends, wore dark blue suits and ties. During the week the wives took dance lessons, and on weekends they showed off their fancy new rumba steps to their husbands.

We teenage kids took dance lessons too. One of the instructors had a little crush on me and asked me to dance as often as he could, but he also was paid to dance with my sister. Jackie had no sense of rhythm and sort of had to be pushed around the floor, but she loved it. I had to promise the instructor that I would give him one dance for every dance he gave Jackie. Otherwise she just would mostly have sat on the sidelines.

In my senior year at Birch Wathen, the subject turned to college. I wanted more than anything to go to Wellesley, a renowned all-female college then and now, on the outskirts of Boston, and I applied there. Some of the smartest women I would come to know later in my life graduated from Wellesley—women like Hillary Clinton, Lynn Sherr, and Diane Sawyer. I also applied to Pembroke College in Rhode Island as my "safe" choice. My third application went to a small college located in Bronxville, a town in nearby Westchester. The college was named Sarah Lawrence.

Sarah Lawrence was an all-female college, barely twenty years old, and considered to be very avant-garde and progressive in its education. There were no exams, no required core curriculum, and no actual grades. You took only three major subjects per semester and worked closely with a professor who, following the British tradition, was known as your adviser, or "don." It was a college that attracted the adventurous, the arty, the self-starter scholar, and the debutante. I was none of the above, but I applied because my then best friend, Shelby, was applying.

Sarah Lawrence had a unique admissions process. When you applied you were sent a form and asked to write answers to specific questions, such as, "Name two books you have read recently which you disliked. Tell why." And "Are you concerned with any problem in the fields of government, politics, or economics about which you would like to learn more? Why?" These questions are actually lifted verbatim off my own fifty-year-plus-old admission application, which at my request, Sarah Lawrence recently sent me as research for this book.

I did fine on the two books I disliked—*Eminent Victorians*, by Lytton Strachey, whom I criticized for his lack of "color and realism" in his characterizations, and *The Snake Pit*, by Mary Jane Ward, for being "repetitious" and "not offering the slightest hint as to how to remedy the sorry conditions in mental hospitals." I also did fine on the government question, waxing on and on in my cramped little handwriting about the battle of Labor vs. Capital, about which I cared little, to be honest, but was prompted by reading about a series of recent strikes: a teachers' strike and one targeting AT&T.

However, my hair stood on end when I read the barefaced lies I proffered to Sarah Lawrence so many years ago. My response to "What has meant most to you in your education outside of school?" was: "Sunday school, which helped me appreciate the force of God and enabled me to increase my faith and understanding in His power." Well, I never *ever* went to Sunday school! Did I think a nun was going to read my application? And then absolve me of my sin? I must have, because I can come up with no other explanation.

Another whopper came in my answer about the experience I had had in the arts. While part of my answer was true—I was indeed "particularly fond of dramatics" (I had been in several school plays since my debut as a bird)—what was unbelievable was my claim that I had worked in a summer stock company in Connecticut and "so gained much valuable technical experience." Good heavens! I never worked in summer stock in my life. Thank goodness Sarah Lawrence never checked the facts.

But what was really myth shattering was the portion of the admission forms assigned to my parents. All my life I thought my mother had filled it out and that my father had added one withering, dismissive line: "Barbara is a very normal girl with normal interests." Period. I thought he hadn't given the whole thing much thought. But no. Looking at the original admission forms, it turned out to be my father who had written the entire four-page evaluation and it was immensely tender.

Asked about my high school experiences, he wrote that I took a "good interest" in my schoolwork; that I was proud of my "good work and good marks"; that I make "friends easily and hold them." Asked about my interests, he described me as being "literary-minded" and backed it up by saying that I read "a great deal." He also wrote that I was interested in "dramatic theatricals," had both "initiative and creative ability," and that I expressed myself "clearly and tersely." As to what present interests, if any, he would like me to outgrow, he replied that I had "no trait" that upset him, nor did I appear to him to have "any bad habits."

All this he summed up at the end in that one sentence about my being a "normal" girl. (That's probably what got me into Sarah Lawrence.) But he was no normal, average American father. I held that against him for years and judged what I had always thought to be his one-sentence contribution to the application as proof that he didn't know me at all. Reading now what he actually wrote, I realize that it's quite the opposite—I didn't know him.

In any event I went off to visit Wellesley and was immensely impressed. Along with Shelby, I also visited Sarah Lawrence for a personal interview. The school seemed small, which I liked, but my heart wasn't there.

This is what happened. Wellesley put me on the waiting list. I would not know until late summer whether they would have room for me. Pembroke, my "safe" school, turned me down. Sarah Lawrence wanted me. I was back to the insecurity of Kappa Pi versus Lambda Pi. What if Wellesley didn't accept me after all? Where would I go? I had applied to only those three schools. I didn't have the confidence to wait to see if Wellesley might take me or the courage to call the school and try to convince them that I would be a perfect candidate. So Sarah Lawrence it would be.

Sarah Lawrence

I NEVER TOOK A science course at Sarah Lawrence College. I never took a comparative religion course or a language course or a math class. For years afterward I used to say I didn't learn a thing. And I would jokingly add that if I had, I might have made something of myself. But when I read the course material Sarah Lawrence recently sent me, I realized that was not true.

Part of the reason I didn't delve into the more important academic subjects was that I took a course called "Theater" for my entire four years. At Sarah Lawrence you signed up to take three major subjects in three different areas. One of the majors was Theater. This was amazing to me—one could really just study theater? It was also a solution to a real dilemma: I had absolutely no idea what I really wanted to do "when I grew up." Perhaps because I had spent my whole life in the world of show business, going to clubs and plays and meeting performers and behind-the-scenes people, I thought "Theater" was where I belonged. For me, lacking any other direction, it certainly seemed like a promising course to take. I liked the idea of learning how to construct scenery, familiarizing myself with costume design and lighting techniques, but most of all it was the idea of acting that interested me. I could imagine losing myself in the role of a totally different person. Somehow I felt I would be able to do that.

We were also assigned great plays to read, among them *The Glass Menagerie* by Tennessee Williams, *A Bill of Divorcement* by Clemence Dane, T. S. Eliot's *The Cocktail Party*, and plays by Anton Chekhov and Sean O'Casey. I was especially moved by *The Glass Menagerie*, because it reminded me so much of my sister's situation. In the play there is a rather frantic Southern mother who is trying desperately to find a "gentleman caller" for her emotionally and physically fragile daughter, who spends her days playing with her tiny glass animals. There is also a son, and when the mother too often forces him to find "gentlemen callers," he abandons the family and is then racked with guilt. Although the situation was not exactly like mine, it was similar enough to resonate with me then and even today.

To my joy, in my freshman year, I auditioned for and won the part of Mary Boyle, the lead in Sean O'Casey's *Juno and the Paycock*. We performed the play for three days. The audience was made up of students and any residents of the neighboring towns who might want to come. I remember the thrill of hearing applause and the joy of getting laughs, especially when the laughs came where they belonged. In many of my future interviews with actors, I so often heard that it was in college or university that they first got the acting bug. That was the case with me. I was going to be an actress. I had found my calling.

I did take other courses. I was told that I should consider a science course, so I took something called Psychology of Art, in which I learned that the color red attracts more people than does blue. (That, at least, was helpful later on in deciding what to wear for interviews.) I also took a superb literature course and, in one spring semester alone, read Tolstoy, Thurber, Dewey, and Freud. I took a class taught by Joseph Campbell on the importance of mythology, and I took writing courses because I thought if I didn't make it as an actress I might be a writer. I remember writing a very somber paper on death.

I guess I was trying to explore some of the mysteries of being alive, because in addition to writing about death, I also wrote a term paper on love: Is romantic love a genuine emotion . . . is it something chemical . . . is it an invention of Western society? I still haven't a clue. But now one reads that a possible source of romantic love is chemical and the result of a particular scent. So perhaps love is about taking the right nose drops. Who knew?

Sarah Lawrence was a wonderful environment in which to learn. The classes were very small, anywhere from six to twelve. We didn't sit in orderly rows but around tables. What we did was talk. And discuss. And talk some more. I learned to ask questions and to listen. I learned never to be afraid of speaking up. Every student's point of view was taken seriously, and no one ever said, "That's stupid" or "That's irrelevant."

Our dons oversaw all of our courses, addressed any personal or academic problems we might have, and in general kept us on the right track.

We were also expected to write very lengthy reports on an area of our particular course that most interested us. (I didn't know how to type in those days, and my handwriting is small and cramped. How any of my professors waded through my reports is a miracle to me.) Once written, these reports were dissected and discussed with each of us. All this required a great deal of original thought, research, and organization, which I am certain has helped me with my work, even to deciding which stories I chose to do.

I lived in a dormitory called Titsworth, named after an early benefactor of the school, Julia Titsworth. You can imagine the jokes, but I loved the name. We even had a song I can sing to this day. It goes: "My girl's from Titsworth. She's really down to earth. I get my money's worth . . . from progressive education."

We all lived in suites—two bedrooms with a bathroom in between. I was very fortunate, my first year, to have a brilliant roommate named Myra Cohn, who later became a poet and an author of children's stories. Myra was a senior who had asked for a freshman to be her suite mate, and the college picked me. Myra was the sort of person who wrote impassioned political letters to the school newspaper but also, incongruously, played the tuba. Why? To develop her lower lip, she said.

My four years in Titsworth spawned other enduring friendships. One was with Marcia Barnett, who called me Bobbie, a nickname that stuck for four years. In turn I called her Mike. Another was with a tall, awkward, funny lady named Anita Coleman, to whom I remained close until the day she died of cancer. Her daughter, Liane, is my godchild. Then there was—and is—Joan Rosen, whose father was a judge in Maine. Joan went on to marry Dr. Paul Marks, the longtime president and CEO of Memorial Sloan-Kettering Cancer Center in New York. Joan decided in our junior year that our little group at Titsworth wasn't serious enough, so she moved to another dorm. That same year I was elected president of Titsworth, an office that came with a seat on the college student council. I had no interest whatsoever in the student council but I loved "getting" Joan because I, the unserious one, served on the student council for two years and she did not. Nonetheless Joan and I have been friends for life. She is a very special and accomplished woman who for twenty-six years directed the graduate program in human genetics at Sarah Lawrence (which many universities used as a model) and founded and directed the first graduate program in health advocacy, also at Sarah Lawrence. Both graduate programs bear her name.

Sarah Lawrence was particularly conducive to forging relationships. None of us needed a psychiatrist because we lived in group therapy every day. There were no secrets among us, no privacy. There was one payphone per floor, and when it rang whoever answered it would scream the girl's name—as well as her caller's.

For almost two years I mostly dated doctors. Usually they were young residents. Through one, I would meet another. Marcia Barnett, aka Mike, was going out with someone at Yale Law School, so eventually I switched from doctors to lawyers. I spent a lot of time at Yale. I hated the football games I had to attend, but I definitely enjoyed the stirrings of my sexuality.

One law student boyfriend would take me back to my hotel room after the evening's major activity, which was usually drinking rum and Coke from paper cups. There was no question of his spending the night—those were very innocent days—but I remember pretending to fall asleep so that he could touch my breasts under my sweater. Though kissing was okay, God forbid you should act as if you enjoyed what we called "petting." By feigning sleep, I reasoned, he wouldn't think I enjoyed it. But I did.

Sarah Lawrence was only half an hour from the city, and I went to New York on most weekends. So that you don't think that sex was the only thing on my mind, I sometimes went to Greenwich Village to listen to the lectures given by one of my professors, William Phillips. Phillips, the cofounder of the *Partisan Review*, was an intellectual of the highest order, and I was all puffed up when he took a liking to me. The college's proximity to New York also lured people who otherwise might not have wanted to teach at a far-off campus. One was the noted British poet Stephen Spender. I loved listening to his voice and the way he used language so easily and melodiously.

It was easy to go home for the weekends, but the situation there was still depressing. My father was hardly ever there. Not only was he moving back and forth between Miami Beach and New York, he was also traveling extensively through Europe in search of new acts and talent. That left my mother and Jackie on their own. Almost every single night, my mother took Jackie to the movies. When they ran out of new American movies to see, they went to French or Spanish films, even though Jackie had difficulty reading subtitles—*anything* just to pass the evening hours. Then, a miracle! I passed along a suggestion from Bobbie Altman, a friend at Sarah Lawrence, that my parents buy a television set for Jackie. Television, relatively new, had been a lifeline for Bobbie's sister, who had cerebral palsy. And so a bulky black-and-white Du Mont television set became the center of my sister's life. Television was particularly entertaining for her because she knew so many of the popular performers, like Milton Berle and Jackie Gleason, both of whom had worked for my father. There were several variety shows on the air at the time, and most of them featured the same jugglers, plate spinners, and singers who had appeared at one Latin Quarter or the other. Television provided great entertainment for Jackie, but I don't think any of us realized the impact it would have on our lives. I don't mean just on my own future. It wasn't only Jackie who loved to stay at home to be entertained. Soon it would be the rest of America, which meant that people would not be going out to see showgirls, no matter how extravagantly they were dressed or undressed. The rise of television was the beginning of the end of my father's success.

IT WAS ALWAYS with a sense of relief that I returned to my new life at Sarah Lawrence. President Harold Taylor and his rather haughty wife, Grace, often invited teachers and students to their off-campus house for meetings, lectures, and stimulating conversations. We'd sit on the floor in their house with their big sheepdog, Ben, talking, talking, and talking.

Much of the talk at the Taylors' was political. The country was in the midst of the tense period with the Communist Soviet Union following World War II. The cold war had spawned such paranoia that Congress was investigating anyone suspected of having even the slightest connection to the Communist Party. The House Un-American Activities Committee was targeting the motion picture industry at the time, blacklisting any actor, writer, producer, or director who wouldn't cooperate or name names. A Senate subcommittee was investigating subversive activities among college faculties, and progressive Sarah Lawrence was a prime target. The American Legion had pointed the finger at the college, specifically at Harold Taylor for harboring suspected Communists on the faculty. Soon after I graduated, some faculty members were called to testify before the Senate subcommittee.

I must admit I hadn't felt terribly involved until this took place. Then the witch hunt hit home. Those faculty members were people I knew and respected. This was not something happening in someone else's world. It was happening in mine. But all this occurred after I left college. In the meantime, like most of the rest of the country, I was a bystander.

On and off campus, we watched with fascination the Commie-baiting tactics of Wisconsin senator Joseph McCarthy, who was busily accusing members of the State Department and, later, even the army, of being Communists. Along with my friends, I was appalled at the obsessive destruction of people's lives by the small, powerful cadre of accusers. One of them was Roy M. Cohn. He burst into the Sarah Lawrence consciousness in 1951 as the relentless twenty-four-year-old assistant district attorney in New York who was successfully prosecuting a couple named Ethel and Julius Rosenberg for allegedly conspiring to pass secrets about the atom bomb to the Russians. It was primarily Cohn's cross-examination of Ethel's brother that cemented the Rosenbergs' guilt. Not content with obtaining a prison term, Cohn pressed the court for the death sentence—and got it. The Rosenbergs were sentenced to die in the electric chair at Sing Sing prison, a maximum security facility not far from Sarah Lawrence.

I can't begin to tell readers who are too young to have lived through the Rosenberg trial what firestorms it set off. Tens of thousands of people around the world protested the death sentence. The papers were full of pictures of the Rosenbergs' about-to-be-orphaned young sons, then six and ten. Arguments raged as to whether the Rosenbergs were framed or whether they really were traitors. And Roy Cohn was at the epicenter. He quickly became public enemy number one on the Sarah Lawrence campus as he relentlessly pursued supposed Communists. He had already become a key player in the successful conviction of one suspected Communist, a former member of the Commerce Department, for perjury, and had zealously prosecuted eleven members of the Communist Party for sedition. But the death sentence in the Rosenberg case made Cohn a living Satan.

It was the talk of the campus, the country, the world. Yet I don't remember having a single conversation about the Rosenberg case, Roy Cohn, or Senator McCarthy with my mother or father. Politics were just not a part of their life.

As for me, I was becoming more and more absorbed in my desire to be an actress. I began to doubt that college was the right place for me, and in my junior year I came close to dropping out of Sarah Lawrence altogether. I had been sick that fall with mononucleosis and had missed quite a lot of school, so perhaps my bonds to the college had been weakened. I had loved my leading role in *Juno and the Paycock* and, later, playing the major part in George Bernard Shaw's *Candida*. This was a wonderful role for a woman, although she should have been played by someone more mature than I. The play's director had his problems with me because I was very shy about onstage physical contact with the actor I was supposed to be married to. My character, the wife of a preacher, was having a love affair with a young poet. In the meantime her husband was beseeching her to stay with him. "You're supposed to have some signs of a sexual relationship with your husband," the director said in frustration. "Stroke his arm. Put your hand on his knee." But I was so uncomfortable at the prospect that I could barely touch him. I think I still had to pretend to be asleep to have any physical contact. But I did well enough so that I received, if not a standing ovation, at least healthy applause at my curtain call.

I was now certain that greatness lay ahead of me on the stage. So I went to see Esther Raushenbush, the dean of the college, and told her I was thinking about leaving Sarah Lawrence to pursue my acting career. To my surprise she was supportive. "College isn't for everybody," she said. "If you're really serious about this, then you should try." I had expected her to say, "How can you possibly think of leaving? This school can't get along without you." But she didn't. So I took her advice and I tried.

My father, who knew every producer and theatrical agent in town, arranged some auditions for me. Most of the agents said I needed more experience, but one of them, a very well-known agent named Audrey Wood, set up an audition for me to read for a part in an upcoming production of Tennessee Williams's *Summer and Smoke*. I was incredibly excited. Debuting on Broadway in a Tennessee Williams play was a sure ticket to stardom.

But then, two days before the audition, I panicked. What if I didn't make it? What if I failed? I knew I would take it personally if I didn't get the part, and I couldn't face the rejection. It was just like being back in high school with the same fear I had of being turned down by a sorority or by the popular girls who didn't want me in their group. I knew then, in my heart, that I didn't have the courage or the confidence to face being rejected, perhaps over and over. I was forced to face the fact that I wasn't going to be a great dramatic actress. I had the pull because of my father's prominence in show business, but I didn't have the push. I never went to the audition. Instead, relieved, I went back to Sarah Lawrence for my last year and graduated. I was even chosen to speak for my classmates at the final class dinner for them and their parents.

I realize now that Esther Raushenbush was very wise. If she'd said to me, "Oh no, you can't drop out. You must stay here," I would always have thought she'd prevented me from following my calling. By supporting my youthful yearnings, she'd allowed me to find out for myself that I didn't have what it takes. One of my professors already knew that. "Bobbie came a long way in developing her talent as an actress this term," she wrote. "But she must learn to evaluate criticism." She obviously knew more about me than I knew about myself.

For all the help my father had given me in arranging auditions, I held on to my resentments. Perhaps because I still barely knew him. How could I? I hardly ever saw him. I knew, too, that his relationship with my mother was strained, which didn't help endear him to me. I couldn't forget that he'd almost left us.

In the summer of my junior year at college, my father took my mother, Jackie, and me on a "grand tour of Europe." It should have been a fabulous trip—Paris, the South of France, the Swiss Alps, Venice—but it wasn't. Even though we stayed in the best hotels, the George V in Paris, the Carlton in Cannes, I wanted to be in New York with some new doctor boyfriend, not with my family. Jackie didn't much care where we were, she was just happy that we were all together.

I made some friends on the ship, dated a Persian boy a few times in Paris, and also managed to acquire a French boyfriend, so I couldn't have been all that miserable. In the evenings my father took us to the Lido, the world-famous nightclub with its sensational topless revues. The Lido's owner, Monsieur Guerin, used to swap shows with my father, so he made sure we had the best table in the house. The trip was an extraordinary experience and why I didn't recognize it as the dream it was is beyond me.

We went to the South of France and spent three weeks in Cannes. I got hit on there by the notorious playboy actor Errol Flynn, but I paid him no mind. He was way too old. Far more fun was the group of people my age who were staying at the hotel, the sons and daughters of Hollywood moguls; we went swimming together at the nearby Hotel du Cap during the day and went out together every night.

The big fashion then for us American young women was circular felt skirts, with big felt poodles pasted on them. They came in all colors and looked great when you were doing the Lindy. We wore two-piece dresses during the day—a little top and skirt—to show off our midriffs, but unlike today, no belly button was ever revealed. And we wore panty girdles or garter belts to hold up our stockings. The stockings all had seams running down the back, and you were forever stretching out your legs and looking over your shoulders to make sure the seams were straight. (Seamless stockings and panty hose, a great invention, came later.)

Our bathing suits were one piece, and white was the favorite color. Bikinis were unheard of. It's amazing to me now that we never wore pants. Shorts, yes. But no pants. I remember my mother buying two pairs of red plaid shorts in Cannes—one for me and the other for Jackie. But even though Jackie and I were sometimes dressed alike, she remained isolated. As much fun as I and the rest of the kids were having, my sister, as ever, was not included, which, also as ever, tinged my good times with guilt. I am so bored with saying this, but that feeling was pervasive and rarely faded.

I look back now, and think, "Oh, my poor father!" That trip must have cost him a fortune. He did everything possible to make us all happy. Except for when I was off with my friends, he was with us all the time. He tried to make conversation at dinner, bought us anything we desired. He even danced with us when we were in the nightclubs. (I could have lived without this, though my father was a nice dancer.) He tried. He really did. I, in turn, remained mostly sullen. How I wish I'd thanked him. And I broke up with my latest doctor boyfriend anyway when I came home.

I ENTERED MY senior year of college with some trepidation. All my friends seemed to know exactly what they were going to do after graduation. Anita was going to work in an art gallery. Joan was going to be a social worker. Other friends were going to graduate school or to Europe. That left me. What was I going to do with my life? My problem was that there was nothing that I really wanted to do, and nothing that I thought I was particularly good at.

For two minutes I considered being a teacher, but that required getting a master's degree, and I didn't want to do that. In retrospect I should have, because if I had, Sarah Lawrence would have had to send the graduate school my numerical grades instead of relying on its progressive no-grade system. To be honest, not knowing my numerical grades and how I stacked up compared to others has bugged me ever since. Was I an A student? A B student? Was I smart? Am I smart? Don't laugh. I still wonder.

I wound up taking the path of least resistance and headed home to New York to try and get some kind of job. I had seen an ad somewhere, probably in a bus, that read: "If u cn red ths, u cn ern mo pa." And so while my friends went on to worthier futures, I went to Speedwriting school on Forty-second Street to prepare to be a who-knows-what.

Television 101

*I*ACED SPEEDWRITING SCHOOL. Out of eighty-three students, I am proud to report that I ranked number one, absolute proof that I excelled at something. The fact that what I had mastered was jotting down baby shorthand that used letters rather than symbols didn't bother me. I also learned how to type on a manual typewriter, a machine that has become so obsolete it's probably displayed now in the Smithsonian.

Both skills would serve me well over the years to come, though they didn't get me my first job. My legs did. So said the pink-faced advertising man in search of a secretary who followed me up the stairs to an employment agency—and hired me on the spot. He'd be all but arrested today for such a bald assessment of female anatomy, but it was SOP in the fifties. I did have good legs, and I needed the job. Well, I didn't exactly need a job. My parents would certainly have continued to support me, but I still didn't know what I wanted to do except that I didn't want to go to graduate school. So a job it was.

What a ridiculous caper it turned out to be. Not only did he hire me, but I managed to get him to hire my friend Anita Coleman, and she in turn brought in another friend. So there we were, the three of us, at a little advertising agency whose name I can't even remember. The agency placed mail-order ads to sell vials of perfume. The ads read "Big and Inexpensive." We called the agency "Small and Cheap." And though I excelled at typing and taking dictation, I failed carbon paper big-time. How to make copies of letters had evidently not been part of my curriculum, so when asked to make six copies, I dutifully typed each letter six times. We were wondrously inefficient.

I lasted there around a year. The novelty of working in the Small and

Cheap advertising and direct-mail office cooled off at the same time as my boss was heating up. To show his affection he even gave me a dog named Raul who never obeyed me because I couldn't pronounce my *r*'s too well. I didn't see any future with the pink-faced man with blond hair who seemed to be perpetually surrounded by the vials of perfume he was promoting, and when he became overly amorous I decided to leave. Besides, I had a lead on a job in a much more interesting business.

Television.

I didn't know much if anything about the television business then, but I sure knew of the importance of television in people's lives. My mother and Jackie spent hours watching programs like *I Love Lucy, Arthur Godfrey and His Friends, Texaco Star Theater,* and *The Jack Benny Program.* Television was their main source of diversion. There were four networks to choose from—ABC, NBC, CBS, and the short-lived DuMont, all of which started their network programming in the late afternoon. The rest of the day and some of the night belonged to local stations, which did their own programming, and where I had a lead for a job.

A friend of mine, Rhoda Rosenthal, was working at WNBT, NBC's affiliate in New York, and she told me there was an opening in the publicity department. "I got my job," she coached me, "by telling them my father had contacts in show business," a rather startling claim since her father manufactured dresses. In my first job search I had deliberately avoided using my father's name, wanting to get a job on my own. But pull was pull. So, besides listing my Speedwriting and typing skills on the job application, plus basic French, I added that I was Lou Walters's daughter and personally knew most of the Broadway columnists.

That was true. Sort of. I had shared many a table at the Latin Quarter with columnists like Hy Gardner, Leonard Lyons, and Earl Wilson, but I had always been in the role of my father's daughter and not of a personal friend. Still, all's fair in love, war, and job applications—and it worked. After a meeting with Ted Cott, a vice president at NBC and the station's general manager, I was sent to meet Phil Dean, the director of publicity, promotion, and advertising, who immediately hired me as his assistant.

The two of us were the entire publicity department, which gives you some indication of the infancy of the television industry. Phil was kind and easygoing, but he spent a whole lot more time at Toots Shor's restaurant than he did at the office. Phil claimed he was doing research at the noted hangout for show biz celebrities and athletes (Yogi Berra, the New York Yankees catcher, once remarked, "Toots Shor's is so popular nobody goes there anymore"), but the reality was that he rarely got back to the office before 3:00 p.m., and when he returned he was rarely sober. So I wrote nearly all of the WNBT press releases, sometimes a half dozen a day.

Learning to write those releases was invaluable experience. Television was considered such minor entertainment at the time that newspapers did not have TV critics. Instead sports and gossip columnists were expected to add television to their regular beats. As a result most TV press releases were tossed into their wastebaskets. Some papers even punished a columnist who'd erred in some way by assigning him (there were no "hers" then) to cover TV. So I learned fast to start each release with a startling fact or a provocative anecdote to catch their attention, something I still do today with my interviews. I remember one release I sent out: "WNBT to feature a star-studded panel on sex." Sex worked just as well then as now, and it got great pickup.

When I wasn't writing releases, I was calling the columnists I knew and planting items about the station's talent. All those years of sitting silently at my father's table at the Latin Quarter really paid off when I actually started talking. The columnists all took my calls, and I got an amazing number of items about our local shows into nationally syndicated columns. I also began to truly appreciate my father's positive reputation and popularity.

Then there was another development: I was soon going out with my boss, Ted Cott. Ted, who had two small children and was in the middle of a divorce, was the head of the station and had the reputation at NBC of being brilliant and innovative. Both were true and were what attracted me to him. (I was then, and still am, attracted to men who are smart and powerful. I'm not sure why. I think it's because I'd always hoped there would be a strong, successful man to take care of me so I wouldn't have to take care of myself.)

Ted was at least ten years older than I, balding and short, with a little bit of a belly. Even with the belly, he was the first man I slept with. In his "bachelor" apartment in Greenwich Village. To be honest it wasn't really passion that made me take the plunge—I just thought it was time. I was in my twenties and still a virgin while many of my friends were not only married but having children. I don't remember many of the details of that night, so it couldn't have been either very wonderful or terrible. I do remember thinking rather sadly that from that moment on, whatever happened, for the rest of my life I would never again be a virgin.

But then I told myself to shut up. "It's time already," was my silent mantra.

Ted, the protégé of RCA's pioneering chief, David Sarnoff, knew everybody in the media in New York and entertained quite often at his apartment. I sometimes acted as his hostess, and learned the value of networking. Through Ted I met Tex McCrary and his beautiful model and ex-tennis-star wife, Jinx Falkenburg. They had a long-standing radio show, *Tex and Jinx*, and an extremely popular TV show, *At Home*. I also became friendly with Eloise McElhone, a very attractive and funny woman who was making the transition from radio to her own show on television. Though I didn't know it then, Eloise would play an important role in my career.

Ted was a very creative boss. About a year after I started there in the publicity department, he launched a training program to teach the younger employees how to produce television shows. I drew a daily fifteen-minute children's program named *Ask the Camera*. The director was a young redhead named Roone Arledge. Years later Roone would become head of ABC News and a legend in both the sports and news businesses, but then he was just a friendly guy who drove his convertible every day to the studio to direct various programs.

The format of *Ask the Camera* was simple. People sent us questions, and we answered them with film clips from our archives. Because we had a relatively small film library, I would often have to make up questions that matched what film we had available. We had a good clip of hippopotamuses, for example, so I wrote the question: "I've always wondered, how does a hippopotamus eat?" Though the ethics may have been questionable, I felt it was okay because I was acting as a producer, not a journalist. I also wrote the voice-over narration for the show's host, Sandy Becker, and edited the film to fit the time. I got so good at it that eventually I didn't need to use a stopwatch. I could both write copy and edit film almost to the second. I still can.

I didn't physically cut the film myself, the film editor did. But we worked it out together, hunched over a machine called a Moviola and going through the film clip frame by frame. I'd tell him exactly which scenes I wanted, and he would cut and splice them together into a cohesive whole. I also learned the fundamentals of what made a good story in that tiny editing room. If you have a strong beginning—a must—and a powerful ending, then you don't really need a dramatic middle. That is the formula I still follow today.

The production work somehow landed me in one of the first issues of *TV Guide*. I guess I was a novelty, being both female and the daughter of Lou Walters. I was pleased by the little piece titled "Young Producer," which cited me as an example of the "bright young people in responsible jobs" in television and suggested I was the youngest producer in the field. I still have a copy of that *TV Guide*, dated May 15, 1953.

My father was proud of the piece, but he didn't take television very seriously. By 1953 half of all American homes had at least one television set, and more than seven million new sets would be sold the next year and again the year after that, but he didn't recognize television as a rival to his nightclubs. When I pointed out to him one night that more people watched the Tex and Jinx TV show *At Home* in a day than came to the Latin Quarter in a year, he acknowledged the numbers, then countered: "But my customers *pay* to see my show."

I was, of course, still living with my family. Young single women didn't have their own apartments then. And the penthouse was so huge we certainly weren't on top of one another. At one point my cousin Selig lived there as well. He, too, was working in television, producing a local cooking show called *Josie's Kitchen*. One of the segments featured South African lobster tails, which resulted in the South African Lobster Tail Institute, or some such organization, gratefully sending him a huge crate of frozen lobster tails. My parents and Jackie were in Florida, and Selig and I lived on that lobster for weeks. It didn't matter if either of us was eating alone or was having people for dinner; we ate South African lobster tails. For all I know the people who are currently living in the apartment are still eating South African lobster tails.

I'm not going to say that everything I know about television I learned during my tenure at WNBT, but I certainly learned a lot. One lesson was—and is—not to assume anything, especially on live television. I learned that from a famous society gossip columnist at the time, Igor Cassini, who wrote for the *New York Journal-American* under the pseudonym Cholly Knickerbocker. Ted had given Cassini his own talk show, and I was asked to produce it. My job was to write Cassini's introduction on a cue card as well as the questions he would ask each guest. But we never got past the introduction. I assumed, fool that I was, that Igor Cassini would know his own name, so I simply wrote his initials on the cue card for the introduction. "Good evening," he intoned when we went on air. "I am I.C."

For all the fun I was having working at WNBT (which would become WNBC in 1960), I was increasingly *not* having fun with Ted

Cott. I wanted to go out with other men. Ted was jealous and possessive. He repeatedly asked me to marry him, which made me pull away even more. I wasn't in love with him. I was still waiting for the man of my dreams, but Ted persisted to such an extent that he began to wait outside my apartment building on Central Park West for me to come home on nights he knew I was out.

It came to a head when I started dating Joe Leff, a highly eligible young bachelor whose family owned a successful knitting business and whose cousin and sister had both gone to Sarah Lawrence. I liked Joe a lot, which sent Ted over the edge. One night when Joe brought me home, Ted suddenly emerged from the shadows and challenged him to a fistfight, right there on the street. To my horror they began to struggle and hit each other. Believe me, having two men physically fight over you is not the exciting fantasy some women harbor. Fortunately they had the good sense to stop attacking each other and to walk away. Needless to say the incident ended my relationship with Ted. And my job at WNBT. Ted had become so obsessive and controlling that I had no choice but to quit. And Joe, whom I really liked, evidently didn't like me all that much. He stopped calling.

Ted must have regained his senses after that because he went on to marry a beautiful woman named Sue. Joe, too, moved on and married a beautiful woman named Joyce, who would later become my best friend. After the sidewalk confrontation on Central Park West, however, I was left high and dry.

Luckily a new job quickly materialized and I went to work at another local New York station, WPIX, on the *Eloise McElhone Show*. I knew Eloise from those parties at Ted's apartment and liked her a lot. She was a little outrageous, a little overweight, and very, very funny. My official title was executive producer, but in reality I was also associate producer, writer, script girl, guest booker, and coffee maker. Multitasking was the norm in those early days of television when the programs were so understaffed that it never dawned on me to question the workload. We had to fill a half hour every day with anything we could find: interviews, cooking lessons, fashions, exercise demonstrations, pet advice, even a segment called "Answer Your Male," about relationships. I wrote many of the letters Eloise would supposedly "receive" as well as the answers to those letters, her introduction of her guests, and the questions she would ask them. I also prepared the graphics, chose the music for each segment, and then sat in the control booth when we went on the air and prayed that somehow it would all work out. To the second. That is why my answer to all the young people who ask me how to get into television is: go to your local television stations, take any job that's offered, and work your fanny off. Volunteer for everything without looking at the time clock. Learn how it all works. Crises happen. Producers don't show up. Guests don't show up. Scripts are lost. Be in place.

Make no mistake: television is a demanding business. To be successful in it you have to be somewhat obsessive and, as a result, it is hell on your social and romantic life. Eloise McElhone paid a price back in the fifties when her husband, perhaps wearying of the hours she was spending away from him and their children, upped and left her for another woman. Eloise went through a very sad time, but I have to admit I was relieved when the show went off the air for the summer.

And what a summer it was! I went to Europe with my dear friend from Sarah Lawrence, Anita Coleman. The ostensible reason for our trip was to visit Anita's boyfriend, Warren Manshel, who was working temporarily in Paris, and get him to propose marriage to her, but what I wanted was adventure. We both got what we wanted.

Paris. The South of France. Italy. Anita and I each had brief flings with two Italians—hers was tall, mine was short. These were sun-filled days and starry nights. It was divine. When Anita got back to Paris, Warren proposed and she accepted. Her parents flew over and there was a fairy-tale wedding on the isle of Capri.

As for me, I was free, free, free! In mid-July I stopped by an American Express office in Rome to see if I had any mail (American Express was the customary mail drop then for travelers) and found a letter from WPIX informing me that the *Eloise McElhone Show* had been canceled and I was no longer needed. I was thrilled. I jumped up and down on the Spanish Steps. I had the rest of the summer to myself. Maybe the fall, too. Maybe my whole life. My parents, always generous, sent me money to stay in Europe.

I went back alone to the South of France, where I had friends, and then moved on to Paris, where I decided to live for a while and try to get a job. I found an inexpensive hotel on the Left Bank, had my hair cut short with bangs like Audrey Hepburn. Young, thin, and American, I got a job modeling for the House of Carven. "Vous avez une bonne taille," Mme. Carven told me, which meant I was the right size for the petite clothes she was introducing.

Can you imagine? Me! A model in Paris. With Audrey Hepburn hair. There weren't too many American girls in Paris then, and I was a popular novelty. I had many friends and several boyfriends. I even thought I was in love. Fred, a Frenchman, was funny, charming, and somewhat elusive. It was Paris. We had a little affair. He liked me but he didn't love me, and he sure didn't want to marry me. "Tant pis," as they say in Paris. Too bad. My heart hurt a little, but it wasn't broken. It's hard to have a broken heart when you're having the time of your life.

I remember walking to the flower market one beautiful, early morning and sitting on a bench, surrounded by bouquets of brilliant flowers and thinking, I'm happy. Utterly and completely happy. As a reminder of that moment of perfect contentment, I later bought a small Childe Hassam painting of that same flower market. It hangs in the front hall of my apartment in New York, where I see it every time I come in or go out.

My father, however, finally put an end to my French idyll. "It's time for you to come home," he wrote to me in November 1954. "Meet me in London."

I dutifully went to London, where he was producing a command performance of a Latin Quarter revue. (A command performance was, and is, a stage show put on at the request of a monarch or a head of state.) In London I looked up friends I had made in the South of France and I was gloriously wined and dined, which made it somewhat easier not to miss Fred. What wasn't easier, however, was when I realized, to my shock and deep fear, that I had missed my period. I was woefully ignorant of birth control and suddenly terrified that I was pregnant.

I remember sneaking off to see a surgeon in London (where they are called "Mister"), but he wasn't sure whether or not I was pregnant. It was too early to test (and the at-home, early pregnancy tests of today had not yet been developed). I didn't know what to do. Abortion was illegal. If indeed I was pregnant, how would I go about getting one? What would I tell my mother? I was frantic. It was a wrenching time for me and one that has made me even more supportive of women in similar predicaments and their right to choose their own fate.

Soon after my father left London to return home, I followed, sailing on the ocean liner the SS *United States*. My spirits were decidedly low, my fears high, until suddenly, on the second day at sea, I got my period. I was euphoric during the rest of the voyage, which is probably why I recall so fondly my assigned seatmates at meals—Bob Hope's mother-in-law, Teresa Kelly DeFina, and a young Greek shipping heir named Alexander.

When I got home I went down to Florida to visit my parents and Jackie. They were staying at the new, very popular Fontainebleau Hotel, with its lush twenty-acre grounds and legendary "lagoon" pool. I know I should have been agitating to get back to New York and find a job, but I was enjoying my lazy tropical life.

I especially enjoyed it when Alexander came to visit me from Palm Beach, where he was staying, but whatever romance there might have been vanished over lunch. My father had a poolside cabana overlooking the ocean, but Alexander, whose taste ran to caviar and champagne, rapidly lost interest in me when he saw the people in the adjacent cabana digging into their corned-beef and pastrami sandwiches. Maybe it wasn't just the pastrami. Maybe it was also a bit of anti-Semitism. Either way I never saw Alex again.

I did meet two other men during that idyll in Florida, however, who would play pivotal roles in my life. I remained steadfastly loyal to one of them in the face of enormous criticism. The other I married.

Bad Choices

ROY COHN and Bob Katz. An improbable pairing. They never met each other, but I met both of them, for better or worse, during that leisurely time in Florida. My first meeting with Roy was brief, and for me, quite unpleasant. He was evidently a frequent visitor to the Palm Island Latin Quarter, because when I went to the club one night, there he was, sitting with my father. "This is my daughter Barbara," my father said by way of introduction. "She said she wanted to meet you." I immediately corrected him. "I *am* your daughter," I said. "But I *never* said I wanted to meet him."

Why would I want to meet Roy Cohn? I detested everything he stood for. After the Rosenberg trial in 1951, he had become even more notorious as chief counsel to the Senate subcommittee investigating American Communists, headed by the Communist-obsessed Senator Joseph McCarthy. By 1955, the year I met him, Roy had become a national celebrity of sorts from the Army-McCarthy hearings the year before, the first congressional hearings to be nationally televised.

Twenty-two million people had watched the gavel-to-gavel coverage of those hearings during the thirty-six-day live television marathon in the spring of 1954. Twenty-two million! It was high drama. There was Roy with his distinctive slicked-back hair and dark circles under his eyes—I thought he looked like a lizard—sitting by the side of the glowering, satanic McCarthy, leveling charges at everyone who came into their sights. And then, on June 9, McCarthy went too far.

He was in the midst of impugning a young associate of the army's chief counsel, Joseph Welch, when Welch uttered the famous words that triggered McCarthy's downfall—"Until this moment, Senator, I think I never gauged your cruelty or recklessness," he said. "Have you no sense of decency, sir? At long last, have you left no sense of decency?"—and the gallery in the Senate hearing room burst into applause. So, unseen, did many in the television audience and others wept happy tears. It was an extraordinary moment. It was as if the bully everyone was terrified of were suddenly stripped naked and people realized there was nothing left to fear. McCarthy's popularity immediately began to plummet, and his reign of ideological terror was over. When the hearings ended inconclusively, Roy resigned but McCarthy was soon censured by the Senate. He would die, three years later, of alcoholism-related hepatitis.

Roy, however, managed to rise from the ashes. He was only twenty-eight when I first met him in Florida, and on his way to becoming one of the most powerful and feared lawyers in New York. He also remained one of the most unpopular men in America. No, I did not want to meet him.

The man I did enjoy meeting in Florida was Bob Katz, an eligible bachelor considered a catch by many eager young women in Miami. I didn't disagree. I also thought, after my carefree time traipsing around Europe for months, that it was time for me to get married. Bob was ten years older than I, good-looking in a dark, smoldering way, well-mannered, a good athlete, and a good dancer. If he wasn't powerful, he was certainly an attractive prospect. His father, for whom he worked, was the largest manufacturer of children's hats. Hardly an exciting business but a very successful one—most children wore hats then and everybody had new Easter bonnets. Unlike show business, it was also a stable business, which appealed to me for obvious reasons. So I started going out with Bob, whom I immediately nicknamed (for my friends) "Katz Hats."

I was seeing another man at the same time, Henry Epstein, who was almost the opposite of Bob. I had met Henry in France, and I enjoyed his company enormously. He was very intelligent and intense, unlike Bob, who was quite phlegmatic and didn't seem to have any passion in any direction. But Henry was short and squat, and not half as physically attractive as Bob. To me, then in my early twenties, short and squat was a turnoff. Though Henry was much more interesting than Bob and a shrewd businessman—he'd made a small fortune in New York real estate and lived in a penthouse on Fifth Avenue—I thought I was supposed to marry a man my friends and I agreed was attractive and sexy. Most of my pals thought Bob was. So I turned Henry down when he proposed and said yes to Katz Hats.

The truth is, no matter whom I married in those days, it wouldn't have worked out. As I'm sure you can tell by my decision-making process, I didn't know who I was, what I wanted, or where I was going, if anywhere. Young women like me graduated from college, got their first jobs, then left to get married. I'd already had *three* jobs, unlike my friends who'd all followed the unspoken timetable and been married for several years. And so my rather dreary engagement to Bob Katz began.

We spent time with his family. We spent time with my family. My father certainly didn't have much to say to Bob or his father, Ira Katz, manufacturer of children's hats, but then again, neither did I. The boredom grew so heavy that after a couple of months I broke the engagement.

Then two things happened. Instead of pleading with me not to leave, Bob agreed easily with my decision to call off the wedding. That bothered me tremendously. I could understand perfectly why I didn't want to marry him, but how could he not want to marry me? I felt rejected and somehow a bit frightened. What was wrong with me?

Then there was the bookkeeper at the Katz family business. She hated me. Plain and simple. Bob's mother was dead, and the bookkeeper had assumed her maternal role. She zealously looked after Bob's father, as well as Bob and his brother, and called them "the boys." I was evidently "the girl" who was going to upset her family, and she made it very clear, in her coldness and sometimes downright nastiness toward me, that I was not welcome.

I couldn't handle the rejection, so I overruled my misgivings. I told Bob that I was fully content with him and that I was looking forward to living in his one-bedroom apartment on Horatio Street in Greenwich Village, a far cry from our penthouse on Central Park West. He must have believed me because I won him back. And I must have believed myself because I tried to woo the bookkeeper as well. For some reason I thought I had to prove myself to her, to convince her that I was a good person and not some shallow, hedonistic flibbertigibbet. She was constantly warning Bob that I was a spendthrift, so I went to the other extreme. I called her one day to tell her I had bought my entire trousseau wholesale at the designer Anne Klein, and my wedding dress on sale at Bergdorf Goodman. I even sent her the receipts to prove my thriftiness. So peace was declared, a formal wedding was planned, as was a return trip to Europe for me, where Bob would also buy supplies for Katz Hats.

Looking back it all seems insane, but I know I did it. Maybe it was the fifties you-must-get-married mentality. Maybe it was my strong desire to stabilize my life. In any event I was determined to marry Bob Katz—until two days before the wedding. Then reality set in. I was marrying a man to whom I had nothing to say. I felt trapped and scared. My mother understood and sent me to talk to my father at the Latin Quarter. He was sympathetic, too, but, as so often, removed. He pointed out that the invitations had long since been sent out. The rooms had been booked at the Plaza Hotel for the ceremony and reception. The caterers were lined up, as was the orchestra. There were even matchboxes with our names and the date printed on them in gold script. "My darling, this happens to every bride," he said. "You'll feel better when it's over."

And so, in June 1955, my father walked me down the aisle. My sister, Jackie, was my maid of honor. There were several hundred guests, some of whom, I'm sure, shed a few tears. But I was the one who really wanted to cry. My heart had never felt so heavy, but then again, my heart would feel just as heavy every time I married (I've been married three times), which is why, as I write this, please know that I will *never* get married again!

Years later, when I gained some celebrity on the *Today* show, stories about me would refer to my marriage to Bob Katz as "Barbara Walters's Secret Marriage!" Well, it was hardly a secret, but it was quite miserable. Or at least I was.

I won't belabor you with all the details, but I remember that when we weren't sightseeing on our honeymoon, we had little to talk about. I knew in my heart and in my mind that I was not at all in love with Bob. And even though he was physically attractive, I felt little sexual desire for him. During many of the days, Bob was busy buying straw and ribbons for the next season's crop of children's hats. In those times I did whatever sightseeing Bob wasn't interested in by myself. I was not unhappy then.

I was also not unhappy when our honeymoon was over and we returned to New York to what was now "our" apartment on Horatio Street. It was time to play wife. I spent my days cleaning the small apartment, walking around the neighborhood, which was new to me, watching television, and burning the spaghetti sauce. I didn't look for a job, nor did I socialize much with my friends.

My mother came down to the apartment soon after I moved in to help me fix it up, but the dark, tweedy gray bedspread I picked out on Fourteenth Street only made the apartment gloomier. She had tried to convince me to buy a hot pink bedspread, but I was trying to be practical and reasoned that the dark gray bedspread would last much longer and wouldn't show the dirt. That dull bedspread seemed like a perfect symbol of the marriage.

Bob was a decent man, but it became clearer every day that we had nothing in common. I wanted to shake my despondency, and I tried. I shopped, more or less cooked dinner, asked him about his day at work, spent time with his family, and watched television with him at night. Bob left the apartment very early and didn't like to go out once he returned home. We both knew the marriage was in trouble and decided things might be improved if we moved uptown nearer my parents and friends. We applied a temporary Band-Aid by renting a small but cheerier apartment at Eighty-first Street and Madison Avenue. I decorated it and had a small dinner party or two, but I was still depressed. It would be years before the book and then the film *Diary of a Mad Housewife* elicited such recognition from housewives like me, but in the fifties, women thought their unhappiness was *their* fault, and their fault alone. So I did what so many other women did: I went to a psychiatrist.

He was a young man with a placid face and, in true Freudian fashion, rarely asked me a question and rarely made a comment while I prattled on about my failures as a wife. What I needed then was some advice on how to either live in this marriage or how to get out of it. He was no help at all.

One possible solution, Bob and I agreed, was for me to go back to work. I was pleased to have his support. At that time very few reasonably well-off married women worked outside the home. It was seen by some as a failure on the husband's part to make enough money. But Bob liked the idea that I'd be able to buy my own clothes and be more financially self-sufficient. And so it was, in 1955, that I got another job in television, this time at CBS as a writer on the year-old *The Morning Show*.

Early-morning television had become a phenomenon with the debut of the *Today* show on NBC three years before, and CBS was trying to play catch-up. At the outset few had thought anyone would want to watch television between 7:00 a.m. and 9:00 a.m., but the creator of the *Today* show, NBC vice president Sylvester "Pat" Weaver (Sigourney's father), had proved them wrong. In spades. Within eighteen months of its debut, "Weaver's folly," as skeptics had called it, became one of the most profitable programs on the air, and, of course, remains so to this day. There we were at CBS, trying to challenge the highly popular host of *Today*, Dave Garroway, and his even more popular sidekick, a chimpanzee named J. Fred Muggs. You know the old show biz adage about never following an animal act? Well, we weren't following J. Fred

Muggs, we were trying to beat him. It was a near-impossible task. That chimp got more fan mail than Dave Garroway and even made a highly publicized world tour.

This is not to say *The Morning Show* did not have its share of talent, even if they were *Homo sapiens.* A young Walter Cronkite and Charles Collingwood were the first cohosts, with future Olympics broadcaster and *Wide World of Sports* legend Jim McKay doing the sports reports. By the time I arrived Collingwood had been replaced by the actor Dick Van Dyke, who would go on to win three Emmys for his own long-running TV series with Mary Tyler Moore. The program then, as with the morning shows now, was a mix of news and entertainment; the boundary lines were already somewhat blurred. But in 1955 Dick was up against it at CBS. We all were.

My job was to write and produce segments, mostly fashion shows using live models, which would help attract women viewers. There was no thought of my appearing on television. The only on-camera job for a woman then was as a weather girl.

Speaking of weather, we used our reports primarily to boost viewership of *The Morning Show.* One gimmick followed another. First we tried cartoons. Then, for a short time, the national weather report featured a young woman supposedly underwater in a glass tank drawing circles on a map with a grease pencil to show the area being forecast. Then we tried an archery champion shooting arrows into a straw map. But no matter what we did, nobody watched the show. Looking back on those segments, perhaps it was understandable.

A new production team was brought in, with extraordinary talent: Fred Freed, who would later move to NBC and hire me for the *Today* show; his associate producer, Robert "Shad" Northshield, who would also move to the *Today* show; and the show's talented director, Av Westin, who would stay at CBS for twenty years before moving to ABC to become executive producer of—guess what?—*20/20!* I had no way of knowing then that I had joined a fraternity of colleagues and friends with whom I would work for the next thirty years. All I knew was that the show was fighting for its life.

Replacing Dick Van Dyke with Will Rogers Jr. and renaming the show *Good Morning!* did not help. While Junior had the easy smile and familiar twangy voice of his famed cowboy-humorist-columnist-entertainer father, he didn't have his father's common touch. Or any touch at all. Behind his back we added a clause to Will Rogers Sr.'s famous quote that he'd never met a man he didn't like—that is, until he met his son. Will Jr. didn't have his father's humor, either, despite the efforts of his young writer, a fellow named Andy Rooney. Even Andy couldn't instill much spontaneity into Will, but every bit of wit or wisdom he uttered came out of Andy's typewriter.

For all the show's floundering, there were memorable moments, at least two of which involved me. I made my on-camera debut on *Good Morning!*—in a bathing suit. When one of the models for a bathing suit segment called at 5:30 in the morning to say she wasn't coming, Av Westin drafted me to take her place. "Go out there," he told me. "Put on the suit and talk about what you're wearing." So I did, praying I'd remember to hold in my stomach. To this day I have the photograph of my first and last television appearance on *Good Morning!* and I don't look half bad, though nobody ever called me from *Sports Illustrated* for their bathing suit issue.

The second memorable moment came from a tragedy: the collision on July 25, 1956, of the Italian luxury liner *Andrea Doria* and the Swedish ship *Stockholm* in a dense fog bank off the Nantucket Light. Fifty-one people were killed, but many others survived, thanks to the ships that answered the distress calls, including the *Ile de France*. A thousand passengers from the sinking *Andrea Doria* were brought to New York during the rescue, and Av Westin ordered me to go down to the pier, in the middle of the night, to see if I could persuade some of the survivors to be on the show. This was my first hard-news story, and an invaluable experience in dealing with chaos. Many of the passengers were in shock, others hysterical. "What a horrible experience you've been through," I said to one after another. "You must be feeling terrible. But could you come into our studio tomorrow morning at 7:00 a.m. to tell us about it?" A surprising number—at least to me—said yes, and I preinterviewed them so I could help plan the broadcast. The next morning we went on the air with what proved to be an exclusive report on the collision. As horrible as the accident was, I had a sense of genuine satisfaction that we beat the *Today* show to the story.

It is always a difficult call when you are interviewing people caught in a tragedy. We all cringe when we see reporters shoving a microphone under a victim's nose and asking, "Did you lose anyone? How do you feel?" But sometimes, as with the case of the *Andrea Doria*, the questions must be asked so that the viewer can appreciate the extent of the misery. There are times when you want to put your arms around a distraught person but you must restrain yourself. It isn't considered professional. Tact, sensitivity, and common sense are all important. Maybe the right word is "judgment."

But there are the times when your own emotion does take over. Not long ago I was doing a story on transgender children. I was talking on camera with a ten-year-old girl, born biologically a boy. As she was describing her deep sadness, she burst into tears. Instinctively I took her in my arms to comfort her. When the program was actually aired, my producers felt that I was not behaving as a reporter and might be criticized. We cut that section out.

The *Andrea Doria* experience was the first of many such situations I would face with people in genuine distress, and even though we celebrated the scoop, it was short-lived. Not long afterward *Good Morning!* folded. So did the subsequent writing project CBS assigned me to. It was a good concept, a series titled *The Day That . . .* We made two pilots, "The Day That FDR Died" and "The Day That a Plane Crashed into the Empire State Building." (The accident, a chilling precursor to the terrorist attack on the World Trade Center fifty-six years later, took place in July 1945, when a B-25 bomber, lost in a dense fog, flew into the seventy-ninth floor of the then-tallest building in the world, killing fourteen people.) But neither documentary ever went on the air, and the project died, leaving me without a job.

It was later written that I went on welfare after I was let go, but that's not true. I did, however, go on unemployment for the first and only time in my life and collected the benefits I was entitled to while I looked for another job.

I was also looking for a place to stay. My parents were living in Florida. Bob Katz and I had decided that our three-year marriage had died a natural death, and I wanted to move out of the apartment. Bob could afford the rent better than I could, so I moved in with a kind friend from my school days at Fieldston, Marilyn Landsberger. I went down to Alabama and got a divorce in one day. I felt empty and defeated. Oddly enough I also felt as if the marriage had never taken place. I didn't miss anything about my relationship with Bob. As I look back now, I can barely remember it.

I never saw Bob again, except for one strange experience more than twenty-five years later. I was on my way to a dinner party in New York and my escort and I were entering the building just as a vaguely familiar-looking man was exiting. He said hello. I said hello. And he left. "My God," I said to my escort. "That was my first husband!"

What I do remember vividly is that at the same time I was getting a divorce, another far more devastating "divorce" was taking place in the family, this one the business partnership between my father and E. M. Loew. I knew the blood had been bad between them for years. Loew continued to challenge every penny my father spent on costumes, on scenery, on talent, until my father couldn't stand it anymore. So he walked away from the gold mine he had founded and sold his share in the Latin Quarter to the partner he had long detested.

My mother, when he told her, frantically tried to talk him out of it, but my father was adamant. She was beside herself with worry, as was I. The Latin Quarter had been the family's life support system for more than twenty years and suddenly it was gone. "What's going to happen?" I asked my father, barely masking my own long-standing fear that I would end up supporting the family. But he reassured me. "Don't worry," he said. "I'm opening another nightclub that will be even more successful."

That was my father's dream—to have nightclubs all his own, with no business partner to rein him in. Even bigger, more lavish nightclubs than the Latin Quarter. First, one in Miami. Then another in New York. He'd call his new clubs the Café de Paris. As for the money it would take to open the clubs, well, that was no cause for concern. My father had sold his share of the Latin Quarter to E. M. Loew for $500,000. He could borrow whatever else he needed from friends, from his family. No problem.

The Café de Paris opened in Miami in the fall of 1957. It was struggling, but my father began making plans for the new club in New York. "The Café de Paris will be everything you can imagine," he announced to the press. "We'll take the audience on a tour of Paris, the Moulin Rouge, cancan girls. Stars from France, Italy, London, ice-skaters, and, best of all, a mermaid swimming in a huge supposedly champagne-filled crystal goblet."

He rented the former Arcadia Ballroom on Broadway and Fifty-third Street, a huge space with seating for twelve hundred. He spent a fortune turning it into the largest nightclub in New York, with six stages, all done up, as he described the color scheme, in "shocking pink and golden white."

My mother and Jackie moved up from Florida to a suite of rooms in a medium-priced hotel in New York, the Navarro on Central Park South. Every dollar was going into the new Café de Paris. If my father had any worries about the Miami club, he didn't show them. He should have. Miami was having one of the worst winters ever—freezing cold, lots of rain—resulting in far fewer snowbirds. Not only was the season a disaster, so was the economy. The country, still reeling from a recession in the early fifties, was entering another. The result was that the Miami Café de Paris was forced to close at the end of its first season.

But neither the gloomy news from down south nor the downturn in the national economy bothered my optimistic father. He'd been there before. "Recession?" he scoffed. "I've never had any trouble with that before. Back in Boston in '32, people were selling apples on the street. The week Roosevelt closed the banks was the biggest week I ever had at the old Cascade Roof." To my father the recession was not a problem but a plus. "When things are tough people are likely to go out at night," he said. "They need a first-class escape, and I'm going to give it to them."

Missing from his thinking was the realization that television was taking over New York nights. The performers he presented to the public for a price could be seen on television for free. The era of the great nightclubs was ending.

He also didn't anticipate the vitriol E. M. Loew was leveling at him for opening up rival nightclubs so close to both Latin Quarters. Loew went to court and won a temporary injunction prohibiting my father from using his own highly recognizable name, "Lou Walters," on the marquee for the Café de Paris. Then came trouble with the unions, which many suspected Loew had a hand in—electricians, carpenters, painters, sound and light men began not to show up on schedule. Next the suppliers—linens, food, liquor—staged their own slowdown. Even the club's liquor license was held up, until the very afternoon the Café de Paris was due to open. But open it did, on May 22, 1958. My mother, Jackie, and I were at my father's table, as ever, when the extravaganza got going. The headliner was Betty Hutton, the exuberant blond singer/actress who had soared to fame in the films *Annie Get Your Gun* and *The Greatest Show on Earth*. "Welcome to Lou Walters's rent party," Betty quipped to the packed house on opening night, a reference to the exorbitant rent my father was paying, supposedly the highest in New York.

Betty remained a terrific draw and filled the club for the duration of her weeklong contract, but even at that, the impressive $70,000 the Café de Paris took in was still $10,000 less than my father needed to meet expenses. And it went downhill from there.

First, Betty turned down a two-week extension of her contract, an extension my father had been counting on.

Second, my father's frantic search for a new headliner to replace her ended with a complete loser: the controversial rock-and-roll singer Jerry Lee Lewis, best known for tearing up pianos and marrying his thirteen-year-old cousin. The café was practically empty on Lewis's opening night. Lewis himself didn't show up for his second night. And the "goblet" containing the swimming mermaid cracked and shattered, drenching some of the patrons and sending the mermaid to the hospital.

My father was by now desperate. He had the nightclub's high rent to pay and a huge payroll to meet. He tried to borrow more money from his family in New Jersey, but they turned him down. I remember my father's brother finally telling him: "Look, Lou, we'll loan you money for yourself, but we're not giving you any more money for your nightclub."

The staff at the Café de Paris was more sympathetic. The maître d' lent him money. So did the maître d's wife and the waiters and the busboys and the cigarette girls. And so did I. I had a new job by then, in public relations, and I emptied my savings account and gave my father all I had, $3,000.

It wasn't nearly enough.

It Gets Worse

*I*N JUNE 1958 my father tried to kill himself.

It happened several weeks after I had moved in with Marilyn and her parents (two of the sweetest people I've ever met). Marilyn and I were having breakfast one morning when my mother telephoned from the Hotel Navarro. "I can't wake your father up," she said, her usual matter-of-fact voice sounding close to panic. "He just won't wake up!"

I knew that the Café de Paris was in serious trouble, but the idea that my father would try to take his own life was not something I had ever imagined. Or had I? Was this the nightmare I had always dreaded? Everything over? Everything gone? I had no time to think. I grabbed a taxi and raced to the hotel to find my father, in bed, ashen and unresponsive. I tried to shake him. Nothing happened. I screamed, "Daddy, Daddy!" No response.

Somehow, despite my own panic, I called an ambulance. Paramedics arrived almost at once and took my father out of the hotel on a stretcher. I knew my sister shouldn't come to the hospital; it would traumatize her. But she certainly couldn't stay alone at the hotel. So my mother stayed with Jackie, and I went with my father in the ambulance. Please, dear God, I kept repeating to myself, don't let him die.

I knew as we sped to the hospital that our lives would change drastically whether my father lived or died. But for the first time I had the most overwhelming feelings of love and compassion for him. I kept stroking his face and saying, "Daddy, Daddy, Daddy." All my resentment was gone. My poor, miserable father. So in debt. His beloved new nightclub a failure. His heart so heavy that he didn't want to live. Yet he had never discussed his grief with my mother, and I had been too involved with my own problems to explore his.

The ambulance took my father to Mount Sinai Hospital, where the doctors and nurses saved his life. He had taken a heavy overdose of sleeping pills, the kind he had been taking in far lesser amounts almost every night for years. They pumped his stomach and did whatever else they needed to do to bring him back from the brink. Eventually he was wheeled into a private room and put into a bed.

His room was on the first floor of the hospital. I learned that this was where the hospital put people who had attempted suicide. I guess they were afraid the patient might try to jump out the window. But when my father was conscious, he just lay in the bed, weak, pale, and mostly silent. By this time my sister understood what had happened, and both she and my mother were there with me. My father was out of danger and slept most of the time. We never left his side. We hovered around him, but he didn't say a word to us about his suicide attempt. Not then, not ever.

Did he do it to spare himself the humiliation of his failure? Was it because he was so deeply in debt and hoped the insurance policy he always talked about would support my mother and Jackie? If this was his thinking, was it possible that he didn't know there would be no money from insurance? My father, it turned out, had borrowed heavily on the policy. There was nothing left for the family. Whatever his reasons, we never asked why. We were just happy he was alive.

This is the first time I have ever revealed that my father tried to kill himself. It was a deeply personal matter, and I felt we had to protect his reputation. Not even his brothers or sisters were told what had happened. I knew the newspaper columnists would learn from the staff at the Café de Paris that my father was in the hospital. I had to reach them before that happened, so I called the most influential of them all, Walter Winchell, who, in addition to his column, had one of the most listened-to radio programs. If he didn't like you, he could be a ferocious enemy, but from my father's earliest days in New York, he had been kind. We even occasionally had dinner with him. I told Winchell that my father was suffering from exhaustion and had suffered a mild heart attack. I was giving him the story first, I said, an "exclusive." Whether he believed me or not, that is what he reported, and that's what was picked up in all the news stories and columns that followed. Looking back as I write this, I wonder how I had the wits to prevent the real story from coming out. But I did. My father's honor and privacy were preserved.

My father stayed in the hospital for about a week.

While he was hospitalized his friends in the business and the staff at the Café de Paris made superhuman efforts to keep the club going. In an extraordinary gesture of support, some of the biggest stars of the moment offered to appear at union scale wages—$125 a week. Singer Dorothy Lamour, who had skyrocketed to fame in the *Road* movies with Bob Hope and Bing Crosby, performed for four days. Others played for one night, famous comedians like Henny Youngman and Joey Adams. Joey's widow, Cindy Adams, is today a well-known columnist. She and I are good friends, and if people sometimes wonder why we're so close, they should know how long my relationship with Cindy and her late husband goes back.

My father also got support from other columnists who always liked his soft-spoken manner. "Seems like everyone is pulling for the game little fellow lying on his back at Mount Sinai Hospital, suffering from exhaustion and a heart attack," wrote Lee Mortimer, in the *Daily News*. Lee had a reputation for being a real SOB, but not where my father was concerned. My father, such a gentle man in such a rough business, was liked and respected by all the Broadway columnists.

For all the goodwill, however, the club could not regain any momentum, and barely a month after the Café de Paris opened, it closed. The vultures descended. Creditors appeared out of the woodwork, some demanding to be paid back the money they'd loaned my father, others demanding to be paid for outstanding bills. Everything at the club was up for grabs: the tables, the chairs, the fancy decor. I went down to the disaster scene and asked for only one memento—my father's old typewriter.

The days of the penthouses were over. My parents could no longer afford the Navarro Hotel, and I realized I could no longer impose on my friend Marilyn. Living with my parents and Jackie was also out of the question. Not only did circumstances preclude it, I was a grown-up divorced woman. I couldn't and wouldn't retreat into my past. So I had to look for my own apartment, the first I would ever live in alone, and it had to be cheap.

When my father was released from the hospital, the solution to several of my parents' problems was for them to move back to Florida, where my father could regain his strength and convalesce. They owned a very nice house on North Bay Road, one of the best locations in Miami Beach. My mother hoped the sunny weather would begin to lift his deep depression. There was no thought of his seeking professional help. My parents were of the generation that would never have considered a psychiatrist. Instead there was gin rummy.

To my mother's everlasting credit, she, the determined noncardplayer, played gin with my father every day. It helped him keep his mind sharp, and she even became pretty good at it. While she had not always been supportive of her husband in the past, she was a mountain of strength during his emotional breakdown. Slowly he improved and the black fog began to dissipate, but he was still in no shape to deal with the reality he was facing in New York. Which was rapidly getting worse.

"What's wrong?" I asked my mother, hearing the fear in her voice when she called me one morning from Florida. "Taxes," she managed to say. "Your father owes taxes in New York and he can't pay them." And so the next horror began. In his need for money to keep the Café de Paris open, my father had failed to report or pay various business taxes, including the payroll taxes which he had put back into his floundering business. The IRS was coming after him.

The government put a lien on the Florida house. My parents had to sell everything—their car, the house, and the entire contents of the house. The tax agents even took the chandelier off the dining room ceiling.

In all the times my mother had worried about reversals in her husband's finances, I don't think she ever thought things would be so dire that they would lose the only home they owned. But despite all her past complaints, she was a very strong woman. When things were the worst, she was the strongest. So she packed up the few things she was allowed to keep and began to look for a small apartment in Miami Beach that they could rent. It was important that the apartment be in walking distance of a supermarket, as neither my mother nor father could drive at that time. During all this my mother did not blame my father. It was too late for that, and she was concerned about his fragile emotional condition. My sister understood everything but knew there was nothing she could do but try to help my mother pack. Poor Jackie. She was exposed to all the vicissitudes of her parents' life with no personal life of her own into which to escape. As for me, I talked twice a day to my mother, assuring her that things would get better, even though I had trouble assuring myself. What a dark period for us all.

As all this was going on I became obsessed with finding the money to pay off as many of my father's debts as I could. I had from early childhood felt responsible for my parents. Hadn't my mother always told me of her problems with my father? I grew up sharing her concerns about his financial state. What was happening may have seemed like a nightmare, but I had dreamed it all before. I didn't know where I was going to find this money. We were not really in touch with my father's family, and remember, they had already refused to loan him money for the Café de Paris.

Into my life at that time came a saint, or at least I thought he was. His name was Lou Chesler, a Canadian with a rather dubious reputation as the czar of gambling casinos in the Bahamas. He had been a habitué of the Latin Quarter (both the Florida and New York clubs) and was fond of my father. I had met him several times, but we barely knew each other. When he learned that my father was ill, he telephoned me to ask about him. I didn't mention the suicide attempt, but I did tell him that Dad was in bad shape. However, I said quietly, I was sure we would be all right.

Wise man that he was, Mr. Chesler wasn't so sure. He gently asked me if my father had debts. Did he need money? I said he did and that I was trying to pay them off. I certainly was not thinking of asking *him* to pay them off. And then came the amazing offer: With no more questions asked he lent me $20,000, a very substantial amount of money at that time, or any time for that matter. "You don't need to pay me back," he said. I was grateful beyond words and I certainly didn't refuse the loan—my pride was not stronger than my need. But I wasn't a charity case. I wanted to repay it. And I did, little bit by little bit over the years, until I paid back the whole thing.

It still seems incredible that this man, almost a total stranger to me, came to my family's rescue. Perhaps my father had treated him with the respect others had not. Or perhaps he was touched by the sense of responsibility I, as a young woman in her twenties, had for my father. Whatever the reason, like something from a corny movie plot, he gave me the money. I never forgot Lou Chesler, and it gives me pleasure to write about him today.

My parents left the big house on North Bay Road and moved into the small, inexpensive rental my mother found in Miami Beach. It was off-season, which was a very good thing, because I had now become the sole support of my mother, father, and sister. Everything I had always dreaded might happen *had* happened. There was no time to cry and I was too busy to feel sorry for myself.

So here is the big question: If my parents had not descended into financial ruin, would I have had the success I have had? Would I, after my divorce, have moved back in with Mom and Dad, perhaps taken a vacation, hung around until I could get another job in television? Was all this, in a strange way, my destiny? (By the way, my daughter always says that one of the first things I taught her was that she must always be able to support herself.) I guess it's really impossible to know the answer about the whole destiny business. But my feeling is that the answer is yes. Very definitely yes.

I couldn't find a job in television, which was what I really wanted. I didn't have the luxury of holding out for a job I loved, so I took the closest thing. I went to work in the so-called radio and television department of a public relations firm called Tex McCrary, Inc. Remember the *Tex and Jinx* radio and television shows from my days in the publicity department at WNBT? Well, Tex was now a partner in the growing PR firm. I heard that there was an opening, and Tex was receptive to my joining the company.

Tex had formerly been a very good newspaper editor, and although I never liked public relations, I learned a great deal from him. He taught me how to put together a story. "Get them with the first line," he would say. "Put your facts in the second line." He was a good teacher to me, and to many others. Another of his "pupils" at the time was a young man named William Safire, a junior partner in the firm in charge of the radio and television department. To be accurate, Bill was in charge of me. Because, except for his secretary, Bill and I were the entire staff of the radio and television department.

Bill, who became a Pulitzer Prize–winning columnist for the *New York Times*, had grilled me during my job interview about what was going on in the New York scene and who was what to whom. The job entailed getting positive stories about the products of the firm's clients into newspapers, radio, and television, so knowing the players in the media was essential. And of course I did, because of my father and the work I had done at WNBT, WPIX, and CBS.

When I got the job, I also got my own apartment, in a Manhattan building owned by friends of my parents. It was a rear apartment overlooking the backs of several other buildings, at Seventy-ninth Street and then-unfashionable Second Avenue. It was rather like the apartment I lived in when I was married to Bob Katz—one bedroom, a living room, and a tiny kitchen. Most important, it had a frozen rent. That is, a very low rent that would not be raised every year. It was a godsend.

Cousin Shirley helped me fix up the dark little apartment. We bought a thirty-nine-dollar yellow rug for the floor, which helped somewhat, but the few pieces of old furniture I'd gotten from my parents' apartment didn't look right. Shirley decided we should paint some of the pieces black and cover the rest with black contact paper, which we did, unaware that what seemed old-fashioned to us was indeed antique.

But Shirley still wasn't satisfied. She went out, came back with a pink dish, plunked green grapes on it, and said: "There. That spruces up the whole apartment." I just adored Shirley.

My life settled into a routine. I took the bus to and from work every day. There was a supermarket across the street from my apartment, and most nights, I would go there, buy a package of sliced bologna and a big roll, head home to make some coffee, and have what I thought was a delicious dinner. I rarely cooked except for an occasional scrambled egg.

I had a very good friend from college, Dorothy Sheckman, who had worked in Paris after graduation and had a wardrobe of magnificent couture clothes from fashion houses like Dior and Balenciaga. She gave me two divine outfits she had grown tired of wearing. From Dior, a pale blue-gray fitted wool dress, and from Balenciaga, a black satin cocktail gown, cut low in the back. How I wish I had both dresses today! I've probably never been as chic as I was back then. So, if I was alone, it was bologna sandwiches, and if I had a date, Parisian couture.

I wore one of those dresses when I turned thirty. But neither the dress nor I went out that night. I was supposed to go out with a dashing young socialite stockbroker I'd met by the name of Gianni Uzielli. I washed my hair, did my makeup, put on my lovely dress, and I waited. And I waited. And I—well, you get the picture. Gianni stood me up. I never found out whom he went out with that night since he never called again, but years later he married a lovely young woman, Anne Ford, granddaughter of Henry Ford.

Not an auspicious beginning to my fourth decade. But then, neither was my first date with guess who? None other than Roy M. Cohn. Roy had somehow tracked me down and kept calling to ask me out. I kept turning him down. My extremely negative opinion of Roy Cohn hadn't changed, but finally, perhaps out of curiosity (after all those weeks of watching him on television, I wondered what he was really like) or, more probably, needing to take a break from the bologna sandwiches, I said yes.

Roy picked me up in his car. People then drove around New York more than they do now. We were going to the "21" Club, the most exclusive restaurant in New York at the time, which was a tonic in itself. But it wasn't "21" that made our first date so memorable; it was how we got there.

The traffic on West Fifty-second Street ("21" is still there, just west of Fifth Avenue) was at a complete standstill. The traffic lights changed from red to green and to red again, but nothing moved. Except for Roy.

"Come on," he said suddenly. "We're getting out." And with that he simply got out of the car, slammed the door, and started walking toward the restaurant. I scrambled after him in disbelief. He had abandoned the car. Just like that. In the middle of the street. I remember thinking he had to be the most arrogant, inconsiderate man I'd ever met, but then again, I was an accomplice of sorts, even though I couldn't drive. I was so startled, so caught up in the sheer chutzpah of his bolting from the car, I just got swept along. I have no recollection of how I got back to my apartment after dinner. He probably called some flunky to pick up his car, and took me home in a taxi. Anyway, that was my real introduction to Roy Cohn.

He called again, and then again, but I ducked him as much as possible and saw him very infrequently. When I did see him, I must admit I found him interesting. He seemed to know everything about everything and everyone who was somebody. He was also very funny in a sardonic way. I was never physically attracted to him, nor, evidently, was he to me—outside of a quick kiss on the cheek, he never asked for more. So now and then, when he called, I said yes and we went out. Nothing close to serious. Besides, I had a new beau who, in his way, was every bit as unlikely as Roy: "Philippe of the Waldorf."

Claude Philippe had for years been the very well-known head of the catering and banquet department at the Waldorf-Astoria Hotel, hence the unofficial title. He was in charge of everything from weddings to all special events. I had met him some years before when my father and I went to the Waldorf to check out the hotel as a possible setting for my wedding to Bob Katz. Philippe himself met with us because the bride-to-be, me, was the daughter of Lou Walters of Latin Quarter fame, but for all Philippe's personal attention, my father had chosen the Plaza because he thought it was classier.

I remet Philippe at Tex McCrary, Inc. He had become a client of the agency after his falling-out with the Waldorf, caused by a highly public indictment in 1958 for income tax evasion. He had been loudly proclaiming his innocence ever since and still had a great reputation as a rather flamboyant manager and a connoisseur of food and wine, so I guess his indictment didn't bother me too much—or many others, for that matter.

Despite the charges against him, Philippe had been snapped up to head the food, drink, and catering business at two other hotels, the Summit and the Americana, and both hotels became clients of Tex McCrary, Inc. I was assigned to get publicity for their star attraction.

Claude Philippe and I had a delightful lunch. He had been born in Paris, was enormously charming and very witty. He knew all about wine, food, restaurants and was the epitome of sophistication. He started to call. I was thrilled. And so began two of the most romantic years of my life. That he was married to an actress in Paris did not bother me. They were separated. She lived in France. He rarely saw her, he said. There was talk of divorce. I wasn't thinking of marrying again, so his being married somehow didn't bother me. Neither was I bothered by the eighteen-year difference in our ages. Philippe was elegant, worldly, exciting, and a master of the intimate gesture—bouquets of yellow roses, love notes in French, a sprig of fresh lavender for my lapel. I was mad for him.

I never told my parents I was seeing Philippe. The reaction of Shirley, who kept referring to him as "the headwaiter," was bad enough. But I didn't care. Philippe and I were both so busy we didn't see each other much during the week. The weekends, however, belonged to us, and they were magical.

Philippe owned a big, rambling house in Peekskill, New York, and we went there almost every weekend. He was an avid gardener, and my job was to plant new beds of pachysandra. Gardening is not my strong suit—I didn't know pachysandra from poison ivy—but I dutifully spent hours on my hands and knees mucking about in the dirt. And I learned how to plant pachysandra. I wish instead I had learned about wines, but education was not on my agenda with Philippe.

The magical parts were not the daytimes but the evenings. Philippe had an old, quite crotchety but warm-hearted housekeeper who tended the house, along with a humorous young man who helped out on the estate. Philippe would cook us the most delicious meals, complemented always by a bottle of the finest wine, and we would linger at the table, in front of a roaring fire, talking and laughing. Then we would go to bed. Philippe, older and more experienced than the men I had known, was a great lover, tender and passionate. I grew up sexually. We never spent the whole night in the same room, however, because I didn't want the housekeeper to think that we slept together, so I would jump up every morning and tiptoe into the guest room. (What can I say? It was a different era.)

There was never company. Our weekends were just for the two of us.

After a year or so Philippe and I occasionally did talk about getting married, which I may have done had he pursued it. I was in love, probably for the first time. But Philippe dragged his heels about getting a divorce. Instead he decided it would be a good idea if we rented two apartments next to each other. I didn't think that was a good idea at all. So we meandered along with no real goal and, as so often happens, the relationship eventually cooled. Philippe finally did divorce his wife, but by then it was over between us. For a couple of years, however, our time together had been extraordinarily romantic and very sophisticated. Like the Cole Porter song, it was "Just One of Those Things." And looking back, I have only two regrets. One, my French didn't improve. And two, I never did learn a thing about wine.

Throughout my relationship with Philippe, I would from time to time still hear from Roy Cohn. Roy didn't take well to rejection, so he was trying a typical ruse. He was attempting to take control of my life by buying his way in.

Roy had taken over Lionel trains in 1959 from a distant relative, the inventor Joshua Lionel Cowen. Owning the wildly popular electric train sets and their many accessories, like smoke pellets and operating grade crossings, had been the dream of almost every American child for decades. But sales were declining at the end of the fifties as children turned more to model cars and airplanes. Lionel needed a PR boost and Roy, because of me, gave the account to Tex McCrary, Inc. I was still trying, in general, to avoid him, but I was grateful because the account gave me a huge boost in prestige at the firm. (It didn't, however, give me a bonus. The agency never offered and, afraid of losing my job, I never asked.)

The trains also gave me yet another boost—with the *Today* show. The host of the popular morning show was still Dave Garroway, with the ubiquitous J. Fred Muggs. And guess what Dave Garroway loved above all else? Lionel trains. At Christmas he accepted from us an elaborate train setup, and then he played on the air with the new locomotives and cabooses and whatever other Lionel products I kept supplying for free. In those days before payola became a no-no, he'd then take them all home. Nobody cared, least of all me. The publicity for our client was worth all the free cabooses he wanted.

Beyond Dave Garroway's obsession with Lionel trains, the *Today* show was one of the most receptive outlets for all our clients' products. For most of the time I worked at Tex McCrary, *Today* had to broadcast three hours of live programming every day, although it was on the air for only two hours in the morning. Videotape technology didn't arrive until 1958, and the first hour in the East had to be repeated for the Midwest and the West. Few guests on the show were willing to wait around for an hour to repeat their interviews or demonstrations or whatever for the third hour—a very different mind-set from today, when TV publicity is all-important—so *Today* needed every gimmick it could find to fill the time. I supplied many of them.

The agency's biggest coup, however, was orchestrated by my boss, Bill Safire. The setting was the American Exhibition in Moscow in 1959. Bill's client was All-State Properties, Inc., a mass manufacturer of affordable tract homes. And the principal characters were none other than Nikita Khrushchev, the premier of the Soviet Union, and Richard Nixon, vice president of the United States.

Are you old enough to remember the famous "kitchen debate" between the number one Communist in the world and the number one capitalist? Well, it took place in Moscow because Bill Safire somehow managed to maneuver Khrushchev and Nixon, who were touring the exhibition, into All-State's model all-electric kitchen. There, against the backdrop of our client's ideal kitchen, complete with stove, refrigerator, dishwasher, and washing machine, with flashbulbs flashing and television cameras whirring, Nixon extolled the quality of affordable housing for workers in America. The images ran on the front pages of every newspaper the next day and led the television news. Brilliant.

I had nothing to do with Bill's coup in Moscow, but it certainly made it easier for me to get our clients' products into the media and on television. It was not very satisfying work, but I was not in a position to be choosy, since I desperately needed the paycheck for my own expenses as well as to send whatever I could to my parents. I liked Bill Safire enormously, but I felt I was underpaid for all my hard work, so I worked up the nerve to ask him for a raise. He turned me down. Instead of money he gave me a lecture about supply and demand. Women looking for a job, he said, were in large supply. The demand for such women, however, was slim. Therefore I should be grateful for what I had. I was. No raise.

He understood me in a way I didn't understand myself. My insecurity led me to be a workaholic, to eat lunch at my desk, never to miss a day of work, to make more and still more phone calls on behalf of our clients. I rarely relaxed, which he obviously noticed. That is why, at an office Christmas party, his gift to me was a sheer, black, shorty nightgown with matching lace panties. I was somewhat embarrassed but also delighted. Today when we are so concerned with sexual harassment such a gift might not be well received. But given my relationship with Bill, I knew that he didn't mean the gift as a come-on. We never dated, rather it was a sweet way of noting that underneath my no-nonsense veneer I was still a female, maybe even a sexy one, and I should enjoy it.

Save for my time with Philippe, however, I rarely indulged in enjoyment. I couldn't. I worried constantly about my family and the tax case hanging over my father's head.

It took a year but my father gradually regained his strength and somehow remained the showman he'd always been. While the tax case in New York dragged on in the courts for two years, he was hired to produce lavish shows at the fashionable Deauville Hotel in Miami Beach. That led to a five-year contract at the Tropicana Hotel in Las Vegas, where he imported the entire Folies-Bergère from Paris beginning on New Year's Eve in 1959. The Folies-Bergère was an enormously popular French extravaganza with beautiful showgirls, elaborate costumes, and entertainers who sang, danced, juggled, and in general put on a terrific show. It was just up my father's alley. He knew the managers of the Folies-Bergère and his introduction of it to Las Vegas was a big event. The audiences, accustomed primarily to just one big attraction, loved the whole show. My father now was definitely back on his feet, even if no longer his own boss. But he still owed a great deal of money to the IRS.

Before he found work in Las Vegas, my father had occasionally come to New York. When he did, he stayed in my small apartment, sleeping on the other twin bed. I didn't like this. I had never shared a room with either of my parents, and it made me uncomfortable, but there was no extra money for a hotel. The one time my father did stay at a hotel I got such a scare when I telephoned him and there was no answer. I kept calling. No answer. Terrified that he had attempted suicide again, I ran to the hotel and banged on the door. My father, rubbing sleep from his eyes, opened it. He was fine. Just sleeping late, by habit.

He spent a lot of time trying to work out his tax problems, and I thought he had succeeded. He certainly made it sound as if everything was working out. But then, in the fall of 1960, came another frightening phone call from my mother.

I was expecting my father in New York when my mother called from Las Vegas to say he wouldn't be coming. When I asked her why, she said, in that tone of voice I had come to dread: "He can't. Or he'll be arrested."

Arrested!

I sat down hard while she told me that he had missed the latest in the endless series of court dates in New York and a warrant had been issued for his arrest. He'd told the court that he couldn't afford any more trips to New York, but the judge was evidently unmoved.

I couldn't believe it. My father a criminal? Unable to return to the city he loved and to which he had contributed so much joy? I felt sick. I didn't know what to do. I realized I was shivering and drew a hot bath. I was in the tub, crying, when the phone rang. It was Roy Cohn.

"What's the matter?" he asked. Lord knows why, but I was so upset I told him what my mother had said. "Get dressed and come meet me and we'll talk about it," he said. I did. For years my friends have wondered why I became a loyal friend of Roy's. I remember Walter Cronkite once asking if he could put a very personal question to me. What was the question? "How could you possibly have had Roy Cohn for a friend?"

I understood—and still understand—how people ask such a question. Here is the answer I have never given before. When I got out of the bath and dressed, I met with Roy and told him exactly what was happening. A week after that meeting, the charges against my father were dropped. Did Roy perhaps pay the back taxes himself? I doubt it. He had strong connections and friendships with most of the major judges in New York. Roy's father, Albert Cohn, had himself been a judge. Over the years, for one reason or another, Roy had done a lot of favors for various judges and politicians. So a much more likely scenario is that he asked for a favor in return. And got it.

I don't know exactly how he did it. I asked but Roy would never tell me. All I know is that, because of Roy, the arrest warrant against my father was dropped and the court case was settled. My father's reputation was restored. He was able to come back to New York. Forget the ethics of the matter. We are talking about my father. After what he did, Roy had my gratitude and loyalty from then on.

Television 102 and a Strange Marriage Proposal

*D*o you believe in fate? Luck? Timing? All of the above? Well, I must, because today I might well be the president of an important head-hunting employment agency recruiting executive secretaries and prospective CEOs. I think I might have been really good at that job, but fate, luck, or timing intervened. Here's how it happened.

By 1961 I had more or less had it at Tex McCrary. I was tired of trying to sell clients who were not suitable for television. My pal and boss, Bill Safire, had left the agency to open his own PR firm. (He would later fold that company to go to work as a speechwriter for then president Richard Nixon.) There still seemed to be nothing for me in television, so I took myself to a top employment agency, deciding it was about time to start a new career. Instead of sending me out to other companies, they offered me a job right there to go to work for them, screening and hiring secretaries. They gave me a couple of days to decide, and I was on the verge of saying yes. Just think of what a good interviewer I would have made, probing prospective secretaries. Instead, while I was trying to make my mind up, I got an offer from *Redbook*. The magazine had heard about my work at Tex McCrary, Inc., and was offering me more money to publicize their articles. So I said okay, thinking, I'm back in the public relations trap again but at least it's a trap I know.

So off to *Redbook*, where I was bored and somewhat unhappy, but it didn't matter. Working was not a choice for me but a necessity, and this was the best job I could get. I often think of all the men—they were mostly men at the time—who had to work at jobs they really hated until they got to the next step, the next promotion. Unlike some of my women friends who had jobs but could quit or get married if things got tedious, the men and I *had* to work. It's all changed now, of course, and many women face the same need to earn an income. But back then the burden fell mostly to men, whether or not they enjoyed what they were doing.

I didn't much enjoy what I was doing at *Redbook*, but it wasn't torture. Then, one absolutely wonderful day, I got a call from the new producer of the *Today* show, Fred Freed, saying he needed a writer. It wouldn't be a long-term job, he told me, it was for a limited time on a limited segment, but if I wanted to try it, it was mine. Did I want to try it? Is the pope Catholic?!

I realized I was giving up a steady job for something that was short-term, but I loved working in television—the creativity, the interesting people, the whole atmosphere. And unlike in PR, I wasn't constantly selling. Moreover, I felt if I worked hard and did well, I just might be offered a permanent position on the staff.

I should remind you that I had known Fred Freed back in my CBS days. He was one of the producers on the morning show I wrote for. Fred would go on to be one of the great creators of television documentaries, but then he had been brought in to revitalize the *Today* show, which was getting slightly draggy. Another footnote about Fred: He was also the father of a young producer I would later work with on ABC's newsmagazine, *20/20*. Her name is Kayce Freed Jennings. She is also the widow of Peter Jennings. When I worked for her father, I remember Kayce as an adorable little girl. Now she is a strong and talented woman. Anyway, back to 1961.

In order to get new advertisers on *Today*, the NBC brass decided to actually sell a piece of the program to a single sponsor. Rather than having a string of commercials from different companies, they wanted to be able to say: "The next half hour is brought to you by so-and-so." The so-and-so they got was S&H Green Stamps, which was owned by Sperry & Hutchinson, a successful consumer-marketing-rewards business. S&H, in turn, wanted to attract a female audience to their product, so they hired a beautiful ex-model, socialite, and former actress who had won the hearts of many of her leading men, including, it was said, Clark Gable. Her name was Anita Colby, and she was so lovely that her nickname was "The Face." A perfect match for S&H, she had class and looks and was of a certain age, something that was much admired in those days before television wanted everyone to be young, young, young.

My job was to be the producer-writer on the five-times-a-week, five-minute segments with Anita. I was to create material revolving around fashion, trends, beauty tips, how-to advice on such crucial matters as properly tying a scarf, entertaining at home, preparing for the holidays, and so on. Occasionally I would throw in a quickie interview, write some funny patter, and we would fill up the five minutes quite easily. Anita was very much a lady and a nice one, too, but she was limited as a performer. She had done little television, and all this was extremely difficult for her. Her life was dinner parties and supper clubs. We could never do a cooking or food feature, for example, because Anita could barely find her way into her own kitchen. She once told me that when she had to cook bacon, she put the strips into hot butter. Yuck. Even I, a lousy cook, knew better than that.

The schedule was grueling. Five mornings a week I showed up at the studio at 4:30 a.m., having taken a taxi (not always easy to find at that hour) from my apartment on Seventy-ninth Street. Anita would arrive an hour later to be made up and get her hair done, which, in those pre-blow-dryer days required sitting under a hot beauty-parlor hood for an hour. The early hours were a big problem for Anita. The poor woman got so exhausted that one day, just after finishing her five-minute segment, she fainted. We weren't sure that she would return the next morning, but she did. Not only that, the segment was renewed after the first three months, as was my contract.

I was thrilled. I was making only a few hundred dollars a week, but I was back in the business I loved. I enjoyed writing the scripts and scouting for new ideas that Anita could talk about. Once Anita left the studio, I spent the rest of the day planning the fashions, writing more scripts, booking the guests, the sort of thing I had been doing for years. This was "mother's milk" for me. And then it was over. After the second three months of our segment, S&H Green Stamps decided that The Face wasn't exactly the face collectors of S&H Green Stamps could relate to. So Anita got axed. I think she was relieved that she could go back to her life of dining at the Stork Club and dancing at El Morocco. As I said, she was a very nice lady and we stayed in touch for quite a while, although I never let her make bacon for me.

Anita may have been fine with being fired, but I was distraught. I thought the ax was going to fall on me, too. No Clark Gable was going to whisk me away to El Morocco. For me it would be back to the employment agency.

But just before the ax fell, lightning struck and my life changed, never to be the same again.

There were eight writers on the *Today* show then, who also produced the interviews and features. Of the eight, only one was a woman. There were never two. It wasn't until that woman left the program voluntarily or died that she would be replaced. But to my very good fortune (here comes the luck) the one female writer who was there chose that moment to decide to get married. And there I was, ready, willing, and on the spot.

Fred Freed hired me full-time. I was given a small office in the RCA building in Rockefeller Plaza, which I shared with one of the seven male writers, a delightful Englishman named John Lord. We had a great relationship, as indeed I had with all the other writers. They couldn't have been more helpful, though our assignments were very different; the female writer's job at that time was limited to writing specifically for whoever was the so-called *Today* Girl.

How Neanderthal it seems now to look back to the era of the *Today* Girls, who were only assigned the features geared for women, and, of course, the weather. By the time I joined the staff there had been at least nine of them. On air, they could ad-lib with the other cast members and look pretty, but that was it. I called them "tea pourers," though it was through no fault of their own. Some were accomplished actresses like Betsy Palmer and Estelle Parsons. Others were fine singers like Florence Henderson and Helen O'Connell, or beauty pageant winners like Lee Ann Meriwether, a former Miss America, and Robbin Bain, a former Miss Rheingold. (The Miss Rheingold competition was a staple in New York for twenty-two years, an ingenious interactive promotion for Rheingold beer, which plastered posters of the six gorgeous finalists all over subways, buses, and stores and invited the public to vote for their favorite. And vote they did, making the Miss Rheingold race second only in number of votes cast to that for U.S. president.) That the *Today* Girl's major requirement on the *Today* show was to look wide awake and pretty at 7:00 a.m. was not surprising. In that "don't worry your pretty little head" era, the popular culture on television mirrored the sweet and subservient image of the good wife; it did not include women who were doing anything with their brains. *I Love Lucy* had wound down its spectacular run, and one of the most popular entertainment shows at the time was *Leave It to Beaver*, the sugary portrait of a perfect happy suburban family doted on by a perfect happy wife and mother. The women's movement had yet to be born. John F. Kennedy was president in 1961, and more women aspired to wear Jackie Kennedy's pillbox hats and sleeveless linen sheaths than to enroll at MIT. Still, change was in the air at the *Today* show. Once again the timing was on my side.

The catalyst was Dave Garroway. He has been somewhat forgotten, but in those days he was a huge star. For nine years he had been the urbane and witty host of the *Today* show, and he still held all the reins. Very little happened that he didn't control or approve. He had to sign off on me when Fred Freed decided to hire me. But first, so did his ferocious secretary. Only after I got her approval was I ushered in to see Garroway. That first meeting was a little odd. While we talked, he kept sipping something out of a bottle in his desk. He vaguely remembered me as the person who used to supply him with Lionel trains, and he was slightly flirtatious. He asked me a few questions, seemed mildly interested in the answers, and that was that. After I was hired I had little actual contact with him.

Garroway's talent was an ability to appear laid-back and relaxed. He seemed to be talking directly to the viewer. He always ended the program holding his hand up and saying, "Peace." Nice and calm. He knew a lot about a lot of things, and the network backed him for years. But by 1961 he was becoming increasingly demanding and his behavior more eccentric and erratic, which may have been the result of whatever was in that bottle he referred to as "the Doctor." Garroway said "the Doctor" gave him energy. No one ever asked him just what was in the concoction, but whatever it was, it no longer seemed to improve his performance or disposition.

He had started to bawl out writers for simply writing a sentence he didn't like (mercifully, because I was writing for the *Today* Girl and not for him, I wasn't on his radar). Sometimes he would upend the carefully planned show and move all the guests from the second hour into the first, throwing off everything—the teleprompters, props, the lighting. Poor Fred Freed. No wonder he was beginning to count the days until he could leave the show.

Garroway's personal life had also just taken a terrible blow. His wife, Pam, mother of his three-year-old son, had committed suicide in April 1961, just before I arrived at the show. That would have devastated the strongest of men, and Dave was already somewhat unstable. Three years before, he had collapsed into the arms of the *Today* Girl just before they went on the air. The medical diagnosis had been "physical exhaustion," and he returned to the air a month later, but there was continuing concern that he was taking downers to sleep and uppers to cope with the show's cruel hours. It all came to a head during his contract renewal negotiations with NBC that same spring of '61. Dave lay down on the floor of his office just before airtime and refused to get up unless NBC honored his demands. By then the powers that be were so worried about his behavior that they wouldn't humor him. Just as NBC had retired J. Fred Muggs some years before (the chimp became too aggressive), so they decided to retire Dave Garroway. His last show was on June 16, 1961.

Garroway would go on to produce or appear on several other television shows over the years, but he never regained the prominence he had on *Today*. He would remarry. In January 1982 he made a nostalgic appearance on the *Today* show for its thirtieth-anniversary broadcast. He seemed his old, upbeat self, but six months later he shot himself in the head. Garroway's stepson, Michael, ascribed his suicide to postoperative complications from open-heart surgery. What a sad end for the man who had been the brilliant father of morning television.

Garroway's departure from the helm of the *Today* show set in motion a whole sequence of events. One change affected the program more than it did the audience (which didn't even know the difference). The *Today* show had been under the auspices of the entertainment division, but the news-oriented president of NBC, Robert Kintner, decided to transfer the program from entertainment to the news department and replace Dave Garroway with a more sobersided journalist—male, of course.

Veteran correspondent John Chancellor became the new morning host and, to my great delight and surprise, he brought in Shad Northshield as *Today*'s new producer. Fred Freed had recently left to start his new career as a producer of documentaries, but I wasn't affected. I had worked with Shad at CBS, and I liked him enormously. He was a big bear of a man with a great sense of humor, which is just what we all needed after Dave Garroway's latter-day reign of terror. All should have been well. But it wasn't.

John Chancellor was attractive, bright, articulate, and completely wrong for the show. He was a serious journalist and stood in sharp contrast to Garroway. Viewers were used to watching him playing with trains and making jokes about the girls in bathing suits. In a million years John Chancellor would never have tolerated working with a chimpanzee.

The *Today* show's ratings dropped. The program was no longer lighthearted and cozy, so a lot of people simply stopped watching. It wasn't John's fault. He was the wrong guy in the wrong place in the wrong time slot. And he knew it. Years later, in an interview with Larry King, John, who would go on to anchor *NBC Nightly News* for twelve years, described his fourteen-month stint at *Today* as "simply awful. I found myself introducing musical acts at 7:45 in the morning and that was just too much for me."

I, on the other hand, benefited mightily from John's uncomfortable tenure—because of Shad. Enlightened Shad. "I don't see what Barbara is doing just writing women's features," he said one day at a writers' meeting. "She's perfectly capable of writing any of the stories for the show." Did the world stop? Did anyone realize what was happening? No, but for the first time in the program's history, I, a female, was cleared to write stories about science and finance, even world news, as well as, of course, the tea-pouring features. As far as I know there was no revolt from the show's viewers or any of the daily guests, and there didn't seem to be a serious protest from the other writers—although no one volunteered to write the tea-pouring stories with me.

Even with all the extra work, I was very grateful. My day still began at 4:00 a.m., but the work was much more interesting. Once in the studio, I would meet with John Chancellor and go over the interviews I had prepared for him. Then I would meet with the guest who was to be interviewed and discuss the area of questions to make sure we were all on the same track. When the program was over at 9:00 a.m., we would have a postmortem meeting to discuss what did or didn't go right. At 10:00 a.m. I would go to the food counter at the drugstore in the lobby of 30 Rock. As I had by then been up for five hours, I would have a BLT or perhaps a hamburger, followed by an order of chocolate ice cream. Then it was off to my nice office, where I manned the phone, booked guests, wrote features and future interviews. There were meetings, conferences, private rages at the guests who canceled and cheers if someone we really were trying to book came through.

I rarely went to lunch, as I had already had my lunch at 10:00 a.m. About 6:00 p.m. I took a bus home, often stopping at the supermarket across the street from my apartment to buy bologna and a roll, still my favorite dinner. If I wasn't going out, I was in bed by 9:30 p.m. It was all fine. And it got better.

Shad was the first producer at NBC to put me on the air (at least in something other than a bathing suit). My mini debut in July 1961 was from a bicycle seat in Central Park. Shad's hope was to give a female slant to what was most often a very male-oriented broadcast, so I produced and introduced a piece for him about biking in Central Park. I couldn't drive but I did know how to ride a bike. That appearance was followed the next month by a more substantial debut—covering the fall fashion collections in Paris.

I couldn't believe my good fortune. I had suggested the feature to Shad and there I was, being sent to Paris to cover the ever-so-chic couture fashion shows. What an assignment! I still have the grainy black-and-white film of my debut at the *Today* desk on August 29, 1961, and though it sounds so immodest to say it, I can see now why Shad put me on air. I still had the then-fashionable short-with-bangs Audrey Hepburn haircut, so I looked like almost every other young woman in the country, which meant they could relate to me. Most of all, I was funny. I was introduced by Frank Blair, who was doing light features for the program. I remember complaining with a wink, "Oh, Frank, it was awful. First of all, every day I had to go look at fashion shows. And then I had to have lunch at Maxim's and drink champagne. And then I had to smell all the perfumes at Dior. I mean it was so trying that I took absolutely the last plane home."

I loved doing my little segment on the air. But it never occurred to me that I would ever have a regular on-air role myself. Glamour, not humor, and certainly nothing intellectual, was the requirement if a woman wanted to be in front of the camera. All I wanted was to do whatever I was asked to do so I wouldn't be replaced by some other female writer. I just wanted to keep my job.

For the next twenty years, thirty years, maybe even forty, I would feel the same way. No matter how high my profile became, how many awards I received, or how much money I made, my fear was that it all could be taken away from me. It doesn't take a rocket scientist to link that insecurity to my father's roller-coaster career or to my mother's constant anxiety or to my sister's needs. I have, as I've said, always felt I was auditioning, either for a new job or to make sure that I could hold on to the one I had.

And that's not all bad. Though I've lived in varying degrees of anxiety throughout the course of my career, I've never really changed my attitude. I've worked as hard or harder than anyone else, accepted most every assignment, done my homework, kept complaints to myself, finished the job, and moved on. That is not a bad formula for success.

To my relief, my family was stable during that first whirlwind year at *Today*. My parents and Jackie were settled in Las Vegas, where my father continued to produce his lavish shows and assemble the most gorgeous line of showgirls and dancers. Unlike in Miami or New York, in Vegas these beauties could leave their breasts exposed. The costumes, as usual, were exquisite. So were the breasts. The owners of the Tropicana, which, up until then, had mostly big-name stars as their headliners, were delighted with my father's work, particularly with his version of

Paris's Folies-Bergère. They gave him a contract, and more and more of the other hotels began to follow his formula, using big production numbers as the main attraction.

My parents bought a small house in Vegas. My father even planted a rose garden. It wasn't Broadway, but it wasn't a low floor in a hospital, either.

Professionally he was having a second wind. He was flying to New York, Miami, and Europe looking for acts and inspiration. The Tropicana's owner rode hard on my father's extravagant impulses and they were paying him a nice salary. I myself was making pretty good money then, some five hundred a week, and I continued to repay Lou Chesler. I never told my father about the loan; I thought it would humiliate him. Mr. Chesler often offered to forgive it but I didn't want him to. He was there when I needed him, and this was my way of showing my gratitude.

I was also relieved that Jackie seemed happy. As usual she'd made friends with some of the chorus girls and soon found a brand-new friend in one of my father's headliners: Carol Channing, the irrepressible Broadway star of *Gentlemen Prefer Blondes* and, later, *Hello, Dolly!* Carol's father, George Channing, had been a serious follower of the Christian Science movement, and she had grown up with many "Jackies" around her family's house. She seemed to truly enjoy my sister's company. Carol invited Jackie to her every show, telephoned her regularly, visited her when she could, and their friendship lasted until the day Jackie died. I will always love Carol Channing.

During this period I spent a good deal of my vacation time with my family in Vegas, but I was always happy to get back to New York. I was in my early thirties, I had a great job, I was single—and, finally, I had a personal life.

From time to time I would still see Roy Cohn. I knew all his faults, but I could never forget what he had done for my father. We never, ever, discussed politics. Though he claimed to be a Democrat, his views were so conservative that, had we discussed them, I probably would never have been able to see him again. Instead I just concentrated on the fact that Roy was very smart and could be very good company.

In spite of his despicable role in the McCarthy hearings, he seemed to have a million friends in all walks of life. For all his tough reputation and his questionable favor swapping, Roy had a whole side of life that was legitimate and attractive. He was a close friend of my old friend Bill Safire, and of William F. Buckley Jr., the founder of the conservative political magazine *National Review*. Another very good friend was Si Newhouse, the head of Condé Nast publishing, and also Si's parents,

Mitzi and Sam, to whom Roy was very loyal. On the political side he was a friend of President Ronald Reagan, of the Catholic cardinals, and of the New York political boss Carmine De Sapio. Roy was like a godfather. You do a favor for me, I do a favor for you. He was also one of the toughest divorce lawyers in New York.

On our rare dates Roy would take me to dinner and then on to the Stork Club, where we would be seated at the best table. Sherman Billingsley, the owner, would sit down with him. So would the leading columnists of the time: Walter Winchell, Leonard Lyons, and Jack O'Brian, who was the most important and toughest television critic of the time. (Today, Kate O'Brian, Jack's youngest daughter, is a vice president at ABC News. I've known her since she was a baby.) If all these people seemed to accept him, I guess I thought I could, too. I'm not trying to justify my friendship; I'm trying to make it more understandable. Partly, I suppose, to myself.

I really didn't know that Roy was homosexual, though I had heard the rumors about his sexual orientation during the Army-McCarthy hearings. (There was no such word then as "gay.") There wasn't a lot of talk about homosexuality back then. There were obviously plenty of gay people, but their sexuality was never written about in the press or, for that matter, even in private. As I've mentioned, when I saw Roy, the extent of our physical contact was a peck on the cheek. Since he wasn't a real beau, and I didn't want him to be, that suited me fine. I never probed. When I look back, I am not sure that Roy admitted to himself that he was homosexual. Until his mother died.

I thought his mother was a dreadful woman. Her name was Dora Marcus Cohn, and she came from a prominent German Jewish family in New York. Roy called her "Mutti," a leftover from his childhood, and the German diminutive of *"mutter"* for mother. She doted on Roy's male buddies. But she sure didn't dote on me. She had no idea if and when I saw her son, but she did know of my existence, and she quickly decided I was hardly what she wanted for her beloved son. I was the daughter of a nightclub owner. Roy was the son of a judge. I had no money or social background. Roy had plenty of both. He once brought us together for dinner, and Mutti could barely hide her disdain for me. I wish now that I had told her that I had no interest in her son, but I was raised to be polite and I kept my mouth shut.

My relationship with Mutti improved ever so slightly when I began appearing on the *Today* show. She then started treating me with a grudging respect. I still wasn't what she wanted for her son, but people were beginning to talk nicely about me, so when we did occasionally meet at a birthday of Roy's or a special occasion, she would then give me a cool hello.

Roy lived with Mutti in an apartment on Park Avenue until she died in 1969. On that day, to my surprise, because I hadn't seen him in a while, Roy phoned me and asked me to come to the apartment to meet with the rabbi. I went. It was the first time I had ever been to his apartment. I could only imagine that it was important to Roy that the rabbi thought he had a girlfriend.

From time to time over the years, Roy asked me to marry him. I think he thought he *should* be married. Plus he liked children, and he obviously liked me, so why not marry? Of course I never seriously considered it. But I became Roy's claim to heterosexuality. Whenever a reporter asked Roy why he never married, he always said he had wanted to marry me but was too busy and was married to his work.

For one fleeting instant, though, I did think about the possibility. It was when Roy bought a large town house. It had four floors, and Roy said my parents and Jackie could have their own apartment on the top floor. The idea of having my parents and sister safe and protected was such an incredible inducement that for one moment I thought maybe. But "maybe" never became "yes." I just couldn't.

I knew there was a lot wrong with Roy, and not just sexually. I had witnessed his terrible temper, having heard him scream at people, presumably subordinates, over the telephone. I was appalled. I was also haunted by the lives he had destroyed during the McCarthy era. To many people, among them my friends and colleagues, the memories were still raw. I understood that but could not explain my relationship with Roy to them.

I stopped seeing Roy almost totally during my second year at the *Today* show. By then I had met someone else I'll tell you about later. Over the years Roy would occasionally call and say, "How are you? Want to have lunch?" We'd then go to one of the fashionable restaurants and catch up on his life. He was never very curious about my life, which was fine with me. His homosexuality became more and more obvious as time went on, but he never admitted it publicly or, for that matter, privately, to me. He was, however, becoming quite reckless, and I used to worry that I'd get a phone call in the middle of the night from the police telling me Roy had been murdered by some young "trick."

As he got older he had his face lifted several times, and he made no effort to hide that fact. Once, when I saw him for lunch, the stitches were showing. It was a strange and contradictory example of both his vanity and lack of concern for what anyone thought about him. But Roy's quirks didn't seem to hinder him professionally. He still had some very important clients, not to mention all those divorce cases. He bought a yacht, which he kept at the Seventy-ninth Street Boat Basin in Manhattan. I never visited. He bought a house in Connecticut where he gave big parties to which I was invited but also never visited. He must have made a lot of money, but I heard over the years that he never paid his bills. I later learned that he charged everything to his business and constantly owed money to the restaurants and clubs he patronized.

And then he got AIDS. In retrospect it seems inevitable. All the parties on his yacht and in his various houses. All those boys, those endless, young, one-night stands. Did they rob him? Blackmail him? Is that where the money went?

Roy never admitted he had AIDS. But the rumors were there. I remember having lunch with him at a very chic restaurant, Le Cirque, and being horrified when he kept sneezing and wiping his nose with a linen napkin. It was so like the thoughtless, selfish Roy who had simply abandoned his car in the middle of the street the first night we'd gone out all the years before, but this might have had much more dangerous consequences. After we left the table I took the maître d' aside and told him to throw out the napkin.

With everything, though, I remained loyal to Roy, just as all those years ago, he had been loyal to me. When, in 1986, he asked me to testify on his behalf before the New York Bar Association, which was moving to disbar him for unethical and unprofessional conduct, I did. I knew that Roy was dying, and I asked the committee to spare him so that he could die with some dignity. Roy's close friends Bill Safire and William Buckley also testified, all of us supposedly in secret, although our testimony leaked to the papers. But the committee had had it with Roy's arrogant and clearly unethical behavior, and they did, indeed, disbar him.

In 2003 Mike Nichols directed the brilliant HBO miniseries *Angels in America*. It was a devastating dramatized version of Roy, adapted from Tony Kushner's equally brilliant 1990 play by the same name. In the TV version Al Pacino played Roy and captured all of his complexities and cruelties. I recognized parts of the portrayal and could not disagree with it. But I could also not dismiss my own memories of Roy.

Shortly after he was disbarred, Roy died. It was August 2, 1986. He was fifty-nine.

Passage to India

ACKIE KENNEDY TOOK A TRIP to India and Pakistan in March 1962. The White House billed it as a "semiofficial" trip, but officially the administration cleared forty-five reporters to cover the first lady. I was one of them.

I was a neophyte among much more senior newscasters from NBC, CBS, and ABC, all male of course, and veteran print journalists from almost every newspaper and magazine—the *Washington Post*, the *New York Times*, the wire services, *Time*, the since-defunct *Saturday Evening Post*—almost all of whom were also male. There were only seven women assigned to cover Jackie's "goodwill tour," which was actually quite a lot, there being so few women in journalism. Six of them were print journalists: Fran Lewine for the Associated Press, Marie Ridder for the Ridder newspaper chain, Anne Chamberlin for *Time*, Gwen Morgan for the *Chicago Tribune*, Molly Thayer for the *Washington Post*, and Joan Braden for the *Saturday Evening Post*. I was the only one from television.

How did I get to go? Because Shad Northshield and John Chancellor realized that the story would be perfect for the *Today* show audience. A woman's story, reported by a woman. Why not send me? I could write and report. I couldn't pack fast enough.

I didn't know Jackie Kennedy at the time, but, like millions of other Americans, I was dazzled by her fabulous good looks, poise, and style. John F. Kennedy, the young, handsome president, and Jackie, his elegant wife, stood in sharp contrast to their elderly predecessors in the White House, Dwight and Mamie Eisenhower. America was young and vibrant again and, as a result, full of promise and potential. It was an intoxicating time.

It was also an exhausting trip. Everything was carefully planned to move the press corps as quickly as possible from one photo op to the next. We all had to lug our baggage and whatever other equipment we had, including our typewriters, which, in those prelaptop days, weighed a ton. I should either have taken weight training—or been Joan Braden.

Joan was a fascinating woman. The mother then of seven, with another yet to come, she was married to Tom Braden, a syndicated columnist, who would later write the best-selling book about their family, *Eight Is Enough*. Joan, with whom I shared a room and later a tent (along with Marie Ridder), was very slim and rather wrinkled from too much sun. She'd supposedly had a fling with Bobby Kennedy, for whom she'd worked on JFK's presidential campaign in 1960, and she was a friend of the whole Kennedy family. She was also an extremely close friend of the famed journalistic brothers Joe and Stewart Alsop. Joe wrote a highly influential syndicated column and was a trusted friend of both President Kennedy and, later, President Johnson. Stewart was an editor at the *Saturday Evening Post*, which is how Joan got assigned to Jackie's trip. In years to come Joan would act as Defense Secretary Robert McNamara's so-called traveling companion, after his wife's death. They had an affair, and she went with him all over the world while still married to her husband, who didn't seem to object. It was the topic of conversation for years in Washington. Whatever Joan had should have been bottled and sold to every woman.

I tell you all this because every man on the India trip turned out to be mad for Joan. The hard-bitten male reporters fell all over one another offering to carry her bags, her typewriter, her anything. I was not exactly a dog at the time, but nobody offered to schlep any of my bags. I was my own Sherpa, trundling from place to place.

I remember that on that trip Joan didn't wear stockings and she got blisters on her heels. The reason I remember this is that some of the guys not only volunteered to carry her bags, they offered to carry *her*. The amazing thing is that I liked her. Joan was funny, sweet, and very feminine. (I did tell you, didn't I, that on that trip, Joan was the married mother of seven children?)

I learned a few things from her that I never seemed able to put into practice. First of all, she liked to sit on the floor, not on a chair or on a couch. That way she could look up at whatever man she was talking to. She was all eyes and had the ability to look fascinated at will—so there she'd be looking up in awe while the guy was looking down at his obviously devoted subject. Then, too, she laughed at every joke someone told, and rarely talked about herself. Almost everything she said seemed to come out as a question that would produce an answer. And every conversation, whether with a man or woman, included a compliment.

As a result of her social skills and ability to be ingratiating, during the Ford and Nixon administrations Joan was to become one of the most important hostesses in Washington. She was Henry Kissinger's great friend when he was single and in Washington. She and her husband, Tom, gave a dinner almost every month. Everyone came. The Bradens didn't have a lot of money—after all, they had all those children to support—but nobody cared. Joan kept the lights very low, served spaghetti, and sat on the floor.

She was also the only person on the trip to get an exclusive interview with Jacqueline Kennedy.

Of course I myself was hoping to get an interview with the first lady at some point during the two-week sojourn. The White House had sanctioned all of us. Their various employers, as usual, had paid the White House for our passage. But no.

I failed in Rome, our first stop, where Jackie had an audience with the pope and chatted with him in French. I failed again in India, where she and her sister, Lee Radziwill, escorted by John Kenneth Galbraith, the U.S. ambassador to India, floated around a lake in Udaipur and watched divers plunge into a fifty-foot pool at Fatehpur Sikri. My hopes were still high when Jackie visited Gandhi's tomb in Raj Ghat, rode on an elephant in Amber village, and lingered in Agra at the spectacular Taj Mahal. But nothing.

I pinned my hopes on Pakistan, the last leg of the trip, where the smitten president, Ayub Khan, laid on a horse show for the first lady (with two thousand men carrying flaming torches), gave her the astrakhan hat off his head, and arranged for her and her tagalong press entourage, including me, to traverse the famous Khyber Pass right up to the dangerous border with Afghanistan. But though Jackie left a wake of charm on the president, she did not bestow any on the reporters following her every step. No interview for me then, nor for anybody. She didn't even hold a press conference.

I did have one momentous breakthrough in Pakistan when Jackie was visiting a monument. "Mrs. Kennedy, there's a bobby pin falling out of your hair," I said to her. She turned, smiled at me, and said: "Thank you." That was it. My exclusive interview.

But I was plenty busy. I had to film a daily segment about the trip for the *Today* show and do live radio reports as well. Difficult because there was nothing much to say except where Jackie had been that day and what she was wearing. At one point she had to take off her shoes to enter a holy temple. We all then excitedly reported that she wore a size 10 shoe. I am sure she could have lived without this rather unappealing piece of information being circulated. But that was already big news for this trip. Things were so slow that the members of the press traded rumors, which were impossible to check, a hot one being that Jackie had brought twenty-six trunks with her as well as two maids. Mercifully I did not report that as fact. It turned out she took only three half-filled trunks, leaving room for presents, and one maid-hairdresser, who'd been working for the Kennedys long before they moved into the White House.

I was further handicapped by not being included in the small pool of rotating reporters. I didn't even know what a pool was until I went on this trip, and quickly learned that it usually was made up of one newspaper reporter, one magazine journalist, and one broadcast journalist who were allowed closer access to whatever Jackie was doing and then briefed the rest of us. Obviously if you went with her yourself to any of the events and saw them with your own eyes, you would be able to do a better job of reporting. But I was stiffed by my colleague Sander Vanocur, who was way above me in rank at NBC. He never once let me take his place in the pool, though I was reporting daily on film and radio while Sandy was gathering material for a special broadcast that wasn't going to air for weeks. Would it have killed him to let me once be the broadcast pool reporter?

In India, with so little material to work with, I went afield for interviews and scored a big hit for the *Today* show when Indira Gandhi, the daughter of Prime Minister Jawaharlal Nehru, agreed to see me in the prime minister's official residence in Delhi. Before I left for India, I had written to Mrs. Gandhi, asking for an interview, and while I was there her people contacted NBC to say she would indeed meet with me.

When we got together she was acting as her father's official hostess and, as such, showed me and my cameraman around the cavernous residence, and drove home for me yet again the connection that unites all women—closet space. Her biggest complaint about the mansion was that there weren't enough closets. Also, the kitchen was so far away from the reception rooms, she said, that any food for guests was cold by the time the servants brought it.

So here was a woman who, four years later, would become prime minister of India and one of the great world leaders, and she and I had the same complaints. I also didn't much like my kitchen and, in my three-room apartment, I certainly didn't have enough closets. Strangely, those remarks are what I most remember from that long-ago interview, as they made Mrs. Gandhi very human to me. I was shocked and saddened when she was assassinated in 1984 during her fourth term in office.

Let me digress for a minute to tell you of my encounter with one of India's more exotic leaders. His name was Shri Morarji Desai, and he was prime minister of India from 1977 to 1979. During that time I was at ABC trying to work my way back from a disastrous period in my professional life. (More about that later.) Between December 29, 1977, and January 6, 1978, President Jimmy Carter made whirlwind visits to Poland, France, Belgium, Saudi Arabia, Egypt, Iran, and India. I was sent by ABC to cover them and do general reporting. Also assigned were Ted Koppel, then ABC's chief diplomatic correspondent, and Sam Donaldson, our chief White House correspondent. It was love at first sight for me with those guys. We became great buddies—still are—and we spent all our free moments of that trip together.

As I had on the Jackie Kennedy trip, I requested in advance the opportunity to interview Prime Minister Desai. He fascinated me because of a regime he publicly proclaimed for his health, which included the imbibing of his own urine for medicinal purposes. The prime minister granted my request. He was a thin, ascetic-looking man who answered my questions easily and frankly. After we had discussed Indian and American relations, I asked him about his use of urine as a cure-all. "I do consider urine therapy as a cure for almost all diseases, but the person who does it must have faith in it," he proclaimed. Urine is a helpful cure for cataracts, he went on, "if you catch them right at the beginning and continue washing your eyes with it."

I couldn't wait to send back my report to ABC News. But while *I* thought I'd gotten astonishing quotes, ABC News thought the whole thing was disgusting and wouldn't run the piece. Let me point out, however smugly, that several weeks later CBS's Dan Rather also visited New Delhi, interviewed the same Prime Minister Desai, asked the same urine questions, and his network *did* run the interview. So finally, then, playing catch-up, ABC ran my footage. The network urine wars. But that is not what I want to tell you about. I want to share with you my favorite Ted Koppel/Sam Donaldson anecdote.

They were both amused and amazed that I had the nerve to ask such personal questions of Prime Minister Desai. That evening the three of us went to a restaurant in New Delhi for dinner. We ordered a bottle of white wine. When it arrived Ted poured a bit of the pale liquid into his wineglass, swirled it around, took a small taste, and gravely pronounced, "It's a good urine. It's not a great urine. But it's a good urine."

That was a dinner I will never forget.

Back to Jackie and her visit to the ancient "pink city" of Jaipur, where she had friends, the maharaja and maharani of Jaipur. The royal family received Mrs. Kennedy and her party in their enormous city palace—as compared to their several country palaces. It was drop-dead gorgeous, with treasures dating back thousands of years and a more recent towering seven-story temple dedicated to Krishna, one of the most beloved Hindu deities, who was born, tradition says, five thousand years before Christ.

The *Today* audience was riveted by the wonders of the palace, among which was a large crystal dining room table designed and handcrafted by Lalique, the famed French glassmakers. Just to eat at that table, we all thought, must be thrilling. We were also thrilled to meet the maharani, Gayatri Devi, known to her friends as Ayesha. The maharani was considered one of the world's great beauties, who, for all her over-the-top background—she had been raised in her family's palace with five hundred servants—was a respected elected member of India's parliament and founder of several progressive schools. She was also a great hostess and owner of the most exquisite saris, so elegant in her draped silk that I entertained the notion of trading in all my sleeveless wrinkle-proof dresses for silk saris.

Perhaps my sari obsession came from delirium because, uncharacteristically, I got really sick over there. I get sick so rarely that once, much later on, when I phoned my grown-up daughter and told her I had a slight temperature, she told me she was coming home immediately to see me, presumably before I died. But I caught a cold sleeping in a tent in Jaipur—there weren't enough hotel rooms for all of us—and I felt so rotten I missed a big ball at the palace.

A "small world" story. At the time of this visit we met the eldest son and heir of the maharaja. Years later, in March 2005, I traveled again to India, this time to conduct an interview with His Holiness the Dalai Lama for a *Special* on heaven. After the interview, as a treat, I took my tiny staff for a few days of sightseeing. I hadn't been back to India except for that one brief visit with Ted and Sam. Anyway, one of the high points of our whirlwind tour was a visit to Jaipur. There, our guide told us, he had special contacts and could arrange for us to dine with the current but now titular maharaja (royalty had gradually lost its power in post-colonial, independent India) at the city palace. Another of the royal palaces had been turned into an exquisite hotel, where we were spending the night. For two hundred dollars each, our guide promised us a memorable visit back to the glory of old India. How could we resist?

Eight hundred dollars later, we arrived at the palace courtyard. There were a few elephants rented for the occasion with painted foreheads lumbering around. They were obliging creatures and could also be found at other tourist attractions where tourists could pay for a ride high atop their backs, which you reached with the help of a small ladder. I did this at one of the temples, but I didn't at the palace, where, along with the elephants, there were a couple of young and very attractive dancers in beautiful bejeweled costumes who whirled and swayed for our benefit. After this brief entertainment we entered the main salon, where waiting to greet us was an old and obviously very tired gentleman in a blazer and ascot. Lo and behold he was the same prince and heir I had met all those years ago on the Jackie trip! He was now the maharaja. I told him we had met before. He certainly remembered Jacqueline Kennedy's visit, but now he had his own heir to worry about, and money was sometimes in short supply. As it turned out, you didn't need special contacts to dine with him; two hundred dollars a person would do it no matter whom you knew. For that amount you could also have dinner in his company at—remember?—that wondrous crystal table with its original Lalique designs. I was so touched to meet him again after all those years that I told him he really didn't have to sit through dinner with us. "Do go to bed," I said to him, and he gratefully trotted off.

I had another experience on the Jackie trip, which I remember for the wrong reasons, at the Taj Mahal: I almost missed the private train to our next destination. I can remember the panic I felt forty-five years later as I sit here, writing this. I was delayed by a phone report I had to make to the office in New York, which left me no recourse but to set off at a dead run for the station. En route I tripped and badly cut my hand. I had to keep my hand bandaged for weeks, and although I waved it around when I got back to New York, so I could say, "I cut it running by the Taj Mahal at sunset," no one ever asked.

My last interview of the trip was with Ayub Khan, the president of Pakistan. My first with a head of state, and I can't remember a thing about it. My memory may have been obliterated by my allergy to horses. Jackie's visit to Pakistan, and therefore ours, included a horse show which left me red-eyed and sneezing. (Knowing the first lady's love for horses, Ayub Khan even sent her home with a four-legged gift named Sardar.) I turned out to be allergic to camels, too, one of which Jackie rode in Karachi. While the other reporters watched and took pictures, I sneezed.

On the last day of the trip Jackie finally gathered the women reporters and gave us each a little painted box I have to this day. "I know it's been a difficult tour, and I want you to know how much I appreciate it," she said in her breathy voice. That was as close as we came to a press conference.

Years later Jackie and I became sort of friendly and would occasionally have lunch or meet at dinner parties. She was very funny and told me naughty anecdotes about her sisters-in-law, none of which I ever talked about publicly. She said she could never keep up with their athletic pursuits and hated the competitive waterskiing, tennis games, and so on. I sympathized. Did I want to interview her? No answer necessary. I tried and tried over the years, requesting an interview with her about her various causes—her favorite books or the preservation of historical landmarks, for instance. We wouldn't have cared if she just read the yellow pages of the phone book. But she always refused. The truth is, against my own desires, I think she was absolutely right. Her silence kept her mysterious and gave her an aura that she might otherwise have lost. And there would have been so many questions she wouldn't have answered.

The only scoop I got on the first India trip I couldn't use. President Kennedy's philandering is well known now, but at the time his extracurricular activities were treated as state secrets. The press didn't touch them. I had met the head of the United States Information Agency in India at that time and he told me in great secrecy that as soon as Mrs. Kennedy returned home from India, Angie Dickinson, the actress with whom the president was rumored to be having an affair, was arriving to take exactly the same trip. But though the USIA, members of the State Department, government officials of India and Pakistan, and several members of the press corps, including me, knew about Angie's carbon-copy trip, it remained a secret. Try that these days.

Since I'd had zero luck getting Jackie to talk, what I could do was invite Joan Braden to appear on the *Today* show. She'd gotten the only direct interview with Mrs. Kennedy when Jackie invited her to sit beside her on the plane trip home. This had been prearranged by Stewart Alsop so that Joan could use it for her *Saturday Evening Post* article. Joan came to New York, where we did a pleasant and not particularly newsworthy interview, but, true to form, she charmed both John Chancellor and Shad Northshield. "Good piece," they both said. Bah, humbug!

A Funeral and a Wedding

OR ALL THAT MY first trip to India had been exotic, I was happy to be home. One key reason was that shortly before I'd left, I'd met a man named Lee Guber, on a blind date. My friend Joyce Ashley had been going out with him and thought he was terrific but felt there was no chemistry between them, so she had orchestrated our meeting. "He's nice," she told me, "but you'll never marry him."

So I had little expectation when Lee and I met at the Friars Club in New York. Joyce was right: Lee was very nice. That was no surprise. He was also very attractive. Blue eyes, dark hair, very well built. More surprising, we *did* have chemistry. We went for a long walk that night and talked about our lives. He was divorced with two teenage children. He had recently moved to New York from Philadelphia. That all sounded fine until he told me what he did for a living—he was a theatrical producer.

Oh no. Not another one! After my experiences with my father, I had sworn to myself that I would never get involved with anyone in show business.

It became clear, however, that Lee was quite different from my father. He and two partners had a company called Music Fair Enterprises that owned and operated very successful summer theaters—the Westbury Music Fair in Long Island and "tent" theaters in the suburbs around Philadelphia, Boston, Baltimore, and Washington. Lee was the producing partner, and staged versions of Broadway musicals like *The King and I* and *Gentlemen Prefer Blondes*. One of the reasons the tent theaters were so popular was that the stage was round, guaranteeing a good seat to everyone in the house. Another, of course, was that the tent shows brought Broadway to the suburbs as great summer entertainment.

Lee also produced Broadway shows, the first of which, *The Happiest Girl in the World*, had a three-month run at the Martin Beck Theater in 1961. It was not a major success, but it won a Theater World Award for one of the actors and a Tony nomination for best choreography. So Lee was no slouch. Even so his Broadway connection made me very anxious. As they say, "Been there, done that." And not only done it, hadn't liked it.

But I really liked him. The only hang-up was his profession. After several months, however, I managed to convince myself that Lee wasn't the same kind of showman as my father. Where my father was a dreamer, Lee was a realist. Where my father was extravagant, Lee was practical. And Lee didn't gamble. He ran his production company like a business. That's what I decided he was—a businessman. Big difference between businessman and producer, so with that reassuring definition in mind, after I got back from India I began to see Lee seriously.

While my personal life was relatively smooth, the *Today* show was in turmoil. My reporting from the subcontinent had temporarily boosted *Today*'s viewership, but the audience was declining steadily. The serious, news-oriented slant of the program was obviously not the way most people wanted to greet the day. So, within a few months of my return from India, John Chancellor was reassigned to hard news, and into the anchor's chair went a game-show host by the name of Hugh Downs.

Hugh was one of the most popular talents at NBC. He had been the charming, unassuming sidekick to the complicated and charismatic late-night talk-show host Jack Paar, and had for years also been hosting *Concentration*, a highly successful quiz show. Hugh was unflappable and perfect for the morning slot—soft-spoken, intelligent, very much the neighbor-next-door. I liked him immediately. Who could have imagined that I would work with Hugh for the next nine years at the *Today* show and, later, for another fifteen years at ABC as cohosts of *20/20*? I certainly didn't when I, a staff writer, was assigned to write the segment introducing Hugh to the *Today* show audience.

At first NBC wasn't too sure they wanted a game-show host as their new morning leader. After all, he had no real news experience and, as I was to come to know all too well, network news was a boys' club that didn't welcome newcomers. But Hugh had a gentle way about him and was a serious, thoughtful man who later wrote several books on topics ranging from astronomy to psychological maturity. He also got a master's degree in gerontology. He could certainly conduct a respectful and intelligent interview, so NBC News swallowed their snobbery and hired him. It was the beginning of a most successful, sunny chapter for the network and for me as well.

Everything changed. When John Chancellor left, Shad Northshield was out and a new producer, Al Morgan, was in. I got along very well with Al. He had a witty, sardonic sense of humor and had written a best-selling novel called *The Great Man*, which was a thinly disguised and not overly flattering book about the radio and television star Arthur Godfrey.

Shortly after Al took over, he moved the program from Studio 3K in the RCA Building across the street into the ground-floor offices of the Florida Development Commission. He wanted to restore the interaction with the public that Pat Weaver, the *Today* show's creator, had called for way back in 1952. It had worked brilliantly for the six years the *Today* show spent behind a big glass window on the ground floor of the RCA Exhibition Hall on West Forty-ninth Street, dubbed the "window on the world," drawing ever larger, more exuberant, sign-waving crowds in the morning. But the program had been forced to move upstairs inside the RCA Building after complaints from a rival TV manufacturer that RCA's products in the exhibition hall could be seen on television.

The Florida Development Commission office, however, was hardly an ideal location. During the day it was decorated with fake palm trees and mannequins wearing shorts, all designed to lure visitors to Florida. By night all of it, including various cages with mynah birds in them, had to be gathered up and stored in a back room so the *Today* show set could be ready for early morning. This led to some interesting interactions that Pat Weaver had never envisioned. For Hugh it meant an early-morning review of his material while secreted in a storage room. The mannequins were creepy enough to deal with, but one day soon after he started, he leaped out of his chair in terror when a voice behind him suddenly said: "My name is Jungle Jim." It was a mynah bird, of course. And it was a mynah bird that greeted Bobby Kennedy, one of the show's guests, in the morning. The storage room was our "green room" then, and that's where the attorney general was waiting.

"Who are you?" came the voice from behind a palm tree.

"I'm Robert Kennedy," Kennedy replied.

"Who are you?" the voice asked again.

"I'm Robert Kennedy," the president's brother repeated.

"Who are you?" the voice persisted, causing Bobby Kennedy to whirl around and snap: "I told you, dammit, I'm Robert Kennedy!" And with that Kennedy stormed onto the set, his face red, his hands shaking, as he sat for his interview.

Al Morgan was a very hands-on producer. He watched the show from his home every morning so he could see it as the viewers saw it. Then he'd come into the office and make changes. One of his mandates was that *everything* had to be live, which was easier in our new location. If we had time to fill, the cameras could pan the crowd outside with their ever-present signs—HI, AUNT TILLIE; HAPPY BIRTHDAY, MOLLY; MOM, SEND MONEY. If a guest was late or didn't show up at all, we could take the cameras out into the crowd and interview people. It was called, then and now, "Man on the Street."

I was supremely happy with my job. For one thing, I loved writing for Hugh. In those days the writer was also a producer. We contacted the guest, preinterviewed him or her if possible, wrote the on-camera introduction to the interview, and wrote suggested questions. I never thought there was a possibility I'd get on the air regularly. I understood that an occasional treat like the trip to India was just that—a treat. I had no real, substantial on-air experience and no following. I kept in mind the exchange I had when I met Don Hewitt, the celebrated CBS producer who eventually created *60 Minutes*. I told him I was working as a writer on *Today*, and he acknowledged that it was the proper job for me as I could never make it on the air. "You don't have the right looks," he said. "And besides, you don't pronounce your *r*'s right. Forget about ever being in front of the cameras."

Don and I often retell this story. Except he adds that he also told a young manager named Marty Erlichman to forget about forging a career for his then young, unknown singer. "She'll never make it," Hewitt told Erlichman. "She's funny looking. Her nose is too big." The singer was Barbra Streisand. Marty Erlichman is still her manager.

So I continued to write for the show, including scripts for the new tea pourer, Pat Fontaine, a onetime weather girl in St. Louis. She was a very nice woman in her late thirties and the mother of five children. There was a flaw, however. She had a drinking problem. Unfortunately no one found that out until after she'd been hired. Still, she lasted for a year and a half, and for the most part was pleasant and professional. But there were mornings when she'd arrive at the studio in no shape to go on the air. One such morning became the beginning of the end. We were broadcasting the show for a week from Mackinac Island off Michigan's Upper Peninsula, for no apparent reason other than that the hotel we were staying in had the longest porch in the world and Queen Elizabeth had stayed there once. After being there a few days, we said, "Well, now we know why she never came back."

There were so many bats on the island that we were advised to walk in the middle of the street to avoid them as they dived from the buildings. They sometimes got into the hotel, and we quickly learned to gird ourselves with brooms and badminton rackets. One small bat got caught in my toilet and I nearly fainted. I screamed until Al Morgan and some others rushed in and flushed the bat down the toilet, which upset me even more.

No wonder Pat Fontaine drank herself silly one night. But sadly for her, she chose the wrong night. We had to leave the hotel by 4:30 a.m. to broadcast the show live from a place that could be reached only by ferry. The show was going to be a big deal for Michigan tourism. The governor was coming, as well as various other state officials, including the director of tourism and a jovial priest we called Father Chuck.

There were about one hundred people gathered in the hotel lobby at 4:15, but not Pat Fontaine. Al dispatched a crew member to her room, who quickly reappeared to report that Pat was passed out in bed. "I couldn't wake her up," he announced. So Al sent two women to haul poor Pat into the shower, pour coffee into her, and dress her, all in twenty minutes. Her wobbly appearance at the top of the stairs did not inspire our confidence, but it did inspire her to break into a grin when she saw the priest below. "Father Chuck, you are one swinging mother priest," bellowed Pat to her drinking companion of the night before. Pat managed to get through the program. Father Chuck was very quiet on the ferry.

In spite of my limited on-air experiences, to my joy when we got back from the bat capital, Al assigned me to broadcast features at least once every few weeks. And slowly, slowly, I honed the skills that would sustain me in this business from then on.

I learned to speak more slowly and to smile more. I was far too intense during interviews. I had to learn to lighten up on camera, which I eventually managed to do.

All the stories I did then were about women—reporting on the rise of political conservatism at several women's colleges, reporting from a reform school for young women in Michigan and from a school for policewomen in New York. I can still do the "bunny dip" from an insider report I did as a bunny at the Playboy Club in New York, "A Night in the Life of a Playboy Bunny." I was not very recognizable, and the customers thought I was a real waitress. We used only one hidden camera to record my stint as a rabbit. The other bunnies and I wore the same uncomfortable but flattering costume—a tight-in-the-waist sort of corselet (that pushed up the almost-exposed bosom), black stockings, and very high black heels. The sexy effect, depending on how you looked at it, was either enhanced or diminished by the bunny ears and bunny tails we also had to wear. But the trick was to master the "bunny dip" while serving drinks without dipping your boobs into the wineglasses. Here's how you do it: keeping your legs together, slightly bend your knees and shift a bit to the right while leaning slightly backward. The squared-off position protected your cleavage but it was murder on the thighs. I didn't really enjoy doing that story, which took two days of filming. But I can still do the "bunny dip." Hugh Downs said it was the first time he knew I had legs.

I learned a more sobering lesson at a Catholic convent just outside New York. The nuns invited me inside their peaceful, quiet world so that viewers would understand that giving up a secular life did not make them freaks. A young novitiate was assigned to show me around, and, to my discomfort, she began to talk to me about the deep conflicts she was feeling. The poor young woman was so desperate that when she drove me to the train station at the end of the day, she suddenly turned to me and asked: "Do you think I should stay here and become a nun?" I didn't know what to say. Clearly she was looking for someone to make the decision for her, but clearly I didn't want that person to be me. I think she was extremely disappointed when I told her the answer to her question required a lot more wisdom than I possessed, but that I was sure she would find her own way. On the train back to New York I could still see her troubled, young face and felt that somehow I had let her down.

That was one of the first times I truly began to understand the power of television. Because people saw me and others on their TV screens, they automatically assumed we must have some sort of special wisdom. Otherwise we wouldn't be on the air. Television not only validated our opinions, it made us all-knowing. The truth is that while we may be more articulate, we may be just as confused about things as the people watching at home.

Television imbues us with an authority that often makes me uncomfortable. On a political panel much later, I told the audience, "Please remember, just because we're on television, we are not gods." That prompted John Chancellor to say with a smile, "Speak for yourself, Barbara."

By the way, the novitiate wrote me a few weeks after our encounter to say she had left the order. I felt terrible and tried desperately to remember what, if anything, I'd said to her that may have influenced her decision. I felt so responsible for her life, while I was having difficulty figuring out my own.

Lee and I got engaged in the summer of '63. All the old terrors about marriage returned, but this time I was determined to overcome them. What I wanted more than anything was to have a baby, and I knew Lee would make a great father, having seen his close relationship with his two children, Carol, who was then seventeen, and Zev, sixteen. I became especially close to Carol, who was in that awkward adolescent stage. Today she is an accomplished nutritionist who wrote a highly acclaimed book in 2002 on controlling diabetes (she has diabetes herself), and we are still in touch. I sign my e-mails to her "the wicked stepmother," which I called myself from the earliest days of our relationship. Obviously, she doesn't agree—at least I hope not. Lee's children were a bonus in the relationship and in no way a detriment. Then, too, there was the stability (that word again) that I envisioned marriage would bring.

My parents were changing their lives again, through no fault of their own. The owners of the Tropicana in Las Vegas had decided they didn't need my father anymore. The Folies-Bergère he'd brought from Paris were firmly established and the hotel executives decided they could produce the show themselves. So they let him go.

It would have been nice if my parents and Jackie could have stayed in Las Vegas, where they had established a good life. My father was almost seventy, and he should have been able to retire, but he didn't have enough money. So he accepted a job producing shows at the Carillon, a popular modern high-rise hotel in Miami Beach, and moved my mother and sister back to Florida.

I began to dread the sound of the phone, anticipating my mother's unhappy words. But though I hated the litany, her complaints were valid. Without consulting her, my father had gone off and bought a house way outside the city. My mother didn't drive. She had no friends. She and Jackie were stuck there, left to spend the whole day in front of the television set.

It was on one of my trips to that cheerless house in the summer of '63 that my father came up with yet another grandiose scheme: an aquacade. The last successful aquacade had been almost twenty-five years before at the 1939 World's Fair, a musical extravaganza in a huge swimming pool with fantastic synchronized divers, a water ballet, and fireworks. Others had since tried—and failed—to mount similarly successful water shows. This did not discourage my always optimistic father. "A show is a show," he told me. "You give the people something spectacular and they'll come."

There we were—again. My father and a new dream but no money. And there I was, with his dream and $5,000 in savings in the bank—$5,000 he wanted me to invest. As Yogi Berra would say, it was déjà vu all over again. I didn't know what to do.

So I turned to Lee.

We had dinner with my father in Florida. Lee listened carefully while my father raved on about his plans: a Latin Quarter revue in the water with pretty girls, lavish costumes, music, color, excitement—the best water show ever in America.

"What would you do if you had only five thousand dollars to your name?" Lee asked him.

"I'd invest it in the aquacade," my father replied. Well, that was no surprise to me, but it seemed to satisfy Lee.

"Give your father the money," he said.

I was still clinging to my definition of Lee as a businessman, so I did as he suggested and handed over my savings to my father. What I refused to acknowledge was that my father and Lee were more alike than they were different. Both of them lived for the next show. Their attitude was, and I suppose had to be, "This time, surely, it will be a hit." They felt it. They knew it. All they needed was the money to produce it.

The aquacade flopped. It didn't create a ripple. My $5,000 was gone, as was all the money my father had scraped together to invest in his new dream. But with it all, in retrospect, I'm glad I loaned him the money. I wouldn't have been able to forgive myself if I hadn't let him try. And I was working. I could start to save money again.

I also didn't blame Lee. Many people had been seduced by my father's dreams. Some of those dreams had paid off spectacularly, just not this one.

But I was becoming increasingly uneasy about our engagement. It had nothing to do with Lee and the aquacade. It was about my own dream that somewhere out there was the perfect man whom I would deeply love. That person just wasn't Lee. Although he was indeed handsome and kind and I couldn't find any real faults, somehow it wasn't enough. Once more I felt hemmed in. So, at the end of the summer of 1963, I broke our engagement.

Here we go again.

Naturally I wasn't at all sure I'd made the right decision. There were days when I missed Lee, and days when I didn't miss him at all. I didn't think we'd be happy together, but I knew I wasn't happy without him.

Then came Friday, November 22, 1963. The day no one who was alive at that time will ever forget. I was eating lunch in the little office at

NBC that I shared with another writer, Bob Cunniff, when Hugh Downs suddenly burst in.

"Have you heard?" he said. "There's a report that President Kennedy has been shot." The next report confirmed his death.

Within hours the breaking news was of the arrest in Dallas of Lee Harvey Oswald, an ex-marine, for allegedly killing the president.

Television came of age that dark day. All entertainment programming was canceled, and for the next four days NBC and the other networks carried live saturation coverage of the national tragedy. During what became known as Black Weekend, television turned from being the "boob tube," as it was sometimes known, to a cohesive national gathering place for a shocked nation.

NBC needed every able body it had to cover the young president's state funeral, beginning on Sunday, November 24, two days after the assassination. So I became an on-air reporter. I was assigned to a position outside the Capitol to cover the arrival of the horse-drawn caisson carrying the president's coffin from the White House. There was profound silence all along Pennsylvania Avenue that day, broken only by the muffled roll of funereal drums and the clip-clop of the horses' hooves pulling the caisson.

Hugh Downs was anchoring the *Today* show from an NBC studio in Washington, and he had to coordinate and comment on every report that came in from the various reporters in the field. He also had to deal with the surreal pictures coming in from Dallas, which only NBC captured live, of Oswald being shot to death in the basement of the police station by a local nightclub owner, Jack Ruby. As the footage of the murder was played over and over again, interspersed with live images of the funeral cortege, Nielsen, the television ratings service, estimated that 93 percent of all television sets in the nation were tuned in to the coverage. Ninety-three percent. There hasn't been anything like that since.

I remained at the Capitol where President Kennedy was lying in state in the rotunda. My job was to report on both the dignitaries and the long lines of everyday people arriving to pay their last respects. I found an old film clip from that day. I'm wearing a black coat. I have long dark hair, and I am saying, "These are the honor guards who have been guarding the casket of President Kennedy. If I feel or seem a bit choked up, it is because I have just left the last guard."

This was the first time I'd reported a national news event. But aside from that small piece of film, which brings back a moment of the event to me, I went through the day—and the night—in a fog. I was at the

Capitol, it seems, for at least eight hours. More than 250,000 people filed past the casket, and the viewing hours had to be extended late into the night and the early morning. Eventually we moved inside the rotunda, where we reported live from 2:00 a.m. to 4:00 a.m. The lines of people paying tribute to the president seemed never to end.

When we went off the air and other correspondents took over, Hugh and I went back to our hotel, completely wiped out physically and emotionally. The next day I returned to New York and watched the rest of the funeral on television—the caisson carrying the president's coffin from the White House to Saint Matthew's Cathedral, followed on foot by Mrs. Kennedy flanked by Robert and Edward Kennedy. The images remain indelible: little John-John Kennedy, turned three that very day, saluting his father's coffin from outside the cathedral; the expressions of such wrenching sorrow on the faces of the Kennedys that you wanted to turn away.

Like everyone else from coast to coast, I shared the same state of depression and shock. One single, sunny day in Texas. One deranged man. And suddenly Kennedy was gone, his assailant murdered, and his vice president, Lyndon Johnson, the new president.

A few days later I was in my apartment washing my hair when the doorbell rang. I went to the door with a towel wrapped around my head and there was Lee. "Life is too short," he said while water dripped from my head to the floor. "Let's get married right now."

I understood completely. What did it matter that we hadn't talked for the three months since I'd broken the engagement? Every doubt I'd had, every reservation about this or that, now seemed so petty compared to the glimpse into the brevity of life we had all just experienced. I can only imagine how many women got pregnant during those few days or how many couples decided not to divorce or got married. I was one of them. "Yes," I told Lee. "Let's get married."

The whole thing happened so quickly this time I didn't have time to get cold feet. My father flew up from Florida while my mother stayed behind with Jackie. Marilyn Landsberger, my wonderful friend who had welcomed me into her home after my first marriage broke up and was now married to a very nice man named Seymour Herskovitz, offered their apartment for the wedding. And on December 8, 1963, just two weeks after the Kennedy assassination, I became Mrs. Lee Guber.

Thirteen Weeks to Thirteen Years

*I*T PROBABLY WON'T SURPRISE YOU by this point, but the marriage did not get off to a great start, at least my half of it. We hadn't had the time to plan a honeymoon, so one of Lee's friends lent us his small house in East Hampton for a week. But it was winter. And freezing. Much too cold to walk on the beach, or anywhere, for that matter. East Hampton today is a very popular summer resort on Long Island, and many people go there all year round on weekends. But back in the sixties it was mostly home to self-sufficient writers and artists, and just about every restaurant was closed for the off-season. The one movie theater in town ran the same feature every night. Television had barely come to East Hampton. There was just one fuzzy channel out of Connecticut.

Lee was very sweet and cooked delicious meals—he was a gourmet cook—but all my old demons surfaced. He was a kind man and I loved him, but I wasn't passionately in love with him. Again, and this won't be a shock either, I felt trapped and restless. Perhaps I just wasn't cut out for marriage. I remember when Lee produced our marriage license and told me he had to mail it to state officials for everything to be legal, I had an immediate urge to grab it, tear it up, and tell him to forget the whole thing.

If I was bad at marriage, I was even worse at skiing. It was almost Christmas and Lee had promised Carol and Zev that he would take them to Stowe, Vermont, for vacation. Therefore, our more-or-less official honeymoon took place two weeks later in that well-known ski resort. As I've said, I liked his children, and it was a chance for the four of us to bond as a new family. Once at Stowe, Lee and his kids whizzed down the taller mountain while I took lessons on the beginners' hill.

I was miserable. My ski boots hurt my ankles. I was chilled to the bone in spite of my new and fashionable parka and ski pants. I couldn't figure out how to handle my poles, let alone the skis themselves. I saw little kids taking off and moving up to the next class while I was still plodding along, trying to navigate up and down a baby slope. When my first hour lesson was finally over, I limped off to the lodge, took off the damned boots, and sat by the fire in tears. I tried again the next day but then, while standing stock-still, I lost my balance and fell over. What a klutz! It did not help that there was a sign on the ski school blackboard reading WELCOME TODAY SHOW'S BARBARA WALTERS. It somehow made me feel even more inadequate. Sure I could talk, but I obviously couldn't do anything else. I went back to the lodge—for good. By the way, since my decision to give up skiing, I've always had a wonderful time at ski resorts. Après ski is my favorite sport.

My attitude improved when Lee and I returned to New York. I gave up my rent-controlled apartment and moved into Lee's small but charming apartment in the West Fifties near the Museum of Modern Art. I have a touching memory of him carrying me into the bedroom on our first night together. We didn't stay there too long because we were able to find another rent-controlled apartment, this time with six big rooms, across from Carnegie Hall. The comfortable old building, dating from before World War II, was owned by the same friend of my parents who owned the apartment I lived in before Lee and I married. The walls weren't in great shape when we first moved in so I had them painted a pale shade of gray and bought gray velvet drapes. I thought it looked pretty attractive, especially the way the gray walls set off the red furniture I'd recently bought, some of which I still have in my apartment today. But my mother saw things differently. "The walls match your complexion," she said, on a visit from Florida. But then she went out and bought me a lovely red crystal vase and had it filled with gorgeous red anemones, my favorite flowers. She set the vase atop the baby grand piano she and my dad had given us. (I still have the vase and the piano.) "Now," she said, "everything looks wonderful." Ah, well.

By this time, Lee and I had more or less settled into our marriage. We were both busy, had lots of friends and little to be unhappy about. At the office, however, another major shift was going on. Pat Fontaine had been let go and left the program in February 1964. Once again the *Today* Girl slot was open. Al Morgan got all excited about a well-known movie actress named Maureen O'Sullivan. He had been captivated by her performance when she appeared on Broadway in a comedy called *Never Too*

Late. We had interviewed her on the show, during which she was articulate and witty. That cemented it for Al. Without further ado he decided that Maureen would be the next *Today* Girl. He had great difficulty persuading the actress to take the job, but he finally prevailed by persuading her that it would be steady and secure, unlike the stage. Maureen, who had something like seven children (including a daughter who would grow up to be Mia Farrow), took his advice and signed on.

There were immediate repercussions. Hugh had made it very clear to Al that, after the Pat Fontaine fiasco, he wanted to have a voice in the selection of the next *Today* Girl. Hugh had to share two hours a day with her on the air, after all, and he had cause to be concerned. He had not been consulted when Pat was hired and, on more than one occasion during her erratic, boozy tenure, it had fallen to him to carry the show. But Al didn't consult Hugh about Maureen. He just went ahead and, while Hugh was on vacation, hired her. So you can imagine how Hugh felt when he came back to work to discover someone he had never met was now about to share the morning desk with him. That made for some uneasiness between Hugh and Maureen and didn't do much for the relationship between Hugh and Al. They had been at odds for some time, but now it boiled over—on both sides.

Hugh was furious at Al for hiring Maureen behind his back. Al was furious at Hugh for challenging his authority and began to develop a real dislike of him. Hugh was perfect in the morning slot, easily projecting the viewer-friendly image of a good-natured neighbor, but Al felt that Hugh was pompous and pretentious. The bad blood between them grew to such an extent that in 1968, NBC was forced to make a choice: keep Al as the producer or keep Hugh as the host. (Hugh refused to sign his renegotiated contract if Al remained on the show.) There was no contest. Hugh Downs was popular and beloved by millions. Al was a force behind the scenes. Guess who stayed and who left?

But that was in the future. The clear and present problem in 1964 was Maureen. Al had fallen into the trap that a great many producers still do. He saw someone who was charming and funny while being interviewed, so assumed that the same qualities would carry over to the role of interviewer. But it rarely works. Asking questions is very different from answering them, and a good deal tougher. Especially so early in the morning.

The morning shows, I think, are the hardest to do. You have to be very versatile. One minute you'll be interviewing the secretary of state; the next minute you'll be cooking cheese fondue with a guest chef.

Because most of these shows are live, you can't afford to make many mistakes. You've also got to be able to get in and out of a commercial, in and out of a newsbreak, in and out of whatever unexpected situation presents itself. For the most part, you have to know what you're doing. Maureen didn't.

It wasn't really her fault. She had absolutely no experience or training in television, and no one took the time to work with her. She was thrust into a situation that was anathema to an actress. Her talent was to take a script, study a character, memorize the lines, and deliver them in a winning way to a live theater audience. Now, suddenly, there was no audience to play to, just the light on a camera, and there were no lines. The role she was expected to play was not the character in a script but herself. Very, very tough for her. Things did not get better with time. Maureen continually missed cues. She couldn't control her interviews. She'd see a stagehand waving time cues frantically to her and she'd ask, on camera: "Am I supposed to end here?" Maureen couldn't get the hang of our man-in-the-street interviews, either. These had to be, by their nature, unplanned and unrehearsed. Too often she cut off the person answering a question before he or she even had time to finish a sentence. When in doubt, or out of fear, Maureen would simply throw the segment back to Hugh or sometimes even to a commercial. She began to appear more and more confused on the air. The ghastly hour she had to awake to do the program didn't help.

What we didn't know until years later, when she wrote about it, was that Maureen was on a steady diet of prescription drugs. Anyone with a drug dependency, however slight, just can't work well under such pressure. You've got to be very disciplined and well grounded to do one of these shows. And you really have to have a sane life. All we knew then, however, was that she was a terrible mistake.

DURING THE TURBULENT MAUREEN PERIOD, I had a miscarriage. We were broadcasting the program from California, and I was working very hard, too hard, perhaps. I wasn't feeling very well, which led me to hope I might be pregnant. I cannot tell you how much I wanted a baby and how exhilarated I felt when I came home and my gynecologist told me that indeed I was pregnant. I was over the moon. So was Lee.

Then I lost the baby.

I blamed myself for the miscarriage. If I hadn't been working so hard, perhaps I could have continued that pregnancy. I was devastated. I was then in my early thirties, and though most women at the time had their children at a younger age, I was still capable of childbearing. But I could hear the biological clock ticking. So I tried everything to get pregnant again. For two agonizing years Lee and I went to one doctor after another, and I took test after test. The fertility treatments available today were not even thought of then. There was no in-vitro fertilization nor surrogate mother. The very idea would have been considered science fiction. Getting pregnant was reduced to a combination of hormones and timing.

I was told to check the exact days after my period to determine when I would be most fertile. At those times I was to take and record my temperature and make sure that Lee and I had intercourse during the hours the doctor thought best according to my temperature. If the time was right, no matter if Lee was getting home very late from one of his shows or I was getting up at the crack of dawn for my show, we dutifully made love. Then we hoped and prayed. Finally it worked. But only briefly.

I suffered another miscarriage. Then, six months later, still another. Anybody who has been through a similar experience knows what an emotional seesaw it can be. You're ecstatic at the high point, then you all but fall apart when you drop to the low. Looking back now, a part of me wonders if it was some sort of sign. I feel guilty even saying it, but the truth is that I'm almost thankful I didn't have a baby. I think of my sister. Was her condition hereditary? Was nature sparing a child of mine the fate that befell Jackie? I'll never know. And I realize how harsh it might sound now. But back then my hunger for a child did not abate even a little, and Lee and I would finally adopt a baby. But I'm getting ahead of the story.

The concern in 1964 continued to be Maureen O'Sullivan. In August we all went to Atlantic City to cover the Democratic National Convention that would select Lyndon Johnson, JFK's replacement, to be the presidential nominee, and Hubert Humphrey, the senator from Minnesota, to be his vice presidential running mate. It was only nine months since John Kennedy had been assassinated, and his death hung heavily over the convention.

Robert Kennedy, who would be assassinated himself four years later during his run for the Democratic presidential nomination, somehow summoned the composure to deliver the "unity" speech at the conclusion of the convention. There wasn't a dry eye on the floor, including the eyes of the hardest-boiled politicians, when he remembered his brother in a quote from Shakespeare's *Romeo and Juliet:* "When he shall die, / Take him and cut him out in stars, / And he will make the face of heaven so fine / That all the world will be in love with night, / And pay no worship to the garish sun."

Maureen O'Sullivan cried, too, but for a different reason. She got fired. There were political interviews to be done with campaign experts, critics, and pundits, not to mention prominent congressmen and senators. Hugh couldn't do all of them, and even though we writers gave Maureen plenty of research and carefully wrote her introductions, her questions, and even probable answers, she was lost and frantic. It was obvious that she just couldn't cut it. With a fierce campaign ahead between LBJ and Barry Goldwater, the Republican nominee, the on-air future for Maureen O'Sullivan looked pretty grim. Al Morgan finally bit the bullet and told her, in the middle of the convention, that he would have to let her go.

Maureen was furious and felt betrayed by Al, who had leaned on her so heavily to take the job in the first place. But I think she was also relieved. "I was nothing but a bookend on the show," she later told reporters. The official word was that she had left the show by mutual consent, and Maureen went back to being a successful actress.

ONCE MORE the *Today* show was without a *Today* Girl. Al began his usual search for a star but he had a problem. He still had to pay off Maureen's contract, which ran for another year and a half. She made a good deal of money, and he didn't have enough left to coax a new performer into getting up each day at such an ungodly hour and taking on the task of learning the ropes of a difficult-to-do early-morning program. He had to hire someone who knew the ropes and would work for relatively little money. And he had to do it fast.

Well, like the ingenue in a corny movie, there I was: the patient and long overlooked understudy. Hugh was all for trying me out. By this time I was a known and trusted colleague. Plus I was no threat. And I could certainly perform adequately, if not spectacularly.

"Why not Barbara?" Hugh asked.

The NBC bosses knew why not. In essence their unanimous response was: She isn't known. She isn't beautiful. Sponsors won't take to her. But there was another response, too, and this one resonated as deeply as all the drawbacks they saw in putting me on the air: She'll work cheap.

Hugh persisted, and this time Al, who rarely agreed with anything

Hugh said or wanted, joined forces with him. The trick, they decided, would be to give me some on-air support. I would be on the program three days a week. The other two days there would be two different women, both well known to our viewers. Sometimes, when appropriate, I would also appear with one of them.

I was very fond of both these women. One was Judith Crist, the witty and acerbic movie critic for the now-long-folded newspaper the *New York Herald Tribune*. She was already appearing on the program giving her film boosts and pans. The other woman was a brilliant and delightful art historian named Aline Saarinen. Aline had, for quite a while, made art exhibits and other cultural matters not only understandable to our viewers but entertaining. She was the only person I have ever seen on television who was able to do this effectively. The widow of the renowned Finnish-born architect Eero Saarinen, she had graduated Phi Beta Kappa from Vassar and gone on to become managing editor of *Art News* as well as an award-winning art editor and critic at the *New York Times*. Aline had caught Al Morgan's eye in 1962 when she appeared on a CBS special about Lincoln Center, then under construction. She was an intellectual without being pretentious, so NBC executives agreed with Al's decision to hire her as a contributor. However, they didn't think she could carry a show alone.

In those earlier days of the program, both Hugh and the *Today* Girl of the moment did the commercials. It went with the job. But the sponsors didn't want Judith or Aline to do them. Judith was too caustic, they thought, and Aline so erudite and elegant that she might turn off the audience. On the other hand, I was neither caustic nor erudite, and in those days certainly not elegant. So the commercials fell mostly to me. One of the program's biggest sponsors was the canned dog food Alpo. These commercials were done live and featured real dogs panting away and licking their chops waiting for the bowl of Alpo to be placed between their paws. While the dog gulped down the yummy glob, the person doing the commercial would extol the virtues of this dog food above all others. My first week on the air, I was assigned the commercial. The famished dog, on a leash but with a mind of his own, practically dragged me across the studio floor along with his bowl. The dog howled with pleasure. I howled with laughter. The sponsors howled with satisfaction.

There would be conjecture that Al's upgrading to brains over beauty was fueled by the growing women's liberation movement and the consciousness of women's inequality in the marketplace. But I doubt it.

Though Betty Friedan's classic call to arms, *The Feminine Mystique*, had been published to great acclaim in 1963, and Congress had just passed the Civil Rights Act of 1964, prohibiting job discrimination on the basis of race and gender, I think Al's motive was more self-serving: If one of us was sick or didn't show up or bombed, he'd have two other women waiting in the wings. The three of us were his insurance against disaster, much like the story of the advertising producer who hired triplets for a Johnson & Johnson diaper cream commercial to ensure that at least one of the babies wouldn't have diaper rash on the day of filming.

Here's how the setup worked. Judith Crist was *Today*'s movie and theater critic. Aline was *Today*'s art critic. I was just me. No one knew exactly what my role really was, including me. "I'm a Lord-Knows-What," I would tell *TV Guide* three months later. In the meantime I was, thank heaven, no longer to be called the *Today* Girl. That airhead title and role was finally retired. If asked, I was to be referred to as a *Today* reporter.

I started in my new role in October 1964 with no big fanfare, no publicity, and no official announcement. Because there was no hoopla, there were no expectations from viewers. I was on the air regularly before anybody realized I was there, three mornings a week and then, slowly, five times a week. Soon I was on even when Judith or Aline had their scheduled appearances. I conducted a lot of the celebrity interviews, introduced and narrated the fashion shows and other so-called women's features, and, where I had the most fun, sat at the desk and ad-libbed with Hugh, Jack Lescoulie, *Today*'s sportscaster, and the program's newsreader, Frank Blair. I began to feel that I was doing well, and even though my future was far from assured, I was exhilarated.

I quickly discovered an odd disparity in my on-air and off-air persona. On camera, from my very first appearance, I felt calm, composed, and confident. Almost nothing threw me. I was an eager extrovert. Off camera, I was an introvert. If Lee and I were invited to a party, and he was out of town, I wouldn't go alone. I was that self-conscious and still am, though less now. I won't dance alone either. To this day I sit out the fast dances where dance partners do their own thing. Flailing around on my own makes me feel like a broken umbrella. I wait to dance until the music is slower and my partner can hold me securely in his arms. But I am not alone in this split personality. Many performers, and, to a degree, on-camera journalists are performers, are open and easy on television or onstage but very shy in private life. Robert De Niro comes to mind. A great and expressive actor on film, he's almost tongue-tied in person. On the other hand there are people who in private life are exuberant and even exhibitionists, but who suffer from such excruciating stage fright that they can't even rise to give a toast.

At one point Al sent me to a voice specialist to try and overcome my problems with pronouncing *r*. Lazy *r*'s are often a product of being born in Boston, with its particular accent. So I tried to fix it. These days I've all but conquered the problem. But then the new speech pattern the specialist prescribed sounded phony and stilted. When several viewers wrote in asking why I was sounding so funny, I abandoned the specialist and went back to my natural way of speaking. Although I did try, no kidding, to avoid sentences with too many *r*'s.

Hugh was wonderful to work with. He was always very generous in the assigning of interviews and didn't just grab the good ones for himself. He was confident and didn't have a jealous bone in his body. Over the many years we would work together, we never had a cross word. My relationship with Hugh, in fact, was one of the most satisfying of my life. Not only was I his protégée in a way, but we became great friends. He had a wonderful wife, Ruth, and at that time two small children, a girl, Deirdre, and a boy, nicknamed HR. When the *Today* show traveled abroad, Ruth usually accompanied Hugh and included me in their dinners, so I never felt alone.

Hugh and I had different personalities and different styles, yet we complemented each other. He was more contemplative and thought of himself as something of a philosopher. His questions during interviews were gentler than mine, but he never restricted me from asking what I wanted. In short he was, and is, one of the truest gentlemen I have ever known.

One of my first interviews on *Today* was with Lee Radziwill, Jackie Kennedy's glamorous sister, who attended Sarah Lawrence College at the same time I did back when she was Lee Bouvier. We lived in different dormitories, and she didn't stay long at Sarah Lawrence, but still, I thought she might remember me, if not from college, then perhaps as one of the few female reporters tagging along on the India trip with her and her sister. But she didn't remember me at all. By now she was married to an exiled Polish prince named Stanislas Radziwill. When I asked Lee what I should call her in the interview, she replied, with a bored look, "Just call me Princess." Okay, Princess.

These early interviews highlighted another difference between my professional self and my private self, a difference I've never understood. It emerged in the editing process, a critical phase of almost every story in which I've always been very involved. To my surprise I discovered I was, and am, as decisive as anyone can be. I knew precisely what should be left in and what should be taken out. Just like that. (I have always been a terrific editor, if I do say so myself—and I do say so myself.) But in private life I can barely make a decision. I second-guess everything from if I should wear the red or blue dress to where to go on vacation: Europe? South America? the Bahamas? Maybe I should just stay home. My daughter says my flip-flopping is because I am a Libra, the astrological sign whose good traits include being "diplomatic and urbane," and my favorite, "romantic and charming," but whose not-so-good traits start with being "indecisive and changeable." On my gravestone I want inscribed: "On the other hand, maybe I should have lived."

For quite a long time Lee (my husband, not the princess) got up early every morning to watch me on *Today*. This was no small gesture on his part; he was a "night person," as are most theatrical producers, and he usually stayed up till the wee hours going to Broadway plays and then on to Sardi's or Lindy's with all the other theater people. He also often had to go to one or the other of his theaters. Getting up at seven was torture for Lee. After a few months he started to check to see what time my particular spot was on and then set the alarm so he could catch just me. But even that wore thin, and after a while Lee stayed gratefully asleep while I greeted the rest of the country as it awoke. I totally understood Lee's sleeping, although it gave us less and less to talk about when I came home for dinner.

Our polar opposite schedules were not as difficult for me as they were for Lee. True, the hours were ghastly, but over time, they became a habit. I used two alarm clocks to make sure I woke up at 4:30. I wanted to be in the studio by 5:30. In order not to disturb Lee, I used to get up in the pitch black, tiptoe into my big closet, turn on my light, close the door, and dress there.

In the early days I washed my own hair every other day at home. On those mornings I got up even earlier, at 4:00. Once I was in the studio, my hair would be set in big rollers and dried under a large hair dryer. Then, and during all my ensuing years on *Today*, I would be made up by a wise and kind woman named Bobbie Armstrong. Years later, when I left NBC to go to ABC, Bobbie continued to work with me and was the greatest makeup artist, as well as the greatest comfort, I could have.

Back on the *Today* show, the hour or so before I went on the air was some of the happiest time I would spend. If Judith, Aline, and I happened to be on together, we gossiped away, shouting over the noise of the hair dryers. We all, including Hugh, got made up in the same large room, and it was there that we read scripts, made changes, and wrote notes for ourselves. Although the writers wrote the introductions to the interviews and suggested questions, I usually changed the introductions to suit what I thought sounded most like me, and I often rewrote my questions. The writers didn't mind. After all, I had been one of the writers myself. The atmosphere in the makeup room was warm and happy. We all genuinely liked one another.

Sadly, little by little, things were getting to be less congenial at home. There were those times when Lee, quite naturally, wanted me to go to the theater with him. Otherwise how could I share things in his life? I tried, though sometimes I would leave the theater after intermission. He understood, of course, and was very gracious about it, but he certainly would have preferred to have his wife by his side. To Lee's credit he never asked me to give up my job. And we never competed with each other. I was in television, but was certainly not famous then, and we took pleasure in each other's successes, even if we rarely shared the actual experience. We also, of course, were still trying to have a baby, and that didn't make our lives easier.

On the air things were only getting better for me. The viewers seemed to like me, the sponsors liked me, the Alpo dogs really liked me, and more and more I was on along with Judith and Aline, not just on my specifically assigned three days. After a few months it was decided that things were getting confusing and that it would be best if I became the only woman at the desk with Hugh while Judith and Aline went back to their specialty roles. Judith became NBC's freelance theater and movie critic. Aline, in addition to occasional appearances on *Today*, became NBC's general correspondent on the arts and, later, the host of NBC's local daytime program *For Women Only*.

At the beginning of my new job as a five-day-a-week full-timer on *Today*, I made the unbelievable-to-me salary of $750 a week. It was union scale, but I was thrilled. Maureen O'Sullivan might have been paid a far heftier salary, but it was more money than I had ever made.

NBC gave me a thirteen-week contract.

I stayed for thirteen years.

Becoming Barbara Walters

I WAS EXHAUSTED most of the time I was on the *Today* show. I learned how to go to sleep anywhere, anytime I had a few minutes. That sometimes included three-minute naps on the set during a commercial or while someone else was doing an interview. I was often so tired that if someone touched me, it felt almost like pain. To this day I can nap anytime, almost anyplace, and if for some ungodly reason I receive a phone call at 5:00 a.m., I am instantly wide awake and make perfect sense.

There were some things about waking before dawn that I liked. I really enjoyed drinking my morning coffee at the kitchen table when everything was still and quiet. It was the calmest time of my whole day. I liked the short drive from my apartment to the NBC studio. There was no traffic at 5:00 a.m. The light was just breaking. It was, in its way, so peaceful. Within ten minutes, though, I would be in my dressing room, everyone hovering over me. The peace was over.

Sometimes the whole show traveled.

Al Morgan loved to take *Today* on the road. The expense was huge, involving not only the whole entourage of writers, producers, makeup artists, and the on-air people but all kinds of technical support and equipment. But then, as now, foreign locales boosted the ratings. So, the show would travel almost every year to one country or another.

The most ambitious broadcast, in fact a historical first, took place on May 3, 1965, when *Today* broadcast live from Europe, via Early Bird satellite. This was the inaugural telecast over the satellite, the first time an event taking place in Europe was seen live in the United States. Al ran the show from Brussels, Belgium, and orchestrated the feeds from Hugh Downs in London's Westminster Abbey, Jack Lescoulie in Amsterdam, Aline Saarinen at the Forum in Rome, Frank Blair on the Capitol steps in Washington, and me in Paris, with the singer and actor Yves Montand on his balcony overlooking the city. My job for this broadcast was to add some glamour by reporting on French cuisine, French couture, and French men. Not a bad assignment.

This first satellite broadcast was so significant that it was introduced by Pope Paul VI speaking from the Vatican. (Morgan said later he'd never forget saying, "Cue the pope.") A tough act to follow, but it was almost topped by live shots of adorable little girls in their respective countries saying "Good morning," "Bonjour," "Buongiorno," and "Goedemorgen—this is *Today!*" The next cut was to London and live coverage of the Changing of the Guard at Buckingham Palace.

The satellite broadcast was widely celebrated as a breakthrough for the future of television. The print media started to take more notice of television—and of me.

There were at that time only two other significant women in television network news. One was Pauline Frederick, NBC's veteran United Nations correspondent, who was a highly distinguished reporter of some twenty years' standing. Pauline truly was a trailblazer, but she was rather stern and unglamorous and got very little media attention. The other was a stylish figure named Nancy Dickerson who had been at CBS before I started appearing regularly on *Today* and was hired away by NBC to be their Washington correspondent. She was a good friend of the Beltway establishment. Lyndon Johnson was particularly fond of her. Nancy sat in for me several summers during my annual vacation and evidently set her sights on my job. She organized a letter-writing campaign suggesting that she would be better at the job than I, which hardly endeared her to me. It also made me quite anxious. I was still very insecure, and Nancy, in truth, was far better known than I. But then she shot herself in the foot.

She was married to a very wealthy man and used to arrive at the NBC studios in a Rolls-Royce, which set some people's teeth on edge. But it was her tendency, when she didn't get the assignments she wanted, to go above the producers' heads and complain directly to David Sarnoff, the chairman of RCA, NBC's parent company. This practice slowly eroded the support she might have had among the people she worked with. Both the producers of the evening news and the *Today* show began using her less and less and finally closed her out altogether. Her career continued for many years, but she never regained the prominence she had had in her early years at NBC.

So that left me, a new face on the air, and the object of curiosity.

To the delight of the NBC publicity department, one article followed another. "That Barbara Walters is a girl no one can deny," began a full-page profile of me in the *New York Herald Tribune* on August 22, 1965. The women's movement had not yet rammed home the substitution of "woman" for "girl," but no matter, I was happy with the media attention, especially the article's title—"They Love Her in the Morning." But not just for my ego. For my status with the brass at NBC.

I'm not sure the top guns at NBC had much confidence in me during my early months on the program until they read the mounting number of articles about me, including one of my favorites, also in 1965, in the *New York Times*, "Nylons in the Newsroom," by the beautiful and, later in her career, extremely influential feminist leader Gloria Steinem. Gloria nailed the television industry's long-entrenched assumption that, as one male executive said, "Women didn't want to watch other women except on girl-type subjects," and used me, as the most visible, nongirly woman on television, to mark a step forward for womankind. I like my quote in Gloria's story, which, more than forty years later, seems so prescient. "If I wear anything below the collarbone, the viewers write shocked letters. I'm a kind of well-informed friend. They don't want me to be a glamour puss and that's fine. It means I won't have to quit or have face lifts after 40. I'm in a different category." (By the way, Gloria and I remain friends to this day. We even performed together at a charity event in Carnegie Hall. Gloria tap-danced and I sang "For Me and My Gal." We received great applause—but no one has asked us to repeat the performance.)

The reaction of NBC's executives to all this media coverage was predictable. Suddenly I was their "baby celebrity," as *TV Guide* put it back then. Before the media onslaught I'd been working in a windowless office. After a feature in *Life* magazine quoted me as saying, "There are days when I don't see daylight"—which was true, given the studio, which was also windowless, and the literal dawn-to-dusk hours I worked—I was given an office with a window. I was also given a secretary, Mary Hornickel, whom I didn't have to share. Wonderful Mary stayed with me for the next twelve years. My picture even went up on the corridor leading to the *Today* office, and NBC executives, including the CEO, actually said hello to me in the elevator.

The network had two radio programs, *Monitor* and *Emphasis*, and I was asked to start contributing to both, which I did, five days a week until I had to cut back my workload to three. Meanwhile the media continued to feed off one another and the brass fed on the media, and there I was, if not the toast of the town, at least a good bite.

In actuality my life didn't change very much. I never asked for and was not offered a raise. I had the same rent-controlled apartment and the same friends. Unlike people in the entertainment division, newspeople did not have a retinue of agents, publicists, personal managers, and hangers-on. I was happy just to have a secretary. I did get invited to premieres and opening nights of plays that I was usually too tired to attend and there was the occasional glamorous party I went to, but basically my life stayed the same. My friends didn't envy me because they knew how hard I worked and how tough the hours were. Unlike Hollywood, where an actor can make one smash film and his or her career can take off overnight, working in television news was, and is, a long and, if you're lucky, steady climb. I had begun that climb.

The ripple effect grew beyond NBC. Within a year or two of my debut, I was asked to write a monthly column for the *Ladies' Home Journal*, *Vogue* asked me for "twenty-five beauty secrets" ("Get enough sleep" probably headed the list), *Cosmopolitan* asked me to model Pucci towels, and my name started to crop up in the columns. I got offers to lecture, to write a book—nobody much cared what the subject was—to contribute personal items for charity auctions. Then came an invitation that really excited me: to appear as a guest on *The Tonight Show* with host Johnny Carson. If *Today* owned the beginning of the day, Johnny Carson owned the end of it. Nobody touched his ratings for thirty years. I was a nervous wreck before I walked out on the set, and I can't remember a word I said, but I must have done all right because he asked me back and, a few years later, even asked me to be a guest host while he was away. (I don't smoke, but just before I was about to walk on Johnny's set, I used to bum a cigarette and take one puff. It made me slightly dizzy but relaxed.) The night I guest-hosted I started with a monologue, as Johnny did every night. I talked about the difference between being a morning person and a night person like Johnny—how I had three breakfasts by noon and lived mostly on bagels. I had a vitamin deficiency, I said, for lack of vegetables. If it wasn't hilarious, it had the benefit of being true. Then I launched into my own tap-dancing routine. I wasn't as good as Gloria Steinem, but I must have been passable. After all, I'd taken tap as a kid, remember? And this time, at least, the audience didn't boo.

I even got invited to the White House. Not to an intimate dinner with the Johnsons, who were then in residence, or even to a state dinner.

But I was invited, nonetheless, to a celebration of the Head Start program. I wish I still had the invitation telegram from Lady Bird's secretary, the savvy Liz Carpenter, instructing me to present the telegram at the southwest gate of the White House. Was I ever pleased! That first invitation to the White House felt like one kind of award. Others were not quite so august. The Fragrance Foundation honored me at their annual "Give Thanks for Women" luncheon. *Harper's Bazaar* included me in its list of "100 Women of Accomplishment," Brandeis University gave me an award for achievement, and the National Father's Day Committee named me "Woman of the Year." All these awards sound like big deals, but the truth is, as we know, that organizations use celebrities, even minor ones as I was, to sell tickets. It didn't matter too much what you had accomplished. Still, it beat being "Miss French Club" or "Most Improved Athlete."

In the meantime there was another and welcome shift in the cast of the *Today* show. Sportscaster Jack Lescoulie, who had gotten rather sour, left the show in 1967 and the upbeat and witty Joe "Tell It Like It Is" Garagiola arrived. Joe had been a professional baseball player and a sportscaster for the St. Louis Cardinals and the New York Yankees before he came to *Today*. Everyone was crazy about him, including Hugh and me. Joe stayed on the program until 1973 and, in retrospect, those four years with Hugh and Joe were among the happiest years of my forty-years-and-counting tenure on television. The three of us appreciated one another's respective talents, and rather than compete, we made one another look good. This would not always be the case for me with other partners in the future, which is why I remember those years with such fondness.

Over all this harmony on *Today*, however, loomed the shadow of my family. When I look back now at my father's life from the safe distance of so many years, I am filled with admiration as well as compassion for him. His highs were so high, his lows so touchingly sad.

While I was enjoying a brand-new success, my father was suffering through what must have been such humiliation. Las Vegas was over and behind him. The aquacade venture was a total failure, another reminder of his talent and imagination gone awry. He had almost nowhere to turn professionally, so he agreed to something that would have seemed beyond reason just a few years back. In 1965 he returned to the New York Latin Quarter, but this time he was neither an owner nor a partner. He was an employee. Not only that, he was working for the man he detested. Hat in hand, pride diminished, he accepted E. M. Loew's offer to produce and direct the Latin Quarter shows. My mother packed their belongings and began the search for a new apartment in New York.

How hard it must have been for my father. The program of the Latin Quarter now, which a customer could buy, was all about E. M. Loew. It told how Loew, who was described as "soft-spoken" (you could hear him from one end of the nightclub to the other), *founded* the club in Florida, and then, with a minor mention of my father, *founded* the New York club. But the dancers and staff knew better. When my father returned to the Latin Quarter and began rehearsals, the chorus girls cheered. Even the waiters had tears in their eyes as they set up the tables for the evening and saw Lou Walters back in what had been his home.

This time, however, it was a very different situation. Loew wasn't overly generous as an employer, and even though I was making more money than I had thought imaginable, I could only help so much. I took my mother and sister shopping for clothes and bought my father the new, warmer suits he would need for New York. The days of the penthouses were long gone. Instead, my mother rented a two-bedroom apartment on Eighth Avenue and Fiftieth Street, a decidedly unfashionable neighborhood. But the apartment was close to the Latin Quarter and was in a relatively new and clean building. Most of all, the rent was low. My mother moved whatever furniture she could from Florida, once again unpacked the dishes, glasses, pots, pans, and clothes, and settled in.

Having my parents and my sister in New York was a mixed blessing. I got to see a lot more of them, which pleased us all. And they were very fond of Lee, which made our get-togethers easy and relaxed. But they didn't exactly bask in my success because they were always nervous that I would lose my job. They were proud and happy that I was doing so well, but it was pride tinged with the fear that my success might end as it had for my father. Their fears often made me fearful, too.

I remember there was also a dog. My mother felt that my sister needed something of her own to love and care for, so she and Jackie went to an animal shelter and brought home a small, sad mutt named Angel. Angel was a sweet animal but scared of everything: thunder, lightning, even traffic noises. Because my mother was usually the one to feed her, Angel became more attached to her than to Jackie. It was my mother who walked Angel because my mother didn't want Jackie to go out alone, and saw no reason for Jackie to have to go out with her, especially on cold and rainy nights. I still have a vision of my mother, wearing her heavy coat, walking up and down that dismal street with that poor scared animal. It was not a happy existence for my mother, my father, or my sister—or even for poor Angel. I found it all so sad.

My father continued at the Latin Quarter until 1969. That's when the union representing the chorus girls, the American Guild of Variety Artists, advised them to strike. The fourteen girls, reduced in numbers from a high of thirty-six, wanted a not-outlandish raise of thirty dollars a week. Loew, true to form, refused. My father was caught in the middle. One newspaper quoted him as saying, "The demands really have been a little excessive, but Loew could have settled the strike. He didn't." So the girls walked out. The Latin Quarter, a slightly shabbier version of its once-glamorous self, temporarily closed its doors shortly before Christmas, losing all the profitable holiday business, then closed for good. And that was the end, in New York, not only of the last nightclub chorus line but of my father's long-ago dream. Shortly thereafter my family returned once more to Miami Beach. Their life was going downhill. Mine was on the way up.

Now that I was becoming recognized, it made it easier for me to entice the big stars like the British actor Peter Ustinov and the incomparable Fred Astaire to do interviews with me. Great names do not guarantee great interviews, I soon learned. The absolutely worst interview I ever conducted was with the actor Warren Beatty in the midsixties. I had done all my usual preparation about Warren, who was coming on *Today* to promote his latest movie, *Kaleidoscope* (Warren had become a first-rank star a few years earlier, with his performance in the film version of Willam Inge's play *Splendor in the Grass*). I should have known when he appeared, rumpled and bleary-eyed, that trouble lay ahead. I pressed on, however, while he sat slumped in his chair, yawning, and either grunting at my questions or giving monosyllabic answers.

I finally resorted to the boring but necessary question—"Tell me, Mr. Beatty, what is your new movie about?" Silence. He scratched his chest, rubbed his hands through his hair, yawned again. More silence. "Well," he finally said, "that's really a very difficult question." That did it. "Mr. Beatty, you are the most difficult interview I've ever had," I said on national live television. "We'll go to a commercial." And we did.

Warren has since become a very good friend, but by his own admission he is a tough guy to interview.

Despite the disaster with Beatty, the amount of positive press I was getting made it easier for me to get interviews with politicians as well as movie stars. If I couldn't always get the politician, I would usually interview the wife, and often they were more interesting than their husbands.

Among them was Mamie Eisenhower, wife of former president Dwight David Eisenhower, who told me the secret of her fifty-year marriage: "We have absolutely nothing in common." I also interviewed the first lady, Lady Bird Johnson, who gave me my first tour of the White House and indirectly afforded me an unforgettable meeting with her husband.

I was at the White House in the winter of 1968 preparing for the interview with Mrs. Johnson, when Liz Carpenter, Lady Bird's press secretary, asked me if I'd like to meet the president. He had a spare moment or two and had evidently asked Liz if I would drop by the Oval Office. I was somewhat taken aback. I had never met a U.S. president before and had not prepared in any way to meet him. But suddenly there I was, being ushered into that famous office, and there he was, all six foot three and a half inches of him, looming over me. He swallowed my hand in his and asked if I wanted a Fresca. I'd never heard of the soft drink and thought wildly that it might be the name of a new dance, so I politely declined. President Johnson, who'd had his gallbladder removed a few years before (if you're old enough, you'll definitely remember the photos of him showing off his scar) and suffered from recurring heart trouble, then told me why he drank a lot of Fresca and other soft drinks. His doctors had told him he had to give up smoking, and drinking soda helped him fight the nicotine cravings. "It's god-awful," said the president. And with that Lyndon Johnson, who liked to shock people with his sometimes coarse behavior, made a chopping motion over his groin. "I would rather they had told me to cut off my sex," he said.

I was momentarily speechless. "So happy to meet you, Mr. President," I finally managed. And left the Oval Office.

I never interviewed President Johnson, but I've always wished I could have. However, there were many other people to interview for *Today*. I usually did two to four interviews a program, five days a week, and continued to do so, year in and year out, for thirteen years. That's hundreds and hundreds of interviews. I obviously can't write about or even remember them all, but certain of the early interviews have stayed in my mind, and I think they stand the test of time. These particular people fascinated me forty years ago. They still fascinate me today.

Garland, Capote, Rose Kennedy, and Princess Grace

*I*F EVER THERE WERE two brilliant, mixed-up, hugely talented artists, they were Judy Garland and Truman Capote. I interviewed each of them on *Today* in 1967.

Garland's career was already in decline. Her drinking and pill addiction had long since caused her to be abandoned by Hollywood. But music halls still loved her, and she was performing to standing ovations at the Palace Theater on Broadway. During one of her afternoons off, I went to do our interview. I was told to be in her hotel suite at noon. I was there. She was not.

By 3:00 p.m. Garland had still not appeared. If it had not been the legendary Judy Garland (Elizabeth Taylor, another legend, would make me wait just as long), I would have left hours earlier. But finally Garland emerged from the bedroom—tiny, only four feet eleven inches, wearing a dress she said she borrowed from her teenage daughter Lorna Luft—and proceeded to bowl me over with her charm, her humor, and her pathos.

Daughter Liza ("Liza with a Z") Minnelli had just married Peter Allen, a singer-songwriter her mother had discovered in Hong Kong and who opened her acts for her. Allen, a talented performer himself, although never in either Judy's or Liza's league, was rumored to be gay, and the marriage ended five years later. But back then Judy was rapturous about him. "He's a marvelous boy who is mad about her," she gushed to me, "and Liza is a lovely lady. I'm just terribly happy, terribly proud."

The marriage was later called a "mistake." (Liza would go on to make at least three more marital "mistakes," following the same pattern as her mother.) Judy, who'd had four marriages by the time of our interview and would have another brief one in 1969, attributed her marital failure rate to her assorted husbands. "The minute they get entangled with me, they say how difficult it is to be married to me," she told me. "Well, why didn't they think of that before?"

"The only mistake I ever made," she went on to say, "the only harm I ever did was sing 'Over the Rainbow.' " And then she laughed, although she wasn't entirely kidding about her signature song from *The Wizard of Oz*. She must have been sick of singing it night after night, year after year, whenever and wherever she performed.

But what a tough life she'd had. Though much had been written about her background, it was chilling to hear her tell it in person. She had been performing, she told me, for forty-three years, pushed onstage by her mother when she was a very small child. "My mother was a witch," she stated. "She would stand in the wings of the theater in which we were performing and if I didn't feel good, if I was sick to my tummy, she would say, 'You get out and sing or I'll wrap you around the bedpost and break your ass.' So," Garland said, "I would go out and sing."

Then came the movies, over two dozen for MGM alone, including the classics with Mickey Rooney, whom Garland described as "the most marvelous gentleman and the world's greatest talent." For the child star, however, life in Hollywood was not marvelous in any way. "We worked night and day," Garland told me. "I never went to a real school. You worked six days a week, sometimes seventy-two hours at a time. I could go weeks without a day off."

And what did it get her? Sitting there, tiny and curled up in the hotel chair, dressed in her daughter's outfit, she was pathetic. "Today I am broke," Garland admitted. "So I better just go out there tonight and do what I always do—sing."

It would be her final run at the Palace. Two years later Garland died in London of an overdose of sleeping pills. She was forty-seven.

TRUMAN CAPOTE HAD A LIFE that was, in its way, not terribly dissimilar from Judy Garland's. The author of *Breakfast at Tiffany's*, Capote began working for *The New Yorker* when he was just seventeen. He achieved fame with his first book, the best-selling *Other Voices, Other Rooms*, when he was only in his twenties. Capote, a notoriously heavy drinker, died of liver disease in 1984 at the age of fifty-nine. But back in 1967 he was riding high.

He was being celebrated for his brilliant 1966 so-called nonfiction novel, *In Cold Blood*, which was being made into a movie starring Robert

Blake (whom I would interview years later when he was accused of murdering his wife). Truman had also made social headlines just a year before our interview by hosting a legendary masked ball in the Grand Ballroom of the Plaza Hotel honoring Katharine Graham, the publisher of the *Washington Post*. It was referred to as the "Black and White Ball" and was packed with what were dubbed "the beautiful people." Scores of celebrities—journalists, society people, politicians, and movie stars— covered their faces with elaborate masks, the women in black or white ball gowns, the men in black tie. It was a triumph. (By the way, I wasn't invited. I wasn't a big-enough celebrity, and I was hardly considered a member of "the beautiful people," thank goodness.)

In 2006 Philip Seymour Hoffman won an Academy Award portraying Capote in his prime in the film *Capote*. To my pride and pleasure, Hoffman told me at a party that he had watched my interview something like fifty times to capture, as he did so well, the personality quirks of the character he would play.

There was much for him to draw on.

"Are you ever bored?" I asked Capote. "No, because I'm terribly curious," he replied. "It's very hard for me to get bored because even when somebody's being actively boring I'm interested in how they are boring me. I'm analyzing that, and so that keeps me entertained."

"What do I do when I feel blue? Read. I hardly ever feel blue. But I have a great sense of tragedy. I take a tragic view of life, and it's really that which accounts for the frivolous things that I do. It's sort of a compensation for having this completely dark view all the time."

Another of Capote's answers from my interview forecast his eventual decline.

"The only thing I couldn't do without is my own conviction about my own creative gifts. If I didn't have that, I think I would feel very desolate. You see, the thing about me is that I'm really several people. I spend a great deal of time alone and I work very hard. Then there's this other side of me that is constantly keeping up with everything. I need people."

Ten years later Capote wrote too honestly and bitingly about the "beautiful people" who were so important in his life. When they abandoned him after he exposed them in print, he went into the despair and desolation he had described in our interview and all but stopped writing.

His last memorable quote from the interview has to do with art and God.

"I happen to think that art is a form of religion and a way of reaching God. Occasionally and very rarely, in sudden moments, one feels in art a state of grace. It is as though a voice from a cloud is speaking to you and dictating to you what is transmitted through your hands to art. It is a religious experience."

Years later I had the opportunity to interview the great actor Sir Laurence Olivier. When I asked him how he wanted to be remembered, his answer was very similar to Capote's. "Something like an expert workman," he said. "A workman?" I repeated. "That sounds so prosaic." "Does it?" said Olivier, reflecting for a moment. "Well, I think a poet is a workman. I think Shakespeare was a workman. And God's a workman. I don't think there is anything better than a workman. Or workwoman."

THEN THERE WAS MY INTERVIEW with Rose Kennedy. God was not a workman to Mrs. Kennedy. He was central to her whole being. She attended Mass every day. Her faith in God gave her courage, conviction, and most of all, solace. I quote her now because of what it says about her remarkable sons.

Mrs. Kennedy, the wife of Joseph P. Kennedy, the very wealthy and controversial businessman and onetime U.S. ambassador to the Court of Saint James's, was the mother of President John F. Kennedy, Senators Robert and Edward Kennedy, and six other children. Two of them, Joseph Jr. and Kathleen, were killed in plane crashes in the 1940s. Another daughter, Rosemary, was brain damaged and lived in a special home where she was cared for most of her life. Then, in the 1960s, President Kennedy and Senator Robert Kennedy were assassinated. It must have been agony for a mother to bear. But Mrs. Kennedy never lost her verve, her courage, or her faith.

Growing up in Boston and having summered on Cape Cod, both places where the Kennedys had homes, I felt a special kinship. As I've already told you, Joseph Kennedy Sr. had spent a good deal of time at the Latin Quarter in Florida. Mrs. Kennedy, however, never set foot in the club. To a very large degree husband and wife lived separate lives. For a long period of time Joseph Kennedy conducted an affair with the motion picture actress Gloria Swanson. He even produced several movies for her. Mrs. Kennedy, by all accounts, both knew and accepted this arrangement.

She was a good-looking woman herself, dark hair, a dazzling smile, very thin, and very chic. It seemed almost natural to her that her husband had other romantic interests, a trait his sons inherited if the hundreds of stories are to be believed. Mrs. Kennedy remarked that her husband had rarely been with her when she gave birth to her nine children. "No matter," she said with a smile and a wink. "A diamond bracelet makes up for the loss."

But what could make up for the loss of so many of her children? The following is what she told me in November 1968. (That month would have been the birthday celebration of her son Robert, who had been assassinated just five months before. It was also the fifth anniversary of the assassination of her older son, Jack.)

"I just made up my mind that I was not going to be vanquished," she told me. "If I collapse then it would have a very bad effect on the other members of the family. So I think I owe them a certain calmness and encouragement and that's what I try to do."

She continued, "I am interested in a lot of things. I have children and grandchildren. I have this motto which I found in one of Jack's favorite books. It was actually said with regard to England but I adopted it as my own motto. 'I know not age or weariness of defeat.' And I don't analyze my feelings. I just keep on being interested."

I went on to ask Mrs. Kennedy whether, when her children were young, there was talk of one of the sons being president. She replied: "Well, I think their father always had that idea. But I wasn't conscious of it when they were growing up. I was just very much occupied in seeing that they were mentally, physically and . . ." Here Mrs. Kennedy paused, and I threw in, "Psychologically?" "No," Mrs. Kennedy said, "morally all right."

She went on. "You know, they talk about a Kennedy dynasty but I'm quite sure that there will be another family who will come right along and that is what makes life exciting." Then Mrs. Kennedy laughed. "That and the absurdity of life also makes it exciting for everybody."

Four children dead and she could laugh and talk of the absurdity of life? A remarkable woman.

I ended the interview by asking if she ever gave her sons advice. She said she had told Jack, during his presidency, that he should not stand with his hands in his pockets and that he would look much better if he held his hands behind his back as the British did in photographs. She also recalled giving Bobby some advice in a letter but ended it by saying that it might be the last time she would write such a letter because "Socrates, who used to give a lot of advice, was finally given hemlock to drink."

No wonder Rose Kennedy was one of my favorite interviews.

. . .

THE KENNEDYS in those days were considered American royalty. But we actually had our own royal princess, though my interview with Her Serene Highness, Princess Grace of Monaco, didn't give me quite the pleasure that the Rose Kennedy interview did.

The interview with the beautiful ex–movie star, which I recently watched again, took place in Monte Carlo in August 1966. It isn't one of my happiest memories, nor, I daresay, was it hers.

The 1956 marriage of the cool, patrician Grace Kelly to the eligible bachelor Prince Rainier was called "the wedding of the century." Monaco, the tiny principality on the French Riviera, is chiefly known as the home of one of the most picturesque and well-known gambling casinos in Europe. It is also known as a tax haven for millionaires who can save money while they moor their yachts, play blackjack, or just sun themselves at the topless Monte Carlo Beach Club. Monaco, and its principal (and I think only) city, Monte Carlo, is smaller than New York's Central Park. But no matter. Prince Rainier was European royalty. And with her perfect features, blue eyes, and blond hair, Grace was our version of American royalty. Most of her leading men, from William Holden to Ray Milland to Bing Crosby to Clark Gable, all of them huge stars at that time, were said to have been in love with her. But one day, while she was in Cannes filming *To Catch a Thief* with Cary Grant, she was introduced to the bachelor prince and *voilà!* as they say in French-speaking Monaco, an engagement was soon announced.

She was the Princess Diana of her time, and for weeks reporters covered every aspect of the engagement and wedding. The public couldn't get enough of it. Who were her bridesmaids to be? What was she going to wear? They showed copies of the hats Grace was supposedly going to take on her honeymoon. I think I even bought one.

It was a fairy-tale wedding. Escorted down the aisle by her father, Grace, wearing a gown designed by MGM costume designer Helen Rose, presented a picture as elegant as Hollywood could create. But this wasn't Hollywood. This was real. Grace Kelly, our golden-haired princess, then disappeared behind the walls of the palace in Monte Carlo, and we only read about her or saw photos of her from then on. She never made another film.

Her Serene Highness had also done no television interviews, and for years I had written letter after letter trying to get her to sit down with me. Finally, ten years after her marriage and three children later, two girls and the proper male heir, the palace authorities must have felt that it was time for their royal sovereign to be interviewed, and a date was arranged for me to come to Monte Carlo. This was to be her first television interview since the wedding.

Princess Grace greeted me in the garden of the palace just fifteen minutes later than our appointed time, which was certainly a leg up on Judy Garland. It is considered appropriate by most Europeans to curtsy to royalty. It is not appropriate for Americans to curtsy. I didn't. Nor did I shake hands. I just sort of bowed a bit from the waist and smiled. The princess was in a casual dress and flat-heeled shoes, and we walked together to the palace swimming pool, with a tiny rowboat in the middle of it. There we sat and talked. Some excerpts:

> BARBARA: Most of us think of a princess as sleeping in bed until noon. Having breakfast in bed. Ladies in waiting. Many servants. Is your life anything like what I have just described?
>
> GRACE: People always romanticize my life. To a great deal my life is not much different from any woman who works and has a great many obligations and a great many things to do. And three childen to look after.
>
> BARBARA: Do you think it is a very different life than if you had remained an actress and married someone in the motion picture business?
>
> GRACE: Yes, I believe so. Because when I was acting, my private life was very much my own. And now my private life is very public.
>
> BARBARA: And people like me come and sit and ask you all kinds of questions.
>
> GRACE: Which are very difficult to answer.

So far, I thought, I was asking rather banal and boring questions, not at all hard to answer.

> BARBARA: What was most difficult for you to adjust to as a princess and a monarch when you first came here?
>
> GRACE: That's a big change in anyone's life . . . different culture, different language. I spoke a little bit of French but not much. I could ask the questions, but I couldn't understand the answers.
>
> BARBARA: Is a European husband very different from an American husband? Is Prince Rainier very different from your own brothers?

GRACE: A European husband is definitely the head of the household. There are no two ways about it. I know European men are always shocked by the relationship between an American man and wife. For instance, if an American wife contradicts her husband in public, which often happens. American women are outspoken and forthright and honest and say what they think. This shocks European men quite a bit. I mean, you would never find a European woman correcting her husband in front of other people.

BARBARA: In the early days of your marriage, did you find yourself doing it? Did you learn quickly?

GRACE: I learned a lot of things. [*Laughs*] I think the thing that has helped me most in my marriage and adjusting to life here is the fact that the prince and I share the same religion. It's been a great bond between us. And I think that has helped us overcome any of the differences of our backgrounds and culture.

Note that there was no mention of the word "love."

BARBARA: How many rooms are there in the palace here?

GRACE: I don't know. I suppose there are over two hundred. I think I read that once.

We went on to talk of how the people regarded her. She thought many people in Monaco still considered her to be a foreigner. She continued to think of herself as an American. I asked if there was any role that tempted her to come back to films. She said, possibly Ibsen's *Hedda Gabler* (who, by the way, kills herself at the end of act 4).

BARBARA: If one of your daughters wanted to be a movie star, would you object?

GRACE: I think so, yes.

BARBARA: Why?

GRACE: I don't think it is ever a career or life one chooses for a daughter.

BARBARA: And yet you chose it for yourself. So what if your child says: "Mother, you did. Why not me?"

GRACE: I'll face that problem when or if it comes.

BARBARA: [my final question] Your Highness, I must ask you what most Americans want to know about you. Are you happy?

GRACE: I suppose I have a certain peace of mind, yes. And my children give me a great deal of happiness and my life here has given me many satisfactions.

(Ye gods! "A certain peace of mind"? No joy? No pride? And no mention of her husband? "A certain peace of mind"? That is the best definition of happiness for Her Serene Highness Princess Grace of Monaco?)

She must have realized how this sounded, because when I thanked her most courteously, she had tears in her eyes. True, it might have been because she had never done a television interview before and answering questions that were not part of a script might have bordered on torture for her. Still, after meeting her, I always felt that she was living an unexpected life of disappointment.

It would end in 1982 in an automobile accident with her seventeen-year-old daughter, Stephanie. The car, which Grace was driving, plunged off the steep, hairpin-turn road above Monaco, fatally injuring Grace but sparing her daughter, who was only bruised and would be treated for shock. Grace was only fifty-two, and there was conjecture that she might have suffered a stroke before the accident. (Strange, the other two most beautiful and interesting women of that generation, at least to me, Audrey Hepburn and Jacqueline Kennedy Onassis, also died way before their time.)

I have my own rather weepy little postscript to this story. I had always heard of the enchanting and beautiful hotel La Réserve de Beaulieu, which is on the Côte d'Azur halfway between Monaco and Nice. I had friends who had gone there and had a wonderful time. So I decided to treat myself to a few days of luxury there when my interview with Grace Kelly was over. I would get some sun and relax and maybe meet a new friend or two.

I arrived in time for cocktails and was given a small table in the lovely garden. I ordered a glass of wine and sipped it alone. There were Americans at adjoining tables. No one looked in my direction. I was just a single woman sitting alone, and they obviously didn't recognize me, if indeed they had ever even seen me on TV. I finished my glass of wine, and when cocktail time was over I sat on the restaurant's terrace and had my dinner alone. The next morning I went down to the area of the small swimming pool. All around me were smiling couples, chatting away. I sunned alone, had a large lunch alone, more cocktails alone, and yet another dinner alone. The next morning I canceled the rest of the weekend and took the first plane home to New York.

I don't know who was more lonely, Princess Grace or I.

Born in My Heart

Y HOMECOMING WAS A happy one, made all the more so because Lee and I were about to begin the most joyous chapter of our life together. After three miscarriages, too many hormones, and way too many thermometers, Lee and I came to a conclusion that was both exciting and scary.

We would adopt a child.

Back in the sixties it wasn't as difficult to adopt a baby as it is today. *Roe v. Wade*, the landmark decision by the Supreme Court upholding a woman's right to abortion, would not become federal law until 1973. We thought we were pretty advanced in our thinking, but single mothers were neither cherished nor applauded. Babies born out of wedlock were called "illegitimate." Pregnant unmarried women were said to be "in trouble" and had a hard time making a go of it. They were often sent away on a seven- or eight-month "vacation" by their anxious parents so they could have their baby away from neighbors' judgmental eyes, and then many times the baby would be put up for adoption. As a result of society's stigma, there were more unwanted babies available than there are today.

Lee and I went to an adoption agency. At the interview, I expressed my concern that I might not be considered the best candidate because I worked full-time, but the counselor told me that wouldn't be a problem. She also told us that there was a long waiting list. We put our name on the list and said we would wait.

And then this miracle occurred. Lee and I were going to the theater one night with a couple who weren't exactly close friends, more like acquaintances. I used to double-date with the woman occasionally before she and I each married. When we ran into each other one day, we said, "We must get together." This was the night we got together.

The woman, let us call her Jane, was now married to an extremely wealthy man, whom we shall call John. His family owned a very large lumber company. After the theater, over supper at Sardi's, a popular theater-district restaurant that catered to a show business clientele, Jane told us that she and John had, two years earlier, privately adopted a baby girl. They now wanted to adopt a boy. And not just any boy. A tall, blond, fair-skinned boy to mirror their blond, blue-eyed, fair-skinned daughter. Since they were short and dark-haired, they obviously weren't thrilled with their own looks.

Jane and John were so determined to find that tall blond boy that they were once again pursuing private adoption. Most adoption agencies at the time divulged few details about a child's natural parents; even basic facts like health and family background were kept secret. So Jane and John had asked their company's lawyers to locate prospective unwed mothers of suitable backgrounds and physical characteristics who planned to give up their babies for adoption. The lawyers also met, if possible, with the fathers. The lawyers had a checklist of what to look for when interviewing the parents—for example, had they attended high school, had they graduated? The lawyers were also instructed to find out if the parents had any possible genetically inherited diseases, like diabetes.

I remember being shocked at their calculated approach toward custom-tailoring their children, although in these days of "designer babies" it doesn't seem that strange. But then all I could think of was Nietzsche's belief in a superior being and Darwin's theories about the survival of the fittest. Lee and I didn't care what the sex of our child would be or his or her hair color or height. We just wanted a healthy baby.

Then came an offer we couldn't refuse.

Jane and John wanted a boy. Period. Again, back in the sixties, there was no way of knowing before the baby was born what sex it would be. So they were looking for a couple who would absolutely agree to take the baby if the child was a girl. Lee and I looked at each other and said, almost simultaneously: "We will."

We told no one. We did not decorate a nursery. We did not buy a layette. We waited quietly.

Jane called from time to time to say the lawyers had met this woman or that couple, but no one who fitted their specifications. Finally they felt they had found just the right candidate. The mother-to-be was single and came from a good family. The parents did not know their daughter was pregnant. She was living in a different state, and was only nineteen, so she did not feel she could take on the responsibility of raising a child. Both she and the father-to-be were tall and fair-haired. No known hereditary diseases.

We continued to wait.

Then came the unforgettable day. I had just gotten off the air and was myself being interviewed by a print journalist when my phone rang. It was Lee.

"It's a girl," Lee said. "She's ours!"

I looked at the woman who was interviewing me and burst into tears. "I'm a mother," I sobbed happily, and swore her to secrecy.

Actually I swore everyone in the office close to me to secrecy. I didn't want the word to reach the papers for fear our baby's biological mother would learn we were the parents. But what I really wanted to do was to rush up and down Rockefeller Plaza and shout out the news, "We have a baby! We have a baby! Hallelujah!" I was out of my mind with joy and couldn't wait to see her.

That night Lee and I laughed and cried. We made love without worrying whether or not it was the right time of the month. We bought airline tickets to fly to the state where the baby was born. The hospital told us we'd have to wait until the infant was four days old before she could leave the hospital. The birth mother was fine. She had no idea who we were and had no desire to meet us. Nor did we want to meet her.

Remember, this was long before the idea of "open adoptions" became a reality or even an option. The identity of adopted children and their birth parents was kept sealed and not available to the child or the new parents. This was considered the best way. The adoptive parents could handle the situation however they wanted and tell their child whatever they wanted.

I don't know if Jane and John ever found their fair-haired, blue-eyed, very tall son. After the birth of the baby, we lost touch. But let me just tell you that my daughter has blue eyes, fair hair, and today she is slightly over six feet tall.

I immediately told my parents and sister, who were living in New York at the time, about the baby's birth. They were ecstatic. We decided to name the baby Jacqueline after my sister. This was fine with Lee. For my sister this naming was truly meaningful. She was now in her early forties. She would never have her own child, and baby Jackie would help to fill that need.

Right after I told my family I told my producer, but I also said that I would not mention the baby's birth on the air, nor would I send out announcements. Again, I was afraid the birth mother would put two and two together and realize that I was the woman who now was parent to her baby and I didn't want her to be in touch with me—or eventually with Jackie. To this day, she never has been. She must have wanted secrecy, too.

All we knew about our baby was that she was healthy. We knew there was no diabetes in her family. We were also told the mother had a high IQ and that she was not Jewish. In turn the birth mother knew almost nothing about us except that we were married and would be loving parents. She didn't care in what religion her baby would be raised. We paid all the birth mother's hospital expenses and her lawyer's fee. That was that.

The same day as the wondrous phone call, I called my cousin Lorraine in Asbury Park, New Jersey. She had followed her father into the clothing business and owned a children's store. Lorraine, who knew much more about what I would need for the baby than I did, immediately sent me a complete layette—bibs, diaper covers, undershirts, one-piece jumpers, blankets, sheets, towels. She also sent a bathinette and a changing table with compartments for diapers, everything I would need. A close friend loaned me her own baby's bassinet and, later, her crib.

The new baby would sleep in what had been our library. It had dark brown fake leather walls. Very chic for a library, very grim for a nursery. No time to paint. Our creative set designer on *Today* made us huge pastel butterflies. We hung them on the walls, and the room was suddenly enchanting. We hastily called a domestic employment agency, did some quick interviewing, and hired an experienced baby nurse.

Four days after the baby's birth, we flew to pick her up. On the one hand I was impatient with desire to hold her in my arms. On the other hand I was nervous. Would I even know how to hold her? I hadn't had much experience with babies and had no parenting lessons. Maternal instinct would have to make everything all right. I had brought with me a soft, flannel one-piece pink bunting for our new daughter, along with a white cuddly blanket, diapers, a bottle, formula—whatever I was told was necessary. I was more or less prepared.

I didn't want to go to the receiving floor where the baby was to be delivered to us because I was afraid of meeting the birth mother. Lee went upstairs with the bunting. A nurse then dressed the infant and put her into Lee's arms. He came downstairs and put our baby in my arms.

Even as I write this, I get tears in my eyes. I cannot properly express my joy as I welcomed this tiny pink bundle. Her face was partially covered by the blanket, so I gently pulled it back. My daughter, Jackie, was the most beautiful baby I had ever seen. Perfect features. One little dimple in her left cheek. My cousin Shirley, when she first saw Jackie, said: "She has a mouth like a rosebud." No hair, just some blond fuzz. Blue eyes. Perfect hands and feet. Perfect.

According to the baby book I immediately began to keep, our daughter weighed seven pounds and was twenty-one inches long, a little longer than average. Later on I also noted in the book that she smiled spontaneously at the age of one month. (Could it have been gas?) She discovered her hands and feet at twelve weeks and recognized Lee and me easily by four months. She crawled by eight months and was, of course, the most brilliant baby ever born. Not only that, she may well have been the only baby born that year who had to lie about her age.

After receiving Jackie, Lee and I went immediately to the airport. "How old is the baby?" we were asked at the check-in counter. "Four days," we said proudly. "Too young to fly," said the ticket agent. "A baby has to be eight days old to be allowed to fly."

We turned in our tickets and went to another airline. "Eight days," we said, and we boarded a plane with our sleeping infant.

I changed her diaper on the plane. Awkwardly. Diapers were cloth then and fastened with huge safety pins. I stabbed myself several times before I got the hang of it. I fed her a bottle. I held her to my chest, to my face, to my lips. "She is ours," Lee kept saying. "She is ours." Seven days earlier we had no way of knowing if we would ever have a child. Now we were parents.

And my parents were grandparents. My sister was her aunt. From the time of the baby's birth, there was no thought in their minds that she wasn't their flesh and blood. I don't think they ever used the word "adoption" to me. Their newborn granddaughter was theirs, and by "theirs" I mean all three of them. And that was fine with me. I wanted them to feel that the child was as much a part of them as she was of Lee and me. Judging from the way they doted on her, they did. All three couldn't get enough of her.

When Jackie was born, Lee's son and daughter were in their late teens. They were very sweet with her, but they had their own interests as well as other younger half sisters and brothers, for their mother had also remarried. So although they held their new baby sister, made the proper cooing noises, and never expressed any jealousy, Jackie was not really a part of their lives.

You can read all the baby books on the care and handling of an infant, but nothing prepares you for the reality. I remember the sweetness of the smell of a newborn. It is the purest, most delicious scent. I remember how teeny she was, and my fear that I wasn't supporting her head properly when I bent over to take her in my arms. I remember testing the water of her little bathinette with my elbow as I had been told to do, to make sure the water was not too hot. Both Lee and I diapered her. In those days you scraped the diapers clean into the toilet before you rinsed them out and put them in a big hamper for a diaper service to pick up. Nothing was too much. Everything about this beautiful little creature was wondrous. In particular I thought my Jackie had beautiful legs. Now, almost forty years later, she still does. I also delighted in that one little dimple on her left cheek. How adorable.

In the months after Jackie's birth, I didn't say a word about her on the air. When I finally began to talk about her, I got letters from some viewers saying that they had known all along that I was pregnant. They could see it. By the way, had I actually been pregnant, I would not have been allowed to appear on the air unless I disguised my pregnancy. Pregnancy was hidden then. In her stint as a *Today* Girl in the fifties, a pregnant Florence Henderson was always shot from behind the desk. But then again, there were few women on live TV at that time, pregnant or not.

When Jackie got older I didn't bring her into the studio, the way many working mothers do today. Now, if you are on television and have a child, you can carry the baby in, change it, nurse it, put it down to sleep, and everybody oohs and ahhs, as they should. Some cast members on daily talk programs even negotiate a special room for their babies and nannies. When Rosie O'Donnell was doing her own daytime talk show at NBC, she had a whole nursery set up, not just for her own children but for the small children of members of her crew. It was like a daycare center. But when Jackie was born, children weren't welcome. It would have been like bringing in a puppy who wasn't housebroken.

I tried to stay home as much as possible. On the nurse's day off, Lee stayed with Jackie until I got off the air at 9:00 a.m. and raced back to the apartment. I loved to give Jackie her bottle, although the pediatrician told me that she was what was known as a "spitter." After she was fed her bottle, she would regurgitate quite a bit of the formula when you burped her. I became an excellent burper, but my clothes were getting ruined. My mother solved the problem by buying me a bunch of cotton dresses called Swirls. You tied them around you and they covered whatever you were wearing. Jackie finally grew out of her spitting phase, but to this day she has a bit of a weak stomach. Only she won't let me burp her.

Jackie was never with an occasional babysitter. During her first two years of life, we hired two different women who were qualified, experienced infant nurses. They didn't want to stay with a family for more than a year, as they deliberately resisted getting to love the child too much. I'd heard of nurses who resented the fact that the mother wanted to be a mother, and I made certain that mine allowed plenty of time and space for Mommy. I wasn't nursing Jackie, so it was all the more important for me to feed her her bottle as often as I could. That included her 5:00 a.m. feeding. After all, I was already awake myself.

When Jackie turned three, two amazing women came into her world. They were so integral to her life, and mine, that I want to introduce you to them. One was a vivacious, extremely intelligent French woman named Thérèse de la Chapelle. She asked us to call her "Mademoiselle," which we shortened to "Zelle." Everyone who ever came into our house knew Zelle.

I could write a book just about Zelle. She came from a distinguished family who had an old but still very-much-lived-in château close to Lyons in France. Her father was a baron, her mother a baroness. When her beloved *bonne maman* died, Zelle herself became a baroness. Not that it did her any good. She was the eldest of fourteen children, and as her large family needed the money after World War II, she was sent all alone to this country to take care of relatives in Chicago. There she learned English and stayed until her relatives said they no longer needed her help. She then moved to New York and helped to raise a little boy, whose mother was an alcoholic, until he was ready for boarding school. I heard about Zelle from friends of the boy's mother. Zelle remained close to this child all his life. Ours was only the third position Zelle had ever taken.

I remember the first day she came to us. Jackie was barely three, and it was time for us to hire someone who we hoped would take a permanent position. I was on the telephone (of course) when Mademoiselle de la Chapelle arrived. While I was talking, Jackie toddled up to Zelle and put her tiny hand in hers. It was love at first sight for both of them.

Zelle never took a day off until the summer months. Then she would return to France. I was usually on vacation during that time and could take care of Jackie myself. Zelle would return to us in New York in late summer. Practically every nickel she made went to her family to keep up the ancient château. But the reality was that in short order Zelle became part of our family. Our home was her home in every sense of the word. She was involved with all aspects of Jackie's life, and when Jackie was grown Zelle more or less became *my* governess.

She was a great character. She was teeny tiny skinny and never seemed to eat. She hoarded every present she ever got, a result, I think, of her wartime experience and having to do without. In all the years she lived with me, she never called me by either my first or last name. If she came into my room, she would say simply, "Knock, knock," and if she had to take or give a message, she would simply say, "Your friend said," and so on. After Jackie outgrew needing a governess, Zelle ran the house. She did the marketing, checked all the bills, answered all the phones, ran errands (everyone in the neighborhood knew her), helped out if we entertained. She was a bundle of energy, running, running, running.

Zelle stayed with us for thirty-four years until she became very ill and felt she should return to France for good. She missed us terribly, and I missed her more than I can adequately express. I made sure she had the best medical care, but Zelle died in her family home in 2004. Jackie was, by then, long grown up, but she and I cried together when we got the news about Zelle's death, and to this day we tell each other Zelle stories.

By the time Jackie was a toddler, I was making pretty good money so I could afford two helpers. Zelle took care of Jackie. Another amazing woman did everything else. Her name is Icodel Tomlinson, and she and I have lived together now for almost thirty-five years.

Icodel came to live with us shortly after she left her native island of Jamaica (she is now an American citizen). During our years together she managed to raise a daughter and three sons. Her son Phillip graduated from the Columbia School of Journalism. Her daughter, Yvette, got her master's degree from the Tisch School of the Arts at New York University. We all rejoiced at Yvette's wedding a few years back when she married one of my tape editors, Mark Burns. Icodel's children are part of my life, too.

Icodel brought into our home her great humor, special wisdom, and the most loving heart, and she became the backbone of our small family. I have never heard her raise her voice or criticize anyone. She did most of the cooking and cared for our home, although she had her own apartment. When Zelle didn't interfere, she also played for many happy hours with Jackie.

They were an interesting pair, Icodel and Zelle. Icodel, cozy, always good-natured, and Zelle, elegant as only a Frenchwoman can be, cultured, high-strung, often jealous of Icodel's easygoing ways, but totally loyal and responsible.

What they had in common was that each loved Jackie as if she were her own child. Between the two of them, especially because Zelle was always there, I could travel anywhere in the world and know that Jackie would be all right, no matter what the circumstances. An enormous relief. And, in spite of the fact that each woman blamed the other for any small crisis, we all lived together quite happily for more than thirty years. Jackie was fortunate to have these two women as constants. So was I. I count my blessings that they found their way into our lives.

Still, did I feel guilt? How do I count the ways? Is there a working mother on earth who doesn't? Mine was compounded in the sixties and seventies by the fact that working mothers like me were still a minority. These days the pendulum has swung so far the other way, toward work, that sizable numbers of mothers are leaving the workforce to stay home with their children. There is no perfect solution. Just exhaustion. And, my favorite word, guilt. I am known for saying that you *can't* have it all—a great marriage, successful career, and well-adjusted children—at least not at the same time. It's a bit easier today because there are employers who are more flexible, who may let you work part-time, and there are BlackBerries so you can work wherever you are, and there are husbands who will change diapers. But it's still a balancing act and probably always will be.

I cherished every moment I could spend with Jackie. We would sit on the floor many an afternoon and play with her "mouse house," a sort of doll's house I had bought her with little Mommy and Daddy mice and their mousy children. We spent every weekend I was home together, often with Shirley, who adored Jackie almost as much as I did. Summers, Lee and I rented a house in Long Island. My parents and my sister, Jackie, visited and couldn't keep their hands off our baby. They would play with her all afternoon in the sandbox or the little rubber tub we kept in the backyard. God knows how she ever learned to walk, because one or the other of them, my mother, father, or sister, was always holding her or wheeling her around the block in her stroller. Jackie rewarded them by being the most adorable girl imaginable. Almost from babyhood Jackie would give my father what he called her "show business smile." This was a big broad smile the toddler somehow knew delighted her grandpa. My heart melted seeing my father so happy around his grandchild.

Lee was also a loving and devoted father. As in many cases when a man has a second family, Lee could and did spend more time with his little Jackie than he did with his other two children when they were young. First of all, he had been very busy establishing his career, and second, his marriage to their mother wasn't that happy. Although it was usually the weekends when he and I could play with Jackie together, Lee was home most mornings when I was at work, and I was with her in the evenings when Lee was at one of his theaters. There was no doubt that she was the darling of our lives.

As baby Jackie grew older, she loved being with her aunt Jackie. They would do coloring books together, and the little girl particularly loved brushing and combing my sister's long blond hair. But there gradually came the time when the little Jackie outgrew these activities with the big Jackie. Without our ever articulating it, she knew that her aunt wasn't as bright as she was. I can't remember when this actually occurred, probably when the child was about ten or twelve. But my sister always loved her namesake, and little Jackie was unfailingly kind to her.

My biggest concern was when and how I should tell Jackie she was adopted. There was no question in my mind that I would. At that time there were two popular and quite different theories. One was to wait until the child was old enough to understand and then explain that she was a "chosen" child. The alternative was simply not to tell the child at all.

For advice I turned to Haim Ginott, a delightful, commonsense Israeli child psychologist who appeared regularly on the *Today* show and had a great sense of humor. (I once asked him whether it was all right to spank a child when he or she was really naughty, and he replied: "I've always felt that if it's a choice between spanking the child or killing the child, spanking is better." But I never did spank Jackie.)

He suggested I should just let the adoption come up naturally with Jackie, with no timetable.

Dr. Ginott was very big on parents bathing with their young children of the same sex. I thought this made sense. I looked forward at the end of almost every day to taking a bath with Jackie. The tub became our adoption forum. I loved soaping her up and splashing away with her. She would sometimes touch my breasts and my body. Jackie was curious, and I felt that here would be my opportunity. I held her little body against me. "Some babies come from their mommies' tummies," I would tell her to make things understandable. "But you, my darling, you were born in my heart."

I meant it then. I still do.

Dean Rusk, Golda Meir, Henry Kissinger, and Prince Philip

THERE WERE TIMES when I wondered why, as the mother of a small child, I would allow myself to work in dangerous surroundings and circumstances. The first time I questioned this was just two months after we'd brought Jackie home, when I was being teargassed at the infamous Democratic National Convention in Chicago. It was August 1968; the Vietnam War was tearing the country apart, and the rift came to a head that terrible week. And it was all being televised for everyone to see.

All of us from *Today* were staying at the Conrad Hilton Hotel, right across the street from Grant Park, where there were multiple and furious confrontations between the baton- and tear gas–wielding Chicago police, the Illinois National Guard armed with automatic weapons, and the thousands of antiwar demonstrators who had come from all over the country. Our production office in the hotel became an informal infirmary for some of the bruised and battered demonstrators. One of our production assistants was beaten with a billy club by a member of Mayor Daley's riot police, as were twenty-one other journalists and photographers. Our press credentials were no protection during the riots. I wasn't beaten, but I was reporting from right in front of our hotel, filming the police clubbing people and dragging them into paddy wagons. I will always remember the sickeningly sweet smell of tear gas spreading through the crowds and permeating the Hilton.

In spite of it all there was a challenge and a thrill reporting such a story. When a reporter is in danger, he or she usually loses all fear. I know I do. For a time you put your real life aside—or maybe this *is* your real life.

The year 1968 had already been a violent one: Martin Luther King Jr. had been gunned down in Memphis in April and Bobby Kennedy had been shot to death in California in June. Overseas, American soldiers were dying in increasing numbers in Vietnam. We documented the escalating casualty rate, which had reached more than 36,000 dead, every morning on *Today*, with no end in sight.

President Lyndon Johnson was a political casualty of the war. He had announced at the end of March that he would not seek reelection. Thus, five months later, this chaotic Democratic convention had drawn many groups in support of the antiwar presidential candidates, Senators George McGovern and Eugene McCarthy. They also came to protest the potential nomination of LBJ's vice president, Hubert Humphrey, and his presumed continuation of Johnson's war policy. Those four days in Chicago were a nightmare for America, but for the reporters it was where the news was, and where we wanted to be.

Humphrey won the Democratic nomination despite the protests, though he didn't win the presidential election. He was narrowly defeated in November by Republican Richard Nixon, thus marking the end of the Democratic administration. That included Secretary of State Dean Rusk, who had served under both President Kennedy and President Johnson, making him the second-longest-serving secretary of state in history. (Only Cordell Hull, under FDR, had held that position longer.) Rusk, considered by many to be a stubborn architect of the Vietnam War, kept his own counsel and did few interviews. Knowing he was going to leave the government, everyone wanted to interview him. I did, too, but I didn't think I had much of a chance. There were too many senior political and diplomatic correspondents vying for the chance, including veteran journalists Eric Sevareid and Walter Cronkite at CBS. Plus I hadn't done any really important political interviews. But I had a curious advantage over the other correspondents.

I'd met Rusk at a Washington cocktail party in the summer of 1967. Hugh was on vacation, and I was heading the morning show alone, which the secretary of state evidently took note of. A week into my assignment I got an unexpected fan letter from him, which still hangs, framed, on the wall in my apartment. This is what he wrote:

The Secretary of State
Washington

August 28th, 1967

Dear Miss Walters,
    As a regular viewer of the Today Show, my spirit moves me to
write you a little note to say how much I admire and appreciate
the job you are doing. Perhaps I was moved to do so by your
splendid handling of the show in August.
    If NBC Vice Presidents ever begin to bother you, show them
this letter and others like it and tell them to leave you alone.
    Cordially yours,
                    Dean Rusk

I was surprised and delighted with this personal and rather humorous letter from a man not known for being personal or humorous. I
immediately wrote him a thank-you note and asked for an interview. He
declined politely, and that was that. Then, wonder of wonders, soon
after he left office, he chose me to sit down with him for his first interview. His fan letter to me had obviously been a sincere one, but still, his
choosing me was very important to my career.
    My first serious and exclusive political interview took place in a room
at the Hay Adams hotel in Washington. Secretary Rusk and I talked for
four long hours, and covered everything from Johnson's, and his, controversial Vietnam policy to his own personal reminiscences of life
inside the Kennedy and the Johnson administrations. When we finished
he thanked me for not asking him any frivolous or naive questions that
would have "embarrassed" him, to which I replied that *I* would have
been embarrassed to ask them. Then we went outside to go on to our
next appointments. And it is the next moment that has stayed in my
memory all these years.
    I had a car waiting to whisk me to the airport so I could start editing
the film in New York. I presumed that the former secretary of state
would have one waiting for him as well, but he didn't. "I no longer have
a government car," he told me. "I'll just grab a cab." I was stunned. Here
was this man who had been one of the most powerful people in the
world with cars and planes at his disposal. Here was I, a reporter, offering a lift to the former secretary of state, a man to whom the whole
country had looked. All the trappings of power and success were gone.
He thanked me for my offer but went off in a taxi.

The interview was a great success. It contained so much new and historically interesting material that we cut it into five segments and *Today* ran one of them every day for a week. Newspapers across the world picked up Rusk's comments and wrote stories about them. Editorials followed. It was an important milestone for me.

Two years later I was pleased when Rusk chose me again for another headline-making interview. The top-secret Pentagon Papers had just been leaked to the *New York Times*, documents that chronicled the government's internal planning and clandestine actions during the Vietnam War. Rusk, then a professor of international law at the University of Georgia law school, blamed television for much of the opposition to the Vietnam War, but he seemed beaten and heartsick as he admitted to mistakes he had made. "I, myself, underestimated the tenacity of the North Vietnamese and may have overestimated the ability or willingness of the American people to accept a protracted struggle of this sort," he told me. "They're an impatient people and they like this sort of a thing to come to an end." (How prescient his words seem today in the clamor over Iraq.) I didn't interview Rusk again, but he and I stayed in touch over the years until his death in 1994 at the age of eighty-five.

Though the first interview with Rusk helped to give me credibility as a serious political journalist, I continued to interview people in the arts—Ginger Rogers, Andrew Wyeth, Leopold Stokowski, Lauren Bacall. (I particularly loved Bacall's tough candor. When I asked her about Frank Sinatra, who had proposed to her some years after the death of her husband, Humphrey Bogart, only to dump her after their engagement was leaked to the press, she pointed to the floor and snapped, "Frank is as dead and dry as this floor." Remember that phrase, "Hell hath no fury like a woman scorned"? Bacall was living proof.) But now I wasn't limited to those sorts of interviews. I could move in different directions. One very important interview was with Golda Meir, then prime minister of Israel.

American women, especially those in the throes of the women's movement, were fascinated by the very different lives of Israeli women. Women over eighteen were required to serve in the Israeli armed forces, many did manual work in collective farms, or kibbutzim, and one of them, Mrs. Meir, had risen to the highest political office in the country.

The prime minister seemed an unlikely role model when she arrived in the studio with her sister, who lived in Connecticut. The heavyset, stern-looking seventy-one-year-old woman seemed more like a rather forbidding grandmother than a head of state. Like my grandparents,

Mrs. Meir's parents had emigrated from Russia. The prime minister was eight when the family settled in Milwaukee, Wisconsin, where she had gone to school and then to college.

She had been a teacher in Milwaukee, she told me, before she and her husband immigrated in 1921 to Palestine, where she lived on a kibbutz raising chickens. "Before that," she said, "I was afraid to be in the room with one chicken." One of the founders of the State of Israel in 1948, she had gone on to serve as Israel's first ambassador to the Soviet Union and as Israel's minister of labor and then foreign minister before becoming Israel's first—and to date, only—female prime minister. All this as a single mother of two. (She and her husband had long since separated.)

I was always interested in how women balanced their work life and their children, so I asked whether she, as a mother, had had to make "great sacrifices." Her answer did not reassure me or American feminists who were clamoring for child-care centers modeled on Israeli child-care collectives, so they could work outside the home. "There's no doubt the mothers pay for it with pangs of conscience," the prime minister said wearily. "I suppose the children do, too." She quoted her grown daughter as saying she'd felt "sad" and resentful as a child that her mother was away from home so much. But there was a trade-off, which every working mother, including me, hoped for: Her daughter also said, in retrospect, that her mother's work had added "something to the home." It had given her a "much broader aspect" and "interest."

"Naturally one has a feeling that it's done wrong to the children, but it turned out all right," Mrs. Meir said. "They don't hold it against me at any rate." (Years later, when I left NBC for ABC, I interviewed Mrs. Meir during my opening week. Sadly, it would be my last interview with her.)

Another early interview, this one with Kathleen Neal Cleaver, the spokesperson for the militant Black Panther Party, was chilling. Married to Eldridge Cleaver, a revolutionary and convicted felon, author of the best-selling autobiography *Soul on Ice*, and then a fugitive living in Algiers, Kathleen articulated the racial fury among many young urban blacks at the time, which had led to riots in the Watts section of Los Angeles, Detroit, Cleveland, Newark, and nationwide after the assassination of Martin Luther King Jr. The Black Panther ten-point program, however, did not reflect Dr. King's nonviolent philosophy.

"If black people can't have the freedoms of life, liberty, and pursuit of happiness, cannot have the fruits of their labor, then we will take the position that no one can have them," she said. "We will have them or the earth will be leveled by our attempts to gain them."

I tried to strike a common bond with the twenty-four-year-old revolutionary, pointing out that she was pregnant, that I had a baby, and that both of us shared the hope that our children would grow up in a free and good society. "Is there any way that the people like me and the people like you can come to some agreement, or does it have to be only a revolution?" I asked.

"I don't see any solution other than a total change of the existing relationships in society," she replied. "A total change of the economic system, of all the institutions which are not only oppressive and exploitative, but anachronistic and out of keeping with the times."

We finally reached some shaky common ground when she agreed that the struggle was not restricted solely to race but to class as well.

"Slave against master," she said. "The lower classes against the upper classes. The classes of the ruled against the classes of the ruler."

The revolution she called for never came to pass. Many of the Black Panthers succumbed to internal squabbling or were killed or imprisoned. The movement, which FBI director J. Edgar Hoover called the "greatest threat to the internal security of the country," gradually imploded. But Kathleen Cleaver went a very different route. She would go on to Yale University on a full scholarship and graduate summa cum laude and Phi Beta Kappa. After graduating from Yale Law School, she worked in the prestigious New York law firm Cravath, Swaine & Moore before joining the law faculty at Emory University, where she remains today.

In the midst of all this I also had an unexpected interview with Queen Elizabeth's husband, Prince Philip, and with Henry Kissinger, President Nixon's national security adviser—both courtesy of the president himself.

Nixon, in fact, turned out to be one of my greatest champions. I met him in 1969 at the White House while I was filming an interview with his daughter Tricia in the Rose Garden. He had the reputation of being reserved and socially awkward, but to my surprise, he seemed relaxed and, to my bigger surprise, almost charming. He was so friendly, in fact, that I kidded him about the stag dinner he was hosting that night at the White House for Prince Philip, pointing out that it seemed a clear case of sex discrimination.

"Is Prince Philip going to do the *Today* show?" Nixon asked me.

"No," I replied. "We've tried to get him, but so far we've gotten nowhere. He's turned us down."

"Tell you what," Nixon said. "I'll speak to him tonight."

I had never thought of the president of the United States as a booking agent, but he turned out to be one. Late that night I got a call from the British Embassy saying that Prince Philip would be available in the morning. Prince Philip must have been angry as hell, but we got the royal interview—and inadvertently raised a furor in England. My question was simple enough: "Might Queen Elizabeth ever abdicate and turn the throne over to Prince Charles?" It was Prince Philip's answer— "Who can tell? Anything might happen"—that created huge headlines in the British press and brought out crowds in support of the Queen. Buckingham Palace had to issue a statement saying the Queen had no intention of standing down.

I quickly wrote Prince Philip a note of apology that I'd put him in such an embarrassing position and received a personal reply from him on Buckingham Palace stationery bearing the crest of the royal coat of arms.

Dear Miss Walters,
   Thank you so much for your kind and thoughtful letter. It was most appreciated by both of us.
   To be the means of unlocking such a spectacular display of cheerfulness and goodwill is a great satisfaction, particularly in this day and age when most demonstrations seem to reflect nothing but anger and provocation.
   I remember the interview very well. It appears that you have forgiven The Queen for not abdicating.
   Yours sincerely,
                         Philip

A year after that President Nixon delivered for me again. This time he persuaded Henry Kissinger to sit down for the *Today* show. I was pleased, but it was hardly a personal favor done out of the goodness of the president's heart. Richard Nixon understood the use of television to promote his administration and its policies. I was well aware of that, but being on the receiving end of Nixon's television savvy wasn't all bad. We used each other, and that's the way it has worked with so many guests I've talked to over the years. People come on TV because they want the exposure and a forum to advance whatever it is they want to advance. And I want something, too—the interview.

So it was that I introduced Henry Kissinger to our audience in December 1970. As national security adviser, Kissinger was controversial, to say the least. Though one of Nixon's campaign promises had been to end the war in Vietnam, the United States was still bogged down there (*Today* had continued to run its roll call of combat deaths.

There had been another 6,164 in 1970). But Kissinger, with his slight German accent, was a curiosity to the public, and a very powerful man. We discussed at length the issues of the day and then, because no one knew much about him, I asked him a few personal questions and got one response I particularly loved. My question was about how fame had changed his life. "The nice thing about being a celebrity is that, if you bore people, they think it's their fault," he said.

I interviewed Henry Kissinger many more times over the years, and we became close friends. Dr. Kissinger and his wife, Nancy, are frequent guests at my home and I at theirs. Of all the interviews I did with him as he went on to be secretary of state for both Nixon and his successor, Gerald Ford, one remains foremost in my mind. It took place when I was at ABC.

When his best-selling book *Diplomacy* was published in 1994, my producer and I took him back to Fürth, his small hometown in Germany, nestled near the larger and more famous city of Nuremberg, where the post–World War II war crimes trials of the Nazi leaders took place.

It was in Fürth, where his father taught at the gymnasium, or secondary school, that Dr. Kissinger spent the first fifteen years of his life. In 1938 he and his family fled the Nazis and came to America. As we strolled the streets during the interview, Kissinger reminisced about his childhood, pointing out his family's old apartment, now a manicurist's parlor, on the third floor of a building. He also took me to the site of his first passion, the town's soccer stadium. As a child Henry was an avid fan of the local soccer club. As a Jew, however, he wasn't welcome in the stadium, so he had to watch every game through the mesh at the end of the field.

When we got to the stadium I asked the cameras to turn off. "Come on," I said to him. "Let's go inside." I took his arm, and the two of us walked into the stadium and quietly sat down. No one expected us. I don't know who recognized Kissinger first, but one after another the people in the stands slowly turned their heads to look at him, until *everyone* was staring. The soccer game stopped, and even the players were looking at him. Then the clapping began and spread around the stadium. Soon the entire stadium was on its feet, applauding its native son. We both had tears in our eyes.

BUT BACK TO the *Today* show and another memory of a world-famous political figure. I celebrated my fortieth birthday on the air. Well, "celebrate" may be too strong a word; "endured" is more like it. There was the de rigueur cupcake with a candle in it and all sorts of funny but affectionate jokes about aging from Hugh and Joe. When the show was over I went back to my office to find my assistant, Mary Hornickel, holding the phone with a quizzical expression on her face. "There's a man on the phone who says he's Lyndon Johnson." "You're kidding," I said, but when I took the phone and heard that familiar Texas drawl I knew that it *was*, indeed, the former president. He was calling from his ranch in Texas.

"Lady Bird and I are lying here in bed watching TV and she said, 'If you had any guts you'd call Barbara and wish her happy birthday,'" he said.

"Thank you very much, Mr. President," I responded. "But the truth is this birthday does not make me very happy."

"I know, I know," he said. "But you know, you really are an inspiration to women all over America."

"That's nice of you to say," I told him. "But I certainly don't feel very inspiring today."

"Well, let me tell you a little story," Johnson continued. "We had a man down here in Texas who ran for Congress ten times, and was defeated ten times. Finally, after twenty years of trying, he ran again—and was elected. So the press asked him, 'What do you think this means, Mr. Congressman?'

"And he told them, 'I'll tell you what it means. It means that if I can make it, any idiot can make it.'"

Then Johnson paused, and said: "And Barbara, when those women out there watch you—"

I laughed, said, "Thank you, Mr. President," and hung up the phone. To this day I don't know whether Lyndon Johnson meant to call me an inspirational idiot or just inspirational, but no matter, I was astonished and touched by his call.

It sure was an improvement over my thirtieth birthday, when I'd gotten all dressed up in my borrowed designer outfit only to be stood up by Gianni Uzielli.

Sad Times in Florida

*I*N 1970 MY FAMILY RETURNED to Florida from New York. It was not an improvement. Aunt Lena was living in Miami Beach, and my parents rented a one-bedroom apartment in a building across the courtyard from her. My sister had to sleep in the living room on a pull-out couch, but it was all they could afford. My father was miserable.

My visit to that apartment was bittersweet. I brought little Jackie with me to lighten up their lives. My mother cherished the baby, and my father lavished attention on her. But one night my parents got into a terrible fight over her. Each accused the other of waking her up and making her cry, resulting in a series of charges and countercharges that got so angry my father walked out of the apartment and didn't come home all night. I don't know to this day where he went. Did he sleep on a park bench? Did he walk the beach all night? My mother and I were terrified that he might once more try to take his own life, but mercifully he reappeared in the morning. As with his suicide attempt, we didn't ask any questions.

Their fight is the bitter part of my memory. The sweet part is that it was the first time my daughter kissed me. I don't know how old babies are when they learn to do that, and maybe she was just imitating a kiss, but she put her lips on my cheek and it gave me the most wonderful feeling of happiness and love.

I knew I had to rescue my parents and sister from that cramped apartment or they would have killed one another. Back I went into my savings and bought them a larger, two-bedroom condominium in a good—I felt I couldn't afford great—building in Miami Beach. It was in a nice-enough neighborhood, and, most important for my mother, it was just a two-block walk from the supermarket.

In retrospect I probably *could* have afforded "great," and I should have bought them a condominium in a better building in Miami Beach. But I was still so afraid of the vagaries of television that I didn't have the nerve to risk more money. So they settled into their new place. My mother and sister slept in twin beds in one bedroom; my father slept in the other. And sleep is what he did most of the time. He found some men in the building to play cards with, but no one he could really talk to. My mother, who always complained that she had no friends, continued her life with, at most, one or two new acquaintances. My parents didn't go out much and were rarely invited to other people's apartments. Remember, wherever they went they took my sister. They didn't want to leave her home alone. And though my sister had perfect table manners and was very sweet, it was difficult to have any real conversation with her.

Lee tried to help out by giving my father some work, but my father's talent was limited. It lay in producing spectacular shows with lots of sexy girls, and that didn't translate to Lee's "family" tent theatricals. So my father's sixty-year career in show business quietly drew to a close.

My sister settled in better than either of them. I got her a made-up job as a teacher's assistant at the Hope School, a local private school for intellectually impaired children. I made donations to the school and continued to do so for a great many years. It was a wonderful place. Jackie was picked up by bus every morning and stayed at the school until noon, filing papers and running errands for the teachers. She loved it and took her tasks there very seriously.

Life in the new apartment, however, continued to be tense. My mother and father argued, mostly about money. I remember one bitter scene when my mother found out that my father had spent some of the money I'd sent them to buy State of Israel Bonds. There had been a fund-raising meeting in the building, and most of the tenants were there. "He has no money," she said to me. "How could he do it? Why does he always have to be a big shot?"

Well, he wasn't being a big shot. I understood that it was important to his pride that he be able to buy a bond, just like his cardplaying friends. Yes, he had been a big spender. But his talent was to see everything in a huge way. If he had listened to my mother, he never would have put his last dime into a nightclub in an old church in Boston and expected it to work. He would have taken a job selling shoes or dresses like my uncles instead of traveling all the way to Nova Scotia putting on little shows trying to earn a living for his family.

So here he was, buying an Israel Bond, saying, "I'm successful and can afford it," and my mother saying back, "Why do you always have to be a big shot? You can't afford it." And there I was, as always, in the middle, as my mother's messenger. "Talk to your father and tell him that he can't . . . that he owes . . ." On and on. But I didn't say a word to him about the Israel Bond. Instead I quietly slipped some cash into his pocket.

Both my mother and father hated being financially dependent on me and constantly apologized about it. I used to respond: "Everything I am, you made me. You sent me to good schools. You allowed me to travel. You taught me to read and be curious. I'm lucky to have the chance to pay you both back." And I meant it.

Oddly, the man who'd always thrown financial discretion to the wind worried constantly that I'd lose my job. "Do your bosses like you?" he would ask. "After that show, did they send you a note?" Here was a man who'd never been the slightest bit nervous about his own future, yet he constantly fretted about mine. He saw my career through the lens of show business, just one bad review from closing. But then again, so did I. Some magazine, I can't remember which, did a profile of me around that time and quoted my father as saying that my childhood years of such financial instability had cast a "halo of fear" over me. It was in that same article that I learned that he had indeed considered becoming a salesman to support us after the death of vaudeville. What a tragedy that would have been. My father cast as the self-deceiving Willy Loman, the doomed, disillusioned character in *Death of a Salesman*.

During this depressing time in Florida, I began more and more to see my father in a different light. Instead of seeing him only as a man who had neglected his wife and children and was never home, I also saw him as a man who stayed with a woman he could have left years earlier, a disappointed woman who had trouble sharing his dreams.

But how could she share his dreams? They had turned into nightmares for her. My father had run through several fortunes, even cashing in his life insurance policy, and was reduced to financial dependency on his daughter. She had had to endure one tragedy after another—one child dying at fourteen months and another child mentally retarded. Yet to her very great credit, she remained a loving mother to my sister, helping her dress every day, doing her hair, being her constant companion. She also remained a devoted wife, in her way, to my father, fussing over him, cooking his favorite foods, brewing his tea in a teapot.

No one can ever really understand other people's relationships, and I didn't try. As much as I loved my mother and my father, I was always relieved to return to my work in New York.

IN JULY 1969 I was given the plum assignment to go to North Wales in Great Britain to cover the investiture of Prince Charles as Prince of Wales. Royal investitures are elaborate, lengthy, and rare pageants. This one, bestowing the title on the twenty-year-old heir to the British throne, was only the second in the twentieth century and followed well-defined traditions unchanged over the centuries. Every movement, every costume and prop, every participant, has some sort of ancient meaning and I had to know every one of them.

I had some help from Princess Margaret's husband, Lord Snowdon, whom I'd interviewed for *Today*, and who was the architect of the elaborate ceremony. We were in Wales for a week, and all I can remember today is that there was a Gentleman Usher of the Black Rod and a Silver Stick in Waiting, but, by God, when we went on the air for five straight hours, I knew every stick and rod there was, and why, and what they were supposed to do with them. I had also memorized every historic name and its significance and could identify virtually every Prince, Princess, Duke, Duchess, Earl, and Lady What's-Her-Face coming out of the thirteenth-century Caernarfon Castle after the ceremony, including Lord Snowdon, who was running about in a green velvet suit looking rather like a little elf. With it all, I loved Wales and had a wonderful time.

After that I just kept going. The *Today* show traveled all over the place—to Jamaica, where I remember getting high on rum with Hugh and his wife, Ruth; to the Greek islands, where Win Welpen, a very funny and beloved producer, writer Barbara Gordon, and I drank ouzo at the local taverna and learned to do Greek dances—we looked like a poor man's version of Zorba. There were trips to Holland, Italy, Portugal, and also to Romania, where the Communist May Day parade thundered right past our hotel, as well as a memorable, freezing-cold trip to Ireland, where our wise "prop" man gave us our early-morning orange juice with a big shot of Irish whiskey in it—some of the happiest mornings I've ever had.

Scotland was more sobering. I went down into a coal mine and it was a devastating experience—the blackness, the utter dark, the feeling of death. I brought home a piece of coal from that mine and kept it for years on a table in my living room as a stark reminder. Our trip to Japan presented another reminder—my gender. The Japanese invited Hugh everywhere but wouldn't invite me because I was a woman, so I spent a lot of time in my hotel room. Hugh had a swell time in Japan. I didn't.

Don't think the gender issue was restricted to Japan. At NBC the men in suits had not undergone consciousness raising either. The women's movement was in full cry by the end of the sixties, but they barely seemed to notice. Women's groups all over the country were holding demonstrations to legalize abortion and to demand equal pay for equal work. Women were picketing the *New York Times* and other newspapers around the country to protest sex-segregated want ads—executive-training openings for men, gal-Friday openings for women—and men-only bars and restaurants, including the Oak Room at the Plaza Hotel in New York and the Polo Lounge of the Beverly Hills Hotel in Los Angeles.

One display of women's determination took place in New York in the summer of 1970 when some fifty thousand women, led by Betty Friedan, marched down Fifth Avenue in what was called Women's Strike for Equality. Fifty thousand is a lot of women and, not surprisingly, the turnout got a ton of press. I wrote a memo to the president of NBC News, Reuven Frank, suggesting a special hour on the women's movement. This is the reply I got from him: "Not enough interest."

The dismissive attitude of many men toward women at the time was certainly not limited to NBC but was pervasive throughout the media. We few women journalists in television were struggling to find our places in the male-dominated newsroom, and none of us knew if it would ever change.

Winning Nixon, Losing Sinatra

$\mathcal{A}$T THE SAME TIME that women were fighting for equal rights, I unexpectedly added a new arrow to my bow. You know that old saw—one thing leads to another? Well, an article I wrote in the late sixties certainly proved that expression true. It provided what I hoped was helpful advice about how to talk to a celebrity. It was prompted by a new trend emerging at the time: celebrity lectures. More and more "names" were traveling around the country to speak (for money) to all different kinds of organizations and charities. The growing business of lecturing meant that more and more so-called ordinary people were meeting these celebrities, searching for something memorable to say or trying to connect personally with the speaker if only for a moment in time—yet not having a clue how to make that connection.

I drew from my own budding celebrity the kinds of things people said to me, which were often mistakes, like: "You look better in person than you do on television." How do I answer that? "Thanks a lot. It took me two hours of makeup and hair and I still look lousy on television?" Or, what was just as well-meaning but worse: "You look so much better on television than you do in person." I still can't think of the right response to that one.

I wrote the article and thought that was it until I shortly thereafter got a letter from Doubleday. It contained, you should excuse the expression, an offer I couldn't refuse. Ken McCormick, the editor in chief, had read the article and thought it could be expanded into a little book for tongue-tied, socially awkward people—the many people who worry that they can't think of the right thing to say to start a conversation.

And so I set to work on *How to Talk with Practically Anybody about*

Practically Anything. The idea was that there were all kinds of situations in which people just didn't know what to say. These situations included not only when talking to a celebrity, but to someone you don't know at a dinner party; to a person who has just lost a loved one; to a child; to an athlete when you know nothing about sports; to a tycoon—even to a bore.

The book was published in 1970. I thought it was a nice helpful little book, but to my great surprise it became something of a phenomenon. It just kept selling and selling. There I am, on the cover, in a bright pink dress with my real dark hair, smiling away. No wonder I am smiling. By now the book has been through eight printings, sold thousands and thousands of copies worldwide, and been translated into more than a half a dozen languages. People still come up to me with old copies to autograph. I continue to be amazed by its success.

In writing the book I drew on my own social awkwardness, because I was still rather shy off camera. To make the book more fun, I also threw in anecdotes from almost every celebrity I knew, and there weren't that many. Mostly there were a lot of mentions of Hugh Downs and Bennett Cerf, the two celebrities I knew the best at the time. Bennett, the head of Random House, the publishing company, was best known for his many years on the enormously popular television quiz show *What's My Line?* He was also known as a great raconteur, and I quoted him throughout the book. But mostly, the advice came from my own everyday experiences. Want to know how to tell if a guy, not wearing a wedding ring, is married? My advice was to admire his tie, jacket, sweater, whatever, and say: "How good-looking. Did your wife choose that for you?" Simple. And you get your answer.

Want to get some tycoon to open up? Just ask for a description of his or her very first job. Trust me: everyone, from presidents and movie stars to policemen and moving men, remembers his or her first job and will relate it in minute detail.

I used as one of my examples my meeting with the Greek shipping tycoon Aristotle Onassis, soon to marry Jackie Kennedy. I had been invited by his press people to meet Mr. Onassis at a lunch in New York. When I arrived (looking better in person than I did on television), Onassis was surrounded by shipping people busily discussing tonnage. I sat silently until there was a momentary lull in the conversation, and then, all wide-eyed with curiosity, I inquired, "I wonder as I listen to you extremely successful gentlemen how you all began? For example, Mr. Onassis, what was your very first job?"

There was no more talk of tonnage. Onassis traced his first jobs, as a young immigrant from Turkey to Argentina (his father had been jailed during the persecution of the Greeks by the Turks), starting as a dishwasher, then becoming a construction worker and finally a cigarette salesman, which ultimately led to his first fortune. By the end of lunch Mr. Onassis was my new best friend and, moreover, had agreed to let me interview him on his legendary yacht, the *Christina*, with its swimming pool and gold bathroom fixtures. Sadly his schedule and the NBC camera crews didn't work out, so I never got that interview. Who knows? Had we worked things out, I, instead of Jackie Kennedy, might have been the next Mrs. Aristotle Onassis. Yeah, right. . . .

From tycoons and VIPs to drunks and lechers, I kept ladling out advice. I wrote how I squelched one persistent knee-grabber at a dinner party by looking deep into his eyes and saying, "You're absolutely right. We *are* meant for each other. Why don't you divorce your wife and marry me?" I never felt his hand again.

I ended the book with "When All Else Fails—Twenty Sure-Fire Conversation Starters." Some came from my friends and colleagues, but others were ones I used in interviews. Here are a few that would still work today.

1. If you were not doing the work you are now doing, what would you most like to be doing?

2. If you could live at any time in history, when would you have wished to live?

3. If you could be any person in history, who would it be?

4. If you were suddenly given a million dollars and told that you had to spend it just on yourself, what is the first thing you would buy?

5. If you were hospitalized for three months but not really too sick, whom—and it can't be a relative—would you want in the next bed?

That last question was one of my favorites because it got so many funny answers.

The comedian Alan King chose the actor Richard Burton because Burton's then wife, Elizabeth Taylor, would come to visit.

Liberace, the flamboyant pianist, chose the secretive, taciturn Greta Garbo so that he could do all the talking.

Johnny Carson didn't miss a beat with his answer: "The best damn doctor in town."

One day I hope to update this little book, with its somewhat useful and sometimes entertaining advice. But first I've got to finish this tome, so let's get back to the early seventies.

My budding celebrity also had its dark side. Most people in the public eye get lots of letters, some from fans, some from crabby critics, still others from prisoners incarcerated in their respective prisons. So I paid little attention to a love letter I received from a besotted fan during my early time on the *Today* show, saying how much he adored me. Then came the second, third, and fourth letters from the same man, and an ominous change in tone. He wanted to kill the pope. He wanted to kill Lee. "I watch you," he wrote. "I see you." It was frightening. Was he watching me leave my apartment in the predawn stillness of New York? Was he planning to throw acid in my face between the building and the car? Was he really planning to kill Lee? It is a federal offense to send death threats through the mail, and luckily my stalker wasn't too bright. He put his return address on the letters. We went to the police and they arrested him in his apartment in the Bronx. He turned out to be a big man who struggled violently to escape arrest, and we breathed easier when he was in custody. Lee pressed charges and he was sent to jail. That made us breathe even easier. My anxiety rose again when some time later the authorities notified us he'd been released from jail, but mercifully, I didn't hear from him. I continue to this day to get letters from fans and nonfans and prisoners, most of whom declare their innocence, but I have never been threatened again. Very scary experience.

On a much happier note, in the summer of 1970 I met a man who would become my adviser and very dear friend. His name was Lee Stevens, and he was an agent with the William Morris Agency, then as now one of the biggest theatrical agencies in the business. The agency represented many top actors, directors, and writers. They represented no one in news. No talent agency did at that time.

None of us in television news had agents; at least I don't think anyone did. People in news were considered too pure to ask for anything as crass as more money. Agents were for entertainers. Those of us in the news division were supposed to treat the industry as if it were a privilege to belong. True, we were far better paid than print journalists, who came close to taking vows of poverty, but still, none of us were getting rich.

People in the television entertainment divisions, however, made tons of money and had agents and managers and publicists and lawyers. In 1970 Johnny Carson, for example, was reputed to be making some $3 million a year. But we journalists were a different species. In my case every time my contract was renewed, I'd simply be called in and told what my salary was going to be, and I'd say, "Thank you, good Lord." It never occurred to me to question my salary.

Then one day Lee Stevens came to lunch along with Hugh and his wife, Ruth, and assorted other people at a summerhouse my husband, Lee, and I were renting for a month. The two Lees were friends. They were both in show business, where even dog acts had agents. Lee Stevens assumed I had an agent as well, and was amazed when I told him I didn't. To make a long story short, by the time that very pleasant summer afternoon was over, I not only had a new friend, I had an agent. I had no idea at the time what a pivotal role he would play in my professional life.

I had already signed a three-year contract with NBC for the 1970–72 seasons and was making what I considered to be a fortune: $2,500 a week with an additional raise of $500 a week annually. That didn't mean I was living high off the hog as much of that money still went to support my family in Florida. But neither was I standing on a street corner with a tin cup. Since I had already signed this contract, Lee told me that he would not charge me the usual 10 percent agents traditionally took from a client's salary. During the term of the contract he would represent me gratis. Should I go on to any new ventures, however, William Morris would receive its customary 10 percent. It seemed like a good deal to me, especially as I could not imagine having any new "venture."

So I didn't give money a thought when NBC came to me in 1971 and asked me to take over *For Women Only*, the local morning discussion show my colleague Aline Saarinen had been hosting, that immediately followed the *Today* show. Part of the local NBC affiliate's public affairs department, it was a thoughtful program that attracted few viewers but provided the station with its proper FCC credentials. (The Federal Communications Commission required all television stations to provide a certain amount of programming dedicated to the "public interest," or risk losing their licenses. The FCC list included children's programs, news, and, relevant to Aline's program, public affairs.) As NBC's cultural correspondent, Aline invited intellectuals and academic authorities to sit on a panel and discuss what *Variety* described as a "deadly serious and icily cold forum of pubaffairs discussions." A small studio audience, experts on a particular subject who were invited to attend, was there to ask questions.

Aline's goal was certainly worthy, but not many women were ready for such an intellectual exchange at 9:00 a.m. Still, the program would probably have plodded along if, out of the blue, NBC had not offered Aline a fantastic opportunity—to go to Paris as its first woman bureau chief. Needless to say, she accepted. (Sadly, she would die a year later of brain cancer.) So now her little morning show was adrift and, floating around, was offered to me.

This meant that, in addition to two hours of national broadcasting five days a week on *Today*, I would be adding to my schedule another half hour of local television. I was hesitant. "How can I do all this?" I thought. "Will I ever see my husband or my child?" Then I was told that we could tape all five programs in one day because that would save the station a lot of money, and it would be my show to host and to book. Still, I hesitated.

For weeks I watched Aline doing her show and decided that the premise was a good one but that the subject matter could be broadened beyond local issues. We didn't have to deal with just a half hour on the city's water supply, we could discuss the hot topics of the day. (Years and years later this simple idea became one of the tenets of my ABC daytime program, *The View*.) I asked NBC if I could broaden the subject matter and, to give the program a fresh start, if we could change the name from *For Women Only* to the rather cumbersome but I hoped more all-encompassing *Not for Women Only*? NBC agreed, and I then agreed to be the host.

The inaugural broadcast took place in September 1971, immediately following the *Today* show. I was worried that there would be more of Barbara Walters in the morning than the audience could bear, but the program was an almost immediate success.

It isn't that I threw the baby out with the bathwater. I simply expanded the subject matter and reduced the purely public service format. When we did go the public service route we tried to make the subjects more personal and more relevant to our audience. Little by little, without making the program frivolous or reducing its intent to provide information, we changed it. Some changes were physical. To make the program more interactive, instead of seating the audience in neat little rows, I put them at round tables. This made the audience feel more relaxed and engaged with the panel. As a result they were not afraid to ask questions or challenge assumptions. Furthermore, the audience was no longer just experts but rather men and women who wrote in for tickets and therefore brought us people who asked questions the folks watching at home would most want asked. Though I didn't know it then, *Not for Women Only* would become the prototype for later women-oriented discussion programs hosted by the likes of Phil Donahue and Oprah Winfrey and, still later, as I've said, my own daytime program, *The View*.

To make the program more meaningful, I tried to choose themes for the show that related to the lives of both the studio audience and the viewers at home—"Is the Family Dying?" "Sensitivity Training," "TV and Children," to name just a few. I threw in some lighthearted themes as well, like "The Hostess with the Mostest," which examined the best ways to throw parties. We had a really experienced panel for that one—the very funny author and Washington hostess Barbara Howar, newspaper columnist and hostess supreme Phyllis Cerf (wife of Bennett), and fashion designer Mollie Parnis, then one of Manhattan's leading hostesses. They dished about what made a great guest and what made a great bore. It was name-dropping with a purpose, another forerunner of *The View*.

I was delighted when the program took off. NBC was even more delighted. Their little local broadcast, buried in the morning before the hugely popular soap operas, was becoming a program to watch and therefore a program to be sold to advertisers. My own schedule was now insane. The addition of *Not for Women Only* meant I not only had to prepare for the interviews I did for the *Today* show, but for the varied themes of the new program.

I had a wonderful producer named Madeline Amgott and a small staff of very hardworking women, but I still did a lot of the booking for *Not for Women Only* and wrote my own questions. The books and magazines piled on my bedside table reached life-threatening heights. Leisurely weekends became a distant memory, as did quality time with Lee. Why I drove myself so hard I cannot imagine. Was it ambition? Was I afraid that my days on *Today* would not last forever? Was it money? It couldn't really have been the latter. NBC paid me only an extra eight hundred dollars a week to moderate *Not for Women Only*, which came to $160 a program. I think it boiled down to the fact that I was grateful for the opportunity to prove myself once more. I had passed another audition.

My past work in public relations was proving very helpful. Just as I'd learned that anything about sex in the lead of a press release caught the attention of its recipient, so also was sex a surefire seller on *Not for Women Only*. Whenever the ratings slipped, we did a program that dealt with some aspect of sex. I remember that for one full week we explored female and male sexual dysfunctions. We had the most dignified and respected experts address these issues, and our questions were also dignified, but we managed to be candid and therefore exciting in a way few shows were in those days.

For example, on one program a sex therapist demonstrated how to discourage premature ejaculation by using a rolled-up towel to simulate a penis and showing the audience where to squeeze it. This was valuable information. Weeks later, I was on a shuttle from New York to Washington, D.C., when a young man approached me and asked me how hard to squeeze a penis. I was about to report him to the flight attendant until I realized he had seen *Not for Women Only* and was seriously asking for my expert opinion.

After several months of taping five programs in one day, we cut down the exhausting schedule. We began to tape three shows on Tuesdays and two on Thursdays. But some of the panels, like the time we had the wives of Nixon's cabinet members, were important enough to run for the entire week. For those we continued to tape all five days in one six-hour marathon.

It was madness. The wives—Barbara Bush (husband George H. W. was then U.S. ambassador to the United Nations), Adele Rogers (husband William was secretary of state), Lenore Romney (husband George headed the Department of Housing and Urban Development), Anne Richardson (husband Elliot headed the Department of Health, Education, and Welfare), and Martha Mitchell (still more or less sane when her husband, John, was the country's attorney general)—arrived in the studio with their clothing changes on hangers so that each day a segment ran, they'd look different. We had a ten-minute break after each half-hour taping session so everyone, including me, could change clothes. All of us chattered away and compared outfits. It was like being back in the dorm at Sarah Lawrence.

Our efforts paid off. Within six months of the revised show's debut, the ratings tripled. NBC's Washington affiliate picked it up, for which I was paid an additional $300 a week. That's when Lee Stevens went to the brass at NBC and suggested that they syndicate *Not for Women Only* with Syndicast, a national media distribution company. NBC did, and within a year or so the program was running in eighty cities. Thanks to Lee I was making $5,000 a week from *Not for Women Only*, twice as much as I was being paid for the *Today* show. NBC was turning a handsome profit as well.

It's pointless to play the "what if" game, but I could kick myself now for not asking to own a piece of *Not for Women Only*. Had I had my own production company then, as I do now (Barwall Productions), I could have owned *Not for Women Only* and had a syndicated program that could have gone on for years. Just call me Oprah. (I tend to exaggerate.) Oprah, who is the best there is, established Harpo Productions, Inc., in 1986, which owns, produces, and distributes the *Oprah Winfrey Show*, the most successful talk show in television history, across this country and abroad. (At last count her program was being broadcast in 132 countries.) She's one smart lady. Yet I'm not sure, as part of the news division, that I could have "owned" *Not for Women Only*. In any event I didn't ask and I didn't get.

Being in the news division dictated a lot of what I could and could not do. It still does. For instance, the women currently on *The View* are provided with clothes every day if they want, and the designers are given credit. But not me. I can't, because as a member of the news division I'm not allowed to accept "gifts" and I can't give credit, which is seen as an endorsement. I almost always wear my own clothes when I'm on the program, or any program for that matter. I manage this with a lot of mix and matches.

In the early days of the *Today* show when I needed a varied wardrobe, designers like Kasper gave me samples to wear. I was a sample size back then, and Kasper was a dear friend. Sometimes, if I liked a particular outfit, I could buy it at cost. I remember I once purchased what I now think of as a quite hideous outfit comprising a purple plaid coat with two skirts, one the same purple plaid and the other a solid purple. I then bought two jackets, one plain purple, the other once again plaid. I could mix and match for days of ghastly outfits. I even found purple leather boots. I was the cat's meow. Or rather, the cats all meowed when they saw me.

I had other designers who were friends and either loaned me clothes or offered them to me at a reduced price. One was Halston, who was then the very hottest designer. All the socialites and movie stars of the time were buying Halston clothes. His muse was Liza Minnelli. Halston made me many mix and matches—a dark red coat with a dark red skirt and dark red pants for traveling, along with a beige skirt and a beige sweater to be worn with a dark red belt and the dark red coat. I took this whole outfit to Romania when the *Today* show traveled there. I didn't need anything else. Halston was very expensive, but his clothes were so basic and practical I wore them for years. Some of those pieces I still wear today, like the deep red pants with the matching coat—and this is more than thirty-five years later.

I never wore provocative clothes on the air. None of us did in the news division. I wore suits or dresses with high necks and long sleeves. My body hardly showed at all, except for my legs in the miniskirt phase. It was an unspoken rule then that the only way for a working woman to be taken seriously was to be sexless.

Things are much more relaxed now, but the basic rule for women anchoring news programs hasn't changed that much. We basically still wear suits. It's only in relatively recent years that I've begun to wear pants instead of a skirt for a serious interview. I distinctly remember one of the first times I did this, and it was to the White House, no less. It was in January 1996, when I was scheduled to interview First Lady Hillary Clinton about her new book, *It Takes a Village*. A fierce snowstorm had closed all the New York airports, but I was determined to get to Washington. (I was worried that Mrs. Clinton, who was facing a new round of scandalous allegations about Whitewater, might not reschedule if I canceled.) So I put on a pair of pants and snow boots and clumped myself to the subway to take the train from Penn Station. When we finally crawled into Washington I clumped my way in knee-high snow up Pennsylvania Avenue to the White House. There was Mrs. Clinton, also wearing pants. I thought she might change for the interview, but she didn't, and for the very first time, she wore pants in an interview. She looked great. Mrs. Clinton is quite small on top but rather large in the hips. The pants flattered her figure, and now one rarely sees Senator Clinton in anything but pants suits.

On an earlier trip to the White House, this one in 1970, the weather was kinder and my outfit far dressier. The dinner was formal, and I wore a black high-necked and long-sleeved dress. No big statement there. Washington is a very conservative city when it comes to fashion. Lee and I had been invited to a dinner for the great American painter Andrew Wyeth. I'd interviewed Wyeth the year before for *Today*, but the central character of this story was not Mr. Wyeth but Richard Nixon.

I hadn't seen the president in the six months or so since he'd persuaded both Prince Philip and Henry Kissinger to sit down with me for the *Today* show, and I didn't know whether he'd even remember. But he did. When I jokingly thanked him for being the best booking agent I'd ever worked with, he laughed and said:

"Who do you want me to get for you next, Barbara?"

"Well, there is someone," I responded.

"And who might that be?" he asked.

"You, Mr. President," I said.

The call came in from the White House almost a year later while

Lee and I were packing to go on a minivacation to Palm Springs. It was Ron Ziegler, President Nixon's press secretary. The president was ready to do an interview with me for the *Today* show. Was I available? Lee and I started unpacking.

For a television journalist to sit down for an exclusive chat with the president of the United States was quite rare at the time. Remember, there were only three networks. Fox, CNN, and MSNBC were still in the future. But Nixon was going into an election year with falling poll ratings, so I guess the members of his administration wanted to woo *Today*'s audience. And with reason. Nixon was seen as secretive, arrogant, and isolated from the public. His enemies had nicknamed him Tricky Dick, and a favorite poster at the time showed a picture of Nixon over the legend: "Would YOU buy a used car from this man?"

The war in Vietnam that Nixon had inherited also continued to divide the country. Though Nixon was steadily withdrawing U.S. troops and replacing them with Vietnamese troops, he had also broadened the war in 1970 by invading Cambodia and Laos to cut off North Vietnamese supply lines. The resulting firestorm of protest on U.S. campuses had led to four students being killed by the National Guard on Ohio's Kent State University campus.

The Nixon White House, particularly its designated mouthpiece, Vice President Spiro Agnew, was blaming the press and "ideological eunuchs" for the antiwar violence. My old friend and former boss Bill Safire, who was by then firmly entrenched in the Nixon administration as a speechwriter, came up with Agnew's famous description of the press as "nattering nabobs of negativism" and topped that by denouncing any critics of Nixon's policies as "hopeless, hysterical hypochondriacs of history." Alliteration games aside, it was a bitter time in America. There was no gray area. You were either a hawk or a dove. The patriotic mantra of Nixon's supporters, the so-called silent majority, became: "America. Love It or Leave It."

No wonder the White House wanted to project the image of a kinder, gentler Nixon to the public. The *Today* show was the perfect vehicle.

The interview, my first with a sitting president, took place in the Blue Room of the White House in March 1971. Nixon seemed very nervous as the camera crew set things up. He kept complimenting me on my knee-length boots—"Those are very nice boots." "They look very comfortable." "Are those boots as comfortable as they look?" When we finally got under way, I asked the usual questions about our involvement in Vietnam, and the president supplied the usual answers about not giving in to dictators. We could not simply cut and run, he said. (Where have I heard that since?) This was important information, but I felt that, for our morning audience, it was also an opportunity to learn more about this secretive and remote man. After dealing with the foreign policy questions, I took a deep breath and said, "Mr. President, there has been a lot of talk about your image and the fact that the American public sees you as rather stuffy and not a human man." I realized that I had just called the president of the United States "stuffy" to his face and I could see his eyes narrow, but I plunged on. "Are you worried about this image, Mr. President?"

Well, I'd opened a Pandora's box. The president went on and on about his lack of interest in his image and polls and press clippings that he professed never to read. "Presidents who do," he said, "become like the athletes, the football teams and the rest, who become so concerned about what is written about them that they don't play the game well." He warned that an elected official "must not be constantly preening in front of a mirror," but should be doing "the very best possible job he can do for this country. And that is what I am doing."

On and on he went, getting more dismissive of any public criticism. "Anybody who takes his temperature with a Gallup Poll," he claimed, "isn't going to be a good leader."

It made for a fascinating interview, a rare glimpse of the man's real personality. We ran the interview almost totally unedited, a precedent, for two full hours on the *Today* show. Today you could never do that. The audience simply doesn't have the attention span. But times were different then, and there was great curiosity about Nixon's character.

The interview didn't help Nixon's poll numbers, but it did enrage the other networks. The custom at the time was that a president never went on one network unless it was a pool broadcast for all three networks. But at that hour of the morning CBS had *Captain Kangaroo*, and ABC wasn't even on the air, so their complaints fell flat. (It would be another four years before *A.M. America* would start, becoming *Good Morning America* ten months later.)

As I was becoming more respected as a journalist, I was also, to my great sadness, becoming vilified by a man whom I loved as a performer and whom I thought of as a friend of the family. Frank Sinatra, no less, became a vehement and vocal enemy. For most of the rest of his life he regularly complained about me publicly and ostracized me privately, for the craziest reason.

First, some background. I had known Sinatra off and on for years. He'd performed at the Latin Quarter back in the sixties when his popularity waned. At that time he was particularly nice to my sister. I'd loved him for that. He'd even written her a sweet personal letter when she asked him for an autographed picture. Jackie treasured that letter all her life. My parents adored him, and although we had heard and read of the angry and occasionally violent side of Sinatra, we thought of him as a kind friend.

Soon after I started on the *Today* show, I remet him at Phyllis and Bennett Cerf's country home, and he was more than nice to me. For example, he told me he would watch *Today* every morning for a week and send me his suggestions via Bennett. Frank Sinatra, that consummate performer, sending me suggestions? His first piece of advice, which I immediately took to heart, was that I was too deadpan when I did interviews and that I should show more expression or reaction. I took his advice to heart and truly appreciated his attention.

And then I made a fateful phone call.

It all began one Saturday. Lord knows how I remember it was a Saturday, but I do. NBC News called me at home. There was a rumor going around that Frank was about to marry Pamela Hayward, the attractive widow of the well-known producer Leland Hayward, and the ex-wife of Winston Churchill's son, Randolph. NBC News, knowing of my relationship with Sinatra, asked if I could call him in California to check out the marital rumor. They didn't want to go with the story if it wasn't true. So I placed the call. I wasn't a gossip columnist, but I thought if I could tell the network what the story really was, both Sinatra and the network would appreciate it.

Frank was out. I got his butler and left the message with a callback number. From that day and for the next thirty years, Sinatra took a hate to me. I had invaded his privacy. I was no better than the worst gossip columnist, all of whom he despised. I wrote him a heartsick letter of apology explaining what had happened and asked Bennett Cerf to give it to him. Sinatra tore it up unopened.

He would not only talk about me with disdain from the stage in Las Vegas, he wouldn't even be in the same room with me. At a tribute dinner several years later for Henry Kissinger, Sinatra, when he learned I was also to be seated there, refused to sit on the dais. Sad and embarrassed, the dinner chairman asked if I would mind not attending because Sinatra was such a big draw. That made me even sadder. Of course, I didn't go.

My father and sister couldn't understand this one-sided, ongoing feud and why the man they admired so much would behave so vindictively. I was hardly the only reporter to feel his wrath, but it hurt more because we had for so long considered him a friend of the family.

Pamela Hayward did not marry Sinatra. She went on to marry Averell Harriman, a former governor of New York and a very wealthy man. After his death she was very active in Democratic politics, and in 1992 she became President Clinton's distinguished U.S. ambassador to France. But long after her marriage and Frank's various marriages, Sinatra's enmity toward me continued.

We finally more or less made up just a few years before he died. He was performing at a charity event for New York's premier cancer hospital, Memorial Sloan-Kettering. The distinguished president and CEO of Sloan-Kettering at that time was Dr. Paul Marks and, as I've told you, the husband of my friend from Sarah Lawrence, Joan Marks. Joan and Paul had remained among my closest friends for all those years, and Paul knew how much pain and embarrassment Sinatra had caused me. So he took a chance and seated me at his own table along with Sinatra and his wife, Barbara. I held my breath waiting for Sinatra to make a scene. But he simply acknowledged me with a nod and a brief hello. I'm sure by then he'd long ago forgotten why I had made him so angry thirty years before. Our one-way feud was finally over.

But if I thought Sinatra's distaste for me was disturbing, it was nothing compared to that of the new man with whom I was about to share a desk on *Today*.

Exit Hugh, Enter McGee

*I*N THE FALL OF 1971, to my surprise and sadness, Hugh decided to leave the show. He had been on *Today* for nine years and wanted to spend more time with his wife in their new home in Carefree, Arizona. He had arranged with NBC to continue doing a series of Specials on newsy, serious subjects that interested him, but unfortunately the Specials, though important, drew such small ratings that after a year or so NBC discontinued them.

Hugh's departure from *Today* left a huge gap. I was very sorry to see him go, but a good deal sorrier when his replacement arrived.

We all thought Edwin Newman, a longtime NBC correspondent, would replace Hugh. Ed had often sat in as host during summer vacations. He had intelligence and a dry sort of humor and he fitted right in. But evidently NBC felt he was either too dry or too intellectual or too something, and started auditioning other men for the job.

Note the word "men." Though I had been at the morning desk for seven years by then, I was not even considered for the job of host, cohost, or any title that would give me a position of equality. I had been hired to fill the woman's role on the program and, although I'd certainly expanded the parameters of the job, it was still the "woman's role." If I left, another woman would replace me and the show would continue. The prevailing wisdom was not only that the men watching at home but also the women would never accept a female in an authoritative role. The host had to be a man.

That man was Frank McGee, a respected journalist, a fine reporter and writer. Frank was personable, with a wide smile and a commanding presence on the air. He had everything going for him, save for one thing—he hated our program.

I didn't realize it at first. No sooner had Frank arrived than I left for

Iran to cover the 2,500th anniversary of the Persian monarchy. Perhaps I was just too busy to pick up any negative vibes. I was swamped doing my homework for the trip and appearing on the *Today* show and *Not for Women Only*, plus taping a whole other week of *Not for Women Only* to run in my absence. In retrospect, my ignorance of Frank's mood was probably good. I needed to concentrate on the upcoming whirlwind week in Iran.

The shah of Iran was throwing a huge anniversary party at Persepolis, the ancient desert capital of Persia. He had invited every king, ex-king, and head of state or government on the planet. And some seventy came, including the kings and queens of Sweden, Norway, Denmark, Belgium, and the Netherlands, Prince Juan Carlos of Spain, King Constantine of Greece, King Hussein of Jordan, President Tito of Yugoslavia, President Ceauşescu of Romania, President Marcos of the Philippines and his shoe-loving wife, Imelda, and my old "friend" Princess Grace of Monaco and her husband, Prince Rainier. There was even an emperor, the tiny, ancient Haile Selassie of Ethiopa (his imperial title included "Conquering Lion of the Tribe of Judah"), who brought along his even tinier Chihuahua, Chicheebeel, in a diamond-studded collar.

Among the high-profile invitees not there were President Pompidou of France, President Nixon, and Queen Elizabeth. Though I didn't find out until later, there was concern about terrorist attacks. The first armed uprising against the shah (which would end in the Islamic revolution and his exile eight years later) had occurred just a few months before the celebration, and others followed. Banks and movie theaters were attacked, police officials were assassinated, and just days before the gala, fundamentalist insurgents threatened "to drown the Persepolis events in a bath of blood." Perhaps that was among the reasons President Pompidou sent his prime minister, Jacques Chaban-Delmas, President Nixon sent his vice president, Spiro Agnew, and Queen Elizabeth sent her husband, Prince Philip, and daughter, Princess Anne. (No one seemed to care about the safety of us journalists.)

If the list of Persepolis guests was newsworthy, the luxuries about to be heaped on them were even more so. The press was having a field day describing the over-the-top lavish, air-conditioned blue-and-yellow tent city that housed the VIPs. Instead of keeping the theme ethnic and Persian, which would probably have been very charming and even meaningful, little in the tent city was Persian. It was wall-to-wall French.

The tents had been designed by Jansen of Paris, the hot interior decorator at the time who did "everyone's" châteaux in France. His firm brought in custom china from France (Limoges, bearing the shah's family coat of arms), custom crystal glasses (Baccarat, encrusted with the imperial crown in gold), and linens (Porthault, the most elegant linen maker in Paris). Even hairdressers were flown in from Paris. So was the food—from Maxim's. The only Persian touches were the handsome carpets on the floors of the tents, the handwoven "carpet portraits" of each head of state, and the mounds of Iranian caviar, two tons, some said, for the banquet, which the chefs from Maxim's served with poached quail eggs.

The lavishness and the emphasis on Western taste turned out to be a major mistake, though no one knew at the time just how great a mistake it was. While the shah was trying to show the world how he was Westernizing Iran, the Shia mullahs in Iran were slamming him for his infidel efforts. Ayatollah Khomeini, who would later lead the Islamic revolution, was already pronouncing the festivities an "evil celebration" and, from his exile in Iraq, warning the shah that "an even darker future, God forbid, lies ahead of you." He was right. But we reporters didn't know that the Persepolis indulgences would become a major milestone in the shah's eventual downfall and bring us the fundamentalist Islamic regime that exists in Iran today. We were there to cover a party.

I was assigned to broadcast the shah's homage to Iran's past, live, from Persepolis. This was primarily a massive parade of some eighteen hundred troops in period costumes along with assorted chariots, horses, water buffalo, and camels. The 2,500 years of pageantry were so promising that our program added an extra hour. That meant I would be on live for three hours. A challenge under any circumstances, and it became more so because no sooner did we arrive in Persepolis than my researcher-writer, Doreen Chu, got sick. Really sick. We were staying in students' dorms in the nearby city of Shiraz, and Doreen repaired to her bed, leaving me on my own with a three-hour live broadcast ahead, no rehearsal, and no one to stand off camera and hand me research notes. Then two good things happened. One, I met a very nice male reporter from the BBC, whose name, sadly, I can't remember, who was also staying in the dorm. And I became friendly with Sally Quinn, a witty, very good feature writer for the *Washington Post*. Sally and I stuck together for the duration, comparing notes and sharing information—the hot water didn't work in the tents, the toilets were sluggish, the tents, all decorated differently, were absurd. Sally was reporting in print. I was reporting on television. Still, we were a big help to each other. It was my new friend from the BBC, however, who saved my life.

When the show went on the air at 7:00 a.m. on October 15, the viewers saw me sitting in a glassed-in booth facing the desert. From there I described the horsemen, chariots, and floats going by. I seemed positively brilliant, rattling off the passing of every dynasty since 559 B.C., including the Achaemenid, the Seleucid, the Parthian, the Sassanid. Here's some more. The Tahirid, the Saffarid, the Seljuk. On and on. What no one noticed, because the camera was basically on the parade, were the earphones on my head, which connected me to my friend from the BBC.

It's not that I hadn't done my own homework. I had, but I couldn't have mounds of notes in front of me with no one to sort them and be seen reading from the notes. My BBC pal, on the other hand, broadcasting for the radio, had all his homework in front of him and could read every fact. So much of what he said I said, with my own additions, ten seconds later. I didn't say it quite in his voice, but there were times in the broadcast when I had a distinctly British accent. The problem was that the BBC did not have commercials and we did. Every time I said, "We'll be back after this message," Joe Garagiola in New York appeared on the screen, at one point promoting Lipton onion soup, at another, Blue Lustre rug shampoo. By the time the camera came back to Persepolis, my BBC friend was way ahead of me and I'd lost at least a century of history.

"When we last left you, you could see the breakup of the individual remote villages in ancient Persia," I'd say. "Well, now they have all been united and it's no longer 1000 but 1100." Sometimes, if the commercial was a minute and a half long or when Frank Blair read the news, the interruption was even longer, and we'd lose five hundred years. I had to keep listening to my friend from the BBC so that when we came back, I could catch up and say: "As I was saying five hundred years ago . . ." What's a century here or there?

On the other hand nobody much cared because what the viewers were looking at were the horses and the costumes and the whole panoply of VIP guests we kept cutting away to. The viewers didn't care whether it was 2,500 years ago or last month.

Did I send thank-you flowers to my friend from the BBC when the last chariot passed by? Did I buy him a rug? I hope so. He literally made my day. For three hours, I was a distinguished authority—and live. I was a great success. The afterglow was short-lived, however. When I returned to New York, the party was over. Hugh was gone and Frank McGee was about to make my life miserable.

Frank considered his assignment to be a comedown. He'd been

partly anchoring the evening news, one of the three rotating anchors who took over the highly respected *Huntley-Brinkley Report* after Chet Huntley's retirement in 1970. NBC assigned him to *Today* when they decided too many anchors spoiled the broadcast, and reduced the anchor slots to David Brinkley and John Chancellor. So Frank naturally felt diminished. And understandably so.

McGee did not consider *Today* to be a serious news program. He was following Hugh Downs, who was, in his opinion, not a newsman, having been host of a game show. To make matters even more unacceptable for Frank, he was now being asked to share a desk, not with a male colleague, but with me, a mere woman, whom he couldn't possibly regard as an equal. Even the beloved Joe Garagiola earned his disdain during interviews on the set. "He asks questions I wouldn't ask out of professional vanity," McGee was quoted in a magazine article.

On camera McGee was pleasant and gave me a tight smile in the moments when we were casually chatting. The audience could not detect anything wrong. Off camera he and I shared the makeup room as Hugh and I had, and there he was distant, bordering on rude, and spent as little time in my company as possible. I could live with that because he was good for the show. The ratings were nearly as high as they were during the high points of Hugh's tenure, and that was enough for me.

To Frank's credit he did add some gravitas to the program by instituting a series of daily interviews from New York with Washington politicians or newsmakers. He and I sat side by side at the desk and asked questions in turn.

But Frank couldn't stand it. He felt *my* questions were interrupting *his* questions, and that his were far more important. The producer of the program, however, liked the two of us asking questions. He wanted to keep things as they were. (The producer by then was Stuart Schulberg, brother of the acclaimed author of *What Makes Sammy Run* and screenwriter of *On the Waterfront*, Budd Schulberg.)

Since he wasn't getting anywhere with Schulberg, Frank decided to take action himself and went right to the top, to the president of NBC, Julian Goodman. He asked me to attend the meeting also so that there could be no confusion about the decision. To my face he complained to Goodman that my participation in these interviews reduced their importance. He felt that my role on the show should be restricted to, as he called them, the "girlie" interviews.

I could continue to sit at the desk, he said, but I was not to join in on the important and newsmaking interviews. Even as I write this, it is hard to believe that such an opinion would be expressed. But Julian Goodman did not seem to be shocked or disturbed. He listened to McGee present his case, and as if I were not in the room, he agreed.

I couldn't believe this was happening, and even though, over the years, I had been grateful to accept any role I was offered, this was too much. I was nervous in front of these two formidable men, but somehow I summoned up my courage and found my voice. I told Goodman that I hadn't been on the program all those years and contributed all the interviews I'd done to go back to the era of the tea-pouring girl. I just couldn't accept his decision. And by the way, although I may have wanted to break down and cry, I didn't shed a tear.

Looking back, I consider that day to be one of the milestones of my career. I cannot imagine what my future would have been had I just swallowed my feelings and restricted my work to the "girlie" assignments.

After my outburst, which seemed to have startled Goodman, we finally reached a compromise of sorts. Frank would get to ask the first three questions in the "Powerful Person" interviews. When he was finished, if there was any time left, I would be allowed to ask the *fourth* question.

Moreover, Frank had the right to conduct any additional interviews he wanted to do—without me. If a guest came into the studio for an interview and Frank wanted to do it, I would be excluded. I had absolutely no rights. From then on I had to do whatever interviews Frank or Stuart Schulberg assigned me. Schulberg, who was not happy with the decision, reacted by having a three-martini lunch each day. We dealt with him mostly from dawn to noon. (I, fortunately or unfortunately, didn't drink.)

Not only did I realize that my fate was in McGee's hands, there was also the reality that NBC was paying Frank twice as much as they were paying me. I knew, in spite of the growing women's movement, that men were almost always paid more than women. This didn't surprise me or make me angry. It just made me feel insecure and replaceable. There were a lot of women who could sit there on the set and smile while Frank held sway, and be happy to do the girlie interviews. So I played my role as assigned, in public and in print. "I'm there to be there if Frank wants someone to turn to for help in an interview," I explained when asked about the situation.

Though I remained superficially loyal and cheerful each day on the program, my new role was so unacceptable to me that I looked for a loophole in the McGee edict. I knew I couldn't come in until the fourth question, and I had no choice in the selection of the guests Frank wanted to interview on the set, but no one had said I couldn't go after my own important interviews and do them *outside* the studio. Stuart agreed.

Therefore that's what I did.

And that's when I got the reputation of being ambitious and aggressive in pursuit of interviews, the "pushy cookie."

I was already reading three or four newspapers a day, as well as assorted magazines, to see who was in the news and whom I wanted to try to interview. I can't say I redoubled my efforts after Frank McGee's edict came down. I was already staying up far too late at night reading, making notes, and reading some more. But I began the practice of sending handwritten letters to the people I wanted to interview. (I hate making phone calls.) What I tried to do in the letters—and still do—is not to tell the people why *I* want to do the interview, but why *they* should want to do the interview. Do they feel they are being misunderstood or maligned? Would they like the opportunity to tell their side of the story?

One of the prime examples was Henry Ford II. He had never given an interview on television, but he was being dragged into the news all over the country by Ralph Nader. Nader, a consumer-protection environmental vigilante, had taken on the automobile industry in his 1965 book *Unsafe at Any Speed*, and was attacking the Ford Motor Company for a variety of dangerous practices, like not installing air bags. He was also attacking Ford, as well as every other corporate CEO, for what he considered the single-minded pursuit of their companies' profit margins at the expense of their social responsibility.

So I wrote Henry Ford, a first letter warmly suggesting, a second, strongly advising, that he take the opportunity to express his own side of the story. Obviously my letters got to him, for he decided to do an interview with me. I filmed it way outside our New York studio in Dearborn, Michigan, and getting him turned out to be such a coup that NBC ran it in separate parts two days in a row.

I remember two specific things from that interview. One, when referring to Nader's criticism about corporate profits, I asked Ford how much money he earned a year, and he replied, "None of your business." "Good for him," I thought, although I didn't say it. I've often wondered why more people don't say that to me. And the second thing I remember was this great advice: "Always give one excuse, never two." So I stopped saying I couldn't come to a dinner party because I wanted to spend time with Jackie and besides, I had a cold. One excuse, I've learned, works just fine, and you are much more believable.

On and on I went, writing letters and making phone calls when it was time to close the deal. As a result I managed to interview Tricia Nixon, the president's older daughter, *outside the studio* in Monticello, Virginia; the celebrated ninety-year-old conductor Leopold Stokowski, *outside the studio* in his apartment in New York; Cornelia Wallace, the young wife of presidential candidate George Wallace, at his campaign office *outside the studio* in Alabama. (Cornelia was of special interest because she had married Wallace, the segregationist governor of Alabama, just a year before an assassination attempt paralyzed his legs and left him in a wheelchair.)

I flew to Atlanta to interview Dean Rusk, then teaching at the University of Georgia, for that second interview with him; to Washington to interview the irrepressible, and now seemingly not so sane, Martha Mitchell, wife of the attorney general, John Mitchell; and again to Washington, on another occasion, to interview the first lady, Pat Nixon, at the White House.

These interviews were getting a lot of attention from the press, Frank McGee wasn't thrilled, but they contributed to the high ratings of the show, so he really couldn't complain. Besides, in the studio the almost daily interviews from Washington continued, and I, like the good obedient girl, continued to wait to join in until the fourth question.

One of the most newsmaking interviews I did took place in Washington in 1971 during the early McGee era. Everyone wanted to get to H. R. Haldeman, who had never done a television interview. Bob Haldeman was Nixon's crew-cut, seemingly coldhearted, and enigmatic chief of staff. (Long hair and sideburns were all the rage then for many men, and Haldeman's retro military hairstyle was a statement in itself.) He was known as Nixon's "Teutonic Guard," and many blamed him for Nixon's cold and isolated image. Haldeman's image was just as cold and distant, and it wasn't helping his boss.

So I wrote and told him why he should want to do an interview with me. It wasn't because he hadn't done one before, or because it would show him to be warm and likeable. Rather, I said, it would be good for the president. Richard Nixon was getting a reputation of being a man with a brutal temper who really didn't care what people thought of him. I told Haldeman that only he could explain the president's philosophy and his reasons for governing as he did. I said that it was important for him, as Nixon's chief of staff, to present that more caring picture.

I followed up with a phone call. I was encouraged when he took it.

"You know, so much of your cold image comes from the way you look," I said, referring to his Germanic-looking crew cut and blue eyes. "People are beginning to refer to you as the 'White House Nazi.' "

"I've heard that," he said with a laugh. " 'Haldeman, *Achtung!*' "

That was good. He was turning out to have a well-hidden sense of humor. After we chatted some more, he suggested I come down to Washington to further discuss the possibility of doing an interview.

I was on the next plane.

Haldeman and I had a pleasant meeting. He told me he would think over my request and get back to me. Later I had lunch with Henry Kissinger. "You're wasting your time," he said. "He'll never do it."

A month later Bob Haldeman sat down with me in his office in the White House (definitely outside the New York studio). The resulting interview, which *Today* ran in three parts on successive days in early February 1972, made national headlines.

What turned out to be my seminal question was innocent enough: "What things, what kind of criticisms," I asked, "upset the president?"

His answer was explosive. The Nixon administration, at that time, was attempting to conduct peace negotiations with the North Vietnamese, and not everyone agreed with their tactics. But, in Haldeman's eyes, and presumably the president's as well, any "people who were opposing what the president was doing were unconsciously echoing the line that the enemy wanted echoed." To drive home his point Haldeman insisted that critics of Richard Nixon were "consciously aiding and abetting the enemy." In short, they were traitors.

I could hardly believe what I was hearing. It was an election year, I pointed out, and various presidential candidates, like Democratic senator George McGovern, were critical of the president's Vietnam policies. Was Senator McGovern "aiding and abetting the enemy"? Haldeman wouldn't name names but he didn't back down. He went on to decry Nixon's political opponents as people who put "partisanship above peace and what needs to be done." (Not very different from President George W. Bush's reaction to critics of the war in Iraq.)

The interview, although it raised a furor in the press, evidently pleased Haldeman, who sent me a warm note. "Thank you for making me a household word," he wrote.

Despite the sorry behavior of Frank McGee and the president of NBC News, my job was going well.

My marriage, however, was not.

Marriage On the Rocks

S o THAT WAS the best of times. Interesting, provocative interviews. My reputation growing. But all the while, my marriage
falling apart. This is, even today, extremely difficult to write
about because there was no crisis, no abuse, no blame. This was simply,
also, the worst of times.

Lee and I had been married for nine years. On the surface, to our
friends, it was a successful marriage. We even looked good together. Lee
would have made any woman look good. He was five foot ten, very well
built, with beautiful blue eyes and a warm smile. He was kind to me. I
was kind to him. We adored our daughter.

We were very pleasant to be with and had a growing circle of friends.
In addition to our close friends like Anita and Warren Manshel and Joan
and Paul Marks, my dear pals from college, we had become part of a
very exciting world. We spent time with the celebrated composer
Richard Rodgers and his elegant wife, Dorothy. Rodgers, who wrote the
music for some of the greatest American musicals, from *Oklahoma!* to
South Pacific to *The King and I*, had a beautiful home in Connecticut.
Dorothy was a perfectionist and everything in her home was exquisite.
Someone once said that when Dorothy Rodgers peed, she peed flowers.
Anyway, they both liked Lee and me, and from time to time we would
drive to their home on a Saturday and return Sunday after lunch. When
you arrived your suitcase was immediately unpacked and your clothes
hung up or folded in tissue paper in the lined bureau drawers. I couldn't
get over such luxury.

Saturday nights there was often a small dinner party with their
friends who lived nearby. People like Walter Kerr, then the esteemed
New York Times theater critic, and his playwright and author wife, Jean

(she wrote the hilarious book *Please Don't Eat the Daisies*), or sometimes a star from one of Rodgers's musicals, like Mary Martin and her husband, Richard Halliday. Lee and I loved those mini weekends. We would have gone more frequently, but we didn't like to leave Jackie, and guests' children were not invited.

There were other times when we would visit Bennett Cerf and his wife, Phyllis, at their equally beautiful estate in Mount Kisco, New York. Bennett had kind of a crush on me and we used to meet occasionally for lunch at "21." I was fascinated by his stories of the brilliant authors his company, Random House, published. Bennett never made a pass at me or even a suggestion of a pass. He just liked me and liked having younger people in his life.

Phyllis (whom friends called "the General" with good reason—she ran her husband's life) was used to Bennett's platonic crushes and made it a habit to incorporate them into their lives. At first she sarcastically referred to me as "Bennett's Mrs. Guber," but when Bennett invited me to lunch one day in the country and asked me to bring my husband, she was charmed by him. Lee and Phyllis became very good friends, and we were often invited to sparkling lunches or dinners. This would end when Sinatra, who was their most treasured friend, took his hate to me. (I've already told you about that.) But the point is that our times together, Lee's and mine, were just fine. The trouble was there were too few times together, with or without friends.

Lee's summer tent theaters were doing well, as was his year-round permanent theater in Long Island. But the musicals he put on and the special performances he presented—Tony Bennett, Johnny Carson, and others—meant that he had to spend most weekends, when the theaters did their biggest business, away from New York. I wanted to be with him, but I also yearned to spend what free time I had with Jackie, and I had so much homework to do for my crazy work schedule that traveling to Maryland or even Long Island was more headache than pleasure.

Even on weeknights Lee often had to visit one theater or another, and I couldn't go with him then either. He would get home long after midnight. I would be getting up four or five hours later. Our schedules began to resemble that of my mother and father when he owned the Latin Quarter and she saw him perhaps one night a week.

There was another similarity to my father that troubled me. Lee wasn't satisfied just producing revivals in suburban theaters. He was ambitious and wanted to produce on Broadway. That was his goal, and during our marriage he produced three shows on Broadway.

One was relatively early in our marriage. It was called *Catch Me If You Can* and featured a movie star named Dan Dailey and Tom Bosley, the actor who would later play the father in the television hit *Happy Days*. *Catch Me If You Can* was sort of a comedy and sort of a mystery but not enough of either to please the critics. It opened in March 1965 to luke-warm reviews and closed in less than three months.

If Lee was discouraged, he didn't show it. Instead he started looking for a new property to produce. That made me anxious. Producing on Broadway meant that he was often asking friends for money to invest in his productions. He said this was par for the course and the way things were done. And of course it was. Lots of so-called Broadway angels wanted to invest in shows, not just because they thought they would make a profit if the show was successful, but because they liked the glamour of being involved in show business.

There is a saying that people have two businesses, their own and show business. I, of course, knew how unglamorous most of show busi-ness was, and wisely Lee never asked me to contribute to his produc-tions. His shows just brought back old memories of my father's failed productions. I dreaded reading the reviews and was demoralized when a play closed. Lee just took a deep breath and tried again.

Lee's greatest challenge and greatest disappointment was with a musical version of a wonderful George S. Kaufman and Moss Hart comedy called *The Man Who Came to Dinner*. It had originally run on Broadway in 1939 and had starred Monty Woolley as an irascible, ego-centric lecturer and critic who comes to a small town to speak, visits a local home, breaks his leg, and stays on and on, driving everyone crazy with his outlandish demands. The play was a huge success and in 1942 was made into a movie, again starring Woolley. His long-suffering sec-retary was played by no less a star than Bette Davis.

Lee felt, with good reason, that it would make a terrific musical. Toward this end he asked, begged, cajoled, and charmed George S. Kaufman's daughter, Anne, and Moss Hart's widow, the divine Kitty Carlisle Hart, to let him acquire the rights. After weeks of negotiating they agreed, in part because Lee had a brilliant idea as to who should play the central character: the acerbic British actor George Sanders.

Sanders, acclaimed for his caustic roles in *The Moon and Sixpence* and *All About Eve*, seemed just right for the part. He was said to be able to sing and dance. The book and lyrics were written by James Lipton, who later became the distinguished host of *Inside the Actors Studio*, conduct-ing interviews with actors on the cable channel Bravo.

Lee's production of *Sherry!*, as the musical adaptation of the play was called, was scheduled to debut in 1967. In addition to Sanders, the Bette Davis part was played by a woman well known to Broadway, Dolores Gray. She was tall, blond, and sexy, with a big voice and a stage mother who had groomed her since she was a young child to get in front of the lights and belt it out. Belt it she did, and as a result Dolores had starred in quite a few successful musicals. All in all it seemed like magical casting.

I was very involved in this production, more than in any of Lee's other shows. I knew how important this one was to him. I attended as many rehearsals as I could, wrote notes, and tried to be supportive while disaster seemed to hit almost every day.

Sanders, it turned out, was not *playing* an irascible grouch; he really *was* an irascible grouch. He was testy, argumentative, and sadly distracted by the serious illness of his wife, actress Benita Hume (he had previously been married to Zsa Zsa Gabor). He was late for rehearsals, if he showed up at all. He couldn't sing, had trouble memorizing his lines, and surprisingly his acting was dreadful. But everybody was still trying to make a go of it when the show arrived for its Boston tryout. Then his wife died, and Sanders walked out of the show. You couldn't really blame him, but it was a major blow.

Lee valiantly tried to keep the production going. He replaced Sanders with a very talented actor named Clive Revill, who was actually much better in the part than Sanders but was relatively unknown to the audience. *Sherry!* opened on Broadway in March 1967 and ran for only seventy-two performances. It was devastating.

Lee had had such high hopes for this musical, his most adventurous production. When the show closed, it took a lot out of him and a lot out of me. I felt that Lee needed me more than ever, but I had less time than ever to give. By then I was appearing on *Today* five times a week.

But Lee, the optimist (like my father), jumped right back into the world of Broadway. Three years after *Sherry!* flopped, he produced a more ambitious and far darker play, *Inquest*, a dramatization of the trial of Ethel and Julius Rosenberg. It was a sympathetic portrayal of the couple who were ultimately executed for spying. (It infuriated Roy Cohn, who had helped to bring about those executions. I saw Roy very rarely by then, and his reaction neither surprised nor disturbed me.) But this drama, too, in spite of a fine cast that included Anne Jackson and George Grizzard, opened to poor reviews and lasted for only twenty-eight days. Lee was heartbroken. And so was I. But for different reasons.

Lee's involvement in the theater was driving me further and further away from him. It wasn't entirely his fault. It was the culmination of all the years with my father's grandiose schemes—the Broadway flops, the failed nightclubs, the aquacade that never got off the ground. I couldn't bear to pretend to be upbeat time and again while Lee read another bad review. I'd lived through enough openings and sad closings for a lifetime.

But there was our little daughter.

Jackie, barely out of her toddler years, had just started nursery school. Zelle would take her to the small school in the morning and I would try, as often as I could, to pick her up when her morning session ended at noon. Then we would go someplace for lunch. Schrafft's was a favorite. It was a popular place for the grown-up ladies who lunched, but it also had great ice cream sodas and sundaes.

Lee, too, loved being with his little girl. His older children, Carol and Zev, were off at college, and Jackie, for him, was a new beginning. He carried her on his shoulders, roughhoused with her, which she loved, and often took her to rehearsals of his shows, just as my own father had taken my sister and me when we were children.

So there we were. A family—caring, but in distress. A family growing further and further apart, doing more and more things separately, not knowing how to come together again. Our disparate hours also affected our sex life. We practically had to schedule appointments to make love, and one or the other of us was usually exhausted.

Both Lee and I were still watching our money. We continued to live in our rent-controlled apartment in midtown New York. Jackie's room was actually a maid's room; Zelle's room was the second maid's room. (The apartment building had been built before World War II when several live-in maids served one family.) I was making very good money by then, but I was also still supporting my mother, father, and sister in Miami. Lee was feeling constrained because he had lost so much of his own money investing in his Broadway shows. But neither of us was a spendthrift. We rented a house only for a month in the summer, took few vacations, and cared little about possessions. Money was not the problem. Time was. But we never talked about that, or any of our problems for that matter. The conversations were unsaid. The problems were unresolved.

I began to write good-bye letters to Lee, and then I would tear them up. How could I leave a man who had done me no harm? When our biggest mistake was that we had no life in common anymore? I didn't feel I wanted to reduce my workload. In fact I had increased it by taking on *Not for Women Only*. Lee couldn't change his lifestyle or ambitions either. I decided once again that I was no good at marriage and that basically the failures were my fault. Perhaps, like my mother, I was looking at the seams. I felt awful, but I didn't know how to make things better.

Then, in July 1971, the newspapers announced to everyone's total surprise that Henry Kissinger had made a secret trip to China, which had been closed to America since the Communists had taken over in 1949. President Nixon, the headlines said, was himself going to visit China. Unimaginable.

Nixon's historic trip was scheduled to take place in February 1972. A small group of reporters was going to go with him. To my utter joy NBC selected me to be one of them.

I decided then that before I went off on this faraway adventure, Lee and I finally had to face our disintegrating marriage. Over a long and teary dinner we decided to separate. At first Lee wanted us to continue to try, but then he admitted that he was no happier than I. We decided that when I left for China, in a month, he would move out of the apartment and find a new place to live. I would keep the apartment, as it was home to Jackie.

I was ending my second marriage. What was worse was that I was taking away from Jackie the daddy she loved. She was only four years old, and even though she would continue to see her father, it would never be the same. She had never met her biological father. Would she now feel in some part of her little being that her second father was leaving her too?

But it was too late to change things. I began to pack for China, and added another notch to my belt of guilt.

My maternal grandparents, John and Celia Seletsky
with their daughters Dena (standing) and Lena

Typical Latin Quarter finale

Mom, Dad, and
the Duchess of
Windsor when the
Latin Quarter
played in Nassau

Mother, father,
and sister Jackie,
around the age
of twenty

My sister Jackie

My adored cousin Shirley and her
husband, Irving Budd

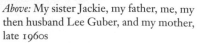

Above: My sister Jackie, my father, me, my then husband Lee Guber, and my mother, late 1960s

Left: (above) With Lee and baby Jackie; *(below)* Jackie and I—sweet memories

Right: Merv Adelson and I on our wedding day, May 10, 1986

Right: With Mademoiselle Therese de la Chappelle ("Zelle"), my daughter's beloved governess and then mine

Left: With Icodel Tomlinson. What would I do without her?

Jackie today

With President Nixon in China in February 1972

Dancing with President Ford at the White House, 1976

Above: Interview with President-elect and Mrs. Carter, December 1976

Left: On President Reagan's ranch in 1981

Below: With President Reagan and his wife Nancy in 1986

With President and Mrs. George H. W. Bush, 1989

On Air Force One with President Bill Clinton, 1996

With President-elect George W. Bush at his Texas ranch two days before he left for his inauguration, January 15, 2001

With Prime Minister Golda Meir on the *Today* show, 1973

My friends Raquel and Moshe
Dyan in 1974

First joint interview with President Anwar Sadat of Egypt
and Prime Minister Menachem Begin of Israel in Jerusalem, November 1977

The shah of Iran in
his opulent palace,
1977

Right: With King Hussein and
Queen Noor in 1978

Below: With Yasir Arafat in
Lebanon, 1996

Above: In Mu'ammar Qaddafi's tent in Libya, January 23, 1989. I was in pink and he was in green and white.

Right: Crossing the Bay of Pigs with Fidel Castro, May 19, 1977

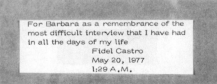

Left: Fidel Castro signed the Cuban Constitution for me the night of our interview.

Top: Prime Minister Margaret Thatcher, whom I admired, at 10 Downing Street, 1987

Above: China's leader Jiang Zemin in 1990

Left: With President Hugo Chávez of Venezuela in March 2007

Left: Henry Kissinger and me when I was not interviewing him

Left: In Riyadh, Saudi Arabia, with General Norman Schwarzkopf for the first interview he did after the First Gulf War, 1991

Below: The note from President George H. W. Bush to General Schwarzkopf on the eve of my visit to Saudi Arabia

Norm —
Careful, Careful; but
she's OK —
Congratulation, again
Gy Bush

One of
many notes
from
Princess
Diana

KENSINGTON PALACE

Tuesday.

Dearest Barbara.

The flowers are just wonderful as you are too!
It was lovely to see you for lunch on Friday & as promised here is a letter for Christopher & I'd be so grateful if

you could kindly give it to him . . . .
My fondest love as always.
Then.

Diana. x

Left: Rubbing noses with the Dalai Lama in Dharamsala in 2005

Below: Interview with Truman Capote, December 1967

My mother, Bing Crosby, and I, May 1977

Having a chat with John Warner and Elizabeth Taylor
at their farm in 1977

Historic Journey:
China with Nixon

*P*RESIDENT NIXON said that the trip to Communist China, a week that changed the course of history, was like going to the moon. He was right. But though it was the trip of a lifetime, like Chinese food it was both sweet and sour. And like the man in the moon I have never felt so lonely.

First the sweet. The fact that I was there at all for NBC was to me a minor miracle. Because of the historic nature of the trip, the television networks sent their heavyweight, politically experienced superstars: Walter Cronkite, Dan Rather, and Eric Sevareid from CBS; Tom Jarriel, Ted Koppel, and Harry Reasoner from ABC. NBC was represented by its number one anchor, John Chancellor, along with two other very experienced correspondents, Herb Kaplow and John Rich, and me.

Why me? One, because NBC didn't want what might look like competition between Chancellor and McGee, had he been chosen to go. Two, which I didn't find out until much later, because all the journalists from every network vying for the assignment were middle-aged white males, Dick Wald, the executive vice president of NBC News, felt that I might bring something different to the coverage. If nothing else I would stand out to the viewing audience in contrast to all the male correspondents. And three, the time difference.

Twelve hours separate New York and Peking, as Beijing was then called. Nighttime in China is morning in the United States, when the *Today* show would be on, the same time slot when I would be reporting from China on the night's big banquets, speeches, important toasts, and cultural events. The viewers of *Today* expected to see me in the morning. And there I'd be, reporting live by satellite, albeit from the other side of the world.

My inclusion in what was really a very small group of journalists ruffled a lot of feathers at NBC. For every reporter who got to go, ten or more didn't. Even John Chancellor, I found out later, was against my assignment. I was relatively inexperienced, for starters, and a woman in a sea of experienced men. John would have been more comfortable with another male correspondent, but Dick Wald was determined to take the gamble, though he confessed to me recently he had fairly low expectations of what I would bring to the NBC team. Dick put my name on the NBC News proposed list, and the White House took it from there. The president's press secretary, Ron Ziegler, said he personally selected the traveling press corps out of hundreds of applications.

I was terrified. Even the list of print journalists was intimidating, including William Buckley for the *Washington Star;* Theodore White, the Pulitzer Prize–winning author of the series The Making of the President, for Time/Life and Public Broadcasting; the prolific, Pulitzer Prize–winning author James Michener, for the *Reader's Digest.* Giants, all.

There were very few women on the trip. One, in the president's entourage, was a very pretty, young blond with whom I would have a nodding acquaintance but no real contact. She was the assistant to Ron Ziegler, Nixon's press secretary, and her name was Diane Sawyer.

There were only two other women journalists in the whole China group, the venerable and fearless UPI correspondent Helen Thomas, and another very experienced journalist, Fay Wells, from Storer Broadcasting. Helen was writing for newspapers. Fay was reporting primarily on radio. I would be the only woman broadcaster. And with Frank McGee's backhanded blessing. "Get Barbara out of the studio for a week?" I learned later he'd said to Dick Wald when he heard of my assignment. "China's not far enough!"

It certainly felt far enough away for me when we arrived on our own press plane a day ahead of the president and his entourage. We were met by a small group of Chinese officials from the Department of Information who all looked exactly alike. Both men and women were dressed identically in navy blue pants and Mao jackets, also navy blue— mandarin collars, shapeless and unadorned except for a round red pin with a silver likeness of Chairman Mao Tse-tung, the leader of the Chinese Communist Party and founder of the People's Republic of China.

I was introduced to my interpreter, Miss Tang, who I later learned was married, but like all Chinese women at that time, she wore no wedding ring and used her maiden name. Miss Tang was serious and sullen.

She always called me "Miss Barbara Walters," never "Miss Walters" or "Barbara." She started every sentence like this, "And so, Miss Barbara Walters, today we will visit a factory." She wore absolutely no makeup, was thirty-one, and looked at least forty.

Her very first question to me was: "How old are you?" I answered that we were around the same age. We talked briefly about children. I told her I had a little girl at home who was almost four. Miss Tang then told me that she had a daughter who was two and a half and lived at a day-care center; she saw her on weekends. After this brief exchange, Miss Tang never expressed any further curiosity about me or Americans in general. Instead she answered every question I asked, and you can imagine how many there were, as if they came from a political hand-book. For example, when I asked her later if she could take me to a beauty salon, thinking that I might be able to find an interesting story there, she replied, "We have no need for beauty salons. We have loftier thoughts." Take that, Miss Barbara Walters!

Even the arrival of the president of the United States attracted little curiosity—and gave me my first anxiety attack. I was reporting from a makeshift studio at the hastily constructed broadcast center at the airport. (All our live broadcasts by satellite would be made from there.) None of us had been given any advance information about who would be in the Chinese meet-and-greet party, or what ceremony there would be, if any. There we were, about to go on the air to report the historic moment to millions of Americans, without a clue as to what was happening.

The answer was: not much. Only a small, official delegation met President Nixon at the airport, one of whom was the seventy-three-year-old premier, Chou En-lai. (In contrast, four months before, the Chinese regime had rounded up more than 300,000 people to greet the Ethiopian emperor, Haile Selassie.) Mrs. Nixon was wearing the bright red coat we would come to know so well, the same color, ironically, as the large signs all around the airport calling the "oppressed peoples of the world" to unite and pay tribute to Marxism-Leninism and the Chinese Communist Party. Her coat and the signs were the only bright spots in the whole scene.

The president's arrival was indicative of the tightly controlled, doctrinaire atmosphere in China. After the brief welcoming ceremony at the airport, the Nixons got into a limousine with the Chinese premier and sped the forty minutes or so into Peking—along empty streets. There were no curious crowds along Peking's "Street of Perpetual

Peace" or in the vast, one-hundred-acre Tiananmen Square, the "Plaza of the Gate of Celestial Peace." Seventeen years later hundreds of freedom-seeking students would be brutally put down by the government in Tiananmen Square, but when Nixon's presidential motorcade swept through it in 1972, the square was nearly empty and silent. There were just people on bicycles going about their business without even looking up.

Some veteran China hands attributed the lack of public enthusiasm to the fact that America and the People's Republic of China had no official diplomatic relations, but I think Bill Buckley got it right. During a roundtable interview I did later with a few of the print journalists, Buckley said he didn't think the Chinese public knew who Nixon was. After all, he pointed out, they still didn't know that we—or anyone—had landed on the moon a few years before. That's how controlled the news was there.

My job in China was to cover the daytime activities of the Nixons, report on any stories I gathered myself, and to describe, live by satellite, the major evening activities, which I could not actually attend. Our cameras were in the Great Hall but I was almost an hour away at the broadcast center watching the banquets on a TV monitor. "On the menu tonight are Spongy Bamboo Shoots, Shark's Fin in Three Shreds, Fried and Stewed Prawns," I would report to the *Today* show audience. "Hear the music? Sound familiar? The large Chinese orchestra is playing 'Home on the Range.' " I ad-libbed much of what I said, just as I had ad-libbed in Persepolis, but this time I didn't have a friendly colleague talking into my ear on a headphone.

When I finished my banquet reporting for television, I was rushed by our radio producer to another makeshift studio to describe to listeners what had just been shown on television. One night about midnight, on my way home from the radio broadcast, I talked with Mr. Ching, one of the interpreters.

"How old are your children?" I asked. "I have three—eleven, seven, and three years old," he replied. "But I have not seen my three-year-old since he was born." Turned out the interpreter had been an office worker, as had his wife. During this decade of the Cultural Revolution, in which millions of Chinese teachers, educated office workers, and intellectuals were forced to live as peasants so as to toe the party line, Mr. Ching had been sent to an adult "reform school" and then to work in the fields. His wife was still working at a different farm. He had no idea when he would see her again. His children were living with their grandmother. He didn't know when his wife would be back to care for them.

We heard similar stories throughout our trip, especially when we visited Peking University, which had been newly reopened after being forced to close during the early years of the Cultural Revolution. It had been one of the finest universities in Asia until it was shut down and its students disbanded. Some of the most prominent professors had been paraded down the street wearing dunce caps and jeered at by teenage members of the Red Guard. Like Mr. Ching, most of the teachers had been sent away to "reform" centers and were then imprisoned or sent to work in the fields. They were just now returning. With this kind of attitude against almost anyone who was educated, it is all the more astonishing to realize what the Chinese have accomplished in the thirty-odd years since the demise of the hated Cultural Revolution.

President Nixon's attempt to bridge the philosophical gap between our two countries was challenging, to say the least, but he was certainly trying. During the days he and his entourage, for the most part, met privately with their Chinese counterparts. We followed Pat Nixon as she visited schools, day-care centers, factories, and communes, all carefully selected by her hosts.

Mrs. Nixon, who seemed shy and remote to most Americans, blossomed in China. She was having a wonderful time, gracious and smiling and particularly good with the children. The Chinese opened up to her as much as they could open up to anyone at that time. How sad that her life in the White House would end in grief and isolation two years later, when her husband was forced to resign his office over the Watergate scandal. I was reminded of the book *Johnny, We Hardly Knew Ye*, written after President Kennedy's assassination. There could easily have been another book called *Pat Nixon, We Hardly Knew You*.

Traipsing around after the first lady, however, had more than its share of challenges for me. I was carrying my own camera and a tape recorder. They looked very much alike and, as I am the least handy person you could find, I often took out my camera when I wanted the tape recorder or the tape recorder when I wanted the camera. Even worse, at one point I found myself almost alone with Mrs. Nixon and, hoping to get a brief exclusive interview with her, I beckoned over the only camera crew I could see and asked if they would film it. They looked kind of startled but did the filming. Only later did I learn that they were a CBS crew, not NBC. CBS was furious that I got this scoop and at first wouldn't release the film. NBC then became furious with CBS for not releasing the film, and it almost became an international incident until I apologized profusely and everyone cooled down. But that gaffe did not go over well with my fellow journalists in China. Instead of thinking of me as a klutz, which I was, they thought I was being a prima donna. It did not add to my popularity.

When I wasn't following Mrs. Nixon or going out to find my own stories, always accompanied by Miss Tang, I repaired to the neat, sparse room I shared with Fay Wells at the hotel. There, waiting for me, was a most comfortable bed with a big puffy quilt. Also waiting, a comb, brush, toothpaste, shaving cream, pencils, pens, postcards with scenes from Chinese ballets, hard candies, hot water for tea, which I could also use to sterilize my contact lenses, and always tangerines. Thank God for the tangerines. On busy days, I lived on them. Herb Kaplow, one of my fellow NBC correspondents, joked that on his first day back home, he woke up, reached for a tangerine, and ate his lightbulb.

We also had big roomy bathtubs, no showers—and unexpected luxuries. One-day laundry service and one-hour pressing, a godsend since we were allowed to bring only one small suitcase, and floormen on each floor to wait on us and bring us food at any hour. Breakfast was the highlight. We could choose Western or Chinese and I chose Chinese, which included delicious chicken noodle soup, a selection of cold meats, vegetables, spring rolls, and, one lucky morning, spareribs with sweet and sour sauce. Who needed oatmeal anyway?

We certainly didn't need a wastebasket. One of the most maddening Chinese habits to deal with made us unable to throw anything out. Whatever we tried to dispose of—a torn pair of stockings, a used Kleenex, an empty bottle of shampoo—was neatly wrapped up and returned to us.

Stories did not come so neatly wrapped. Though we were supposedly free to go wherever we wanted, there was no way to get there. There were no taxis, no private cars, no transportation whatsoever except for the official buses and cars which moved us from place to place. I had seen a department store within walking distance of the hotel, so I asked Miss Tang to take me and my cameraman to film what turned out to be called the Number One Department Store. (Stores had no names. They were numbered as they were built.) My theory has always been: show me a department store and I'll show you how people live.

The Macy's of China was large, crowded, and cold, heated by one coal stove near the entrance. Bicycles, the most prized possession—no one owned a car—cost about sixty dollars. The average factory worker made about twenty dollars a month. Denying himself all the extras, a worker could probably buy a bicycle at the end of the year . . . or maybe a sewing machine, the next most cherished item, which also cost about sixty dollars. Shoes cost a dollar fifty a pair, and face cream and shampoo were sold by the glob. I did a show-and-tell report on the store for broadcast later that evening.

Next door to the store was a pharmacy (the Number One Pharmacy?) that sold the prize souvenirs for foreigners—plastic acupuncture dolls. They were small, white, slimy-feeling dolls with innumerable markings for insertion of the needles. The needles themselves were from three to eight inches long, a sort of do-it-yourself acupuncture kit. The pharmacy also had white, slimy acupuncture ears (Chinese doctors thought that the ears contain most of the nerve endings of the body). The dolls and the ears turned out to be the most popular souvenirs I brought home, along with the large red buttons bearing the face of Chairman Mao that virtually all the Chinese wore.

Dr. Paul Marks, my friend at Memorial Sloan-Kettering Hospital, went crazy over the ear I brought him. Acupuncture techniques had barely reached this country, and the Chinese were boasting that they did operations with no anesthesia, only needles. One afternoon, before we left Peking, some of the reporters were treated to a view of an actual operation. The patient, I was told, was lying on an operating table, had his eyes open, and seemed totally relaxed. I, who can't bear a pinprick, avoided this excursion and settled for bringing home a half a dozen plastic ears. What I didn't bring home, which was also for sale—and would you believe it in that puritanical country where I was told no one married for love, but because they were "politically compatible"?—was a selection of aphrodisiacs.

I managed to get permission to film another story, this one at the Evergreen People's Commune. The agricultural commune was just ten minutes from our hotel, where we enjoyed hot and cold running water and quite luxurious bathrooms. The commune had neither.

We visited the home of a farming family named Kong. It made the spare little coal miners' houses I'd seen in Wales look like Trump Plaza. The Kongs' two-room farmhouse had a mud floor, a brick-and-wood bed heated from beneath by a box of hot coals, an outhouse, and nothing else. Yet the Kongs, too, toed the Communist Party line. Yes, they had enough food to eat, and heat in the winter, and clean, warm clothing, all of which they owed to Chairman Mao, who had taken the farm away from a brutal landlord and given it to the peasants.

It was a good piece, I thought, because it was the only time we were invited into a real Chinese home and could show viewers at home not only how the Chinese lived but how they thought. I sent it off to New York, but somewhere between the Evergreen People's Commune and Rockefeller Center it disappeared. For all I know it may still be en route.

The long days, often stretching from 6:00 a.m. to 2:00 a.m., began to get to me as the week progressed. I realized then, as I do again now writing this, that I was depressed.

And this is the sour part.

All was not well between me and some of my male colleagues. The enmity had begun before we even got to China, when we made an overnight stop in Hawaii. Henry Kissinger and a few others from the White House staff, including Nixon's secretary, Rose Mary Woods, and speechwriter Pat Buchanan, were invited by Clare Boothe Luce, who was living in Honolulu, to a small dinner. (Mrs. Luce was the wife of the founder of Time Inc., and a formidable presence herself.) Dr. Kissinger and I had become off-camera friends following my far-ranging interview with him for *Today*, and he asked Mrs. Luce if I could be invited to the dinner, too. That's what started the sour part.

I wasn't the only reporter invited. John Chancellor was there, as was Theodore White, but being the only woman journalist made me stand out. The reporters who were not invited, and most were not, resented my access to Kissinger and White House staff. In their eyes I was the upstart, unseasoned and spoiled. It didn't help when Kissinger drew me aside for a private chat. The consensus was that he was giving me some sort of advance scoop when in fact he was merely asking me, if I had the time and opportunity in China, to buy some souvenirs for him to take home to his family and friends. (But not for Nancy Maginnes, the woman he was seeing who would become his wife. At that time Nancy, who is quite conservative, wanted nothing to do with the Chinese Communists and had told Henry she wanted no presents from that country. She has since become very fond of China and many of its leaders.) This shopping aside with Kissinger just added fuel to the fire.

The print journalists were already deeply resentful of the large contingent from television in the China press corps. While the White House had limited the print media to one writer per newspaper or magazine and to a pool of photographers, they had permitted the networks to send large crews of TV technicians and cameramen. The Nixon White House cleverly anticipated the public relations value of images of the president in exotic, forbidden China being beamed live, by satellite, into America's living rooms and they were bending over backward to accommodate the television contingent. The television staffers were often provided cars to ferry them around, for example, while disgruntled print journalists had to ride on buses.

The resentment of the newspaper and magazine reporters was well-founded. It was Richard Nixon's television show from beginning to end. He didn't trust the Washington press corps, who he felt were "liberals" and responsible for the public outcry against the war in Vietnam. Nixon wanted to bypass the press and go directly to the American people, and live television was the perfect vehicle.

Unfortunately I got caught in the cross fire.

The print journalists couldn't really take out their anger on seasoned television journalists like the beloved Walter Cronkite or the universally respected John Chancellor. So whom did they single out? Yup, me.

A few photographers went so far as to circulate a story that they had dumped a whole pile of ruined film on the floor outside my hotel room. If they did, I never saw it. They claimed that I had stuck so close to Mrs. Nixon that I was in every one of their images of her. I doubt it. I was usually no closer to Mrs. Nixon than the male reporters. Another story, that some photographers had dumped their smelly long johns in the wastebasket in my hotel room knowing the hotel would return them to me, absolutely did not happen. Just an adolescent locker-room fantasy.

What did happen is that, basically, the print reporters shut me out. When they gathered together at the end of the day for a drink, I was not included. When they sat and chatted on one of the bus rides, I was not asked to join in the conversation.

Even Max Frankel, the future executive editor of the *New York Times*, who would win a Pulitzer Prize for his coverage of the China trip, turned me away. One evening he was going out to eat with a few colleagues, and when I asked if I could join them, Max made up some lame excuse and off they went without me. Years later Max apologized to me and told me how badly he still felt about it, but the truth is they just didn't want me along. I was the upstart. I was the *Today* show, which was getting attention and for which they had no respect.

But I certainly didn't understand that then. What have I done to these guys? I kept thinking. What have I done to make them hate me?

I thought of things like the dinner party in Hawaii and my private conversation with Kissinger, and, while standing with the president, the smiles of recognition he would sometimes give me. I was beginning to look like the teacher's pet. And you know how people feel about the teacher's pet.

Then there was Haldeman, who was running around China with his own movie camera. My interview with him had been just a few weeks before, and he kept smiling at me in China, and even winked at me on occasion. That might have set the other reporters' teeth on edge. They'd never so much as managed to interview Haldeman and here I was, on a winking basis with the president's chief of staff.

Looking back on it now, I can better understand the hostility. Every other television correspondent had worked, at some point, in print. Though the print people considered them sellouts to the vulgar, higher-paying positions in television, they still shared common backgrounds. I didn't. I was a child of television. Plus I was a woman, while they were all members of the old boys' club. But I didn't get it then.

However, my colleagues from NBC, especially John Chancellor, were very friendly and supportive. That helped make up for the others. I was also fascinated by China during that epic week. It was my personal life that was unsettled and contributed a great deal to my sense of loneliness.

Because of the satellite it was easy to call home, but I didn't have anyone to call. I couldn't call Lee. After all, we had just separated. I couldn't call my parents either. They were already worried about me going to so distant a part of the world. A phone call would just lead to all kinds of anxious questions. I was also concerned about leaving my little girl. What if something happened to her or she got sick and I was on the other side of the world? I knew that Zelle was fully capable of handling anything that could go wrong, so that was one call I could make. I telephoned home whenever I could, told Jackie I missed her and loved her dearly and asked Zelle to turn on the *Today* show before Jackie went off to nursery school so she could see her mommy in that strange land called China. Then I hung up the phone, felt even lonelier, and went back to work.

After another long day following Mrs. Nixon, I went to my broadcasting booth to report on the major cultural event of the visit: a special ballet to be performed at the Great Hall of the People. All the Westerners, reporters, technicians—everybody—had been invited to see what was billed as *The Red Detachment of Women*. The theme of *The Red Detachment* had to do mostly with female soldiers kicking the hell out of anyone who opposed the Communist regime. Hardly *Swan Lake*. But the big news was offstage because the invitations to the event had been extended by the most important woman in China, the wife of Mao Tse-tung, who was known by her maiden name, Chiang Ching. She herself was attending the performance.

Madame Chiang was what we would call a piece of work. Everyone was dying to meet her. She was Mao's fourth wife, a generation younger than he, a former actress, beautiful and, many thought, evil. Mao had divorced his third wife to marry her. No one knew if they had children. Probably didn't dare ask.

Anyway, up until the 1960s, little was heard from Miss Chiang. Then, during the Cultural Revolution, she rose like the Dragon Lady to form the infamous Gang of Four, which brutally purged intellectuals, writers, and revisionist government officials. She had many of them put to death. She also took it upon herself to revise China's repertoire of ballets and operas, banning anything that had to do with China's rich cultural past and replacing them with eight revolutionary Maoist works. This ballet was one of them.

Her brutal, dictatorial ways would catch up with her. When her husband died four years later, she was tried, sentenced first to death, then to life in prison, and is said to have committed suicide in 1991. But on the night of the ballet, sitting with her husband between the Nixons, she was an imposing and fascinating figure. In my little booth miles away from the ballet, I could only describe her for the *Today* show audience from my television monitor. We never met.

After the ballet was over at about 11:00 p.m., we were told that a bus would take us to the Friendship Shop, as the store for foreigners in every major Chinese city was called. It was open twenty-four hours a day and you could buy a jade ring for $4,000 or an emerald necklace for $20,000. It was there that I bought the presents for Henry Kissinger and some beautiful silk brocade for myself. (I still wear the skirt I had made from the brocade.) At the shop I became a bit more popular with the other members of the press. Several of them asked my advice about presents to bring back home for their wives or kids. The ice was melting. Back to bed by 1:00 a.m. Up again for the Chinese chicken noodle soup at 6:00 a.m.

The week went by in a blur. Visits to more factories, schools with tiny tots dressed alike in their uniforms, singing the praises of Chairman Mao. Mrs. Nixon told me she thought the children were receiving a surprisingly well-rounded education. She said that in the second grade they were doing math she couldn't do. "I wish I could stay longer," she mused.

But my anxiety level remained high. I had no idea how my live reporting was coming across in New York and whether they were even running the filmed stories I sent back. I felt extremely inadequate, especially when I was broadcasting from the jerry-built communications center. The walls were paper thin, and I could hear Walter Cronkite broadcasting from one small studio, Harry Reasoner in the next studio, and John Chancellor across the hall. How could I possibly compete with those titans?

Ironically it was President Nixon who reassured me that I was doing a good job. We were all at the Great Wall of China, the zenith of Nixon's television week, with cameras positioned to beam his every step back to America as he strolled casually along with the Chinese premier, Chou En-lai. When the stroll ended and the cameras were turned off, he came over to compliment me on a report I'd done on a gymnastics event the night before. "How do you know about it?" I asked the president. "Oh, I get word by telephone every morning," he said. So the canny television-savvy president was keeping track of the ratings during his trip to China. That said a lot about him, but regardless, it was music to my ears.

Yet it almost left me stranded at the Great Wall. The chat with the president left me little time to find the NBC car I was assigned to. I wasn't going to make the same mistake I had made with the CBS crew, but then I wasn't about to spend the next five years trying to get back to the hotel from the Great Wall on my own. To my relief I saw Av Westin getting into a car. I had worked with Av years before at CBS and he was now the executive producer of *ABC Nightly News*. I asked if I could hitch a ride with him and he said sure and squeezed me in next to the chief ABC correspondent, Harry Reasoner, who could not have been more jolly. (I would remember this happy ride years later when I went to ABC and thought I must have dreamt it. But I'm getting ahead of myself.)

That night, our last in Peking, the Chinese press, all twenty-six of them, invited the American press to dinner. I joined the group when I got off the air. Conversation at the table, me to a very bright Chinese journalist on my left:

"We've asked you so many questions. Anything you are curious about concerning America or Americans?"

"No."

"Anything you desire like a car, or another bicycle?"

"No. I have all I want."

"You have two sons. What do you hope for them?"

"That they do not have bad habits and grow up to serve the people."

I mention all this because so many of us have now visited China or read about it and, once more, it is almost impossible to see how that closed, regimented society blossomed into the modern society, albeit Communist, it is today.

On the sixth day of the trip, we flew to beautiful Hangzhou, known as the "Venice of China." In the bad old days, the city was the home of rich beautiful women, of beautiful silk, and of the best tea in China. It was like a picture book, with its lakes, pagodas, and temples. President and Mrs. Nixon took a boat ride on West Lake and so did we. The president was in great humor. It was lovely and relaxing, and as it was the weekend, I didn't have to work that night.

I also attended my first banquet. Since I had been living on the ubiquitous tangerines and breakfast soup, everything tasted so delicious to me that I wrote down every single item we were served. There were small plates of roast chicken, fish in sweet-and-sour sauce, shrimp with green tea leaves, fried duck in spices, fried chicken squares with onions and peanuts, bamboo shoots stewed in peanut oil, bean soup with scallops, chrysanthemum cakes, egg rolls with sugar and sesame fillings, lotus seeds in rock sugar, and fruit. Divine.

After the banquet, another first. The president walked slowly through the room greeting us and finally introducing us to the legendary Chou En-lai, a slim, elegant gentleman who spoke some English. "This is Helen Thomas," the president said, introducing the veteran UPI reporter. "She's been reporting on the White House for sixty years." (The remarkable Helen retired in 2000, just shy of her eightieth birthday.) And then the president introduced me to the premier. "This is Barbara Walters," he said to him. "We're just breaking her in."

At our last stop, Shanghai, President Nixon signed a joint communiqué with his hosts, dealing with delicate future relations with Taiwan and a joint pledge for a gradual increase in American-Chinese contacts and exchange. At the end of the communiqué Nixon announced, "This was the week that changed the world."

It changed the world of news as well. The China trip probably marked the seminal moment in which television assumed superiority as America's primary source of news. The print reporters were furious. *Life* magazine's Hugh Sidey complained that the White House "seemed to treat writers as an unnecessary evil." When we got back, an editorial in the *New York Times* claimed that television had taken control of news coverage.

The week in China also changed me. I learned more about reporting than at any time before or since, and I saw a country, before almost any other Westerners, emerge from the shadows into a new era.

I would return to China several times over the years, including a trip with President Gerald Ford in 1975. But nothing would ever come close to that first visit in 1972. I felt humbled and grateful. What an extraordinary job I had! I was so fortunate. On my last afternoon in that atheist country I said a little prayer of thanks.

Our final night in China, I was again sharing a room with Fay. We were still up at two in the morning throwing away our old notes and trying to figure out a way to prevent the Chinese from returning our trash, when there was a knock on the door. Two grave-looking Chinese men entered and dumped large gift-wrapped boxes into our laps. They weighed about thirty pounds each. "Candy, compliments of the Shanghai Municipal Revolutionary Government," said the one who could speak English. Fay and I burst out laughing. Two in the morning and thirty pounds of candy to take home. We couldn't leave it there. The Chinese would never have forgiven us. Or allowed it.

The next day our American press planes picked us up, and lunch was hot dogs and hamburgers. Heavenly. Not a tangerine in sight.

The visit was over. I had survived and evidently done well. The word had come through from NBC that my reports from China had been given more airtime than any of our news team. Better yet, the NBC team had beaten the ratings of all the competition. I had even made a friend or two, not among the Chinese, but among my colleagues. Especially John Chancellor, who had changed his mind about me during the course of the week, recognizing the hard work I'd done. He braved the disdain of the male chauvinists on the plane by stopping by my seat and planting a very public kiss on my cheek.

Now it was time to go home and face a different challenge.

Life without Lee.

A Dead Marriage
and the Dead Sea

I CAME BACK FROM China totally spent but with the knowledge that I had done a better job than NBC or I ever expected. Still, when I opened the door to my apartment, there was no one there to hug me and say, "Welcome home, I am proud of you." Lee was gone. I had wanted to be free for a long while and now I was. But freedom has consequences. The same person whom you have yearned to leave or to leave you is also the person you miss when you want someone to care and to fuss over you.

Things would have been easier had Lee and I argued or called each other names. But it was never like that. Lee had been there when my on-air career began. I had been there for his Broadway ventures. We had the joy of adopting our baby and watching her grow. Lee was a good father. I, in turn, was a good stepmother to his children, and I wanted to keep that relationship going. I felt sad for Lee and for myself.

I also decided that two marriages were enough, and I vowed never to marry again. (I didn't keep the vow.)

This was an easier decision for me to make than it would have been for many women. I had enough money to continue living in the same style as during my marriage, and I wasn't afraid of being alone. If anything, with a very busy career and a young child, I never seemed to have as much time by myself as I wanted; being alone seemed very desirable.

Lee and I had no financial disputes. There was no alimony and no settlement on either side. Lee gave me minimal child support for Jackie. He wanted to. She was, he felt, his responsibility, too. It all seemed fair.

Lee could see Jackie whenever he wanted. We never had a formal agreement about that, and it never caused a problem. Our apartment was a rental. I kept it, and Lee rented a smaller apartment for himself.

Aside from the fact that we were tearing a marriage apart ("Other than that, Mrs. Lincoln, how did you like the play?"), things were pretty tidy.

My parents, however, were very upset. My father had become especially close to Lee and kept asking me, "Why? Why?" Every answer sounded weak. They felt terrible for Lee but they were also anxious about me. As was Shirley. Shirley, my confidante, my best friend, had always supported my decisions before, and I was sure she would now. But she didn't. It wasn't that she didn't understand how I felt. I had often confided in her my vague discontent which became stronger and less vague as the months and years went on. But like my parents, she was worried about my future. "Lee will be fine," she said. "He'll have no trouble finding someone else. But you're pushing forty. You don't leave one man until you have another."

She worried about Jackie's future—who would pay the doctors' bills, the school tuitions, college? "Who knows how secure your job is?" She pointed a finger at me. "Right now you're doing great, but anything can happen in your business. You lost a job in television before. It could happen again." I listened, but I didn't change my mind. I would take my chances.

One amusing rumor, at least amusing to me, that started circulating was that I'd left Lee for Henry Kissinger. Kissinger never entered my mind when Lee and I separated. I admired him and enjoyed his company, but there was never a romance. I had also been introduced to his future wife, Nancy Maginnes, whom I liked immediately. They would marry in 1974. But to some of the Washington and New York columnists, for Kissinger and me to be an item made great sense. Certainly Shirley thought so. "Henry Kissinger would be perfect for you," Shirley said. "He's nice, he's smart—and he's Jewish."

In those first few weeks after I returned from China, I was not thinking at all of romance. I was much more concerned about my little girl. At first she didn't fully realize that her father was no longer living at home. After all, he'd often been away at his different theaters. But soon enough, though she was only four, the separation began to have its effect.

Lee couldn't have been more devoted to Jackie. He saw her often, never missed a school play, and took her away on vacations. He and I spoke to each other many times a week and never said a bad word about each other. But Jackie often protested and began to cry when Lee came to pick her up. I'm not sure she ever really forgave her father for moving out, although I always told her it was both our decision.

As for Lee and me, after the first few months of pain, we began, little by little, to find our way back, and a real friendship developed, in part because of our love for our little girl.

Lee eventually married a very smart and nice woman named Lois Wyse. Lois was the cofounder and president of Wyse Advertising and the author of more than sixty books, including the best seller *Funny, You Don't Look Like a Grandmother.* I knew Lois slightly. One of the commercials I did for the *Today* show contained a famous slogan she had written for a jam and jelly company: "With a name like Smucker's, it has to be good." Lois sometimes came to the set to check that we were doing right by her client. I liked her then, and later, after she and Lee married, we became friends. Lois adored Lee, seemed to love his show business life, and accepted the fact that he and I had an unusual feeling of warmth for each other. I remember being at a party with the two of them one freezing winter night. The party was around the corner from my apartment, but when it was time to go home, I was nervous about attacking the icy streets in the dark alone. It was Lois who urged Lee to walk me back to my building. He and I walked arm in arm, as old friends do.

Lee continued to follow the siren song of Broadway. The last and very expensive musical he would produce in 1986, *Rags,* closed after only four performances. This time more than his heart was broken. Six months later he was diagnosed with inoperable brain cancer. Lois nursed him devotedly and without complaint through a long siege of chemotherapy. As the disease progressed I visited often. Lois always welcomed me. In the last months of his life, when I am not sure Lee really knew who I was, my visits still seemed to give him some pleasure.

Lee died in March 1988 at the age of sixty-seven. The morning of his death, Lois telephoned me. "Can you come?" she asked. I ran right over and we sat alone and held hands. I realize it may sound strange, but Lois somehow knew, without jealousy, that I meant a great deal to the man she loved and that he continued to mean a great deal to me. For years, until her own death in 2007, we called each other, with a smile, "sisters-in-law."

But fifteen years earlier, although there was nothing as profound in my life as my separation from Lee, there were also separations in my professional life that were making me sad. In January 1973 my on-camera buddy and off-camera support, Joe Garagiola, left the *Today* show. The given reason, which so many people still use to shade the truth, was that he wanted to spend more time with his family. The real reason, I believe, was Frank McGee. Frank never really understood Joe's value to the program. To him Joe was an over-the-hill baseball player and something of a joke. Joe was hardly that. He was very smart and, moreover, very wise.

The tension on the set had eroded the spirit of friendship and goodwill that Joe, Hugh, and I had felt toward one another. We had traveled together, had uncountable meals together. We knew each other's families and celebrated each other's birthdays. Happy, happy years. But with Frank's arrival all that had changed.

In contrast, Frank and I never had breakfast or lunch together, and I don't remember ever having a personal conversation with him. I'd send him a Christmas card or a present on his birthday, but I never received an acknowledgment, let alone a thank-you.

During this hostile period I had felt closer than ever to Joe. We could count on each other for a laugh or help in a tight spot. After all, Joe and I had spent five great years together, longer than some marriages. So his departure caused me real pain. It was even tougher to keep that happy face on camera for two hours every morning.

Enter Gene Shalit, the wild-haired, handlebar-mustached, bow-tied arts critic from *Look* magazine. I adored him from the beginning, though at first the *Today* audience did not. Gene was far more sophisticated and subtle than the down-to-earth Garagiola. And he sure looked different. Joe didn't have much hair, while Gene had more than enough for both of them. But Gene's witty and often biting theater and movie reviews soon won over the viewers. He became one of the most influential motion picture critics in the country and we became lifelong friends.

Working with Frank McGee meant having to continue to go outside of the studio to do my own interviews. In August 1973 I went *way* outside the New York studio. The occasion was the twenty-fifth anniversary of the founding of the State of Israel. I had an interview lined up there with Prime Minister Golda Meir. This was my first trip of what would be many to the Middle East.

Curiously, although I'm Jewish, I had never had any great desire to go to Israel. I'd never felt any special religious or spiritual connection to the Jewish state, perhaps because my parents and I were not religious and none of our relatives lived there. The closest my father had come to identifying with the tiny country's beleaguered population was by buying those Israel Bonds. So I had little sense of expectation when I arrived in Jerusalem.

To my great surprise, Israel overwhelmed me and aroused feelings I never knew I had. No visitor, Jewish or not, can fail to be moved by the stunning history in the ancient, walled city of Jerusalem. I couldn't get over the beauty of the land itself, at once rocky and arid, yet lush where the Israelis had ingeniously brought water to the desert. I felt a startling and quite strong connection. I understood the pride and suffering and the stubbornness that drives Israelis.

While I was there I wanted to interview Moshe Dayan, the Israeli defense minister. A former military commander and chief of staff of the Israeli Defense Forces, Dayan was a dashing and heroic figure in the United States. He was very good-looking, with a strong face and high cheekbones, and an eye patch to cover the eye he had lost to a sniper in Syria. Even though he had been raised as a farmer on an Israeli kibbutz, someone once described him, I think accurately, as looking like an Oriental prince. That's the dashing part. The heroics were his military past and his civilian role as defense minister during the 1967 Arab-Israeli War, which the Israelis won hands down.

The problem, Israeli officials told me, was that no one was authorized to arrange interviews for Dayan. He alone decided to whom he was going to talk, and he usually said no. I put in my request for an interview and prepared to wait.

It was one of the best "waits" I've ever had. In the era before cell phones, waiting to hear from a potential interviewee often required sitting alone in a hotel room all day next to the phone. But not in Israel. The government and the NBC bureau in Tel Aviv knew where I was every second, so I took some time to explore Jerusalem. I roamed the ancient city, home to the three major religions of the world, Christian, Muslim, and Jewish. I traced the steps of Jesus. I poked my nose into the various nooks and corners of the Old City, where everything from spices to watches was sold. The city, still the ultimate source of conflict between Palestinians and Israelis, is one of the most fascinating places in the world.

One memorable night I was planning to go to hear the Israel Philharmonic, but got sidetracked by a very attractive Israeli professor I'd met that afternoon on a tour of Old Jerusalem. "Don't go to the concert," he said. "Let me show you the Dead Sea by moonlight."

The Dead Sea by moonlight. How could one resist? Off we drove that evening to the lowest point on earth, just an hour from Jerusalem. The moon was just coming up, illuminating the still, calm water. I must have brought a bathing suit because I clearly remember going into the very salty, very warm water, which was so dense you could float effortlessly. In fact, that's all you could do. The mineral-rich water is too heavy to swim in. I calmly floated on my back in the moonlight, thinking how ironic it was to find such peace in such a volatile region. I could see the lights of the Kingdom of Jordan on the other side of the Dead Sea. It was so very close, yet it would be another twenty years before Jordan and Israel made peace.

As I still hadn't heard anything from Moshe Dayan I gave myself another treat—a few days at Sharm el-Sheikh, then an Israeli resort on the Red Sea. Since returned to Egyptian control, Sharm el-Sheikh would become first a popular resort and later, the target of vicious terrorist attacks at the beginning of the twenty-first century. But in the summer of 1973 it was lovely and quiet. Then the message came in: Dayan had agreed to the interview.

I had no idea what to expect. I heard from our NBC bureau that he hated to do interviews and could be rude and abrupt. Great. And that's what we became—great friends.

In my living room now, displayed on my bookshelves, are various ancient stone artifacts Moshe Dayan gave me over the years. He was a passionate amateur archaeologist and spent much of his free time on digs in the Holy Land. I, too, collect ancient artifacts, so Dayan and I had a bond. All the pieces he gave me—one of which he was using at the time as an ashtray—are signed by him and are among my most treasured possessions. "To Barbara with all best wishes, Judea BC 4000, m. dayan" is the handwritten inscription on the bottom of the "ashtray."

Our first encounter in the backyard of his small, two-bedroom house on the outskirts of Tel Aviv was not particularly friendly. He had really been forced into the interview by the rising international outcry over Israel's seizure of a Lebanese passenger plane. The Israelis had been tipped off, erroneously, it turned out, that a wanted Palestinian terrorist was on board. Dayan saw no need to apologize. "We are not terrorists; we catch terrorists. When the terrorists stop, we'll stop." All those years ago, and Dayan's words are still repeated in Israel today.

Of the innumerable people I've interviewed, Dayan was certainly one of the bluntest. His best, and occasionally worst, quality was that he didn't care what anyone thought about him. I remember asking him something or other during the interview to which he responded: "That's a silly question." "Okay," I charged back. "If you think that's a silly question, why don't you ask the right question, then answer it, and I'll just sit here and we'll be fine." He didn't expect that response from me. He laughed out loud, and that was the moment our friendship started. I also met his lovely second wife, Raquel, and we, too, became very fond of each other.

My interviews with Meir and Dayan garnered a lot of attention. Even Frank McGee gave me a grudging "Nice work," which was a big deal coming from him. There was so much interest in Israel then, as now, and its ongoing struggle to survive. Less than two months after my visit, the country was at war again. The October war, as the Egyptians called it, or the Yom Kippur War, as the Israelis called it, saw Israel in great danger after a surprise joint attack by Syria and Egypt.

I followed the 1973 war closely, and was relieved when Israel recovered from the initial attack and repelled its Arab enemies. But Golda Meir and Moshe Dayan were held accountable for the loss of Israeli lives and severely criticized for not having anticipated the attack. Both of these giants in Israeli government resigned. (Mrs. Meir remained active politically but would not hold another government post; Dayan would return to the Israeli cabinet in 1977 as foreign minister under Prime Minister Menachem Begin.)

On the domestic early-morning television front, I was having my own little battle. Hardly history making but a field day for the media. CBS decided it was going to revamp the *CBS Morning News* to challenge *Today*. There had never been any real competition for NBC in the morning. But this time CBS decided to hire the young, good-looking, snappy, feature writer at the *Washington Post*, my old friend from the Persepolis days, Sally Quinn.

I liked Sally a lot and was sorry we were going to be competing, but the media was delighted and did its best to create a catfight between us. *New York* magazine ran a cover story with Sally sitting, legs crossed, on a pile of suitcases, and the cover line: "Good Morning. I'm Sally Quinn. CBS Brought Me Here to Make Trouble for Barbara Walters."

At least the magazine printed the letter I'd written Sally when I'd heard of her new assignment. "CBS could not have made a better choice. I mean this in all sincerity and look forward to seeing you very often now that you'll be in New York. I won't be able to catch you on camera, but I hope we'll get together off camera. For God's sake, let's avoid all those people in and out of the media who may try to create a feud between us. We like each other too much." I signed it, "Much luck and affection."

The truth was, however, that I was somewhat anxious because I knew what a good and witty reporter Sally was. I had enough trouble with McGee. I didn't look forward to the daily comparison with Sally. She had a lot of contacts in Washington and qualities I didn't have, the first three being blond hair, blue eyes, and youth. But CBS made the same mistake with Sally that NBC had made with Maureen O'Sullivan. The network assumed that a person who was wonderful being interviewed would be just as wonderful being the interviewer.

Sally's debut in August 1973, teamed with a pleasant veteran newsman named Hughes Rudd, was not a great success. It was not Sally's fault. Not only was she sick and feverish, she later said, but nobody at CBS ever gave her any directions. They just threw her on the air and expected her to soar. It was an all but impossible assignment.

The *CBS Morning News* did not make a dent in the ratings of the *Today* show, which by then was drawing close to four million viewers a day, a huge audience at the time. Instead of being anxious about competition from Sally, I began to feel sorry for her.

About three months after she started on CBS we were pitched against each other for our respective networks on one of the most colorful stories of the year. The occasion was Princess Anne's wedding to Mark Phillips in London's Westminster Abbey in November 1973. The lavish wedding of the only daughter of Queen Elizabeth and Prince Philip was the forerunner to Princess Diana's wedding to Anne's brother Prince Charles. There was the same pageantry, and royalty and political leaders attended from all over the world.

The *Today* show and the *CBS Morning News* both covered the wedding live, starting at 5:00 a.m. because of the five-hour time difference. It's not that I am a saint, but by then I was really feeling compassion for Sally. She was struggling in London while I could still remember, from the time I covered the investiture of Prince Charles as Prince of Wales, much about the royal traditions. I knew who the major players were and who among the guests were the so-called lesser royals, the term used for those royal relatives who were further than tenth in line to the throne. I shared much of this information with Sally. A quick learner, she got through the wedding just fine. But Sally would last just another few months at CBS before leaving to return to the *Washington Post*. Not only did her career flourish there, she married the *Post*'s famous executive editor, Ben Bradlee. They are still happily together, and she and I are still great friends.

When I got back from London, everyone on the program was buzzing about Frank McGee, who had seemingly taken leave of his senses. He had plunged into a flagrant love affair with a young black production assistant named Mamye, and had left his wife to live with her. It was unbelievable. Frank had been married happily, or so we thought, for many years to his wife, Sue. He never took a trip for *Today* without her. She used to travel with him during the times he worked day and night at the political conventions. It seemed the most secure of marriages.

The only possible hint that it wasn't, was when I heard that Frank and his wife used to drink something like a pitcher of martinis a night. Do you drink until you are practically blotto every night if you are really happy? Nevertheless, we who worked with Frank were mystified as to why Frank suddenly upped and left his wife for Mamye. Mamye, who had babysat for Frank and Sue's grandchildren. Mamye, whom we all knew as fun, giggly, inefficient, and not even particularly pretty. How the drama stayed in-house and did not end up in the columns is beyond reckoning. But it didn't. We all kept it a secret. Just try that today. In this day and age it would be front-page fodder for the tabloids, all over the Internet, and with ten-minute updates on cable news shows.

But although it was a secret, we were noticing some changes in Frank. In the past he would have his makeup applied and his silvery hair combed in the large dressing room with the rest of us. Now he insisted on having his own dressing room, even though the other room was small and cramped. There were rumors that his hair was falling out. His skin tone seemed paler.

Although he never said a word, we began to wonder if he was ill. But when a man is ill, isn't that when he most wants to be with his long-faithful wife? Surely this was not the moment to run off with someone less than half his age. Or was it? It all seemed so crazy. But because Frank was more distant than ever, none of us were privy to his thoughts or feelings.

In the midst of all this drama my friend and agent, Lee Stevens, was negotiating my new three-year contract with NBC. It was September 1973, and with *Not for Women Only* now being syndicated in some eighty cities, Lee felt he was dealing from a position of strength. It turned out he was. He got me a substantial raise but was not interested just in getting more money for me. Lee put in the contract that if Frank were ever to leave the program, voluntarily or involuntarily, I was to have the title of cohost with whoever succeeded him.

It wasn't surprising that no one at NBC questioned that clause. The brass doing the negotiations believed that Frank would be doing the program for years to come. Our ratings were solid, and he was only fifty-one. Therefore the chance that they might have to make me a permanent cohost must have seemed ridiculously slim, certainly not within the three years of the contract they were currently negotiating. So NBC included that clause. I signed off on the deal and continued to get my own interviews outside the studio. There were plenty of interviews to get.

A scandal of historic proportions was engulfing the Nixon White House in 1973. Watergate was in full bloom, and all the players in the daily headlines were in Washington. So, for much of that tumultuous time, was I.

Resignation in Washington.
Victory in New York

*T*HE PLACE TO BE in the summer of 1973 was Washington. The place to stay was at the Watergate Hotel. The show to be on was the *Today* show.

The Select Committee on Presidential Campaign Activities, otherwise known as the Senate Watergate Committee, was holding public hearings to investigate the mounting crisis for the Nixon administration and the president himself. One shoe was dropping after another.

What had begun the year before as a curious burglary at the Democratic National Committee headquarters in the Watergate complex had escalated into sensational charges of political spying, sabotage, wiretapping, burglary, and conspiracy. By the spring of 1973 the scandal had reached the highest echelons of Nixon's inner circle: John Dean, the White House counsel, had been fired, and Nixon's top staffers, including his chief of staff, Bob Haldeman—he who winked at me in China—had been forced to resign.

And now the Senate hearings.

I was free to be in Washington much of the summer. My little girl was with Lee, who had taken a summer house in Westhampton, Long Island. My parents and my sister were in Miami, and I spoke to them three times a week. My mother told me some disturbing news about my father. He seemed to be losing strength, she said, and slept most of the day. I felt that it was depression, but I didn't know what I could do about it.

I was broadcasting from the NBC studio in Washington doing features and interviews while Frank anchored the program from New York. Between us we had all the major Watergate players on *Today*. Hardly a day passed when I didn't interview a congressman, a senator, a constitutional lawyer, a pollster, or somebody knowledgeable about the crisis. With so many Washington interviews to do, the McGee edict that I couldn't come in until the fourth question quietly went away. Frank did his interviews from New York and I did mine by remote from the NBC studio in Washington and it was quite a calm period between us. I'm sure he was happy that I'd been reassigned to Washington—somewhat like sending me to China.

Many of the journalists in town for the hearings were staying at the Watergate Hotel, and we gathered in the evening to compare notes. The old boys' club finally had begun to accept me because I had good stories to swap from my morning interviews. (The nightly news programs did not do interviews back then.) The only other news program doing interviews, and taped at that, was *60 Minutes*, but that CBS program was only on once a week. *Today* was on five mornings a week, live, for two hours. It was a huge advantage.

For all of us in news, whether television or print, covering Watergate was one of the most interesting and exciting experiences you could have. The stars were the young *Washington Post* reporters Bob Woodward and Carl Bernstein, who kept breaking one Watergate story after another, but there was more than enough material for all of us. It was a riveting time, particularly for me because I knew Nixon. And the pincers were closing around him.

One bombshell followed another during the hearings, bringing the scandal closer and closer to the Oval Office—the testimony that Nixon had discussed the cover-up some thirty-five times with his counsel; the revelation that Nixon taped all his conversations and phone calls in the Oval Office; Nixon's refusal to hand over the presidential recordings to the Senate Watergate Committee; the court-ordered (backed up by the Supreme Court) delivery of the tapes, which disclosed a mysterious eighteen-and-a-half-minute gap that was blamed on Nixon's secretary, Rose Mary Woods.

It didn't help Nixon when Spiro Agnew, his vice president, was forced to resign following charges of income tax evasion. (Nixon named Gerald Ford as Agnew's replacement.) And it certainly did not help Nixon when the House Judiciary Committee started impeachment hearings in May 1974. I was again in Washington for the three months of those hearings. At their conclusion in July, I remember being with very close friends, Shirley and Dick Clurman. Dick, who was winding up a brilliant twenty-three-year career as a journalist and chief of correspondents at Time Inc., was a close friend of Leonard Garment, John

Dean's replacement as Nixon's special counsel. The Clurmans, Garment, and I were watching the chair of the committee, Democratic Congressman Peter Rodino, preside over the vote that would send three articles of impeachment against Nixon when Len, who had a very dry sense of humor, said, "Come on, Peter. Sink to the occasion." I loved the line and remember it to this day.

Soon afterward, along with the rest of the nation, I watched Richard Nixon resign, the first U.S. president ever to do so. Pat Nixon stood ghostlike behind her husband with their two daughters, Julie and Tricia. Julie, so close to her father, had begged him not to resign, but he had no option. It was Julie who admitted to me in a later interview that she was the one who had to tell her mother that her father was going to resign. For all the excitement and historical importance of the moment, it was also quite poignant.

I thought of all the times that I had been with Nixon, this awkward man who had always been kind to me. I had interviewed him several times. I had covered Tricia's wedding. As I watched him announce his resignation, I felt both anger and pity. Mostly I thought how devastating this must be to Pat Nixon. She never seemed to have had a close relationship with her husband. The fact that they rarely communicated must have made her all the more lonely, grappling with a situation she could not control, which was going to drag her down, too, and this so soon after her triumph in China.

In the midst of this intriguing time, I did interviews with people who had nothing to do with politics. Liza Minnelli, for example, who was wowing everyone in a sold-out engagement at the Winter Garden in New York; Henry Fonda, who was winning accolades portraying the famous lawyer Clarence Darrow on Broadway; Maria Callas, the fiery Greek opera diva who had lost her longtime lover, Aristotle Onassis, to Jackie Kennedy.

The Callas interview had a special appeal. For years people had speculated as to how she felt when Onassis jilted her. Callas admitted in our interview that she and Jackie had never met and that furthermore, she'd never wanted to meet her. She implied that Onassis had actually proposed to her several times (which I didn't believe) but that she was wary of marriage, having been married once before. She kept talking about how all she wanted was for Onassis to be happy, but it was obvious from her protestations that she herself was heartbroken. Her career, which she had given up for Onassis, was all but over, and so was any hope of rekindling her relationship with him. When eventually Onassis and

Jackie split up, Callas came back into his life, but it was, reportedly, never the same.

Most of my interviews, however, dealt with Watergate—with Senator Ted Kennedy; with Martha Mitchell, whose soon-to-be-ex-husband, former U.S. attorney general John Mitchell, would be found guilty of conspiracy, perjury, and obstruction of justice and serve nineteen months in prison; with Jeb Magruder, Nixon's deputy campaign director, who was charged with perjury and conspiracy to obstruct justice and spent seven months in prison; with Gail Magruder, Jeb's wife, who said her husband's prison sentence was an "anticlimax" after all they'd been through. Haldeman, too, went to prison and spent eighteen months behind bars, convicted of conspiracy and obstruction of justice.

The pivotal figure in all this, of course, remained Richard Nixon, with whom I would continue to have a professional relationship. So I will now digress.

After resigning the presidency, Nixon repaired to his house in San Clemente, California, taking with him his press secretary, Ron Ziegler, and his young assistant press secretary, Diane Sawyer. I had no contact with him during this period, though I wrote him often, hoping for an interview. When he finally did do his first interview in 1977, it was not with me but with the British television journalist David Frost.

David, now Sir David and a good friend of mine, paid Nixon a reported $600,000 for the series of taped interviews over a twenty-four-hour period which were then boiled down into four ninety-minute programs. The most interesting, of course, was the section on Watergate. Because of the presidential pardon Nixon was granted by Gerald Ford, who replaced him as president, Nixon never had to stand trial for his role in Watergate, so no one had as yet heard his side of the story. Nixon had approval over the interview with David, which was taped and edited. There was such curiosity about the former president, and David was such a good interviewer, that the programs were syndicated and seen in seventy countries around the world. To this day, there is still curiosity. In 2007 the play *Frost/Nixon*, based on those interviews, opened on Broadway after playing in London. It was a huge success and was then made into a movie.

Nixon came back into my life in 1980, three years after the Frost interviews. He approached the networks to promote a book he'd written about foreign policy and the ongoing cold war with the Soviet Union. It was titled *The Real War.* But Nixon set conditions for the potential interview. He would do it only if it was live and therefore without any editing. Nixon's first choice was *60 Minutes* on CBS, but Don Hewitt, the program's producer, never allowed anything live and he turned Nixon down. It was Don's loss and my gain.

I was at ABC by then, and I sat down with Nixon on May 8 in our New York studio for a live one-hour interview. I had long since developed my own way of preparing for an interview. I wrote down on three-by-five cards as many questions as I could think of, then asked anyone who walked into the office, whether it was somebody delivering the mail, a production assistant, or a hairdresser, "If you could ask any question of [whomever], what would it be?" It was very productive. For this interview with Nixon I had so many questions that I could have done six hours with him. I must have written over a hundred questions on my cards, which, as was my custom, I cut down and cut down again and cut down yet again.

This was my predicament: If I was too tough on the former president, people would feel sorry for him, and those who still had some admiration or affection for him would turn against me. On the other hand, if I was too soft on him, the criticism would be, "Why didn't the news department choose somebody tougher to do the interview?" It was a delicate balancing act. I finally divided the questions into foreign and domestic policy segments, Watergate, and also a more personal segment. I wanted to give him the opportunity, if he wanted, to talk about such things as what faith meant to him, how his family had helped him get through the resignation and his subsequent health crisis with phlebitis. Even though he had resisted personal questions during my very first interview with him while he was president, I thought he might welcome them now. I saved these questions for near the end of the interview.

But the final question was key: was he sorry he hadn't burned the tapes that led to his resignation? For this last question, I told my director to give me a thirty-second cue at the end of the interview. I wanted to give Nixon very limited time to say yes or no, rather than skirt the issue.

We met in the studio. Nixon was his usual awkward self, trying to be friendly to the crew by making a slightly off-color joke. We put makeup on him because he had a propensity to sweat. Some people felt this had cost him the election during a 1960 television debate with John F. Kennedy. (Those who heard the debate on radio thought Nixon had won, while those who saw Nixon sweating on television thought JFK had won.) Then we began the interview, live.

Nixon was superb on foreign policy but reluctant to talk about Watergate. When I asked him whether he felt responsible for the distrust and cynicism Americans now felt toward their leaders, Nixon replied: "I think under the circumstances that with Watergate now six years past, we're at a time when it is time to move forward to the future and not dwell on the past."

I pressed, but it was obvious he wasn't going to talk further about Watergate. But he really stonewalled me toward the end of the interview when I got to the personal questions. When I asked him why "people who have written books about you, who worked for you, people who are close to you in one way or another, say that you are cold, remote, and that they are unable to reach you?" he replied, "Why are you interviewing me, then?" I answered by saying I was not talking about whether *I* found him cold and remote, I was quoting people like Henry Kissinger, to which Nixon curtly responded: "Why don't we get serious."

I went on, saying that I was sorry that he found "these questions unserious" and reminded him that people "are interested in you, the man, and your feelings," but he would have none of it. I next wanted to give him that chance to talk about how he got through the dark days. Was it his faith? Were there friends? I was trying to induce some sympathy for him, but he was not about to allow me to go there. When I asked him if, in the early days after Watergate, there were times "when you thought you might go under, emotionally," Nixon bristled and said: "Not at all." Period. Silence.

There was nothing to do then but to go back to the foreign policy questions, the ones I hadn't asked yet.

But I couldn't find the right cards.

Even today, more than twenty-five years later, revisiting that moment makes my stomach tighten. I couldn't frantically shuffle and reshuffle the cards on live television, so I had no recourse but to wing it. Fortunately, since I write my own questions and I'd written them one hundred times before the interview, I remembered them. We hurtled toward the last segment of the interview, talking about his case for increasing the military budget, the lack of congressional support for it, the upcoming presidential election (which would see Ronald Reagan defeat Jimmy Carter), the downfall of the shah of Iran, and finally—the thirty-second cue.

"In the few seconds we have left now, and there's almost just time for a yes or no—are you sorry you didn't burn the tapes?"

Nixon replied that everyone he'd spoken to in Europe had said to him, "Why didn't you burn the tapes?" "The answer is," he said, "I probably should have."

"If you had to do it all over again, you'd burn them?" I pressed in the last seconds.

"Yes, I think so," Nixon said. "Because they were private conversations subject to misinterpretation, as we have all seen."

There. I'd gotten him to say what would make headlines the next day.

"Thank you for being with us," I said. And the interview was over.

When we took off our microphones and I stood up to shake his hand, I realized I was ice cold from the strain of having done the last ten minutes of the interview without any written questions. There we stood, Nixon perspiring through his makeup, and me frigid. It was then, when I stood up, that I saw that damn pile of questions on my chair. I had put them under my fanny when I thought we were through with the foreign policy segment and had been sitting on them the whole time.

NIXON EVIDENTLY DID NOT object to the interview, and we continued to have a good relationship. I did two other interviews with him, one in 1982 following the death of the Soviet leader Leonid Brezhnev, another in 1985 after the publication of his fifth book, *No More Vietnams*. But then—silence. For a reason not of my making.

Soon after Tom Murphy and Capital Cities bought ABC in 1986, the entertainment department bought Woodward and Bernstein's second book about Watergate, *The Final Days*, to make into a television movie. Nixon did everything he could to prevent the movie from being made. He was protecting his wife, he said. Mrs. Nixon had had two strokes since her husband left office, and he was worried about her. "I, myself, speak about what I've been through, but you know, for a woman to suffer in silence during the difficult last days in the White House and the days thereafter, which were even worse, is much more difficult," he had told me in our earlier interview about his book. He was afraid now that the ABC movie, which covered that exact time period, might cause his wife to have another stroke.

His plea, however, fell on deaf ears. ABC could have canceled the movie but they didn't. It was already finished, and they insisted on running it. (It got very low ratings, by the way.) But Richard Nixon never spoke to me on the air again. When I approached him later for another interview, he turned me down. He liked me personally, he said, but I got my paycheck from ABC.

Pat Nixon did not have another stroke after seeing the ABC movie, but her health continued to deteriorate. She died of lung cancer on June 22, 1993. I covered her televised funeral at the Richard Nixon Library and his birthplace in Yorba Linda, California. Nixon was visibly upset. That supposedly cold, remote man cried uncontrollably at the service.

I recently learned from a young assistant of Nixon's, Monica Crowley, that after Mrs. Nixon's death, he had a change of heart about me and his boycott of ABC. Nixon had written another book, *Beyond Peace*, and had decided to do an interview with me. He talked to Monica about rearranging his study for the camera and lights and told her he was looking forward to talking to me. But it was not to be. Nixon suffered a massive stroke on April 18, 1994, which left him partially paralyzed and unable to speak. He died four days later, at eighty-one. The book was published posthumously.

Ten months after his wife's funeral I was back in Yorba Linda to cover his. Richard Nixon was the first U.S. president I interviewed, and he played an important role in my early career. He had always been considerate toward me. His death marked the end of a painful era for America, but it also touched me in a personal way and made me sad.

End of my digression on Nixon. Back to the 1970s and another death that really did change my life. In April 1974, I was in California when the call came from New York: Frank McGee was dead at fifty-two. Frank *dead*? I couldn't believe it. We all thought he was sick, but we had no idea how ill he'd been. It turned out that he'd had bone cancer. He must have been in great pain, but he did the program almost every morning until the day he died and never said a word about it to any of us.

I immediately flew back to New York and was on *Today* the very next day. We were all in shock, as were our viewers. I received hundreds of letters of sympathy from people all over the country, a testament to the seemingly pleasant—and totally false—relationship I'd had with Frank.

Frank's wife and his children were at his funeral. Mamye was nowhere in sight. Shortly after everyone returned to the office, the drama deepened. Mamye and Stuart Schulberg got into a fight, and he fired her. Though he later apologized and offered to help her transfer to another department at NBC, Mamye decided to sue NBC for racial discrimination. The situation created a terrible rift on the show, pitting Mamye's supporters and friends against Schulberg and the more senior members on the program. In the end the Office of Equal Employment Opportunity dismissed her complaint of racism. Mamye had left *Today* by then to work elsewhere at NBC, and things calmed down. None of this, not even the lawsuit, ever got into the papers.

After Frank's death NBC immediately embarked on a search for a new male host for *Today*. Many names were flung about, including NBC "outsiders" like Dick Cavett and Bill Moyers and NBC News "insiders" like Tom Brokaw, Tom Snyder, Garrick Utley, and Jim Hartz. NBC decided on Hartz, a pleasant and popular local newscaster. They seemed to want someone easy and uncontroversial. There had been enough drama in the country and on the *Today* show. But just before the announcement was due to be made, Lee Stevens called the top guys at NBC and said, "Oh, fellows, by the way, there's just one little thing." He reminded them of the contract he had negotiated with them. "In case Frank McGee leaves the show," Lee pointed out, "Barbara is going to be a cohost."

On April 22, 1974, NBC sent out a press release announcing my new position. "Barbara Walters will be cohost of the NBC Television Network's *Today* program from now on," read the release from Donald Meaney, vice president of Television News Programming. "This is the first time the program has had a cohost and *Today* is now the only TV network news or public affairs program to have a female cohost."

And so it was that I became the official cohost of the *Today* show. Two years later I would leave *Today*, but from that moment to the present, every woman on the morning television shows on every network has been a cohost. This is, of course, not noted in the history books, but it was a very big step at the time. And all because Lee Stevens slipped a clause into my contract that no one at NBC thought they would ever have to act on.

Fun and Games in Washington

ASHINGTON CAME ALIVE after the president's resignation in August 1974. Genial Gerald Ford replaced gloomy Richard Nixon, and the whole city seemed to take a deep breath and relax. As was said then, it was the end of the national nightmare. There was an air of gaiety, of celebration and relief. Unlike today, when foreign nations' embassies are quite serious places with occasional staid dinners, the embassies in the Ford era seemed to vie with one another to be thought the most popular and exciting place to be.

The parties were invaluable to me in terms of making personal contacts. Nothing is more important to a journalist than a phone book full of home phone numbers and a person on the other end who knows and likes you. So these were working parties for me as well as fun.

The number one embassy when it came to extravagance and just plain enjoyment was the Iranian Embassy, presided over by its flamboyant bachelor ambassador, Ardeshir Zahedi. The shah of Iran, in his early twenties, had entered an arranged marriage that lasted a short time but produced a daughter, Princess Shahnaz Pahlavi. Zahedi had been married to the princess. They, too, had a daughter and then later divorced. But the shah maintained his friendship with his former son-in-law.

The ambassador was an imposing figure, tall and dark with a great head of hair, a prominent nose, a ready smile, and a glad hand for everyone. He was also smart, shrewd, and the shah's most trusted adviser in the United States. No one knew if the shah approved, but Zahedi believed in large parties with hundreds of guests, flowing champagne, mounds of fresh Iranian caviar, and a bulging buffet with every kind of treat from hummus to hamburgers. You could eat your fill, mingle and mix, or just stand around and watch. There was plenty to watch. There were belly dancers to clap to, musicians to listen to, bands to dance to, politicians to talk to, and movie stars to ogle.

Elizabeth Taylor was a favorite guest. There were rumors that Miss Taylor and the ambassador were having an affair. But he never seemed to have a real girlfriend. As a matter of fact, when Farah Diba, the empress of Iran, paid visits to New York, Zahedi asked me to be his "date." He usually took over a small, private room at "21" and invited a select group of dignitaries and friends. I had already met the Shahbanou, as she was called, and the ambassador could count on me to mind my manners and follow protocol. The next day I would be the recipient of several pounds of caviar.

NBC would not allow the members of its news department to accept gifts (no network news department allows it to this day), but caviar and candy, being perishable items, were allowed. Zahedi once sent me a Cartier watch for my birthday, which I not only returned to him but wrote a letter explaining why (it was, by the way, a very pretty watch). I also sent a copy to Dick Wald, head of NBC News, and kept a copy for myself. This turned out to have been a very wise thing to do. Shortly after the shah was overthrown in 1979, the new fundamentalist Islamic regime accused American reporters of being on the take. I was one of the reporters they publicly accused, mentioning a Cartier watch they had obviously found a record of in some file or other, but—aha!—I had the letter proving I had never accepted it. But all this was some years away from the swinging parties of the seventies given by the generous ambassador.

Washington had another bachelor ambassador, Alejandro Orfila of Argentina, who had also been married and divorced. He supposedly owned a lot of houses and land back in his home country and he, too, liked to have lavish parties, although not quite in the Zahedi league. Orfila was a serious man, as indeed were all the ambassadors. You didn't get dispatched as your country's chief diplomat to the most important post in the world if you were anything but first rate. I went to quite a few parties at the Argentine Embassy and had a very pleasant dalliance with Ambassador Orfila. We went out several times and I was startled when, out of the blue, he asked me to marry him. Was he kidding? I brushed off his proposal, if that's what it was, and we continued to be friends. Maybe he just wanted an American wife.

Orfila went on to become the twice-elected secretary-general of the prestigious Organization of American States (OAS). We lost touch after he left Washington, but I've always remembered him fondly from that period of gaiety in the nation's capital.

I was also seeing several men in New York. There was Alan Greenberg, known to his friends and colleagues as "Ace," the brilliant banker who made the investment banking firm Bear Stearns the formidable institution it became. I had known Alan (I always called him Alan) ever since he came to New York from Oklahoma in the 1960s and eventually became "Ace." He was extremely smart and funny. Today he's happily married to Kathy, a charming lawyer, and is one of my closest and most trusted friends. Furthermore, he manages whatever money I have. I will always be grateful to have Alan in my life. I don't know what I would do without him.

There was also a fascinating man named John Diebold, who wrote the visionary book *Automation*, which extended the meaning of automation beyond the car assembly lines in Detroit to business machines. He was a techie genius when it came to automating transactions and records in banks and health care. Don't ask me more. That's all I understood. His daughter went to the same school as Jackie, and we were introduced at a parents' conference. John was one of the most considerate men I'd ever met. Of every man I knew then, John was the warmest and sweetest to Jackie.

He had imaginative taste. Jackie, Zelle, and I had both a pre-Thanksgiving and early Christmas dinner at John's beautifully furnished apartment on the East River. (Icodel was having dinner with her children.) John had his wonderful cook make everything a little girl would like, from corn pudding and sweet potatoes with marshmallows to yummy banana splits for dessert. One Christmas, John gave Jackie a miniature horse farm with stables and six tiny horses with separate saddles. She was thrilled. Much better than the mouse house.

Why am I going into all this? Because it was a very heady and happy time for me. I had never had those years in my early twenties and thirties when one dated in a lighthearted way. I was too concerned with my family, trying to keep us all afloat, both emotionally and financially. Then, in my beginning years at NBC, it was work, work, work. It still was, but the rewards were greater, my status had grown, and I was no longer that serious girl who rarely smiled. Finally, there had been my marriage to Lee and the birth of our daughter. Now in my early forties, I was experiencing what I had never really known before—fun and romances.

Please understand, too, that all of these men were not in my life exactly at the same time. And some I saw more than others. Before you say, "Enough already," let me speak of two more.

Just before the Watergate hearings, I had gone to Los Angeles to visit my oldest and dearest friend, then and now, Joyce Ashley. Joyce was married to Ted Ashley (they later divorced), who headed Warner Brothers Pictures. They had a glorious home in Malibu right on the beach, and their neighbors were the actress Jennifer Jones and her hugely wealthy husband, Norton Simon, who had a magnificent art collection. He later gave it to an art museum he built in Pasadena, California, which bears his name. Jennifer was long past her movie career, but she was still a beautiful woman who, however, was so insecure about her looks that she changed clothes at least three times before any party she gave and always made sure the soles of her shoes were wiped clean so that they looked brand new.

Anyway, in spite of all this, or maybe because of all this, I liked Jennifer a lot. She was fey and funny, generous and thoughtful. One night she invited Joyce, Ted, and me to dinner and introduced us to an extremely attractive man named Matthew Byrne, who was a federal judge. Matt was about as appealing a person as I have ever met. A gregarious bachelor, he seemed to have a million friends and was one of the most sought-after men in Los Angeles. However, coming from a very close family (he supported his mother, sister, and nephew) he had never shown any signs of wanting to marry.

At first Matt wasn't too crazy about me. He had become rather well-known because he was the judge assigned to the famous 1973 trial of Daniel Ellsberg. Ellsberg had been accused of espionage, theft, and conspiracy by the government for leaking the secret Pentagon Papers to the *New York Times*. For the first half hour we met, I badgered Byrne with questions about Ellsberg and the trial, when all he wanted to do was have a scotch and relax. He told me later he almost walked out. But I must have calmed down and done something right, because after that we went out almost every night that I was in Los Angeles.

We had a lovely little romance but never quite made it to the point of being deeply serious. I may have been had Matt wanted it, but I can't recall his ever saying he loved me. Did he ever love anyone? Even after his mother died, he never married.

He could have had an even more prestigious career, but he made one big mistake. During the Ellsberg trial, Matt had a supposedly secret meeting with one of Nixon's top aides, John Ehrlichman, to discuss the possibility of him being named head of the FBI. The meeting could have been construed as a bribe at worst and, at best, improper. When it was leaked, it destroyed all chances of the appointment. I discussed this meeting only once with Matt, who swore that the meeting was not about the FBI job, but he wouldn't say what it *was* about, so I don't really know what happened. But Matt remained on the bench for the next thirty years as a very well thought-of federal judge.

We stayed loosely in touch over the years, and I was very touched when in the winter of 2006, I received a phone call from Matt's grown nephew informing me that his uncle was dying of lung disease and would love to hear from me. I called Matt, who was very weak, and we joked about past moments in our lives. Before I hung up, I said, "I love you, dear friend." Matt answered, "I love you too, dear friend." That's as close as we got to the *l* word. He died two weeks later.

Now just one more "gentleman caller," as playwright Tennessee Williams would call him. Toward the end of the Watergate impeachment hearings in 1974, I was in New York for a few days when some mutual friends introduced me to a man I had sure heard a lot about. His name was Charles Revson and he was the multimillionaire founder and owner of Revlon cosmetics, which at that time was the most successful cosmetic company on the planet. Revson had just divorced his third wife by having her brought to his office on her birthday. The story goes that she thought she was going to be given a big share of Revlon stock as a present. Instead, Revson's lawyers handed her a letter advising her that her husband was filing suit for divorce. It was in all the papers and just added to his reputation as a brilliant but hardly sentimental tycoon.

Revson was in his late sixties when I met him, divorced and rumored to be dating Lee Radziwill. So I was very surprised when friends who were in the perfume business and worked with Revson said he wanted to meet me. The things one remembers. It was summer. I was wearing a brand-new yellow silk pants suit. Pants suits were rather avant-garde at that time and I thought I looked pretty snazzy. However, over dinner, Revson told me he didn't like the outfit, yellow was not my best color, and he would be happy to take me shopping. I thought he was out of his mind and told him so. Obviously that didn't bother him one bit because he asked me out the next night, told me his yacht was going to the South of France, and he would like me to join his friends on a cruise. I told him I was going to Washington the next day to cover the impeachment hearings and so could not have dinner. As for the cruise, thanks but no thanks, for in my mind I was planning to go back to Los Angeles to be with my friend Joyce and see more of Matt Byrne. I just wasn't interested in Charles Revson, millionaire or not. The next day, just as I was leaving my apartment for the plane to Washington, an enormous bouquet of roses arrived from him. There must have been six dozen long-stemmed roses, all wrapped in tissue paper. What to do? Nobody was home in my apartment. Dump them? All those roses? Nothing like that had ever happened to me before. So, like a fool, I carried them, along with my suitcase, on the airplane, balancing them on my lap, jabbing the person in the seat next to mine, and schlepping them all the way to my hotel in Washington.

I never did see Charles Revson again. What I hadn't known on that one summer date in 1974 was that he was suffering from cancer. I always wondered if that was why he so unceremoniously decided to leave his wife. (Shades of Frank McGee.) He died the following summer at the age of sixty-eight.

These were just some of the various men in my life during the early and middle seventies. Which brings me to the more important part. There were, during those years, three men who were, then or later, extremely well known. They were all distinguished and accomplished. What they had in common was that they were all in government. That's not really a surprise. After all, people in government were the ones with whom I was most often in contact. Other than that, they were very different.

They did, however, have one other thing in common. I cared about each of them very much.

Special Men in My Life

$\mathcal{E}$DWARD W. BROOKE was the first African American elected to the U.S. Senate since Reconstruction. He served two terms, from 1967 to 1979. He was a Republican from the mostly Democratic state of Massachusetts, so he clearly did not fit a senator's traditional profile. Before going to Washington, he had served two terms as that state's very popular attorney general, and then had run for the Senate at a time when few people expected a black man could be elected to that all-white, very exclusive club. He won, and in the Republican Party he became a star.

One magazine of the time described him as "a model of how blacks could rise through the whole white-dominated ranks of mainstream politics." There was some thought that he might be the first African American nominated to run as vice president or could even rise as high as running for president. A most distinguished man. Anyone can find this information easily. What they will not find, and what only my closest friends knew, is that Senator Edward W. Brooke and I had a long and rocky affair.

Oh, yes. He was also married.

Where do I begin? Where did the affair begin? It was 1973. I certainly wasn't lacking for men in my life, or for romance. I was dating more than I ever had. Why, therefore, did I have a clandestine affair with a married man? A black married man? Though racial tolerance was on the rise—interracial marriages more than doubled in the 1970s—having a romance with a married black senator would have raised more than eyebrows. I had a daughter to think about and a network that would be less than thrilled to see me involved in any kind of scandal. None of that seemed to matter to me.

Ed Brooke was simply the most attractive, sexiest, funniest, charming, and impossible man. I was excited, fascinated, intrigued, and infatuated.

We met first in New York at a restaurant. I was with friends. He was with friends. We were introduced. He shook my hand and smiled. He had a big, wicked smile, more of a grin. "Now just who is this?" I remember thinking.

Months later I was in Washington. We were doing some kind of a panel on Nixon and China, and Senator Brooke was booked on the panel. He asked if I was staying in town that day. I said I was. He asked if he could take me to lunch. I said, "Sure." He took me to the Senate Dining Room, where guests were often invited. Perfectly innocent, and despite a serious expression to fool all onlookers, he flirted excessively.

He told me that he had never stopped thinking of me since the night we met. Really? He told me that he watched me every morning. No kidding? He told me that he was married to an Italian woman who was white and that he had met her in Italy when he served in the army (segregated in those days) during World War II. After the war he came home and sent for her, his young war bride. She spoke no English. Even now, Brooke said, after almost thirty years of marriage and life in America, she had barely learned English. He said sadly that after the novelty of their relationship wore off, they had little in common except their two daughters, by then almost adults. He rarely saw his wife except on holidays or when he was campaigning. She was, he admitted, a very good campaigner, especially among the large Italian American population in Greater Boston. It was a marriage that had long ago run its course, but politicians didn't get divorced in those days, and besides, his wife was used to his absences and never questioned him. Why divorce?

It is very difficult to explain to anyone else why you are attracted to someone. It certainly wasn't because Brooke (I never called him Ed) catered to me or flattered me. Or maybe it was precisely because he didn't do either. I had always liked men who were kind to me. I was not a masochist. But Brooke played with me. He was hard to reach. Hard to pin down. I found it both funny and frustrating. After the initial compliments, Brooke often joked, and sometimes, I thought, wasn't really joking, that I was the oldest woman he had ever been attracted to. I was in my early forties. He was ten years older, but age didn't seem to touch him. He had been attracting women most of his life.

Sometimes when he said that I was the oldest woman he had ever been with, I thought of telling him: "Oh, yeah? Well, you are the blackest man I have ever been with." But the truth is it didn't matter. Not that I was blinded to the fact that if our romance became public, his color wouldn't matter. But Brooke being black just didn't seem important one way or the other. It was also something we never discussed.

Looking back, maybe that was strange. I remember thinking that Brooke, who was light-skinned, didn't truly consider himself black. He never talked about his background or any problems black people might have. If he had felt discrimination, and he *must* have, he never mentioned it.

Part of the attraction was that Brooke wanted to be in control. I wasn't used to that, and at first it was pleasing to me. But then he would try to control me in ways that made no sense except to prove that he could. For example, we once made plans to be together in New York. I sent Jackie to stay at Shirley's. My cousin hated the whole idea of Brooke but loved Jackie and was happy to have her sleep over. Jackie also found a night away from Mommy very adventurous.

Zelle and Icodel, who were at home, loved me and protected me with their silence. Dinner was cooked. Music was playing. And then Brooke phoned to say he had decided not to leave Washington. No excuse. In one way I was relieved. I had felt so guilty sending Jackie away for the night. On the other hand I was furious, and for a week or so refused Brooke's phone calls. But then I gave in and began to see him again. Why on earth? The simple answer was that he excited me.

There was one couple who knew about us, old friends of Brooke's. They had a home in Virginia. Sometimes we stayed there. Sometimes we stayed in Brooke's apartment at the Watergate. We were very careful, and besides, we didn't see each other all that much. I lived and worked in New York. He lived and worked in Washington. And most important, I didn't want to be away from Jackie unless I truly had to.

Summer was a different matter. Brooke had a big house in Oak Bluffs, an elegant section of Martha's Vineyard that, then and now, caters mostly to upper-class, affluent African Americans. My close friends from Washington, Ann and Vernon Jordan, also have a house in Oak Bluffs. I always thought Vernon suspected something, but if he did, he was too much a gentleman to say. I visited Brooke there one weekend. I met his mother (his father was dead), a most charming woman who adored her accomplished son. God knows what she thought of me, but she was cordial. Her son could do no wrong.

The next summer, with three weeks off from the *Today* show, I took a house myself in a different part of the Vineyard. I asked Shirley to stay with me, and she brought her granddaughter who was the same age as Jackie. We were very private. Brooke visited us two or three times a week. Jackie still vaguely remembers him. She rarely saw him on his visits to me in New York. She sort of liked him, but not a lot. He once gave her a present with a note typed on U.S. Senate stationery, her name spelled wrong. The note was dated November 14, 1974. It said, "Dear Jacquie: Here's Raggedy Ann to be your friend. And now you will have 'company for dinner every night.' " It was signed "Love, Mr. B." I wonder now if his secretary typed the note. I wonder, too, when he said that Jackie would have company for dinner, if it was because he wanted me to have dinner with him alone.

I was still seeing other men in a more or less casual way. One was the very kind and gentle John Diebold, whom I've already told you about, and who was as different from Ed Brooke as day and night. He was so thoughtful and dependable. When I wasn't seeing Brooke, I was most often with John. I used to sing a song by Rodgers and Hart that began: "He was too good to me," because it reminded me so of John, who, of course, never knew about Brooke.

In spite of these complications, my relationship with Brooke grew. Politics was his passion and my great interest. We never ran out of things to talk about, and of course there was the fascination of our having to be so secretive. Forbidden fruit and all that. But I was beginning to resent the sneaking around, and I slowly began asking myself if we could ever be married. Would such a marriage destroy his career? Would it destroy mine? We would never know if we couldn't have a public relationship. By this time things were getting serious. That Thanksgiving, when we had been seeing each other for almost two years, Brooke didn't go home. Instead, he stayed in New York with me. He was planning to spend part of the Christmas holiday with me, too. His wife, who had condoned his romances for many years, now suspected that something different was happening.

Washington, at least some people in Washington, also began to suspect that the senator and I had more than a professional relationship. We would occasionally be at the same reception or dinner. We deliberately sought out these parties to which we had both been invited. At these occasions, purposely out loud, Brooke would ask if he could take me home. People were noticing.

There was, at that time, a tough and shrewd gossip columnist for the

Washington Post named Maxine Cheshire. Everyone feared her, as did I, especially when she began to write blind items about Brooke and me seeing each other. Things had to change. I told Brooke that I could no longer live like this. He was married. It had to end. But Brooke was not having just another flirtation. Our relationship had all but reached the point of no return. So he did something neither he nor I had ever imagined he would do. It was something that would put his whole political career in jeopardy. He went home and asked his wife for a divorce.

She was furious. I don't blame her. Not that she would actually miss her husband as he was so rarely home, but she was, after all, Mrs. Edward W. Brooke, a very important woman. She was also the mother of their two daughters. And though she may not have spoken English well, she sure spoke her own language well. The Italian voters would be unforgiving.

She fought back. With inquiries, perhaps to his staff, she found out that I was the woman for whom her husband wanted a divorce. She hired detectives. She knew someone who worked for the tabloid *National Enquirer*. The paper loved the story and assigned its own investigator. Brooke, at that time, owned a vacation house on the Caribbean island of Saint Martin. He often went there on vacation, sometimes with a "guest." Could I have been such a guest? The *National Enquirer* reporter, I heard, was roaming the island with photographs of me hoping a storekeeper or a restaurant waiter would recognize me. I had never been there with Brooke, but their search went on. I was getting very nervous.

Around this time I received a phone call from a very good friend, Pete Peterson, who had been secretary of commerce under Richard Nixon. I trusted Pete and knew he had my best interests at heart. With some embarrassment and pain, he told me that he had heard of my relationship with Ed Brooke and he felt the story would soon burst into the public. It would all but ruin my career, he said. NBC might have trouble standing by me. My divorce from Lee had been very quiet and dignified, and my reputation was solid and aboveboard. Pete thought I had better seriously examine what the ramifications of continuing my relationship with Ed Brooke might be.

I did. So did Brooke. He could not afford to risk his career. He was proud of being in the Senate, and his future could only get better. I also could not risk my career. I had a child and my family in Florida to think about. We decided wisely but very sadly that we had to stop seeing each other. That was that. We stopped.

I missed him terribly at first. He had been so much a part of my life and my fantasies. However, the truth is that after the years of hiding, it was also a relief. But by this time Brooke had burned his bridges with his wife. He decided he still wanted the divorce and hoped that a divorce with no recriminations would not affect his Senate seat. But that was the trouble. The divorce became very acrimonious, and there *were* recriminations.

His wife's fury led to stories in the newspapers about his private life. This undermined his reputation. In the middle of it all, Brooke ran for reelection. He lost the election, and his promising political career ended.

It was by then 1978, and even though it had been several years since we had seen each other, a part of me always felt it was my fault. I still feel that way. Maybe I'm giving myself too much credit, or perhaps too much blame, but before me, no matter how many romances or affairs Brooke had had, he never sought a divorce. His asking for one and his wife's anger led to his political downfall.

But his life went on. He married a beautiful woman. They had a son, who by now must be a young man. In 2004 President George W. Bush awarded Brooke the Presidential Medal of Freedom. Happy news. Not such happy news was the story I read about him in 2003 in the *New York Times*. He had breast cancer and had undergone a double mastectomy. He had gone public with the news, he said, because he wanted other men to be aware that breast cancer, though extremely rare, could happen to men. It was very brave of him. The article gave his age as eighty-three.

I thought of writing to him to say how courageous he was, but I decided not to. Our relationship seemed so long ago. For a time, however, it was a very important one in my life. That is why I am writing about it now.

Now about two of the other men who meant so much to me at the time.

I met Alan Greenspan in 1975, at a tea dance in Washington hosted by Vice President Nelson Rockefeller. In these days of concrete barricades and multiple security checks at government buildings, it's hard to believe the vice president of the United States was having a dance. Well, actually, he was and, as a matter of fact, Vice President Rockefeller and his wife, Happy, hosted several such "dancing" housewarmings at Admiral's House, the newly renovated, official residence for vice presidents and their families on Embassy Row. The invitation list for the different parties included movie stars (Cary Grant), astronauts (Alan Shepard), businessmen (publisher William Randolph Hearst), members of the press (me), and political appointees (Alan). It also included the Rockefellers' friends and members of Congress. (In fact the Rockefellers had their own house in Washington and weren't planning to move into the eighty-two-year-old Admiral's House, but were using the official residence to meet and greet.)

The residence had a particular attraction because of the important pieces of art the vice president had donated from his personal collection. The centerpiece was the famous "cage" bed in the master bedroom, designed by the surrealist artist Max Ernst. It was covered in mink, watched over at the head and foot by medallions of the sun and moon, and had trapdoors to hide lamps, telephones, and electrical gadgets. No one slept in it, but everyone who visited the mansion wanted to see it. Then we would mill around on the spacious grounds for refreshments as a small orchestra played. There was a little dance floor, and some people danced.

At one of these housewarmings, a tall, bespectacled man approached me and asked if I wanted to dance. His name was Alan Greenspan, he told me, and he was the chairman of the Council of Economic Advisers for President Ford. Sounded important if rather dull to me. But Chairman Greenspan was very pleasant and unassuming. After we danced—and, by the way, he was a very nice dancer—he told me that he actually lived in New York on weekends and asked if he could call me. I gave him my phone number and indeed, the next weekend he phoned. I was just coming out of the relationship with Ed Brooke, and I welcomed this call, the first of many, from the tall, quiet stranger.

I had a little problem, which was actually kind of fun. As I have written, I had been going out off and on for many years with the investment banker Alan Greenberg, and I continued to see him from time to time, even during the Brooke years. So when Alan Greenspan would call the house, he sometimes left only his first name. When Alan Greenberg called the house, he, too, often left just his first name. This was very confusing to Zelle and Icodel. Even if they asked either gentleman to please leave his last name, it was not much help. Greenberg. Greenspan. They sounded so much alike that both ladies were in despair. When they gave me the message, I could only ask: "Which one talked louder?"

Alan Greenberg was blunt, jovial, and outgoing. He talked in a normal tone of voice.

Alan Greenspan, on the other hand, was very soft-spoken. He almost whispered.

And that's how I would know whether it was Greenspan or Greenberg.

In the years ahead, when Alan Greenspan was the immensely influential chairman of the Federal Reserve and testifying before Congress, I never heard him raise his voice. He certainly never did with me. Part of it is just the lovely nature of the man. Part of it is an innate reticence. When we first began to see each other, I would often take him to a dinner party. He rarely mingled before dinner, and if he was seated next to a woman he didn't know, it was hard going for her because he was difficult to draw out. He is, by his own admission, an introvert, but even so he has also said he enjoys social events. He was not the sort of man you would notice when he walked into the room, and often I would have to introduce him to friends more than once because they wouldn't remember him. Perhaps because of his shyness, he walked a bit bent over as if not to attract attention. It wasn't insecurity; it was modesty. Even now, in spite of his great fame, Alan still has that quality.

I am now going to quote some of what Alan wrote of those times in his candid, best-selling autobiography of 2007, *The Age of Turbulence*. He remembers many more details than I do.

Here are some of Alan's words. "I am not threatened by a powerful woman; in fact, I'm now married to one. The most boring activity I could imagine was going out with a vacuous date. . . . Before getting to know Barbara, a typical evening for me would be a professional dinner with other economists. Barbara, however, interacted constantly with news, sports, media and entertainment personalities. . . . During the years we dated and afterward (we remain good friends), I escorted Barbara to lots of parties where I met people I otherwise would never have encountered. I usually thought the food was good but the conversation dull. They probably thought the same about me.

"Even so, I did build up a wonderful circle of friends. Barbara threw me a fiftieth birthday party. The guests were people I'd come to think of as my New York friends: Henry and Nancy Kissinger, Oscar and Annette de la Renta, Felix and Liz Rohatyn, Punch and Carol Sulzberger, Henry and Louise Grunwald and David Rockefeller. I am still friendly with many of these people today, more than thirty years later."

Alan also wrote of my introducing him to friends of mine in Los Angeles, where he would "tag along" with me to parties, even though he felt totally out of place. "Business economists are not exactly party animals," he wrote. Today those people, who are still friends of his and mine, probably brag about having met Alan all those years ago.

I didn't know a thing about economics. I didn't have to. Alan and I would discuss the news of the day. We would talk politics, although he was always very careful not to tell me anything I shouldn't know. We would go to the theater or occasionally to concerts. Alan had a fascinating background. We had all read Ayn Rand's *The Fountainhead* with its mysterious and independent hero-architect, Howard Roark. The message of *The Fountainhead* was that laissez-faire capitalism was everything, that government should stay out of all things, and that charity was poison. Ayn Rand was perhaps the most passionate and controversial advocate of free enterprise you could find, and she had a small but devoted and influential following. They called themselves Objectivists. Alan was still a follower of Ayn Rand in those days. He encouraged me to read her other most famous book, *Atlas Shrugged*, which I did. Neither book had a great influence on me, but I do remember wishing that my parents had thought to call me Dagny, the name of Ayn Rand's beautiful capitalist heroine.

How Alan Greenspan, a man who believed in the philosophy of little government interference and few rules or regulations, could end up becoming chairman of the greatest regulatory agency in the country is beyond me. It was a big issue when Alan was first appointed, but he was so brilliant at this job that the Ayn Rand relationship faded from conversation.

Alan, to my great surprise, had been a musician before becoming an economist. He had studied the clarinet at the Juilliard School of Music in New York and, for a time, played with the Henry Jerome band in New York, along with Len Garment, Nixon's future White House counsel, on saxophone. (They became friends, and it is said that Garment later recommended Alan for the job as chair of the Council of Economic Advisers, which is when I met him.)

Through Alan, I remember meeting a very pleasant Dick Cheney, who was then White House chief of staff to President Ford. I also met Donald Rumsfeld, Ford's defense secretary. Nice men, I thought, interesting though unexciting. We occasionally had dinner with them and their wives, evenings that were not noteworthy. I met them again years later when George W. Bush was president. They seemed like very different men to me. They also didn't seem to remember that we had known each other. (I requested interviews with each of them and was turned down.)

Back when Alan and I had a relationship, he lived in Washington during the week and kept a small apartment in New York near the United Nations. His mother, to whom he was devoted, came over every weekend to bring him food and make sure that a housekeeper had come to tidy up. Alan's parents had divorced when he was very young, and he rarely mentioned his father. He was raised by his grandmother and mother, both of whom worked. I liked his mother very much. She was warm, lively, and, unlike her son, an extrovert. She loved to play the piano, and as I had a piano in my apartment, she often played for us when she visited. Years later, when Alan was chairman of the Federal Reserve, and living full-time in Washington, he would come to New York every week to see his mother. We would sometimes have lunch after he visited her. I admired this devotion to his mother very much.

When he was in his twenties, Alan had been married for a short time to a woman who, I think, was also part of the Ayn Rand group. The marriage ended in divorce, and he had long been a bachelor with, it seemed, little desire to remarry. As I, too, had no real desire to remarry, the subject never came up. Furthermore, I never heard Alan express a desire to have children. He was sweet to my daughter but had no real relationship with her. Since I didn't think of him as a prospective stepfather, that was okay with me.

I felt calm and secure being with Alan. The same qualities that made him so admired in Washington were present on a personal level. He was so smart, so knowledgeable, and had little of the dominating ego that many powerful men possess. Although I rarely understood what he was talking about when he testified before Congress, I had no problem understanding him when we were together. He never talked down to me. He could and did listen to my worries and complaints for hours and never talked to me about his own. He never criticized. He had a surprisingly wry sense of humor. He was, in short, the nicest person you could meet.

If I had any reservation, it was that Alan was very frugal, not just with me but with himself. He wore the same navy blue raincoat until it practically fell apart. He was a bit like the classic absentminded professor. He rarely remembered to pick up a check or buy a Christmas or birthday gift. But that is the only small failing I can recall.

After Jimmy Carter defeated Gerald Ford in the 1976 presidential election, Alan left government to return to the economic consulting firm he had founded called Townsend-Greenspan. (I never did find out who Townsend was.) People often asked Alan for advice on buying or selling stocks or bonds. He politely brushed them off. That was not his area of expertise. His mind, so keen, was best at examining long-term trends and financial conditions that would influence all elements of society.

In future years we often laughed about the one time I asked him for financial advice. After we had been seeing each other for a few years, I decided to leave my rent-controlled apartment and buy a co-op. Shirley found a beautiful one for me in the same building that Jacqueline Kennedy Onassis lived in. It had four bedrooms, a huge living room and dining room, and it faced Central Park. It was 1977, and New York City was facing a financial crisis. There were even concerns that the city might be going bankrupt. The seller was asking $250,000, which seemed pretty fair for a big, beautiful apartment on Fifth Avenue. I asked Alan's advice. "Don't buy it," he said. "The way New York City is going, it's not a good investment." So I didn't buy it. Today that apartment is worth at least $30 million.

Alan and I never actually broke up, but when a relationship doesn't grow, it gradually diminishes. We didn't want to marry and in those days we couldn't live together. Still, I was shortly to be going through a very turbulent time professionally. Alan, it should be noted, was at my side throughout that time, and I don't know how I would have gotten through it all without his wisdom and support. You will hear more about that later. Although it was some thirty years ago, my essential feelings about Alan Greenspan have never changed. He is one of the finest people I know.

Eventually I fell in love and married someone else. Alan met and fell in love with the wonderful NBC correspondent Andrea Mitchell, another strong woman. Andrea is a great reporter, and she and Alan have much in common. Alan finally got over his marriage phobia. I was so pleased to have been invited to Alan and Andrea's wedding in 1997. It is the happiest of unions. They adore each other, and I adore being in their company. I am proud to be their friend.

In the fall of 2007 I joined some friends of Alan's in giving him a book party. The book, by the way, is a fascinating read about his eighteen years as chairman of the Federal Reserve and his own life journey (including me and those boring dinner parties). When you finish this book, and I hope you will, do read Alan's.

And finally some words about John Warner, one of the finest and most effective senators in Congress, who, at this writing, is serving his fifth consecutive term as the senior senator from Virginia. I also met

John in the early seventies, years before he became a senator. He was then the head of the Bicentennial commission, preparing to celebrate two hundred years of America's independence. Gerald Ford had appointed him to this federal position after several others had failed to do very much with the job. Actually there wasn't really a great deal of heavy lifting to do. It was mostly making sure that all the states were going to contribute *something* to the celebration.

John took the job very seriously and committed himself to visiting all fifty states. As the spokesman for the Bicentennial, he appeared on the *Today* show, and I was assigned to interview him. He remembered me, he later said, as brisk and attractive. I remember him as having great hair and being rather pompous. Still, when he asked if I would have lunch, I said okay. He talked a lot about himself and his plans for the Bicentennial. I liked his Southern manners. He was definitely from the old school. I asked around about him, and this is what I learned.

John was one of two sons of a doctor in Virginia whom John adored and was close to his entire life. John had finished law school at the University of Virginia after serving with the marines in Korea and cut quite a swath as an eligible young lawyer at the various Virginia debutante balls. In 1957, he married Catherine Conover Mellon, the only daughter of Paul Mellon, one of the richest men in the world. (The Mellon money came from Paul's father, Andrew, who had helped found such companies as Alcoa and the Gulf Oil Corporation.) John was an advance man for Richard Nixon when Nixon was campaigning for president. In 1972 Nixon appointed John to be secretary of the navy. John was secretary from 1972 until 1974 and that's when he was appointed to head the Bicentennial celebration.

In the meantime John and Catherine had three children, two girls and a boy. But Catherine was young and, I gather, didn't enjoy John's way of life. She was more artistic and sought a lower-key and simpler style. The marriage ended in divorce in 1973, and for many years John pretty much raised their children. Paul Mellon had given his daughter and son-in-law a magnificent home in the fashionable Georgetown section of Washington and a huge farm in the horse country in Virginia. In the divorce agreement Paul Mellon gave them both to John, I guess because he was such a good and responsible father.

I remember asking John, when he first talked about the farm, how big it was. I had no idea how large farms were supposed to be, but I knew enough to be staggered when he told me it was almost three thousand acres. It had horses, cows, a tennis court, an indoor swimming pool, and a state-of-the-art kitchen. When I got to know John better, he invited me to visit, along with Jackie and Icodel. We passed acres and acres of corn, which Jackie had never seen growing. We then made ice cream in the kitchen, which had every possible piece of cooking equipment you could want.

The house was only partially decorated. John had a splendid study with a fireplace and a huge desk. Upstairs the master bedroom also had a fireplace and was decorated in a lovely paisley. The interior designer was Billy Baldwin, one of the most famous decorators in America. But John had stopped work on the house when he and Catherine separated.

Anyway, that's how things were when John Warner and I met. He talked of wanting to run for senator from Virginia, but he didn't seem to have much backing from the Republican Party. He also knew few journalists. I remember taking him to a birthday party for the *Washington Post's* executive editor, Ben Bradlee, and introducing him to many of my friends. Although they found him very pleasant, he wasn't exactly their sort, or, at that time, mine. But we grew closer. When the *Today* show went to Hawaii, John arranged to be there, too. I was surprised and pleased by his attention. I had brought Jackie, and John arranged for us to have a special tour of Pearl Harbor and to visit a submarine. We had a fascinating time and even little Jackie was excited. I appreciated John's kindness, but our relationship was winding down.

It drew to a close in 1976 when John was invited to the White House to be the escort of no less a superstar than Elizabeth Taylor. Knowing them both, I could not imagine a less well-suited pair. But each had a fantasy. Elizabeth's career was on the rocks, and she was seeing a series of not very appealing men. Then along came this knight in shining armor. Independently wealthy, handsome—did I neglect to tell you that he was very handsome?—and, I think most important, there was his fabulous farm.

Elizabeth loved horses and perhaps she thought herself back in the days of her childhood when she first appeared in the film *National Velvet*, a classic story about the love of a child for her horse. The film made the exquisite girl a star and Elizabeth had not known a day since when she was not famous. So now, at last, a farm, peace, security. She and John were married in a field at the farm on December 4, 1976. Elizabeth, in photographs, with the cows and horses in the background, is a symphony of rustic elegance. She is wearing a lavender gray dress, a lavender turban, gray suede boots, and a silver fox coat, and is holding a bouquet of heather.

The marriage gave John instant fame, in spite of the fact that this was his new wife's seventh marriage, counting both of her marriages to the British actor Richard Burton. For a moment or two John considered an acting career himself. He even had a screen test. But what he really wanted to be was a senator from Virginia. He finished second in the Republican primary in 1978 to a young up-and-coming politician named Richard Obenshain. When Obenshain was tragically killed in a private plane crash just a few weeks later, John was tapped to be the candidate.

The Republicans couldn't have made a better choice. With his celebrated wife at his side, John traveled the state of Virginia from one end to the other. Elizabeth introduced him and shook so many hands that she later complained that she got ulcers of the hands. John made the political speeches, but it really didn't matter what he said. Everybody wanted to meet his famous wife. In November, John was elected to the Senate and soon became one of the hardest-working and most conscientious politicians in Congress.

That was a problem for Elizabeth. Being the wife of a senator is not a lot of fun. She hated the long, boring dinners. She missed her friends. Elizabeth Taylor has a great, slightly ribald sense of humor, and there were not a lot of people who appreciated it, including, I think, her husband.

I remember going to their farm for a rather bizarre interview with them—my second prime-time *Special* for ABC—just before John was elected to the Senate. Here was my former boyfriend, with a pipe in his mouth, talking about his partner, Elizabeth, and how they were in all this, day in and day out, together. But later, talking with them both in the kitchen I remembered so well, it seemed that what Elizabeth was doing most, day in and day out, was eating. John said she should eat more vegetables. "I do eat vegetables," Elizabeth replied. "Potatoes."

Although she claimed that she was very happy, the marriage was obviously doomed, and they were divorced six years later, in 1982. Sometime later, in yet another interview with me, she confessed that she had been unhappy in the marriage and that is why she ate. But her respect and affection for John remained.

So did mine. I hate to keep using the word "kind" to describe this man or that, but John Warner was one of the kindest people you could find. He was a gentleman, honest and caring. I watched with pride as he became more and more effective in the Senate. I myself, in spite of my earlier vow never to marry, had another marriage, and after that divorce in 1990, John and I began to see each other again, this time quite seriously. That was when I really got to know him. I admired his complete devotion to his job. He was a staunch Republican, but he didn't just follow the party line. He became a maverick in 1993 when he refused to support Mike Farris, the Republicans' nominee for lieutenant governor of Virginia, because he felt he was too controlled by the Christian Right. (Farris lost.) John took on the Republican hierarchy again in 1994 when he actively campaigned against Oliver North, another born-again and controversial figure, who was the Republican nominee for Virginia's other Senate seat. John disliked North so much that he supported a popular state politician who was running against him as an independent. The result of John's political maneuverings was that the Republicans lost the Senate seat. It was won by the Democratic incumbent, Senator Chuck Robb.

John's stature was not diminished. He became chairman of the Senate Armed Services Committee in 1999 and served in that capacity, with a short break, until the Democrats gained control of the Senate in 2006.

John and I saw each other for about five years in the 1990s. He spent many weekends with me during summers in Southampton. My friends became his friends, and they enjoyed him thoroughly. He loves to play tennis and golf and had many spirited games with Pete Peterson and Roone Arledge, both of whom had homes in the Hamptons. Most of all, John loved to paint. I can still picture him sitting in the shade of a tree in my backyard, doing his oil paintings of flowers. Flowers are John's specialty. They are the cover of his Christmas card each year.

Again, however, it has to be said that a relationship that doesn't grow begins to diminish. I could never imagine myself as the wife of a senator living in Washington. And New York life was never really for John. We talked all the time but saw each other less and less. Eventually he met a nice woman, Jeanne Vander Myde, who lived in Washington and shared his interests. They were married in 2003, and when I talk with John I can tell how happy he is.

It is especially important for John to have the companionship and satisfactions he now has. In August 2007, at the age of eighty, John announced that he would not seek reelection to the Senate. He would leave at the height of his power, admired and respected. John continually proved himself a true leader. He was among the first in his party to call on President Bush to reduce the troops in Iraq. He did this although he respects the president and would not want to hurt his own party. He has come such a long way from the man who had originally been known primarily as the husband of Elizabeth Taylor. I think he will be truly missed in the Senate.

Shortly after John announced his resignation, he telephoned me and we had a long, happy conversation. He had always phoned me on the nights when he was reelected to the Senate. This now was a phone call of affection between two dear friends. I told John that I would miss that call on election night, but I thought he had done the right thing. He will leave at the top.

Whenever I think of John, I see him, as I do Alan Greenspan and Ed Brooke, as such a very special man. I consider myself so fortunate to know them.

And now that you know about my late-blooming, delayed love life, it's time to get back to work.

Egypt, Israel, and
¡Hola, Castro!

*C*OHOST. A very satisfying title after ten years of sitting beside the male host on the morning desk at *Today*. Ten years. Seems small by today's standards, but in 1974 a breakthrough. The title did not translate to anything else. I didn't get a raise or a bigger office or more say over the program. But the media took note. *Newsweek* even considered the new title to be worthy of a cover story: "BARBARA WALTERS — STAR OF THE MORNING." (I loved the line that described the questions I asked as "some of the toughest in television journalism— dumdum bullets swaddled in angora.")

The real and only difference in my life was that Frank McGee was gone and so was all the off-camera tension and acrimony. I could interview anyone I wanted to in the New York studio—and ask all the questions. Which I didn't, of course. Jim Hartz and I worked as a very sharing team.

There was another departure from *Today*—Frank Blair, the program's newscaster for twenty-one years. I can't say I was terribly sorry to see him go. He was drinking a lot by then and had become rather sour. He also had quite a reputation. Frank was a handsome man and, though long married, he bragged about chasing every woman on the show, including me. He was the only one on the program, in today's parlance, who hit on me. But that had been years before, and we'd had a cordial truce ever since. A very pleasant fellow named Lew Wood replaced Frank, and the *Today* team became Jim Hartz, Gene Shalit, Lew, and me.

I was still spending a lot of time in Washington, and it was proving to be helpful. Among the many ambassadors I met and became friendly with at the various embassy parties was the Egyptian ambassador, Ashraf Ghorbal. He was intelligent and charming, as was his wife, Amal Amer, and I spent many pleasurable evenings with them. Four years later Ambassador Ghorbal would play a vital role in the Camp David Peace Accords between Egypt and Israel, but in 1974, there was no hint of peace between the two countries.

Egypt and Israel had fought a bitter war in 1973, the war that had caught Israel by surprise and marked the downfall of my friend Moshe Dayan. A Middle East peace conference was scheduled to be held in Geneva, and there was an air of cautious optimism. Having spent a good deal of time with Israeli leaders, I was anxious to interview their Muslim counterpart and official enemy, Egyptian president Anwar el-Sadat. I expressed that interest to Ambassador Ghorbal, who passed it on to the Egyptian foreign minister, Ismail Fahmy, when he visited Washington in the summer of 1974. Through Ambassador Ghorbal I managed to get an interview with the foreign minister (who would later resign rather than accompany Sadat on his historic journey for peace to Jerusalem). He, too, was cordial and, after our interview, listened attentively to my request for his assistance in securing an interview with President Sadat.

"Americans don't know President Sadat at all and, as a result, they fear him and they fear your country," I told the minister. "If your president is considering doing any interview, he would have no better forum than the *Today* show. Please ask him if I can come to Cairo to speak with him. Let me introduce him to the American people."

Several weeks later, to my great pleasure, as Sadat had given no interviews to the American press, I got the green light. Well, half a green light. I would be welcome in Egypt, Ambassador Ghorbal told me, but President Sadat had not committed to the interview. The indication was that I'd get the interview—if Sadat liked me.

I left as soon as I could for Cairo, with a secret plan. I liked the Egyptians I'd met in Washington. I liked the Israelis I'd met in Israel and in Washington. To me they seemed in many ways very similar: strong, intelligent, and proud people. Yet, because their two countries existed in a perpetual state of war, they couldn't even speak to each other. Egypt didn't recognize Israel's right to exist, so therefore the Israeli government didn't exist either. On the Egypt Air flight to Cairo, I saw that Israel did not even appear on the airline's map.

So this was my plan. Assuming I got the interview with President Sadat, I then intended to fly to Israel to pose the same questions to the Israeli prime minister, Yitzhak Rabin. I was going to run both interviews on the same program. Not only would people now perhaps understand the differences between the two countries and their leaders, but the two men might even discover some areas of agreement. So what if I didn't win the Nobel Peace Prize; it would make good television.

It didn't happen.

I sat in my Cairo hotel room for several days, staring at the phone, willing it to ring. I'd already cleared my plan with Prime Minister Rabin, who was a very savvy politician, but there was silence from the Egyptians. To pass the time I talked travel plans on the phone with my producer, who was staying in the same hotel. There were no flights from Egypt to that "country that doesn't exist," so we would have to go via Cyprus or Athens. But it would be well worth it to secure the two interviews and run them back-to-back. Immediately after we hung up, the phone rang.

"It cannot be done," said the Egyptian government official on the line. "If you intend to use an interview with President Sadat on the same hour or even on the same day as Rabin, you will not be allowed to speak with our president."

How could the Egyptians have known my plans? Obviously they had tapped my line. So much for Barbara Walters, peacemaker. I gave the official my word that I would not combine my interview with Sadat with any other interview. But I still wasn't cleared to see him. I would be interviewed the next day by one of his aides, the official told me. Then they would see.

I played it safe. Trying to be sensitive to Muslim conservative taste, I dressed in a black jacket and an ankle-length black skirt that I had bought for the occasion. I had no idea who or what to expect when I arrived at the president's house in Giza. I was taken to a marble-floored reception room and served *chai*—delicious spiced tea—when the door opened and a beautiful woman walked in. She was dressed in a chic green pants suit.

"I am Jehan Sadat," she said.

We talked for an hour, and I discovered what a remarkable woman Mrs. Anwar Sadat was—and is. She was wearing the same pants suit she had worn to the front lines to encourage the Egyptian troops during the 1973 war. No other wife of an Egyptian leader had ever done that, either wear pants or go to see the male troops. She had also enrolled at Cairo University, hoping to encourage other women to seek higher education, and was planning to take her exams on live television. In spite of fierce religious opposition, she was championing birth control to curb Egypt's runaway population crush. She was also spearheading the building of homes for the disabled and for orphans and advocating rights for women going through divorce.

Sadat himself had been divorced, with children, when he met the fifteen-year-old schoolgirl who was soon to be his wife. To Jehan, born of an English mother and an Egyptian father, Sadat was a hero. An Egyptian nationalist and revolutionary, he had been imprisoned for his efforts to rid the country of its British colonialists and their puppet, the corrupt King Farouk. Jehan's family did not approve of their daughter's choice. Sadat was many years older than she, divorced, and penniless. But the couple married anyway, and from what I could see, it was a marriage of respect and affection.

Over the years and over many more cups of *chai*, Jehan and I became lifelong friends. I admired her then and now, and I was cleared for the interview with her husband. Her approval was the one that he needed.

There is an image that has stuck in my mind for more than thirty years. When I arrived for the interview, I noticed a slight, bemused man sitting on one of the empty boxes our television equipment had come in, puffing on a pipe and watching his sitting room being transformed by the crew setting up the cameras and microphones, monitors and lights. There were no security guards, aides, or secretaries around him. The president of Egypt was simply taking in the scene.

Our interview, the first of many over the years, went well. Sadat repeated over and over that he wanted peace with Israel, the conditions being Israel's return of the land it had occupied since 1967 and the formation of a legitimate Palestinian state. "The core of the problem is Palestinian," he said. Most important, he answered the one question everyone wanted to know: Would he consider meeting with Prime Minister Rabin?

"It is impossible now. Impossible. After twenty-six years of hard feelings, violence, wars, hatred, bitterness—suddenly we meet? This is not logical at all."

The answer, however, did not sound entirely final but rather as somewhat hopeful because he had said impossible "now." We parted on a warm note. Bar-ba-ra, he called me. Always those three syllables, with emphasis on the middle syllable. *Bar-BA-ra.* I can hear his voice now as I write this. (Years later, after her husband's death, Mrs. Sadat told me that what she remembered best about her husband was his deep booming voice.)

I had certainly not found Sadat to be the feared ogre so many expected. He was personable, candid, and totally charismatic. So much so that I was concerned he would overshadow Prime Minister Rabin, who, though brilliant, often came over in interviews as taciturn and humorless.

But in our interview in Tel Aviv, Prime Minister Rabin turned out to be extremely talkative. He answered my questions and afterward asked many of his own. Rabin was extremely curious about Sadat, a man he had never met and indeed might never meet. "What is he like?" "What did he say?" "What did you think of him?" I was not presumptuous enough to think of myself as an official intermediary, but I couldn't help but be struck by the fact that as a reporter, I could speak to both men and, in effect, deliver the messages they could not relay in person. So I described Sadat's personality to Rabin and told him my impression that Sadat was a thoughtful and reasonable man. I also told him my feeling that Sadat was not ruling out a meeting but was waiting until the time was right.

Back in New York the two interviews aired on *Today* on two successive days. Large portions of the interviews also ran on the evening news programs. It was the beginning of the fall television season in September, and they were very well received, especially the segments with Sadat. This was his introduction to the American people and they were fascinated by the man who would later become an American hero for being the first Muslim leader to make peace with Israel. I was there for that, too, which I'll tell you about later. Sadly, I would also be in Cairo again for Sadat's funeral, after he was assassinated in 1981, for making that peace.

In 1975 morning television was having its own little war. *Good Morning America* made its debut on ABC in November. It was our first serious challenge at *Today*, but hardly a surprise. Some months before the kickoff of the program, I had been approached by an ABC board member to see if I might be interested in coming to ABC. It was my first contact with ABC, and, at the time, seemed very unusual to me.

The ABC board member was a friend, an older, very nice, and successful businessman named Jack Hausman. He and his wife, Ethel, had a daughter with cerebral palsy, and in the past they had tried to be helpful with my sister. They thought she might have enjoyed visiting and perhaps working in one of the sheltered workshops they ran for people with the neurological disorder. Jackie did visit but felt it was not a place for her. Still, I appreciated their interest and every year, volunteered to host their telethon, which raised money to fund research for cerebral palsy.

Leonard Goldenson, the founder and chairman of ABC, Inc., also had a child, a daughter, with cerebral palsy. I knew him only slightly, but he and Jack Hausman, because of their mutual concern, were close friends and had cofounded the United Cerebral Palsy Association.

Hausman was on the board of ABC. The two of them must have talked because one day, out of the blue, Hausman called and asked if he could see me. It was during that meeting that he inquired if I had any interest in leaving NBC and coming to ABC, which was considering doing its own morning show. He told me that ABC would be willing to pay me a great deal of money.

I gave my answer immediately. "Thank you, but no," I said. Why would I want to leave a successful morning program, where I was happy, for an unproven morning program at a rival network? So *Good Morning America* did not debut with me, but instead with its cohosts (note the "co") David Hartman and Nancy Dussault. (Joan Lunden did not become cohost until 1980.) Though *GMA*'s cohosts were a very attractive team, they never came close to beating us. I didn't give ABC another thought.

I was in my happiest place in years. The *Today* show was bringing in ten million dollars a year in profits, making it NBC's most lucrative daytime program and the envy of other networks. Furthermore, my contribution was being recognized. In 1975 the International Radio and Television Society named me "Broadcaster of the Year," a very prestigious honor. This award meant a good deal to me because it came from my colleagues in the television industry. I also won the Emmy for the "best host or hostess of a talk, service, or variety series." This award, too, meant a great deal to me, but there was a little hitch. Emmy nominations are made by the individual programs, and Stuart Schulberg, *Today*'s producer, also entered Jim Hartz for the award. Jim might have felt insulted, Stu explained to me, if he'd entered my name alone.

That smarted a bit. For all that I was the cohost, on some level I was obviously still thought of as "the woman" and not as important as "the man." I wondered if Stuart would have worried about *my* feelings if he'd only nominated Hartz. Somehow it was acceptable to nominate the man without the woman, as had been done so many times before, but not the reverse.

Both Jim and I made it through the initial vote of the Emmy committee and were on the final list of four nominees. I ended up winning the award, but because Jim and I had been put in competition with each other, I couldn't really savor the moment. "I'm sorry that my partner didn't get this award because he really deserved it," I said in my remarks. "So I accept it for both of us."

That slight aside, the atmosphere on the program was more upbeat than it had been in years. Jim was an easygoing presence. Since the

Bicentennial was coming up, his main assignment was to broadcast from every state in the country, so he was often on the program just to do special reports. This seemed to be fine with him, and I was holding the fort in the studio, conducting the major interviews. For the first time I was also reading the news headlines at the top of the program, a task that had in the past gone only to the male host.

I was exercising another first as well in 1975. Besides inserting the cohost clause into my contract, Lee Stevens had added the provision that NBC would allow me to develop and host a pilot for a new program: my own *Special*. The ratings had been so high for Prince Charles's investiture, Princess Anne's wedding, and the shah's gala at Persepolis that I thought the viewers might want to see more glamour and royalty. NBC agreed, so off I went to Paris with a producer named Lucy Jarvis to pursue additional glitz for the viewers. It was a disaster.

What I know now is that European royalty, unless you're talking about the queen of England and her immediate family, doesn't really sell, because what you're getting are little-known royals. But we clung to hope back then and lined up the duke and duchess of Orleans, pretenders to the French throne. They were a perfectly nice couple who fell under the heading of "Who cares?" We filmed my dinner with them at Maxim's and then went off to see the duke's racehorses running at Longchamps. We did another segment at Versailles, which was also a giant yawn. The curator, who had been there for years, opened Marie Antoinette's private rooms for us. Marie Antoinette, as you know, was the queen of France until her head was chopped off during the French Revolution in 1793, and I almost envied her as the curator showed us every single bauble and bijou in her apartments. It was agony. I mean, how many satin-appliquéd butterflies can you ooh and ahh over? But we had to kowtow to him. It took days and was a royal bore.

In the midst of all this I got an emergency phone call from my mother in Florida. My father was in the hospital, about to have abdominal surgery. I flew home immediately and made sure he was all right. It seemed to be a not-too-serious procedure. Then, as soon as I could, I flew right back to Europe. I had to help my mother, who was frightened, while at the same time, I couldn't leave my film crew and producer in Europe in the lurch. I was exhausted.

At least when I returned, we had real royalty to film—Queen Margrethe of Denmark and her husband, Prince Henrik, a former French diplomat. Her story was more interesting. She was the first woman to sit on the throne of Denmark. The royal couple had two adorable little princes, one of whom fell off a horse while we were filming and was summarily placed right back in the saddle by his parents. That was kind of nice and interesting. Less so was the tour Queen Margrethe gave us of her unprepossessing palace, but at least there weren't any satin-appliquéd butterflies.

We came home without much. The resulting pilot program, which was supposed to morph into a series titled *Barbara Walters Visits*, this first visit being "Royal Lovers," did not do well. NBC chose to run it at 1:30 in the afternoon, hardly prime time. Most of the viewers at that hour were women who were more apt to be putting their children down for a nap than fantasizing about being married to a prince. It got no ratings. I certainly didn't think then that doing celebrity *Specials* of any nature was a good idea. No twenty-twenty foresight for me.

What concerned me more than the ratings flop was the news from Florida. Although my father's operation had been a success, he was quite fragile and needed help walking, dressing, and going to the bathroom. It was suggested that he have a male nurse when he went home from the hospital. But the Miami apartment was very small—two bedrooms, a living room, and a tiny kitchen. My mother shared a bedroom with my sister. A nurse sitting in my father's room or in the living room all day seemed like a very bad idea to my mother. She also worried that my father wouldn't get the care he needed. She was nervous and afraid, and that meant that my sister was nervous and afraid, too.

It was a very bad situation, and so my mother made a drastic decision. She had my father admitted to a well-recommended nursing home. Well recommended though it was, with excellent care and a private twenty-four-hour nurse for my father, it was still a nursing home. If there was any silver lining, it was that there were a few men my father could play cards with. Even so, my father, being my father, hated the indignity of it. What a comedown for Lou Walters. But I think he was too weak and depressed to fight it. As for me, I couldn't fight it either. How could I force my mother to keep my father at home, even if I provided round-the-clock nurses when she herself was elderly and agitated?

My mother made a great effort to visit my father at the nursing home. At least three times a week she got her sister, Lena, to drive her and my sister there, and she would take my father some of his favorite foods—pickled herring or salami. But he was slowly fading away. I visited him several times and religiously called him every Saturday, but he would say very little. I'd do most of the talking, telling him what I was doing, asking him questions, and he'd say, "Yes, darling" or "No, darling."

My visits were too rare and always upsetting. There wasn't a time when I saw or spoke to him that I didn't feel that I should bring him to live with me and little Jackie in New York. He adored Jackie, and maybe she could have brought him out of his depression and back to life. But to my everlasting guilt, I didn't do it. My apartment was fairly small, just two actual bedrooms, one of which we used as a library. We would be too crowded, I thought. Today, though, I wish I had done it. But in truth I was too busy with too little time as it was for my Jackie. So my father stayed in the nursing home.

I know it's boring to look back and keep talking about guilt, guilt, guilt, and I know that many families face the same problem today, especially as parents live longer. But I still feel the guilt so strongly that I have to force myself to write about it. I realize how much I cared about my father and how much I admired him. I am much older now. My childhood resentments are gone. I am able to recognize the parts of him that are in me—his love of books, his enjoyment of writing, maybe even his sense of humor. With this comes the realization that I am my father's daughter—with my mother's fears.

Life went on. My family in Florida, sad and lonely, I in New York, busier than ever. I was on *Today* every morning, followed by *Not for Women Only*. I was also from time to time a substitute host for Johnny Carson on *The Tonight Show*. It was during this period that I persuaded Hugh Downs to come out of semiretirement and alternate weeks with me hosting *Not for Women Only*. That lightened my load somewhat, but I also was accepting some speaking engagements and writing the occasional magazine article. I continued to share my parents' concern that this could all be over tomorrow, so I had better do everything I could to earn money for their future and mine.

"Doing everything" meant first and foremost getting interviews that were exclusive and important. But while I was doing my usual letter writing and phone calls—bonanza! I was assigned to go to Cuba with Senator George McGovern and a bunch of other reporters to see Fidel Castro.

Change was in the air in the spring of 1975. Fourteen years had passed since the failure of the U.S.-funded invasion of Cuba by armed Cuban exiles to overthrow Fidel Castro, and thirteen years had passed since Russian shipments of nuclear missiles to Communist Cuba brought the United States and Russia to the brink of war. There was talk now in the United States of normalizing relations with Communist Cuba or at least lifting part of the economic embargo that had been in place since 1962 (and still is).

Senator McGovern was chairman of the Select Committee on Nutrition and Human Needs. He was in favor of lifting the trade embargo against Cuba on both humanitarian and diplomatic grounds. McGovern hoped to leverage the positive effects of ending the embargo to eventually help with other conflicts with Cuba, including the release of nine Americans jailed there whom the United States considered political prisoners. McGovern was also advocating a cultural and sports exchange with Cuba in the hope that baseball could help break down the hostility that existed between our two countries.

I was just one of about fifteen reporters traveling with Senator McGovern, but while we were in Cuba, for some unknown reason, Castro singled me out from the rest, and for a change my male colleagues were happy about it.

We had all been in Havana for several days, being dragged from factories to medical facilities to schools, all designed to show off the accomplishments of the Communist system. But no sign of the great Fidel. We were staying in what had been one of the finest hotels in pre-Communist Havana, the Nacional. Along with the formerly grand mansions that dotted the Havana harbor, the hotel was badly in need of a paint job, but it had bigger problems: no air-conditioning and no toilet seats. Still, there were salsa bands playing away in the lobby and you could always get a daiquiri, Ernest Hemingway's favorite drink when he lived in Havana.

But we were not there for the daiquiris, and we were all getting pretty disgusted when, on the third day, we were ushered into a convoy of cars and driven some distance to a farm we were told was owned by Fidel's eldest brother, Ramón. We were lying around on the grass when suddenly a half dozen jeeps pulled up. Lo and behold, in the second jeep was the man himself, in full heavy winter khaki uniform.

And here were Fidel Castro's first words: "Dónde está Barbara?" [Where is Barbara?]

How on earth did he know my name? Probably because the *Today* show reached Havana and Castro, who was known to stay up all night, must have watched it as his lullaby before going to bed.

"Here I am," I shouted. "Here we all are," I continued, pointing out my colleagues. "We have been waiting for days, sir, for you to agree to a press conference with us." Castro spoke very little English, but his translator, a pretty woman named Juanita, expressed our urgency and Castro, with a big smile, agreed. That night he held a press conference in Havana at the Palace of the Revolution. His message: Lift the blockade, at least for medicines and food. Treat Cuba with respect. Stop trying to assassinate him. We are neighbors and in one way or another we ought to live in peace. And no, he had nothing to do with the assassination of John F. Kennedy. Pretty much the same words he would be saying for the next thirty years. When, however, we asked him critical questions concerning freedom of the press or the lack thereof, the imprisonment of dissenters, and his role as a dictator who brooked no opposition, Castro's welcoming demeanor disappeared.

It may not have been the most startling press conference, but we were thankful that we hadn't come to Havana in vain, for Castro, although long on words—his speeches often ran for hours—was short on granting interviews, and few journalists had gotten to meet him. Since I had been instrumental in bringing about the press conference, my colleagues were appreciative and that night we toasted one another over generous daiquiris. Now we could return home to toilet seats.

The press conference was okay, but every reporter worth his salt (whatever that means) wanted to secure an exclusive interview with Castro. I thought I had landed one. Just before we left his brother's farm earlier in the day, I had managed a few private minutes with Castro, during which I hurriedly asked if he would do a one-on-one interview with me. He readily agreed and said sometime during the year. But here's the hitch, and I should have paid more attention—he never said what year.

Actually it would be quite a few years later, and when I finally did get that interview with Castro, it would not run on NBC. It would instead help to keep me from drowning at ABC.

The Million-Dollar Baby

*I*T ALL BEGAN with a tennis game, in March of 1976, on a private court in Westchester, New York. The players were Lou Weiss, who headed the television department at the William Morris Agency, and his neighbor, Fred Pierce, president of the ABC Television Network. I don't know who won the game, but I do know that I was part of the score.

"Five years?" Pierce wrote on a matchbook cover and handed it to Weiss. "For five million."

That's what Fred Pierce was offering to lure me away from NBC to ABC. An offer of $500,000 from ABC's entertainment division to do four one-hour *Specials* a year and an additional $500,000 from the news division to coanchor the *ABC Evening News* with veteran newsman Harry Reasoner. It was an astonishing and unexpected proposal.

The money didn't bowl me over. I was already making close to that amount at NBC. It was the historic offer to become the first female coanchor of a network news program. A woman doing the network news was unheard of and certainly not something I had ever considered. The prestigious position had always been a male bastion, and the prevailing thought was that delivering the news about politics, wars, and natural disasters would not be taken seriously if done by a woman.

I was tempted by the prospect, but only tempted. It was not in my nature to be courageous, to be the first. I was the same person who chose the so-called lesser sorority in high school rather than take a chance on not being chosen at all. I was the same person who was afraid to remain on the waiting list at Wellesley College, my first choice, and to choose Sarah Lawrence because it was a sure thing. I had had enough drama and ups and downs in my life to want to veer toward the safe, sure side. Safe was NBC and the *Today* show. I had always thought I would stay until they no longer wanted me. Then they would give me a gold watch and I would go on to do, well, I wasn't sure what—but that was a long time away.

Still, Lou Weiss and Lee Stevens persisted. Why not take a meeting with the ABC folks? What could I lose? It could be interesting to hear their views and might influence what I wanted for my own future at NBC.

So Lee arranged a secret meeting for me in a private dining room at ABC's Century City complex in Los Angeles. I was in LA for the Academy Awards that March, and the feeling was that a meeting there would not be noticed as much as if it were held in New York.

I was flattered that the biggest guns at ABC were present—Leonard Goldenson, the chairman of the board (whom I've already told you I knew slightly); Elton Rule, the president of ABC Inc., the aforementioned Fred Pierce; and Bill Sheehan, the president of ABC News. They sweetened the proposal. They promised to expand the half-hour news broadcast to an hour, an unheard-of first on any network. Were I to become the first woman to coanchor the news, the additional half hour would give me the opportunity to use my strength—interviews. Not only would I be delivering the news along with Harry Reasoner, I would also be able to supplement it in a more personal, in-depth way and in prime time, which had never been done before.

As appealing and flattering as this was, I still did not take very seriously their proposal (which also included serving once a month as the moderator of ABC's Sunday morning public affairs show *Issues and Answers*, and coanchoring or appearing on special news programming such as election-night coverage). I had no desire to leave *Today*. Lee was negotiating my new contract with NBC, and I was sure it would all work out. I certainly wanted it to. I thought NBC wanted it to as well.

Why, then, was Lee having such a difficult time? He had started talking to NBC back in December 1975, so everything would be in place by September 1976 when the new contract would take effect. The men he was talking to were Herb Schlosser, the president of NBC, Dick Wald, the president of NBC News, and its chief negotiator, Al Rush, vice president of NBC's program and talent acquisitions. But the men were balking.

They couldn't really argue with the money Lee was asking for. William Morris had figured out the gross profits the *Today* show and *Not for Women Only* were making from their thirty-second commercial advertisers and calculated what my contribution was worth on those terms. Lee also argued that I was entitled to the same compensation given to the stars of successful network "entertainment" series, like Johnny Carson, especially since, unlike them, I didn't receive residuals for reruns.

The figures Lee proposed were not that meteoric: a gradual annual increase starting at $800,000 a year for 1976 (I was already making $700,000), then an increase of $100,000 a year for the duration of the contract. It was the duration that proved to be the first inflammatory point. Lee and I wanted to extend the three-year contract to a five-year contract. I was unmarried. I had a child and my family to support. I didn't know how long all this was going to last, and I wanted, and needed, some degree of security. But Al Rush would have none of it.

"Over my dead body," was his response Lee told me later. "Three years. That's it."

Perhaps Lee, who was well used to the nasty art of negotiating, did me a disservice by reporting this to me. But he did. As a result, for the first time, it began to erode my loyalty toward NBC.

It eroded further when Lee and I asked to have some control over what interviews and features I would do on the show; perhaps over who the new producer would be, should there be one; and who, in the future, my cohost might be. As things stood, I had no say in anything. Stuart Schulberg assigned me the pieces I did and though he was very flexible, there was no guarantee that he would be on the program forever. Furthermore, although I liked Jim Hartz, the program had already had five male hosts, and who knew what or whom the future would bring. I couldn't bear the thought of another Frank McGee.

The hackles went up again. The very notion that I, as a newsperson, considered "talent" and not an executive, would have the right to say what features or interviews I wanted to do or whom I wanted as a producer or cohost was totally out of the question. What sort of precedent would that set?

I didn't want to make waves, so Lee watered down my request for control to simple participation. Would they agree that I be consulted, that my views would at least be considered in making these selections? That would mean that I had no authority, just the opportunity to suggest. But this, too, caused a furor.

Dick Wald and Julian Goodman, the former president of NBC and now the chairman and CEO, were particularly outraged by my request for consultation. I was surprised by Dick's reaction. Years before, we had snuck out of an NBC Christmas party on a clandestine romp to see *Deep Throat*, a much-talked-about porn film. I liked, trusted, and respected him and thought he liked, trusted, and respected me. But he obviously didn't.

Neither did Julian Goodman, though that didn't surprise me. It had been Goodman, remember, who had backed Frank McGee's edict that I could only come in on the fourth question during a *Today* interview. This time he evidently wanted me gone altogether. I heard that he didn't like the fact that I had appeared as a guest on a nationally syndicated daytime program hosted by the popular Mike Douglas. I enjoyed being on the show, and I also thought my appearance might bring new viewers to the *Today* show. But Goodman didn't see it that way. He disapproved of a member of the news department appearing on such a lighthearted program. To add insult to injury, he had also seen me doing a little soft-shoe on the Johnny Carson show during one of my guest-host appearances. He hated that. Serious journalists did not do soft-shoe or appear on daytime talk shows. (I wonder how he would have felt about NBC's news anchor, Brian Williams, last year doing skits on *Saturday Night Live*.)

The negotiations were further complicated by the frequent absence of the NBC executives at the table. As not such good luck would have it, the network was in the throes of a huge strike by NABET (National Association of Broadcast Employees and Technicians), the broadcasting and cable TV sector of the Communications Workers of America. The engineers had walked off their jobs along with the maintenance workers and newswriters. The strike was serious, and NBC was preoccupied with training its executives to fill the holes left by the union strikers. Therefore my contract negotiations were often canceled or given little attention. Who had time to think about Barbara Walters in the midst of the calamity befalling NBC? Far more pressing were the union meetings at which Herb Schlosser, NBC's then president, was spending most of his days. He never once took the time to meet with me.

As if that weren't enough, there was turmoil at RCA, NBC's parent company. Robert Sarnoff, RCA's CEO and son of NBC's famous founder, "General" David Sarnoff, was suddenly fired by the board for no apparent reason. The prevailing story was that Bobby, as he was known, was spending too much time away from work and using the company plane to accompany his new wife, the famous opera soprano Anna Moffo, on her singing engagements. That was bad for Bobby, and bad for me. Bobby liked me and probably would not have allowed NBC to treat me as cavalierly as they were at the time. I didn't know the incoming CEO, Andy Conrad. I had never met him.

As the negotiations continued to drag on, I began to think more seriously about ABC. One advantage, and it was spellbinding to contemplate, was that I wouldn't have to get up anymore at 4:30 a.m. After thirteen years of getting up in the dark, I could live a normal life. Jackie and I would be able to have breakfast together. I could walk her to school. I would have much more time with her. And if I went out in the evening, I wouldn't have to worry about being exhausted the next day. A whole new world would open up for me.

I was also excited by the expanded news broadcast the ABC executives had promised. There would be ample time for interviews, which were my strength, and would make the broadcast unique. No nightly news anchor did interviews. It would set our broadcast apart from the traditional talking heads and newsreaders.

Also, there wouldn't be the continuous volume of daily homework that was swamping me—the articles that had to be read; the films of celebrities I should really see; the books I had to skim by authors due to appear on the program. I think hosting or cohosting a morning show may be the most difficult, as well as the most rewarding, program you can do. Anchoring the evening news meant being up-to-date on all the major developments of the day, but it didn't require nearly as much advance preparation.

Other options were even more seductive. You could arrive at the office as late as 3:00 p.m. if you wanted to, and work with the managing editor on the news for that night. ABC did three feeds—one at 6:00 p.m., one at 6:30, and another, if there was an update and they had to, at 7:00. By 7:45 you could be at home. In short, a normal life.

But normal or not, after thinking it over, I decided that I was happy, successful, and ensconced at NBC. Why rock the boat?

"Tell ABC no," I told Lee.

ABC, however, wouldn't take no for an answer. The network was determined to beef up its news division, which was a distant third in the ratings to CBS with Walter Cronkite and NBC with John Chancellor. (We considered ABC the schlock news network. The joke used to be if you wanted to end the Vietnam War, put it on ABC and like all their programs, it would end quickly.) Hiring the first female coanchor in broadcast history would, they felt, give the news a needed shot in the arm. It could bring more women viewers, and luring me away from the *Today* show might also help *Good Morning America* gain ground.

ABC's other divisions were on the fast track at the time. Fred Silverman, a programming genius, had been wooed away from CBS to head the entertainment division. With such innovative prime-time programs as the first big TV miniseries, Irwin Shaw's twelve-hour *Rich Man, Poor Man*, and several popular new shows like *Charlie's Angels* and *Starsky and Hutch*, Fred was taking ABC from last place to first in the prime-time ratings. That was before 1977, when he brought the all-time-winner miniseries *Roots* to the television screen.

The other genius at ABC was Roone Arledge, who had left NBC to revolutionize ABC's sports division. He had certainly moved on since our time together at WNBT in 1953 on the children's show *Ask the Camera*. By 1976 Roone was well on his way to becoming a sports-programming legend. He created *ABC's Wide World of Sports* and *Monday Night Football*. He also personally produced the ABC coverage of both the Winter and Summer Olympics and brought his singular "up close and personal" touch to the athletes' stories. Between Roone and Fred, ABC's profits were soaring: more than $29 million in 1975; $83 million in 1976; an astonishing $165 million to come the following year. So offering me a million dollars a year was no big deal to them. They could well afford it, especially since only half that amount would be borne by their news division. The rest would be paid by ABC's entertainment division. In truth it was a bargain for ABC. It wouldn't cost the news department much to bring Harry's salary in line with mine, and the four *Specials* could bring in many millions of dollars. But I still planned to stay at NBC.

Then, wouldn't you know it, in April, a month after my secret meeting with ABC in Los Angeles, the million-dollar figure was somehow leaked to the press. That offer finally got NBC's attention, but it started a nightmare for me.

Overnight I became the "million-dollar news baby," proffered a salary that, on the surface, was at least twice as much as anyone else was making in the news business, including Walter Cronkite. Lost in the barrage of incredulous media reporting was the fact that the ABC offer, which I hadn't accepted, was being split between the news and entertainment divisions. I would in fact be making less at ABC News than I was at NBC News. But nobody cared. Except me.

With ABC's offer now public, NBC began negotiating in earnest. In fact they told Lee Stevens he could write his own ticket to keep me there. An agreement was hastily drawn up. The same salary as ABC was offering with, yes, a five-year contract. A maximum of two more years on *Today* and then perhaps my own *Specials* or a newsmagazine. Everything except for my right to be consulted in the areas that directly affected my work.

Then the new CEO of RCA, Andy Conrad, got into the act.

"What's this all about?" he asked Herb Schlosser.

"Barbara Walters may go to ABC," Herb answered.

"Is it about money?" Conrad asked.

"No. We'll pay her the same money," Herb said.

"Then what's this all about?" Conrad pressed.

"It's about her having the right to be consulted on a new producer. And her right to be consulted on a new cohost. And her right to have input on the pieces she does. Julian and Dick don't think that is a good idea," Herb said.

"Hang on to her," Conrad said. "Give her whatever she wants."

With those marching orders, Dick Wald wrote a letter to be attached to the NBC agreement giving me consultation rights. And Herb Schlosser asked me to lunch. There are a lot of things I don't remember about this time, but I remember so clearly him saying these words: "Barbara, don't leave us. We need you."

Where had he been all this time?

I have never felt so torn, personally and professionally. NBC had stalled so long by then that even with all their adjustments, I already had a taste of what a future at ABC might mean. There was now that real opportunity of having a different, easier kind of life. Thirteen years of a grueling schedule would come to an end. Not just doing *Today* five days a week, but *Not for Women Only* as well. I agonized over the next few weeks going through the pros and cons. I was driving myself crazy. I just couldn't come to a decision.

As my weeks of tortuous indecision went on, Lee Stevens was encouraging me to go. "What an event it will be," he proclaimed. "You'll be making broadcast history. You'll be changing the world for other female journalists." That really got to me. This wasn't just about me. The role of women in broadcasting would be vastly improved. Could I help to bring that about? If so, what a genuine accomplishment.

But what if I was a huge flop anchoring the news? I would be destroying what it had taken me years to achieve. There was also the question, as yet unanswered, about my potential coanchor, Harry Reasoner. I'd first met him many years before at the Democratic convention that nominated Lyndon Johnson. We'd had a rather flirtatious lunch. I'd seen him again on the trip to China with Nixon in 1972. Had he been part of the old boys' club in China that stonewalled me? I couldn't remember.

I couldn't imagine he'd be happy sharing the anchor job with me, a "girl" from the *Today* show. I couldn't imagine him being happy sharing the anchor job with anyone. He'd come to ABC from CBS, leaving *60 Minutes* specifically to anchor the *ABC Evening News*. For a while he'd shared the slot with another veteran newsman, Howard K. Smith, but somehow he'd gotten rid of Smith. And now—me. A woman he probably wouldn't think had news credentials, who had grown up in television and never worked on a newspaper or at a wire service.

The early indications were not reassuring. The *New York Times* reported that Harry had initially threatened to quit when he heard I might be coming to ABC. His attitude had improved only a little bit since. "I am trying to keep an open mind about it," he told the *Times*. Another source, however, was quoted as saying Harry thought the ABC offer to me "seemed in the nature of a stunt rather than a solid journalistic move." Said Harry to *Newsweek*: "I was with her on Nixon's China trip, but I never actually saw her work. All I know about her from that trip is that she rides a bus well." Not very encouraging words.

Heaven knows why, but it didn't occur to me, or for that matter, to anyone else, to arrange a meeting with Harry. That seems insane to me today. Is it possible that, with all the turmoil, I was too busy? Granted I was still at NBC, but it certainly would have been helpful to talk to him personally rather than reading what he'd said in the papers. I didn't know how he really felt, only how ABC executives felt. And the head of ABC News, Bill Sheehan, seemed to me to be a bland, rather ineffectual fellow. I couldn't really rely on his opinion.

So there I was, not knowing what to do.

Back and forth. Forth and back. Almost paralyzed by indecision, I somehow managed to get through the *Today* show and *Not for Women Only* every morning. Then I spent most of the rest of the day answering—or, more to the point, *not* answering—the questions from the media about my decision. *Newsweek* wanted to do another cover story. *Time* was planning a major piece. Then there was Sander Vanocur, the television critic for the *Washington Post*, who called me daily for the answer, and even wanted an exclusive. I'm not one to hold a grudge, but I found it ironic that Sandy, the former NBC reporter who never shared his slot with me as a pool reporter all those years ago in India with Jackie Kennedy, was now asking me for an "exclusive." I talked to him but I didn't give him one. In truth I didn't know what to say.

Thank heaven for Alan Greenspan. Remember I told you he saw me through an agonizing time? Well, this was it. I hemmed and hawed, paced up and down, wrung my hands. NBC was home. ABC was the unknown. What to do? Alan listened to me patiently night after night while I tried to reach a decision. He was a calm and objective friend. He also did a little homework on his own. He was somewhat concerned that ABC might not be able to come up with the five million dollars guaranteed for five years. He did some calculations and determined they could. That was reassuring. ABC could pay the money if I could deliver the goods.

By then a media frenzy was building. It may seem strange today that my staying or going would be such a story. But remember the headlines about Katie Couric when she left NBC for CBS thirty years later? Back when I was agonizing about what to do, no woman had ever been considered as anchor or coanchor on a network news program. Equally important, no newsperson was making a million dollars. There were reporters and photographers staked out in front of my apartment building. We were still living in my rent-controlled apartment on West Fifty-seventh Street, and there was no doorman to hold them at bay. The reporters were making Jackie very nervous.

My indecision had to end. And it did, on Wednesday afternoon, April 21, in Radio City Music Hall, where I'd taken seven-year-old Jackie to see the musical classic *That's Entertainment!* I was totally worn out but I felt that in the past few weeks I hadn't been spending enough time with her. Why I thought this nostalgic review of Hollywood's past musicals would be her cup of tea I don't know, but it was a chance for us to hold hands and be together with no phones ringing and nobody pushing for my attention.

Sitting in the darkened theater, still torturing myself, I remembered Richard Nixon saying to me at some point: "Don't make any decisions when you're exhausted." He was right, I knew, and I was indeed exhausted. But I just couldn't go on this way. And somewhere in the midst of watching Fred Astaire (whom I'd interviewed) and Ginger Rogers (whom I'd also interviewed) whirl so elegantly and gracefully on the screen, I decided to go to ABC. Their evening news had nowhere to go but up. I didn't want to spend the next two years at NBC getting up at 4:30 a.m. I wanted time to be with my daughter. The expansion of the news to an hour would play to my strength. How could I go wrong?

I held my nose and jumped.

I called Lee at 9:00 the next morning, after I did my two hours on

Today, to tell him my decision. Lee said he would call Herb Schlosser and Al Rush. Then I had to rush off to tape a whole bunch of shows for *Not for Women Only* and to tape a few commercials that were to run on *Today*.

That is when it got ugly.

When I returned to my office I planned to call Herb Schlosser to tell him personally I was leaving NBC. But instead the phones were ringing off the hook, with devastating news. A series of "anonymous" spokesmen from NBC had called every newspaper and newsmagazine and the wire services to announce that they had withdrawn their counteroffer, knowing full well that I had been the one to end the negotiations! I guess it was to save face before the public announcement that I was going to ABC, but nonetheless, it was very harmful to me then—and long term.

Citing the "carnival atmosphere" surrounding the negotiations, NBC put out a series of lies. They claimed that I had demanded a private limousine and a full-time hairdresser and makeup person. How absurd! NBC had been providing these services to me, and to many others, for years. But it sounded good and greedy. "These were things that one would associate with a movie queen, not a journalist, and we had second thoughts," one of the spokesmen told the *New York Times*.

I was furious and called Dick Wald. He claimed he knew nothing about the release, which was also a lie. I found out later he had been at the meeting that morning with Julian Goodman, Herb Schlosser, Al Rush, and the publicity people who would be the actual hatchet men. It was Al Rush, the chief negotiator, who entered the meeting saying: "I think the boat has sailed. I think ABC's got her."

Well, it's a long way from "I think" in the morning to "movie queen" by the afternoon. But they had decided then and there, in that meeting, to publicly withdraw their offer. And guess what? They felt it was *my* fault! Not only were they angry that I was leaving, but who did I think I was anyway, that I hadn't called them myself to tell them my decision? No one considered that I was busy doing my job, cohosting the *Today* show and taping back-to-back complete programs of *Not for Women Only*, and the commercials that were so profitable to the network.

Herb Schlosser later claimed they had tried several times to reach me by phone but I was doing the commercials and couldn't be reached. Ridiculous. Is it conceivable that the chairman and CEO of NBC, the president of NBC, the president of NBC News, and the vice president of program talent and acquisitions could not at least have gotten a message to me? We were all in the same building, for goodness' sake. Which brings me back to Dick Wald, who stood in my office that afternoon and claimed he had no knowledge of the contract withdrawal and said that he'd take care of it right away.

According to my assistant, Mary Hornickel, Dick left my office about ten minutes before six. Shortly afterward, John Chancellor came on the evening news and announced, "NBC valued Barbara's service highly, but the negotiations for a renewal of her contract involved a million dollars and other privileges, and this afternoon NBC pulled out of the negotiations, leaving her a clear path to ABC. We wish her luck in her new job." To his credit, John later told me that he was very upset when he found out it wasn't true and that *I* had been the one to end the negotiations. But the damage had been done.

Our mistake, Lee Stevens's and mine, was not to send out our own release with the news that I was going to ABC. Somehow we thought NBC would be gracious enough to work out a joint release or at least discuss what should be said. We couldn't have been more wrong.

When I left the studio at the end of the day, the flashbulbs practically blinded me. The headlines the next day were horrendous. One paper compared me to a Radio City Rockette, a chorus girl reading the news and wanting to be taken seriously.

Then came the drumbeat of the money. The press was relentless on the "million-dollar baby," or, more, the "five-million-dollar baby." Even the foreign press picked up the money story: German newspapers, French, Japanese, Indian, on and on. "Kobieta za 5 mlm dolarow" ran the headline in a Polish newspaper. I was becoming famous practically all over the world. Small consolation then, although it would be helpful years later when I wanted to interview world leaders.

Then there were my television colleagues. Everyone from Walter Cronkite to the head of CBS News to sportscasters was clucking away about the million-dollar death of journalism. "Is Barbara a journalist or is she Cher?" asked Richard Salant, the president of CBS News. Cronkite echoed his boss's views, claiming he had experienced "the sickening sensation that we were all going under." But you know what? Almost every television journalist, including Harry Reasoner, walked into his boss's office, demanded a raise—and got it. Well, you're welcome.

A few brave voices, especially from women, were raised in my defense. "There is, in my paranoid little mind, a vague suspicion that the controversy wouldn't have raged as far and deep if Ms. Walters had been

Mr. Walters," wrote columnist Ellen Goodman in the *Washington Post*. She was echoed by Marianne Means, a syndicated columnist for Hearst newspapers, who wrote: "The controversy over Barbara Walters' whopping $5 million contract to coanchor the ABC Nightly News smells to high heaven of sour grapes. . . . The real shocker is not that a coanchor person has reached the $1 million yearly figure, but that a woman has."

A few men also wrote in my support. One of them was Bill Barrett, the television columnist for the *Cleveland Press*. "Barbara Walters deserves the opportunity," he wrote. "She has come a long, long way—a lot farther than any man would have had to go to get to the big network news chair." I was even the subject of an editorial in the *Charleston Evening Post*. "Barbara Walters is both a gifted journalist and an accomplished showman (we refuse to say showperson). . . . We rejoice, with the merest trace of envy, at the elevation of a reporter to the upper bracket of stardom."

I was grateful for the voices raised in my defense, but I was also uncomfortable being a centerpiece in the gender wars and in the entertainment vs. news wars, the "purist" wars that saw money as the death of journalism. Journalists, I felt, are supposed to report the news, not *be* the news.

I somehow continued to do the *Today* show. My contract with NBC had another four and a half months to run—but I was miserable. It was very tense on the set and in the halls, sort of like staying on in the same apartment with an ex-husband.

The reports coming in about Harry Reasoner didn't help. One article quoted a woman at ABC as saying he was a "male chauvinist pig." What upset me the most came from Lou Weiss. He had seen Harry in a restaurant shortly after the ABC announcement, and Harry was complaining loudly, for all to hear, how he didn't want me. Lou was so taken aback by Harry's public outburst that he told me that maybe we had made a mistake. It was a little late for that observation.

I wasn't long at NBC. The network took me off the air in June. The nation's Bicentennial celebrations were coming up, and they didn't want me broadcasting that major event. But they also didn't let me out of my contract. They would not let me go to ABC, or even to set foot in the ABC newsroom, until my contract expired in September. If I had, they could have sued me for breach of contract, and in their anger they just might have.

So there was no two-hour farewell program of "Barbara's Greatest Hits" over the last thirteen years on *Today* or excerpts from the many interviews I had done. It was good-bye and good riddance. On my last day I was permitted to say a few closing words to the viewers who, by devotedly watching, had so changed my life. This is what I said.

"The *Today* show is twenty-four years old. During the first twelve years, there were thirty-three different women on the program; for the past thirteen years, there has been only one. In the early years of the program, I was sort of a glorified tea pourer, but times have changed. Women in television no longer have to begin as I did, and I'm happy for whatever small contribution I've made toward this change."

And that was that. There was a small party for me with the *Today* cast and crew in Studio 3K at 9:00 a.m. Not the best time for a party. The Alpo people had at least given me a lunch the day before and presented me with a magnum of champagne in a red ice bucket shaped like a fire hydrant. The dogs were seemingly more grateful for the dog food commercials I'd done for them than the humans were for the work I'd done at NBC.

I didn't get a farewell watch at the going-away party, but that was fine. More valuable to me by far was the silver box I got from the *Today* producers with an inscription. "To Barbara. Love. *Today*." Even more gratifying was a gold bracelet with a charm from the program's stagehands and crew members with my name on it and the words "We love you." And it was over. Just like that.

That night I went to Herb Schlosser's fiftieth-birthday party. I'd been invited before the nasty endgame at NBC. All my old friends at NBC were going to be there, including the major players in the failed contract negotiations, Dick Wald and Al Rush. I wanted to see how they would react when I walked in. It was not pleasant.

The room went completely silent when I arrived. Everyone froze, like a still frame in a movie. The tableau resonated with the unspoken, "What is *she* doing here?" Herb rallied through the shock. He alone was a gentleman. "How nice to see you, Barbara," he said, coming up to greet me. I responded, "Well, I wouldn't have missed your birthday, Herb." I smiled, made my manners, and left after ten painful minutes.

As I write this, once again I can't help but contrast my experience with what happened to Katie Couric when she left NBC. There was little uproar over the salary CBS was giving her, a reported $15 million a year. NBC gave her the most glorious send-off—a three-hour retrospective preceded by two weeks of tributes, messages from celebrities and high-profile politicians, special music written for her, and past clips of her work from her years on *Today*. There was a gala going-away party and an equally warm welcome awaiting her at CBS. It is true that even in 2006, there were articles and editorials about whether Katie would succeed, but nothing scathing or mean when she left NBC; no lies and nothing deliberately hurtful.

We did the same kind of send-off for Meredith Vieira when she chose to leave my daytime program on ABC, *The View*, to take Katie's place on *Today*. We gave Meredith good-bye tributes, a going-away party for her whole family, and, most of all, our loving best wishes. We were sorry she was leaving but happy about the new chapter in her life.

Perhaps my experience was the price of being first, and in a very different time. Back in 1976 you could freely attack a woman for wanting to attempt to do a so-called man's job, especially in the holier-than-thou men-only news departments. Many people still believed that women were supposed to know their place—and stay in it. There were few women in front of the camera and fewer still in any kind of executive position. Today, that same attitude would not only be politically incorrect, but the backlash would be enormous.

After I left the *Today* show, NBC made the decision not to renew Jim Hartz's contract. Instead, they quickly announced that the new cohosts of *Today* were to be newsman Tom Brokaw and Jane Pauley, a perky young woman from NBC's Chicago affiliate. I sent Jane a congratulatory telegram: "You are beginning a wonderful new life. . . . Get a good alarm clock and enjoy." One thing she wouldn't need from me was any advice on how to handle the dogs in the Alpo commercials because, in another change, the "talent" on the *Today* show was no longer going to be required to do commercials.

One more thing about my departure from NBC, the most important of all. I did not know back then what I learned when I began to research that painful period for this book. In 2006 I had lunch with Lou Weiss, he of the famous matchbook tennis game in 1976 and now the chairman emeritus of William Morris, and with my former NBC colleagues Dick Wald and Herb Schlosser. (Both were fired within two years of my departure. I have no idea whether it had anything to do with me. Schlosser later went into investment banking; Wald eventually came to ABC News and we became friends again.) Each gave me his view, as best he remembered, of the turmoil surrounding my exit from NBC.

They didn't agree on everything, but they did agree on this. If I had stayed at NBC, I never would have had the same opportunities I have had at ABC. NBC's ratings were in a slump. ABC's star was rising fast. And with Dick and Herb gone, there would have been no one who would have been looking out for me or invested in my future.

"You needed a place where you could create a brand-new career," Herb Schlosser told me. "That would not have happened at NBC," Dick Wald concurred. "You would never have been able to do *Specials* at NBC. They had no plans to do any newsmagazine shows, and you would certainly not have had a chance in hell of being an anchor or coanchor on the evening news."

Well, what an eye-opener! For thirty years I had wondered, even agonized at times, if I had made the right decision. The parting was so difficult and distressing. Now, finally, I know that I did not make a mistake. I can't tell you what a relief, even after all this time, it is to know that. Even though what followed was so much worse.

"Don't let the bastards get you down"

IT WAS A TERRIBLE summer. I was convinced that I had made an awful mistake by leaving NBC. Every day reinforced that opinion. I remember thinking I should go to a psychiatrist so that I would have someone sympathetic to talk to. But there was no point. There was nothing anyone could do for me. A nice relaxing nervous breakdown might have helped, but I couldn't afford that.

Since NBC was holding me to my contract, I couldn't do any work for ABC. I was put out to pasture for the three summer months, and rather than enjoy the luxury, I hated it. It was not that my work was my life—I did, and do, have friends and interests and, of course, my daughter—but once I left NBC, I was completely cut off from what was professionally familiar, rewarding, and fulfilling. The future looked very bleak.

Harry and I finally met with Bill Sheehan over lunch in Los Angeles. I recall feeling as if I were entering an arranged marriage and meeting my fiancé for the first time under the watchful eye of a chaperone. But while some arranged marriages are happy and successful, this one did not look promising. Harry was sardonic and sour. But the die was cast for him as well as for me. For now, neither of us had a way out. We shook hands at the end of the lunch. As I remember, I said something like, "You won't be sorry." Harry smiled a tight little smile, and we went about our day. Poor man, he must have been miserable.

But the misery quickly became mine. We were in Los Angeles for a meeting with the ABC affiliates from all over the country. This was an extremely important meeting. One, I was about to be introduced to the owners and general managers of all the local stations carrying ABC's programming, many of whom were betting on ABC News to rise in the ratings and help to lift the rest of their programs. Equally important, I was going to tell my new colleagues just why it was so peachy that ABC News was going to expand from its thirty-minute format first to forty-five minutes and eventually to an hour.

Remember, the longer news was one of the major reasons that I had decided to make the move. Remember, too, that I had been told emphatically by all the top ABC executives that they were committed to the expansion of the broadcast so that I could supplement the news of the day with brief newsmaker interviews. I assumed that Bill Sheehan had already delivered this message to their affiliates and I was not to be the messenger but the cheering section. So I was excited before the meeting and sure that this expanded program would be well received. But as it turned out, no ABC executive had even warned the affiliates of what was coming, let alone endorsed it.

Bill Sheehan made a few lame remarks at the meeting about the expanded news show being "inevitable" and that ABC would like to lead. Harry, too, put in his two cents about the expansion, but two cents wasn't going to do it. Obviously he was leaving it to me to make the case. Now I wonder: Did the news division know all along that the affiliates would fight this move? Had they offered me the extra time just to get me to sign the contract?

To say that the meeting did not go well is to put it mildly. I gave my impassioned speech about the value of being the first network to lengthen the national news and the time it would give me to do headliner interviews. But instead of applause, there was a chilling silence. They were too polite to boo me off the stage, but I felt they wanted to.

Harry, on the other hand, took the podium to thunderous applause. The adoration continued during his off-the-cuff remarks. "We won't be cutesy, we won't be catty," Harry informed the doting audience. "And if we don't like each other, nobody out there will know it." "Harry, you'll get to like me," I quickly interjected. That, at least, got a laugh from the affiliates, but it was obvious where their affection lay. Because of my strong support for expanding the news, I wasn't ABC's newest star, I was ABC's million-dollar disaster.

And so died the dream of the hour-long news broadcast I'd been promised and with it, my hope of presenting regular interviews that would set us apart from the other news broadcasts. (By the way, the hour-long news program still hasn't happened. The local affiliates then and now have no intention of giving up one second of their lucrative local newscasts.)

One blow followed another during that desultory summer. At some point, after we returned to New York, I went over to ABC News on

Sixty-sixth Street and Columbus Avenue to see where I would be work-ing in the fall. I didn't dare go inside because of the NBC directive that I not set foot in an ABC newsroom while I was still under contract. Looking at the outside of the place was just as disheartening. I found a small, ordinary-looking building in the middle of a bunch of west side apartment houses. Years later ABC would build a huge complex, but now there was just this small building with, from what I could see through the revolving door, only a single elevator. How could I have left one of the world's greatest news divisions and my sunny office overlook-ing the famous skating rink at Rockefeller Center, and at Christmas-time, the giant tree, to come to this third-rate, nothing building? I walked by the place a few times, then left quickly for fear of being seen.

I felt even more lost as the summer continued. The Bicentennial cel-ebrations were in full swing all over the country—without me. My last broadcast on the *Today* show had included a taped piece I'd done on the Bicentennial in my home state of Massachusetts. But after that, because I wasn't allowed to work, nothing. Over the Fourth of July weekend there was a parade in New York Harbor of hundreds of nineteenth-century "tall ships" from all over the world. I would have loved to have covered it, but instead, as I got dressed in the morning, I watched Tom Brokaw and Jane Pauley describe the celebration. Later, as the guest of Alan Greenspan, I went to the ship where the ceremonies were taking place. My sometime date, John Warner, as head of the Bicentennial Committee, officiated. I tried to have a good time and forced a lot of smiles, but my heart was heavy.

That summer the presidential conventions were also being held. The Democratic convention, which nominated Jimmy Carter, began in New York a week after the Bicentennial celebration; the Republican convention, which nominated incumbent Gerald Ford, took place in August, in Kansas City, Missouri. ABC thought I should attend. After all, I would be reporting on election night. But I had no official position. I had worked at every convention since 1964, and there I was, twelve years later, wandering around with no real purpose and no place to go.

One night, feeling so outside things, I ventured into the NBC con-trol room and saw many of my old friends. I felt such a pang. They were pleasant and polite, but they were also very busy, so I wandered back out into no-man's-land. I went into the ABC control room. I knew no one there and they, too, were busy. It was not a time for introductions or pleasantries. I wandered off again.

Between conventions Bill Sheehan offered to set up a tour of ABC's bureaus for me, and meetings with the correspondents. If I wanted, he said, I could go to a few of their European bureaus. But after I talked to a couple of their correspondents in Washington, the trip didn't have much appeal.

The Washington correspondents were totally disgruntled. Bill Sheehan had no power, they told me. ABC News was disorganized and cheap. The cameras were old and outdated. There was no money. They had no suggestions for me other than that ABC should start spending some money on better equipment. I wondered if they resented my getting paid so much when that money could have purchased newer cameras. After I heard their complaints, there seemed no point in going to the London bureau or the Paris bureau to hear more of how awful everything was. So I repaired for a few weeks to a summerhouse I'd rented in Westhampton Beach on Long Island. Jackie was going to a little day camp, and I picked her up every day and took her for ice cream. I smiled for Jackie. I was cheerful for Jackie. But it was an act. My malaise was not helped by our summer neighbor, Howard Cosell. Howard was a very well-known ABC sportscaster but a melancholy and somewhat bitter man. For some reason he took to visiting me almost daily to complain: ABC didn't appreciate him. . . . ABC certainly wouldn't appreciate me. . . . Harry Reasoner paid no attention to him and wouldn't to me. . . . I finally had to ask Howard to please not tell me any more.

The comedian Gilda Radner chose that summer to present her caricature of me—Baba Wawa—on *Saturday Night Live.* Audiences found her mimicry of my pronunciation of *l* and *r* as *w* hysterically funny. I found it extremely upsetting. I was feeling so down that I probably wouldn't have found anything funny. But everyone else loved Gilda's impersonation.

"Hewwo! This is Baba Wawa hewe to say fawewell," Gilda said one Saturday night. "This is my wast moment on NBC and I want to wemind you to wook fow me awong with Hawwy Weasoneh weeknights at seven o'cwock.

"I want to take this oppohtunity to apowogize to NBC," she continued. "I don't wike weaving. Pwease twust me, it's not sowuh gwapes, but, rathaw, that anotheh netwohk wecognizes in me a gweat tawent for dewivering wewevant news stowies with cwystal cwahity to miwwions of Americans. It's the onwy weason I'm weaving."

(By the way, I never had trouble with my *l*'s, only my *r*'s, but it made it funnier.)

People started calling me Baba Wawa behind my back, and even to my face. Sometimes they still do. But because I was so depressed at the time, I felt they were laughing *at* me rather than laughing at Gilda's characterization *of* me.

My daughter, Jackie, set me straight. I was walking by her room one Saturday night when I heard her laughing. "Watch this," she said. I watched. Gilda was doing Baba Wawa, and my young daughter thought it was really funny. I mumbled something about not thinking it was so clever, and Jackie said to me, "Oh, Mom. Lighten up." Hearing that from Jackie made me realize that I was losing all perspective. Where was my sense of humor?

So I was pleased when I ran into Gilda sometime later in New York at an exhibition at the Canadian Mission to the United Nations. She must have been nervous when she saw me walking toward her. "I guess you know who I am," I said to her, pronouncing my words very carefully and leaving out any *r*'s.

She nodded. And waited.

"Well, do me a favor," I said. "Do me. Please go ahead and do me."

We went into a corner, and she sat down and became Barbara Walters. She sat the way I sit, with one ankle tucked behind the other, leaned forward just as I do when I'm interviewing someone, and then she started talking.

It was right on. She was brilliant, and I told her so. She told me that she and I had the same makeup artist, Bobbie Armstrong, who had told her how I sit. Gilda also told me she had studied my way of speaking by watching tapes of *Not for Women Only*. We parted friends and I, along with most of America, was truly sad when she died of ovarian cancer in 1989 at the age of forty-two. I sent a note to her husband, Gene Wilder, which said simply: "She made me laugh. I will miss her. Baba Wawa."

There sure wasn't much else to laugh about during my summer in limbo. The negative stories about me continued unabated, and Harry's attitude toward me began to harden. The not-so-subtle implication in the media was that I had been brought in by ABC to save his job. That put him in a lose-lose position. If the ratings improved, it would be seen as evidence that he needed my help. If they went down, we would both be considered failures.

The countdown began for our debut in early October. We rehearsed for two weeks as soon as my NBC contract expired in September, during which time Harry was civil but hardly friendly. The biggest challenge for me was being handed late-breaking news that had to be instantly incorporated into the broadcast while other stories were just as instantly killed.

This was by far my toughest audition, and the pressure was intense. ABC had invested a lot of money in the new broadcast. The set was new. The executive producer was new. The writers were new. Additional correspondents were being hired, several of them, I was happy to see, women. All in all the national news budget had been boosted by 2 5 percent.

The broadcast was being promoted and advertised in major newspapers all over the country. The picture of me was ghastly. There was Harry looking straight into the camera as any anchorman would. And there was I, looking off into the distance with big, wide eyes, like some sort of starlet. Hardly the image of a coanchor.

The program was called *ABC Evening News with Harry Reasoner and Barbara Walters*. It didn't occur to anyone, including me, to have my name before Harry's. In fact, my name would always be second to a male partner's. For the fifteen years Hugh and I cohosted *20/20*, the sequence would always be Hugh Downs and Barbara Walters. But some people considered that an advantage. Years later, when I was interviewing Bing Crosby for one of my *Specials*, he told me that he always asked for second billing whenever he could, and never wanted his name above the title of a movie. That way, he said, if the film was a success, everyone would realize it was, in great part, because of him. But if the film failed, it would not be regarded as his failure. I thought that was very smart. (Remember this the next time you see an old Bing Crosby film on television.)

No matter who got top billing, Harry and I were being promoted as "television's most dynamic and informative news team," which was pretty dramatic if nerve-racking. I felt my career was on the line. "If the show doesn't make it, I'm finished," I told *Newsweek* the week before the broadcast began. "But if it does make it . . . my God, how fantastic."

Our first broadcast was scheduled for Monday, October 4. What I hadn't realized until it was too late was that October 4 that year fell on the holiest of Jewish holidays, Yom Kippur. Most Jewish people do not work that day. They fast until sundown, then usually go to temple, and afterward break the fast with a big dinner. Even though my family did not celebrate the holiday (we never went to temple or fasted), out of respect for my religion, I never went on the air on that holiday. I still don't.

I was bothered that the Jewish people in our audience would know that I had, indeed, been working during the day when no Jew was supposed to work. I really did wonder if God would forgive me, but there was little I could do about it. October was already late to be starting with a new program but we hadn't been able to begin until my NBC contract had expired, and ABC did not want to wait any longer.

My career hung in the balance. After all the hype and press about my move to ABC, millions of people all over the country would be watching to see if I succeeded or fell on my face. On a much smaller scale the top ABC executives would be watching in an adjacent studio. Their reputations, too, were on the line.

I had taped two major interviews by satellite earlier in the day for the first broadcasts—one with Golda Meir, the former prime minister of Israel, the other with Anwar Sadat, the president of Egypt. I was happy to be getting interviews with the two world leaders and thought they would be the perfect way to show viewers what I had to contribute to the program. Each interview, to run on successive nights, was newsworthy. Golda Meir because the debut of the program coincided with the third anniversary of the 1973 war. Then it was Israelis against Arabs. I wanted Anwar Sadat because now it was Christians against Muslims in a bloody civil war in Lebanon. He would give his insights into the latest threat to peace in the Middle East.

At the last minute, however, the interviews threatened the peace at ABC. I had promised Golda Meir that her interview would appear on our first broadcast so that she could give a special Yom Kippur greeting. She also wanted to appear on the program the day before Israel's enemy, Anwar Sadat. But after Bill Sheehan viewed both interviews, he decided that Sadat's interview would run first. I told him about my promise to Golda Meir and argued vehemently against the change, but he was adamant and as this was my first broadcast, I had to go by his decision. Predictably Golda Meir was furious when she was informed of the change. She said she would never do another interview with me, and she never did.

On our opening night, the top ABC executives were full of smiles, all too hearty. I was strangely calm. I knew I could read from the teleprompter. I'd been doing that for years. I just prayed that tonight I wouldn't stumble over a word. And 5–4–3–2–1: We were on.

"Good evening," Harry said, before outlining the major story of the evening—the resignation of Earl Butz, the secretary of agriculture, for telling an obscene racial joke on a commercial airline. And then, he introduced me. "Closer to home, I have a new colleague to welcome. Barbara?"

"Thank you, Harry," I said. "Well, tonight has finally come for me, and I'm very pleased to be with you, Harry, and with ABC News." And then I introduced the other stories we would be covering, including the Supreme Court decision allowing the death penalty to go ahead in at least three states, the status of the strike at Ford, and my newsmaker interview with Anwar Sadat.

The rest of the broadcast proceeded smoothly—until the end. I signed off with an explanation to the viewers of what they could expect from me, including a closer look at the people shaping the news; an explanation of how the news impacts the viewers' lives (for example, "Why every television news program gives the Dow Jones Industrial Average and what it means to you, even if you don't own any stock"); the airing of issues of particular concern to women, which, I noted, "have been neglected."

And then it was Harry's turn. He admitted he had a "little trouble" in thinking what to say to welcome me that didn't sound sexist or patronizing. Well, that didn't sound very encouraging. And then he topped it off by saying, "I've kept time on your stories and mine tonight. You owe me four minutes." I hoped he was kidding. He wasn't.

My initial reviews were pretty good. The next day the *New York Times* called me a "thorough professional, a remarkable woman who has risen to the top in what was once almost exclusively a man's world," and pointed out that I hadn't "faltered or fumbled embarrassingly on the new job." *Time* magazine's review was also positive, at the beginning, anyway. "Walters' debut was as crisp as a new $100 bill," it began. The rest I could have done without, like the magazine's description of the broadcast "as personalized as Walters' 'weadily wecognizable delivewy,' " and the additional note that I made one hundred dollars for every minute of the newscast. That smarted a bit, but basically so far so good.

Then came the complaints from some critics about my interviews with Anwar Sadat and Golda Meir. Instead of being considered newsworthy figures, which I thought the president of Egypt and the former prime minister of Israel to be, these critics dismissed them as "celebrity guests." That, of course, cast me as a celebrity interviewer and not as a serious journalist. President Sadat didn't help. At the very end when I thanked him for being with us, he thanked me, then said: "How do you like a million-dollar job? I must tell you very frankly, you know the salary of my job. It is twelve thousand dollars only, and I am working night and day."

I laughed and said, "But you know, Mr. President, one does not work for money, one works for love."

Today this small human interchange would probably be welcomed.

But back then it was criticized. My attempt to liven up the news and make it more interesting was pronounced a gimmick more worthy of a talk show than the straight-up delivery of the news. The traditional models of a news anchor remained Walter Cronkite, John Chancellor, and Harry Reasoner, who did not hide his displeasure at my exchange with Sadat.

When I turned to him and said, "But what I should have said to President Sadat is that he has better fringe benefits than we do, Harry," he did not respond. "Reasoner looked less tickled than crazed," wrote one critic. Wrote another: "Harry Reasoner looked pained and rightly so."

Nonetheless, the ABC executives were delighted with the kickoff of the new broadcast and brought out champagne to toast Harry and me. They needn't have uncorked the bottle. Though we drew a huge audience the first night, almost twice as large as NBC and CBS combined, most of the viewers turned out to be curiosity seekers. On Tuesday, the second night of the broadcast, David Brinkley opened NBC's newscast with the words: "Welcome back." And back they stayed. Well, most of them, anyway. ABC was pleased that the broadcast gained more than 700,000 new viewers during my first seven weeks on the air—a jump to 10.5 in the Nielsen ratings from 9.9 during the same time period the year before—so I wasn't a complete disaster. But in the horserace between the networks, Harry and I stayed close to where Harry had been before I'd joined him: in third place.

If the broadcast had been a huge success, Harry might have felt differently about me. But the ongoing gap in the ratings seemed to stoke his resentment further. Day after day I would walk into the studio at 3:00 p.m. to shoot a promo for the evening newscast, and no one would talk to me. The crew, cameramen, and stagehands had been working with Harry for the past six years, and if he didn't approve of me, neither would they. Harry would crack jokes with the crew and they with him. I was invisible. Then he would go across the street to the bar at the nearby hangout, Café des Artistes, to have a few drinks with the guys before the broadcast. They'd have a fine time bad-mouthing me to everyone within hearing. Some of those people with big ears thought they were doing me a favor by telling me the disparaging things Harry and his gang were saying about me, that I was a disaster, that I was dragging the program down. Repeating these remarks was no favor.

The only way I could hold my own was the New York Yankees. I was a big Yankee fan. Still am. In desperation I would come into the studio and make bets on the Yankees with Harry or the guys on the crew, and very often I won. For five minutes or so I could be one of the guys. But there were very few of those five minutes. And the baseball season is short.

I also tried cracking jokes at my own expense. I remember one such attempt during the moments before the broadcast. We were doing a segment on the search for Noah's Ark on Mount Ararat in eastern Turkey. All those *r*'s. So I quipped to the crew, "Mount Ararat? Why couldn't this have happened on Mount Kisco?" The crew laughed. Harry didn't.

ABC did everything possible to placate him. In addition to giving him that raise, they had made sure our offices were the same size and the same distance from the office of the executive producer, Bob Siegenthaler. We each had our own assistants, hair person, and makeup person. Neither of us had a limousine to get to the office. The hours were more reasonable for the nightly news—we weren't due in the office until 10:00 a.m.—so we took cabs or walked. Once the broadcast began we were to have equal time on the air.

The blood was so bad between us, however, that his cronies on the crew took to using a stopwatch to note my airtime. If I did a segment that ran three minutes and twenty-five seconds, Harry would demand that he do a piece three minutes and twenty-five seconds long. To keep things equal he did a long piece on real estate values in Los Angeles, another on the Dallas Cowboys football team. Nobody accused him of being a nonjournalist.

Harry's hostility soon began to show on the air. Frank McGee had managed at least to keep his aversion to me off camera, but not Harry. I remember reaching toward him at the end of one broadcast, in a friendly manner, just to touch him on the arm. He recoiled, physically recoiled, in front of millions of people. The media, of course, picked up on the bad chemistry. "Harry Reasoner . . . seems as comfortable on camera with Walters as a governor under indictment," wrote Roger Rosenblatt in the *New Republic*.

Harry began taking swipes at me on the air. One night we did a profile on Henry Kissinger, then President Gerald Ford's secretary of state. We were talking about his negotiating ability and his popularity with women. At the end of the piece, we had a few seconds to ad-lib, and I said to Harry, "You know, Henry Kissinger may not look the type but he is considered to be rather a sex symbol in Washington."

"Well," Harry responded coldly. "You'd know more about that than I would."

During those long weeks I don't know what I would have done without my assistant, Mary, and Bobbie, my makeup person. They were my confidantes and my daily supporters. But, equally as important, I began to get letters, hundreds of them, from women all over the country who had seen Harry's antagonism with their own eyes. They related their experiences of harassment and discrimination, their own inability to climb the ladder to success in their all-male environments. "Hang in there," they wrote. "If you can make it, we can make it."

I was very moved by these letters and tried to answer as many as I could. We finally made up a form letter and then I would add a personal postscript. When I had a really bad day, Mary would insist that I read the latest batch of supportive letters, and I would keep going.

Bob Siegenthaler seemed paralyzed by Harry's hostility. I'm not sure what he could have done. He didn't want to take Harry on, but it got so bad that Bob began directing the cameramen not to show us side-by-side in what is known as a two-shot. This format would continue when Av Westin replaced Siegenthaler in 1977. The camera was either on me or on Harry.

In the midst of all this tension, the League of Women Voters asked me to moderate the third and final presidential debate between the incumbent president, Gerald Ford, and his challenger from Georgia, Jimmy Carter. (Unlike today, there were very few debates among the candidates.) I don't know whether the league chose me out of pity or because they thought I would do a good job, but boy, did I need that vote of confidence. It also meant a lot of homework. True, the moderator was mostly a timekeeper and the person who made certain that the three questioners kept to the point, but occasionally the moderator could also ask a follow-up question, so I had to be informed on the major issues. All three television networks, CBS, NBC, and ABC, plus public broadcasting, would be carrying the debate.

It was held at the College of William and Mary in Williamsburg, Virginia, on October 22, less than three weeks after I'd started on the news. Afterward a poll declared that Carter came out ahead of Ford, but as far as I was concerned, I came out ahead of both of them. The debate went smoothly. I did not make a flub or misstep. I slept soundly that night for the first time in a long time and flew back to New York refreshed and ready for new battles.

Well, almost ready. The debates were just ten days before the presidential election. I would be joining Harry as coanchor on the biggest political night of the year, indeed of the past four years, and I had never anchored an election night before. ABC had prepared election books for Harry and me. I sat up every night studying which Senate and House races were the most important, which states were possibly up for grabs, which issues were commanding the most attention, which candidate might be expected to win which state, and what was the past history of those candidates and those states. I memorized the names of the senators and the representatives and what their battles were all about. It was a massive assignment. Then there were the anecdotes we were supposed to come up with, preferably based on real political knowledge, to fill the time waiting for the election results to come in. If I had been calm before my first night on the news, I was now terrified.

Harry and I sat at one desk in the special election-night studio ABC had constructed for us. Nearby was Howard K. Smith, Harry's former coanchor, who wanted to prove his value to ABC, having covered election nights for years past. During those long hours on air, he and Harry talked over my head, which, that night, was okay with me. A young researcher named Jeff Gralnick, who later became a top producer, did his best to keep me current, and I only made one glaring error. As I recall I gave the state of Florida to Gerald Ford when, in fact, Carter had won Florida. (What is it about Florida and miscalled presidential elections?)

I did have one advantage. Having just moderated the final presidential debate, I was really up-to-date on the issues. I also knew Jimmy Carter from our interviews for the *Today* show, so I could throw in some personal and politically informed ad-libs of my own. I made it through my first election night, and when eventually Carter was declared the winner and the next president of the United States, what was foremost in my mind was not "Thank heaven this night is over" but could I possibly get Jimmy Carter to be one of the guests on my first ABC *Special*?

Oh! Did I forget to mention that just one month after the election, while continuing to coanchor the nightly news, I was expected to deliver the first of four one-hour prime-time *Specials*? Who had drawn up this contract anyway? Why had I signed it? If I hadn't had that nervous breakdown yet, I certainly deserved to have one now.

Especially since the press continued to have a field day with the drama at ABC News. When there wasn't anything to report, they repeated rumors. One story that crept into the news and was recycled over and over again claimed that I now had a pink office and a pink typewriter! How ridiculous can you get? My office was bland and beige with a regulation black typewriter. Another critic wrote that I had had a special bookcase hoisted up the outside of the building like a piano and delivered through my window. Crazy! Everybody had bookcases in their offices. Mine were no different.

But all that was small potatoes compared to the continuing stories about how this much-ballyhooed partnership with Harry was failing. *TV Guide* wrote an editorial advising me to resign. *New York* magazine ran an article calling the Reasoner-Walters news team a "flop." During those early months, I rarely went out at night but once, when I attended some reception or other, I bumped into Clay Felker, then the editor in chief of *New York*. I had known Clay for a long time. "What you wrote was very painful," I said to Clay. "Well," he answered with a shrug, "you *are* a flop."

More and more, I felt as if I were drowning with no life preserver in sight. The ABC executives, including the president of ABC News, Bill Sheehan, who had all been so gung-ho about my arrival now seemed nowhere to be found. My only defender was my devoted, optimistic, and loving cousin Shirley. Every time I read something awful I'd call her. "What story?" she'd say. "I never saw that story. Nobody I know reads that paper." So I'd feel better—until I talked to my mother in Florida. She read everything about me—and believed it. "Mom, what they wrote isn't true," I'd tell her. She would respond, "Oh darling, if it isn't true, why is it in the papers?"

What even made me sadder was that my father, in the nursing home, also got the newspapers. He was very frail, and when I telephoned him, he struggled with the right thing to say. He had always been afraid that my career might be over. Now that it looked as if it was happening, he tried so hard to cheer me up. He had a television set in his room and would say, "You looked beautiful last night, darling. It will turn out all right." And then he would add in a small voice, "Do you want to come down here for a while?"

The frightening thing was that I agreed that my career might well be over. Everything I had worked for all these past years now was crashing down because of my bad judgment. I told myself that I should never have taken the chance. Was it ego? Was it too much ambition? I wondered if ABC was going to ask me to resign. I posed the question to Lee Stevens, and although he assured me that wasn't going to happen, even he didn't sound too convincing. If I was asked to leave the broadcast, what was going to happen to the family I was supporting, my mother and my sister in their Miami apartment, my father in the expensive nursing home, and my daughter, Jackie?

Jackie. My solace when I came home after the broadcasts. She had no idea what was going on. To her I was the same mommy I'd always been. Zelle and Icodel were also pillars of strength. "You were wonderful tonight on the news," they'd tell me when I opened the door to the apartment, limp with discouragement. I remember being so far down one night that I told Icodel that I couldn't go back to work the next day. "Oh, yes, you can," she said. "You're going back there tomorrow. I said a prayer for you last night. You'll see. You'll win."

There were some female journalists who, bless their hearts, began to rally behind me. I was very touched when Sally Quinn, long since back at the *Washington Post* as a feature writer, leveled her sights at Harry in *Time* magazine. If anyone should be thrown off the show, she said, it should be Harry Reasoner. "He's insulting her on the air. He's being rude and sarcastic and putting her down." Even Richard Salant, the president of CBS News who had questioned at first whether I was a journalist or Cher, was sobered by my negative press. "She's taking an awful licking," he said.

On and on it went for months on end. There was rarely a day without some opinion, pro and con, usually con. But what set me up for quite some time was the telegram I received out of the blue from a man I had never met. It said simply, "Don't let the bastards get you down," and was signed "John Wayne." I felt as if the cavalry was coming.

But the horses weren't fast enough.

Thank Heaven! The Specials

WHATEVER MADE ME THINK I could do even one interview *Special* a year, let alone four, for ABC's entertainment division in addition to my other assignments for the news division, including moderating *Issues and Answers* at least once a month? During the contract negotiations I had been so preoccupied with the whole idea of coanchoring the news that my yes to four *Specials* not only went unnoticed by the press, it went unnoticed by me.

In retrospect the whole idea was insane. No one had attempted hour-long, prime-time interview *Specials* before. For good reason. A one-hour *Special* had to have at least two and, better, three major interviews that were exclusive, otherwise, they wouldn't be special. My agents and ABC had come up with the idea to find a way to pay me the extra $500,000 a year. We all downplayed it because the big story was my doing the news. Now I was stuck. Where would I find the time? More than that, where would I find the people to interview?

I had no idea how hard it was going to be until I had lunch in July 1976 with Sue Mengers, the foremost movie agent at International Creative Management. To this day, although long retired, Sue Mengers is a legend in the business. Smart, tough, and funny, she is also brutally honest. Her major client then was the formidable Barbra Streisand—and that's who I wanted on my first *Special*. Furthermore I wanted to do the interview in Streisand's home.

"It will never happen," Sue said. "Not in a million years. No stars are going to let you and your cameras into their homes. Edward R. Murrow may have done it years ago, but it was a novelty then. Those days are over. No star is even going to sit down and do an interview with you."

In desperation I persisted. As it turned out, Streisand was the executive producer and star of a major film scheduled to open on December 17: the third version of the famous movie *A Star Is Born*. Streisand had recast the movie as a rock musical and was portraying Esther Blodgett, the movie's central character, played twenty-two years earlier by Judy Garland, winning her an Academy Award nomination. The role of Norman Maine, Blodgett's doomed husband, was being played by singer Kris Kristofferson. Streisand had written several new songs for the movie, and most important, her boyfriend, Jon Peters, who had formerly been her hair stylist, was the producer.

For these reasons Sue Mengers convinced Streisand—and Peters— that a big super-duper prime-time *Special* would be just the ticket for her to publicize the movie. Streisand also agreed that we could do the interview from her sprawling ranch in the hills of Malibu. What could be better? Streisand was a huge attraction and rarely did interviews. Her romance with Peters was the subject of much speculation. Everybody wanted to see them together, and now they would.

There was only one precarious condition. Streisand insisted that she have total control over what went into the final piece. Now remember, this *Special* was under the entertainment division. Had it been under news I would not have been able to give her permission to edit it. But ABC News didn't seem to object back then, and I was so thankful that Streisand had agreed to let me do the interview that I wasn't going to take the chance of losing her. I knew that Streisand was considered a control freak, but I was so sure she would be happy with the piece that I signed on. (Yup, just as I was so sure that Harry Reasoner would get to like me.)

On September 25, less than ten days before my debut on the news— and, coincidentally, my birthday—I was in California taping the interview with Streisand and Peters. It would not be aired until December 14, at which point I would be officially at ABC. It was a long, long day but I felt that things were going well. Streisand, as much of a perfectionist about her home as she was about her career, took us all through the house, much of it decorated in the art nouveau style. She showed us the pattern of the rug she had designed herself and then, picking it up, pointed out that the floor beneath had exactly the same design. We also went through her beautiful garden. Streisand knew the Latin name of every blossom and shrub. She was particularly proud of her camellias— *Camellia japonica*.

The interviews themselves, with Streisand and Peters sitting side-by-side, were revealing. She spoke honestly of how cruel people could be to her. "People come up to me and say, 'Hey, your nose is not that big.' They treat performers sometimes as if they're not alive. It's a painful feeling because it's like I'm not a human being." (I could certainly relate to that.)

Peters, too, spoke candidly. When I said that many people felt he was only a hairdresser who had never produced a film before and that he was just a hustler who latched on to a star (I really did say that), he admitted it was true. "I was a hairdresser, and I've been a hairdresser for seventeen years. And I'm also a hustler. I hustled my whole life to get what I want. And as far as latching on to a star, it's true that from the professional side, I could never have produced this movie without Barbra."

The two also professed their devotion to each other. Streisand said she loved Peters because "he deals out of positive vibrations . . . and I'm very negative." Then she sang the theme song she'd written for the movie, "Evergreen," which would win the Academy Award for Best Original Song. All in all I thought the interview came off just fine.

But then, as the old-time comedians used to say, "Folks, you ain't heard nothing yet."

After we finished taping we all sat down together to review the entire unedited interview—Streisand, Peters, me, Marty Erlichman, Sue Mengers, two representatives from the Warner Bros. movie studio (one from production, one from publicity), and my producer, Lucy Jarvis, and associate producer, Joanne Goldberg, both of whom I'd worked with at NBC on the *Royal Lovers Special*. It was then that I realized what torture I was in for. Each person in the room had a different opinion about what should be left in or taken out. Lucy, Joanne, and I sat in Streisand's living room looking at each other in growing despair. This was not going to work.

So I tried a different tack. During the interview I had asked Streisand about her reputation as a perfectionist and prima donna. She'd responded: "It's because I am a woman that they say those things about me. Everybody sets me up to be a target." I reminded her of those words and asked that Lucy and I be allowed to start the editing on our own, promising all the others that we would discuss what we were doing as things went along.

From that time on there was rarely a day or night without a phone call from California. When it wasn't Barbra it was Marty Erlichman, and when it wasn't Marty it was Sue Mengers. What lines was I using? What was in? What was out? Did I get the right close-up of the camellias? When was I going to show them a rough edit?

There is a three-hour time difference between Los Angeles and New York, but nobody in the Streisand camp worried about that. I got phone calls at midnight, at 1:00, at 2:00 in the morning. I argued, debated, cajoled, and finally agreed to whatever I could without hurting the interview. I had to. If Streisand did not approve of the changes we made, she could refuse to let the piece run.

I am a very hands-on editor myself, and I oversaw each line and picture being used. I continued to make the changes Streisand was demanding until the day it went on the air—literally. I would have been frantic had I not already been frantic over the evening news.

Since that time I have done four more interviews with Streisand and had more or less the same experience with the phone calls. She is so talented and so great a star (and besides, I like her personally when we are not working together) that I was happy to do them. But—and this is a huge but—after that first Streisand interview, I learned an extremely important all-time lesson: Never again would I allow her, or anyone else I was interviewing, to have control over anything I was putting on the air. Some would try, citing the Streisand example. Too bad, I'd say. Never, ever, again.

The concept I had of the *Specials* was a format that would feature at least one celebrity and one political figure, a formula similar to some future newsmagazines. So I was very pleased that President-elect Jimmy Carter agreed to sit for an in-depth interview for that first *Special.* After the torture with Streisand the interview with Carter and his wife, Rosalynn, was a romp in the park, or rather, a romp in Plains, Georgia.

I had first talked with Carter back in 1974 on the *Today* show when he was unknown to most Americans but had nevertheless decided to throw his hat in the ring and run for president. He was the governor of Georgia then, a former peanut farmer and naval officer who had risen up the political ranks through state politics.

At first people really did say, "Jimmy who?"—especially since he never used his full name, James Earl Carter. This, too, was rather refreshing. The *Today* interview was brief—most morning-show interviews were and are—but I was impressed. He was a small man who radiated a quiet confidence. He had a friendly smile, although his eyes bulged a bit. After the darkness of Richard Nixon and the awkwardness of Gerald Ford, Carter had an air of simplicity and authenticity. I thought to myself that he might even make it all the way to the presidency.

I followed his race carefully and once, when he was campaigning in Florida, I went there to report on his progress. I tied this to a visit with my parents and brought my daughter with me. I have a sweet photograph of Carter, sitting on the floor with eight-year-old Jackie, talking in a very serious way with her. Jackie promised to vote for him.

So I was looking forward to our interview. It took place a month after the election, in his hometown of Plains, Georgia. The entire phone book for Plains and its neighboring towns was only forty-five pages long, and the listings for Plains itself were just a page and a half. Plains didn't even have a restaurant until the presidential race brought so many journalists to town that one simple eatery opened.

The interview was held in the Carters' unpretentious four-bedroom brick house, surrounded by a wooded grove. Carter said he had constructed much of the living room furniture himself. As we sat on the couch he had built, he told me, "I never have had a doubt that I would be elected. I never have reached a single day in my life when I felt that I would lose." An interesting statement of confidence from a one-term governor of Georgia who had come from such inauspicious roots.

Then I stuck my foot in my mouth. The outgoing president, Gerald Ford, had talked publicly about bringing his own bed to the White House for him and his wife, Betty, and I asked Jimmy Carter if he'd be bringing his own bed. Sounds cheeky, but it didn't seem that way at the time. And neither Jimmy nor Rosalynn Carter seemed the least bit taken aback by the question. So, with some embarrassment, I pressed on. "Do you sleep in a double bed or twin beds?" I asked. "Double bed," Carter replied with a smile, looking at his wife. "Always have. Sometimes we sleep in a single bed . . . but it's much more comfortable in a double bed."

I cringe now at this exchange with President-elect and Mrs. Carter, but it made them very human. It also painted an accurate picture of their close relationship, which would become apparent to everyone over the next four years.

But I was roundly criticized for my Carter bedroom revelation. John O'Connor, the respected television critic for the *New York Times*, called it an "exploitation of personal and intimate details" and pronounced it "pointless, if not ludicrous." But that criticism paled before the wrath that greeted the way I ended the interview.

Carter would shortly be leading this country, which had been so torn apart by the Vietnam War and the Watergate scandal, and I said: "Be wise with us, Governor. Be good to us." "I'll try," he replied.

To this day I don't know what possessed me to say that. Why didn't I just ask him to read us a story each night when he tucked us into bed?

Now, in my faltering defense, if Walter Cronkite had said the same thing in his baronial Uncle Walter tones, people might have said, "What a nice ending." But if I was in trouble before, you can imagine what the reaction to that exchange was. I was killed by the critics. How dare I say something so corny, so stupid, so personal, and, of course, so female?

Here's an example from Morley Safer, of *60 Minutes* fame, who was also doing radio commentary. I think of it even today as kicking a colleague when she is down.

"The interview with Governor Carter is really what ended Ms. Walters' brief career as a journalist and placed her firmly in the ranks of . . . what? The Merv Griffins and Johnny Carsons? What right does any reporter have to issue such a benediction? . . . It is as if Mr. Carter had just become Louis XIV and, without Pope Barbara's admonition, he might be dumb with us and mean to us."

Here's another: "She's bad at it," wrote Sander Vanocur, in the *Washington Post*. "Does she ever let anyone finish a thought?" (Ah, sweet revenge. I can't help but mention that years later Sandy, as he was called, came to work as a correspondent at ABC, and not a top one at that. At that time I was on *20/20*, and Sandy would come by and ask me if the program had any assignments for him. I even helped him when I could. ABC later let him go.)

But what provoked the most wrath was a segment we sandwiched in between the Streisand interview and the Carters: a brief tour I conducted of my own apartment in New York. I really hadn't wanted to, but we were short a third guest. I hadn't been able to get another celebrity to agree to an interview, so against my better judgment—and it really *was* against my better judgment—we filled four minutes of the program with a view of my living room.

We rationalized this by saying that we had shown Streisand's home and Jimmy Carter's home, so why not mine? In came the cameras to my apartment to shoot me among the gray walls and drapes and the red furniture and the fake fireplace. As it turned out, it was a good precedent to set. Most of the *Specials* I would do in the next twenty years or so would take place in the celebrities' homes, and become a trademark of the programs. (Now celebrities are more concerned about their privacy, and want to be interviewed in hotel rooms.) As for my apartment, it didn't make great television, but I thought it was hardly the worst piece of television on the air.

Oh, yeah? More swell stuff from Morley Safer: "Sandwiched

between the white bread of the Carters and the pumpernickel of Streisand, we were treated to the pastrami of Ms. Walters herself." And this again from Sandy Vanocur. "She was interviewing herself," he wrote. "That way, at least, the only person she can interrupt is herself."

Well, you know what? That first *Special* was a runaway smash hit. It significantly beat out both CBS and NBC. More than fifteen million people watched. "It was unlike anything viewers had seen and they loved it," ran an article in *Entertainment Weekly*, written, incidentally, by a woman. "Barbara Walters had to prove she was worth a million dollars, and on the night of December 14, 1976, she did."

I may have been dying on the news, but in spite of the critics I was soaring on the *Specials*. They became the tail that wagged the dog. No matter what happened to me on the news, I continued to do the *Specials* that year and the next and the next and on and on until this very year. I've been doing them now for more than thirty years.

As a matter of fact, in the winter of 2006, we did a tongue-in-cheek *Special* called *30 Mistakes in 30 Years*, which ran for two hours over two nights. It was fun to look back on all the things I said and did I should not have said and done—like the "be wise" admonition to Jimmy Carter. By 2006 I could afford to make fun of myself. But thirty years earlier the *Barbara Walters Specials* were what kept me from being considered a total disaster.

After the first *Special* it became easier and easier to secure famous guests. I continued to mix celebrity guests with newsmakers and recruited a new staff. We lined up a wonderful mix for my next *Special*, which would air in April, just four months later.

This time the celebrity guests were Elizabeth Taylor and her new husband, my old friend John Warner (soon to be elected senator); the newsmaker guests were His Imperial Majesty the shah of Iran and his wife, Empress Farah, and for good measure, Barbara Jordan of Texas, the first black congresswoman from a Southern state and a brilliant orator. Jordan had burst into the national consciousness during the House Judiciary Committee's impeachment hearings of President Nixon in the summer of 1974, where she won national acclaim for her eloquent reaffirmation of faith in the Constitution. I can still hear the way she said, "the Con-sti-tu-tion," before she voted for all five articles of impeachment. The congresswoman herself was much admired but also criticized for being blunt and aloof. I thought she was terrific.

The interview with Elizabeth Taylor and John Warner, which you read about earlier, was strange for me. Even though I was asking the questions, I felt like a third wheel. They were the couple. I was the ex-girlfriend and Elizabeth knew it. The viewers loved it, though, and that's what counted.

It was the interview with the shah of Iran and his shahbanou in Tehran, however, that caused a sensation. First we interviewed the thirty-eight-year-old empress in her own private library with its suede couches, walls of books, priceless Persian manuscripts, sculptures and paintings by Miró, Calder, Picasso, Salvador Dalí, and even an Andy Warhol portrait of Mick Jagger, which she had chosen herself. This was her retreat. I liked the empress very much. In spite of the priceless artifacts, paintings, and her twenty-four-carat lifestyle, I found her down-to-earth and easy to talk to.

We then interviewed the shah in another part of the palace. He was nineteen years older than his wife and had an opulent office with a gilded desk, golden telephones, and windows surrounded by gold-embossed frames. The windows were of bulletproof glass. He seemed arrogant and coldly superior, yet he answered all of my questions honestly, so honestly that there were times when I wanted to say to him, "Don't you realize what you are saying?"

When I asked if he felt that it was God's will that he was born to be king, he said it was, that "it was the whole meaning of my life." (Bear in mind that he came to the Peacock Throne only because his father, a military officer and eventually prime minister, had overthrown the former shah.) When I later asked the shah if a newspaper in his country could criticize him, he said plainly, "No."

"Why not?" I asked, and he replied, "You cannot insult the king."

This attitude contributed to his growing reputation as an autocratic dictator untouched by the needs of his people. Although the shah had made many important reforms in his country—he requisitioned some huge private estates and redistributed them to small farmers, spearheaded the training of teachers and doctors, and gave women more rights—his regime was in great danger. He and his family were said to be corrupt, and the secret security service he'd formed, SAVAK, was undeniably cruel. Indeed it was just two years after this interview that the Islamic revolution took place in Iran and the shah and empress were forced to flee their country.

At the time of our interview, however, the shah did not feel threatened. In private life he was hardly autocratic or fierce. For example, talking about his four children, he said that he still regretted throwing sand in the eyes of his son, the crown prince, when they were on the beach and his son was annoying him. He said he sometimes cried over films with animals or children. But he never cried over himself. He said a king didn't have that right.

Okay. Nice personal stuff about an emperor, but hardly controversial. Then we had a joint conversation with the shah and his wife, the first time they had ever been interviewed together on American television.

In doing my homework, I'd read in a magazine some pretty strong statements about women attributed to the shah. I couldn't quite believe he would be so foolish as to have made them, so I decided to ask him. "Your Majesty, I want to talk a bit with you about women. I quote you: 'You have never produced a Michelangelo or Bach or even a great cook.' So you don't feel that women are in the same sense equal, that they have the same intelligence or ability?"

Now remember, the shah had introduced many reforms for women in his country, including their right to be fully educated and to leave their heads uncovered (which infuriated the mullahs). Many of the growing number of medical students in Iran were young women. But in spite of this he reinforced my question about women not having the same intelligence or ability as men by answering, "Not so far. Maybe you will become in the future."

I then exclaimed, "You have given women in your country equality in their human rights but you do not think they are equal in intelligence?"

SHAH: Well, there are cases, sure. You can always have some exceptions.

ME [sarcastically]: Here and there?

SHAH: Yes, but on the average, I repeat again, where have you produced a top scientist?

ME: Madame Curie.

SHAH: That's one.

ME: But we've had a lot of trouble getting ahead perhaps because of this point of view. Do you feel your wife is one of those exceptions? Do you feel your wife can govern as well as a man?

SHAH: I prefer not to answer that.

ME: But you have made your wife the regent of this country. If you die, your wife heads this country. And yet you are not certain she can govern as well as a man?

SHAH: I can't say; I don't know how she would react in a crisis.

All this time the empress had sat silently by her husband. I then said to him, "Well, I admire you for your honesty, but what you are really saying is women are nice in their place. Nice, pretty creatures." At which point I turned to his wife and said: "Your Majesty, say something, please. How do you feel when you listen to this?"

Her eyes brimming with tears, the empress looked at her husband and said quietly, "I don't think you really believe that." Her voice got stronger as she continued: "But what have men done to the world, really? Have they achieved something that today makes the world so perfect? Politically, economically, relationships, progress? So let us not classify people."

I asked then if she thought she could govern as well as a man and she replied, "Compared to my husband, it is difficult, because there are very few heads of state with thirty-six years of experience behind them and with his intelligence and his capacity. But compared to somebody else, I think, why not?"

I could only imagine their conversation in their bedroom that night. I was also concerned because the next day I was scheduled to talk further with the shah about oil prices, as Iran controlled so much of the world's oil. We could not complete this interview without asking about oil, and I was afraid I had offended him and he would cancel the session. His aides agreed that he was probably annoyed with my questioning, but the next day the shah was smiling and friendly and our interview went on as planned.

The conversation with the shah and empress aired in April 1977, and to this day there are still people who talk about it with me. And here is the truly important part. When the shah was forced into exile and it was later revealed that he had cancer, it was his wife who took over and managed not only his care but every aspect of their lives—where they could travel, how they would live, and the multitude of decisions that had to be made for thousands of their exiled countrymen.

Empress Farah now lives a quiet life. She spends as much time as she can in Maryland, near her grandchildren and her eldest son, who would have been emperor had the revolution not occurred. We still see each other. I admire her courage and dignity, and Iran could have done worse than to have had her as its leader (and, in fact, it has).

Although this *Special* also did very well in the ratings, the Elizabeth Taylor interview drew many more viewers than the one with the shah and empress. Even fewer people watched the interview with Barbara Jordan. It was like asking people what kind of music they like and they reply "Bach"—and then go out and buy rock. The celebrities carried the program. So we made a decision that affected almost all of our future shows—more celebrities and fewer politicians and newsmakers.

The result was that when we did our third *Special*, we featured Bob and Dolores Hope, Bing Crosby, and Redd Foxx, who was starring in the sitcom *Sanford and Son*. We continued to do each interview from the subject's home. This had proved to be a great part of the appeal of these programs. Our viewers loved seeing how the stars lived.

Redd Foxx's house was an eye-popper. Everything had a fox on it—the drapes, the carpets, the lampshades. But in his bedroom there were not foxes—there were live monkeys. His bed faced a glassed-in area, sort of like an aquarium, only with monkeys jumping around. The glass cage was air-conditioned, kept at the right temperature for the monkeys, and they could stare at Foxx and he could stare back. I stared at all of them in disbelief.

The Hope house was lovely, traditional, and undistinguished. Dolores Hope was also lovely, an understanding wife to a husband who more often than not was away. It was a pleasant, uneventful interview.

The interview with Bing Crosby was a surprise. The seemingly affable, easygoing Crosby turned out to be as strict and rigid a parent as one could find. Many young people at the time were beginning to share a room and sleep together without marriage, but when I asked Crosby how he would feel if one of his seven children wanted to share a bedroom with someone they were going with, he said he wouldn't speak to them ever again.

Flabbergasted at his answer, I asked, "If one of your sons said, 'I like this girl and I'm living with her and we're not getting married,' you would *never* speak to him?"

I will never forget Crosby's dismissive answer: "Aloha, on the steel guitar." (My producers and I still use that expression today if we want to get rid of something on a show.)

Beyond that he said if his only daughter, Mary Frances, told him that she was having an affair, he would tell her to take her things and move out and he would never, ever, talk to her or see her again. He seemed to have conveniently forgotten his own reputation as a philanderer in his younger days. But now he insisted that that was how he, a Catholic, had been raised, and he knew of no other way to behave.

Still, in spite of this rigidity, which I daresay some people might agree with, I liked Crosby. I liked the fact that he took second billing on films, and I liked the way he told me he wanted to be remembered as "not a bad fellow who sang a fair song in tune most of the time."

Most of all I liked the way he treated my mother.

For the very first time I had taken my mother on one of my assign-ments, and I took her without my sister. My father was in the nursing home, Aunt Lena had agreed to look after my sister, and my mother had finally agreed to travel with me alone. She loved Bing Crosby from all of his films, and this visit thrilled her so much.

Crosby had a magnificent estate on the outskirts of San Francisco. To take care of it, he had a wonderful English butler named Alan Fisher, who had worked for the Duke of Windsor before coming to America. Mr. Fisher took my mother all over the beautiful house and prepared a special tea for us with buttered scones and little sandwiches. My mother was so elegant and charming that day. She was at her best, and both Crosby and his butler doted on her. I wished that I could have taken her on every interview I did. She deserved the respite, but even during this magical time for her in California, she worried about how my sister was getting along and called home constantly.

The visit with Bing Crosby remains very important in my eyes, not only because of my mother but because it turned out to be Crosby's last interview. He died six months later of a heart attack in Madrid, Spain, after playing eighteen holes of golf. He was seventy-three. After his death, Alan Fisher sent me a pair of Crosby's eyeglasses. He said he thought nobody would miss them and that my mother might like to have them. She did.

After the first two or three celebrity *Specials*, more and more of the biggest stars of the day agreed to be interviewed. I remember Lucille Ball, sitting next to her husband, Gary Morton, and saying bitterly that Desi Arnaz, her former husband and the man who was her partner for so many years on and off camera, drank too much and was never around. Yet it was obvious because she couldn't stop talking about him that she still loved Arnaz.

She went on to tell me she was devastated when her marriage to Arnaz broke up. They had everything, and she couldn't understand what went wrong. "He had to lose," she sighed. "He had to fail. Every-thing he'd built he had to break down. Even our marriage." She'd mar-ried Morton in part, she said, because unlike Desi, he liked to stay home and she never had to worry where he was. But to this day, because *I Love Lucy* is always running somewhere in syndication, millions of people still think Lucy and Desi were the happiest of married couples.

I talked with Muhammad Ali, the former heavyweight boxing cham-pion, in his home on Chicago's South Side. There must have been thirty people sitting around. I had never seen so many hangers-on. No wonder he couldn't hold on to his money. Ali began the interview by teasing me. He said I should look up to him because men are made taller than women. "God made man in his image. He didn't worry about no woman. He made the woman out of his rib." For a moment I felt I was back with the shah again, but then Ali laughed and said, "I'm just having fun." And fun he certainly was in those days.

Then there was John Wayne, the man who had sent the telegram that so buoyed me up during my first terrible months at ABC. He agreed to an interview and we finally met, first aboard his 136-foot yacht, the *Wild Goose*, which had been a navy minesweeper, and later we talked at his home in Newport Beach, California. I expressed surprise at how elegant the house was, and Wayne shot back: "Why not? I've been to school. A lot of us country boys have good taste." I also remember that Wayne, seventy-one, particularly wanted to talk about his young female assistant, Pat Stacey, whom he obviously loved. Separated from his third wife, he wanted to have his devotion to her recognized. "I have a very deep affection for Miss Stacey," he told me. "I have a very pleasant life with her." Up until this interview the public did not know about "Miss Stacey."

"Duke," as Wayne was called, had been ill, so at the end of our conversation, I asked a question I have often posed since and which, in his case, seemed all the more appropriate. "Do you have a philosophy that sums up your thinking today?"

Wayne answered: "Listen, I spoke to the man up there and I've always had faith that there is a supreme being, so the fact that he's let me stick around a little longer or that *she's* let me stick around a little longer certainly goes great with me. I want to hang around as long as I am healthy and not in anybody's way." When I asked if he had any regrets, he said, "If I had to do it all over, I'd do it the same way."

Soon after this interview John Wayne entered the hospital. He died of cancer three months after the *Special* aired.

Though we had learned that interviews with heads of state were not big winners in the ratings, for another *Special* I traveled to Amman, Jordan, for the first American television interview with its longtime monarch, King Hussein, and his very new American wife, Queen Noor. At the time of their marriage Noor became the stepmother to Hussein's eight children from three previous marriages, including Jordan's present king, Abdullah. Queen Noor, née Lisa Halaby and a Princeton graduate, was as blond and beautiful as any movie star. Americans were fascinated by her. (I also did the first television interview with her after her husband's death in 1999.)

Just to be sure that this *Special* would get big ratings, we also included interviews with Alan Alda, who was then a smash in *M*A*S*H;* Diana Ross, who changed all the decor in her LA house from turquoise to red and black literally overnight (since I had planned to wear a pink dress, this was a fashion disaster for me); and finally, a hilarious excursion with Steve Martin, who took me to his supposed home—a crumbling shack with a door that fell off and mold everywhere, including on what he described as his prized "pudding collection."

During the first season of these *Specials,* Harry and I were still plugging along with the third-place news, but everything was about to change for me.

In May 1977 ABC made Roone Arledge the president of ABC News as well as ABC Sports. He turned out to be one of my greatest champions. In an interview with the *New York Times,* he called me a "professional journalist," and said, "She's a great asset who has been mishandled." It was not me but Harry, Roone went on, who was responsible for the broadcast's low ratings. "Harry has been on the program for six years, and the show has been going steadily nowhere," Roone said. "The ratings seem to indicate he doesn't have strength. He has had his shot. It's not that he has been held back."

Roone's words were magic to my ears. After being the butt of so much criticism for the year and a half of coanchoring the news with Harry, my confidence as a journalist was at an all-time low. Roone would become my savior.

Under his direction I was about to do a series of newsmaker *Specials* for the news division that had nothing to do with my celebrity *Specials* for entertainment. The interviews were with the most important, charismatic, and controversial leaders of the time, and they turned out to be more important than anything I had done or would do on the evening news. Little by little they began to restore my tattered reputation.

Finally, Fidel

THE DAY IS BEAUTIFUL, hot, sunny, the blue of the sky reflected in the blue of the water. I am cruising across one of the most infamous bodies of water in modern American history with one of America's most infamous adversaries: Fidel Castro and I are in a Cuban patrol boat, streaking across the Bay of Pigs.

"Is it true that we are the first Americans to cross the Bay of Pigs in sixteen years?" I ask the bearded Communist president of Cuba.

"As I remember, this is the first time," he replies through his interpreter.

"How do you feel when you come to the Bay of Pigs?" I ask him.

"Before the invasion I usually came here to fish and to rest," he tells me. "After the invasion, I continued to come here, many times. I like this place. It is quiet, and there are good places for underwater fishing."

And so began my extraordinary interview with the Cuban leader whose forces had decimated the CIA-sponsored invasion of Cuba in 1961, right here in the Bay of Pigs. Now his recollections are not of the U.S.-led attempt to overthrow him but of the good spot for spear-fishing.

Just how my camera crew and I ended up in this boat with Fidel Castro bears telling. It had been two years since I'd met him in Cuba, two years of trying to pin down the exclusive interview he'd promised me. I had written him countless letters through the Cuban Mission at the UN and through the Cuban delegation within the Czech Embassy in Washington. (The United States did not and does not have diplomatic relations with Cuba.) I never received a response—until May 1977.

I was ecstatic when Castro suddenly agreed to the interview. So were ABC and Roone Arledge. The mysterious Cuban leader hadn't given a television interview in sixteen years, except for little blips about some sports event. We knew it probably wouldn't draw huge ratings. Castro was no movie star. But an interview with him was considered so newsworthy that Roone decided in advance to run pieces of it on the evening news as well as schedule a half hour prime-time news *Special.*

When I arrived in Havana I met with Castro in his office. He was all smiles. "Where would you like to go?" he asked through Juanita, the same lovely interpreter we had met before. "What would you like to see?"

I thought fast. "The Bay of Pigs, Mr. President."

"Yes, we can do that," he agreed.

"And, and I'd also like to go through the Sierra Maestra mountains to see where you started your revolutionary campaign."

"We'll do both," he said. "I'll arrange it."

That is how we came to be on the Cuban patrol boat the next day, skimming across the Bay of Pigs. We stopped at a little island for a picnic lunch of grilled fish and pineapple, during which Castro swapped fish stories with the ABC crew. It was there that we taped our first brief but candid interview with him. In it he expressed his admiration for John F. Kennedy, the American president who had ordered the invasion of Cuba, and his disdain for Richard Nixon, who hadn't. "I never liked Richard Nixon," Castro said. "From the very first moment I could see he was a false man, and, politically speaking, he was foolish."

To say that we were thrilled with the way things were going is an understatement. Our producers, Dick Richter and Tom Capra, had encountered unimaginable hurdles from the moment we'd landed. First they'd been informed that NABET, the same union that had crippled NBC during my contract negotiations, had gone out on strike against ABC. Our union crew had to drop everything and fly home while we had to wait for a freelance crew to arrive. In the interim we had to rent equipment from the Cuban National Broadcast Center, which tried to take us to the cleaners. When Castro learned of this he himself intervened and negotiated a very fair price. After all, who was going to argue with Castro? But another crisis quickly arose.

I had a live interview scheduled for the evening news with Alicia Alonso, Cuba's prima ballerina—except we couldn't get it to New York. There was no direct satellite hookup between Miami and Havana, so the interview had to be fed—can you believe it?—to Czechoslovakia and from there back to New York. The audio hookup, on the other hand, came through Miami, and turned out to be almost impossible to coordinate with the visuals.

The Bay of Pigs was a pick-me-up for everyone, and we celebrated back at the Hotel Riviera. Like the Hotel Nacional where we'd stayed two years before, the Riviera, in the past also one of Havana's great hotels, was in sad shape. Again, there were no toilet seats. The wallpaper was peeling off the walls, the beautiful furniture was chipped, and the upholstery was torn. There were no soft drinks, either. Only rum. Without the Coke.

But who cared? We knew we were on our way to a great story. Unexpectedly, I was also on my way to a new friendship. After we returned from the Bay of Pigs, Castro invited us to join him at a baseball game, and the ABC crew was soon buzzing about a group of American men they recognized at the game—George Steinbrenner, the owner of the New York Yankees, retired Yankee pitcher Whitey Ford, and several Yankee coaches.

I had never heard of George Steinbrenner—he'd owned the Yankees only for a few years—but I was curious about what he was doing in Cuba. He, on the other hand, was not in the least curious about me. He took one look at me approaching him with a camera crew, spun on his heel, and strode away. It turned out that he and his coaches had been secretly invited by Castro to Cuba to give major-league pointers to the Cuban baseball players. Suddenly there was ABC News in his face. We had evidently outed him, and he was enraged. The word got around that Steinbrenner and his entourage were packing up to leave in the morning because of us, which made me feel very guilty.

I saw him sitting at the bar when I got back to the hotel and, with some apprehension, I sat down next to him. I told him we hadn't shot any footage of him and weren't going to. "I'm not here because of you," I explained. "And I'm not going to make a big deal out of the fact that I saw you here." He seemed surprised and was so relieved that he canceled his plans to leave. We began to talk, and thirty years later, we're still friends. Nothing has pleased me more than to have sat in his box at Yankee Stadium and cheered on the home team, remembering that it all went back to that ball game in Cuba.

Back to Fidel. I have a note in Spanish framed on a wall in my apartment. The translation reads: "For Barbara as a remembrance of the most difficult interview that I have had in all the days of my life." It is signed "Fidel Castro, May 20, 1977. 1:29 am." It is the time that is relevant. That's how long our interview ran the following night in his office.

Five hours. Nonstop. During which he smoked long Cuban *Cohiba* cigars, enveloping me in the smoke. It's a wonder I didn't get instant bronchitis.

It would have been worth it, though, for in this lengthy television interview Castro laid out his major concerns and fears. First of all he made it very clear that he was a Communist. Although he came from an affluent family, he had been a Communist from his young years. Nothing was going to change him, which is why, he claimed, the CIA had made more than twenty attempts on his life, a claim partially validated by the recent release of declassified CIA documents.

Castro was also candid about the number of political prisoners in Cuba's prisons—between two and three thousand—and in his response to my charge that the state controlled the media. "You allow no dissent," I said to him. "Your newspapers, radio, television, motion pictures are under state control. People can dissent in their meetings, in their congresses, but no dissent or opposition is allowed in the public media."

"Barbara, our concept of freedom of the press is not yours," he replied. "If you asked us if a newspaper could appear here against socialism, I can say honestly no, it cannot appear. It would not be allowed by the party, the government, or the people. In that sense we do not have the freedom of the press that you possess in the U.S. And we are very satisfied about that."

He was not as candid when I asked him the personal questions no one had asked him before. He clearly did not want to disclose whether he was married. "What is the importance of my being married or not?" he said. I told him it wasn't, but wondered why "such a simple question like 'Are you married?,' not very complicated, raises such an uproar."

He paused, then said firmly: "Formalmente, no." [Formally, no.] That's all.

I was dead tired when our five-hour marathon finally ended, but Castro was just warming up. "Barbara, are you hungry?" he said, and suddenly the whole crew and I were in his kitchen, where he made us delicious melted cheese sandwiches. I've had many gourmet experiences in my life, but having Fidel Castro cook for me at 2:00 a.m. certainly stands out. And we weren't done yet. "What do you want to have for dinner tomorrow night when we're in Sierra Maestra?" Castro asked. "Is roast pork and yuca okay?" I was struck dumb by the thought of another marathon with Castro until Dick Richter poked me in the ribs and I managed to say yes.

It was 3:00 a.m. when we got back to the hotel. Dick called Roone, begged for more airtime, and got it. By the time I collapsed into bed the half-hour *Special* had turned into an hour. At 9:00 the next morning, my phone rang. El Comandante would be sending a car for me in half an hour. To my astonishment, and the wide-eyed amazement of the few tourists in front of the hotel, the car turned out to be a jeep and the driver was Castro himself. This was not to be an ordinary journey. Off we went to board Castro's presidential plane and fly to Santiago de Cuba, the second-largest city in the country, where Castro and his band of insurgents had launched the revolution in 1953 to overthrow the dictator Fulgencio Batista. It took them six years to succeed. Twenty-four years later their guerrilla campaign formed one of the most memorable days of my professional life.

"Come, Barbara. Sit next to me," Castro said at the airport as we got into the second jeep of the day. With Castro again at the wheel, we climbed into the Sierra Maestra, where his revolutionaries had been secretly based. He drove with one hand, waving his cigar in the other. Crammed into the backseat were his translator, Juanita, and two of Castro's former comrades from their revolutionary days. For six hours we drove up and down mountain roads while Castro pointed out the sites of battles and ambushes and guerrilla encampments to me and the camera crew following in other jeeps.

As we splashed through rain-swollen streams, Castro handed me the tin of hard candies he kept on the dashboard to give to the children who swarmed around him at every stop. He also handed me his revolver. My job was to hold the candy and the gun over my head to keep them dry. And to learn the verses of "Cielito Lindo," which he sang loudly and off-key in Spanish. I look back on that trip as the most amazing car ride I have ever had.

At nightfall we reached his mountain retreat, a large complex of cabins, where each of us had our own room, fresh towels, hot water—and a toilet with a toilet seat. We drank much too much Algerian wine over dinner, dined on roast suckling pig with the head still attached, and then, amidst much laughter and goodwill, bartered with Castro, who joked that he wanted payment for the services he'd provided us.

This may be one of those stories where you have to have been there, but it was hilarious. Tom Capra told him we couldn't pay him as an actor because he was a lousy actor. He stopped in the middle of scenes to talk to children. Castro then suggested being paid as a director or a producer, to which I responded that he was lousy at both. "You took us through swamps. If that's your idea of directing, it's not very good. And don't think you're a producer, because we wasted hours and hours seeing absolutely nothing."

We settled on paying him as a driver and offered him five dollars, which he accepted. Tom then wrote out a receipt for his ABC expense account—"Payment to one driver, Fidel Castro. $5"—and Castro signed it with a flourish. I'm sure Tom still has that slip of paper.

As I look back on that visit to Fidel Castro's personal hideaway, I know that it is the kind of experience I will never have again. Few world leaders ever give up this much time or become so open with journalists. Our timing was right. Castro wanted to explain himself. Also, he liked our crew. He appreciated their efficiency and good humor and, I think, the fact that they weren't striking. People in Cuba don't go on strike. I guess he liked me, too. Not that he ever became personal in word or deed, but the mountain trip was not exactly what he treated every journalist to. By the way, Castro knew very little English. Everything he said was translated by Juanita, who never left his side.

We left Havana the following day and I stopped in Florida to see my mother and sister as well as my father. I think it is a shock for any child to see a parent in a nursing home. My father had always been a smallish, slight man, but wiry and strong. Now he seemed shrunken and fragile. I took him outside in his wheelchair and we held hands for a while and tried to talk, but he had almost no energy. I told him I loved him and he told me he loved me, and I left. Somehow I knew it was the last time I would see him, and I couldn't hold back my tears.

Back in New York, Dick Richter, Tom Capra, and I edited the footage of Castro. It was not easy. As much as we wanted to show how charming he could be, we also needed to make clear that he was the absolute dictator of a Communist country, a man who allowed no dissent, a man who imprisoned his enemies and was a staunch opponent of our democratic system. I ended the piece by saying: "What we disagreed on most profoundly is the meaning of freedom—and that is what truly separates us."

Fidel Castro Speaks aired on June 9, 1977, and got high ratings as far as news specials go, but didn't come close to *Barnaby Jones*, a longstanding detective series on CBS, and a movie shown on NBC. I didn't see it because I was in England covering Queen Elizabeth's Silver Jubilee. But the Castro *Special* marked a turning point in my career.

Roone acted on his statement to the *New York Times* that I was being "mishandled" behind the anchor desk and officially made me a roving anchor for ABC News. He realized that I would be far more valuable to the network as a reporter, free to travel anywhere in the world at any time rather than sitting behind a desk. I still coanchored the news, but Roone's solution to the bad chemistry between Harry and me was to keep us separated as much as possible. I was the sole anchor if Harry was away on assignment, and vice versa, but more and more I was the one on the road. That is why I said Roone was my savior.

There was also a negative fallout from the Castro *Special*. While Castro was happily playing the entire five hours of the interview over and over again on Cuban television, leaving out the personal questions, some of the many Cubans living in America were furious at me for giving him airtime. I got hundreds of letters, some benign, from people with friends or relatives in Cuba or in Cuban prisons, asking me to intercede with Castro on their behalf (I forwarded those letters to Cuban officials), but others contained threats against me. I took those threats very seriously in part because my father was being cared for by Cuban nurses in the nursing home. They had been very cool toward me when I'd visited. Did they know I'd just been interviewing Castro? They certainly knew now. I was also very concerned about the safety of my daughter. ABC was as well, and hired a bodyguard to take Jackie to and from school. The letters gradually tapered off, and after I was advised that the threat had passed, we returned to a normal routine.

Just when I thought things were back to normal, my frail father died. He was eighty-one years old. As it happened, I was having lunch with George Steinbrenner on August 15, 1977, when I got the call. I was heartsick but not surprised. I flew immediately to Florida to find that my mother, too, had been emotionally prepared for his death. Perhaps she was even relieved. For a long time she had watched him become progressively weaker and more dispirited and, for just as long, she had felt helpless to do anything about it.

Since we had never really observed our religion, we didn't sit shiva— the seven-day Jewish ritual of mourning—for my father. Instead we had a simple graveside service. I stayed with my mother and sister for a few days, then returned to New York. I had contacted the major papers, and my father's obituary ran in all of them. *Variety*, the only one that would have mattered to him, gave his life a rave review, which included this wonderful line: "He believed in full lighting." What better epitaph for a showman?

I should have had a memorial service in New York, but I didn't. It had been such a long time since my father left New York that I was afraid that no one would come. I envisioned my mother and sister and me sitting alone in an empty hall. Empty seats had always made my father angry. He would have hated not having a full house.

I realize now that that was a mistake. Of course people would have come. Just look at the number of people who came to the dedication of Lou Walters Way, the street-naming tribute arranged by Mayor Bloomberg. My father was finally honored and remembered. I should have done it sooner.

As for Castro, I saw him again two years later when he came to New York in October 1979 to address the United Nations. He invited me to dinner at the Cuban Mission on Lexington Avenue, and I asked if I could bring other members of the media to meet him on an informal basis. He said to bring anyone I wanted. This started the rumor that because I was acting as Castro's hostess, we must be having an affair. I don't want to disappoint anyone, but let me say once again, Castro and I were most definitely not lovers. No romance. Not even a pass. *Nada.*

It was quite a dinner, though. Roone, of course, came from ABC News, as well as friends like Katharine Graham, Ben Bradlee and Sally Quinn, and Henry Grunwald, the brilliant editor of *Time* magazine. I asked the top editors of the other major magazines and newspapers in New York, all of whom came with the exception of A. M. Rosenthal, the managing editor of the *New York Times.* He alone refused, saying he wouldn't be in the same room as Fidel Castro. I didn't invite any correspondents from CBS or NBC because I thought I might get a new interview with Castro out of the evening, and I didn't want any competition. Not a nice gesture on my part, but then again, television is a tough game, and you don't win by always being Ms. Nice Guy.

Well, I didn't get any interview, but after Castro agreed to talk on the record, all my print friends suddenly produced notebooks and for an hour grilled the Communist leader. He was as charming and funny as I remembered him—and just as good a short-order cook. After the interview, he went into the mission's kitchen and cooked us all a delicious lobster dinner. He followed up the next day by having a live lobster delivered to each guest. Lobster diplomacy.

It was to be twenty-five years before I saw Fidel Castro again. I had repeatedly asked for a new interview but never received a response. All I got from him was a Christmas card every year, hand-delivered by an official from the Cuban Mission. The card usually came by April, and I always hoped it would include an invitation to return to Havana. In October 2002 it finally did.

Castro was seventy-six by then. He had outlasted nine U.S. presidents, all of whom wished he would vanish off the face of the earth, and was in the midst of his tenth, Bill Clinton. When we met back in the Palace of the Revolution, Castro told me I looked very well. "You look well, too," I said. "Only you have gotten grayer and I have gotten blonder." His ever-faithful translator, Juanita, was back at his side and I was happy to see her, still lovely but now gray-haired herself. We hugged each other, remembering our wild trip through the Sierra Maestra so many years before.

Back in 1977 Castro told me that he would shave off his beard if the United States lifted the trade embargo against Cuba. In 2002 he still had the beard and, save for some shipments of food, the United States still enforced the trade embargo. The U.S. government also forbade American tourists from visiting Cuba, though some did, illegally. Other countries had softened toward Communist Cuba, and more than a million European and Canadian tourists a year were availing themselves of Cuba's sunshine, beaches, and rum. Tourism is now Cuba's biggest business.

Was that why he was now wearing a business suit, I asked, instead of his trademark military uniform?

"Barbara, precisely in order to seduce you and for you to be kind to me, to have pity on me," he joked. "You have more questions than the U.S. Air Force has missiles."

So his sense of humor remained intact. As did his absolute power. Before our arrival we had requested an interview with Juan Miguel González, the father of Elián González. Elián, you will remember, was the five-year-old refugee from Cuba whose mother had drowned at sea while fleeing to America in 1999, thrusting Elián into the center of a highly publicized, impassioned custody fight between his vehemently anti-Castro relatives in Florida and his father in Cuba, championed by Castro. Elián, whose Miami relatives appealed his extradition to Cuba all the way to the U.S. Supreme Court, had been returned to his father, Juan Miguel, in 2000.

The drama had riveted the United States for months, but our request to interview the father in Cuba had been turned down—until my interview with Castro. The next morning Juan Miguel was sped to Havana in a government car. Elián was "very happy" to be back in Cuba, his father told me, producing a picture of the boy, then just shy of nine. "He's almost as tall as I am. He's doing karate at school. He's a green belt."

That good news about Elián was hardly surprising. He had become a poster child for Cuba and appeared often at Castro's side in film clips of national holidays. Castro himself was said to have five sons and many grandchildren, including a set of triplets, but, as in my past interview, he wouldn't admit to any relationships. When I asked him why, after all these years, he replied, "It's prohibited to go into my personal life. It's not our way."

"What's to hide?" I said.

"It's my human right," Castro joked. "I cling to my human right to defend my privacy."

I kept asking. And finally he admitted. "Yes, we have descendants and all that."

I pressed him about the triplets.

"Well, I think there are some triplets around. I've heard they exist."

That was it for anything personal about Castro.

Castro presented me with a farewell gift when we left Havana—a picture book of old combat photos from the Bay of Pigs, titled *Memories of a Victory*. The text was in Spanish, of course, as was the attached note, translated here: "For Barbara, in whose terrible hands I fell again after 25 years. I promise that I will never try to escape. It's impossible, and I think with affability about our next meeting, arranged for 2027." It is signed "Fidel Castro" and dated October 7, 2002.

Whatever you think of his politics and ideology, he has cut a huge figure in modern history. When he was taken seriously ill in July 2006, no one knew for days whether he was even alive. I was working on this memoir when I heard the news that he was in the hospital for surgery and immediately e-mailed the Cuban foreign minister, Felipe Pérez Roque, to express my concern and ask him to extend my wishes to Castro for his speedy recovery. Lest you think this was a purely beneficent gesture, I also sent a separate e-mail requesting an interview when and if Castro was strong enough.

I received no reply from Fidel Castro and now I never will.

The Historic Interview: Anwar Sadat and Menachem Begin

THE QUESTION I am most often asked is: Of all the interviews you have done, which is your favorite? Well, "favorite" is not a word I would use, but if I had to choose the one that meant the most to me it would be the late president of Egypt, Anwar el-Sadat. He changed the world. At least he tried to. In bringing about peace, if not friendship, between Egypt and Israel, he took the first great step toward compromise in what remains one of the most contentious and complicated areas of the world. Sadat had foresight, courage, and charisma. He was, in physique, a slim, small man, but in his heart he was a giant.

If I also had to choose the time in my professional life that meant the most to me, and of which I am proudest, it would be those same years in the midseventies in the Middle East. I played a small part in those difficult, tumultuous, and now historic times, and I cherish the memories.

A month after my father's death, I went to Beirut to interview Yasir Arafat, the head of the Palestinian Liberation Organization. I had been trying to get an interview with the elusive head of the PLO for years, and in September 1977 he said yes. There was no ABC newsmagazine like *20/20* back then, and so the interview was scheduled to air on ABC's Sunday-morning news program *Issues and Answers*.

At that time in the eyes of the West and Israel, Arafat was the number one Palestinian terrorist for his violent campaign to secure an independent Palestinian homeland. At the same time he was a hero and champion to the Palestinians, many of whom had either fled or been expelled from Israel and now lived in squalid refugee camps in Lebanon. Arafat was a powerful figure in the bitter mosaic of the Middle East.

It was a very uneasy time in Lebanon. To simplify what was a very complicated struggle, the country was winding down from two years of civil war between Christian and Muslim militias. At the same time the PLO was also launching rocket attacks into Israel, and Israel was responding in kind.

Although the situation was volatile, I was concentrating so hard on what I was doing that I didn't consider the danger. I was also in good hands in Beirut. To work with me ABC had sent a very talented and nice senior news producer, David Jayne, who had spent considerable time covering the war in Vietnam. Also along on his own assignment was Larry Buckman, an ABC radio correspondent.

We waited for days in the ravaged city to see Arafat. Once a beautiful and prosperous banking center for the entire Middle East, Beirut had been all but destroyed by the violence. The modern buildings in the city's center stood empty, their windows shattered, as did the abandoned resort hotels along the Mediterranean. (The images of Beirut in 2006 following the Israeli air strikes against Hezbollah, another pro-Palestinian terrorist organization, looked eerily similar.) While we waited to see Arafat, the PLO took us on what Moshe Dayan had told me would be a propaganda tour of some of the refugee camps. We filmed the camps, and propaganda or not, there was no denying that the Palestinians lived in squalor. Human waste ran through the streets and alleys, and there was garbage everywhere. Little children cried out, "Revolution until victory!" the PLO's anti-Israeli slogan, as they ran through the litter with wooden rifles, pretending they were shooting Israelis.

Because there was no satellite transmission at that time between Lebanon and the United States, ABC chartered a plane and David Jayne flew the refugee camp footage to Amman, Jordan, where he could transmit it to New York. Then he returned to Beirut.

Our meeting with Arafat took place suddenly one evening when, without any explanation, we were put in a car and driven by a circuitous route through the city—I know we went down several blocks more than once, occasionally in opposite directions—until we stopped in front of a very ordinary apartment building with washing hung out to dry from the windows. That was the PLO's tactic then (and later, Hezbollah's) to blend in with the civilian population.

Arafat was waiting for us in a heavily guarded apartment up three steep flights of stairs. His head was bare when we entered, and I remember being struck by the fact that he was bald. I'd never seen a picture of him without a cap or his kaffiyeh. When it was time to talk he then put on his kaffiyeh.

The long-awaited interview turned out to be as limp as his hand-shake. He played the same game he always did, coming close to saying he would recognize the right of Israel to exist, then backing off. Arafat always held out the possibility of peace in public interviews, but we knew he took it back in private interviews with his own people. Still, we were happy just to have the interview, and the next day David Jayne set off once again to Amman, taking along Larry Buckman, to satellite the footage to New York. I was going to go with them but at the last minute decided not to. It didn't seem to make sense for me to go to Jordan for one day since I needed to be back in New York to appear on the program on Sunday, so David and I agreed we would meet in Paris on Friday for the flight home.

He never arrived. I waited for hours in Paris with increasing anxiety until I received the terrible phone call. The charter flight David and Larry were on had exploded on takeoff from Amman. They had both been killed along with the two Jordanian pilots. Investigations were launched, but no explanations were ever found.

David and Larry were dead. Gone with them was most of the tape of my interview with Arafat, but that was nothing compared to the loss of their lives. I felt it was my fault. They were in Amman because of my interview. I would get the glory. They got death. I met with their families when I got back to New York. They never blamed me, but I could not help but blame myself.

I spoke about Larry's and David's deaths on the news. "Newsmen and women are supposed to be impersonal on the air," I said. "It's part of our code. But I couldn't come back tonight without talking of my two colleagues who died Friday morning in Amman, Jordan." Larry was "young and witty and the father of three little girls," I told the viewers. David, too, was "young, only forty, and had four children. He was the loveliest man, the best and the brightest. It shouldn't have happened. I know it's the business we're in, but I ache for their widows, their children and ourselves at ABC News."

At the end of our interview in Beirut, Arafat had taken the black-and-white kaffiyeh off his head, written on it in Arabic the words "Revolution until victory." He presented it to me as a gift. My plan was to put it near the small, ancient oil lamp Moshe Dayan had given me to represent the enmities in the Middle East. But when, after I got home, Icodel unpacked my suitcase, she did not see the imagery. She saw an ink-stained piece of cloth and put it in the washing machine. That took care of that souvenir. I didn't give a damn. The symbol had been rendered meaningless by the crash.

David's and Larry's deaths, to me, were two more senseless losses in the morass of hatred in the Middle East. I had interviewed at least once many of the warring leaders in the region—Egypt's Anwar Sadat, Israel's Golda Meir, Moshe Dayan, Menachem Begin, and then the PLO's Arafat. The more interviews I did, the more hopeless things seemed to me.

Until November 1977.

I was in Kansas City, talking with Dolly Parton for a *Barbara Walters Special*, when, during an interview with Walter Cronkite, President Sadat stunned the world by announcing that he was willing to go to Jerusalem on a peace mission. All he needed was a formal invitation from Prime Minister Begin to address the Knesset, the Israeli parliament. The invitation was quickly forthcoming from Begin after CBS News reporters corralled him in a hotel in Tel Aviv and set up an interview with him in a hotel room. Cronkite skillfully knitted the two interviews together, making it appear as if the president of Egypt and the prime minister of Israel were talking to each other—a historical first in itself—and the networks' race to Jerusalem was on.

(Actually, earlier that same day, it was Peter Jennings, ABC's chief foreign correspondent, whom Sadat had first told off-camera about his willingness to go to Jerusalem for peace. It would have been Peter's historic story if he'd had a camera crew with him, but he didn't. So he lost the breaking news to CBS and Cronkite.)

Peter took another blow when Roone designated me ABC's lead reporter on Sadat's journey to Jerusalem. Peter's objection was valid— he had covered the Middle East for a long time. Roone did it, he later said, because of my strong relationship with both Sadat and Begin. Peter held this against me for years. I didn't blame him, but I didn't turn down the assignment. Sadat's sudden announcement that he was going to Jerusalem on November 19, just five days after Begin extended his invitation, set us all scrambling.

I flew to Tel Aviv on November 18 on the same flight as NBC's anchor, John Chancellor, both of us wondering where Cronkite was. I learned the answer late that night, after interviewing Moshe Dayan on the prospect of peace with his former and formidable enemy. Exhausted after the long flight and the interview, I was sound asleep in my hotel room when the phone rang. "Cronkite's in Cairo," Roone announced from New York. "He's got a seat on Sadat's plane tomorrow to Tel Aviv. Chancellor may be on that plane, too. Get on that plane."

Right. I couldn't call the Egyptians I knew in Cairo because there was no direct line between Egypt and Israel, the country that didn't exist for them. So I got out my phone book and called Egypt's ambassador to the United States, Ashraf Ghorbal, at his home in Washington. God knows what time it was, but I had to get a seat on Sadat's plane. I pleaded with the ambassador, and he said he would try but could give me no guarantees. Two hours later he came through. "You will be welcome on President Sadat's plane," he said.

But how to get to Cairo? There were no direct flights between Egypt and Israel, remember. I could take an Israeli plane to Cyprus and then transfer to a Cypriot flight to Egypt, but that wouldn't get me there in time to make Sadat's plane. Fortunately we heard about a French jet that CBS had chartered to fly in their satellite equipment from Paris to Tel Aviv. We paid the French pilots to fly me to Egypt. We would stop very briefly in Cyprus and take off again.

I grabbed our film crew and off we flew. Once in the air, I leaned my head against the window and fell asleep, having not had that luxury in close to twenty-four hours. I woke with a start to see the pyramids directly below us. I thought I was dreaming, but it turned out the Egyptians had not made us stop in Cyprus. Amazingly the pilots got permission to fly nonstop from Tel Aviv to Cairo, a matter of just over an hour. We were the first civilian plane to make this direct trip to Egypt since the creation of Israel in 1948. Historic, but at the time people had more important things to think about.

We landed in an airport that was almost empty. Security was very tight in light of Arab resistance to Sadat's solo journey for peace. I bolted out of our plane and ran toward the main terminal. And there, with incredulous looks on their faces, were John Chancellor and Walter Cronkite. As Cronkite later recalled on the PBS program *American Masters:* "I was boarding the plane in Cairo when a little private plane landed on the field and she hopped out of it and ran across the field like a football player going into the play, holding her hand up—wait, wait, wait for me." The two news anchors were not overjoyed to see me. "I couldn't have been unhappier," Walter confessed. As for me, I couldn't have been more thrilled that I'd made the flight, and in short order we were in the air again, this time to pick up Sadat at his weekend retreat in Ismailia.

Going up against Chancellor and Cronkite was a scary prospect. But, there we were, ABC, NBC, and CBS, in one plane. (The only other American journalist on board was Wilton Wynn from *Time*.) We landed near the town of Ismailia, and there was Sadat, beaming and meticulously dressed in a navy blue suit. He walked slowly along a red carpet past an Egyptian honor guard and his major ministers. (His foreign minister and former friend Ismail Fahmy was not among them. Calling Sadat a traitor, he had resigned in protest of this visit to Israel. Sadat did not seem perturbed.) As he got close to us, I reached out with my microphone and asked, "Mr. President, what are your feelings at this moment?"

I did not get the exclusive, newsworthy sound bite I'd wanted to flash home. "Bar-ba-ra," Sadat exclaimed in his booming voice. "So you made the plane." I laughed, but before I could repeat my question, Sadat turned to Cronkite and asked, just as loudly, "Walter, what do you think of Bar-*ba*-ra making the plane?"

"Well, Mr. President," Walter said dryly. "It's not exactly what I had in mind."

When we were airborne again Sadat invited the three of us into his private cabin for a brief interview. We drew straws en route to see who would get the first question. That seemed very important at the time, but now I can't remember who won, so I suspect it wasn't me. But I had an ace up my sleeve.

Before we entered the cabin, I'd written a question on a slip of paper. "Mr. President, would you agree to do an interview with me after you speak at the Knesset?" To make the request easy to answer, I'd put four boxes at the bottom of the page, reading "Yes"; "No"; "Alone"; "With PM Begin." As we left the cabin, I slipped the note to one of his aides.

ABC was broadcasting live President Sadat's history-making arrival on Israeli soil and as soon as the plane landed, I ran across the tarmac to find Peter Jennings and the ABC setup at the airport. I didn't even have time to look at the note Sadat's aide had returned to me as we landed. I was probably still panting when I went on the air with Peter to describe the plane flight from Egypt and the interview we'd had with Sadat. Only then did I look at the note I'd stuffed in my bag: "Yes," Sadat had checked. And "Alone." It would have been even better if he'd agreed to be interviewed with Begin, but no matter—I'd gotten an exclusive with the man of the hour! (I lost the piece of paper, of course. I lose everything.) The only person I told was my producer, Justin Friedland, who then had to set up the secret interview without my competitors knowing about it. If the word got out, I was afraid that Sadat would have to include them.

With the interview sewed up, I relaxed for a tiny moment to take in the extraordinary scene at the airport. There were hundreds of people waving Israeli and Egyptian flags. I wondered how the Israelis had managed to get so many Egyptian flags so quickly. And how the Israeli army band had gotten the music and learned the Egyptian national anthem. But most of all I remember all of Sadat's former enemies lined up to greet him—Menachem Begin, Golda Meir, Moshe Dayan, Ariel Sharon, Yitzhak Rabin. It was almost too much to comprehend.

(It was certainly too much for the viewers back home who had tuned in to ABC to watch the Ohio State vs. Michigan football game. Instead of seeing the kickoff on their screens, the football fans saw Sadat's dramatic arrival in Israel. They were furious and jammed the ABC telephone lines to complain. After seven minutes ABC went back to the football game, to the fans' great relief. To hell with history.)

Justin and I drove from Tel Aviv to Jerusalem. What a sight! All along the road were people cheering, small children waving Israeli and Egyptian flags. The impossible had happened. The enemy had come to Israel. We all felt optimistic. If Sadat was meeting with Begin, could peace be far behind? It was one of the most glorious days I had ever experienced.

Arriving in Jerusalem, I went directly to an interview I'd arranged with Prime Minister Begin. The prime minister's residence was small and modest. Begin and his wife, Aliza, whom by now I knew quite well, greeted me, and the prime minister took me into his study. It was a very personal room with photos of his family all around. I had expected Begin to talk of Sadat and the triumph of this day. Instead, with great emotion, he talked of the Holocaust and the pictures of his relatives who had died in the concentration camps. Those were the thoughts uppermost in his mind after meeting Anwar Sadat.

After the interview Begin seemed energized. He had a busy schedule the next day, including following Sadat in addressing the Knesset, but he was obviously too excited to go to bed. He still hadn't prepared his remarks to the Israeli parliament. He never wrote anything in advance, he told me. Instead he asked his faithful aide, Yehiel Kadishai, for a Bible to look up some references for the address. He was still talking long after midnight, when Kadishai said, "Mr. Prime Minister, for all our sakes, please go to bed."

Begin left, but like a child who just wouldn't go to bed, he popped out again. "Barbara," he said, "I forgot to tell you something. On the ride from the airport I said to President Sadat, 'For the sake of our good friend Barbara, would you do the interview tomorrow with me together?' And Barbara, Sadat said yes. So we do it in the Knesset, when we're finished speaking."

Richard Nixon may have gotten me an interview with Prince Philip, but Begin had gotten me the most important interview of my career. "Thank you, Prime Minister," I said. "Thank you so much." And off he went to bed.

The next day Justin had a small room off the main chamber of the Knesset all set up for the joint interview. There was no football game that day, so ABC broadcast live Sadat's extraordinary address to the Israeli Knesset and Begin's speech as well. Shortly afterward the two leaders arrived at the room to meet me amidst a great commotion of Israeli security guards and Egyptian soldiers, followed by a few incredulous members of the Israeli press.

I had stayed up most of the night preparing questions for this first-ever joint interview with the leaders of Israel and Egypt. I talked with them for forty minutes—two tape cassettes' worth in TV time—during which the difficulties on the road to a finalized peace quickly emerged. Both men expressed their admiration and even liking for each other, but the devil of an actual peace agreement was in the details. Sadat had said in his address to the Knesset that although everything was negotiable, the Arab people would not concede one inch of occupied land. And he reiterated his position when I asked him whether he would give up any of that land for peace.

"Not at all," he said. "Not at all."

"Well, I'm afraid I don't understand," I said. "If you will not give up any of the land, if none of it is negotiable, then what will you be trying?"

"We can sit together, we can talk; no one knows what will happen in the next week or so."

I pressed on until Sadat said, "Barbara, politics can't be conducted like this."

"I have to keep trying," I said to him.

I then tried a lighter question and asked President Sadat if he planned to invite Prime Minister Begin to Cairo.

"I am planning to invite him to Sinai," Sadat replied with a mischievous smile. Sinai was, of course, still occupied by the Israelis.

"Well," Begin shot back. "I invite you." And they both laughed.

We covered other topics as well, including the sensitive subject of a possible Palestinian state. Begin said very firmly, "My position is no." We also talked about Sadat's visit earlier in the day to the Holocaust Memorial at Yad Vashem. "I was very moved," he said. "I never thought it reached to such an extent like I saw today." I also asked Sadat, remembering other Egyptians who considered him a traitor, if he was at all concerned for his physical safety.

"Why should I be? I will not be taken one minute before God wants it," he replied. Four years later, as a result of this quest for peace, he would be assassinated.

What some American people didn't understand then, and may still not, was the significance of Egypt's place in the Middle East, and why Sadat's unilateral quest for peace with Israel had drawn such condemnation from the other Arab leaders, including King Hussein of Jordan. The answer was in the numbers—Egypt had two-thirds of the Arab population in the Middle East, counting the Sudan, and by far the greatest military capability. What Egypt did greatly affected all the other Arab countries in the region.

"Is it true that there cannot be war or peace in the Arab world without Egypt?" I asked Sadat.

"This is a fact," he replied. "War or peace is decided in Egypt because we are forty million people."

I was very proud of this interview. It made headlines around the world the next day—and started a firestorm at CBS.

As soon as my interview with Begin and Sadat ended, Justin grabbed the tape cassettes and rushed to the Israeli Television Broadcast Center to edit the conversation and satellite it to New York. The word quickly spread, prompting an Israeli driver for CBS to run to his producers and say: "ABC has Sadat and Begin!" And the chase was on.

CBS staffers frantically tracked down the two leaders and pleaded with them to do another interview, this time with Walter Cronkite. CBS News was so determined to beat the upstart, third-place ABC News, not to mention the possibility that I might personally upstage the much more authoritative Cronkite, that they instantly transmitted Cronkite's entire unedited interview back to New York and directly onto *60 Minutes*. That turned out to be a mistake. Not only did ABC get my interview on the air seconds before CBS ran Cronkite's, but at the end of his interview Cronkite is clearly heard saying: "Did Barbara get anything I didn't get?"

I returned to New York, having slept the entire way home in a "nest" the El Al steward made for me on the floor, to find my status greatly improved in the news division. The back-to-back interviews with Castro and Arafat, followed by the interview with Sadat and Begin, had put me back on the map as a serious journalist. It didn't hurt that I'd gone head-to-head with Chancellor and Cronkite, the top men in broadcast journalism at the time, and, you should excuse the expression, beaten the pants off them. From that time on I was more or less accepted as a member of the old boys' club.

But I had unfinished business. I had a major plan in mind. At the end of my interview with Begin and Sadat, I had asked them if their respective ambassadors in Washington "could at least now meet and talk, which they've never done before?" Sadat thought for a minute and then replied, "Why not? I say, today we are ready." Begin then also agreed. "I hope that starting from tomorrow the ambassadors of Egypt and Israel all over the world will give common interviews and meet with journalists and express their opinions."

I immediately phoned Simcha Dinitz, the Israeli ambassador to the United States, and his Egyptian counterpart, Ambassador Ghorbal, to invite them to do a joint interview with me on *Issues and Answers* when I returned home. Dinitz agreed but Ghorbal refused. He didn't want their first exchange to take place publicly on television. So instead I invited them to an off-the-record dinner party, which they both accepted. This was, believe me, a major event. Even today the Egyptian and Israeli ambassadors are rarely at the same dinner.

I hosted the dinner, a coming-out party of sorts, at the Madison Hotel in Washington just a few weeks after I'd returned from Israel. Though both diplomats were assigned to the United States and both lived in Washington, they had never met. They couldn't, for Egypt and Israel were still technically at war and had been, actively at times, since 1948.

What a euphoric time it was for all of us. I carefully planned the party. Among the guests were Katharine Graham, Ben Bradlee, and Sally Quinn; the humorist Art Buchwald; President Carter's close adviser Hamilton Jordan; Carter's press secretary, Jody Powell; Carter's national security advisor, Zbigniew Brzezinski; the outgoing secretary of state, Henry Kissinger; and my old friend Bill Safire, by then a columnist at the *New York Times*. I also asked Sam Donaldson, our incomparable White House correspondent, Peter Jennings, and about thirty others.

All eyes were on the two ambassadors, who stood and chatted for the first time during predinner cocktails. They later recalled that their first exchanges were meaningless pleasantries. "We even discussed the weather," Ambassador Dinitz said. "But then we talked more substance, and it was a good feeling."

Luckily Bill Safire took notes that evening, because I never would have remembered exactly what their toasts were to each other during the dinner. Ambassador Dinitz praised Ambassador Ghorbal "for his ability and professionalism—and sometimes I wasn't too happy about that," and then went on to recall the smiling faces of the children he had watched on television welcoming President Sadat to Israel. "It is incumbent on us to give them a reason for their smile," he said.

Ambassador Ghorbal responded in kind. "For the first time, Ambassador Dinitz has spoken for both Israel and Egypt," he said, and went on to pledge his government's commitment to a full, comprehensive settlement "and not leave it to the next generation." He then raised his glass to the prospect of peace, to the ambassador of Israel, and to President Carter.

The party was a great success. As Henry Kissinger said in his brief and amusing remarks, "I have not addressed such a distinguished audience since dining alone in the Hall of Mirrors," referring to the hall in the Palace of Versailles outside Paris, where the treaty was signed ending World War I.

Everything at the party was supposed to be off-the-record, but the next day, to my horror, I read an item in the gossip column in the *Washington Star* about the incomprehensible behavior of Hamilton Jordan at the party. The president's soon-to-be chief of staff had evidently had too much to drink and insulted his dinner partner, Amal Ghorbal, the Egyptian ambassador's wife, by staring down the front of her décolletage and announcing, "I've always wanted to see the pyramids."

I nearly fainted when I read it. Sam Donaldson was at the table and was asked if it happened. He wouldn't admit it publicly, but he told me privately it had. I had been so busy being a hostess that, perhaps luckily, I didn't see or hear any of this. But the sorry story made the rounds of the newspapers, including the *Washington Post* and the *New York Times*, leading Bill Safire to feel free to write about the more gracious part of the evening in his *New York Times* column. He titled it "Barbara's Dinner Party," and it was a very nice piece that mercifully left out the Hamilton Jordan story. Even more mercifully, Ambassador Ghorbal did not seem upset.

For all the hopes for peace at the time and the feelings of goodwill between the Israelis and the Egyptians in 1977, the peace talks didn't progress until Jimmy Carter essentially locked up Begin, Sadat, and their respective delegations from Israel and Egypt at Camp David in September 1978. I was assigned to cover this. A news blackout was imposed on the press, leaving us hanging around the outside of the presidential retreat (we weren't allowed inside), waiting for any news droppings and chasing down rumors. One of the most persistent was that Jordan's King Hussein was about to fly to Washington from London to join the talks. I can't tell you how many times I was told, "Jordan's coming in." The rumor was so persistent that several people began reporting it as the truth. I had King Hussein's private phone number in London where he was staying, and when I, alone, got him on the phone, he denied categorically that he was heading to the United States. (Hussein in fact was dead set against Sadat making a separate peace with Israel.) Further, he told me that no one from the White House had even been in touch with him. So I went on the air and reported that, quoting King Hussein, and the next day someone else would again report that he was coming to Camp David.

It made me very uneasy. I'd spoken to the only person who knew whether or not he was coming to Washington—the king himself—and I believed him. Yet something inside me wondered whether the print reporters knew something I didn't. I was struck once again by the power of the printed word. It reminded me of my own mother believing the lies the papers printed about me when I started at ABC. But Hussein, as he had told me, did not come to Camp David. My reporting was correct. Sadat himself almost left, frustrated with his supposed partners for peace. Jimmy Carter had to keep intervening between the two delegations until finally, after thirteen days (and setting aside the thorny issue of Jerusalem), they reached an agreement. On September 17, 1978, Sadat and Begin, shepherded by Jimmy Carter, signed the Camp David Peace Accords at the White House.

This again was a huge story, and I hoped to have another joint interview with the two leaders. Begin said yes, but Sadat said no. His representatives would not say why. Therefore the next day I interviewed each in his respective embassy. I remember the interviews clearly, mostly because many of the questions I asked them were deliberately identical. One was about the status of Jerusalem, to which Begin replied that 99 percent of Jews worldwide considered Jerusalem the capital of Israel, while Sadat said that seven hundred million Muslims and Arabs would disagree. Another question was about Israeli settlements in what the Palestinians considered their land in Gaza and the West Bank. Begin said he considered the settlements essential to the security of Israel, while Sadat insisted that Israel had no claim of sovereignty over either.

It is stunning to review those questions today and realize that although Israel has given up its settlements in Gaza, there is still no resolution on the West Bank or Jerusalem. At the time of Camp David, however, it truly seemed as if Israel and Egypt were going to work out their differences and achieve a lasting peace in the Middle East acceptable to the Palestinians and the other Arab countries. Thirty years later peace remains elusive.

In the historic spirit of the moment, I did something I'd never done before and haven't since. At the end of my respective interviews, I asked both Begin and Sadat to autograph my copy of the questions I'd put to them. "To Barbara, with admiration," Begin wrote. "Best wishes," Sadat wrote, followed by something in Arabic, then the word "Peace." I had the questions framed and they hang still on that long wall in my apartment. (Yes, it is a very long wall.) They are dated September 18, 1978. I finally remembered to keep something.

For all the celebration, the Camp David Peace Accords were not a final peace treaty. They were merely the framework for one. Egypt and Israel were supposed to work out the remaining issues within these guidelines by the end of 1978. Of course they didn't.

I'm going to fast-forward now to March 1979, when I made another seminal trip to the Middle East. Because the Egyptians and the Israelis had failed to resolve the differences between them, Jimmy Carter decided to intervene again by commuting between Sadat in Egypt and Begin in Israel to try to bring the peace process to closure. A large press corps, including me, went with him.

We started in Cairo, where Carter was negotiating privately with Sadat. Once again we were in a news blackout. Nothing is more frustrating to a reporter—and there was a huge contingent of us, 194 journalists and technicians—angling for the smallest scrap of information. ABC alone sent 13 correspondents, 14 producers, 24 technicians, 2 editors, 2 unit managers, and almost seven thousand pounds of equipment to cover the peace agreement—if it ever happened.

I interviewed Jehan Sadat. She wouldn't comment on the talks. I interviewed Jody Powell, who said, "Nothing is happening." It was a disappointing stalemate. I worked the phones, which is an often insurmountable challenge in Egypt. I was scheduled to make several on-air live reports a day on the most important news story in the world, and all I could report was that I had nothing to report. But nobody else did either, although I worried constantly about Cronkite and Chancellor.

After three no-news days in Cairo and a side trip to Alexandria, we all flew to Jerusalem where Carter was to meet with Begin in the King David Hotel. We were jammed behind security guards at the hotel entrance, when I saw the arrival of another Israeli friend, Defense Minister Ezer Weizman. "Mr. Minister," I yelled at him. "Nobody will say anything. Please give me two minutes!"

Ezer walked toward me, and I thought I was finally going to get something to report, but no. "Two minutes I will gladly give you, but like this, without words," he said, giving me a big hug. Thanks but no thanks.

To lift our collective spirits, several of us decided to give Sam Donaldson, my very good pal, a surprise forty-fifth-birthday party. Sam loves to tell the story of how I lured him to the party by inviting him to my room—alone. Whether or not he really means it, Sam insists that he thought I was inviting him to a tryst and went into a schoolboy tizzy of picking just the right red tie. (He always wears a red tie.) Fifty people gathered in my room, including Cronkite, Dan Rather, Chancellor, and Jody Powell. When Sam knocked on the door, we all screamed, "Surprise!" No tryst, but Sam had a very good time anyway, especially when the belly dancer arrived.

Sam's surprise party was the highlight of the no-news peace offensive that week. Many of the White House press corps returned to Washington, calling Carter's peace mission a complete failure. Cronkite stayed behind, as did Chancellor. So did I, because I had lined up an interview with Prime Minister Begin. I was going to ask him why the mission had fallen apart, whose fault it was, and so on. I then planned to go to Cairo to ask the same questions of Sadat.

This is where it finally became interesting.

My interview with Begin was scheduled for 4:00 p.m. at his home in Jerusalem. We were there and ready to go, but there was a complication. Carter had unexpectedly returned to Cairo the day before to talk further with Sadat—and twenty-four hours later they were still talking. Nothing seemed to be conclusive, but we didn't want to do our postmortem with Begin until Carter officially gave up and was on his way home.

We managed to finagle an extra hour from Begin, during which Aliza Begin served us all orange drinks and chocolates, then more orange drinks and more chocolates, until Begin finally said, "Enough." We sat down to start the interview, in which we thought he was going to blame Sadat for the peace effort's collapse, when the phone rang. Begin took the call in the kitchen. It was Carter calling from the Cairo airport.

The smile on Begin's face was a yard wide when he came back into the living room. "I can tell you that the president gave me good news," he said. "But that's all I can tell you."

We knew we were at the center of a big story, but we didn't know what it was. We were frantic. Bob Frye, my producer, took his walkie-talkie and contacted the ABC bureau in Jerusalem. He was told that

Carter had read a statement to the press at the airport that was being transmitted to New York. "Get it from New York and read it to us," Frye told the bureau. So there we all were, including Prime Minister Begin, huddled around the walkie-talkie listening to Carter's statement: "Sadat has agreed to"—and the walkie-talkie went dead.

We grabbed Begin's phone and called New York. My assistant on this trip, Shirley Craig, took down the wording of Carter's announcement in shorthand, then knelt beside Begin to read it to him. He listened silently as Shirley read, occasionally nodding his head in agreement. It was an unbelievable moment.

We immediately started the interview with Begin. He didn't yet know the details of the agreement, so we focused on his feelings. Begin was as animated as I'd ever seen him, and although he tried to be calm and statesmanlike, it was obvious he was thrilled. It wasn't a very long interview—he had to get to his office—but it was a portrait of peace in the making. Hooray! We had a scoop.

As soon as I finished I flew to Cairo, through Cyprus this time, to get the other side of the portrait of peace. There my luck ran out.

It was almost 11:00 p.m. when we finally got to Sadat's residence in Giza, overlooking the Nile. I tried to persuade a security guard to take him a message that we wanted to have a few words with him, but the guard refused. So we were reduced (no kidding) to throwing pebbles at Sadat's windows, trying to get his attention. Why we weren't arrested I can't imagine, but finally another guard consented to take a note from me to Sadat. The answer came back that he would not see us then but would be pleased to see me when he came to Washington to sign the final peace treaty.

That in itself was news. So at 2:00 in the morning I did a stand-up report outside Sadat's house, announcing that the Egyptian president would be going to Washington for the official signing of the peace treaty. I was so tired that we had to do at least six takes. We were all delirious by then and grateful for a one-bedroom suite, the only hotel room available. Four of us piled into that one room and slept on the twin beds—Shirley, Bob Frye, and a reporter from *TV Guide*, John Weisman, who was doing a story on how television was covering the Sadat visit. He couldn't get a room, so we said, "Join us." I remember thinking that I hadn't washed my hair in a week, so while they slept I showered and washed my hair with Egyptian soap. The funny things that stay in your mind. Finally, on March 16, 1979, we returned to New York.

It is said that journalists have to be objective and fair, and I like to think we are. But there is no doubt that the television networks were part of the peace process. During this whole Carter, Begin, and Sadat shuttle, television was able to run with the story much faster than the newspapers and way ahead of the newsmagazines. The print journalists were not happy. The new and not-very-complimentary phrase they used was "video diplomacy," starting with Cronkite's doctored split-screen interviews with Sadat and Begin and continuing through my interview with the two leaders at the Knesset and, later on, with Begin in Jerusalem.

But like it or not, television had become the dominant purveyor of news by the late seventies and was central to the story in the Middle East. As John Weisman later wrote in *TV Guide*: "From the very beginning, from Anwar el-Sadat's historic trip to Jerusalem in November, 1977, the story was a TV story. Indeed, if Vietnam had been the world's first TV war, the Israeli-Egyptian agreement was the world's first television peace."

Golda Meir's observation was more cryptic. "I'm not sure in the end whether Begin and Sadat will get the Nobel," she said. "But for certain, both should get the Oscar."

They did indeed get the Nobel Peace Prize. And on March 26, 1979, Anwar Sadat and Menachem Begin finally signed the formal Egyptian-Israeli Peace Treaty in an elaborate ceremony on the South Lawn of the White House. I went as a guest of Senator John Warner. Finally I wasn't working and could savor the moment, but not for long.

I had yet another interview lined up with President Sadat at the Egyptian embassy at 4:30. This was a little nerve-racking in that we had to get the interview taped and edited in time to make the seven o'clock broadcast. We made it by seconds, but there was little joy at the Egyptian Embassy. Sadat's courageous act was already being condemned throughout the Arab world. The Arab League would shortly suspend Egypt's membership, and the leaders of Egypt's former Arab allies would sever diplomatic ties with the country.

The atmosphere was very different in the Israeli camp when I interviewed Begin later that night. I remember the festive celebration in Begin's hotel suite, where he and his staff were singing Hebrew folk songs.

What a golden time it was, full of hope and heroes and the promise of peace.

I would stay in touch with both Sadat and Begin. I spoke individually to them with some frequency, sent them cards on all the appropriate occasions, and did several more interviews with each of them. But events moved on. Sometimes tragically.

In October 1981 Anwar Sadat was shot at a military parade in Cairo by Muslim extremists who had infiltrated the army. The assailants considered Sadat a traitor. I was stunned and grief stricken when I heard the news. ABC asked me to help to find out about Sadat. Had he survived? Was he dead? I called the hospital in Cairo and managed to talk to one of his aides. I knew the answer when he told me that Jehan Sadat had left the hospital. She would never have left her husband's side if he were still alive. Eight hours later the Egyptians officially confirmed his death.

Peter Jennings and I covered Sadat's funeral in Cairo. Though dignitaries from the Arab countries were conspicuously absent, many other leaders came, including Menachem Begin and three former U.S. presidents—Jimmy Carter, Gerald Ford, and Richard Nixon. Instead of the streets of Cairo being lined with mourners, they were empty and eerily quiet. Peter and I couldn't decide whether people had stayed home because they were afraid or because they had turned against Sadat. Whatever the reason, it made for the strangest, saddest funeral procession.

Afterward I went to President Sadat's house, as a friend, not a reporter, to offer my condolences to Jehan Sadat. We embraced, and then sat together and shared our memories of her husband. "You know, you were the only one I was ever jealous of because Anwar liked you so much," she told me with a smile. (What a lovely compliment from a lovely woman who remains my friend to this day.)

Mrs. Sadat talked movingly about her husband in an interview with me three months later. She had asked him to wear a bulletproof vest to the parade, but he refused. "When God is ready to take me, he'll take me," he had said to her. "Okay," she'd replied, "but you don't have to help."

He'd also had a premonition of his death. Their son, Gamal, was leaving on a trip to the United States a few days before the military parade, and after his father said good-bye to him, he called him back. "Gamal," he said. "You must take care of your mother." Jehan told me this with tears in her eyes. "My husband knew," she said. "He knew."

I felt depressed and discouraged when I flew home from the funeral. Another loss, another senseless death. I had no idea that I'd be back in the Middle East just a week later to attend yet another funeral, this one of my friend Moshe Dayan. Moshe had been sick for a long time with colon cancer and was even losing sight in his one remaining eye. The cause of his death was given as a massive heart attack. Personally I think the cause of his death was his life.

He had been denounced in Israel for his failure as minister of defense to anticipate the 1973 Yom Kippur War. Many Israelis had never forgiven him—until his funeral. Thousands of people now turned out to pay their final respects and file past his coffin. To Dayan's widow, Raquel, they were hypocrites. "Where were they all when he needed them?" she said bitterly to me.

I was very close to Raquel and even lent her a black dress to wear to the funeral. (She didn't have a proper one in her closet.) When the streams of people paying condolences left her house after the burial, I and a friend from America, Lola Finkelstein, helped tidy up and wash the dishes. My heart ached for Raquel and was heavy for myself as well. Moshe and I used to make the rounds of antiquity dealers in New York when he came to give lectures. He spent whatever extra money he had on ancient artifacts and had a remarkable collection at his home in Israel. Moshe Dayan was a man far ahead of his time. He was convinced that the only way to solve the Palestinian problem peacefully was to grant them autonomy, a controversial position then. He was one of Israel's chief negotiators with the Egyptians at Camp David in 1977. He was also the author of several history books, including one on the Bible. Dayan was loved and hated, but he never cared what others thought of him. Like Sadat, he had an enormous personality, great humor, and charm when it suited him. He was an extraordinary general and totally original. I knew no one quite like him, and I am grateful that I got to know him as a friend.

Of the three people I admired most in the Middle East, only Menachem Begin was then still alive, but our cordial relationship eroded in 1982 during an interview in which I questioned him pointedly about the wisdom of Israel's invasion and subsequent occupation of southern Lebanon. Although Begin was being roundly criticized in both the Arab and Western press, and his popularity had dropped sharply in Israel, he obviously hadn't expected such criticism from me. After the interview he looked straight at me and said, "And you, too, Barbara?" He was very angry and never really forgave me for asking. To Begin, I was now just one more adversarial reporter.

After Sadat and Dayan died the chapter of my life in the Middle East more or less came to a close. I would interview Yasir Arafat again, this time in Cuba at a conference of nonaligned nations, and I would interview other Arab leaders: Jordan's King Hussein, Libya's Colonel Mu'ammar al-Qaddafi, more recently, Hussein's heir, King Abdullah of Jordan, and another Abdullah, the king of Saudi Arabia. But nothing would ever come close to recapturing the excitement of covering the peace process between Egypt and Israel in the midseventies and of meeting and knowing the great men of that time.

That is not to say there was no more excitement in my life. It just moved to a different hemisphere.

Exit Harry, Enter Hugh

THE OTHER QUESTION I am most often asked is whether being a woman in what was, and still is to a degree, such a predominantly male profession has been a hindrance or a help? The answer, of course, is both. On the negative side there were the Frank McGees and the Harry Reasoners, who were threatened by the thought of a woman as their professional equal. On the positive side there have been plenty of men and women who had no concerns whether it was a man or a woman interviewing them.

That is usually the case, I have found, even in countries like Saudi Arabia, where women are so severely discriminated against. In 2005 King Abdullah chose me from among all the American journalists who had requested to do the first interview with him after he inherited the throne. The king evidently had no trouble being questioned by a woman, and furthermore by a woman whose head was only partially covered. It may be that Arab leaders welcome the modern image of them it projects. Or it might be as simple as their recognizing that Western female reporters have different customs and therefore not expecting them to adhere to the same strictures as their own female citizens.

There are other times when being a woman can be an advantage. Sex rears its happy little head, and a sought-after male subject chooses you to do the interview in the hope that somewhere along the line, the romantic side—or at least the flirtatious side—will surpass the professional.

Though, as I've said, Fidel Castro never made the slightest pass at me, I felt he liked me. Did he give me more of his time than he might have given a male journalist? Possibly. But there was no "possibly" about the intentions of the Panamanian dictator, Gen. Omar Torrijos, whom I interviewed in 1978. He saw me, liked me, and decided to give me special access. (Listen, folks, it sometimes works the other way. Nancy Reagan, for example, had a crush on, and friendship with, Mike Wallace and saved several of her post–White House interviews for him.) Considering that Torrijos's attraction to me worked to my advantage, it was fine with me.

I was in Panama in April 1978 because the U.S. Senate was about to vote on whether to ratify a treaty negotiated by Jimmy Carter and Torrijos that would transfer the sovereignty and eventual control of the Panama Canal to the Panamanians. This was a very controversial issue at the time—and had the potential for danger. I had wanted to bring my assistant, Mary Hornickel, with me but my producer, again Justin Friedland, said no, it wasn't safe. If the Senate vote went against the return of the canal, Americans were not going to be very popular in Panama, and if we had to get out of the country in a hurry, he didn't want to have to worry about anyone but the smallest possible crew. So Justin and I went alone with one cameraman, a sound technician, and an ABC photographer.

General Torrijos, whose formal titles included "Maximum Leader of the Panamanian Revolution" and "Supreme Chief of Government," was a charismatic man with chiseled features that spoke of his Indian ancestry. He was said to have "the walk of the hunter," meaning that he could come upon you silently from behind without your knowing it.

The future of the Panama Canal was the top story of the time. Everyone wanted to hear from Torrijos. Roone Arledge had dispatched me to try to get him to do an exclusive interview. It was an important assignment, but I was conflicted about being away from New York at what was a pivotal time for me and for ABC News.

Roone was about to alter the face of the news radically. It was obvious that Harry and I were not going to make it as dual anchors. Something had to be done to relieve us of our mutual discomfort, which was getting closer to agony. So Roone's very creative solution was to abandon the idea of two anchors or even one sitting behind a desk. Instead, he said, the position of a sole anchor was dead. (It was not, but his proposal then seemed to placate the naysayers.) He was going to have not one, not two, but *three* anchors to bring the news from their separate locations. He would have as the primary anchor in Washington the very experienced and professional Frank Reynolds and in Chicago he would have Max Robinson, the first African American network news anchor.

The new boy in town, Peter Jennings, would be based in London. The name of the broadcast would be changed to *World News Tonight*.

As for Harry Reasoner, he was going back to CBS. After much deliberation, Roone had decided that I had a greater future at ABC than Harry did, so he released him from his contract. Roone was betting that I would earn my salary and, although some in the company felt he was making a mistake, Roone had his own vision—and that vision included me. He gave me a new title, not just "roving anchor" but "chief correspondent for special events," with the authority and, he hoped, the ability to travel the world and land the big newsmaker interviews. Roone was trying to work out the timing of this important announcement about the changes in ABC News, and I was very nervous about exactly how this would affect me. In the meantime Roone sent me off to Panama.

When I arrived I immediately sought out Torrijos's advisers and pressed my case that, as with Fidel Castro, Sadat, and Begin, I would be best able to bring the most attention to their general and his cause. They agreed and promised a brief interview before the Senate vote. That was the best they could do. At the moment Torrijos was on the resort island of Contadora, where he went to relax and where, by the way, the deposed shah of Iran was brought a year later for temporary refuge after he was forced into exile.

I was told to be ready at 7:00 a.m. to fly to the island in Torrijos's private helicopter. I landed slightly flustered from lack of sleep and with bloodshot eyes. But Torrijos didn't seem to care, and although he didn't speak a word of English and I speak no Spanish, we obviously got through to each other in more ways than one. In the interview the general warned Congress that he would not take lightly a defeat of the proposal to return the canal to Panama. But the big question was, What would he do if the vote did *not* go his way? Torrijos would not tell me. The U.S. Senate vote on the canal was scheduled for the next day, April 18, and because Torrijos was so, shall we say, taken with me, I asked him then and there for a second interview right after the vote. He agreed.

We were certainly off to a good start. There were hundreds of journalists in Panama all vying for Torrijos's exclusive attention, and we'd gotten it. Justin and I felt quite smug as we choppered back to the mainland. Our smugness didn't last.

We waited all the next day for our promised interview with the general. Nothing. The Senate debate was dragging on and on, postponing the vote, and our exclusive interview. The word finally came from one of the general's aides that he'd changed his mind and there would be no interview. Swell. That left me with nothing for the evening news, so we did the next best thing. We did a stand-up in front of the house where it was thought Torrijos was listening on the radio to the debate.

That's where the adventure began.

A uniformed man suddenly appeared. "The general wants you to join him in the house," he directed.

I looked at Justin. "Go," he said. "I'll feed this piece back to New York and catch up with you."

Immediately I was escorted past an incredulous and unhappy group of correspondents from NBC and CBS into the house to spend the rest of the day and most of the evening in the company of General Torrijos.

There were no other women in the house. Only I and Torrijos's inner circle of military aides and friends. They were all listening to the debate in Washington. The general's interpreter was translating for him, and it occurred to me that if the vote went against Panama, Torrijos might not be very pleased with his now-favored American correspondent. What might he do with me? Hold me hostage? Not a happy thought. But not a crazy one. I was by now fervently hoping that the vote would favor the occupants of the room, especially the general, who made sure that I was by his side. We were inseparable through the rest of the debate and then on the ride to the Panamanian television broadcast center, where he was going to monitor the actual vote.

I searched for Justin in the crowd outside the broadcast center, and to my relief saw him waving at me. I also saw the amazed faces of reporters from around the world who were patiently waiting for a simple statement from Torrijos, while I was being firmly escorted inside the building by the general himself. We went into a conference room where, again, I was the only woman. The vote was being broadcast in Spanish by Panama radio. Torrijos and his men hung on every number. Most of the time they cheered, so I knew the vote was going as they had hoped. Their cheers broke into wild applause when the result was announced. The canal would be returned to Panama.

An overjoyed Torrijos then revealed the real reason he had been keeping me so close to him. He told me, through his interpreter, that if the vote had ended up going against Panama, he had instructed the Panamanian army to destroy the locks on the canal. He had planned to take me up with him in his helicopter to witness the canal's destruction! That would have been quite a coup for me, but one I am glad I didn't get. Who knows how my own country would have reacted? But the agreement was passed, and I felt that I was now free to find Justin and do my big report.

The general, however, wasn't through with me. Taking my hand, he led me outside through cheering, jostling crowds to the National Guard Headquarters, where he gave a press conference. Then we went on to several other celebrations. I don't know how Justin did it, but every time I emerged from some building with Torrijos, Justin was there. At one point the crowds were so huge that I found Justin waving at me—halfway up a tree.

It was all very exciting but embarrassing. Here were all the networks and the world press chronicling this historic moment and there was I, smack in their lenses. But there was nothing I could do about it.

I begged the general to do an interview with me then and there. He didn't want to but promised to do one with me the next day. What I had to do then, and as soon as possible, was to get the story of this day on the air, especially his threat to destroy the canal. I finally did, late that night. The other correspondents in Panama were quick to discredit the story, claiming that it was impossible to blow up the canal, and that I'd made it up. That really stung. Especially because they inaccurately reported my words. What he had said, and what I reported, was not that he would have blown up the canal, but that he planned to blow up the locks controlling the entrance to the canal, thereby flooding it and rendering the canal useless.

I'd barely gone to bed that night when it was 5:30 a.m.—time to get up to report live for *Good Morning America*. Once again I was sleep deprived when we left on a small military plane to fly back to Contadora, Torrijos's Camp David by the sea. I was so anxious about the press conference Roone was holding that very day in New York at "21" to announce the change in format for the nightly news that, en route, Justin and I considered patching a phone feed through Torrijos's house to the restaurant so I could participate in some way, but we gave up the idea as impractical and disruptive. So, instead of being greeted by my colleagues at "21," I was greeted by Torrijos, in a jumpsuit, lounging in a hammock under his shaded portico.

His staff had prepared a breakfast that even "21" couldn't equal—fresh orange juice, mounds of mangoes, pineapples, and grapefruit, eggs however we wanted them, ham, bacon, muffins, coffee. All this against the backdrop of the waves breaking on the beach, a bright blue sky, warm sun, and a balmy tropical breeze. I just wanted to stretch out and sleep for three days.

But I was there to work and we did the interview, during which I asked him to confirm the threat I'd reported.

"General," I asked. "When you said you would destroy the canal if the treaty were not ratified, were you serious?"

"Yes, I spoke seriously," he replied. "It was a decision very painful, but there was no other alternative to take."

I asked him how he intended to do that. "It is very simple," he said. "The canal is as indefensible as a newborn baby. We know every critical point of the canal."

"And you were going to take me with you last night if you had done this, so I could watch?"

"I thought of taking you along so that they would have proof that we did it," he said.

I was vindicated. And very eager to get back to New York. The *New York Times* had tracked me down in Panama to ask me about Roone's pending reorganization. I didn't want to jump the gun on Roone's press conference, but I did make clear that what I didn't want to do was to be anchored to a news desk and what I did want to do was what I was doing at the moment—covering stories and doing reporter's notebook pieces. "I was very unhappy last year coanchoring with Harry," I told the *Times*. "This year I'm very happy." My idea of happiness, however, did not jibe with that of General Torrijos.

"Stay here for a few days," he said through his jolly interpreter.

"I can't possibly," I said. "I don't even have a bathing suit."

"We will get you one," he countered.

"I have a flight to New York," I said.

"Stay," he insisted. "Later I'll have my plane fly you back."

It's hard to argue with someone who has his own country, including the bathing suit concession and a fleet of planes. I thanked him for the invitation and the offer of a private plane to return me to New York but explained that for business reasons, I simply had to get back to New York right away. I was so insistent that he relented and actually made it possible.

I would never have made the Braniff flight I was booked on without his help. Not only did Torrijos send me off in his private plane, he called the airport and had the commercial flight to New York delayed. The general's plane landed, taxied right up to the Braniff plane, I rushed from one to the other, and we took off. That was the last contact I ever had with the romantic dictator, who died in a mysterious plane crash three years later.

WORLD NEWS TONIGHT debuted three months later on July 10, 1978. The new three-anchor format worked well. Within a year the broadcast was tied with *NBC Nightly News*. ABC was doing just as well in the morning. *Good Morning America* was closing in on the *Today* show and trailed my old alma mater by just 1.06 rating points.

More important to me was the debut in June 1978 of an ABC newsmagazine program called, you guessed it, *20/20*. Roone Arledge had put *20/20* together to challenge *60 Minutes* on CBS, but it didn't get off to a good start. The inaugural broadcast, hosted by journalist Harold Hayes and art critic Robert Hughes, was a disaster. Much too highfalutin. But from disaster rose a solution. A desperate Roone, who had uncharacteristically paid little attention to the initial program, was in a panic. Would *I* want to be the anchor? he asked. If I hadn't just gotten over my own recent anchor disaster, I might have said yes. But I just couldn't bear another audition and perhaps another disgraceful defeat.

As luck would have it my old colleague Hugh Downs, who was semiretired (he was doing a program on public television for senior citizens called *Over Easy*), was substituting for a day as the host of *Good Morning America*. There he was for Roone to see, perhaps a bit bland but experienced and, most of all, available. By the end of the day Roone had hired Hugh Downs to host *20/20*. The opportunity for me to anchor the program went away, or so I thought. As it turned out I would eventually join Hugh as cohost, and together, we would preside with great success over *20/20* for fifteen years, and I would continue on the program after he left.

At first, however, I was not officially attached to *20/20* or any specific program. In a way this was a very good thing. I was able to do a variety of stories that appeared on *World News Tonight*, *Good Morning America*, *20/20*, and for the first few years, *Issues and Answers*. (*Issues and Answers* would be replaced by *This Week with David Brinkley* in 1981 when David came to ABC from NBC to host what became the most popular Sunday-morning TV program.)

Some of the stories I did back then were big scoops. For example, in October 1979 when Jimmy Carter enraged the Iranians by allowing the deposed and cancer-ridden shah to come to New York Hospital for treatment, no journalists were permitted to see him. It was rumored that the shah wasn't really sick and indeed wasn't even in the hospital. Because of my past relationship with the shah, I was given permission by his aides to visit him in his hospital room. He looked very pale and ill. Over his bed was a big poster of a gorilla clinging to a branch of a tree with the caption "Hang in There." I wondered who among his aides had the courage and the humor to put the poster up.

I was not allowed to bring a television camera or even a tape recorder. All I had was my own Polaroid camera. I asked an aide to take my photo with the shah and we got just one picture. It was a Thursday. *20/20* was then aired on Thursdays and so, photo in hand, I raced to the studio and we showed the proof that the shah was indeed in the hospital in New York and exactly how ill he looked. I still have the tiny Polaroid photograph.

Twelve days after the hospital meeting, on November 4, 1979, radical Islamic students stormed the U.S. Embassy in Tehran and took more than fifty Americans hostage. (My photo of the shah had nothing to do with it. The new Iranian government was well aware he was in New York.) The hostages would be held for 444 days and lead Roone to create *Nightline*, hosted by Ted Koppel, to chronicle the crisis. The hostages would finally be released in January 1981, six months after the shah died in Egypt. (I caught the wrath of the fundamentalist government as well, though on a greatly reduced scale. While pillaging the shah's offices, the revolutionary students found a taped interview I'd done with the shahbanou and declared me persona non grata.)

Another early story for *20/20* was one of the strangest interviews of my career. It took place on a lake in upstate New York in the middle of the night. The subject was Abbie Hoffman, a former anti–Vietnam War activist turned fugitive from the law. Hoffman had been arrested in 1973 for selling three pounds of cocaine, a charge that could have brought him a life sentence. He had jumped bail the next year and been in hiding, under an alias, for six years. In September 1980 he decided to surrender, but in style. Several of his friends had called me in whispered conversations to ask if I would like to meet with Hoffman. It would have to be kept secret until he actually appeared.

His appearance, it turned out, would be at dawn on a lake near the tiny town in which he'd been hiding on the Canadian border. At the appointed hour my camera crew and I were in one boat, waiting, as Hoffman gradually emerged out of the early morning haze in his own boat. It was like a slow-motion dream, all very mysterious and theatrical. I did an interview with him at his hideout on land, in which Hoffman spoke about all the good works he'd done for the local environment while using an assumed name. He obviously thought it would help his case—and it did. He turned himself in the next day and ultimately served two months in prison, followed by ten months in a work-release program at a drug rehabilitation center in New York.

By the time I did that interview, 20/20 had been on the air for two years. It had been doing reasonably well with Hugh as the genial and well-informed host, and his number one correspondent in those days, Geraldo Rivera. Geraldo did strong investigative pieces full of high drama. He and Hugh did a good many outdoor adventure features as well. But Roone evidently felt that the program could do even better if I, instead of just contributing pieces, joined up as Hugh's cohost. This time I agreed. I wouldn't be doing the program by myself, and it was time for me to find a "home" at the network. Most important, I was fond of Hugh and knew I would not have another Harry Reasoner experience.

For all our friendship and mutual professional respect, however, Hugh didn't want me as coanchor. He didn't want *any* coanchor. He'd been doing the show solo from its outset and, he felt, doing it very successfully. So at first he resisted Roone's insistence that the show would be better with me there. To his credit, Hugh told me exactly how he felt. But Roone was the boss and Hugh finally agreed. Once he did we never had a bad day.

As with the *Today* show, I did the tough booking of the high-profile guests and Hugh continued to do the kind of lower-key and easygoing but often dangerous features he did so well—very popular features like swimming with sharks, maneuvering a glider, or instructing viewers on how to sail a small boat.

Hugh wanted and got top billing. That was fine with me. (I remembered Bing Crosby's advice.) Hugh therefore opened the program and I closed it. "We're in touch, so you be in touch," was our warm and cozy sign-off. The show was undeniably stronger with the two of us. "I don't know when I've been happier to have been wrong," Hugh told me.

In time 20/20 became one of ABC's most successful weekly programs. On occasion we even topped *60 Minutes* in the ratings, although 20/20, first on Thursdays, then on Fridays, was in a much more competitive time slot.

I also continued to do four prime-time *Specials* a year. They were so time consuming that I wanted to fold them into 20/20, but they were too popular for ABC to give up. Instead Roone took them away from the entertainment division and put them under ABC News, where they remain to this day. This meant increased revenue in Roone's budget.

My permanent place on *20/20* and the continued *Specials* meant more hard work. But at long last I felt I could stop auditioning week to week or, more often, day by day.

Things were smoother professionally, but they were more complicated at home.

Heartbreak and a
New Beginning

M Y MOTHER AND MY SISTER continued to live in Miami after my father died. Their life without my father should have been peaceful, but they were more and more alone, totally dependent on each other, and, I think, frightened as well. My mother worried constantly about what would happen to Jackie when she died. Jackie, I think, worried too, and the unspoken question was whether I would take her to live with me.

I ached, knowing that I just couldn't do to myself what my sister, unwittingly, had done to my mother. The two women, instead of cherishing each other, constantly argued—tears from Jackie, doors slamming, phone calls to me, each complaining about the other. Their discontent tore at me. One of the problems was their isolation. My mother would not go out without Jackie, which meant she was rarely invited anywhere. Other widows and single women lived in their building in Miami, and I urged my mother to make some coffee, buy some danishes, and invite a few of them to the apartment to watch my *Specials*. She'd reply, "It's too much effort," or "They want to play cards," or "They don't want to come." So she and my sister would watch the *Specials* alone.

There's an old joke that every woman in television knows: You do an interview with the president of the United States and your mother says, "I didn't really like your hair." My mother was true to form. But to her credit, she was no stage mother. As proud as she was of me, she never said to friends or acquaintances, "Did you see my daughter on TV last night?" or told me that "so and so wants a picture for her niece." She never used me to enhance her life.

I did my best, however, to enhance her and Jackie's life. I visited them whenever I could, and if I went to Florida for work I would try to include them in whatever I was doing. I was a guest on a show Phil Donahue did in Florida, for example, and I took my mother and my sister. They had a wonderful day, and Donahue could not have been kinder to them. I enjoyed opening the world up to them, even if just a little bit.

I also invited them regularly to New York, but that was often a trial. My mother didn't want to pack and make the trek for less than three weeks. So this meant a stretch of almost a month of hearing them argue and cry, while I became the unwilling referee. They were each right. They were each wrong. And they were both so sad. I hated to come home at the end of the day.

At least we had more room at home. In 1978, thanks to the job at ABC, I bought an apartment on Park Avenue and Sixty-second Street and hired Angelo Donghia, a brilliant and much-sought-after interior designer, to decorate it. Since my old apartment had been so dark, I asked him to make everything white—my bedroom, the living room, everything white. The apartment was lovely and airy and bright, except for the kitchen. The prior owners had painted the kitchen bright orange. It would have taken four coats of white paint to cover it up, and I didn't want to spend the money. So orange it stayed.

It was the first home I'd ever owned and, the kitchen aside, I loved it. My daughter, Jackie, finally had a proper bedroom, and there were large rooms for Icodel and Zelle. We also had a guest room where my mother and sister slept when they visited.

The high point of everything for my mother was seeing her granddaughter, whom she adored. By 1981 Jackie was entering a very troubled adolescence, but to my mother she could do no wrong. Where some people talk about the problems or complications that may arise with adopted children, I never, ever, heard my judgmental mother say anything but the most wonderful things about Jackie. This was her grandchild. Period.

It was during one of my mother's visits to see us that she had a terrifying health scare. She woke me up in the middle of the night because she was having difficulty breathing. We rushed her to the hospital to discover that her heart was failing and she had fluid in her lungs. She spent some time in the hospital and eventually recovered, but for a long time she was frail and depressed.

When she was released from the hospital, I couldn't let her go back to Florida, so I experimented with putting her in what I thought was a nice home for senior citizens in nearby Riverdale, New York. She and my sister had their own little apartment and any supervised care that was needed. The bonus was that the director of the facility found work for my sister at the nursing home on the grounds. Bless him. He told Jackie that she was to be a "secretarial assistant," and she seemed quite happy spending a few hours a day running errands, filing, whatever she was capable of doing.

I thought this might be a perfect solution for my sister in the future. If anything happened to my mother, Jackie could continue to live in the residence. All her meals were served in the dining room. She had begun to make friends among the women she worked with. She would have a life there and still be close to me. I never discussed this with my mother, but I hoped she would realize the possibilities on her own. She didn't. My mother disliked the home, and that killed any chance for the conversation to take place. She insisted there was no one there with whom she had the slightest thing in common. What she really wanted to do was live with me and, in retrospect, perhaps I should have found them a small apartment nearby. But then, what would happen to Jackie if my mother died?

Then came the second health scare. My sister had a small lump in her breast, and it turned out to be malignant. My mother and I decided not to tell Jackie she had cancer. The diagnosis would have terrified her. We told her that the lump was harmless but should be taken out. Jackie was fine with that and asked very few questions. I took her to the best doctors to determine the course of treatment. One suggested a mastectomy. Another said a lumpectomy would be just as effective, and there seemed to be growing evidence that that was true. I could not discuss any of this with Jackie. I thought it would have frightened and confused her. My mother left the decision entirely in my hands, so I decided on the lumpectomy.

It was terrifying to hold my sister's health in my hands. My decision could literally be a matter of life or death for her. To my everlasting relief the treatment worked out. Jackie had the lumpectomy at Memorial Sloan-Kettering, the world-renowned cancer center in New York, and followed it up with radiation. The hospital suggested a very fine and understanding radiologist in Riverdale near where Jackie and my mother were living, and my mother took her there every day for the many weeks of the treatment. Things went smoothly and Jackie never realized that she had had breast cancer.

My mother continued to be unhappy in New York, though I suspect she would have been unhappy anywhere. What she saw as the burdens of her life had robbed her of any joy. She had been such a loving mother when I was growing up, and I still loved her dearly, so I kept trying to find things that would give her pleasure. It was a difficult task. One Thanksgiving I put together a dinner at the Friars Club. There were twelve of us at the table: my daughter, some cousins, and a few of my friends who were alone for the holiday. I had bought new dresses for my mother and sister, and they looked lovely. Henny Youngman and Red Buttons, two comedians who were old friends of my father, came over to our table and made a big fuss over my mother. I thought she was having a good time until I suggested that everyone at the table tell the rest of us in turn what he or she was most thankful for. When it came to my mother, she looked around the table and said: "I have nothing to be thankful for." My heart sank.

My mother missed the warm weather in Florida and, after Jackie's radiation treatments ended, they returned to Miami. I found them very nice accommodations at a small spalike residence that provided meals and social programs. Jackie loved it and happily attended painting and dancing classes. My mother, too, seemed more or less satisfied.

Although I often thought, when I heard them arguing with each other, that I would never be free, I felt now that perhaps I could relax. But over the next months, when I telephoned my mother, she often seemed disoriented. Sometimes she didn't recognize my voice or even my name. My sister said Mother was often like that, and spent more and more time in bed. I called Aunt Lena, my mother's sister, who was still living in Miami Beach, and she confirmed that my mother was forgetting things. She did not even want to get up for meals and seemed to be losing track of time and place. My aunt had been worried but didn't want to bother me, hoping that my mother would get better on her own.

I phoned my mother's doctor. He also confirmed what Aunt Lena had told me. One thing was clear: My mother needed full-time care. I flew down to Florida. I took her in my arms and brought her to the same nursing home to which she had brought my father. My mother barely knew what was going on.

Could I have brought her to New York and, with nurses, kept her with me? Of course. But I didn't. I struggled with that decision. I remembered when I was a child telling my mother that when I grew up, I would build her a house and we would all live together. That house was not a nursing home. I knew other children of aging parents were facing this kind of terrible predicament, but their dilemma didn't help mine. Shirley also tried to make me feel better. She reminded me of what I knew, that my mother had put my father in a nursing home, and Shirley had put her own mother, my aunt Rose, in a nursing home. "She wouldn't have gotten the level of care at home with me, the outcome would have been the same, and it would have destroyed my life," Shirley said. "It will destroy your life, too."

Shirley's advice was particularly apt. My personal life had entered a new stage. I was in my early fifties and had been single for twelve years. My work was stable, and I was going out more and more with Alan "Ace" Greenberg, now the CEO of Bear Stearns. He wanted very much to marry me. He was dear to me and I felt I should take the plunge and marry him. The problem was that although he was the nicest, smartest man, I didn't think I was in love. Then, in the summer of 1984, I unexpectedly met another man, Merv Adelson. Wham! I thought, at last this is *it*. I was really attracted to Merv and knew that if he felt the same way, my indecision would be over. It soon was.

We met on a blind date. Our Cupid was an advertising man named Leo Kelmenson, my neighbor in Westhampton, where I rented a summer house. Leo told me he had just sold his advertising agency to a very successful man from California. He was one of the founders and owners of Lorimar Productions, a television company that had a string of huge hit shows like *Dallas, Knots Landing,* and *The Waltons.* He'd also co-founded La Costa, a fabled spa and resort in Carlsbad, California.

"Merv is going to have to come to New York often now for the agency," Leo told me. "He's recently separated from his wife and very attractive. Would you like to meet him?"

Why not?

Merv called and we had dinner. Leo was right. He was very attractive. His hair was silver, his eyes were blue, and he had a year-round tan. He was sexy, funny and charming and, to me, very California—just the sort of man I'd seen in Vegas when my parents were living there and who didn't have any interest in me. Nor, I'm sure, would Merv have been interested if I hadn't become Barbara Walters. Not that he was interested in celebrities. He was after all in the television and movie business and had dozens of beautiful actresses working for him. But I was something different, not an actress, yet someone who understood his world.

No sooner had we sat down than Merv, to my surprise, launched into a confession. The money that he and his partner had used to develop La Costa, he told me, had come in part from the Teamsters Union Pension Fund. The Teamsters Union at the time had a reputation of being involved with organized crime. *Penthouse* magazine had run an article in

1975 that implied that Merv, too, was associated with the Mob. That charge was untrue, Merv insisted, and he had sued *Penthouse* for libel. He had lost the libel suit in 1982, two years before our dinner, but the judge had granted him a new trial. He wanted me to know this up front because the legal issue was not yet resolved and the rumored Mafia connection was a blot on his reputation.

All this before the main course. I appreciated his frankness. I also found it endearing that Merv was being protective of me and my reputation when his libel case didn't really affect me. We were just having dinner, after all, a delightful dinner, which ended on a funny note.

Merv had no cash for a taxi to get back to the Pierre Hotel, so I loaned him five dollars. I guess he was so used to having his car and driver pick him up in Los Angeles that, like Queen Elizabeth II, he didn't have to carry any money. A week later he sent my five dollars back with a cute note. And we made another date.

We began to see each other a lot over the summer, and I realized I was falling in love. It was a wonderful, rare emotional experience, and despite my family problems, I was happy. Merv seemed bigger than life. He skied, rode horses, played golf and tennis, sailed. He wore jeans and T-shirts when every man I knew in New York was wearing navy blue suits and ties. And he lived as if there were no tomorrow.

Merv had a beautiful estate in Bel Air which I visited and where, later, we would live. We spent time at his ranch, called the Lazy Z, in Aspen and his house on the beach in Malibu. He also owned an apartment in a hotel in New York, though more and more often he stayed with me. Which is the major reason I didn't bring my mother to New York to live with me. I anguished about it but decided there was no way I could continue my new relationship with Merv and have my mother along, with round-the-clock nurses in the apartment. And what would I do with my sister?

So, in the summer of 1984, my failing mother went into the nursing home in Florida while my sister continued to live at the small residence with the social programs. I tried to find Jackie a roommate as a companion, but it proved close to impossible. I then approached the Hope School for the intellectually impaired (which they were now called), where Jackie had done some limited work years before. The school had opened a residential home where she could live in one of several two-bedroom suites and be supervised and cared for. Jackie could also resume her activities at the Hope School, filing and running errands for the assistant to the principal. That's where Jackie went.

She didn't like it. She wanted her own apartment in Miami Beach. "Why can't you find me a roommate, Barbara?" she would ask over and over again. I would try to explain the difficulties, but she wouldn't listen. "Where there's a will, there's a way, Barbara," she'd tell me.

They were always on my mind, my mother and sister, but I didn't discuss it very much with Merv. We were beginning a romance, and I didn't want to inflict all this on him. From the little I did tell him, he was very kind and supportive. He also was developing a special relationship with my daughter. When Jackie met him, she instantly adored him. Merv was fun and hip and outdoorsy, as was she. He had three children himself, one of whom, Ellie, wasn't too much older than Jackie. There was the possibility—dare I say it?—that we might become a family.

I had met Merv in May. That October, after I moderated the first presidential debate between Ronald Reagan and Walter Mondale, we went on safari to Africa with another couple who were dear friends of his, JoAnne and Gil Segel. We laughed our way all through Africa. Never in my wildest dreams did I imagine I would be camping in a tent in the African bush—for fun!—but there I was. And it was magical. Elephants, wildebeests (I'd never heard of a wildebeest before), zebras, and lions by day; vodka in our tent by night. Who wouldn't have fallen in love?

Merv and I got engaged while walking on the beach in Malibu in June 1985, a year after we met. By this time I had eased out of my relationship with Alan Greenberg. He is now married to a terrific woman, and remains my friend to this day.

So there I was in 1985, engaged to be married, with more than a full-time job at ABC, a rebellious adolescent daughter, and an ailing mother and dissatisfied sister always on my mind.

"My stomach hurts," my sister told me one day over the phone. I didn't think much of it. Jackie tended to exaggerate a cold into pneumonia. Nonetheless I called the school and asked them to make sure she saw a doctor. The second call from Florida was devastating. Jackie's test results had come back. She had advanced ovarian cancer.

I was heartsick. It had never occurred to me that Jackie might die before my mother. I flew immediately to Florida. To my relief the doctors told me that this cancer had nothing to do with her breast cancer. I don't know how I could have borne it if it had turned out that this cancer was a result of the decision I had made when she had her lumpectomy.

Ovarian cancer is a secret killer. There are some tests you can take, but they're often inconclusive. A woman rarely knows in advance if she has the disease. The doctor told me that he wanted to operate right away to remove Jackie's ovaries. Her condition was that serious. I quickly called my friend Dr. Paul Marks at Memorial Sloan-Kettering. My instinct was to have my sister flown to New York to be operated on, but I was torn. The doctor who was treating her in Florida had a warm bedside manner and had established a rapport with Jackie. She would need more than medical care, and I thought she was more likely to get loving personal attention in Florida than at the large, more impersonal Sloan-Kettering. Paul Marks agreed. He knew Jackie and understood that she needed a doctor she trusted to supervise her postoperative care and the intense chemotherapy she would require. So we went with the doctor in Florida.

I stayed with Jackie for the surgery. It went well, although there was a strange side effect. I sat with her in the recovery room after the operation, and she kept repeating, "I'm so sick, I'm so sick"—but she never stuttered. Not once. The stutter had disappeared. To this day I don't know why.

I remained with Jackie for two days after her operation. Then I had to leave for Milwaukee to make a long-scheduled speech, after which I planned to return immediately to my sister in Florida. I was backstage at the convention hall, waiting to go on, when I got a call from Jackie's doctor.

"I have terrible news," he said. "Your sister got out of bed to go to the bathroom and had an aneurysm. There was nothing anyone could do. She didn't suffer at all."

My God. Jackie was dead? It couldn't be! She had seemed weak when I kissed her good-bye, but all the signs were that she was recovering well. I was numb with shock. And guilt. What was I doing in Milwaukee instead of staying by my sister's side? She'd died all alone. I, too, was alone in that dreary backstage room as the waves of guilt and sorrow hit me simultaneously. I sobbed, trying not to make any noise. No one heard me. And then I dried my eyes and went onto the stage to make the speech.

What does that say about me? I don't know. Maybe I don't want to know. I just did my job, which seems to be what I do no matter what the circumstance. Maybe it's the way I cope. I didn't tell anyone in the convention hall that my sister had just died. I gave a terrible speech and was criticized for it. I didn't give a damn.

Jackie was dead. My difficult, temperamental, tragic, loving sister who had played such a huge role in my life. I remembered all the mean thoughts I'd had about her as a child and the frustration I'd felt toward her as we grew older. Then there were the decisions I had had to make for her as we became adult women. Had I made the wrong decision having her surgery in Florida? Would she have had better treatment in New York?

Merv sent his plane to Milwaukee to take me back to Florida. We buried Jackie in the same cemetery as my father. We have a family plot there, and it is where I'll eventually be buried as well. My cousin Selig and his wife, Marvel, flew down from New York for the graveside ceremony performed by a local rabbi. My aunt Lena came, as did my cousin Shirley, along with her two sons. A few people came from the Hope School as well. It was a very small, sad group.

I decided not to tell my mother that Jackie had died. Her mental state was confused enough, and I knew that my sister's death would be too difficult for her to deal with. As it turned out, to my surprise, my mother rarely asked me about Jackie and when she did, I lied. I told her that Jackie was staying with Carol Channing in California. My mother, knowing that Carol had always been very kind to Jackie, accepted that and seemed satisfied. To make sure that my mother did not find out about Jackie's death from anyone else, I told only my closest friends and asked them to keep it a secret. I was afraid the media would find out and report it, and that could lead to someone in the nursing home saying something to my mother. I gave up consolation for discretion. It was a poor substitute.

My mother's condition continued to deteriorate, and her periods of lucidity grew shorter and shorter. I flew down to see her once a month and brought along my daughter as often as possible. Sometimes my mother knew who I was, other times she didn't. "Who are you to me?" she'd say over and over. And I would say, "I'm your daughter. Barbara." Somehow she always knew that Jackie was Jackie. She had a very strange kind of selective memory. Sometimes she didn't even know who she was. "Who am I?" she would say. "Well, Grams, who do you think you are?" Jackie would lovingly tease her.

When she did recognize me, she would beg me to take her out of the nursing home and bring her back to New York. I spent hours discussing it with Shirley and finally decided, now that my sister was gone, I could do that. But I decided not to move her into my apartment. Merv and I were engaged. He was virtually living with me, and I worried about the strain on both of us if we lived with my deteriorating mother and round-the-clock nurses. Instead I took a suite for her in a hotel across the street from the apartment, staffed it with nurses, and visited her every day. But she was unhappy there.

It was a decision I still go over in my mind. I think, Perhaps, perhaps, perhaps I should have brought my mother into the apartment. These are ghosts that don't go away.

In the midst of all this, Merv and I got married. True to form, I had twice postponed the wedding. The first time was in the fall of 1985. I began to have doubts and didn't go through with it. Then we were supposed to get married during the Christmas holidays in Aspen. Again, I couldn't go through with it. I had growing reservations about Merv. He was wonderful company for the most part, but he could be very moody, and that cast a cloud over our relationship. I also worried again about the instability of marrying someone in show business. I tried to convince myself that Merv was primarily a businessman, the same rationalization I had adopted before marrying Lee. But just as Lee had produced one Broadway flop after another, Merv had already branched out into making forgettable and not very successful movies. There were rumors that his company might be in trouble. How could I repeat that mistake?

But my biggest concern was the bicoastal life we would have to live. In spite of the fact that my friends all truly liked Merv and he seemed to like them, he really didn't like New York. He had been born in California and lived there all his life. It was home. As for me, I didn't think I could move full-time to California. I couldn't do 20/20 from there. It would have meant giving up my career. So we decided we would spend ten days together in New York, ten days together in California, and ten days apart. I was able to make arrangements with 20/20 to pretape the program the weeks I would be in LA. I rationalized that for two busy people our schedule might even make for a better marriage, but in my heart I worried. The arrangement might work for a year or two, but for a lifetime? Planes? Plans? Time differences? Separations? How many years could we go on like that?

As it was, Merv was already beginning to come to New York less and less. And I was staying less often in Los Angeles. When I was there we spent most of our free time with his grown children, whom he wanted me to really get to know. I liked them very much, but it meant that Merv and I had little time to really sit down and talk. The truth is, we didn't have that much in common. He was a great athlete. He liked to play golf, tennis, and ski. I did none of those things. I liked to read and see friends. Merv had few friends and reading was not a great pastime.

On Tuesday, May 6, 1986, I flew to California to break off our engagement. Why do I remember the date? Because we got married four days later. The sun was shining when I arrived, the garden was blooming, and Merv was charming and funny and tan and handsome. What was the matter with me? Jackie already considered herself his daughter. Her feelings for Merv meant a great deal to me and might even have tipped my decision.

So on Saturday, May 10, 1986, I became Mrs. Merv Adelson. Just like that. Fast, so I couldn't change my mind again. I didn't even have a dress. I borrowed one from a friend, swallowed a Valium (which I never take), and more or less zonked my way through the wedding.

Actually it was a very sweet ceremony. We got married in Beverly Hills at the home of good friends, the noted film and television producer Leonard Goldberg and his wife, Wendy. A few other friends scrambled to make it from New York, and there were quite a few pals from California. My dear and trusted agent, Lee Stevens, gave me away. Jackie was my maid of honor. Beverly Sills, the famed soprano, who was very close to me, read Elizabeth Barrett Browning's sonnet "How Do I Love Thee?" Jackie and a friend of hers sang "That's What Friends Are For." It was all extremely touching and lovely.

As it turned out, the marriage was nice, too, for quite a few years. Because we had gotten married so quickly we decided to have a big party that fall in New York at the Pierre. I spent our entire honeymoon in the South of France seating and reseating the tables. Every time I finished a table somebody dropped in or dropped out and I had to redo the table. What honeymoon? All I was doing was tables. (I have learned since that you seat the tables no earlier than the day before the party.)

It was the grandest, most elegant party anyone could ever have had. We hired a party designer who turned the hotel's grand ballroom into an arbor of beauty, festooned with garlands of sweet-smelling flowers and centerpieces of roses, orchids, and tulips on each table. Three hundred people came, from Brooke Astor and Mary and Laurance Rockefeller to my old girlfriends from college and their husbands. All my New York friends and colleagues came, as did Merv's pals and business associates from Los Angeles and, of course, both of our families. Everyone got along. There was singing and dancing, champagne and laughter. Howard Keel, the great baritone and onetime star of *Kiss Me, Kate* was then appearing on Merv's show *Dallas*, and he sang a beautiful love song dedicated to me that night. Only he sang it to the wrong person. He sang it to my cousin Lorraine, who looks a lot like me and was sitting at the same table. She was thrilled.

The only shadow over the wedding party was provided by the *Wall*

Street Journal, which, two weeks before, had run a front-page story dredging up all the old stuff about Merv's association with the Mafia. But it was only a tiny shadow. Merv and his partner had settled the libel suit against *Penthouse* out of court before we married. Merv even had proof that the allegations of his links to organized crime were false. Bob Guccione, the owner of *Penthouse*, had written him a letter saying the magazine had not meant to imply that Merv was a member of the Mob.

Nonetheless I had to deal with the article, and I did, with my toast at the party. "I would like to thank the *Wall Street Journal* for underwriting tonight's party," I said. "I wish they'd had to arrange tonight's seating." Everybody laughed and everyone then accepted Merv.

Merv sold his apartment at the Pierre after we married, and together we bought a beautiful apartment where I live to this day. I finally got away from the orange kitchen.

As for my poor, ailing mother, her health continued to slip away bit by bit. Sadly, she wasn't even able to come to the party in New York. She barely knew me. Yet she was still the mother I adored, the mother who put bows in my hair when I was a child, who cooked breakfast, lunch, and dinner for my sister and me and lavished love on both of us. This is the woman who used to tell me when I was a child that she wished she had six of me. As I grew older, whenever I had to leave her, she would hold my face and kiss me over and over again and tell me how much she loved me. Yes, she became a depressed, unhappy woman in her later years. Yes, she wasn't easy to be with. But with all the sadness in her life, I could never really blame her. She saw the cup half empty. She made me determined to try to see it half full.

She died in June 1988 at the age of ninety-one. I was in California for my daughter's twentieth birthday. Jackie was going through a very difficult time, and Merv and I were giving her a party. I felt it important that I be there, but I was terribly torn. My mother seemed to be getting weaker, although her doctors didn't consider her condition critical. Then, while I was in California, she slipped into a coma. My cousin Selig, of whom my mother was very fond, went to see her, and he advised me not to fly back to New York. "She won't even know you're here," he said. So, against my better judgment, I stayed in California for my daughter's party. Maybe my mother wouldn't have known I was there, but *I'd* have known I was there. I'm sick of telling you how guilty I feel. Suffice it to say that to this day I can't bear to watch a film in which an older person dies in his or her child's arms. I dream about my mother all the time.

We buried her in Florida. Standing in the cemetery, looking at my father's and my sister's graves and then burying my mother, I realized that, after all those years of worry and responsibility, I was finally, finally free. But it didn't give me a sense of exhilaration. There was a touch of relief, but mostly there was sadness and regret.

I look often at a favorite photograph I have of my parents and sister that sits on a table in my apartment. It was taken many years ago at the Latin Quarter. Jackie is blond and smiling. My mother and father are smiling, too. It was a happy moment, before the series of sad and difficult events that followed. I treasure that moment. When I think back on my family life, there were not nearly enough of them.

The Hardest Chapter to Write

O F ALL THE CHAPTERS in this book, this is the hardest for me to write. I think it should be a chapter of its own because if my sister, Jackie, was the centerpiece of my youth, my daughter, Jackie, is the centerpiece of my adult life. There is another, perhaps more important reason.

I love my daughter more than I love anyone in the world, always have, but when she reached adolescence our life together became extremely difficult. I would probably not have written about this at all, but Jackie feels that it is very important for people to understand what she and I went through because, she hopes, it may help others. Her thought is that if *we* could make it, and we did, it may give hope to other parents who are struggling with their own adolescents' hard-to-understand emotions and rebellion. It may also help working mothers feel less guilty, because when your child is in trouble, the first thing you do is blame yourself. A troubled child can be from any family, but I think working mothers, like myself, feel the pressure even more keenly. And so I am sharing our most painful years—which, in truth, I would rather not remember.

I am not sure how Lee and I getting divorced affected Jackie. She was only four at the time and says she does not remember how she felt. She never heard us arguing, because we never did. It was just that suddenly her father wasn't living at home anymore. We carefully went through the rote that most divorcing parents do. "We both love you, darling. Our separation has nothing to do with you. You did nothing bad. We both will continue to see you, etc., etc." Jackie seemed to take all this in stride.

What actually happened was that her relationship with her father was never the same. Lee loved Jackie very much and saw her at least twice a week. He took her on wonderful vacations, skiing trips in winter, pretty houses in the summers, and one August, he even took her to Venice, Italy. But she never felt close to him.

Jackie was nineteen when Lee died. Today she says she regrets that she didn't know her father better. His photograph is in her home, but although I never remember saying a bad word about him because there were no bad words to say, I could not help her accept and enjoy him. "He tries too hard," she would tell me. "He lectures me." Indeed, the time came when there was a good deal to lecture her about.

As a little girl Jackie could not have been more adorable. We played games together in the afternoon, took baths together. We spent almost every weekend together, often with Shirley, who adored her almost as much as I did. Summers, when Jackie wasn't with Lee, I, too, rented a house on Long Island. My parents and my sister visited, and they couldn't keep their hands off her. My father took Jackie for walks in her stroller and enjoyed his little granddaughter as I don't remember him enjoying my sister and me. It gave me great pleasure.

I never did know how little Jackie felt about being named after big Jackie, especially when my daughter was old enough to realize that her aunt wasn't as smart as she was. But I thought my Jackie had a pretty happy childhood. She doesn't seem to think so.

Jackie was never with an unfamiliar babysitter. If I was away either Zelle or Icodel—or both—were with her. But in spite of all the continuity of this love and attention, Jackie grew up with no sense of self. Her theory is that almost every adopted child feels a sense of loss and suffers from what she describes as "inner abandonment." This is something, she thinks, an adopted child lives with her whole life.

Add to this, Jackie was exceptionally tall. When she was about two, my then assistant, the aforementioned Mary Hornickel, measured Jackie's height and said if you double the height of a two-year-old, you will know how tall she will be. Jackie measured more than three feet then. I was furious with Mary. But indeed Jackie is now almost six feet one. She is also very beautiful, with those big blue eyes, a glorious smile with one dimple in her cheek. We used to joke with Jackie that we could only afford one dimple. But striking as she was, Jackie only felt big and awkward.

In addition to the effects of the divorce, there was my traveling not only around the United States but to France, Germany, the Middle East, China—everywhere. True, Jackie always had Icodel and Zelle to come home to from playdates or school, but did my working and traveling make a difference to her sense of security? When she was a little girl I would take her in my bed many nights, which we both loved. Then I would carry her into her own bed at 5:00 a.m. when I went off to work. I never saw her at breakfast time, except on weekends, and never took her to school, but I also never missed a school event or any special occasion. Every birthday was celebrated with great love and attention. Still, I will always have the doubts most working mothers, certainly of my generation, felt.

There was also the question of my growing celebrity. I never realized that it would make a difference to Jackie. I had the same friends, none of whom were celebrities. We lived comfortably but not luxuriously. Our home, it seemed to me, was very normal. Still, Jackie now says she never really knew if a school friend liked her or liked the fact that I was her mother. It took her almost her whole life, until she had accomplished so much on her own, to come to terms with her identity.

I may have unwittingly contributed to her confusion. From the time Jackie was a tiny baby, I vowed to myself that I would not burden her with any of my problems or frustrations. I would not be like my own mother, who confided in me probably too much. I would keep my problems to myself. And I did. But you know, it is probably true that as much as you try to profit from your parents' mistakes, you make others they didn't make. By not telling Jackie my problems, challenges, hurdles, I perhaps did her harm, for she didn't realize that I, too, suffered sometimes. Instead she grew up feeling that she just couldn't begin to compete with what she saw as my accomplishments. She didn't know until she was an adult that there were also prices I had to pay. She certainly didn't know that as a child.

When it came time for nursery school, I sent her off to one in the neighborhood so that either Zelle or, when possible, I could pick her up at noon at the end of the school session. Jackie seemed to like the little school, although I have this very clear memory of one Christmas celebration. Parents were invited to hear a chorus of about a dozen little ones sing songs of the season. Jackie had a sweet voice, and Lee, Zelle, Icodel, Shirley, and I all looked forward to hearing her. But when the children started to sing, Jackie, and only Jackie, turned her back on the audience. All we saw was the back of her head. When I asked the teachers why this had happened, and if Jackie needed special help or attention, I was told that this occurred very often and that Jackie was just shyer than some of the other children. Nothing to worry about. Today I think it was something to worry about.

Getting a child into private school in New York is notoriously horrendous, so I was very happy that I had good contacts at the Dalton School, considered to be one of the best in the city. It was also coed, and I thought that Jackie, coming from our all-female house, should get to know that boys existed. Dalton was large for a private school. It went all the way through high school, and the kids more or less had to be self-starters. It was also known as a place that gave special attention to each individual child, and Lee and I thought that would be good for Jackie. So we applied and Jackie was accepted. Not only that, she was chosen to play the number one angel in the kindergarten Christmas play. This time she faced the audience. By this time, too, Lee and I had separated, but we came to the play together. All seemed fine.

As the years went on, however, things did not seem so fine. Jackie had a few friends, but she said, wistfully sometimes, that she was not really accepted by the girls considered the most popular. (This reminded me of my own childhood and, though I never showed it, I worried for her.) Occasionally she would invite one of the so-called popular girls to the house for a sleepover, but they never seemed to invite her back. Jackie acted as if it didn't matter. On Valentine's Day she sent a valentine to almost every child in the class. She received few back. I ached for her. Again, Jackie said it didn't really matter. Of course it did. I went to see her teacher and the school psychologist. Not to worry, I was told. Girls were cliquey. As for boys, Jackie was inches taller than any of them. If she went to a party and the kids played Spin the Bottle and the bottle happened to point toward her, the boys would often say, "Ugh." Today I think that is why those popular girls shunned her. The boys didn't want my big awkward daughter around, and the girls wanted the boys. None of this did I know. None of this did Jackie tell me until much later.

As for schoolwork, she did okay in general and excelled in art. Unfortunately neither the school nor Jackie considered that a very important accomplishment. When I talked with Dalton about possibly transferring Jackie to a smaller school where she might do better, I was told again and again that next year, she would do better at Dalton. Was this because I was a celebrity? Did the school just want to keep her name on the roster?

Could I have done more? If I had not been concentrating so much on my own work, the tough hours, the necessary travels, would I have known more?

When Jackie got to be fourteen, in 1982, it was as if a teenage warning bell went off. Her grades fell sharply. Up until then Zelle had helped her with French, and I struggled to help her with the math, but that didn't seem to be enough. We hired special tutors for both subjects. Then Jackie, who could walk home from school to our new Park Avenue apartment, started to come home later and later. One day I went to surprise her by meeting her after school only to be told by one of the girls that she had left early. The girl looked at me kind of funny and said: "She's with the boys on Eighty-fourth Street."

I ran to Eighty-fourth Street. There I found my daughter with a small gang of tough-looking boys, smoking and leaning against the cars on the street. They disappeared when I appeared. I took Jackie home, and in tears she told me that she was in love with one of them and she saw them every day and there was nothing I could do about it. The boys, or rather, young men, were called the Eighty-fourth Street Gang.

The next day, while Jackie was in school, I revisited the Eighty-fourth Street Gang. I told the leader that if Jackie was ever seen with them again, I would have them arrested, and that this was something I could do. They later told Jackie what I said and told her to go home. Jackie promised me that she wouldn't see them again. It was a promise she never meant to keep. I never told Lee. Jackie was barely fourteen. I couldn't imagine that things would get worse. They did.

Jackie began to sleep later and later each morning. I couldn't get her out of bed. By this time I was no longer on the *Today* show, so I was home in the mornings. I would shake her, sometimes pour cold water on her. Nothing woke her. Drugs? Not my child! (There was even a television special with that name.) If I mentioned drugs, Jackie swore she wasn't on any. I never found marijuana in the house, but I probably wouldn't have known as I had no idea what marijuana looked or smelled like. But it wasn't pot I had to worry about. Much later I learned that Jackie was on amphetamines. She was swallowing all kinds of pills. No wonder she couldn't get up in the morning. Fortunately she didn't like cocaine and never got into hard drugs. But the pills were enough.

Remember this was more than twenty-five years ago. We didn't know about kids and drugs the way we do today. Besides, I had never touched pot or any kind of a pill except the Valium I took before I married Merv. I couldn't recognize the symptoms.

Jackie barely finished Dalton that year. I made plans for her to go the next fall to a small girls' school in the city that seemed to be so desperate for students that they said they would accept her. But her behavior got worse. When she finally did wake up in the early afternoon, she would scream at Zelle and me, bang out of the house, and return when she felt like it. She dressed all in black with tons of makeup. She would not tell me who her friends were and, short of having her followed, I couldn't find out.

Our relationship was coming apart. Some days she all but refused to talk to me. Yet with it all, she never, ever said to me, "You're not my mother." She never touched one of my things or stole anything to buy drugs. In calmer moments she would hug me and tell me she was sorry and that she knew how much I loved her and that she loved me.

By this time, though, I knew we were in desperate trouble. I went to a child psychologist for advice on how to handle my daughter. I also wanted Jackie to go to the doctor and get the help she needed. She kept one appointment and absolutely refused to go again. All this time I was appearing on television, the picture of composure and tranquillity. It was a nightmare.

Finally I realized that Jackie needed to get out of New York City. Lee and I agreed to send her to an all-girls boarding school in Connecticut (since closed). On the surface it was a lovely place. Pretty buildings. Lots of trees. The headmaster was out of a movie—English accent, tweeds, charming, sure he could help our little darling. He couldn't.

Jackie started to refuse to come home on weekends. She had a new friend, let us call her Mary, whom the school kicked out midterm for bad behavior. She and Jackie had been found in the nearby town, high on God-knows-what. My daughter, though, was not told to leave. The school obviously didn't want to lose Barbara Walters's daughter.

After Mary was expelled, we heard that once or twice, on a weekend, Jackie had gone to Boston to visit her. When I got the name of Mary's parents, her mother seemed not to know whether Jackie visited or not and said that Mary, then fifteen, lived her own life. I told the school that Jackie was never to be allowed to visit again. I didn't know what else to do. If I took Jackie out of the school, where would send her?

It was around this time that I met Merv. He and Jackie immediately took to each other. She said that she could talk to him. This gave me some hope. I was so grateful to Merv.

The school year finally came to a close. It was now 1985. Merv and I were engaged. What to do about the summer with Jackie? I heard that the Parsons School of Design, a well-regarded school with all kinds of artistic programs, had a summer session in Los Angeles for high school students. Great. Merv and I would be spending time at his home in Malibu. I had a close friend in Los Angeles with a daughter Jackie's age, and they knew and liked each other. So we made plans for the two girls to take a summer course and live at Parsons. Jackie liked art and agreed to go. For a moment or two things seemed as if they would work out.

Two weeks into the course, Jackie disappeared. She had run away from the school with someone who, I later learned, was Mary. Frantic, I got in touch with a wise and experienced friend, Dr. Mitchell Rosenthal, who runs Phoenix House, the foremost drug rehabilitation center in the country. "Don't call the police," Mitch advised me. He said I would end up on the front page of every newspaper, which would make Jackie hide even further or perhaps induce someone who saw her to kidnap her. Could there be a greater hell?

Days went by with no word. That was neither good news nor bad. I was going crazy. During that time Mitch and I made a plan. When we heard from Jackie, because I had to believe I would soon hear from her, he would arrange to have a "transport" person pick her up and help us decide what next would be best for Jackie. Transport men and women are brave and experienced people whose business it is to find wayward or difficult children and, usually against their will, transport them to either what was known as an "emotional growth" school or, if necessary, to a lockup facility where they could be treated. Mitch put me in touch with one such man. His name was Mike. I will forever be grateful to Mike.

During this short time I visited three schools, as well as Mitch's own facility, Phoenix House, so that when we did find Jackie, we would know where she should go. The one I liked best was in the Midwest, about a two-hour drive from the nearest city. It had no train station, no airport. It was hard to get to and hard to run away from. It has since closed, but it was one of the first such schools that primarily treated adolescent boys and girls, like Jackie, who had no mental illness or criminal behavior but were suffering from severe problems ranging from drug abuse to general rebellion.

The school didn't stress academics. It had no psychiatrists or even psychologists. Instead, by strict rules, many hugs, outdoor wilderness activities, and a great many group experiences, it attempted to inspire in the kids a feeling of personal identity and self-esteem. It was a three-year program. The school felt it couldn't really accomplish much in less time than that. Three years seemed a lifetime to me, but the kids I met there seemed relatively happy and told me the school was helping to change their lives. When Jackie was finally found, I decided, I would send her there.

By now, almost four days had passed with no word from Jackie. I decided, front page or not, that I had to call the police. Then the phone rang. It was the sister of a man Jackie was hitchhiking with. Her brother had stolen Jackie's wallet and gotten our home number. He was a bad man, she said, and told me not to give him anything. She did not give me her own name but told me where Jackie was, thank God, and gave me a phone number. It was in a Midwestern state.

My heart in my mouth, I telephoned. After a great many rings, a woman answered. I asked for Jackie. She got on the phone and said she was fine and didn't want to talk to me. Did she need money? I asked. Yes, she said. She and Mary wanted money to go back to Boston. "Fine," I said. "Give me your address and I will send you both airline tickets."

Maybe Jackie was tired of running. She told me later that they had hitchhiked across the country, ending up in the home of some guys they met. They were all stoned. How she was still alive, I will never know. She says she doesn't know either. Anyway she gave me the address of where they were staying. I was all sweetness. Immediately I called Mitch Rosenthal. "Don't do a thing," he said. "I'll send Mike."

Jackie told me later that Mike, who was a very big man, bigger than Jackie, arrived at the run-down house in the early morning hours. The door was open, and Jackie barely protested as he carried her off to his waiting car. He took her to a place where other transport counsellors brought their runaways and spent a good day and a half talking with her. He then called Mitch and Merv and me and said that Jackie was essentially a good kid. He didn't feel she needed any kind of a lockup facility. Indeed, he said, she almost seemed relieved to have been removed from the house she was in, and he thought the school I had chosen would be a good place for her. We arranged for Mike to bring Jackie there at once. (Jackie later told me she was actually glad to go with Mike. She was becoming afraid of Mary and didn't want to see her again. She never has.)

As I said, the school was a hard place to run away from. The path leading into town was long and forbidding, and the town itself was so small that any new face would be quickly noticed. The kids lived in wooden dormitories, boys and girls separated. As the school got larger, the older kids helped to build some of the structures for the newer kids. The counsellors, many of whom had themselves graduated from the three-year program and decided to stay on, seemed to know just how much toughness and how much affection to give the kids.

All the music the children listened to was carefully chosen. Only selected television programs or movies were permitted. If a child lied or misbehaved, he or she was considered not to be "clean." Appropriate steps were taken. Mostly the students were forbidden to talk or be talked to for a matter of hours or days. The regimen was strict but supportive. Parents could take their children out at any time, and some did, but the school advised strongly against this. "Give the program a chance," they advised.

Above all the children were told they had to be totally honest, both with the counsellors and, most important, with their parents. For the parents this was often torture. It certainly was for me.

When Jackie was first brought to the school she was allowed one phone call to me. Sobbing, she told me how sorry she was, how she would never, ever do anything like this again. She had learned her lesson, could she come home, please. "Don't leave me in this horrible place, please, please, please." I was shattered. But I knew, I just knew, she needed more than I could give her at home. Sobbing myself, I told her she had to stay. She hung up.

As bad luck would have it, the day Jackie telephoned was the day Merv had arranged for the whole cast of *Dallas*, Lorimar's huge television hit, to go to the city of Dallas itself. There a big celebration was planned. Merv had begged me to participate and to make the cast introductions. All I wanted to do was to stay in bed and pull the covers over my head. The last thing I wanted was to take a plane to Dallas and fake a smile all day. It brought back to me the day my sister died and I was far away making a speech. But Merv had been kind and concerned about my daughter, and if this celebration was important to him, I felt I had to go. I went with the brightest lipstick and the heaviest heart.

I must digress, now. Please, parents, if you are having an experience like this, I know it may be the most difficult decision of your life to force a child to stay in a place where you can't be totally assured that it will truly make a difference. Your own heart may be breaking, and the easiest thing is to remove your child from the program. But if you have *any* confidence that it will work, hang in there. It may be your best, and perhaps only, hope.

For the first three weeks after Jackie entered the school, I was not allowed to talk to her. Her adviser-counsellor, who had herself gone to the school, told me Jackie was adjusting. She also said she knew what I was going through and to call her own mother, who would tell me of her experience and perhaps make me feel better. I did so, but I don't remember feeling any better.

My first phone call to Jackie, three weeks later, was not much more successful. After a few calm minutes, she again began to cry and to tell me that everything was all my fault. "Par for the course," said her counsellor.

A month after that, along with other mothers and fathers, I went to visit Jackie for the first time. Lee was already suffering from brain cancer and wasn't well enough to go. Later Merv would come with me on his own plane, and we brought Lee and his wife, Lois, with us.

When I arrived that first time Jackie greeted me with a smile and a hug. I had not seen her in three months. She looked healthy and happy but said she still wanted to come home. I told her that wasn't possible. Then, over a two-day period, she made her required confession and told me things about herself I never wanted to hear and have tried sometimes to forget. She told me of her unhappiness, of her continued drug use with uppers, downers, and marijuana (even if I couldn't smell it). She had tried LSD and didn't like it. She also told me that she had not stopped seeing the head of the Eighty-fourth Street Gang. He made her feel wanted, she said. She stopped seeing the gang only when one of them went to jail.

I was in shock. How could I not have known that all this was going on? How could I not have known how unhappy she was? And yet, finally I was hearing the truth and there was relief in that. I didn't know what would happen next, but I believed that Jackie was on her way to a brighter, better chapter in her life and my eyes were finally opened, whether I liked it or not. We could proceed with honesty and we have ever since.

While Jackie was at the school, Merv and I married. The school gave Jackie permission to come to our wedding. My memory of my wedding day is all tied up with Jackie.

She stayed at the school until she graduated three years later. When she turned eighteen, she could have legally left. At first she wanted to, but Merv, whom she loved and trusted, wrote her a long letter. Jackie had told us of an experience she'd had when as part of the school's program, she had climbed a mountain. She said it was very tough but she had felt great when she accomplished it. Merv wrote that if she stayed at the school, it would be another mountain climbed and an even greater accomplishment. She chose to stay.

As for me, the experience at the school was almost as great as it was for Jackie. We had our own parents' weekends where we listened to the counsellors and the children. I learned how to love my child without being judgmental. I learned what buttons not to push. I never missed a weekend when parents were allowed to visit. I became very close to the other mothers and fathers who knew me as another parent, needing to hear and share experiences. Yes, they knew I was "Barbara Walters," but most of all, I was "Jackie's mother."

During those years I saw Jackie slowly change. She developed self-reliance, especially, she said, during days and nights spent alone on wilderness experiences. She learned that there were other kids whose grief was similar to her own. She could cry and rant and rave about how unfair life was to her and no one was shocked or critical. She learned that some of the other children did not have the support or love from their parents that she had.

In her last year at the school, she was elected vice president. She was also helping some of the new kids adjust, who were as defiant and frightened as she had been. A fairly large number of these children, she told me, were adopted, adding to her theory of their special feelings of inadequacy.

Jackie's graduation day, when she was eighteen, was glorious. She wore a white dress and big smile, and it was as joyous a day as we could have had. I couldn't have been happier if she had just graduated Phi Beta Kappa. What a road we had traveled.

Jackie still had a long way to go. Everything wasn't hunky-dory. But I supported her in every possible way from then on, and our relationship became closer and closer. She never lived in New York again. Jackie feels the city is too big and too cold for her. A great place to visit me, she feels, but not to live in. For a while she lived in Seattle with a girl from the school. She tried marriage, but it didn't work.

Finally Jackie moved to Maine, because it seemed to have the same climate as Seattle but was closer to me. You will never guess what she did—or maybe you will. With her former counsellor from the school, she opened a small residential outdoor therapy program for girls called "New Horizons for Young Women." Her partner didn't want to stay in the East so Jackie eventually bought her out.

With little business experience, Jackie read everything on the subject she could get her hands on. She obtained the proper licenses needed to open such a facility, raised the money to buy the land and build the dormitories, and hired the proper counsellors, psychologists, nurses, guides, on and on. Jackie had her own idea of what she wanted the place to be. Small. All girls. Not a program where you had to walk miles before you were given a glass of water. A place of warmth and affection but with structure and strict rules. All the girls were given clothing to wear. No competition in that regard. No makeup. No iPods. No TV sets. Close supervision. Outdoor activities all year round but also areas for artistic expression, hobbies, interests. It was, in many ways, unique.

Jackie did the advertising and marketing necessary to let schools and counsellors know the place existed. She went to the necessary conferences and did all that was required to make such a difficult project a reality. And it is. New Horizons offers a six-to-nine-week program, and when a child ends those weeks, the counsellors advise the parent on the next steps to take.

Along the way, besides creating and running the whole establishment, Jackie became an accomplished business executive. She is not a therapist and does not work directly with the children, although she has told me laughingly that when she is with the girls and one of them says, "What would you know, anyway?" she replies, "Everything." And tells her why.

Again, it seems that a fairly large number of the girls who come to Jackie's program are adopted. Jackie thinks this is no accident.

Jackie now has a longtime boyfriend to whom she is very devoted. They share many interests and seem happy together. Jackie doesn't want children. She feels she already has so many in the program. Once, when I complained and said, "I want grandchildren," Jackie replied, "Get a dog." So I did. The world's most perfect dog, a Havanese named Cha Cha. She isn't a grandbaby, that is true, but nobody has everything.

I am more proud of my daughter than I can possibly express. She is a beautiful, delightful, funny woman. She marches to her own drummer. It may not be my music, but I guess, in a way, I marched to my own drummer and it wasn't necessarily Jackie's music.

A few years ago Jackie felt that it was important for troubled parents, especially mothers, to know what she and I had gone through. I couldn't tell the story myself on my own program. It would have looked too self-serving. So we asked NBC's magazine program, *Dateline*, if they were interested in the story. They sure were, and they assigned Jane Pauley. Jane visited New Horizons and spent several days with Jackie and some of her girls, who, with their parents' permission, agreed to tell their experiences. Jane was sensitive and compassionate. She interviewed Jackie alone and, finally, the two of us together. Jackie and I sat side-by-side and told our own parts of the story. People still talk to Jackie and me about our appearance.

One more thing. I keep reading about children who, as adults, want to find their biological mothers. Jackie has never expressed a desire to learn who her birth mother is. I thought she might be afraid of hurting my feelings, so one day I asked her if she would like to find out. If so, I told her, I would help her.

"Why should I try to find my biological mother?" Jackie said with a grin. "Haven't I had enough trouble with you?"

Yes, darling. Likewise.

9/11 and Nothing Else Matters

B Y THE LATE 1980s things had greatly calmed down with Jackie. She was by then living in Seattle and had begun to find her own way in life. We stayed in close contact, and I was so relieved and grateful to have my daughter back.

I was doing just fine professionally as well. There were hardly any major politicians, world leaders, and others in the headlines whom I didn't interview for 20/20. Meanwhile the show business celebrity interviews on the *Specials* continued to draw enormous audiences. From 1985 to 1989 the programs were viewed, on average, in more than seventeen million households. And who knows how many people were watching in those households?

If things were going swimmingly in my professional life, I was treading water in my marriage to Merv. Beginning to sound familiar? The bicoastal arrangements were getting more and more difficult and to add to that, Merv's company, Lorimar, was in disarray. He and his partner, Lee Rich, had split and Merv took on three new partners, one of whom was a very smart young man, Les Moonves, who is today the president and CEO of CBS. Nevertheless the company floundered, and Merv decided to sell it to what is now Time Warner. Although this gave him a great deal of money, it also meant that he felt somewhat lost. All of a sudden he had no real place to go. The beautiful buildings, the lavish offices, the huge staff of producers and writers were gone. So here it was again, my worst fears confirmed. Another show business marriage. Another theatrical empire vanished. Merv then started a mergers-and-acquisitions business and opened an office in Los Angeles and another in New York, although he had little desire to go there. He still felt out of place and unhappy when he came east.

The marriage sputtered along, but by the summer of 1990 we decided it had simply run out of steam. We were profoundly sorry, but we had both known it was inevitable.

Merv and I separated in September of that year. There were no arguments, no bad scenes. To draw from T. S. Eliot, our marriage ended "not with a bang but a whimper." On my birthday I came to Los Angeles and had dinner with Merv and his three children and their spouses, and, knowing we were separating, they gave me a beautiful gold charm bracelet with their names on it. It was very sweet and touching. I liked my stepchildren a great deal and knew I was about to lose the day-to-day contact with them. The thought of that saddened me. I also knew that Jackie, who loved Merv, would take the divorce very hard.

I didn't want the news of our separation to dribble out in the press and to read the gossip and speculation, so I wrote out an announcement and gave it to my friend Liz Smith for her nationally syndicated column. The day before she published it I went to a spa with a friend so I wouldn't have to deal with all the phone calls. This, in part, is what Liz printed.

It is with great sadness that Barbara Walters and Merv Adelson are announcing that they will be having a trial separation. For the past five years, this glamorous and very nice couple has lived a high-intensity, bi-coastal wedlock, with each traveling from coast-to-coast at least once a month. But now, Merv's business interests require his spending most of his time in Los Angeles and Barbara's television assignments, instead of lessening, seem to have multiplied so that she is traveling all over the world or operating primarily from New York. The twain meets—but the effort is gigantic.

Our friends were shocked. They thought we'd had the happiest marriage. It is a cliché but true: one never knows what is going on in another's private life.

Our divorce was amicable, but even so, a divorce has its confusion and its difficulties, especially if you have depended on your spouse to make the major financial decisions, as I had done. I had never paid much attention to my own affairs and had happily turned them over to Merv when we married. When we split up, I decided to take responsibility for my own financial well-being. I was fortunate to have a wise friend, Linda Wachner, who at that time was the president and CEO of a large public company called the Warnaco Group. Linda took me by the hand

Left: John Wayne
with me on his boat
in 1979

Below: Dancing with
George Burns in
1979

Katharine Hepburn on the Broadway set of *The West Side Waltz* in 1981

Katharine Houghton Hepburn

XII - 17 - 1992

Dear Barbara -
I'm having your letter
framed - You're sweet - Thank you -

K. Hbf

A note from Katharine Hepburn,
December 1992

Above: Jimmy Stewart and I riding an elephant in 1983

Left: Sylvester Stallone and his motorcycle, 1988

With Audrey Hepburn on the beach in Acapulco in 1989

Working out with Arnold Schwarzenegger in 1990

With Clint Eastwood in 1992

With Christopher Reeve in 1995

With Bob and Michelle
Smithdas in 1998

With Will Smith in 1998

A note from Monica Lewinsky three months before our interview

My questions for the Monica Lewinsky interview,
February 20, 1999

MONICA LEWINSKY

10. You testified that, shortly after your internship began, you and the
President began 'intense flirting.' When did you see him? What did
he do? *Love monica*

11. This photograph was taken at a birthday party for the President. *before relationship*
(PHOTO #1) When you see this photo - what do you remember?

12. November 15, 1995. The Government was shut down. Interns took
on greater responsibilities in the White House. On that day, you found
yourself alone with Bill Clinton in the Chief of Staff's office and you
lifted the back of your jacket to show the President the top of your
thong underwear. *new fired* How did that happen? How did Bill Clinton react?

13. That evening, the President invited you to see him privately. What did
you say? Who made the first move?

14. What did you think when Bill Clinton first kissed you?

Interview in Attica Prison with John Lennon's murderer, Mark David Chapman, December 1992

Interview with convicted murderer Jean Harris after her release from prison, December 1993

Opposite: Oprah, Cha Cha, and I in 2004

Interview in prison with Robert Blake, February 2003

I'm second from the left, on the day the bathing suit model didn't show up at CBS, 1956.

My only advertisement, done for Citgo Gas in the 1960s. And I don't even drive.

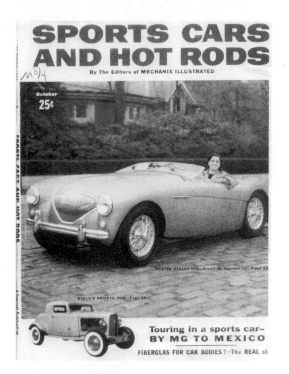

With Hugh Downs and Joe Garagiola on the set of the *Today* show, 1967

On the set of the *Today* show with Joe Garagiola, Frank Blair, and Frank McGee, 1971

With an unhappy Harry Reasoner in 1976

Above: In 1990 I was inducted into the Academy of Television Arts and Sciences Television Hall of Fame along with Roone Arledge, Don Hewitt, and Joan Ganz Cooney

Left: With Hugh Downs on the set of *20/20* in 1999

Below: With John Stossel on the set of *20/20* in 2003

With Diane Sawyer—just kidding!

The original ladies of *The View:* Meredith Vieira, Joy Behar, Star Jones, Debbie Matenopoulos, August 1997

Ladies of *The View:* Elisabeth Hasselbeck, Rosie O'Donnell, Joy Behar, 2006

Current ladies of *The View:* Elisabeth Hasselbeck, Whoopi Goldberg, Sherri Shepherd, Joy Behar, 2007

Left: With my Maltese, Pudgy, in front of the pistachio house in Florida, 1940s

Right: Modeling in Paris for Carven, 1954

At Longchamps racetrack for a *Special* on NBC. I love the pictures of the men.

Norman Parkinson took this photograph—my favorite

In front of a painting in
my living room

The world's most perfect
dog—Cha Cha Walters

and introduced me to an expert accountant and another expert in insurance. She also helped me make some basic investment decisions. I was fortunate, but I empathize with the new divorcée who may have to make such decisions without someone savvy to help her.

I will always be grateful to Merv for his love and support of Jackie throughout her years of difficulty. He later married a much younger woman and they adopted two children. They are now divorced.

Since Merv lives in California and I in New York, our paths did not cross for many years. When they finally did, I found myself pleased to see him, and today we are friends.

I think that is enough about my personal life.

THE MOST POPULAR of my celebrity *Specials* was, and is, the Oscar Night program, which we started in 1981. Since then I've interviewed almost every big star who graced a movie screen, from Elizabeth Taylor, Robert Mitchum, and Audrey Hepburn to Denzel Washington, Tom Cruise, and George Clooney, to Helen Mirren and Eddie Murphy.

Most people think I'm actually at the Academy Awards when I'm interviewing the stars, but I'm not. My producer, Bill Geddie, who has been producing the *Barbara Walters Specials* since 1988 (as well as being the co–executive producer of *The View*), always finds some wonderful location for me in which to do the opening and closing. Often, for the sake of a grand look, this involves climbs up and down staircases. (I'm terrified of heights.) I remember once we used the set of the epic musical *Sunset Boulevard*, and I had to walk down this long staircase that was supposedly in the home of the Gloria Swanson character. I was wearing spike heels and some long, billowy gown. I couldn't cling to the banister and I couldn't look down because I was talking to the camera. I thought I would never make it.

Another time, in another billowy ball gown, I had to glide down a very long escalator in a movie theater while the cameras recorded my descent. The escalator was so high and steep that what you couldn't see on camera was a stagehand crouching in front of me so I would feel secure that someone was there to catch me if I fell. We did this descent four times. The stagehand, I think, deserved an Academy Award for valor.

Interviewing celebrities is often harder and much more time consuming than interviewing newsmakers or world leaders. People seem to think I just pick up the phone and get right through to Michael Douglas or Julia Roberts. Not so. Over the years there have been endless back-

and-forths with agents, public relations representatives, lawyers, and managers. Sometimes it has taken months to confirm an interview. One of the most elusive stars was, you won't be surprised, Katharine Hepburn. After pursuing her for months we finally settled on a Tuesday in October for our conversation. And wouldn't you know it, the weekend before our interview I got a call from the League of Women Voters asking me to be on the panel that same night for the presidential debate between Ronald Reagan and Jimmy Carter. I phoned Miss Hepburn in Connecticut. "Would you mind changing our interview from Tuesday to Thursday?" I asked her. She was so thrilled to get out of the interview that it took us ten months to get her back.

The preparation is also much harder for the celebrity interviews. If you read the newspapers every day, which I did, and do, you're basically up to speed on what a politician or world leader is up to. But there's much more homework to do when you're talking with a celebrity. Interviews with politicians and world leaders are about issues, but interviews with celebrities concern their lifestyle and their emotions. I scour every clip written about them, plumb their childhoods, watch the movies they've been in, pick up bits and pieces about them wherever I can. If I've done my homework well, at some point during the interview the celebrity may be surprised by what I know. Julia Roberts was very startled when I said, "You write poetry." "How do you know *that*?" she asked. By reading, reading, reading, and then talking to anyone who might have some personal insight into the particular star I am talking to. The conversational format of the celebrity interviews almost demands that I know more about the subjects than they do.

I've already told you about writing every question I, and anyone around me, can think of. Working this way means that by the time I am ready to do the interview, I know every question and really don't need the paper. It is actually just my security blanket. It also means that no matter what my subject says, or in what direction the interview goes, I can be on top of it. For me, however, asking the right questions has always been less important than listening to the answers. "What do you mean by that?" "How did you feel then?"

While I am on the subject, the biggest mistake interviewers make is to be tied to their questions, sometimes, unfortunately, questions they haven't written themselves. The next biggest mistake is not to listen. And try not to interrupt. Earlier in my career, interrupting was my biggest failure.

Most often a big star wants to do an interview to plug his or her latest movie. Fine. But I try to get that out of the way as soon as possible, often in the introduction. Sometimes the person is trying to clear up a misconception. I make that easy by asking one of my favorite questions, "What is the biggest misconception about you?" These days, there's a whole new trend—the interview as a confessional. Drive under the influence, cheat on your wife, take too many pills, go into rehab, make an apology—do an interview. You can fill in the names. That seems to be the daily fodder of syndicated entertainment news shows. On the Academy Award programs, however, we make an effort to go for the stars whose careers and personal lives are so interesting that they bear the test of time. We try to have at least one Oscar nominee.

Once we sit down for the actual interview, I try to get the subject to forget the lights and the cameras and just talk to me as if we were alone in the room. I ask everyone to leave the setting except for the camera crew, and, if the celebrity is a comedian, I ask the crew to please not laugh. I don't want the sound of laughter to go out to the viewers.

This worked fine until I was interviewing Jerry Seinfeld in 1992, and he got going on some riff about a laundry detergent that had ads boasting it could remove bloodstains. "If you've got bloodstains, you know, laundry should not be your biggest concern," he said. "There should be something else you're doing if you're bleeding, besides the wash." The crew and I were almost bursting keeping it in and I finally said, "Okay, you can laugh." We just about exploded, whereupon Seinfeld shouted, "You're all fired. All of you. Clean out your desks." So there went that rule—and our jobs—until we all rehired ourselves.

Over the years I amassed so many interviews that we started putting together compilation *Specials* that drew on segments from my earlier interviews. The first, *The 50th Barbara Walters Special,* ran in 1988 and was a huge deal at the time—two hours of excerpts from seventy interviews. Bill Geddie did a terrific job putting it all together, with me peering over his shoulder the whole time. Bill loves to tell the story of the "rule" I laid down when we first met. "If I feel strongly about something and you don't, I win. If you feel strongly and I don't, then you win. But if I feel strongly and you feel strongly, I win." We have been together for almost twenty years. And sometimes I really am right.

The old interviews turned out to be gold mines. The original, uncut interviews were at least an hour if not two, but what we'd run on air was only eight or ten minutes long. So we had all sorts of unused material to merge into theme compilations, like love and humor and fame. The one I particularly liked was called *The Price of Fame.* Here we plucked whatever the star had said about being a celebrity, the up- and the downsides. The line I remember best came from Paul Newman, who told me when he had stopped signing autographs. "I was standing at a urinal . . . ," he said.

I did more serious theme programs for 20/20. In 1985, for example, we devoted an hour to a program about the transmission of AIDS. There was a general feeling of panic at the time following the AIDS-related death of actor Rock Hudson. To give light, rather than heat, we aired a *Special* the night after Hudson died titled *AIDS—Facts Over Fear.* To prove that AIDS could not be transmitted through perspiration or tears, which was a widely held myth at the time, I held and kissed a two-year-old child with AIDS, who was clearly perspiring. Many viewers were horrified. But that was just the point. The doctor we had on the show assured us that he had been in close physical contact with more than six hundred AIDS patients over the years and never contracted the disease. I was very proud of that *Special* because I think it had an impact and helped to dispel some of the myths.

`Perhaps my personal favorite was a one-hour *Special* on adoption in April 2001 called *Born in My Heart.* (You may remember that's what I told my daughter, Jackie, when she was a little girl.) The idea for the *Special* came to me because there were so many of us at ABC, and especially on 20/20, who had adopted children. Our hope was that sharing our stories might make a difference in someone else's life as it had in ours.

The *Special* touched many people's hearts. It was a lesson of love told by people who were expressing their most intimate thoughts, often with humor. Connie Chung, who is Chinese-American and was then a correspondent on 20/20, and her Jewish husband, Maury Povich, told the story of their original request for a half-Chinese, half-Jewish baby and the adoption agency's response: "By the time we find such a child, you will both be dead." They ended up adopting a beautiful Caucasian boy they named Matthew.

Dr. Tim Johnson, our medical adviser, appeared with his grown son, Nolden, whom he and his wife, Nancy, had found abandoned years before in Indonesia. One of our producers who had done heartbreaking stories on the thousands of neglected orphans in Romania introduced us to the two Romanian little girls she had adopted. Sherrie Rollins Westin, the wife of ABC News president David Westin, appeared with her then six-year-old Chinese daughter, the enchanting Lily.

To me, however, the highlight of the program was my own daughter, Jackie, then thirty-three, who had agreed to be interviewed by ABC correspondent Cynthia McFadden, herself adopted.

Jackie told Cynthia how much she'd always resented being referred to as my adopted daughter. "I mean it's like here you have a parent who loves you to death and you feel so close to. Yet everybody else is saying, 'Don't you want to find your *real* parents?' Or 'What if your *real* parents find you?'"

A "real" parent, she continued, had little to do with giving birth. "It's the one who wipes your butt; it's the one who takes a tissue and cleans up your tears; the one who is there for the good times and the bad."

"Who is your real mother?" Cynthia asked.

"Barbara," Jackie replied.

Interestingly Jackie insisted that it was much harder being the child of a famous woman—"hands down," she put it—than being adopted. As a child, she said, she had skirted the issue of my celebrity by first telling her friends that I was a teacher, and then eased closer to the truth by telling them that I was on TV and "kind of famous." When one friend responded, "Wow! Your mom is Oprah Winfrey!!!" Jackie said, "I about lost it. And I thought, Well, she could be."

I'd always felt that Jackie was born to be mine and, at the end of the interview, it was lovely to hear that Jackie felt the same way. "I was supposed to be in her life," Jackie said. "I can't imagine myself with anybody else."

FIVE MONTHS after the adoption *Special* aired, the World Trade Center was attacked. I was at home on the morning of September 11, 2001, and saw the planes crashing into the towers on television. I raced to the office, where Peter Jennings was already on the air. I was a huge fan of Peter's on the air but not always a fan out of the studio. I thought he was one of the best journalists in all of television but inside the company he had the reputation of being short-tempered and rude to correspondents, including me. He could also be dismissive and abrupt while broadcasting and pretty much hog the airtime. When this was brought to his attention, especially in my case because we often worked together on special events, he would write notes to me apologizing. Then it would happen again. He almost couldn't help himself. But he will always have my deepest respect for the magnificent job he did on 9/11 and the days after. They would be his finest hours, his finest days. He never left the studio, bringing in interviews and reports from all over the country and indeed from all over the world.

To this day I remember the acrid smell of smoke that drifted the five miles north from the destroyed World Trade Center to ABC on Sixty-sixth Street. I was too busy to be frightened. Jackie kept trying to call from Maine but all the circuits were busy, and she couldn't get through. When she finally reached me, I told her I was fine, and that was the last personal call I could have for two weeks. The news department gave out assignments. Mine was to try to interview any survivors, a very difficult task because they were in such a terrible state of shock. I did manage to interview the owners and the chef of Windows on the World, the restaurant on the 106th and 107th floors of the North Tower; more than seventy staff members and close to ninety guests were missing. The owners were crying, so was the chef. Nobody knew at that point who had died or who might have lived. Over the next days I was deluged with phone calls and pictures from the relatives and friends of the people who had been in the restaurant, hoping against hope that someone might have seen them alive. I, along with a great many other correspondents, went into the studio with Peter and presented our reports. But tragically, in my case, it soon became apparent that everyone at the restaurant that morning had been killed.

Six days after the attack I sat down with one of the heroes of 9/11, the mayor of New York, Rudolph Giuliani. It was late at night and he was exhausted, having spent his days and nights post–9/11 visiting firehouses, police stations, the morgue, the first responders at the hellish site, comforting the families of the fallen, updating the death toll at a daily press conference.

The mayor was determined to return the city to normalcy, to rally New Yorkers to go about their everyday lives while trying to cope with his own anguish. "You feel terrible and you cry, or you want to cry and then you say to yourself, 'I can't. I've got to figure out how we encourage people to figure out some way to get beyond this,' " he said. If he was comforting millions of New Yorkers and, indeed, people all over the country, who, I asked, was comforting him? This was not an idle question. I had noticed Judith Nathan, his then so-called companion and now his wife, standing in the shadows. (Giuliani was in the midst of a bitter divorce.) "Judith Nathan, who I care for very much and who cares for me and understands me, is an enormous source of strength," he said. It was the first time he had identified her in such terms.

Giuliani went on to draw lessons from the Battle of Britain and how the people of London had taken "terrible casualties, terrible losses," but never given up. He quoted Winston Churchill: "Courage is rightly esteemed the first of human qualities because it is the quality which guarantees all others."

A year after 9/11, we aired a special memorial program, *Grief Hour,* with a group of widows and children of men who had died in the attack. We taped it over the year at a counseling center on Long Island where therapists were helping family members, some of whom were very young, to rebuild their lives. One could not help but feel great pain listening to them. Some of the youngest children still refused to believe that their fathers were gone. After a year of denial, several of the widows were just now experiencing the pain of reality. As one young widow put it: "A friend of mine said, 'Oh, we miss you.' I said, 'I miss me, too. Don't be looking for me anytime soon.' "

I stayed in touch with some of the widows, a few of whom remarried. The children, too, over time, recovered, at least to some degree. Children are often more resilient than one feels possible. Gradually I lost contact with them, but when you become involved in people's lives, even for a short time, you can't help but be affected. I feel this way whenever I do an interview with people who have suffered through a tragedy. It affects you, it stays with you. You don't remember it every day, but it is part of what makes you appreciative of your own life and sensitive to the enormous difficulties that others face.

IT WAS THE CELEBRITY *Specials,* however, that continued to make the network happiest. People just couldn't get enough of the stars. They were also a huge financial engine for ABC. The *New York Times* suggested that between 20/20 and the *Specials,* I was bringing in more profits than any other broadcast journalist. Yet I can't forget that, in 1991, fifteen years after I had come to ABC and long after I'd begun creating those profits, my contract came up for renewal, and when ABC failed to act within its exclusive renegotiation period, I seriously considered leaving the company.

I know it sounds ridiculous, but I couldn't get Roone Arledge's attention. Roone had a reputation of never answering phone calls and letting matters just drift until the person either gave up or agreed to whatever negotiation Roone wanted. My concern wasn't money. It was personal. I felt that, even though I was supposedly a huge success, Roone didn't care whether I stayed or not. At least that is how it seemed to me. Roone loved the courtship of adding a new personality to the ABC roster. Though I knew that if you asked him, he would tell you that he and I were great friends, I simply wasn't on his radar. He was busy catching other fish. In the meantime I was on another network's hook. I had an astounding offer from CBS.

I had been approached by Howard Stringer, then president of the CBS Broadcast Group (now Sir Howard Stringer, chairman and CEO of Sony Corporation), and Laurence Tisch, the CEO and president of CBS. We had a secret meeting, which I realize now I should not have kept secret. I should have met with them in the most popular restaurant in town so that it would come to Roone's attention. But I didn't, so only I knew the tempting offer they made to me: my own newsmagazine program in a great prime-time period—10:00 p.m. on Mondays—with the best possible producers (one of whom, Andrew Heyward, would later become the president of CBS News). And the salary? A staggering $10 million a year!

I discussed all this in confidence with my very close friend Suzanne Goodson, during our regular weekend walks around the Reservoir in Central Park. Suzanne is one of the least judgmental people I know, and the only criterion in her advice was whether or not I would be happy. My wise and most trusted adviser, Lee Stevens, had died, and my new agent, Marvin Josephson, had been in Israel for weeks because his daughters were there learning Hebrew. I called him about the CBS offer, but he was reluctant to return. I should have insisted that he come back. I didn't. (I have never been as aggressive in real life as I can be in trying to get interviews.) So Suzanne was my sounding board and let me talk things out.

"Do I want to climb another mountain?" I mused to her aloud. "Just think of the furor over the $10 million salary. Do I want to go through the same scrutiny by the press and have my ratings put under a microscope every week?" I'd been anxious about anchoring 20/20 by myself and turned down that offer, so did I really want to take a chance on anchoring a brand-new newsmagazine at a new network with new producers, no matter how good they were? I joked, "I don't even know where the ladies' room is." And I said to Suzanne and myself, "The devil you know is better than the devil you don't."

I cannot figure out to this day why I didn't tell Roone about the CBS discussion. (I didn't even ask my faraway agent to see if Roone would match the offer.) Roone continued to be very remote, but he must have known something was up because he asked his closest aide, Joanna Bistany, to take me to dinner and discuss the matter. By that time, I had all but made my decision. I would stay in the place with the ladies' room I knew. Then and there, I told Joanne I was staying. She spilled her wine. Just like that, with no further negotiation, I turned down CBS. The very next morning, practically at dawn, a new letter of intent arrived at my home from ABC and I signed it, agreeing to stay for another five years.

Actually I know why I didn't tell Roone about the competitor's offer. And I know why I turned CBS down. The truth is that I couldn't audition one more time. It is as simple as that.

And so the years at ABC rolled on.

The network wanted more and more celebrity *Specials*, be they Oscar night or compilations, with or without a theme, but there were only so many really big stars around for the shows we were already doing. So in 1993 Bill Geddie and I came up with the idea for an annual *Special* called *10 Most Fascinating People*. The hope was that we could mix serious interviews with politicians, doctors, and business executives along with movie stars, sports stars, and recording artists. The key was in the length of the interview. The days were long gone when people would watch half an hour in prime time with Congresswoman Barbara Jordan, for example, but we hoped that people would sit still for a serious four- or five-minute interview if they knew there would be a TV star or a recording artist in between. And they did.

The first year we mixed Clint Eastwood, K. D. Lang, and Shaquille O'Neil with, among others, business tycoon Barry Diller, Jack "Doctor Death" Kevorkian, the writer Maya Angelou, and the most fascinating person of all (which we try to keep secret each year), Hillary Clinton. The *Special* did very well, so well that *10 Most Fascinating People* is still going strong today. Last year, we talked with, among others, Will Smith, Rush Limbaugh, and Tina Fey. After fourteen years, the program was still a great success.

I would love to tell you that we do an extensive poll to determine the ten most fascinating people of any given year. But the reality is that the list is put together by the tiny staff at the *Barbara Walters Specials*, primarily Bill Geddie, the executive producer; Brad LaRosa, the coordinating producer; two young producers, Betsy Shuller and Jennifer Joseph; and, of course, me. This "Gang of Five" does all my *Specials* (unlike a newsmagazine like *20/20*, which has close to a hundred people on its staff).

Although I'm pleased with all the retrospectives, there are times when I look at them and shudder. I have sometimes said that the *Specials* are primarily a retrospective of my hairstyles. How many hairdos can a girl have? And what a serious, sobersided interviewer I was in the early days. I've certainly learned to lighten up and put my best face forward. By the way, I learned which was the best side of my face to put forward from the late, great British actor Sir Laurence Olivier. After I interviewed him in 1980, he held my face in his hands and told me that the left side of my face looked better than the right. From then on I have tried, whenever possible, to be shot from the left.

I had never thought about lighting, either, until Merv told me mine was awful. "Every Hollywood star always worries about their lighting," he said. So we went out and hired a superb lighting director named Chuck Lofthouse and from then on I have had lighting from the floor shining up at me—or directly at me—rather than shining down. Good for all of us, even in our living rooms, to remember.

Though I may have come late to what many in television enjoy today, like having their own lighting directors, I've had a fantastic run, and to think I get paid for having fun! Well, the *Specials* do take work but I've laughed a lot with every comedian from Bob Hope and George Burns to David Letterman and Robin Williams. I've danced a lot with such varied partners as Bing Crosby, Patrick Swayze, and Al Pacino. I've baked cookies with Martha Stewart, ridden on an elephant with Jimmy Stewart, flown on a helicopter piloted by King Hussein, and sped through streets on a motorcycle driven by Sylvester Stallone, while wearing his leather jacket. The cookies crumbled. I don't get to ride too many elephants, and I'm not crazy about motorcycles. But I still have the leather jacket.

Presidents and First Ladies: Forty Years Inside the White House

NOW I WILL BRAG a little. I have interviewed, at least once, every U.S. president (and first lady) since Richard Nixon. So here now, various impressions blended by time and modified by the events of history, with some special moments that have remained in my head all these years. And, by the way, in some cases, I found the first ladies more interesting than their husbands.

As I said, I never did a formal interview with Lyndon Johnson, although we had occasion to meet several times. What particularly struck me when we did meet was that he, who was outgoing and gregarious in private, had so much trouble communicating with the American people. In part this was because he never became comfortable with the teleprompter attached to the cameras. He seemed stilted and cautiously afraid of losing his place. We talked about this one time, and President Johnson asked if I had any advice to give him. I said that it was important to be very familiar with what you were going to say so that if you lost your place, you could ad-lib until the prompter caught up with you. Also I told him that unless you were really comfortable with the prompter, you should not stray from your script, as you would most likely lose your next lines. (This is good advice, by the way, for anyone using a teleprompter.) My suggestions were probably the same as he got from others, but it didn't seem to make a difference. With his glasses perched on his nose, staring stony faced into the camera, he came across as awkward and ill at ease, not at all the way he was in person.

I knew Mrs. Johnson better. Like her husband she was warm and easy to talk with one-on-one, but these qualities also seemed to disappear when she had to give speeches or make public appearances. I did several interviews with Mrs. Johnson. The first time I angered some of her friends when I raised the question of her husband's predilection for attractive women. I felt I had to ask because the rumors persistently swirled around him. I tried to couch the question by putting the blame on others, as in "Mrs. Johnson, many people wonder, etc. etc." If Mrs. Johnson was upset by the question, she certainly didn't show it. Answering serenely, she said: "Lyndon loves people and 50 percent of those people are women." Great answer. But my question was considered so impertinent that some years later when I was at a dinner in New York, a great friend of Mrs. Johnson's, when we were introduced, refused to shake my hand. I remember feeling as if I had been slapped in the face, but I understood her reaction. To her I was one more of those pushy, rude journalists. Maybe I was.

In another interview, this one in Austin, Texas, many years after her husband's death, Mrs. Johnson talked about the fact that during their marriage, she practically waited on her husband hand and foot and never minded when he bellowed, "Bird, get in here!" She told me, "It was a different world then. That was your husband. You lived his life, pretty much. You had your own life, yes, but many things you put on the shelf and many things I have done since his departure were on that shelf."

Mrs. Johnson was so wise that I have often thought that if this were now, rather than then, she might have run successfully for political office after her husband's death.

At the end of our last interview, I asked Mrs. Johnson if she ever felt anger or bitterness toward her husband's detractors. Her reply has stayed with me ever since, and I try myself to live by what she told me: "I am too close to the great departure from life to harbor anger." Mrs. Johnson died at the age of ninety-four in July of 2007. A much-loved first lady.

I have already written a good deal about Richard Nixon, but Nixon's two daughters' paths also crossed mine. There was the elder, blond, reticent Tricia, and the younger, more outgoing brunette, Julie.

In 1971 I reported, along with NBC newsman Edwin Newman, on Tricia's wedding to lawyer Ed Cox. Tricia, with her demure white wedding gown and long blond hair, looked like Alice in Wonderland, young and innocent. But this is what I really remember about the wedding: The reception was in the White House and at one point, while dancing with her husband, Pat Nixon tried to give him an affectionate hug. The president stiffened and almost seemed to recoil. The following night, we aired the wedding again in a special program, so I had a second chance to see this poignant and telling moment. I wondered what Mrs. Nixon thought when she viewed the wedding footage? I know what I thought. I felt sorry for her and angry at him. Where were his emotions? Was he incapable of publicly showing affection?

Evidently his aides also noticed Nixon's lack of attention, let alone affection, toward Mrs. Nixon and found it a political liability. Years later, when Nixon's private archives were turned over to federal control, a telling memorandum surfaced from Roger Ailes, then Nixon's television adviser, voicing his concern. "From time to time he should talk to her and smile at her," Ailes wrote. "Women voters are particularly sensitive to how a man treats his wife in public."

Julie was the Nixon daughter I knew best. We are still occasionally in touch. Julie and her husband, David Eisenhower, grandson of President Eisenhower, have a son, Alex, and two daughters, Jennie and Melanie. Jennie has visited me and is the image of her mother.

Not too long after her father's resignation as president, I was at LaGuardia Airport waiting to board a shuttle for Washington. There I spotted Julie looking lost. She had never in her whole young life had to take a commercial flight by herself and had no idea how to get a ticket or where to board. I helped her, realizing once more how life changes when power and privilege disappear.

After ending his postpresidential retreat in San Clemente, California, President Nixon moved to the East Coast. I saw him now and then at the home of a grande dame named Mildred Hilson. He played the piano at her birthday celebrations. Once he showed me how to make sure that I wasn't cut out of a photograph. "Put your arm through the arm of the person you are next to and then they can't cut you out because your arm would still be there." I have sometimes taken that advice.

In 1976, the year I came to ABC, Gerald Ford, who had never been elected president, or vice president for that matter, lost the election to Jimmy Carter. Shortly after the New Year I sat down with President and Mrs. Ford for what was to be their farewell interview before leaving the White House. What I remember most about that interview was not the president but First Lady Betty Ford. Before the interview began Mrs. Ford took me on a tour of the living quarters of the White House. It was meant to be a charming, personal portion of our visit, but it wasn't. Mrs. Ford, it turned out, could hardly put a sentence together. She was slurring her words and was obviously inebriated or on drugs or both. Later, when she sat down with her husband to do the actual interview, she had a glass of some pale amber liquid at her side. "Can't you put that away?" the president asked with both concern and annoyance. Mrs. Ford answered that she really needed a sip or two. We barely directed any questions her way.

When the interview was about to air, I had a decision to make. Should I show the part of the interview in which Mrs. Ford was obviously inebriated, or should I be considerate and humane and delete that section? My executive producer said he would go with whatever decision I wanted to make. It was my interview, my decision.

Well, I was probably a lousy reporter, because I made the decision to omit Mrs. Ford's slurred voice. We showed the visuals of Mrs. Ford taking us around the rooms, but I did the voice-over description of what we were seeing. If she had a drinking problem, I wasn't going to be the one to expose her. In retrospect, exposing her problem might have helped her. But at the time I didn't feel I could add to her obvious despair.

Some years after leaving the White House, a sober and reflective Betty Ford sat down with me again and for the first time publicly discussed her struggle with addiction. She had been on pills to ease back pain and drank to ease the stress of being first lady. Her husband and four children finally confronted her with her condition and explained how devastating it had become for all of them. Grateful but frightened, Mrs. Ford agreed to go into a rehabilitation program at the Long Beach Naval Hospital. We took Mrs. Ford back to that hospital for our interview in 1987. She had not been there since her release. She walked the halls with us and, with tears in her eyes, described her condition before her rehabilitation.

"I couldn't remember anything," she confessed. "Telephone calls from one day to the next, plans we had, I wouldn't remember having heard of them."

"So if you have physical pain, you take a pill?" I asked. "If you have emotional pain, you take a drink?"

"I used the pills and alcohol to help me cope," Mrs. Ford said. "It was like an anesthetic."

Right after New Year's of 2007, I covered Gerald Ford's funeral. He had died at the age of ninety-three. All eyes were on his grieving widow. They had been married for fifty-eight years. I remarked then that I thought the lasting legacy of the Fords was Mrs. Ford's founding of the Betty Ford Center for Alcohol and Drug Abuse. Few people understood the problem of addiction better than she did, and she used that knowledge and influence to help thousands of others. Betty Ford made her own kind of history. But here is my postscript. If I were interviewing a first lady today and she was obviously inebriated, I would certainly air it. Times have changed. My interview with the Fords was thirty years ago. Today we let it all hang out, no matter who it is—and that's how it should be. We do have the right to know. Too much is already covered up.

Jimmy Carter was elected as this country's thirty-ninth president one month after I came to ABC. His was the election night I stumbled through with Harry Reasoner.

In addition to talking to Carter for my first *Special*, I had other opportunities to spend some time with him. Here are two memories. The first was during the Christmas holidays in 1978. The Carters invited my daughter to spend the day and evening with their daughter, Amy, at the White House. It was enormously thoughtful of them. At age eleven Amy was one year older than Jackie. I was not invited. This was to be Jackie's day, but I could bring her and pick her up after dinner. Jackie had a happy time. She told me she really liked Amy and found her friendly and unspoiled.

There was a party that night for the children of White House employees, and Walter Cronkite had been asked to read *A Visit from Saint Nicholas*. " 'Twas the Night before Christmas," Walter intoned to the delighted children in that famous mellifluous voice. I was invited to that part of the festivities. When the performance was over and Walter and I were preparing to leave, President Carter asked us to stay for coffee. Walter and I have often laughed at what happened then. Each of us had hoped the president would say something newsworthy that we might use on a broadcast—some pithy kind of a Christmas message. Instead the president took the opportunity to tell us about his hemorrhoids. "Very uncomfortable and painful," he said. He might have to have an operation. Merry Christmas: I have hemorrhoids.

My last anecdote about Jimmy Carter took place in the Oval Office in January 1981, just weeks before he was to vacate it. Roone Arledge and I, perhaps because we'd had so many encounters with Carter, asked if we could pay him an informal, off-the-record visit. I can't imagine doing that with a sitting president today, but that's what we did and Carter, dispirited and depressed, seemed happy to see us. All his negotiations for the release of the American hostages in Iran had proved fruitless, and a U.S. rescue mission, nine months before, had failed miserably. The newspapers, in recapping his presidency, were not only dwelling on the hostages but dredging up his encounter with an angry swamp rabbit some months before while fishing in a lake. The rabbit had attempted to board the president's small boat (I didn't know rabbits could swim), and Carter had had to shoo it away with his paddle. It was a silly incident but the report of the "killer rabbit" had been carried on the evening news of all the major television networks, making Carter look very foolish. And here it was being rehashed again.

Roone and I were more interested in the election than in rabbits. When we asked Carter if he blamed the Iranian hostage crisis for his defeat, he said yes, but then surprised us by saying, "That and the Cubans in Florida." Why the Cubans? Because in 1980 Castro had allowed, and Carter had permitted, the influx of more than 100,000 Cubans, among them convicted felons and psychiatric patients. The Cubans had flooded into south Florida, particularly Miami, overwhelming immigration services and infuriating the resident "Anglos" and African Americans. The economy was in a recession, and the non-Cuban population deeply resented the havoc caused by the influx of refugees and the millions of U.S. tax dollars being spent on them. "It was costly in political popularity," Carter later admitted in his presidential memoir *Keeping Faith*. As a result Carter, who had won the state of Florida in 1976, lost it in 1980. But as history has recorded, Carter has become a more admired ex-president than president.

As for Rosalynn Carter, I found her distant and chilly but I applaud her attention, while first lady, to those suffering with the misery of mental illness. She brought about greater understanding and helped millions to seek assistance. It was an important contribution. Congress even passed legislation she had introduced, the Mental Health Systems Act of 1980, but it was never implemented by the incoming Reagan administration.

In spite of his great success in negotiating a peace treaty between Israel and Egypt, and returning the Panama Canal to its rightful owner, Jimmy Carter never really recovered from the series of crises that plagued his later years in office, not the least of which was the 1979 energy crisis that resulted in gas rationing and long lines at the pumps. In what became known as his "malaise speech," Carter called on the country to carpool, drive slower, and turn down their thermostats to reduce our dependency on foreign oil. It was a message Americans didn't want to hear or heed. But, if Jimmy Carter's presidency ended on a note of despair, his successor, Ronald Reagan, began his presidency on a high note of hope.

When Reagan came into office in 1981, the country entered into a state of near euphoria. No sacrifices were called for with the arrival of good-natured, optimistic Ronnie and his ever-so-stylish wife, Nancy. The American people much preferred this optimistic view of the world.

I had interviewed Reagan as a candidate. He was certainly affable, but I couldn't help but be struck by his lack of knowledge in specific important areas. For example, there was a lot of talk in the press back then, as now, about Israel achieving peace with all its Arab neighbors by returning the land it had occupied since the 1967 war. Much of the arguing back and forth had to do with an important United Nations Resolution, number 242, which outlined the formula of "land for peace." But when I questioned Reagan about it, he looked at me blankly. Not a clue.

In the summer of 1980 I reported on the Republican convention in Detroit that nominated Reagan. It was an unusual convention. There was some concern that he might not be a strong enough president and the convention was debating the possibility that Gerald Ford might be chosen as Reagan's vice president. As an ex-president, Ford would then have been a kind of copresident, an unprecedented position.

Here is my own sideline experience at the time. I was in a room off the convention floor, doing special reports with Sam Donaldson and columnist George Will. The three of us weren't anchoring; Frank Reynolds was. Frank would call on us from time to time for special reports or when we had some news. My friend Alan Greenspan, a former adviser to Ford, was also attending the convention in an unofficial capacity. He wasn't giving me any secret information, but knowing him did give me good access. It looked as if the Ford nomination wasn't going to happen, and George H. W. Bush's name was beginning to surface. This was a surprise because Bush had run against Reagan in the primaries and had been quite critical of him.

I knew George Bush fairly well, and I was on the phone with him in the midst of all the speculation about who would be the VP nominee. Suddenly he told me to hold on, that Ronald Reagan was calling him. I shouted to my producer that I was about to get big news and to tell the director to put me on the air instead of just on the phone. But the attempt to do this disrupted the call, and I lost Bush. As I was trying desperately to get him back, NBC's Andrea Mitchell reported that she had just heard that George Bush was going to be Reagan's running mate. Good for Andrea, but I nearly went crazy. I had lost the scoop of the whole convention. At this point George Will looked at me with disdain and said, "It's only television, Barbara." Well, although I enjoy listening to George and reading his insightful columns, he has also for many years earned a very good living from "only television."

The Reagan years, especially during the first term, were a great contrast to the Carter era. Hollywood stars attended the state dinners along with the other guests all gussied up in diamond necklaces and fur coats. The wine flowed. The orchestras played. Except for Jacqueline Kennedy, Nancy Reagan was the most fashionable first lady we ever had. She was applauded by her friends but criticized by most of the press for her extensive and costly wardrobe. She loved the color red, and her favorite designers were Bill Blass and Adolfo, whose outfits cost thousands of dollars. Mrs. Reagan claimed she paid for them herself, but there were investigations and she didn't get off the hook until her performance at the Gridiron dinner, an annual roast given by the Washington press corps. I was there when she came onstage looking like a bag lady. Singing special lyrics to a Barbra Streisand song, "Second Hand Rose," Mrs. Reagan crooned, "I'm wearing secondhand clothes." She was a smash and had an easier time of things after that.

Then, only sixty-nine days after Reagan took office, he was shot by a mentally ill twenty-five-year-old named John Hinckley Jr. In a later interview Reagan described to me what happened to him. "When we got to the hospital, I got out of the car first and walked into the emergency room and a nurse was coming to meet me. And I said, 'I'm having trouble breathing,' and just then my knees began to get rubbery and the next thing I knew I was on a gurney. Incidentally, I was wearing a suit for the first time, a brand-new tailored suit. I had to lie on the gurney while, with the scissors, they cut the suit off of me."

Reagan also told me that the doctors went crazy trying to find a missing contact lens in his eye. It seemed he only wore one contact so he could see both close up and farther away. I particularly remember this because I, too, usually wear just one lens so I can both look at my questions close up with my nearsighted eye, and with a contact lens in the other eye, read the teleprompter at a distance.

The president seemed to put the assassination attempt behind him very quickly. In a remarkably short time he returned to work. The first lady had a harder time adjusting. I interviewed her two months after the attempt on her husband's life, the first time she talked publicly about her fears and anxiety. She said the president slept soundly, but she often woke up in the middle of the night, and then, wide awake, wanted to eat something, maybe an apple. But, she said, she was afraid the crunching sound would awaken the president and instead she ate a banana. I thought that was very funny and very human.

Perhaps this is the place to talk about the parents of the would-be assassin, John Hinckley Jr. After a seven-week trial, Hinckley was found not guilty for reasons of insanity. Doctors said he was schizophrenic. His motive, it turned out, was his infatuation with the actress Jodie Foster. He felt that by shooting the president he would impress her. After his trial he was sent to Saint Elizabeth's, a hospital for the mentally ill in Washington, D.C. There were many people, however, who felt that he should have been found guilty and sentenced to life in prison.

After what I thought was a suitable time, two years, I wrote to Hinckley's parents and asked if they would consider sitting down and talking with me. I told them that it would be an opportunity to have people understand the disease of schizophrenia and might help other parents determine if their child had severe mental problems or was just going through a difficult adolescence. I promised them a dignified interview. The Hinckleys considered my request and agreed. This was the first and only time they did such an interview. It was aired in April 1983.

John Hinckley Sr. had been a successful businessman in Denver, Colorado. He and his wife, Jo Ann, had three children: two boys and a girl. John Jr. was their youngest child. He was, they said, "a beautiful and happy little boy." The family was very close, took trips, and spent all their weekends together. But things began to change when John dropped out of college and came home. He used to sit and stare out the window, his father said. He was very depressed and, in his father's words, "could not seem to cope with the outside world."

Eventually, after having John Jr. tested to make sure that there was nothing physically wrong with him, Jo Ann and John took him to a psychiatrist, who told them to stop pampering their son, make him leave the house, and force him to get a job. They were not to help him. He had to learn to be independent. It was a form of "tough love," and the Hinckleys weren't sure it was the right treatment. When, at one point, their son wanted to come home, the psychiatrist told them: "Well, if he were my son, I would send him a hundred dollars and tell him good-bye."

The Hinckleys were in anguish about what to do, but when their son did come home, unshaven and wanting to stay, his father said no. Jo Ann Hinckley protested, but her husband said they had to follow the psychiatrist's advice. There seemed no other choice. "I gave my son all the cash I had," John Hinckley told me, "and said, 'You are on your own,' and that was the last I saw of him until the shooting."

Then, with tears brimming in his eyes, Hinckley Sr. said, "It's my fault. I sent him out when he couldn't cope. It's my fault."

The Hinckleys have since moved from Colorado to Washington, D.C., to be near their son, who is still incarcerated there. They devote their lives and funds to promoting research into the causes and treatment of schizophrenia and other mental diseases.

To this day I consider my interview with the Hinckleys to be one of the most important that I have ever done. I am indebted to those brave and honest people. As the mother of a child who had her own teenage troubles but, thank goodness, was not mentally ill, I sympathize with their confusion and grief.

The main victim of their son's shooting spree was the president's tough, husky, funny press secretary, James Brady. His nickname was "the Bear." One of the bullets meant for the president landed in Brady's head, and for a while he was at death's door. When he recovered I also did the first interview with him and his courageous wife, Sarah.

It was devastating to talk to this man. After the shooting Jim could express himself somewhat, but his sentences usually ended—and he could not help this—with a wailing sound, like a loud, moaning cry of despair. He continued to make an amazing recovery, but there were ongoing effects of the brain damage.

Sarah Brady, when she was not devoting her time to her husband and son, tirelessly lobbied Congress for a gun-control bill. In 1993 the Brady Bill was passed. It requires licensed dealers to enforce a waiting period and do a background check of anyone purchasing a handgun.

Just before Thanksgiving of 1981, eight months after he'd been shot, Ronald Reagan agreed to let me interview him. Furthermore he invited me to conduct the interview at his secluded ranch in the hills near Santa Barbara, California. No television cameras had ever been invited to the ranch where the president spent his happiest private times. Mrs. Reagan didn't love it there, and I could understand why. The main house didn't have proper heat, and she often complained of the cold. The bathroom was small, and it was more like a camp for a young couple than a vacation home for a president. As I recall, there were just a few books in the house. But this was just what the president liked. He wanted a comfortable, unpretentious home surrounded by hills and valleys where he and Mrs. Reagan could ride their horses and just relax, watch a little television, and go to bed early.

There was a small lake on the property with a canoe called "True Love," the name of the love song in the movie *High Society*. The film had starred Grace Kelly and Bing Crosby, both of whom Reagan knew well from his acting days. Most of all the president wanted plenty of trees on the property that he could prune and chop into firewood. This was what he was doing when I arrived. I couldn't get over the fact that he was strong enough to saw logs when just the past spring, he had been in the hospital struggling for his life.

This was my favorite interview with the president. It was vintage Reagan: charming, amusing, and even poetic. As part of our report the president drove me around the ranch in his jeep. I sat next to him in the front seat. His dog sat behind us, thrilled to be with his master. The jeep was all but falling apart. "Forgive me, Mr. President," I remarked. "I don't want to hurt your feelings, but this is the scroungiest jeep. The upholstery is coming out." The president answered, straight-faced: "Yes, but, remember, we have an austerity program going on."

Later in the day, as the sun was setting, I stood with the president atop one of the hills on his property. He gazed at the valley before him for a while, and then he said quietly, "I've always believed that there was some plan that put this continent here to be found by people from every corner of the world who had the courage and the love of freedom enough to uproot themselves, leave family and friends and homeland, to come here and develop a whole new breed of people called American. You look at the beauty of it. And God really did shed his grace on America, as the song says." He was not reading from a script.

I went on to conduct three more interviews with Ronald Reagan while he was president and shortly after he left office, and I probably conducted more interviews with Mrs. Reagan while she was first lady than any other television reporter. She often said to me that her life began when she was introduced to Ronald Reagan. The president, too, once told the same thing to me: "I think my life began when I met Nancy."

The Reagans' love for each other was never more apparent than when, during the president's second term in office, Mrs. Reagan discovered she had breast cancer and made the decision to have a mastectomy. Five months later she talked with me about that decision, the first time she had publicly commented on the operation. She had been criticized by some women for having a modified radical mastectomy instead of a lumpectomy, the far less invasive procedure that my own sister had. Mrs. Reagan defended her choice. She had told her doctors, "I want it over and done with." And then she added with a smile, "I told them it wouldn't take them long because I was never Dolly Parton."

Her biggest concern, she said, was not the feelings of other women but her husband's feelings. He assured her, she told me, that her decision would make absolutely no difference in their relationship and his love for her. She then went ahead with the operation.

The Reagans moved to Bel Air, Los Angeles, after they left office, and I continued to stay in touch with them. When Merv and I married, we also had a house in Bel Air. "What fun," Mrs. Reagan wrote me. "Who borrows the cup of sugar first?" We often had the Reagans over for lunch or dinner, and Mrs. Reagan and I became personal friends. After Merv and I divorced and I was spending all of my time in New York, Mrs. Reagan and I had long talks on the telephone. She had plenty of time then, as her husband had Alzheimer's disease and had entered what she described as "the long good-bye." I was invited to Ronald Reagan's funeral in 2004. I attended it as a guest and also reported on it. It was symbolic of the many years during which Mrs. Reagan and I shared both a personal and professional bond.

I have chosen to write more about Reagan's personal side rather than the historic events of his presidency because others can do and have done the latter far better than I. I wanted to give my own impression of President Reagan because, unlike several historians and indeed, the common thinking, I never found him cold or hard to reach. True, he told too many jokes, several of which he had told me before, and though I may never have found him brilliant, I certainly didn't find him stupid or, after he became president, uninformed. I didn't agree privately with him on some issues, like his pro-life stand on abortion, but he was not a man who minded if you confronted him. He did indeed inspire pride and patriotism and confidence. At that time in our history, those were no small things.

It may seem odd to some that, though I say openly that I am pro-choice, I rarely if ever give my political opinions on camera. I have interviewed politicians on the Left and on the Right, but I doubt if anyone watching me knows my politics. Although this doesn't seem to be the style these days, I would like to keep it that way. Part of the reason is that ABC News expects its correspondents to behave with objectivity. Although I care very much about the issues facing this country, you would not know which candidates I favor in presidential elections or whether I am a Republican, a Democrat, or a freethinking anarchist.

Of all the presidents I've interviewed, George H. W. Bush was the one I knew best on a personal level. We met way back in the sixties through his younger brother, Jonathan, a friend of my then husband, Lee. (Jonathan had for a short time been in show business and their paths had crossed.) I got to know Bush much better in 1971 when he came to New York to begin a three-year appointment as the U.S.

ambassador to the United Nations. He had just lost his race for the U.S. Senate in Texas (he was beaten by Lloyd Bentsen) and at first, was not overly enthusiastic about his new post. He was having "withdrawal symptoms," he wrote me in a note. "I believed in what we were doing. I thought it was fair and reasonable, but we didn't win. The U.N. will be an exciting place—and we must not look back." Barbara Bush was not always in the city during his years at the U.N., and George Bush and I occasionally had dinner with mutual friends. I liked him a lot. He was smart, experienced, and had a sense of humor that followed him from the U.N., to China, where, from 1974 to 1976, he served as chief of the United States Liaison Office. (He did not hold the official title of ambassador because the United States did not establish formal diplomatic relations with the People's Republic of China until 1979.) I must have written him there about the latest shockers in the Watergate scandal and the impeachment proceedings against Nixon because his response took note of it. "Boy, are we isolated from the hot dope," he wrote. "We are loving Peking. There is a certain luxury in being out of the crossfire and turmoil at home." That luxury was short-lived. Bush came back from China to become director of the CIA, then to run for the Republican presidential nomination in the 1980 primaries. I never felt he had the fire in his belly that would propel him to run for the presidency. Obviously, I was wrong.

One morning, after he had just done an early morning TV show, he called and woke me up, asking if he could come by my apartment for breakfast. He would be over in a few minutes, he said. I threw on a bathrobe and, over coffee, he told me that he had definitely decided to throw his hat in the ring. I was surprised and doubted that he had a chance. (An inside note here. When I did the first draft of this section on presidents, I wrote that before Bush arrived "I threw on some clothes." I thought it sounded strange to say that I was in a bathrobe. But in the summer of 2006, I was at a party that he and Mrs. Bush attended and I mentioned that I was writing a memoir. "Did you say that I came over to your house and you were in a bathrobe?" he asked. I told him I thought that might embarrass him. "Not at all," he said. "It's the truth. Write it." So I just did.)

Bush didn't win the presidency that time, but he did in 1988, after serving eight years as vice president to Ronald Reagan. In the early days of his presidency I went to a dinner at the White House and afterward sent a thank-you letter. I received back a photograph of the two of us with the inscription: "Souvenir time. George Jr. told me he had a nice time sitting next to you at dinner." I barely remembered the conversation. Little did I think that my jovial dinner companion would one day become president himself. Thank heaven I didn't yawn over dessert.

I also remember a very special dinner in the private family dining room at the White House. It was March 1991. President Bush had invited a small group of people in honor of Margaret Thatcher. I was delighted to be included, but the reason I particularly remember the dinner is that I was leaving the very next morning to fly to Saudi Arabia to conduct the first interview with our victorious general in the Gulf War, Norman Schwarzkopf. When the president learned of this, he took his place card, which read, "The President," and wrote on the back of it, "Norm, careful, careful; but she's OK. Congratulations again, George Bush." He then handed me the card to give to the general.

Those were good days for George Bush. The bad days were to come when, in the last year of his presidency, in spite of winning the Gulf War, his popularity was falling. The race for the presidency was heating up. Ross Perot, the eccentric independent, was nipping at his heels, and the governor of Arkansas, named Bill Clinton, was throwing darts at Bush and becoming more and more popular. In addition both President Bush and Mrs. Bush had been treated that summer for a condition known as Grave's disease, which is a dysfunction of the thyroid gland. They were both taking thyroid pills, but Bush claimed he was in very good health and no longer had any symptoms. Still, he had been turning down all requests for television interviews. I did my usual push, writing and repeatedly calling his aides, especially his media affairs assistant, Dorrance Smith. Dorrance had previously worked at ABC, and I knew him well. Finally, in June 1992, the president agreed to sit, with Mrs. Bush, and do what is called an in-depth interview.

Dorrance told me I had an hour for the interview, which was plenty of time. Then I did something I had not done in any other interviews with presidents. The question that kept dogging Bush was that he had no vision for the future of America. His critics were pouncing on what was being called the "vision thing." Dorrance knew it. We never tell our questions in advance, but I thought the "vision thing" was extremely important, and as I have said, I had known George Bush a long time and liked him a great deal. So I gave Dorrance a heads-up and said the president should be thinking about his answer. This was a rather dangerous thing to do, giving any politician a heads-up about what you're going to ask. But I thought, "I have nothing but difficult and critical questions to ask him, starting with his being at the height of his popularity just a year ago and now being perceived as indecisive, weak, and a loser. So I'll give him a little break."

In the interview Bush blamed the failing economy for his growing unpopularity, and we drudged along. I finally asked, "Again and again, what you hear people saying is, 'We don't know what the President's vision is.' So Mr. President, what is your vision for this country?"

Despite the advantage I'd given him, Bush's answer was long, turgid, and uninspiring, without anything to give the public real confidence in his leadership. He seemed to lack drive or energy. No wonder some people thought he was ill. My interview certainly didn't help him.

He is thought of very differently today. With the passage of time, George H. W. Bush has become a popular ex-president.

As for Barbara Bush, the country's view of her has also changed over the years. After Nancy Reagan, with her slim body and designer clothes, Barbara Bush, with her white hair, ample body, and signature three-strand fake pearls, represented the good-natured, unthreatening grand-mother we all wished to have. During her husband's term in office she brandished that image, but when he left office, her truer personality emerged. In both private and public conversations she showed a dry wit and a willingness to give her opinions. She spoke out forcefully on mat-ters that were controversial, and even disagreed with her husband. In the fall of 1994, two years after her husband was voted out of office, she published a memoir and gave me the first interview. The interview was conducted in Kennebunkport, Maine, their vacation residence.

First she took on career women, saying that if a woman opted to have children, the children must absolutely come before the career. Okay, not too controversial, but these days when so many women must work, eas-ier said than done. Then she confessed that when it came to the ques-tion of abortion, she was pro-choice. This was not something she had ever admitted when her husband was in office. When I remarked that some people felt her husband had been pro-choice and then changed his position to pro-life, she said no, he was always pro-life, never pro-choice. They agreed to disagree. I wish she'd had the courage to give her opinion when her husband was president. It would have carried far more weight in the controversy.

Also in this interview, she spoke frankly about a severe bout of depression she suffered at the age of fifty-one, shortly after her husband returned from serving as the unofficial ambassador to China. She was ashamed, she said, and told no one but her husband. At his insistence she got help. The depression never returned, and now she told me, "When I hear about depression, instead of saying, 'Well, pull yourself together,' I say, 'Get help.' "

These days Mrs. Bush is seen more accurately than in her White House years, especially because her son, the current president, so often describes her as the tough, no-nonsense woman she is. Whenever our paths cross privately now, I feel I can say whatever I want and so does she. We go back a long way, as she pointed out in a note to me in 2002. "You and I have known each other for a *long* time—starting in 1971 or 1972 with *Not for Women Only*," she wrote. "A cabinet wives program. It was fun." Yes, indeed, Mrs. Bush, it was.

So now, Bill and Hillary Clinton. One of the best things about Bill Clinton was that though he would keep you waiting forty-five minutes for a scheduled hour-long interview, he'd stay for *another* hour. Maybe even longer. It was great.

Still, I never felt that I really got through to Clinton. I never experienced his renowned sex appeal. He never sparkled with me. I remember from Katharine Graham's superb autobiography that she felt President John Kennedy more or less overlooked her because she wasn't young. I felt the same way about myself and Bill Clinton. I interviewed him in September 1996. (It was three years before I conducted my interview with Monica Lewinsky, the White House intern with whom he had an affair.) Our conversation was not memorable to me.

However, I've seen Bill Clinton quite a few times since he left office, at dinners or charitable events. Now, whenever we meet, he is warm and friendly. Maybe, when I am not asking questions, he feels more comfortable. At private dinners he talks and talks and talks. He rarely takes questions from the other guests. Fortunately what he has to say is always worth listening to.

Still, to me, the most interesting member of that family is Hillary Clinton, with whom I've conducted several interviews both in and out of the White House. If I didn't feel back then that I got President Clinton's message, I certainly felt I got hers. Besides my own interviews, I'd watched her address groups, small and large, and never use notes. She has a great throaty laugh that is contagious. I remember going to a very private birthday dinner for her when she was in the White House. One of the toasts was delivered by the late Peter Stone, a successful writer of Broadway shows and movies. Peter raised his glass, and looking around the room at the many Jewish guests who were friends of Hillary's, said: "Please join me in toasting the nation's First Shiksa." We all laughed, Hillary the loudest.

This is what I remember most. It was June 2003. The big "get" that late spring was Hillary Clinton. Her autobiography, *Living History*, was about to be published. The book was being kept under heavy wraps, and nobody knew what areas it would cover, where it would begin, or how much Mrs. Clinton would say about her relationship with her husband. Everyone at every network and cable news program wanted to do that first interview with her. I wanted to get it for *20/20*, but because I had done the interview with Monica Lewinsky, ABC didn't think I stood a chance. "Stay out of it," I was told. "You will only muddy the waters." The reasoning was that if I tried, I might offend Clinton's people and jeopardize the possibility of the Hillary interview going to any ABC correspondent. Accordingly my name was not on the list of correspondents ABC sent to the Clinton camp. I accepted that.

The only conversation I had concerning the book was with someone I knew slightly who had worked with Mrs. Clinton at the White House and had been retired for many years. She and I met at a baby shower, and in the course of conversation I remarked that whoever got the interview should try to take Mrs. Clinton back to her childhood home in the suburbs of Chicago to see what her life was like there. Then I thought we would really understand her. It was a casual remark, and I didn't give it another thought.

So you can understand why I almost literally fell off my chair when, two weeks later, Mrs. Clinton's very able lawyer, Bob Barnett, telephoned and said: "Can you and your ABC people meet with me tomorrow, someplace private, to discuss the terms of the interview with Senator Clinton?" Lo and behold, I was the chosen one! It created some ripples within the news division, but at least ABC got the interview.

When I read the book I realized why I might have been chosen to conduct the interview. The first third of the book was about her childhood in the town of Park Ridge, Illinois, and the influences that made her the woman she is. I think it's likely that my chance remark at the baby shower had been passed along to her decision makers.

Whatever the reason, I thought the fact that Mrs. Clinton chose me said miles about her. I was, after all, the reporter who had done the interview with the woman who had caused her and her husband such pain, but she didn't hold that against me.

I did indeed ask her to take me back to her hometown. There we had a chance to spend the kind of time that is not possible in a formal sit-down interview. We visited the house in which she grew up with her staunchly Republican father and closet Democrat mother, and we had "olive burgers" at a little tavern next to the town's only movie theater.

Mrs. Clinton was happy to talk about the little girl she had been and the more grown-up girl who would fall in love with Bill Clinton. In my past interviews with Mrs. Clinton I hadn't really liked or disliked her. She was smart, crisp, often evasive, and fairly formal. Now as we laughed together and talked about how much she had loved Bill Clinton's hands, I really liked her. But I had a job to do.

When we finished this part of the interview, we made arrangements for our next session at her home in Chappaqua, New York. There we were going to have to deal with Monica Lewinsky. "It won't be as easy a conversation the next time we meet," I told her. "I know," she said. "I'm dreading it, but I realize we have to talk about it."

And we did. She talked about how furious she was with her husband when he finally told her the truth about Monica. How she considered leaving him. How in the end she could only trust her own judgment in deciding what to do because "your friends won't be there at three in the morning."

"How could you stay in this marriage?" I asked. "Because," she said, "no one understands me better and no one can make me laugh the way Bill does. Even after all these years, he is still the most interesting, energizing, and fully alive person I have ever met."

She expected me to ask those questions, but she didn't expect, and didn't like, what came next. Nor, I heard, did her husband when he watched the interview. I had mulled over just how and when I was going to ask: "What if he does it again?" I knew it would be hard for her to answer, but I had to ask. Her answer was a nonanswer. "That will be between us, and that will be the zone of privacy that I believe in. But right now, I am very, very hopeful and very committed to our marriage."

Passage of time: In the fall of 2007, I had the opportunity to interview Bill Clinton again, this time for our *10 Most Fascinating People Special*. His wife was now a presidential candidate. Clinton, at least to me, seemed a changed man—warm, friendly, smiling, and seemingly very much at peace with himself. Our interview was conducted in his spacious office in Harlem. On the walls are a broad array of photographs, ranging from Dr. Martin Luther King and Nelson Mandela to old-time jazz musicians and family and friends. There are books everywhere, many of them first editions.

The interview had its light moments, such as when I asked if he planned to take over the traditional role of first lady should his wife become president, like presiding over the White House Easter egg hunt or showing off the Christmas decorations. Clinton replied: "Sure. We love the holidays. Chelsea still comes home every Thanksgiving and cooks a Thanksgiving meal for us and a bunch of her friends, and we take in strays who are a long way from home or don't have a family. So if I am asked to be involved in any of that Christmas celebration or Easter stuff, I'd love to do it."

The more moving part of my interview, however, was when I asked what impact, if any, his quadruple bypass surgery had on him. Evidently, it had had quite an effect. "I think it's made me more grateful for every day I have alive," he said. "All the things that used to bother me don't seem very important anymore. I think it made me more determined to use my time in a way that gives other people the chance to live the life I've had. A lot of people might have thought it was tragic if I had perished at a young age, but the truth is I would still have had a life more full, more rich, than the vast majority of people who have ever lived. I look at flowers more than I used to. I notice how the air smells when the seasons change. Those things mean something to me again, like they did when I was a boy. I both love the small things in the world and I sweat the small things less."

His answer might seem predictable and maybe corny but at last he got through to me.

George W. Bush may also seem predictable and not always wise to me, but he certainly has been good to me. I had little recollection of him from our dinner together at the White House when his father was president, and I wasn't sure what to expect when I first met him as a presidential candidate. He was visiting New York, and Karen Hughes, then his trusted communications adviser, invited me to come up to his hotel suite. He bounced into the living room, confident as all get-out. He told me he was sure he was going to be president, gave me a strong handshake and a wink (he likes to wink), and that was pretty much it. I was surprised at his certainty. From what I had heard, he was more or less wishy-washy. I sure didn't feel that.

When he was nominated, I started my usual writing and calling for an interview, and hit a home run right after the election. I was invited down to his ranch in Crawford to talk with him just two days before he left for his inauguration in Washington in January 2001.

The interview was done in the barn, which was very wet and soggy, and my boots (no high heels here) were drenched and caked with mud. Whenever I saw Bush in the future, he would take delight in reminding me of the mud on my boots.

Was he nervous about being president, I asked. Not a bit. "I can't wait to get up there," he said. "I can't wait to get started." This was not an uncertain governor. This was the next president of the United States, and we'd better know it.

Unlike my open-ended interviews with the freewheeling Bill Clinton, my first interview with Bush—like other interviews with him in the future—were all strictly timed. I would be told, for example, that I had twenty-nine minutes and no more, and then I would have all kinds of time to walk around the White House with the dogs trailing or, as in the case of this first interview, to tour the ranch with Bush driving his jeep—shades of my interview with Ronald Reagan. Not only were interviews precisely timed, so were social events and White House dinners. Clinton liked to schmooze and perhaps even dance after a dinner; Bush believed in early to bed and little socializing when the meal was finished. During his eight years in office, I was invited to three Bush White House dinners. Each time the entertainment ended at 10:00 p.m. The president then took to the stage, thanked everybody for coming, and by 10:10 we were out of there.

Back to the ranch. To my eyes it wasn't exactly a ranch, more of a "ranchette." It was in the middle of nowhere. Well, actually not exactly nowhere. It was near Waco, Texas. Bush drove me over a few small hills, the area being almost completely flat, and by some small streams and a tiny waterfall. On the way back to the house he pointed out the small artificial lake in front of the house, which he had stocked with fish.

The house itself was quite modest. Mrs. Bush was just furnishing it. The president-elect took me into his small office. There was a painted stove, which, he said, was a gift from his father. When he opened the door of the stove, there were rifles. The office also had a computer, but Bush told me that from this day forward he would send no e-mails. "Too dangerous," he said.

I interviewed President Bush four more times during his eight years in office. Our interviews, now held in the White House, were substantive, although Bush rarely strayed from his well-known opinions and fairly rigid script. Same questions about Iraq. Same answers. But what has stayed with me the most is what he had to say about his faith. His faith is an intimate part of his life, and what I wanted to know was how much, if at all, his beliefs affected his decision making. I brought up the subject in two separate interviews. In 2005 he told me this: "Faith is a very important part of my being able to handle the pressures of the job. Other presidents might feel differently about it. I don't. I am sustained by prayer, my own prayer and the fact that others pray for me."

Another time when I asked how accepting God in his life motivated his decision making, he said, "I don't think it necessarily makes the decisions of war and peace any different, but it makes me as a person different than I was." He went on, "I'm a fierce competitor. I want to win. But if it doesn't work out, I will have accepted my fate here and part of that acceptance, part of the calm that I feel, is a result of my religion."

There has come the day when President Bush went back for good to that ranch in Texas. When he did finally return home, I daresay, he did it with a feeling of calm. However his presidency ended, he will no doubt have "accepted his fate."

Heads of State: The Good, the Bad, and the Mad

EADS OF STATE. Oh, the power! Oh, the glory! Oh, the climb up! Oh, the fall! From the democratically elected to the chosen by birth, chosen by coup, chosen by war, chosen by edict, chosen by hook or by crook. I have tried to think of what each has in common with the others. One quality stands out: belief in yourself. The conviction that only *you* can do the job. The shah of Iran felt he was born to be emperor. Fidel Castro told me that if he wanted to resign, his countrymen would consider it treason. Anwar Sadat and Menachem Begin both were fatalists. Each thought God had endowed him with the wisdom to lead, though their gods had different names.

Over the years I've interviewed at least thirty heads of state, from the obscure, like Poland's last Communist prime minister, Gen. Wojciech Jaruzelski, to his better-known successor, Poland's first democratically elected president, Lech Wałesa. Some were women—Golda Meir of Israel, Margaret Thatcher of Great Britain, Indira Gandhi of India, and most recently Dr. Michelle Bachelet, president of Chile—but the majority were men. Some were Christian, like Chancellor Helmut Schmidt of Germany and Czech president Václav Havel (I interviewed him so early in his administration that his office didn't have enough typewriters and I left him mine); others were Muslim, like King Abdullah of Saudi Arabia, President Hosni Mubarak of Egypt, and the Hashemite kings of Jordan. I interviewed three Jewish prime ministers of Israel, two Hindu prime ministers of India, and at least two atheists—China's General Secretary Jiang Zemin and Fidel Castro.

I always felt privileged to interview world leaders, though I certainly didn't like all of them. Some I liked in spite of myself. Vladimir Putin had a good sense of humor. Hugo Chávez poured out his heart in a very personal way, all in an effort to reach the hearts of Americans. Most were friends of the United States. One, like Saddam Hussein, was at one point considered to be more or less a friend and, as we all know, later became a fierce enemy. Another, Mu'ammar Qaddafi, was a fierce enemy who has now become, more or less, a friend.

When I am doing an interview with a so-called enemy, I keep my personal opinions to myself and let my questions tell the story. If the person hangs himself or herself with the answers, I have also done my job. In any case I consider it important for a journalist to be able to present the views of people even our own government can't, or won't, talk to. It is a way to learn what we are up against. And yes, if Osama bin Laden wanted to do an interview with me, I would jump at the chance. I think any reporter would.

An interview with a head of state used to be considered a great coup and received a good portion of time on television newsmagazine shows. But since the Britney Spearses of the world and sensational crime stories became the big ratings draws, international political leaders, with few exceptions, have come to be considered dull fare, and their time on the air has been cut short. We really seem to care only if they are outrageous and call our president a devil or declare that the Holocaust never existed. Stand up and scream and we will interview you, or be reasonable and unheard.

World leaders have changed as well. They have become much more ratings savvy. Now before they agree to an interview they want to know how much actual airtime they will be given and what the ratings of the program are. In some cases they'll refuse to talk unless their interview is presented unedited. Most network newsmagazines won't agree to that.

Don't panic. I'm not going to subject you to every one of the heads of state I have talked to. Even I glaze over at the prospect. I'm just going to pick a few sound bites (or book bites, in this case), about some of the most important or interesting leaders I've interviewed.

Let's start small, with one of the more entertaining—I hate to call it entertaining, but that's what it was—an interview in 1986 with the recently deposed dictator of Haiti, Jean-Claude Duvalier, known as "Baby Doc," and his glamorous wife, Michèle, disparagingly known as the "Dragon Lady." The couple was being accused by the new government in impoverished Haiti of stealing as much as $400 million from the national treasury, and the Duvaliers wanted to refute those charges from, of all places, a villa in the South of France.

I knew that Mme. Duvalier was hardly going to dispel the charge of thievery when she sat down for the interview wearing a designer suit, a diamond brooch, diamond earrings, and a diamond ring. Hardly a great public relations move. Baby Doc sat there like a big lump of lard. He barely opened his mouth. But Michèle was like a little buzzing bee—buzz, buzz, buzz, talk, talk, talk. "It is said that I have a collection of furs, that I refrigerate my apartment because of the furs, but how can one wear furs in a tropical country?" she trilled. She didn't have a special room for her furs, she said, the entire palace was air-conditioned, "because one cannot live in Port au Prince without air-conditioning."

I almost felt sorry for her when she said that. Almost. Did she not know or care that many Haitians had no running water or electricity, let alone air-conditioning; no jobs; no future? Did she realize what she was saying? But when I asked her these questions, she just looked perplexed. And on we went.

A source inside the new Haitian government had provided us with her bills from jewelers all over the world, as well as canceled checks drawn on the national treasury. After the air-conditioning conversation, I showed these to her one by one and, without blinking an eye, she insisted that all the hundreds of thousands of dollars had gone to decorate the airport in Haiti for a visit from Pope John Paul II in 1983! That must have been some airport.

It astonishes me how many celebrities and even heads of state consent to be interviewed, or seek out an interview, and then don't realize what they sound and look like. As Mme. Duvalier dug herself into an ever deeper hole, I kept thinking, "Why is she talking to me?" But if she didn't get it, the viewers certainly did. For weeks after it aired, Haitians stopped me on the street in New York to thank me for exposing the Duvaliers. And while it was true that I certainly wanted to expose their extravagance and their disregard for their own people, it was the couple who damaged themselves.

From an interview with a petty woman to conversations with a woman who was by far the most meaningful to me, a woman whose place in history is assured as one of the most important leaders of our time. I am speaking of Great Britain's first and only female prime minister, Margaret Thatcher. She held the office from 1979 to 1990, longer than any other British prime minister in this century, including Winston Churchill. I interviewed Mrs. Thatcher more than any other head of state, starting—and this is important—*before* she became prime minister. I had been interested in talking with her when she was not in a position of great power, which perhaps accounts for all the interviews she later gave me.

She was a leader in every sense of the word—direct, articulate, and authoritative. She was also very opinionated and to many, tough, which earned her the nickname "Iron Lady." That was hardly surprising, as she was, for the most part, the only woman in a sea of suits and ties. I can still conjure up images of her at this international conference or that economic summit without a hair straying from her bouffant hairdo, wearing a tailored suit, pumps, pearls, and carrying a purse.

Like her or not, she transformed the social system of Great Britain, the ultimate Conservative. She was, however, a prime minister and not a queen, and as such, she lived surprisingly modestly.

In 1987 she gave me a tour for *20/20* of 10 Downing Street, the prime minister's official residence in London. The downstairs was very grand and imposing. Up a flight of stairs were her living quarters. She and her husband, Denis, a retired chemist, lived, as she described it, "above the store."

Her living room was small and undistinguished. She was a great admirer of the modern sculptor Henry Moore, and had one of his smaller pieces prominently displayed, as well as some sketches his niece had sent her. "You must conserve your heritage, but some of the modern design I think is fantastic," she said. She showed me the book she was reading: *Seeds of Change: Five Plants That Transformed Mankind.* The first, she told me, was actually a tree, whose bark produces quinine and cures malaria. "I'm in the middle of tea now," she said. "I haven't got on to the potato."

Speaking of potatoes, the kitchen, where the prime minister cooked for her husband on the weekends, was tiny. "In Britain there is no domestic staff provided for prime ministers. They are expected to have wives," she said.

Out of the kitchen, she had her own definition of leadership. I sometimes quote her when I am speaking to audiences on the subject. The advice came from her father and an early lesson he taught her: "You never just go and do something because someone else is doing it. That is wrong. You never just follow the crowd for the sake of following the crowd because you don't like to stand out. You make up your own mind about what is right. And then you try to persuade other people to follow you. It was quite a tough thing for a child, but it was very, very firm in my father's upbringing. It has stood me in very good stead since."

Well, Mrs. Thatcher certainly did her own thing, maybe too much so, because she was finally turned out of office in 1990 after a bloody fight within her own political party. Her country didn't turn against her. Her party did. But unlike in our country where an ex-president and first lady receive Secret Service protection and expenses for an office staff, a former prime minister in Great Britain receives nothing. When she was ousted, Mrs. Thatcher had no living quarters. She ended up in an apartment lent to her by the widow of Henry Ford II, and she paid for her own secretary and assistants. For a while she was deeply depressed, not surprising after all those years of power.

She articulated her feelings in a poignant interview with me four months after she left office. "It's the habit of years which get you," she told me. "The telephone goes and immediately you think, 'Oh goodness me, the United Nations is sitting. I wonder what's happened.' You jump up to answer the phone. And then you realize that it's no longer you anymore."

This was a very important lesson, one, however, which I think I already knew. There does come that day for most of us when "it's no longer you anymore." That is why you must have good old and loving friends who are truly there when fame and celebrity are gone.

My last interview with Margaret Thatcher was in 1993 when she was in New York promoting her memoir, *The Downing Street Years*. Her official title by then was Margaret, Lady Thatcher, Baroness of Kesteven, having been elevated to the peerage by Queen Elizabeth. She was her same outspoken self, even criticizing President George H. W. Bush for not pursuing Saddam Hussein during the first Gulf War. "When you've embarked on something, it's best to finish it and finish it properly," she said. Saddam Hussein should have been "publicly humiliated" and "made to surrender." "If you tackle an aggressor or a dictator, which is what Saddam Hussein is, they've got to be humiliated," she said. "They've got to be seen as defeated in battle." Obviously Bush didn't take her advice.

Since I saw her in triumph as prime minister when her advice was usually taken and in despair when she was turned out of office, it has left me with a particularly soft feeling about her. I feel privileged to have known her as I did.

My interview with Saddam Hussein took place ten years before the first Gulf War. The year was 1981. Israel had just bombed Iraq's fledgling nuclear reactor, and I went to Baghdad to interview the Iraqi president. It was his first interview for American television, and I did it for ABC's then Sunday news program, *Issues and Answers*. I wasn't frightened of Saddam Hussein, but I was anxious when we came in for a landing to find virtually no lights on the runway. Iraq was in the middle of a war with its neighbor, Iran, and Baghdad was in a blackout. Our interview was conducted in the darkened presidential palace in Baghdad, which would be taken over by coalition forces after the invasion of Iraq in 2003.

What do I remember about Saddam Hussein? He wore a black suit and looked serious and imposing. He spoke calmly, rarely raising his voice as he condemned the United States for the Israeli bombing of the reactor. "This aggression was carried out by an American armed weapon," he said through an interpreter. "And that's why all the reactions, all the criticisms, and all the decisions to express this anger and this hatred are legitimate. I consider them as aggressors." He did not even support a Palestinian state in Israel because, to him, there was no Israel. It was all Palestine, and who were the Israelis? Palestinian Jews.

I guess one might ask how I, being Jewish, felt hearing these remarks. The truth is that I felt great concern for Israel but nothing personal. I'd heard similar remarks from Arabs before and would again. To me it went with the territory or the person.

So I was not surprised to hear similar remarks from another bitter enemy then of the United States and Israel, Col. Mu'ammar Qaddafi of Libya. He and I talked first in January 1989. I had tried for ages to get an interview with him, so I leaped at the offer when he finally agreed.

I had to get a special waiver from the U.S. government to go to Libya because it was then considered a terrorist state and, as such, out of bounds to Americans. The United States had linked the country to the 1986 bombing of a West Berlin nightclub that killed two U.S. servicemen. We responded by launching retaliatory air strikes. Qaddafi's house in Tripoli, Libya's capital, had been all but destroyed, his sons wounded, and his fifteen-month-old adopted daughter, Hana, killed.

The exact time and place for the interview had not been set but my producer, Martin Clancy, and I had barely gotten off the plane when uniformed men approached us and said that the colonel wanted to do the interview right away. It is interesting to me how many heads of state wanted to do interviews with me at night, and then usually kept me waiting. Maybe it was when they had the most time or maybe it was a matter of control. But in Libya, our camera crew, mostly coming from London and Italy, had not even arrived. We promised to be ready the next day. "Where," we asked, "would the interview take place?" "In the colonel's tent," we were told.

The colonel's tent, it turned out, had thick carpets covering the sand

and was in a small oasis smack in the middle of Tripoli. You would never have found it except for a guard sitting under a palm tree. Inside the property were more palm trees and adult and baby camels wandering around. (Qaddafi evidently relived his nomadic Bedouin childhood by drinking camel's milk.) The tent was set up close to the shattered house the Americans had bombed, which was preserved as a kind of shrine. His daughter's broken crib was still there in the second-floor bedroom, and near the entrance were the helmets of two American Air Force pilots whose planes had been shot down.

The inside of the tent was bright orange and green, green being Libya's national color and the traditional color of Islam. I was wearing a pink knit suit. Qaddafi arrived wearing a white suit, a green shirt, a white cape lined in green, and white alligator mules. He looked absolutely stunning but all I could think of was that between his white suit with the green, the green-and-orange tent, and my pink suit, the viewers were going to have an awful headache.

I disliked Qaddafi because of his support of terrorist groups and his determination to drive Israel into the sea, but in the two hours we spent taping the interview, he answered every question and betrayed no hostility toward me. Neither did I to him. He did, however, have a curious posture. Never once did he look at me. Occasionally he would look to his left, where his interpreter was sitting (though he seemed to understand a good deal of English and sometimes would correct the interpreter). Still, I would look him in the face, and he would look to the left or down or up, but never once did he meet my eyes. I thought it might be because I am a woman, but my colleague George Stephanopoulos, who interviewed him some years later, told me he had the same experience.

I began my questioning of Qaddafi by asking simply, "What do you think is the greatest misconception about you in our country?" He answered in a long, rambling diatribe against the Western media, which, he claimed, would "show pictures of me next to skulls, to dead bodies, and they're not reflecting the true picture of me." I politely disagreed. "Your misconceptions about us," I said, "are as great as our misconception about you."

The misconception theme continued, which gave me the opening to ask the question that so many people in my country were wondering about: Was he insane? Seems to me that whenever we don't like a foreign leader, we question his sanity, but I had to ask. I tried to phrase it so it wouldn't sound too hostile. "While we are talking about misconceptions, can I ask you something directly which may seem rude? In our country we read that you are mad. Why do you think this is?"

Instead of taking offense he threw back his head and laughed. His convoluted answer about being loved by "the majority of ordinary people in the four corners of the globe" was not necessarily reassuring, but at least he didn't kick me out. Indeed, he seemed quite satisfied at the end of the interview and asked if there was anything else I wanted. I said two things. First, I wanted to visit what had been reported in America as a factory for creating chemical weapons and other WMD, but which his people told us was making medicines; second, I wanted to meet his family, particularly his wife. "No Westerner has seen them on camera," I said, "and meeting them might help people understand you."

On the first request he said that he himself did not have the power to make those arrangements. Oh, yeah? Instead, he would ask the commissioner in charge of the plant if it was possible to visit. It turned out, although we asked again and again during our three-day stay, that it wasn't. So much for that. As for meeting his family, Qaddafi said he would think about that and let me know.

I waited for five hours in my hotel room, passing the time by eating Libya's delicious blood oranges. (Tripoli is in fact a beautiful city with a busy bazaar, welcoming people, and beautiful beaches.) Then came the knock on the door. "Come immediately," said one of Qaddafi's aides. And back we went to the tent, where Qaddafi's wife, Safiya, and four of their six young children were waiting.

Safiya Qaddafi, his second wife, was a tall, stunning woman. Her children, lined up on either side of her, looked at me with hatred and fear in their eyes. I was the dreaded American from the country that had killed their little sister. "Our children consider all Americans like monsters, like Dracula," Safiya said to me. "When the people here want to get their children's attention, they say, 'Look out or the Americans will come for you.'" Safiya, a former nurse in a Tripoli hospital, had met Qaddafi during his recuperation from an automobile accident. They fell in love and married after he left the hospital, and became the parents of five sons and one daughter. "If my husband was really such a villain," Mrs. Qaddafi said to me, "do you think I would have stayed with him until now?"

At the time of this interview Qaddafi was, as I have mentioned, our sworn enemy. But he has done an about-face. In a dramatic shift in December 2003, our former terrorist foe became our new best friend when Libya announced it would give up its nuclear arms program along with other WMD. Among the reasons for Qaddafi's change of heart, one columnist wrote, was the killing of Saddam Hussein's sons by U.S. forces in Iraq, and Safiya Qaddafi's demands that her husband do more to protect their now grown sons from the same fate. I don't know if that is true, but if it is, it wouldn't be the first time that a strong wife influenced her husband.

The interviews with Saddam Hussein and Mu'ammar Qaddafi may have been two of the more exotic conversations I have had, but with Jiang Zemin, the general secretary of the Chinese Communist Party and chairman of the Central Military Commission, I met another leader who at the time was hardly considered a pal of the United States. I sat down to talk with him in Beijing in May 1990. A year had passed since the famous fifty-day student demonstration for democratic reforms had been crushed in Tiananmen Square by Chinese security forces. It became known as the Tiananmen Square Massacre, though no one was sure how many people had died. Heads had rolled in the Chinese leadership, and Jiang Zemin was the new man in charge.

It had taken us a great deal of time to get this interview. Henry Kissinger had been very helpful because he had had good relations with the Chinese hierarchy since his first and historic visit to that country. Dr. Kissinger put me in touch with the proper people who put me in touch with the proper people who put me in touch, etc., etc. After many, many letters, we got the go-ahead, probably because Jiang Zemin wanted to persuade Congress to continue America's favorable trade agreement with China.

We met on the beautiful grounds of the official state guesthouse in Beijing. We conducted the interview through an interpreter, though Jiang Zemin understood some English and even spoke a bit of it. He had a pleasant smile but cold eyes, and was given to quoting Shakespeare. When I asked him how he would describe the primarily student rebellion on Tiananmen Square the year before, he replied, in English: " 'Much ado about nothing.' "

It was hardly much ado about nothing, but he wouldn't budge and even said he didn't "have any regret" about the way the army sent its tanks against the students. He would, however, have handled it differently—by banning assembly on Tiananmen Square and thereby avoiding the use of lethal weapons. " 'A fall into the pit, a gain in the wit,' " he said, citing a Chinese proverb.

One of the enduring images from the siege was that of a young man standing in front of a column of tanks, blocking their progress toward the square. We had run the famous photograph of this lone figure, dressed in a white shirt and carrying a plastic shopping bag, over and over on ABC News. No one knew what had happened to him.

I had brought a copy of the photograph with me and I showed it to Jiang Zemin, full in the face. It took him by surprise, and his eyes became even more steely. He did not like the surprise or my question.

"Do you have any idea what happened to him?" I asked. "We have heard he was arrested and executed."

"I cannot confirm whether this young man you mention was arrested or not," he said. He answered, unexpectedly, in English.

"You do not know what happened to him?" I pressed.

"I think never killed," he said.

"You think he was not killed?" I said.

"I think never killed," he repeated.

That was it. We never did find out what happened to the man who braved the tanks.

When the interview was over and transmitted to New York, I wanted to travel a bit. Although I had been in China from that earliest visit with President Nixon, I was always working and had little opportunity to explore that vast country. This time I had my own plane ticket, but sometimes it can be very hard to get from one province to another. The flights can suddenly be canceled, delayed, or overbooked, as was the flight I had a ticket for. "Sorry, full," I was told at the airport. So I went to the ticket agent and showed him a photograph of me with Jiang Zemin that had been on the front page of one of the Chinese newspapers. I felt sure he would say, "Come this way," but he couldn't have cared less. The plane took off without me.

A revolution of a different sort in the USSR drew me to Moscow in January 1991 to interview Boris Yeltsin, then chairman of the Russian parliament. One Soviet republic after another was declaring independence, the latest being Lithuania, and the Soviet Union's president, Mikhail Gorbachev, had sent Soviet troops into the capital city, Vilnius, to shut down the television station. (By the way, my maternal grandmother came from Vilnius.) Fourteen unarmed Lithuanians had been killed and scores injured.

That was a story in itself. But then, so was the power struggle under way between Yeltsin, who supported independence for the Baltic states, and Gorbachev, who did not. I met with Yeltsin in Moscow in his ornate gold-encrusted offices in the building that houses the Russian parliament, called, curiously, the White House.

Yeltsin didn't hold back in his criticism of Gorbachev. He accused him of "losing his common sense" and being "dangerous." "How can it be possible to use troops against civilians at this time?" he said. And he chided the United States for turning Gorbachev into a folk hero. "You are blinded to certain things," Yeltsin said. "You see only the personality of Gorbachev and an aura around him." He was right. To this day Gorbachev is far more popular in this country than Boris Yeltsin.

It was widely rumored that Yeltsin had a drinking problem. He had evidently slurred his words during a lecture he delivered at Johns Hopkins University in 1989, and there were other private reports about his excessive drinking. So I felt I had to ask, "Do you drink too much?"

It was one of those moments again, much like my questioning Qaddafi's sanity to his face. Would Yeltsin take offense? Would he throw me out? To my relief he simply answered the question. "No. And I believe that, judging by the way I look, you can see that it's not true."

He was not, however, the portrait of health and fitness. His face was puffy and florid, and he sure looked like a drinker to me. But though I was pleased that he'd answered the question, I myself was in such distress that I'm not sure I was seeing straight.

I was suffering from severe lower back pain, and the almost-ten-hour flight from New York to Moscow hadn't helped. I was therefore sleeping on the floor of the bedroom in my hotel. I was traveling, as I often do, with my hairstylist/assistant, Bryant Renfroe. After I finished this interview with Yeltsin, we were planning to take two days off and go to the glorious city of St. Petersburg, where I'd never been. We had a late-morning flight. I'd given Bryant a key to my suite, and suddenly I looked up from the floor and there he was. He had been watching television in his own room. "The Gulf War has begun," he told me. "We're bombing Iraq." The only television set was in the living room, but when I tried to get off the floor, my back went into spasms. I couldn't stand up, so Bryant slipped the bedspread under me and dragged me into the living room. Watching the images of the war was so upsetting that my spasms seemed minor. Bryant helped me off the floor. Forget St. Petersburg; we flew home immediately.

A year later I returned to Moscow for another interview with Yeltsin. By then he was the president of Russia, the first freely elected president. Gorbachev was gone, and so was much of the former Soviet Union. In December 1991, the month before this second interview, it had collapsed into fifteen separate countries.

The date of this interview was January 31, 1992. Yeltsin, who had survived several assassination attempts, was about to come to America to meet with George H. W. Bush.

Concerns about his health were higher now that he was president. By his own admission he suffered from insomnia, migraine headaches, and depression. He'd go missing in Russia for days, even weeks, without official explanation and the stories about his drinking bouts were escalating. Some observed that his speech was slurred even when he took the oath of office as president.

So I put the same touchy subject to him that I had the year before. "What is being said in some of the American papers and magazines is that you have been drinking too much as a result of pressure."

Far from being offended, Yeltsin seemed happy to answer the question. His defense, I thought, was rather original. "Sports and liquor just don't go together," he said, detailing his physical exercise regimen: long workouts twice a week and shorter daily ones combined with a cold shower.

"Do you think it's your enemies who are spreading these stories?" I asked him.

"Or maybe it's just people who are looking for sensational stories," he said, perhaps meaning people like me. "First they spread rumors and then they wait for a reaction."

Despite at least one attempt to impeach him, Yeltsin would manage to hang on to the presidency for another seven years. He resigned in December 1999, after selecting a former KGB agent, Vladimir Putin, to succeed him. (Yeltsin died of heart failure in April 2007.) Putin was later elected president in his own right, and in 2001 I returned to Moscow to interview him. Our interview was held late at night, and he was late. No matter. I was used to that.

The plan was for President Putin and me to walk down one of the Kremlin's endless marble hallways while we casually exchanged pleasantries in English. But Putin had not advanced very far in his English lessons. "How are you?" I asked him as the cameras followed us. "What, please?" he responded. "How are you?" I tried again. "I am what?" he replied. Not a great beginning to the piece.

The interview itself, in another elaborate room with marble floors and gilded furniture inherited from the czars, went quite well. After much trial and error, my producers and I had devised an efficient way to work with interpreters. In times past we had had the interpreter sitting by the non-English-speaking head of state, but inevitably the head of state would turn to face the interpreter instead of me. So we came up with a better game plan. We put the interpreter in a separate room where he or she listened to my questions through earphones and then repeated them into a very small earpiece in the head of state's ear. The answers were then repeated into my ear. Because the interpreter was not seen, the head of state looked at me.

A lot had been made of George W. Bush's remark on meeting Putin for the first time—"I looked this man in the eye. I was able to get a sense of his soul." (I understood, because when I do an interview I look straight in the person's eyes and I can tell by the slightest expression, a squint or a flinch, where I have hit home. Good thing for journalism students to remember.) In any case, I agreed with Bush's assessment of Putin. He had friendly eyes and, in person, hardly seemed formidable (though he held a black belt in judo). He was small and lithe and easy to talk with, even through the interpreter.

I questioned him, first of all, on Bush's statement about his soul, a remark which by then had been ridiculed in the United States. Putin smiled. "It's difficult for me to say what he saw in my soul, but I can respond to those who smiled in response. I believe it's not accidental that he, not they, became president of the United States. He sees better and deeper and understands the problems more accurately."

What concerned him the most then was Russia's failure to prevent the 9/11 attacks on New York. "I had the feeling of guilt for this tragedy," he said. "We had talked about the possible threats to the United States, to other countries, but [our special services] were not able to determine who, where, and how they would strike."

Putin was, in fact, the first world leader to phone President Bush after the attack. "I expressed our solidarity with the American people," Putin told me. "Because of acts of terrorism in Moscow, perhaps I understood better than many people what the Americans felt. The American people understand that in this dire moment in time, they are not alone."

As the interview went on, I wanted to know more about Putin's personal side. If I'd had the nerve to ask Qaddafi if he was insane and to ask Boris Yeltsin about his drinking problem, I had to ask Putin a question that had gone through my mind from the moment I knew I was going to do the interview. I hadn't written it down on my list of questions, in case any unfriendly eyes saw them. The moment came toward the end of the interview when I felt our conversation was comfortable enough so that he wouldn't be insulted. We all knew that Putin was a former KGB officer. Here was my question:

"Did you ever order anyone killed?"

"No," he replied. "In fact my work was more intellectual, political information gathering, analysis, and so forth. So thank God, nothing like that happened to me."

These days, as the list of the murders of some of Mr. Putin's critics grows longer, the question is being asked again. Putin and his administration, of course, deny any involvement.

In the late winter of 2002 I had the most interesting foreign experience in years when I had the opportunity to travel through Saudi Arabia and interview pretty much anyone I wanted. Saudi Arabia's image in America was very shaky after the violent events of 9/11, when it was revealed that fifteen of the nineteen hijackers were Saudi citizens and that the mastermind of the attack was another Saudi, Osama bin Laden.

Soon after the attacks, the Saudi royal family hired Qorvis Communications, a PR firm in Washington, to cast a better light, if possible, on the kingdom's image. I had been asking the Saudi government for permission to go there for quite a while, and suddenly the permission came through. So I packed two long black skirts, a black scarf to cover my head, and off I went with Martin Clancy, a camera crew, and a Qorvis representative, Judy Smith.

I wanted to interview then Crown Prince Abdullah, who was the de facto leader of Saudi Arabia during the long illness of his half brother, King Fahd. I was told I could meet him but not interview him on camera. If he ever did an interview, however, he would do it with me. Well, good luck and fat chance. But I was glad to be introduced to him anyway in the royal palace in Jeddah on the Red Sea with its magnificent sculpted gardens.

What an eye-opener. Lest anyone think the Saudis are insular and out of touch, consider the entire wall of television monitors—I counted thirty-four—in the main reception room. Everything was on, from CNN and Al Jazeera to all three of the American morning shows—and even *The View*! In fact, I was a celebrity of sorts in the hotel beauty parlor because the manicurist watched *The View*.

Aside from the noninterview with Abdullah, we were given extraordinary access to travel across the kingdom. We not only went to Jeddah but to Riyadh, the capital of Saudi Arabia, and to the southern region of Asir. The Saudis hoped that we would show an enlightened country with a fairly well-educated population. Indeed, we found that to be true in some of our interviews, especially with members of the royal family who spoke perfect English, as they had been educated in the United States or Great Britain. The princes were charming and sophisticated as were their wives, who wore *abaya*s (long black robes) outside their homes and low-cut gowns by Yves Saint Laurent and Oscar de la Renta inside. Their homes were exquisite, many with indoor fountains and air-conditioning—outdoors! Some of the living rooms were as large as hotel lobbies. Though alcohol is forbidden by Islam, they drank the best French wine, and, though satellite TV was forbidden by the government, they watched whatever they wanted.

There were, in fact, satellite dishes on the roofs of houses all over Saudi Arabia. Perhaps the government looked the other way because more often than not, the images on Al Jazeera were of Israelis attacking Palestinians and bulldozing their houses.

I know this chapter is supposed to be about heads of state and here I am, going on about what would become our one-hour television *Special* on Saudi Arabia. But without the *Special*, I would not eventually have gotten the interview with King Abdullah (King Fahd died in 2005), even though much of what we found in Saudi Arabia was hardly complimentary.

We had begun our journey in the southern part of the country, where we met with two fathers of three young men who were among those accused of participating in the 9/11 attacks. Obviously none of their sons had returned home, yet each of the fathers, interviewed separately, said that his son, and in one case, two sons, were just away and would certainly shortly be back. No amount of conversation on my part about documented accusations made a difference. If there were documents the United States was lying and so was Saudi Arabia.

The high school textbooks we saw were particularly disturbing in the repeated depiction of Jews. One, for example, had a story about a talking tree behind which a Jew is hiding. "Muslim, come forward," the tree calls out. "There's a Jew hiding behind me. Come and kill him." When we asked a government minister why the textbooks contained this kind of material, he said he, too, deplored the fact and the books were being corrected. To my knowledge they have not been.

Equally disturbing were the university students I interviewed. One told me he considered George Bush as great a terrorist as Osama bin Laden. Another claimed that Zionists must have attacked the World Trade Center because four thousand Jews stayed home from work that day. Furthermore, the student said, the Jews were responsible for every war throughout history. I countered with the facts, but I did not argue with the students. Their harsh prejudiced views revealed so much about aspects of the country's culture.

Then there were the religious police, the *mutaween*, who prowled the streets and malls to make sure not one inch of a woman's flesh was showing. It is well known that women in Saudi Arabia are not allowed to drive, nor can they travel or be admitted to a hospital without permission from a male relative. They can't even have a cup of coffee in public with the opposite sex. Neither could I. I deliberately sat in the men's section at Starbucks in Jeddah to see what would happen and was politely but firmly escorted to the women's section.

We ended our visit to Saudi Arabia with a brief interview with Abdullah bin Laden, thirty-five, one of Osama bin Laden's fifty-four siblings or half siblings. Abdullah holds a Harvard law degree and was living in Boston until after 9/11, when he was spirited back to his own country. This interview had been arranged by Saudi Arabia's influential ambassador to the United States, His Royal Highness Prince Bandar bin Sultan bin Abdulaziz Al-Saud. Prince Bandar thought it would help the reputation of the bin Laden family, still one of the wealthiest and most important in that country. The ambassador practically had to drag Abdullah in front of my cameras and we got almost nothing out of him. He denied, of course, that he and the rest of the family had anything to do with his half brother, but the man was too nervous to say more than that. Still, we had talked with a bin Laden, which was more than anyone else had done at the time and it made for great on-the-air promotion.

The one-hour *Special* on Saudi Arabia aired in March 2002. It did extremely well. It was exotic, and people were curious to hear from brother bin Laden. Because it presented a good deal of material critical of Saudi Arabia, I wasn't surprised that I didn't hear about the interview King Abdullah had promised me. Time passed. Katie Couric went to Saudi Arabia for the *Today* show and was able to do a brief what we call "walk and talk" three-question interview with King Abdullah. I gave up any thought that I would ever get an interview with him until, out of the blue, a Saudi official called in October 2005. If I was still interested in interviewing the king, the official said, I should put in my request right away. The king evidently remembered his promise to me, and although he had had many other requests, he was willing to honor mine. I was impressed and back I went to Saudi Arabia with my long black skirts and scarf.

On our first trip to Saudi Arabia in 2002, we neither asked for nor needed security. The U.S. invasion of Iraq the following year changed all that. On this trip in 2005, there were armed guards in front of our hotel and security outside my room. We traveled in armored Mercedes-Benzes provided by the king's security force. The government was taking no chances with our safety. Indeed, it was concerned with its own vulnerability to possible terrorist attacks.

King Abdullah is a tall, imposing man in his eighties with dyed black hair and a matching dyed beard. Unlike most of the Saudi royal family, he doesn't speak English. But even through an interpreter, he had a sense of humor and a twinkle behind his glasses. He only gave us half an hour of his time, and he held us to the second. He could see me getting my time cues and knew exactly when the time was up. That left me with a great many questions I wanted to ask but couldn't. I did manage to question him on the delicate matter of women's rights, or lack thereof, a subject of great interest back home. The king seemed to champion expanding rights for women. "My mother is a woman. My sister is a woman. My daughter is a woman. My wife is a woman," he said. "I believe the day will come when women drive."

I'd gotten more or less the same answer three years before from several Saudi princes, yet nothing had happened. "Can you not just make a decree that women drive?" I asked him. "You are the king." Here was his reply, which I still can't figure out. "I value and take care of my people as I would my eye," he told me. (That said, as of this writing women in Saudi Arabia still are not allowed to drive their own cars, even though the government has said the ban will be lifted this year.)

His Majesty was less enigmatic on the subject of Al Qaeda's terrorist acts inside Saudi Arabia, saying they were "Madness. Madness and evil. It is the work of the devil."

Has the threat been eliminated? I asked him.

"No," he said.

No wonder we had so much security.

He said he was against the U.S. invasion of Iraq and the war in Afghanistan, and was very concerned about the unresolved Palestinian problem. "I believe this may have negatively influenced the opinion of the Saudi public toward the United States," he said.

Israel. The Palestinians. The incendiary issue kept coming up over and over again as the prime source of Muslim hatred toward America. I remembered the optimistic interview I'd had in 1999 with young King Abdullah of Jordan, who'd been thrust onto the throne by the deathbed wish of his father, King Hussein. Abdullah, then, was convinced that peace was at hand. "Maximum two, three years," he had said. "We've gone too far in the peace process to go anywhere but forward." But that was before 9/11. That was before the American invasion of Iraq and before the Palestinians in Gaza voted into power the militant Hamas party.

Troubled times then. Just as troubled now.

Which brings me to Venezuela's maverick president, Hugo Chávez. I interviewed the highly controversial leader in the spring of 2007. Chávez, who considers Fidel Castro his mentor, is trying to create a socialist revolution in Latin America, starting with his own country. He has fertile territory. Almost 50 percent of the population of Venezuela lives in poverty. That there is poverty in much of Latin America is not big news, and we might not have paid too much attention to yet another left-leaning leader there were it not for Chávez's bombastic name-calling of George W. Bush. In September 2006 Chávez visited the United States, and on the floor of the U.N. General Assembly, he condemned Bush's invasion of Iraq and called the U.S. president *"el diablo"*—the devil.

He certainly got everyone's attention. The media was more interested in his tirade than his actual criticism of the president. I didn't know Chávez, but suddenly we were told by the Venezuelan Embassy that if I was available, he wanted to do an interview with me. I'm not sure why. Maybe because he knew of my conversations with Castro. Anyway, as bad luck would have it, his few days in New York coincided exactly with the days I was in Australia interviewing Terri Irwin, the widow of the crocodile hunter Steve Irwin. Chávez said he wouldn't do the interview with anyone else at ABC. He did do one with Tavis Smiley of PBS, but that was all, and home he went to Venezuela.

From October on we tried to reinstate the interview. In December, Chávez was reelected by a huge majority to a second term as Venezuela's president, and we renewed our efforts. Finally our opportunity came. President Bush decided in March 2007 to visit five Latin American countries: Brazil, Uruguay, Colombia, Guatemala, and Mexico. Chávez then decided to do his own tour of some of his neighbors, culminating with an interview with me upon his return home. So on Saturday, March 10, 2007, with my faithful producers Martin Clancy and Katie Thomson I left for Caracas.

Our interview with Chávez wasn't scheduled until Tuesday. What we had hoped to do in the interim was go around Caracas with Chávez and get footage of him in various parts of the city, but he was still out of the country doing his own Latin American tour, so we explored the city without him.

Caracas is relatively uninteresting to visit. There is no true old section, few museums, little to do except to take the cable car up Avila Mountain for a scenic view of the city. This did not appeal to me (heights scare me, remember?). We stayed at a very well-serviced hotel and tried to get the feel of the country. I was introduced to some affluent citizens who lived in luxurious homes behind high walls topped with barbed wire. They traveled with bodyguards in armored cars for fear of being kidnapped. Venezuela has a reputation for kidnappings. Crime in Caracas is rampant, and Chávez either cannot or does not want to do anything about it.

Many of the leaders of Venezuelan industry had already left the country. Others feared that Chávez might one day confiscate their property as Castro had done to much of the middle and upper class of Cuba. One of the sons of a man in the housing business introduced me to his friends, who told me they felt they would all have to leave the country in a year or two, for there would be no jobs for them and perhaps no home to go to.

We also visited a barrio called Santa Cruz del Este, a typical area with houses of the poor stacked practically one atop another. You wonder how those houses don't collapse into the street. Here the people, proud and friendly, told a different story. Chávez, they said, had helped them get running water and toilets. Venezuela is oil rich, the fourth-largest supplier of oil to the United States, and Chávez has been handing out money to many of the poor to help them in community projects. They love him.

The people in the barrio were welcoming, perhaps because we had set up our visit in advance. Nevertheless I traveled in an armored car with two bodyguards supplied by ABC. We were advised by people who knew the conditions to take no chances. We, too, could be targeted for kidnapping. We were told never to leave our hotel without our body-guards. God knows why I wasn't more afraid.

We planned to leave the country on Wednesday after our Tuesday interview with Chávez so we could hurriedly prepare pieces to air on *Good Morning America*, *20/20*, and *Nightline*. But at 1:00 a.m. Tuesday (again, nobody seemed to worry about late hours), we got a call that Chávez was hoarse from his travels and was "postponing" the interview. No word on when it would now take place. We were in a panic—all that time, all that money spent on transportation, hotels, camera crews, all that homework, writing of questions—all for nothing. Before I jumped off Avila Mountain, I got good news: Chávez would do the interview on Wednesday. That meant we could grab the first plane out on Thursday and crash our pieces for Friday.

So what was he like? By now Chávez had added "donkey," "liar," "coward," "murderer," and "a drunk" to his list of adjectives describing

Bush. I couldn't wait to meet this loud, rude sworn enemy of the United States.

Wednesday came. The interview was taking place in what had once been, a hundred years ago, an ornate private home. Now it was the closest thing Caracas had to a presidential palace. I expected to be greeted by the president in his trademark uniform of open-collar red shirt and cap. Instead, when I was ushered into his private office, I found a smiling, round-faced man dressed nattily in a navy blue suit, white shirt, and tie. He shook my hand warmly and was welcoming and gracious. He obviously wanted to please. Twice married and now divorced, he showed me photographs of his children and complained sadly, as he would also say later on camera, "I had to abandon them because my life is devoted to the poor of the earth." He would also say, "It is also very hard for me to be married but I have got a heart here. I've also got blood running through my veins." Good to know, I guess.

I had begun the actual interview by asking him, on a scale of one to ten, ten being the highest, how he would rate President Bush's visit to Latin America. Not surprisingly he gave it a one, saying he had done that only because he wanted to be generous; he really thought it should be a minus five. He had called Bush a devil and then a donkey, he said, because "he is very ignorant about the things that are happening in Latin America and the world." If he, Chávez, had been "excessive in his language" (his words), he said he might apologize. Moreover, he proclaimed that he himself would win a U.S. election if he ran because of his "respect for human rights." "George Bush does not struggle for this," Chávez went on to say. "He struggles for other things. He bombs people, villages, and he invades nations."

Chávez accused Bush of trying to assassinate him. He seemed actually to believe it. However, reassuring the United States, he also said there were no circumstances in which he would cut off oil except "in case of any other aggression by the U.S. administration." Then and only then would he cut off the supply.

He complained that the U.S. media demonized him by showing only photographs of him with Saddam Hussein, Fidel Castro, and Mu'ammar Qaddafi. They never showed pictures of him, he said, with Pope John Paul II or with Bill Clinton.

At the end of our interview Chávez spoke a little broken English, assuring "the people of the United States, all the women, all the men, we Venezuelan people love you. We want to be your brother. I love very much a great leader of you. Martin Luther King is my leader. His dream, Martin Luther King's dream, is your dream, is our dream, is my dream."

When we left his office, he pumped the hand of every member of our group, cameramen, bodyguards, and producers.

In December 2007, he lost a referendum that would have given him an indefinite term in office and even more power. Still, as things stand now, Chávez may have many years ahead to accomplish whatever his dream may be. Like his mentor Castro, he wants a socialist Latin America, thinks our democracy is a mistake, and will try to prevent it from happening in the other countries of his hemisphere. He has already begun to nationalize some of Venezuela's industries like telecommunications, electricity, and oil. He says he will leave private property alone. Perhaps. And he says he looks forward to good relations with the next president of the United States. One more thing: he drinks twenty cups of coffee a day.

Adventures with the Most Mysterious Men

*T*HE INTERVIEW that got me in the most trouble began innocently enough in the summer of 1986 on a yacht in the South of France. Merv and I were on our honeymoon, and through a friend of Merv's, we were invited for lunch aboard the *Nabila*, the opulent yacht owned by Adnan Khashoggi. Who knew that within months Khashoggi would become a central figure in the Iran-Contra scandal that tarred the Reagan administration—and almost cost me my job?

At the time we knew Khashoggi only by reputation. He was a rich, very rich, Saudi wheeler-dealer who had made millions brokering the multibillion-dollar sale of American weapons to Saudi Arabia in the sixties and seventies. That, plus other deals, had earned him the reputation of being one of the world's richest men—and the biggest spender. Judging from his yacht, it was true.

The seventy-million-dollar, 280-foot floating palace he'd named after his only daughter had its own helicopter and landing pad, marble bathrooms with gold fixtures, eleven VIP suites, each named for a semiprecious gem like garnet or topaz, a barbershop, and mirrored massage rooms. The ship was wired with cutting-edge technology that might not seem like much today but back then was unheard of. Everything in the master suites was operated by remote control: a button to lock and unlock the door, a button to unveil the TV, a button in Khashoggi's own stateroom that swung open the back wall of the shower to reveal a secret staircase leading, presumably, to a safe room. The *Nabila* even had a state-of-the-art operating room with a closed-circuit TV system that enabled the doctors aboard to be in visual contact with doctors anywhere in the world.

At lunch, we learned one way he'd managed to accumulate such wealth. Would I or any of his other guests, Khashoggi asked, like to visit his onboard Hindu mystic, Shri Chandra Swamiji Maharaj, or, for short, Swamiji? Swamiji could see into the future, Khashoggi told us, and read people's minds. I bit, having never met a true swami before, and was escorted after lunch to a much smaller cabin where the swami was sitting on the floor in the lotus position, playing with his toes. There was another man in the room in an ill-fitting suit who was described as the swami's translator, but I paid no attention to him. The swami had such an aura of calm about him that I poured out all the trouble I was having with my daughter at the time, hoping for some swami wisdom.

Well, I didn't get much wisdom. Nor, I discovered months later, did anyone else Khashoggi dispatched to the swami. Turned out that he offered an audience with his guru to anyone with whom he was doing business in the hope that he would eventually reveal his personal and business concerns. The so-called translator would then relay them to Khashoggi.

Merv and I liked Khashoggi. He was pleasant, quite small and plump, and looked somewhat like one of those blow-up toys you push over that bounce right back. We accepted his invitation to return for dinner that night, where among the guests was the flamboyant former prime minister of Canada, Pierre Trudeau. We had another luxurious meal on the *Nabila*, but that was that. We didn't see Khashoggi again.

Four months later the Iran-Contra scandal burst into the headlines and threatened to severely damage the Reagan administration. Reported first in a Lebanese newspaper, then on the front pages of every U.S. newspaper, was a labyrinthine tale about the Reagan administration violating its own policy by secretly selling weapons to Iran in return for the release of American hostages being held in Lebanon. Soon afterward it was disclosed that proceeds from the covert arms sales were secretly and illegally going to support the anti-Communist insurgents in Nicaragua. And who was the mysterious middleman who was thought to have brokered the arms deal? Khashoggi.

What a story! Since I knew him I started tracking down Khashoggi all over the world to see if I could interview him for *20/20*. Finding him was a challenge. He had a huge ranch in Kenya as well as homes in Marbella, Paris, Cannes, the Canary Islands, Madrid, Rome, Beirut, Riyadh, Jeddah, Monte Carlo, and a thirty-million-dollar apartment in New York. When I finally managed to reach him, he was pleasant enough, but noncommittal. He didn't say yes, but he also didn't say no. So I'd wait a bit, then phone him again.

He called me back, unexpectedly, while Merv and I were at La Costa, Merv's spa and golf resort in California. Khashoggi told me he was sending me some material by air that he wanted me to read. His personal messenger hand-delivered the package the next day. Enclosed was a copy of a letter he'd sent to Robert McFarlane, Reagan's national security advisor, in 1985, suggesting that there were "moderate" elements in Iran that wanted to open communication with the United States. Most interesting was that McFarlane personally answered him, thanking him for his interest. Lots of people sent ideas about a lot of subjects to the White House, but few received responses from such a senior member of the administration. Khashoggi was confirming to me his personal relationship with the highest level in the Reagan administration. I got the message.

What I didn't understand was a copy of a lecture he also sent me, presented by former CBS News president Fred Friendly at Columbia University. This lecture dealt with the dilemma faced by reporters who uncovered information that might prove dangerous to the country if made public. Was Khashoggi warning me? Or was he asking me if I could keep a secret? I didn't have a clue.

The next time I called him, I asked him about the lecture. Instead of answering me he agreed to an interview. "I'll come see you," he said. Three days later he arrived at La Costa.

"Do you have a secure phone?" he asked, after we had exchanged pleasantries. The answer was no. We weren't in the business of state secrets. But we were about to be.

"We have our own phone line in the cottage," I told Khashoggi.

"Is there an extension?" he asked.

"Yes," I said. "In the bathroom."

"I'm going to call someone. You don't need to know who," he told me. "Listen on the extension, but don't make a sound."

So there was Khashoggi on the phone in the living room and there was I, on the extension in the bathroom, sitting on the lid of the toilet. And he was talking arms sales with another mystery man.

"How much did we get for this? Seven million? Good. And how much did we get for the TOWS? Two million. . . ."

I didn't have paper or a pen with me, so I grabbed an eyebrow pencil, ripped the top off the tissue box, and started scribbling notes as fast as I could. (I didn't know from TOWS then but I now know it stands for "tube-launched, optically tracked wire-guided" missile. I wrote "toes" in my notes and wondered what feet had to do with all this.) The conversation lasted far longer than the tissue box, but I got the point. Khashoggi was proving to me that he was indeed the middleman in the U.S.-Iranian arms deal. The interview, he now said, would have to wait.

"Someday I'll take you to meet the man who is behind the whole thing," he assured me. "Then you'll have your story."

"Someday" is a horrible word to a journalist. Too much can happen waiting for someday, mainly that someone else will break the story. So I stuck close to Khashoggi. After we both returned to New York from California, I spent hours with him and his then wife, Lamia, in their vast Fifth Avenue apartment—sixteen apartments folded into one, including an Olympic-size swimming pool. In December, after I had spent weeks courting his confidence, Khashoggi suddenly told me he was ready to do the interview.

And the adventure began that got me in so much trouble.

It was all very tidy at the beginning. We scheduled the interview for a Wednesday afternoon in Khashoggi's apartment, which would give me and my producer, Martin Clancy, ample time to edit the piece for Thursday night's *20/20* broadcast. But the night before the interview Khashoggi phoned from Las Vegas to announce a change in plan.

"I've decided I don't want to do the interview in New York," he said. "I'm going to Monte Carlo and I'll take you with me on my plane. We'll do the interview there."

"Okay," I said, "but I'll be bringing my producer and a crew of six."

"Good," Khashoggi replied firmly.

Merv then weighed in. "I don't like the sound of the whole thing," he said. "I'm going with you." And the crew became seven.

Very early Thursday morning, 3:00 a.m., in fact, we took off from Newark Airport aboard Khashoggi's private DC-8. The plane turned out to be an airborne version of his yacht. The seats were covered in cream-colored chamois and silk, the seat belts had gold-plated buckles, and Khashoggi's private chef served us breakfast on china monogrammed with the initials *AK* in gold.

The first part of our interview with Khashoggi took place on the plane on December 11. (We planned to do the second part at his apartment in Monte Carlo.) We had no time to spare because Martin and I intended to feed the complete interview by satellite back to New York for the 10:00 p.m. broadcast that night. And so the explosive interview began at thirty thousand feet, the jet engines whistling in the background, with Khashoggi dressed in a caftan.

For the first time a face was put on the arms-for-hostages scandal rocking the Reagan administration. An Arab face with an Arab accent describing the clandestine deal between Robert McFarlane and "moderates" in the Iranian regime trying to get the U.S. hostages in Lebanon released in exchange for U.S. weapons (Iran was six years into a bloody war with Iraq). He also confirmed the establishment of a Swiss bank account to shelter some thirty million dollars received from the Iranians for the weapons. The account was controlled by top national security officials in the Reagan administration, who were siphoning the money off to illegally fund the Contra rebels fighting the Communist regime in Nicaragua.

I was totally amazed by what I was hearing. But there was still a missing piece. The actual arms dealer was an Iranian businessman named Manucher Ghorbanifar, a shadowy figure who operated so far below the radar no one even had a photograph of him.

"I'm taking you to see Ghorbanifar," Khashoggi said when we landed in Nice, France.

Now I was really flabbergasted. The interview with Khashoggi was a coup in itself, but Ghorbanifar, too? The man whose telephone conversation I'd listened in on in the bathroom at La Costa? The man with the "toes"? Merv looked quite nervous about the whole thing but without skipping a beat we immediately boarded Khashoggi's waiting helicopters (we needed two to transport us all) and flew to Monte Carlo.

Ghorbanifar was startled, to say the least, when he arrived at Khashoggi's apartment. He was expecting to see Khashoggi privately, not an American television crew. Heaven knows what power Khashoggi held over Ghorbanifar, but basically he told the arms dealer to do the interview, and Ghorbanifar immediately sat down with me, sweating profusely.

His motive behind everything was no more complicated than making a sound business deal, he told me. New weapons for Iran would help secure a victory over Iraq and a potentially profitable peace from which both he and his business partner, Khashoggi, would benefit. "Two billion a day," he projected. According to Ghorbanifar, the weapons-for-hostages deal had worked. He claimed he had negotiated the release of three hostages, including Benjamin Weir, a Presbyterian minister. (What he did not mention were the new hostages being captured as replacements.) With this news the interview came to a close.

Martin and I raced back to our hotel to edit the interviews. He edited Ghorbanifar and I edited the Khashoggi interview we had done on the plane. We'd been up for more than twenty-four hours by then and were punch-drunk with exhaustion. We finally finished at 3:00 a.m. Monte Carlo time, which made it 9:00 p.m. in New York. We had to wake up a grumpy French technician to transmit the interview, the final portion of which arrived fifteen minutes before *20/20* went on the air. There was obviously no time for ABC to promote it or even preview it. They just ran it cold. And it made a huge splash.

Ted Koppel picked up the interviews on *Nightline*, and the story made all the newspapers the next day. I was sleeping it off in Monte Carlo. Merv was wonderful. When I finally came to, he proposed spending a romantic weekend in Paris. A lovely idea that never happened.

Khashoggi called and said in a rushed voice that Ghorbanifar was coming to his apartment at 2:00 p.m. with an urgent message that he wanted me to deliver to President Reagan. We must meet with him, he said. Our flight to Paris wasn't until the late afternoon, so I agreed. I assumed the message would be in a sealed envelope I could easily get to the White House.

It wasn't.

And this is where I got into deep trouble.

Ghorbanifar, very composed without a television camera on him and not sweating at all, opened the conversation with a startling projection: "I am going to tell you everything because I might be killed and someone must know the true story," he said. "I know your president is being pressured not to have anything to do with Iran, but I want you to tell him that he must keep the door open. If he does I believe I can have another hostage released on Christmas Eve, maybe even two. As this is a matter of life and death, no one except the president must know about it. If the story gets out, the hostages will not be released, I will be killed, and my family in Iran will be killed also."

I swallowed hard and all but choked. I couldn't believe it. Ghorbanifar was going to tell me the entire story of his role in Iran-Contra, or Irangate as some were calling it. This big scoop was falling into my lap.

I got out the little notebook I always carry to take notes, and Ghorbanifar launched into an endless story of high-level deceit and betrayal. Part of it concerned his ally, Ayatollah Montazeri, a moderate, who was among those in line to succeed the ailing Ayatollah Khomeini (who had led the Islamic revolution against the shah). Unlike the West-hating Khomeini, Montazeri wanted to restore relations with America and the West. The arms deal, which had been struck with McFarlane and Lt. Col. Oliver North, then an aide to the National Security Council, would have given the pro-Western Montazeri enough prestige to cement the succession. Three or four arms shipments had taken place, but some included faulty parts. The deal had temporarily fallen apart, Montazeri had been discredited, and Ghorbanifar's own life was in danger. Adding insult to injury, when the shipments resumed, the Americans tried to cut Ghorbanifar out of the deal. It was then, he said, and only to protect himself, that he had personally given the sensational story of the arms-for-hostages scheme to the Lebanese newspaper.

These tidy paragraphs do not represent in the slightest the time it took Ghorbanifar to tell me the saga. (At one point I thought, "What the hell am I doing here?") I filled my little notebook, then moved on to Khashoggi's stationery. When my pen went dry, I began using pencils. When Khashoggi's stationery ran out, I started writing on whatever scrap of paper I could find. And still Ghorbanifar went on.

Merv sat there silently next to me as afternoon became evening and evening became night, getting up only occasionally to cancel plane reservations to Paris and make new ones. Finally, finally, Ghorbanifar finished telling his story. It was 4:00 a.m. By that time Merv and I were so exhausted we'd given up any thought about spending a romantic weekend together. We checked back into the hotel and slept for an entire day.

I pieced together my notes as best I could when we got back to New York. What a fantastic story, but how much of it could I use? Ghorbanifar had made it clear that if I publicly revealed certain portions of it or identified him as my source, the hostages would not be released and he and his family might be killed. I understood now why Khashoggi had sent me Fred Friendly's lecture. How much of what Ghorbanifar had told me did I have to tell ABC? And what about the message Ghorbanifar wanted me to deliver to the president: Resist pressure. Keep talking to Iran. Send more arms. The hostages will not be released if you don't. There are other lives at stake.

I knew the rules: a reporter is not supposed to become personally involved in a story and certainly not be allowed to act as a messenger. But, like it or not, I *was* involved. I didn't want anybody's blood on my hands, so I decided to honor Ghorbanifar's demand for secrecy. But how to get to Reagan? Though I'd interviewed the president several times, I really had no personal relationship with him. I couldn't just call the White House and say, "I'd like to talk to the president, please. I have an important message for him." Well, I suppose I could have, but I was afraid that I'd have to speak to six aides along the way who would want to know what this was all about.

And then it came to me. Nancy Reagan could be the conduit to her husband. I couldn't call Mrs. Reagan cold at the White House, but we had a mutual friend, Jerry Zipkin, who was very close to her. They talked, I heard, almost daily. I telephoned Jerry. "I know this sounds odd, Jerry, but I need to talk to Mrs. Reagan. I'm involved in a very serious matter, and I need to talk to her as soon as possible. Can you telephone her at the White House and ask her to call me?"

An hour later Mrs. Reagan called. "I'm in a very strange position," I said to her. "I have some important information for the president." I told her the entire story, concluding: "I have no idea how accurate this material is, but I was asked to make sure the president got it himself." While we were speaking I heard a click on the line. "Ronnie? Is that you?" Mrs. Reagan asked. It was, so I repeated the story to the president. He then gave me specific instructions about how to send my written material to him at the White House. I followed those instructions, and that was the last I heard from anyone in the administration.

A week or so later Merv and I took my daughter to Hawaii for Christmas. On Christmas Eve I sat in front of the television set waiting for a news bulletin announcing that a hostage had been released. There was no bulletin. Someone, somewhere along the clandestine line, had failed. Was it our side? Was it Ghorbanifar? I never knew and could not find out.

I thought I was through with my part of the Iran-Contra scandal. Two investigations had been launched. One a congressional committee headed by former Senator John Tower, and another by a special prosecutor, Lawrence Walsh. But a month or so after I'd spoken to Reagan, a story appeared in the *New York Times* about the release of unspecified documents pertaining to the arms-for-hostages deal. Concerned that my name might eventually surface, I sat down with Roone Arledge and Dick Wald, the senior vice president of ABC News, and went through the entire saga from beginning to end. I gave them a copy of the memo I'd relayed to the White House about Ghorbanifar, that he'd said his life was in danger, that a hostage might be released if Reagan acted on his message. Roone and Dick decided I would report key elements of the story on the evening newscast, without naming Ghorbanifar as the source. So I did, enabling ABC to scoop the other networks on the story.

That would have been that had the *Wall Street Journal* not picked up the story again in March 1987, this time naming me. Titled "Iran Arms Dealer Used Barbara Walters to Secretly Pass on a Message to Reagan," the story reported that my memo about Ghorbanifar had been circulated among the editors at ABC News and that I had sent the memo to the White House "without prior approval from the network."

The phone rang.

"Please come to my office," came the cold voice of David Burke, an ABC News executive who was more or less the official watchdog for policy and procedure. "We'd like to talk to you."

It was not a pleasant meeting.

Burke was stern and angry. In front of a very uncomfortable Dick Wald, Burke told me the network was going to publicly reprimand me for violating ABC News regulations that prohibit any employee of the news division from giving material to any government agency without the prior knowledge and approval of ABC News. The only exceptions were life-and-death situations, in which correspondents were allowed to use their own judgment.

I was stunned. "As far as I'm concerned, David, this was a matter of life and death and I did use my best judgment," I said. "Why don't I just explain to the press that Ghorbanifar told me his life was in danger and that, if Reagan acted, a hostage was supposed to be released."

But he would have none of it. I was publicly reprimanded.

"Barbara Walters' transmission of her information to the president was in violation of a literal interpretation of news policy," read, in part, ABC's statement to the press. "ABC News policy expressly limits journalistic cooperation with government agencies unless threats to human life are involved. Miss Walters believed that to be the case."

Just about every newspaper and magazine in the country carried the story. "Barbara Walters Gave Reagan Papers on Iran," headlined the *New York Times*, as if I'd been a major participant in the Iran-Contra affair. "Walters as Courier Criticized," chimed in the *Los Angeles Times*, while a slightly kinder *USA Today* headlined its story: "Walters Takes Heat for Iran Memo to Reagan." A cartoon in the *New York Post* even had Ayatollah Khomeini sitting behind a desk over the words: "Good evening and welcome to *20/20*. Barbara Walters and I have swapped jobs."

In retrospect I should have showed Roone and Dick and also David Burke the Ghorbanifar material sooner. At the time I was worried that somehow it would leak out, possibly leading to Ghorbanifar's death. But I still would have sent that report to the White House in the hope that a hostage would be released.

I also think that ABC was wrong in reprimanding me, and I was hurt, especially because neither Roone nor Dick Wald defended me. They said it was David Burke's territory and left the decision to him. From my point of view the news department certainly had no qualms about using the material I provided. I honestly believed that lives were at stake, which justified the exception in ABC's news policy. I eventually made my peace with Roone and Dick. As for David Burke, we rarely talked, and eventually he left ABC News to head CBS News.

Ironically there turned out to be more than the lives of the hostages at stake. Robert McFarlane, who had resigned as national security advisor in 1985 but privately continued his role in Iran-Contra at President Reagan's request, attempted suicide in 1987 by overdosing on Valium. Shortly after he was released from the hospital, I was the first to interview him and his wife, Jonda. McFarlane told me he felt he had "failed the country."

Charges were leveled at several members of the Reagan administration for their roles in Iran-Contra, including McFarlane, who pled guilty to withholding information from Congress. Oliver North and Adm. John Poindexter, McFarlane's successor as head of the National Security Council, were convicted of various offenses but their convictions would be overturned on technicalities. Reagan's secretary of defense, Caspar Weinberger, would also be indicted, but George H. W. Bush, who succeeded Ronald Reagan as president, pardoned him before he stood trial. Bush would also grant pardons to McFarlane, to former assistant secretary of state Elliott Abrams, and to three high-level members of the CIA. So everyone involved in the Iran-Contra scandal got away with it, including Khashoggi and Ghorbanifar.

I remained in occasional touch with Khashoggi, who continued to wheel and deal. I would interview him again in 1990 when he was indicted, along with Imelda Marcos (whom I would also talk with), for helping to conceal hundreds of millions of dollars in assets she and her husband, Ferdinand Marcos, the deposed president of the Philippines, had allegedly stolen from their country. Both were subsequently acquitted. Khashoggi would have other scrapes with the law, but the last I heard he was living quietly in Monte Carlo, perhaps with his swami but definitely without his yacht. He had sold it years before to Donald Trump, who subsequently passed it on to a Saudi businessman.

I never heard from Ghorbanifar again, though he, too, may still be playing his international games. At one point his name surfaced in connection with the Pentagon and his ongoing quest for a "regime change" in Iran. (According to *Newsweek*, Ghorbanifar claimed to know where

Saddam Hussein hid $340 million in cash, half of which, he said, could be used to overthrow the ayatollahs.)

As for the American hostages held in Lebanon, one of whom, journalist Terry Anderson, was held for nearly seven years, they were finally released in 1991. Along with every other American, I was happy their ordeal had ended. That also ended my foray into global diplomacy.

Murderers

*I*N MY BUSINESS, crime always pays. Give us a good rape, give us a good murder, and we are guaranteed a successful broadcast. I don't mean to sound frivolous or coldhearted, but the more sensational the crime, the higher the ratings. So you won't be surprised to learn that during my twenty-five years at 20/20 I interviewed almost every important murderer, alleged or convicted, if a murderer can be considered important. Almost all had committed such horrifying crimes that they made sensational headlines.

Consider Arthur Seale, who, in 1992, along with his wife, Irene, kidnapped Sidney Reso, the president of Exxon International, locked him in a box in an unventilated storage unit in New Jersey, and demanded ransom. When Reso died four days later, the couple secretly buried him and continued to press for the ransom. Or Jeremy Strohmeyer, a handsome eighteen-year-old former honor-roll high school student, who in 1997 sexually molested and strangled a seven-year-old girl in the ladies room of a gambling casino in Nevada. Or Rabbi (Rabbi!) Fred Neulander, who had been widely respected at his well-attended affluent temple in New Jersey until he had an affair of *Fatal Attraction* proportions in 1994 and hired two hit men to kill his wife of twenty-nine years. They bludgeoned her to death with a lead pipe. The rabbi is currently serving thirty years to life; Arthur Seale and Strohmeyer are incarcerated forever without parole. Seale's wife, Irene, is serving a lesser sentence of twenty years because she cooperated with the police and led them to Reso's grave.

The process of securing an interview with accused murderers or convicted murderers like these is often long and arduous. First of all you can't do it unless the prisoner agrees and makes it known to the proper authority. On our part this then requires a lot of petitioning and many phone calls for official permission to whoever is in charge, be it the warden, the sheriff, or the state superintendent of prisons.

Once at the prison you have to leave whatever you are carrying—pocketbook, wallet, mirror, and so on—before you enter the restricted area. You are not allowed to bring in gifts, even books or magazines. Sometimes you can bring in a certain number of quarters that the prisoner, provided he or she is in the common visiting room, can use to buy candy, hamburgers, or soft drinks from vending machines. These are eagerly accepted.

I've visited many prisons all over the country, once touring an execution room with its equipment for lethal injections. Whenever I make one of these visits, for whatever the reason, I am haunted for days after. I hear the noises in my head from the prisoners as I've walked down the halls, the shuffle of the shackled legs, the clang of the lockup gates behind me. When I leave the prison, I take deep gulps of fresh air. I never say, "There, but for the grace of God, go I." But I do say, "Thank God I am free." The prisoner I've just interviewed, no matter how hideous the crime he or she has committed, has become a real person to me, and I have to clear my head.

The fact that I can sometimes feel empathy for someone who has brutally killed another human being doesn't mean that I can understand the murder. But at the time I am sitting opposite the killer, I am not judgmental. I don't say, "How could you be such a monster?" I do, however, say, "There are people who think you are a monster. How do you respond to that?" During the actual interview I am not feeling a lot of emotion. It is when I leave that the force of the crime hits me. Why? I ask myself. Most of these killers, when you meet them, are mild-mannered, polite, articulate. Some, like the rabbi, still claim their innocence, but most of the convicted murderers I've interviewed express great regret.

OF THE MANY MURDER CASES I've been involved in, five stand out in my mind.

The most intriguing murderer turned out not to be one. When I first sat down with the mysterious and debonair Claus von Bülow in 1982, he had been convicted one month earlier of twice trying to murder his very wealthy wife, Sunny, who was then in a coma. His weapon was a hypodermic needle, which the jury believed he had used to inject Sunny von Bülow with insulin, a potentially fatal drug for his wife, who had a serious low blood sugar condition.

The case had ignited worldwide attention, given Sunny von Bülow's fortune of $75 million, the testimony against von Bülow by his stepchildren (a prince and a princess of Austrian nobility), and Claus's attractive lover, Alexandra Isles. (Isles had cut off her relationship with von Bülow on the advice of her attorneys when he was indicted.) Von Bülow himself had not testified at the trial and everybody in the media, both print and television, was scrambling for an exclusive interview with him to hear his side of the story. I had no particular entrée to von Bülow and never thought I'd get the interview, were he to give one. So I was surprised when I received a call soon after his conviction from Andrea Reynolds, von Bülow's adviser and current lover. She had something to tell me, Mrs. Reynolds said. Would I please come see her at the von Bülows' Fifth Avenue apartment?

I was cool in more ways than one when I arrived. I didn't know what the "something" was Mrs. Reynolds wanted to tell me, plus the fact that it was a foul, cold day and I'd ruined my new suede boots in a puddle of slush. Von Bülow's apartment was opulent and in one of Fifth Avenue's grandest buildings, but I'd seen opulent before. Mrs. Reynolds invited me to have tea in the library, and while I was sitting there, mourning my boots, in walked the tall, smiling Claus von Bülow. He shook my hand, sat down, and began to talk about a mutual friend of ours, an Englishman. He acted as if we were dinner partners who were meeting for the first time, so I did, too. "Uh, how is he and how is the family?" I responded politely about our friend. And yes, I'd like another cup of tea. Then he very calmly, quietly explained what his situation was.

His sentencing was two weeks away, his appeal of the guilty verdict, if accepted, even further away, and the prosecution, fearing he was a flight risk, wanted to imprison him. He impressed upon me that he was very devoted to his and Sunny's only child, Cosima, that he had no intention of skipping bail and abandoning her, that he wanted to correct the misrepresentations about him in the media and remain at home.

I realized then I was auditioning for an exclusive interview. Why me and not everyone else clamoring for the opportunity? Because Andrea (who now asked me to call her by her first name) told me later that she had called the William Morris Agency, where she had a connection, and asked who the best person would be to interview her lover, and the agency had said that I was. Von Bülow must have felt confident enough of her opinion and comfortable enough with me because I got the interview.

The prosecutor who'd won the murder conviction was furious that I was going to give von Bülow his moment in the court of public opinion. Indeed, von Bülow seemed sincere and convincing during the interview about his loyalty to, if not love for, his wife, whom he described as "the most beautiful woman" yet also "a deeply unhappy person . . . with virtually no self-confidence." He admitted that the conflict they'd had over his work schedule had brought them in recent years to the brink of divorce (Sunny wanted him to spend the entire summer with her at their "cottage" in Newport, Rhode Island, as well as a month in Europe). He was also candid about the sexless relationship they'd had at Sunny's instigation ever since the birth of Cosima, by then a teenager, and their agreement that he could do what he wanted "but be discreet." But there remained the issue of his conviction for attempted murder. "One final question, simply this: Mr. von Bülow, did you try to kill your wife?" I asked him. "No, I did not," he replied. Our interview was over.

I don't know whether this interview had anything to do with the outcome, but von Bülow was allowed to stay out on bail. Even better for him, after hiring the famous Harvard law professor Alan Dershowitz, he was granted a new trial. In June 1985 the second jury declared von Bülow not guilty, based on new medical evidence and inconsistencies and conflicting testimony in the first trial. The onetime murderer was a free man, and soon afterward I interviewed von Bülow again.

He was as elegant and formal and mysterious as ever as we rehashed the trials. He reminded me of those British actors in old movies playing the master of the house wearing a smoking jacket and velvet slippers. But what struck me the most about von Bülow was that at no time during our meetings and interviews did I hear him say, "This is a terrible thing that's happened to me." In all the time I spoke with him, he never complained. He never raised his voice. He never got emotional. He was a very cool character.

He was not above the fury of his stepchildren, however, who remain convinced to this day that he "murdered" their mother. Alexander von Auersperg and Ala Kneissel (now Isham) launched a civil suit against him after he was exonerated, and von Bülow, evidently fearing a loss this time, capitulated to their demands. He renounced any claim on their mother's estate and basically got out of town. Von Bülow now lives in London attending dinner parties and occasionally writing theater and art reviews. Sunny lived in a vegetative state untill she passed away in 2008.

An aside. In the subsequent film about the von Bülows, *Reversal of Fortune*, Glenn Close played Sunny and Jeremy Irons played Claus. Irons, whose portrayal earned him the Academy Award for best actor in 1991, told me he watched my interviews with von Bülow again and again to capture that sort of suave charm and reserved hauteur he had. Among the rumors about the mysterious von Bülow at the time was that he was a necrophiliac, which led to this exchange toward the end of the movie. Ron Silver, who played defense attorney Alan Dershowitz, says to Irons, "You're a very strange man," and Irons, aka von Bülow, responds: "You have no idea." And that's the way I felt about him . . . indeed, a very strange man.

The most dramatic prison interview I conducted was with actor Robert Blake, who was also charged with murdering his wife, but, unlike von Bülow, was denied bail and had to spend almost a year in prison awaiting trial. When I interviewed him in Los Angeles County Jail in February 2003, the preliminary hearing had just begun on whether to free him on bail. The former Emmy-winning star of the seventies television series *Baretta* looked gaunt and seemed emotionally drained. Handcuffed and wearing a prison-issue orange jumpsuit, the seventy-year-old actor had spent most of every day of the last year in solitary confinement, supposedly for his own protection, in the cell formerly occupied by O. J. Simpson. No wonder he looked as awful as he did.

He was charged with shooting Bonny Lee Bakley, his wife of less than six months and mother of his baby daughter, in the head on May 4, 2001, while she waited for him in a car after dinner near a restaurant in Studio City. Though he claimed he was still in the restaurant at the time she was shot, a year later, Blake was arrested for her murder. The incriminating evidence had come from two former stuntmen, both heavy drug users, who claimed Blake had hired them to kill her.

Blake had been desperately trying to get on television ever since, not to plead his innocence but to talk to his little daughter, Rosie, whom he hadn't seen in a year. Two sets of his defense lawyers had quit his case, fearing that he might incriminate himself if he spoke in public. His third attorney also strenuously objected but had not resigned. The last stumbling block was the Los Angeles County Jail, whose sheriff, Leroy Baca, had steadfastly refused to let any journalist, with or without the lawyers' approval, do an interview from the jail. But I had a reason to believe I could make him change his mind. (By the way, this was the same Sheriff Baca who was in charge of Paris Hilton when she was sent to jail in

2007.) I called him and asked if I could meet with him the next time I was in Los Angeles. We did, and the sheriff could not have been nicer, but said, "I can't give you permission. It's against regulations." And here is where I played my trump card.

I'd interviewed prisoners there before, I pointed out. "Who?" he asked, startled. "When?" "In 1996. The Menendez brothers," I replied. (You'll read about them later.) He hemmed and hawed and finally agreed to check it out. He had trouble believing I was right, but I was. And he relented. "There *is* a precedent," Sheriff Baca told me. "In that case, you can do it." Even though I was trying so hard to get his permission, I was still surprised when he gave it.

So the scene was set for the sensational, touching, hilarious, wild, peculiar interview with Blake. He cried at times, was hostile at others, talked directly to his two-year-old daughter, and, in general, acted as if he were still acting.

Blake was convinced he'd be convicted and never see his daughter again. When I asked him what he wanted to say to Rosie, his eyes brimmed with tears. "Life is a spectacular gift, Rosie," he said directly to the camera. "Don't ever sell it short. And I'll always be there with you. I'll never, ever leave you." And then this wasted man started to sing to her. " 'You're the end of the rainbow,' " he sang, tears spilling down his cheeks. " 'My pot of gold. You're Daddy's little girl to have and hold.' " On and on he went. It was as pathetic as it was unbelievable.

When I asked him, "What if you are found guilty?" he angrily shouted these lines at me: "What do I care? How do I kill a dead man? What are they going to do to me that they haven't done already? They took away my entire past. They took away my entire future. What's left for them to take? They're going to take my testicles and make earrings out of them?"

You can't top that.

After the interview aired, the judge granted him bail and released him. Blake looked so pale and thin the judge might have been afraid he would die in jail. Blake thought our interview was the reason he was released. He still says so.

In March 2005, Blake was found not guilty of murdering his wife. There was no physical evidence linking him to the murder and the drug habits and contradictory statements of the retired stuntmen discredited their testimony. Our interview may also have played a small role in his acquittal; parts of it were played at the trial. At the press conference afterward Blake publicly thanked me.

As for his little daughter, Rosie, she has been adopted by Delinah

Blake Hurwitz, Blake's older daughter from his first marriage, a professor of developmental psychology. I met her and she was lovely. Blake did something right.

Of all the convicted murderers I interviewed, I was closest to Jean Harris. Too close, in fact, but I'll get to that. She was the most improbable murderer. Harris had been the prim and proper headmistress of an elite school for girls, the Madeira School, in McLean, Virginia. Her victim was her longtime and unfaithful lover, Herman Tarnower, a well-known cardiologist and author of the best-selling book *The Scarsdale Diet*. Harris was fifty-six when she shot Tarnower. He was sixty-nine. Hardly the age, one would think, for a crime of passion, but that's what it was.

Harris, who had been "seeing" Tarnower, as she would put it, for fourteen years, began to come apart on a Saturday morning in March 1980. An insomniac, she hadn't slept a wink. The day before she had expelled four popular students for smoking pot, the girls' furious parents were at the school berating her, and there was a student protest going on in support of the "Madeira Four" outside her window. She had also run out of the antidepressants Tarnower had been supplying her with for ten years, but when she phoned him for a new shipment, he added more stress. At one point in their relationship he had promised to marry her and then backed off. She knew that the lifelong bachelor was having an affair with his young assistant, but Tarnower rubbed salt in the wound when he now told Harris that she would not be seated on his right at an upcoming tribute to him nor, indeed, would she even be seated at his table.

It was all too much for the already fragile Harris, and after writing Tarnower a furious letter about the young assistant, she said she prepared to kill herself. But she wanted to have one last conversation with Tarnower before she died. And the fatal sequence began.

On March 10 Harris put a loaded gun in her purse, bought a bouquet of flowers, and drove five hours from Virginia to Tarnower's house outside New York. It was 10:00 p.m. and raining when she arrived. He was in bed, told her he didn't want to talk, and to make matters worse, he turned his back on her. Then she saw a negligee and a pair of slippers in the bathroom and lost it completely. What happened next became the central point of the trial. The defense claimed Harris held the gun to her head, Tarnower intervened, and in the ensuing struggle the gun accidentally went off, fatally wounding the cardiologist. The prosecution claimed she had shot the doctor on purpose. Either way, Tarnower lay dying on the floor from four bullet wounds. Harris was arrested, convicted of second-degree murder, and sentenced to fifteen years to life.

This bare-bones recital of the facts in no way conveys how sensational this case was at the time, and the ripples it caused for years to come. Feminist groups cast Harris as the victim of an uncaring man who threw her over for a younger woman. In their eyes she shouldn't have been convicted of anything when clearly, Tarnower had been the SOB. Her imprisonment raised such passion that an ad hoc group formed called the Jean Harris Defense Committee, which orchestrated a letter-writing and signature-gathering campaign to petition Governor Mario Cuomo to grant Harris clemency. Every year, as regular as clockwork, he refused.

I had written many letters to Mrs. Harris and her lawyer asking for an interview so that she could tell her side of the story. Nearly two years after her conviction she finally consented to sit down with me at the Bedford Hills Correctional Facility, a maximum-security prison for women in New York.

I'll never forget my interview with Harris, the first she'd given. When I met her in prison, she was wearing the same good-little-girl leather hair band she'd always worn, a white shirt under a beige cable-knit sweater, and still looked very much the schoolmistress. Though she had lost an appeal for a new trial just two days before, she was calm and dry-eyed when she sat down with me. Until I asked her about Tarnower.

"Do you still love him?" I asked.

"Yes," she said.

"Do you think about him?" I asked.

And then she crumpled and completely broke down. "Don't. Don't," she sobbed, pushing me away with her hands.

"I won't. I won't," I quickly responded, not wanting to cause her any more pain. "Let's talk about your life here a little bit, all right?"

But Jean Harris wanted to talk about Tarnower.

"I think about him constantly," she said through her sobs. "It's one of the reasons I don't care if I get out. I can't imagine what it would be like out there, without him. Isn't that stupid!?"

She recovered and we went on with the interview, but her wrenching outburst stayed with me for a long time. Here was a woman who was going to spend at least the next thirteen years in prison and didn't care about getting out because "he" was not going to be there. I had rarely witnessed that kind of love and was very moved by it.

Harris put her life to good use in prison. In a subsequent interview she and I did at Bedford Hills, she showed me a child-care center she'd helped set up where the inmates could read stories or play games with their children when they came to see them. Along with a visiting nun, she taught a class in prison parenting for pregnant inmates and young mothers so they could cope better on the "outside." With the nun, she also started the Children of Bedford Foundation to give better educational opportunities to the children of prisoners. Some of those children went to college and even on to law school.

Harris suffered a heart attack in jail, and the Jean Harris Defense Committee intensified its efforts to secure her pardon. I signed every petition that came my way and joined the letter-writing campaign to Governor Cuomo, who still refused to release her.

Was I the impartial journalist? Yes, in terms of my interviews with Harris, but on my own time definitely not. I cared about her and thought her fifteen-year prison sentence was an injustice. ABC, however, and rightly so, did not support my personal involvement in the pardon effort, and soon after a newspaper columnist wrote about my participation, ABC News told me that I was no longer permitted to report on the case. I continued to visit Harris from time to time, but I was silenced professionally for the last nine long years of her incarceration, during which she had another heart attack.

It was not until December 1992, when Harris was in the hospital about to undergo quadruple bypass heart surgery, that Governor Cuomo finally pardoned her, citing her health. She was sixty-nine years old by then, and had spent twelve years in prison. Finally she was a free woman, and so was I to talk on camera with her. Our last interview was in March 1993, three months after her heart surgery and her release from prison.

Harris looked tired but had lost none of her spunk. Her answer to my question about what she had found hardest to adjust to in prison was not the strip searches she had been subjected to every time she had a visitor but rather "the lack of logic." For example, her visitors' names had to be submitted in advance and checked off a list by a guard before they could visit her. But some visitors were turned away or had to wait a very long time because the guard couldn't find their names on the list. "I kept saying to them, 'Please let me have the list and I'll arrange it alphabetically for you,' " she said. "And the guard said to me, 'It won't do any good because they don't come alphabetically.' "

When I asked her whether she felt the years in prison had been wasted, she answered, "Not for a minute." She said she was much stronger than when she'd entered prison. "I didn't have a very strong will to live when I went in," she said, "but I have a very strong will to live now."

What impressed me the most was the contrast between this interview and our first one, when she'd broken down at the mention of Tarnower's name and said she thought about him all this time.

"Yes, I did, but I don't anymore. That was twelve years ago, and it's over and it was very painful. What I think about now is all the things that ought to be done to improve the lives of children in this country, and that consumes me."

Harris, whose story was portrayed in several books and movies (the most recent was the 2006 HBO film *Mrs. Harris*, starring Annette Bening and Ben Kingsley), is in her eighties now and lives in an assisted living home in Connecticut. She is close to her two sons by a former marriage, pre-Tarnower, and has friends. She still raises funds for the Children of Bedford Foundation. I send a contribution. She sent me a little note in the spring of 2007, asking warmly: "When are you going to stop working? And so hard? I'm pretty rickety—wish I had your energy." I hope that her life is peaceful. I think she has a right to that.

Mark David Chapman was not the most famous murderer I interviewed, but he had certainly murdered the most famous person—John Lennon. I had tried for over a decade to get an interview with him, writing him a letter on each anniversary of Lennon's death. It took twelve years for Chapman to say yes and another few months for the warden, after determining that Chapman was now sane enough, to also agree. I finally met with Chapman in 1992 at Attica Correctional Facility in upstate New York.

What made Chapman's interview worth such a long-term effort was that no one had ever heard in his own words why he killed Lennon. There had been no trial and so no testimony because Chapman had instructed his lawyer to withdraw his insanity plea and instead plead guilty. The court had sentenced him to twenty years to life and, for his own protection, he was being held in an isolated part of the prison. This first television interview with him in 1992, along with the simultaneous publication of a book about him, would break his silence.

I remember Chapman, somber, wearing glasses, shuffling toward me in leg irons, his hands cuffed, wearing the bright orange prison jumpsuit I had become very familiar with, and flanked by two burly prison guards. (Prison guards always seem to be burly.) When he reached the small, bare room the authorities always seemed to assign me and my crew in every prison, he seemed relieved, as would every murderer I interviewed, to sit down and have his cuffs and shackles removed. Like all the others he was eager to talk. But while Chapman was cogent, very quiet, and seemed perfectly sane, what he said was not.

His hatred of Lennon had begun, he told me, when he chanced upon a book about the former Beatle in a library and learned that Lennon was living in an elegant landmark building in New York. "I got very, very angry," he told me. "I used to love the Beatles. Their idealism meant a lot to me and I saw that, at the time, as a sellout." Chapman, who had been abused as a child, suffered from depression, and had once attempted suicide, bought a gun and a ticket to New York from Hawaii, determined to kill Lennon. "Why?" I asked him. His reply: "John Lennon fell into a very deep hole, a hole so deep inside me that I thought by killing him I would acquire his fame."

On the night of December 8, 1980, Chapman waited outside Lennon's apartment building for Lennon to return from a recording session. Chapman had, in his pocket, a gun and his "bible," J. D. Salinger's *A Catcher in the Rye*, whose alienated central character Chapman identified with. Somehow Chapman thought killing Lennon would make him feel better. "I see this real somebody who I perceived, at the time, to be a phony," Chapman told me. "My nobody was wanting to strike down that somebody."

This was a man who was deemed mentally sound enough to withdraw his insanity defense?

Chapman told me he had asked Satan to give him the power to kill John Lennon. "I turned to Satan, because I knew I wouldn't have the strength to kill a man on my own," he said. "So I went through what I thought was an appropriate Satanic ritual and took off all my clothes and chanted and screamed and howled." Satan spoke to him later as Lennon's car drew up. "I heard this voice saying, over and over, 'Do it, do it, do it, do it.' "

And he did.

Chapman pumped four bullets into John Lennon as the former Beatle walked toward his apartment building. Chapman then leaned against the building and read *A Catcher in the Rye* until the police arrived and put him in the back of a police car. He didn't seem perturbed by the sight of Lennon lying bleeding on the sidewalk, but was very disturbed by the policeman who was holding Lennon's head and cursing him. "It frightened me to death," Chapman told me. "Here's this police officer mouthing these horrible words at me."

Lennon died in the back of a police car as he was being rushed to the hospital. Chapman went to prison, where, he told me, a priest standing outside the prison walls finally expelled his satanic demons through an exorcism.

Chapman concluded the interview by apologizing to Lennon's wife, Yoko Ono, and their son, Sean, who was five years old at the time of the murder. "I'm sorry and I mean that," he said. "I'm sorry. I'm sorry."

Our interview was finished, but when the guards put the handcuffs and the leg irons back on and started walking him back toward his cell, he kept turning his head back toward me and saying, "I'm sorry, I'm sorry, I'm sorry." His words echoed down the long hall and faded as he neared his cell. I can still hear them.

A great many people were upset by this interview, and after we ran it, ABC felt that I had to be very careful about security. I was told to come into the building through a separate entrance because there were so many protesters outside, people who loved John Lennon and were furious that we had given his assassin airtime. But the interview didn't do Chapman any good. As of this writing, he is still in Attica, where he is said to have become an evangelical Christian. He has been denied parole four times, due partly to Yoko Ono, who, in November 2006, nearing the twenty-sixth anniversary of her husband's death, wrote in the *New York Times:* "I don't know if I am ready yet to forgive the one who pulled the trigger." Nor, it appears, are others. During one parole board hearing, close to two thousand people signed an online petition threatening retribution were he to be released. Chapman is safer in prison.

Finally, the Menendez brothers, who came to me in 1996 via Leslie Abramson, their fiery defense lawyer. The public's fascination with lurid crimes had spawned Court TV in 1991 and like millions of other Americans, I closely followed on my television set the drama Leslie was staging in a Los Angeles courtroom. Her client, Erik Menendez, and his brother, Lyle, represented by another attorney, were charged with first-degree murder for brutally shooting their parents in 1989 while they were watching television in their opulent Beverly Hills home. Erik had been eighteen and Lyle twenty-one at the time of the double murders. Their joint trial began four years later, but Abramson tried to recapture the brothers' youth by dressing them in sweaters and khaki pants every day of the trial so that they looked younger than their ages. What a drama. We all watched the "boys," as Leslie always called them, cry when they testified about the sexual abuse they claimed their father had inflicted on them, and their shared fear that if they told, he would kill them. Instead they killed him and their mother. It was clearly self-defense, Leslie laid out in the course of the five-month trial. The jury ended up deadlocked between those who believed her and pressed for a verdict of manslaughter, and those who pressed for first-degree murder, convinced that the boys had killed their parents out of greed to get their hands on the family fortune. The mistrial was a spectacular, though temporary, victory for Leslie and her "boys." Their second trial began in 1995 and lasted seven months.

I talked with Leslie throughout both trials. She was a piece of work, small with masses of curly blond Orphan Annie hair and a tiger both inside and outside the courtroom. She infuriated some lawyers and journalists with her shenanigans, but she and I hit it off. Leslie was in the process of trying out for a TV show of her own with one of the networks (it never came to pass), and I gave her some suggestions. What I ultimately wanted, of course, as did absolutely every television journalist, was an interview with the brothers. But I also genuinely liked her. My relationship with her served me well when, after the second trial ended, she advised Erik and Lyle to go with me for the interview. By then the Menendez brothers had been found guilty of first-degree murder and sentenced to life in prison without the possibility of parole.

This is why they were convicted. The brothers already had two strikes against them. One, the spending spree they had gone on after their parents' deaths with their father's life insurance policy (Lyle had even bought a gray Porsche 911 Carrera for sixty-four thousand dollars). Second, Erik's confession of the murders to his therapist, which was overheard by the therapist's girlfriend and eventually reported to the police. Third, and the tipping point in the second trial, a sharp change in the attitude of the judge. Stung by the criticism of Judge Ito in the controversial O. J. Simpson trial, which had ended in Simpson's acquittal just a week before, the judge in the Menendez trial this time didn't allow television cameras in the courtroom. He also limited testimony from family members and expert witnesses on the boys' claim of sexual abuse on the grounds that no evidence of such abuse had been proved in the first trial. That gave the jury only two options: first-degree murder or acquittal. With self-defense no longer an option, first-degree murder it was. Leslie Abramson was so upset about the conviction and so exhausted by the trials that for a period of time she left criminal law. Still, she urged Erik and Lyle to give me their first and exclusive interview.

I talked with the Menendez brothers in the Los Angeles County Jail. It was the first time Erik and Lyle had sat next to each other outside the courtroom and told their stories. What awful stories they were.

On the night of the murders, Erik told me, "I said to myself, I'm never going to let him touch me again, and just before the shootings, my dad told me to get to my room and that he would be there in a minute and . . . there was going to be sex and it was like an explosion in my mind."

I reminded him that he and his brother had already bought shotguns, but Erik insisted that the guns were for their own protection. "When it was revealed I had told Lyle the secret, my dad said to Lyle, 'You're going to tell everyone and I'm not going to let that happen.' "

But why had they killed their mother? Because, the brothers said, she knew and did nothing. "There was anger on my part," said Lyle. "My mother was aware and had to lie to herself about my father." Said Erik: "She told me that she knew, that she had known all my life what my father was doing . . . At that point I just saw Dad and Mom as the same person. I saw them as a single person."

So they shot their parents and, with their inheritance, went shopping. "There are people who think you are spoiled brats, that you are evil, that you are monsters. What do you say to them?" I asked. And Erik responded with what became my favorite line. "I'm just a normal kid," he said. "Oh, Erik," I said back to him. "You're a normal kid . . . who killed his parents!?"

The interview took place just before the formal sentencing and the subsequent decision as to which state prison or prisons the brothers would be placed in. They were very anxious to be imprisoned together. "The family that Erik and I grew up in, we had to be there for each other throughout, and it really created a bond that gets us through a very rough period," said Lyle. Erik seemed terrified at the possibility of separation. "If we're not put in the same prison, there is a good probability that I will never see him again. With everything taken away, it would be the last they could take." But their pleas didn't sway the authorities. Lyle was sent to the California Correctional Institution near Tehachapi, and Erik to the California State Prison in Sacramento County. "I gather you know the disaster that occurred a few weeks ago," Erik wrote me in October 1996. "Lyle and I were separated. I won't dwell on this unfortunate and cruel decision that was made by whatever powers that be. I am sad." The brothers remain in separate prisons to this day.

This was not the first letter I received from Erik. Almost from the time I interviewed him, he had begun to write to me. At first I didn't answer, but his letters were so intelligent and he seemed in such emotional pain, stressing again and again how tortured he was by what he had done, that I began to answer him. He told me he had received hundreds and hundreds of letters from people who had been abused by their parents. He tried to answer them and hoped he could do something to help them, though of course he couldn't. He also had thoughts about prison reform, but the authorities were not interested, he said, and his views were getting him into trouble.

Which brings me to an aside I find intriguing. While they were incarcerated, Erik and Lyle both married women on the outside who were among the hundreds, maybe thousands, who wrote to them during the trials and their subsequent years in prison. Lyle married, divorced in less than a year, and married again. Erik married in 1999 and, as of this writing, is still married to one of his prison correspondents, Tammi Menendez. What makes these marriages particularly astonishing is that prisoners like Lyle and Erik are not allowed conjugal visits. In plainer English—no sex. So when Erik wrote to me in 2002, three years after his marriage, and suggested that I might want to do an interview with Tammi, I immediately answered that yes, I did. Erik said that his wife was very afraid of talking—she had been asked to leave her volunteer job when her colleagues found out she was Mrs. Erik Menendez—but he would tell her that it was a good idea. He kept hoping and trying to get his case reopened, this time using the restricted material relating to his parental abuse. Perhaps he felt an interview with the sympathetic Tammi would help win him a new trial. So I flew to California to meet Tammi. Ten years Erik's senior, twice married and a mother of two daughters (one grown and one six years old), Tammi was fragile, blond, very pretty, and shy. After we got to know each other a bit, we went together to visit Erik in prison.

It was a bizarre meeting. I had been in enough prisons by then to know to bring quarters for the vending machine, and we sat there, the three of us, eating hamburgers and having a conversation as if we were in McDonald's. I remember thinking how well Erik looked. He had been incarcerated for twelve years by then, but he was tanned and fit. It turned out he was a night janitor in the prison and by day worked out with plastic bags filled with water as weights. He and Tammi were very sweet together. They could hold hands during the visit, but no other contact was allowed.

I later interviewed Tammi outside the prison. (We couldn't film the couple together because on-camera interviews with inmates weren't allowed.) Tammi told me that it was during the brothers' first, televised trial that her "heart went out to Erik," that she "could understand what he went through." Had she been abused herself? I asked. "In my marriage I was emotionally starved," she said. "He was just not there for me at all." (Tammi would later disclose in a book about her relationship with Erik that her then husband had been molesting her older daughter, his stepdaughter. He subsequently committed suicide.)

Tammi wrote to Erik in prison during the trial. To her surprise he responded. After her husband's death in 1996, she waited several months before she wrote again. This time, she says, she needed support from him. When I asked her why she trusted Erik when she had never met him, she replied, "Maybe because he was incarcerated. He was very safe for me."

They met for the first time the following summer, when Tammi went to California to visit Erik. "I was scared," she said. "I'd never been in a prison before." Sparks flew. "I was just thinking, 'I am really attracted to this person. And it's not a good thing because he's incarcerated.' And we visited again and things just kept getting more intense." She finally moved from Minnesota with her younger daughter to be near Erik's prison. The couple married in 1999 in a cinderblock conference room next to the prison's visiting hall. Erik's grandmother came, as did two of his aunts, one from each side of the family. They weren't allowed to have a wedding cake. "We had Twinkies from the vending machine," Tammi said. But the prison did make one concession. "They allowed us to kiss each other after the wedding, so that was nice," Tammi said.

Erik seemed as devoted to Tammi as she was to him. We were able to interview him by phone though we couldn't show him. "I can't offer her most of the things another husband can in terms of being with her physically and being able to hold her," he said. "What I can offer her is unconditional and complete devotion and love. She is everything to me."

The interview seemingly got Erik in more trouble. Both he and Tammi wrote me that soon afterward he'd been taken away in handcuffs and locked in "the hole." He spent four days in an isolation cell, Tammi wrote, "with blood, feces and food scattered about," before he found out why: he'd been charged with "conspiracy to escape." He passed a polygraph test and was eventually released from lockdown. But there were other repercussions.

Erik has since been transferred four hours away to Pleasant Valley State Prison in Coalinga, California, and Tammi can only visit him on weekends. Lyle has been moved, too, to Mule Creek State Prison in

Ione, California. Each brother has appealed his sentence but to no avail. Erik's worst fears have played out; the brothers haven't been allowed to see or speak to each other in more than a decade. They can write to each other, but the letters are opened and read by the authorities.

Erik writes to me to this day. He is the only convicted murderer I've stayed in touch with. Do I think what he did was hideous? Yes, of course. Does he think what he did was hideous? Yes. At least he says so. His letters are intelligent, sensitive, and uncomplaining. Erik will probably never be released from prison, and I wonder again and again how this man I have just described as intelligent and sensitive could have cold-bloodedly shot both of his parents to death. As I've said before about Erik and all the murderers I've interviewed, I can feel empathy toward them as human beings, but I just cannot comprehend their crimes.

Uncommon Criminals

*N*OT EVERYONE WHO MAKES the headlines and draws big television ratings is a convicted murderer. Other big hits are convicted white-collar multimillionaires like Martha Stewart and Michael Milken, the so-called "king of junk bonds." So, in high-profile cases, are the families of both the accused and the victims. When there is a trial as sensational as that of O. J. Simpson, practically everyone involved is someone you want to talk with. Sometimes, too, the criminals turn out not to be criminals. That makes for particularly intriguing stuff.

Let's start with a case in point, Patricia Hearst, the daughter of Randolph Hearst, chairman of the Hearst publishing empire. To this day no one is really certain whether Patty Hearst was a criminal or a victim.

Nineteen-year-old Patty Hearst burst into the headlines in February 1974 when a homegrown armed revolutionary group called the Symbionese Liberation Army kidnapped her from the Berkeley town house she was sharing with her fiancé, and stuffed her, in her nightgown, into the trunk of their car. A week later the SLA released an audiotape on which she was heard pleading for her life. However chilling, that was to be expected. What was unexpected was the image caught on a security tape two months later of Patty at a bank robbery, cradling a machine gun in her arms. "I am Tania," Hearst said, using her new *nom de guerre*. "Up against the wall, motherfuckers." And so the rich, privileged heiress was transformed from being a sympathetic kidnap victim to an obscene wanted felon.

Hearst was finally captured in September 1975. Her trial, in the days before Court TV, filled the newspapers day after day. Her defense tried but failed to cast her as a victim of brainwashing and intimidation; the jury found Hearst guilty of armed robbery and she was sentenced to seven years in prison. I visited her there soon after I started at ABC. She wasn't allowed to give an interview, but I wanted to meet her in the hope she would give me one when she got out. Seeing her in federal prison was a surreal experience. Hearst had completed her reversion back to her pre–urban guerrilla days. Gone was her signature military beret, the dyed red hair, the cocky aggressiveness she had assumed with that machine gun in her arms. She was quiet and polite.

Visiting her in prison led to my interview with her in 1981, the first she gave after her early release from prison. (Hearst spent only twenty-two months in prison because President Jimmy Carter commuted her sentence to time served. Later President Bill Clinton would grant her a full pardon. The country seemed to agree that it was the right thing to do.) Our conversation was both chilling and puzzling. The chilling part included the fifty-seven days she spent blindfolded and locked in a closet after she was kidnapped, the sex she was forced to have with the members of the SLA, their threats to kill her. The puzzling part was why, given many opportunities, she didn't escape or even phone home. "At one point you found yourself in a motel in Las Vegas. You were alone, absolutely alone, for several days. You could have picked up the phone and called your parents, just to say, 'I'm okay.' You never did. Why?"

"I just couldn't," she answered. "It seems not only improbable, but it just seems so implausible. It never crossed my mind to call them. After everything they [the SLA] had done to me, my thinking was so twisted that I really believed that I could not go and turn myself in without being killed."

What I remember most from that interview was not what Patty Hearst said, but how dead voiced she was. Here she was describing the horrific things that had happened to her in an expressionless monotone with no emotion. I was more emotional than she was. There were no tears, no guilt. It was as if the memories had been wiped out of her consciousness and she was reading from somebody else's text. Was that her way of coping? Had she gone through so much that any emotion was too much? I couldn't tell.

What also stands out was her absolutely beautiful baby, Lydia. After her release from prison, Patty married a San Francisco policeman, Bernard Shaw, one of her bodyguards. They were living a quiet life then in a well-protected, unpretentious house in an upper-middle-class sub-urb of San Francisco. They are still married, now have two grown daughters, and live in Wilton, Connecticut. The last time I saw Patty was of all places at a polo match that Camilla Parker Bowles invited me to on the outskirts of London (her future husband, Prince Charles, was playing). Patty was there with her beautiful, now grown daughter, the adorable baby I remembered so well. Lydia is a model, and Patty, for the most part, leads a quiet suburban life. She did not take her experience and say, "I'm going to spend my life doing something important." It's as if it never happened.

Now, one of the most sensational stories I ever covered. In 1996 and throughout the next year, television viewers were glued to their sets to get the latest news about a beautiful, blond little six-year-old girl named JonBenet Ramsey, who was murdered on Christmas Day in her family's Boulder, Colorado, home. The tragic murder of the girl was even more lurid because there was so much footage of her parading around at child beauty contests wearing lipstick, mascara, and suggestive adult clothing. (The images sparked a national tut-tut about the child beauty contests and the adult sexuality they overlaid on JonBenet and her fellow prepubescent contestants.) The discovery of her strangled body in the family's basement, her skull fractured, and her neck bound with nylon cord twisted tight with a paintbrush handle, was horrifying. So was the blood in her underpants and on her Barbie nightgown. Was it a botched kidnapping? A ransom note was found on the stairs. Or was that a coverup for the sexual molestation that ended in her violent death? And if so, who did it?

Her parents were a respected couple named John and Patsy Ramsey, who, by all accounts, were loving parents. They insisted from the beginning that an intruder had entered their house, hid until they were asleep, and then hideously murdered their daughter. But accusatory fingers were immediately pointed at JonBenet's mother, Patsy, a former beauty queen herself (Miss West Virginia). Had she, the papers screeched, lost her temper after JonBenet wet her bed on Christmas Eve and in anger killed her? John Ramsey was also a target. Did he sexually assault and kill his daughter? Even JonBenet's nine-year-old brother, Burke, drew early attention but was discounted as a suspect because the police believed he didn't have the strength. For months and then years, the focus was on JonBenet's parents. Grieving for the daughter they professed to adore, they also had to live with constant investigations and accusations of guilt of this most awful crime. (It was only later disclosed that thirty-eight registered sex offenders lived within two miles of the Ramseys.)

In 1998, two years after the murder, the case against John and Patsy

Ramsey went before a grand jury. The jurors deliberated for thirteen months. Their decision finally came down in October 1999. There was insufficient evidence to indict either one—or both—in JonBenet's murder. But the rumors and accusations continued. Even today some think the Ramseys were guilty.

Everyone of course wanted to interview them. I followed my usual route, writing letters and talking to them several times over the phone. I told them that they could finally let people see them when they were not looking harassed and cornered. They could calmly present their case. They had seen many of my past interviews and said they would think about it. Another year passed, and finally the Ramseys agreed to be interviewed. (It often takes this long, or longer, to obtain an interview.)

The Ramseys didn't reveal any new information. They had none to give. But just listening to them was wrenching. "I saw her lying on the floor on a white blanket," John Ramsey said in a tight, tortured voice. "Her hands were tied above her head. She had tape over her mouth. Her eyes were closed. I immediately knelt down over her, felt her cheek, took the tape off her mouth. I tried to untie the cord that was around her arms. I couldn't get the knot untied."

John Ramsey said he ran upstairs with his little girl's body, screaming. "It was like a dream, when you scream but you can't say anything." He said he laid JonBenet on the floor of the living room, and Patsy Ramsey rushed in.

Mrs. Ramsey, in anguish, then told me, "I remember seeing her lying there in front of the Christmas tree and I looked at John and he said, 'She's dead.' It felt like my life was in slow motion, and that this was not really happening. I kept saying, 'No, no, no,' and I asked God to raise her."

By the time we finished the hour-long interview, I was convinced, and am to this day, that they had not committed the murder. The Ramseys, it seemed to me, were still in extreme pain, devoted to each other, and adoring of their daughter. They would have had to have been the greatest actors in the world to behave together as they did, if one or both of them were guilty. You could see it in their body language, in the way John Ramsey consoled his wife at times during the interview. Most of all, neither had any record of violent or untoward behavior in their past, and there was no motive for killing a child they had treasured. You don't strangle a little girl because she wets her bed.

Patsy Ramsey was also a survivor of stage four ovarian cancer. She seemed to be in remission but she knew her cancer could return. At the end of our interview, she talked about her faith in God. "If it weren't for our faith, there would be no hope of ever seeing JonBenet again. But we know that we will see her again in heaven." I then quietly asked, "Do you think that JonBenet is in a better place?" Mrs. Ramsey answered, "I would have liked to think that my arms were the best place for JonBenet to be. But she's in a place where I hope to be one day. I know I will be there."

The year 2006 marked the tenth anniversary of JonBenet's still-unsolved death. Patsy Ramsey died of ovarian cancer in June of that year at the age of forty-nine.

Six months later I talked to John Ramsey once again. There seemed to have been a break in the case. A teacher named John Mark Karr had been arrested in Thailand, after confessing to being with JonBenet when she died. "I didn't want to get my hopes up, even though it was easy to let that happen," Ramsey told me. The publicity surrounding Karr was enormous. "Ironically, at some point I started feeling sorry for the guy, because he was getting convicted, basically, as we were early on," Ramsey said. But no conviction ever took place. Karr was subsequently freed because his DNA didn't match any samples from the crime scene.

Today John Ramsey lives quietly in Atlanta, still hoping that the person who murdered his daughter and all but destroyed his and his wife's life will finally be apprehended. At the end of this last interview, I asked, as I had asked his wife, what faith meant to him. Here was his answer. "Because of my faith, I know the end of the story. I will be in heaven and I know I will be reunited with Patsy and JonBenet. Finally our story will have an end and a beginning." In 2008 new DNA samples were finally obtained, which proved once and for all that John and Patsy did not kill their daughter.

Murders are not the only stories that draw huge ratings. People also love to see the high and mighty fall from their halcyon heights and show up in police mug shots. One who took such a plunge from the top in 1989 was Michael Milken, a billionaire financier who was a highly controversial promoter of what were called "junk bonds." (Junk bonds are high-risk bonds that, because of their risk, could and often do pay very high dividends.) In many cases the junk bonds Milken advocated helped a lot of businesses, especially smaller ones which otherwise might not have gotten off the ground. But Milken also made serious mistakes along the way in his zeal to promote the bonds and was charged with ninety-eight counts of racketeering and fraud by none other than Rudy

Giuliani, then a district attorney in New York. Milken was a huge name in the investment banking business, and he rapidly became the prototype for what were considered the excesses of the eighties. His photo was in the newspapers almost every day, looking gaunt and wearing a toupee. (That fact didn't much help his image.) The details of the major charges were extremely complicated, but they were sufficiently understood for a federal grand jury to indict him. After a plea bargain to six lesser securities violations, Milken was sentenced to ten years in jail, a sentence that was later reduced to two years with three years' probation.

I knew and liked Michael Milken. He was a friend of my then husband, Merv Adelson, and one of the companies he helped to finance was Lorimar, Merv's production company. Merv and I had spent time in Los Angeles with Milken and his wife, Lori, his high school sweetheart and mother of their three young children. He was brilliant, a visionary, and very much a family man. Though he was a billionaire, he had a relatively modest lifestyle. I remember having hamburgers at their rambling ranch house, which had been built for Clark Gable and Carole Lombard. The ketchup bottles were on the table and we all used paper napkins. Those were early evenings. Milken got up at 3:00 a.m. so he could be in his office by 4:00 because it was already 7:00 a.m. on Wall Street in New York. That all came to a halt, obviously, when the court sent him to a minimum-security work camp in Pleasanton, California, in 1991.

I visited him there, as I had visited Patty Hearst in prison, in the hope of securing an exclusive interview with him when he was released. He said then that his biggest regret was letting the press define him. His lawyers had not permitted him to do any interviews. He felt that had he been allowed to, he could have explained what his motivations were and what good he had done. Lawyers, in their caution, often shut their clients up. I think it is a mistake; too often they make their client look even more suspicious.

If you have to go to prison, Pleasanton isn't the worst place to be. We sat outside on a bench in the warm sunshine. Milken was sharing a room with seven other prisoners. They slept in double-decker beds. I noticed he was wearing a baseball cap, but not just to keep the sun out of his eyes. The prison didn't allow him to wear his toupee, so he was covering his head. "Why don't you take the cap off when you get out of here and get rid of the toupee?" I said to him. "Let people see you the way you are." Others must have told him the same thing because when we did the interview in 1993, three months after he was released from prison, he was toupee-free.

His homecoming, however, was clouded. Less than two months after his release his doctor diagnosed him with advanced inoperable prostate cancer. He was told he had twelve to eighteen months to live.

I didn't dwell on the cancer in our interview. He called the news "devastating," and we moved right on to his time in prison. Like Jean Harris, he had used it well. After a stint as a janitor—"I cleaned toilets, washed windows, took out the trash"—Milken was allowed to be an "educational tutor." "Out of all the inmates I taught, only one did not get his high school diploma," he said. This was in keeping with the educational programs he had endowed through the Milken Family Foundation long before his indictment. One, called Mike's Math Club, attempted to make math fun for fifth and sixth graders. After his release he expanded the program to include other subjects as part of the full-time public service he was required to do for three years with inner-city children. Even today Milken is involved with education for children.

At the time of our interview, Milken felt he had little time left to live. The challenge at hand was to beat his cancer, and, against all odds, he did. He set up and funded the Prostate Cancer Foundation and a think tank he named FasterCures. He completely changed his lifestyle and diet. The hamburgers we'd gobbled together were replaced with soy and vegetables. He became a devotee of Eastern medicine: yoga, aromatherapy, and meditation. Who knows what worked and what didn't, but to this day, more than fifteen years later, Milken is not only alive but well. I run into him from time to time and have sent several friends who have been diagnosed with prostate cancer to see or talk with him. He always gives generously of his time and knowledge. Milken took a dreaded experience in his life and turned it into a force for good.

Martha Stewart also came out of prison seemingly stronger and better for it. Stewart was the richest "homemaker" in America—she was worth more than one billion dollars—until she was indicted for securities fraud and obstructing justice in 2003. "Little Miss Perfect has fallen on her face," one reporter summed it up. And all, the government charged, to avoid $45,673 in stock market losses, which would have been petty change to her.

I knew and liked Martha. I had decorated cookies with her for one of my *Specials* in her perfectly appointed kitchen at her home in Westport, Connecticut. We had lunch afterward and compared our private lives—two divorced and ambitious women, each with a daughter. We became more or less friendly. Not close, but friendly. When Martha was indicted, I called her lawyer, Robert Morvillo, to see if I could arrange an interview. Somewhat reluctantly he agreed to meet with me, bringing with him several of Martha's other advisers.

At that point Martha Stewart may have been admired in some circles, but she was not liked. She was considered arrogant and cold. My argument at that meeting was that an interview would be an opportunity for her to show people another, more human side. I told them I would like to take Martha back to the small town in New Jersey where she grew up so that viewers could see the warm and family-oriented life Martha came from. Seeing her family home, her old high school, the library where she studied, would humanize her. (Remember, I later did this same kind of visit with Hillary Clinton.) Her advisers finally got the picture and agreed to the interview.

The first part of the interview, which aired in November 2003, was the "Martha at Home" section. We went back with her to Nutley, New Jersey, to the house in which she grew up, with one bathroom for her parents and five siblings. "I had to get up really early to use the bathroom," she said, which in my mind, at least, explained why she still gets up at 5:00 a.m. Her mother taught her how to cook, sew, iron, clean, mend, and tailor. Her father taught her gardening, and, she said, "everything else that had to do with keeping a home, like the plumbing, the electrical, the carpentry." She joined every single club in high school. "Did you ever do nothing?" I asked. "I don't think so," she replied.

Martha as a child was turning out to be every bit as formidable as Martha the adult. But at least you could understand her drive and her huge accomplishments.

We did the rest of the interview on a chilly fall day in her house in East Hampton. I remember the kitchen being all different shades of green and thinking how "Martha" it looked. The dishes and napkins were green, even the floor was green. There was a fire in the entrance hall, and all was very cozy, but the major question in my interview was anything but comforting. Still, it had to be asked. Martha, at that time, was at the lowest ebb of her popularity. She knew it.

"Martha, why do so many people hate you?"

Her answer was straightforward.

"I think sometimes I may be insensitive," she said. "But I have a job to do. And I may sometimes really think that others should work as hard as I work or concentrate as much as I concentrate. But those traits and that behavior, if applied to a man, would be admirable. Applied to a woman, you know, 'She's a bitch.' "

Well, there was truth to that, God knows. Her indictment had in fact spawned much discussion as to whether she was being treated more harshly because she was a successful woman. Her many supporters started a "Save Martha" campaign on the Internet, selling T-shirts, mugs, and the like. And indeed, if she was being punished for being more successful than most men, it was working. The value of the stock in her company had fallen sharply.

"I hear the figure you have lost is between 400 to 700 million," I said.

"Something like that," she said.

The questions and her answers that made all the evening news broadcasts, however, were about the possibility of her going to prison. Her answer was the first time in the interview that she really got to me. She was then sixty-two and realized that her life was getting shorter. I sure could relate to that. The most painful thought to her, therefore, was the waste of time. "At my age, there's no time for an unexpected, undesirable, unwanted hiatus," she said. When I asked her whether she was "scared" she replied, "Of course I'm scared. Who wouldn't be scared? The last place I would ever want to go is to prison."

She did, of course. Three months after she had calmly folded those green napkins in the kitchen, she went on trial. I went to the court on the last day of testimony and thought her lawyer's summation was terrible. Morvillo was rambling and unconvincing. He also did not put Martha on the stand, which may have been a mistake. The prosecutor, on the other hand, made a compelling case with not too much actual evidence. On March 5, 2004, the jury found Martha guilty on all counts. She was sentenced to five months in prison, five months of home confinement, and two years of supervised probation.

By this time we were friends, and I went to visit her at Alderson Federal Prison in West Virginia. It was not unpleasant. You could take a walk outside, and there were tables to sit at. I'd brought a supply of quarters for the vending machine, and we sat outside eating yogurt. (Martha had gotten the prison to put yogurt in the machines.) She had adjusted well. She introduced me to her fellow inmates, all of whom seemed to like her.

I wanted to do a new interview with her when she got out of jail in March 2005, but Martha was soon on to a whole new career at NBC. Producers had also visited her in prison and were convinced that she now had the sympathy of the country. They felt they could present a very different Martha, forceful, yes, but also warm. They arranged for her to do a version of Donald Trump's big success, *The Apprentice*, as well as a morning five-day-a-week, one-hour syndicated celebrity and cooking show with a big, beautiful studio and a relaxed atmosphere for the "new, fun-loving Martha." Unfortunately *The Apprentice: Martha Stewart* only lasted one season, but the daytime show is still on the air. It is currently programmed opposite *The View* in New York, the major market. But we are not worried about the competition.

Martha and I are happy to be easy friends again. I think she is a terrific lady. She has radio shows, new magazines, all kinds of different projects. There is nothing this woman can't do, unlike me, whose daughter once said, "My mommy can't cook. My mommy can't drive. My mommy can only do television."

If we all think that the Martha Stewart trial became a media sensation, nothing, no, nothing, compared to the arrest of O. J. Simpson in June 1994 and his subsequent trial. I have saved this saga, the best, or rather the worst, for last. Need I remind you that Simpson was tried for the murder of his ex-wife, Nicole Brown Simpson, and a young man of whom no one had previously heard, Ron Goldman? *Ninety-five million* people watched the live pictures of Simpson's white Ford Bronco proceeding along an LA freeway trailed by the police on the day he failed to turn himself in. The slow-speed car chase occurred on a Friday while I was on the air with *20/20*. Along with the rest of the country, we watched in fascination. Peter Jennings then joined us as the chase became more and more bizarre. Finally, after miles of being followed by the police, O.J. surrendered and spent the next seven months in prison awaiting trial.

My personal involvement began two months after the murder, in August 1994. I was on vacation, cruising off the coast of Alaska on a friend's boat, when I got a phone call from my office in New York. "A Mr. Fred Goldman is trying to reach you," my assistant said. I thought hard but couldn't place him. "The name sounds familiar," I said. "Who is Fred Goldman?" "We think he's Ron Goldman's father," was the reply.

Good Lord! I jumped off the boat in the middle of nowhere, found an airport where I could charter a plane, and flew to Los Angeles, where I sat down with Fred Goldman, his wife, Patti, Ron's sister, Kim, and two stepsiblings, Lauren and Michael. With all the emphasis on Nicole, the Goldmans were distraught, not just because their beloved son was dead but because people knew nothing about him. The family wanted people to know that twenty-five-year-old Ron was not just a waiter in a restaurant that Nicole Simpson frequented but that he worked by day in a home for people with cerebral palsy and was working nights so he could eventually open his own restaurant. What was breaking their hearts was hearing Ron reduced to "Nicole's male companion" or simply a "waiter." "I hear reporters talking about the victim, not victims," said Kim. "And I yell at the TV and scream out his name. 'Ron! His name is Ron! He has a name, he has a family, he had a life!' "

This was the first of a series of interviews I did with the Goldmans. I was sad for Nicole and her family, but the more I got to know the Goldmans, the more I ached for them. Ron's father, Fred, had been divorced and for many years until he remarried, had raised Ron and his sister, Kim, as a single father. The whole family adored the easygoing Ron. They showed me home movies of him with his younger stepsiblings, laughing, hugging them, singing with them, teaching them tennis.

Ron was not part of the complicated relationship between Nicole and O. J. Simpson. He had simply been delivering the eyeglasses she'd left behind that night at the restaurant. He was in the wrong place at the wrong time.

Kim and her stepmother, Patti, attended the Simpson trial every day. It was particularly difficult emotionally for Fred Goldman to attend that often. Kim, by her presence, became the conscience of the trial, reminding everyone of her murdered brother. To this day, whenever Kim or her father mentions O.J., they refer to him as "the killer."

I have stayed in contact with the Goldmans over the years. Fred and Patti moved out of Los Angeles and settled in Arizona. Kim wrote to me when she got married, when she had a baby, and later when she divorced. Among other things she works for an organization that aids victims of crime, something she understands all too well.

O.J.'s televised trial lasted nine long months, from January to October 1995. "The Trial of the Century," as it became known, was the greatest soap opera there ever was and turned millions of people into courtroom junkies. Even foreign leaders were transfixed. "Do you think O.J. did it?" was Boris Yeltsin's first question to Bill Clinton when the Russian president arrived in New York in October 1995 for a summit.

You can imagine how intense the competition was among television journalists to interview anyone connected to Simpson and the trial. Of course, we all wanted to talk to O.J. himself. I got the home number of his personal assistant, Cathy Randa, and she arranged for Simpson to phone me at my home. His story back then is now familiar. Nicole was the villain. He had tried to break up with her but she would keep coming back. He would never harm Nicole, the mother of his children. He laughed, strangely, during our conversation but was charming and I must admit, somewhat convincing. He didn't want to do an interview but he wanted me to repeat our conversation on the air. I hung up, unsure whether this smooth-talking man was guilty or not. I did report on our conversation, but he never did agree to an interview with me or any other reporter. His superskilled legal team saw to that.

The Goldman family was talking almost exclusively to me. Nicole's family had become close to Diane Sawyer. We respected each other's territory. Everybody else was up for grabs, and it was a matter of phone calls, letters, contacts, the usual procedure. The trial made stars of many lawyers who flooded the airwaves, among them Cynthia McFadden, who did a superb job reporting for ABC, and a very smart ex-prosecutor named Star Jones, who would later come into my life on *The View*.

I managed to secure interviews with many of the people who became household names and faces during the course of the trial—the most important being Brian "Kato" Kaelin, the flaky blond would-be actor who lived in Simpson's guesthouse and saw him the night of the murder. I interviewed Simpson's devoted assistant as well as his ex-wife, who swore that, during their twelve-year marriage, Simpson never raised a hand to her. "O.J. is a big talker," she said. "He likes to shoot off his mouth but with little action. I'm here. I'm living evidence." I talked to Simpson's friend, a chiropractor, who spoke to Simpson the night of the murder and said he sounded fine and was a good guy.

But then I talked to close friends of Nicole who claimed Simpson stalked her after their divorce. " 'I'm so scared of O.J.,' " one friend claimed Nicole told her. " 'I'm so scared of O.J.' "

For months, like the other reporters, I was caught in the whirlwind. The interviews everyone also wanted were with the legal teams in the courtroom—Marcia Clark, the dark-haired (now blond) prosecutor who dressed in short skirts; Chris Darden, the young African American assistant prosecutor; the members of Simpson's legal defense "Dream Team," headed by Robert Shapiro and the now-deceased Johnnie Cochran Jr., a brilliant and theatrical African American lawyer. No reporter, and I include myself, went away on vacation.

Finally, on October 3, 1995, after deliberating only four hours, the jury, composed of nine African Americans, one Hispanic, and two Caucasians, reached a verdict. I was in LA and rushed to the hotel suite that we were using as a makeshift studio. I had arranged for Kato Kaelin to be with me, and he almost fell off his chair in astonishment when the jury found Simpson innocent. (Although he has never directly accused Simpson of lying, most of us feel that Kaelin knew a lot more than he has ever expressed.) If Kato was astounded by the verdict, so were millions of others. The verdict divided much of black and white America.

In any event O. J. Simpson left the courtroom that day a jubilant, free man.

If Simpson was jubilant, one of O.J.'s leading lawyers, Robert Shapiro, was anything but. I got to him right after the trial and talked to him live for a headline-making interview. Rather than rejoice over the not-guilty verdict for his client, Shapiro was bitter at the way his colleague, Johnnie Cochran, had used Simpson's race as a defense strategy. "My position was always the same, that race would not and could not be a part of this case," Shapiro told me. "I was wrong. Not only did we play the race card, we dealt it from the bottom of the deck."

Shapiro was "deeply offended," he said, by Cochran's summation to the jury comparing racism to the Holocaust. "To me the Holocaust stands alone as the most horrible human event," said Shapiro. The race issue had become so divisive among the Dream Team that Shapiro said he would not work again on a case with Cochran. "He believes that everything in America is related to race. I do not."

An aside: Shapiro had, for the duration of the trial, basked in the fame that came with his being appointed one of Simpson's lawyers. At sporting events he was often introduced and cheered by the fans. But the night of the Simpson verdict was also the first night of the most holy Jewish holiday, Yom Kippur. After talking with me, Shapiro, who is Jewish, went to his synagogue. He later told me that this was one of the most painful nights of his life. He was booed.

The verdict continued to be a divisive issue between blacks and whites. No one illustrated that racial divide more than Chris Darden, who had been shunned and even threatened by blacks for prosecuting Simpson. When Darden sat down with me for his first interview five months after the trial, he told me he agreed with Shapiro that it was Cochran who had enflamed the race issue. He'd already been marginalized in his old neighborhood for taking on the case. "Some people walk up to me and express pride in what I've done and others, shock and outrage," he told me. The bar had been raised during the trial when Darden objected to Cochran using the *n* word to illustrate the racism of one of the prosecution's witnesses.

"It is the filthiest, dirtiest, nastiest word in the English language," Darden had protested. "It has no place in this case or in this courtroom. . . . It will blind the jury to the truth." That gave Cochran the opportunity to discredit Darden to his own race. "His remarks are demeaning to African Americans as a group, and so I want to apologize to African Americans across the country," Cochran said.

I asked Darden what he felt when he heard Cochran's apology on his behalf. "What he was really saying to African Americans was that I was a sellout. I was a race traitor. I was an Uncle Tom." Darden was devastated. "People wanted to kill me. People spit at me. Life changed for me drastically."

When the jury found Simpson innocent, Darden told me he felt like he'd been "struck in the stomach with a baseball bat." But he wasn't surprised. He said that his father, a retired welder, had warned him of the outcome at the start of the trial: " 'Black folks will never convict O. J. Simpson.' " Darden said he knew his father was right the moment he saw the jury. "From the first day I didn't believe we had a snowball's chance in hell of convicting O. J. Simpson," he told me. "I sensed it was payback time and that we had no chance."

A year or so after the trial, I also interviewed Marcia Clark, the lead prosecutor in the case. Her agents were predicting a big career for her, possibly on television. She, like Darden, had written a book that I found pedestrian, with no real insight. After reading it and interviewing her, I felt that she didn't have the brilliance of mind to have been the prosecutor at so dynamite a trial. Her future career has borne that out.

Simpson may have beaten the murder charges, but he didn't beat the civil case brought against him by the Goldmans. In 1997 the jury found Simpson guilty of causing Ron's "wrongful death" and ordered him to pay some $8.5 million in compensatory damages. He hasn't.

Fast-forward to the summer of 2000. O.J. had come up with a money-making scheme. He was launching a Web site that would charge Internet visitors for him to answer their questions. He was looking for publicity for this new venture and wanted to come on *The View*. "What ratings!" I momentarily thought. But when I mentioned on the show that Simpson might possibly be on the program, the viewers and even our production staff protested. What was I thinking? We canceled O.J.

Fast-forward again to the summer of 2006. I was working on this book when I got a call from a representative of the ABC branch that produces special programs. My own *Specials* are under the umbrella of ABC News, but rather than confuse you with the different departments, let me just tell you that the phone call was about another book, a sort of nonfiction piece of fiction, called *If I Did It*. The book was purportedly by O. J. Simpson. Would I be interested in a two-hour interview with him? If so, ABC would produce it. I was told I would shortly receive a chapter or two from the book, which was under a strict embargo. I read what was sent to me. O.J. described everything up to the actual stabbing. He said he had a friend who gave him a knife. It was chilling and filled with details I thought only the killer could know. But it was fiction, remember? And with the title *If I Did It*, I felt there was no way Simpson was going to confess to the crime on television. ABC was not so sure. They wanted me to do the interview because they felt that only I could get Simpson to break down and confess. If I managed to do that, it would be sensational television. There would be huge ratings, and the case would finally reach closure.

I was tempted, but it didn't take me long to make up my mind. Challenge or no challenge, confession or no confession, I couldn't have lived with myself if I were to give Simpson airtime to sell his book. I turned down the interview, and ABC decided to drop the proposal.

Fox later scheduled an interview with Simpson to be done by Judith Regan, the book's publisher. (Rupert Murdoch owns both Fox and HarperCollins, where Regan had her imprint.) A spate of angry editorials followed, decrying the deal. Fox withdrew its offer. Judith Regan was later fired. The saga continued in 2007, when a federal judge awarded the rights to the book to Ron Goldman's family to do whatever they wanted with. They published it under a new title, *If I Did It: Confessions of the Killer*, and it became an instant best seller.

As I write this chapter, O.J. has been arrested yet again, this time for his involvement in an armed robbery in Las Vegas. I don't know what will happen to him, but I'm sure this will not be the last time we will hear from O. J. Simpson. As far as I'm concerned, however, it's the end of any interest I have in him or will have in the future—unless he wants to sit down and really confess to murdering Nicole and Ron. In which case I am ready.

Over Again, Never Again

*E*VERYONE SHOULD HAVE a chance to be an interviewer. You get the opportunity to ask all the questions you would never have the nerve to ask in real life. It's a chance to get to know the most interesting, accomplished, and famous people in the world. I, of course, have had that blessed opportunity, although, believe me, not all of my interviews have been a success. There are a small number of people I have had great trouble interviewing over the years. There are others whom I have talked to again and again and never felt I could run out of questions, for they always had something new to say. I also think of the people I wish I'd interviewed, but either couldn't or didn't.

First the difficult ones. This doesn't mean I don't like or admire them, it just means that it's difficult to sit down with them in front of a camera. When conducting an extensive interview, it is necessary to talk on a personal level, at least to some degree. Otherwise you are just plugging a movie or TV show. That's fine for a brief conversation but not if you are trying to do something special. My problem in these interviews is that I wanted the person to reveal him- or herself, if only a little bit, and my subject wanted to reveal little or nothing. So here are three of my bigger frustrations.

Warren Beatty. Although he has much to say and is informed, with very strong opinions, he is so obsessed with answering questions exactly the way he wants or thinks they should be answered, that he is tongue-tied. And while I am talking about his mouth, it is like pulling teeth to get him to talk.

The first time I interviewed Warren was my ghastly experience way back on the *Today* show. Later, when I knew him better, he explained that he had just flown to New York from Los Angeles and had never done a television interview before. He said he must have fallen asleep during the interview, which was live. Well, thanks a lot. What I remember and have already written about is that I stopped asking him questions and went to a commercial. I have noted many times that it was the worst interview I ever did. Not long after, Warren more or less swore off doing any television, not just because of our interview but because he didn't think his appearances particularly helped sell his movies. I remember when he made the film *Reds*, about an American communist buried in the Kremlin, I was told that he considered for a moment or two sitting down with me but then decided not to. Then in 1990 he directed and starred in the film *Dick Tracy*, about the popular cartoon detective. There was a great deal of hoopla about the film. It had been fifteen years since Warren had done a TV interview, but by this time we had been at several dinner parties and he was warm and forthcoming, so I asked if he would finally like to sit down with me again. "Well," he said very slowly, then drew out the one word "y-e-s." Bill Geddie, who would produce the interview for a *Special*, was thrilled. "Not so fast," I warned him. And our troubles began.

It took weeks before we could get a date out of Warren, more weeks until he could decide where he wanted to meet, and days and days before he decided if and where he would like to place the police car that supposedly belonged to the fictional Dick Tracy. By the time we sat down to do the interview I hated the damn police car. I hated the interview even more. Warren hemmed and hawed before answering any question. At that time, he had not yet married the divine Annette Bening and settled down to being a devoted husband and father. He was still known as a great ladies' man and, in particular, a man who often had, shall we say, "relationships" with his leading ladies. In this case Warren's leading lady was none other than Madonna. How could anyone do an interview with him without dealing with this? So I tried.

ME: You have a history of falling in love with your leading ladies. Is it part of the excitement and the creativity of working, or do you work with someone to whom you are already attracted?

I thought my question was broad enough so that Warren could answer it in any number of ways. Here is what he said:

WARREN: Well, as you know, I'm not going to answer that kind of question. I think as a journalist, you should ask the question, and as a human being, I should decide what I talk about and what I don't, because I don't want to say the wrong thing.

ME: What could you do to yourself that's the wrong thing?

WARREN: Well, I don't know. I just think you have to be prudent.

ME: What could you do to yourself that would be so terrible if you opened up a little bit?

WARREN: Blake said, "Prudence is a rich, ugly, old maid courted by Incapacity."

Here's another selection from that interview:

ME: There are certain adjectives that one reads about you. Warren Beatty, recluse.

WARREN: Recluse?

ME: Yeah.

WARREN: Here I am.

ME: Okay. But you know, first interview in fifteen years. So you are hardly outgoing.

WARREN: Well [said almost like a three-syllable word], I'm very slow. I'm very slow.

Then Warren brought up that first and only other interview I had done with him. "Did you think I was trying to give you a hard time?" he asked.

ME: I thought you were simply terrible.

WARREN: Do you remember that you cut me off in the middle of the interview? It was then that I realized that I was not doing well. But then, I don't think I said five or six words to you for the whole interview.

ME: But you know, that interview had special meaning for me because when people would say, "What's the worst interview you ever did," I would say, "Warren Beatty." And now I feel bad.

WARREN: Was there anybody up there alongside of me?

ME: There wasn't even anybody close. You were it.

Now history was repeating itself. This new interview with Warren was almost as bad as our first one. Not only that, but when it was over, Warren rose from his chair with a happy face and said, "Now that I've had a chance to relax, let's do the interview all over again."

No. No. No. Let me say it plainly. I do not want to interview Warren Beatty again. But I certainly am glad we are friends.

Mel Gibson. In 1990 I flew all the way to London just to interview Gibson for an Academy Award *Special*. He was playing Hamlet in a film directed by Franco Zeffirelli, and I give him a lot of credit for stretching himself and trying new things. I really looked forward to talking with him. We drove an hour to the Shepperton Studios outside London, where he was filming. To accommodate him we planned to do the interview right on the set. We arrived early in the afternoon and said we could talk whenever Gibson wanted. He was working hard and we waited hours, during which I curled up on a bench and fell asleep. When he finally showed up at almost 11:00 p.m., Gibson looked as if he wanted to do the same. He wasn't rude. He just wasn't forthcoming. When I pointed out that a few years back he had received very bad press, he said, "Doing films back-to-back and not knowing how to cope with this new lifestyle or things that were expected of me. I was running into all these preconceptions from other people. So I changed my life and went back to Australia. I thought I'd exit for a while."

I found that very honest, and I understood. But the interview still had no passion although in real life, Gibson is a passionate Catholic. Remember his remarkable film *The Passion of the Christ*? Here is how our interview ended:

ME: Do you ever have trouble reconciling the violence, the sex outside of marriage, the nudity in some of your films with your strict religious views and your own personal morality?

GIBSON: Hmm.

ME: So what do you do?

GIBSON: I don't know.

ME: Did you ignore it? You do it anyway, obviously.

GIBSON: I did it, so?

ME: Does it bother you, though?

GIBSON: No.

So I decided enough of that and asked if he had any lines from *Hamlet* he would like to do for us. Here is what he said.

"O most pernicious woman! O villain, villain, smiling, damned villain! That one may smile, and smile, and be a villain."

I decided to think that was pretty funny and told him I would not take it personally. We flew home the next day. Did we become friends as with Warren Beatty? We didn't even become acquaintances.

Al Gore. First of all, let me say that I like and admire Al Gore a great deal and perhaps one day will interview him again—even though he isn't a movie star . . . although, in a way, he is one now as a result of his Academy Award–winning documentary, *An Inconvenient Truth*. I'm including some thoughts about the former vice president in this chapter because my last encounter with him was very discouraging.

For two years after his devastating loss to George W. Bush, Gore did no television interviews. Then, in November 2002, we heard that he and his wife, Tipper, had written a book. The publishers said that they wanted the Gores to do an interview. We assumed that the book would be something personal, so we arranged to do it, expecting to talk about the 2000 loss. However, when we got an advance copy, the book, titled *Joined at the Heart: The Transformation of the American Family*, turned out to profile the experiences of various families around the country. Almost nothing personal and not a word about the controversial election (so controversial that it ended up in the Supreme Court). Our producer found the Gores' joint literary effort a well-meaning but tedious read and asked me to explain to the vice president that it was not what we had in mind, that we'd like him to let us out of this commitment and that we would do an interview with him in the future. When I phoned Gore's people with this message, Gore himself got on the phone and was furious. I mean *furious*. He shouted at me, and I guess he should have. I had promised, he said, and I had to keep my word. The mild, bland Al Gore was nowhere to be heard. In a way, that pleased me. If I could somehow capture that passion on television, it would make for an important piece. So we agreed to go ahead with the interview, but we told Gore that he would have to talk about his cliffhanger loss to Bush.

Okay. I went to Nashville, to the Gores' house, which looked rather like a miniature version of the White House. Before we sat down for the filming, Gore took me for a car ride. Along the way he sang a bit for me ("On the Road Again") and we stopped off at a local college, where he introduced himself to the students with the words, "I'm Al Gore. I used to be the next president of the United States of America." When I remarked that he was really quite funny, he thanked me and said, "I benefit from low expectations." So far, so good. When the interview began, the segment about the book was interesting enough (we'd also spoken on camera with one of the families featured in the book), but what everybody really wanted to hear was Gore's true reaction to the election. Well, forget it. That section of the interview, in which we talked to Gore and Tipper along with two of their four children, daughters Karenna and Kristin, was even more placid than the conversation about the book. Pleasant might be a better description than placid. Gore's answers to my questions conveyed no conviction, no introspection, no emotion. He should have had *some* kind of reaction to what had been such a trumatic defeat. But no. "My attitude," he said, "was that you win some, you lose some. Then there's this little-known third category. You flip a coin and it lands on its edge." A flip of the coin? No more, no less? In contrast, Kristin readily expressed her anger and disappointment. Of all the family members, she seemed the most bitter—and the most real. But Gore kept repeating that all was and would be fine. He would find other things to do. No explanation. No regrets. Everything would be hunky-dory. Smile. I didn't believe a word of it.

I have since been delighted to see the Al Gore I thought I knew reappear as he's taken on the task of educating us all to the dangers of global warming. I wish he had shown more of that passion when he was doing our interview or, for that matter, when he was running for president.

PEOPLE OFTEN ASK me whom I wish I could have interviewed or still want to. It's a small list made all the more exclusive because, with the exception of one, they didn't (or don't) do interviews. They are the late Jacqueline Kennedy Onassis, the late Pope John Paul II, the present pope, Benedict XVI, Queen Elizabeth II, and the late Princess Diana.

The Queen doesn't do interviews. Prince Philip occasionally will sit for questions, as he did with me in 1969 at President Nixon's urging, especially if they have to do with his favorite wildlife and environmental charities. Prince Charles, like his father, will occasionally also do an interview if he is touting one of the many charitable projects in his Prince's Trust. I haven't talked to him since I interviewed him in Kensington Palace in December 1984. He told me then that so many people kept telling him how "marvelous" he was that he sometimes had to do a "little self-kicking" to keep from getting "big-headed." He went on to have a rather disastrous interview in 1994 with British journalist Jonathan Dimbleby, in which he admitted he had been unfaithful to Diana, but only after the marriage had "irretrievably broken down." He has not sat for an in-depth television interview since then.

The big attraction to me, though, is not the prince but his wife, Camilla Parker Bowles. We chose her as our "Most Fascinating Person" of 2005, the year she married Prince Charles. We accomplished this with footage of her but no interview. She obviously fascinated him. She still fascinates me. We had met several times and once, as I've told you, she invited me to a polo match in England, and was extremely gracious and easy to talk to. I have dangled the interview bait to her saying we would talk about her favorite cause, the disease osteoporosis. So far she has resisted the bait. Too bad. It is an important subject and she could shed a lot of light on this debilitating disease.

Talking about Camilla Parker Bowles brings me to the subject of Princess Diana. I sure wish I could have interviewed her, and almost did. Before I actually met her I had been writing her representatives requesting an interview or at least a meeting. Her press secretaries kept changing. The one constant employee seemed not to be her butler, Paul Burrell, who after she died claimed a very close relationship with the princess, but her private secretary, Patrick Jephson. (He had held the same position when she was married to Charles.) The private secretary is extremely valuable to his royal charge. He is the person who, among other duties, helps to plan royal visits to other countries and then accompanies the royal personage. He often decides which events his charge should attend at home and abroad. He keeps the appointment book and helps decide who should or should not be invited to dinners. He is, in short, in many ways the personal adviser and buffer. When Diana and Charles separated, it was decided that Jephson should go with her. So he was the man I was most often contacting.

When the princess made one of her first visits to America, he was with her and we met and talked. He was very stiff-upper-lip in that "veddy" British way, and extremely protective of his princess. However, we had a chance to chat and, as they say, we "got on." After he and Princess Diana returned to England, he would from time to time ask my advice on an American charity event that was inviting the princess to attend. One such dinner involved the princess being asked to receive something called the Humanitarian of the Year Award from United Cerebral Palsy. I knew the charity very well because I had emceed past dinners and was to emcee this one too. (I was involved because the chairman of the event was my old friend Jack Hausman.) I checked and found that Gen. Colin Powell was also going to be honored and that if Princess Diana attended, Henry Kissinger had said he would present the award to her. I told Jephson that the princess should absolutely accept and she did. She looked dazzling in a clingy black gown, made a charming speech about compassion, and got a standing ovation. Another time Jephson asked if I thought the princess should attend a certain fashion award dinner. I said I didn't think it was the best idea. She came anyway. She was criticized for being frivolous but it did her no real harm.

Anyway, little by little Jephson began to trust me, and so did the princess. At another large charity dinner in Washington (Diana was coming more and more often to America) to raise money for breast cancer research, she and I sat one away from each other at the head table. I remember she was next to Ralph Lauren, who was chairing the dinner, and she danced the first dance with Oscar de la Renta. We had a chance to talk informally and the princess, now divorced from her husband, teasingly asked if there were any eligible men in the room. I pointed out a few. "Too old," she said. "Too short." I felt as if I were talking to my daughter. These different events brought us closer. Princess Diana sent me personal Christmas cards with photos of her and her sons and handwritten notes in her big round penmanship.

I had another connection with the princess. One of her closest friends was a woman quite a bit older than she, named Lucia Flecha de Lima. Her husband, Paulo Tarso de Lima, had been Brazil's ambassador to Great Britain and now held the same post in the United States. Diana, who knew the couple from London, considered Lucia a surrogate mother and telephoned her constantly for advice. This was especially true when, after her divorce, Diana fell in love with a Pakistani cardiologist named Hasnat Khan and seriously considered marrying him. Lucia was very concerned and tried to advise Diana of the consequences. As we all know, Dr. Khan and Diana never married. She was not of his religion, and he, if not she, understood the potential consequences. He was also uncomfortable in the limelight. While this romance was going on, I was also quite friendly with Lucia, and we had many confidential conversations about the relationship, which at that time was little known. I never betrayed this confidence. I hoped Diana knew that, thinking it might make it easier for me to get the interview with her that I and every other journalist wanted.

In 1995 I was visiting London and once more requested a meeting. The princess invited me to lunch at her home in Kensington Palace. This palace is actually a group of small town houses connected to one another in a blocked-off area. On one side of Diana's house was the home of Princess Margaret, the Queen's sister. On the other side was the home of Prince and Princess Michael of Kent, the Queen's cousins. Diana was not particularly friendly with either of her neighbors.

I arrived for lunch on time at 12:30 and walked up a flight of stairs to the living room. On the landing was a lovely portrait of the princess, who was waiting at the landing. The living room was pale yellow. It was recently painted, she told me. As it happened I was wearing a yellow suit. Diana laughed and said how thoughtful it was of me to match the room.

This was a particularly trying time for her. She was separated from her husband but not divorced. Her unhappiness, which manifested itself in various ways including bulimia, had been written about in a block-buster book by Andrew Morton. At first Diana disavowed any participation in the book, but later it came out that she had been interviewed on tape for it. At our lunch she said rather calmly that her husband and his family were trying to make it look as if she were mentally ill so they could send her away somewhere. These accusations had been rumored in the British papers, but it was very disturbing to hear the princess claiming them over the chicken salad. I thought she was exaggerating, but she believed they were true. She was certainly not mentally ill, she said, but the accusations were wearing her down. She also com-plained about her brother, Charles, Earl Spencer. She had needed a place to go in the summer, she told me, and had asked if she could take one of the houses on the family estate at Althorp Park (where she was later to be buried). Her brother refused her request. "There would be too many paparazzi," he said. She was angry and hurt. I re-membered this when the earl was giving his emotional speech at Diana's funeral and proclaiming his great devotion to his sister. I recounted what she had told me on the air after her death, and Earl Spencer was furious and threatened to sue. But it was true and he knew it, so no suit followed.

Before I left Diana on that now-long-ago lunch, I asked once again if she would consider doing an interview with me, perhaps to explain how she felt at present and how she saw her life in the future. She didn't want to do one now, she told me, but when she was ready, which would be soon, I would be the first. I left elated. She walked me down the stairs, not just to her entrance but to my car, where she shook hands with my dazzled driver. It was such a simple but thoughtful gesture—the beauti-ful Princess of Wales, walking outside her home to greet a driver she had never met. I could see why she was beloved by so many of the so-called ordinary people. As soon as I got back to my hotel, I called my office in New York and said I might very well be doing an interview with the princess. A half hour later they called back to say that news had just hit the wires. Two days before my visit the princess had evidently sat down to do an interview with a little-known BBC reporter named Martin Bashir. Martin, by the way, a fine journalist, now works for ABC in New York and we are friends. But at the time I was angry and extremely disappointed, to say the least. What I didn't know was that Martin, being of Pakistani birth, was a friend of Dr. Khan, and this gave him special entrée to Diana, who trusted him. In a quiet, low-key way, he did a sensational job. This would be the bombshell interview in which the princess said there were three people in her marriage: herself, her husband, and Camilla Parker Bowles. This was also the interview that was said to have convinced the Queen that her son the Prince of Wales and Diana should get a divorce. One more thing: this interview was kept secret from her private secretary, Patrick Jephson, and was one of the major reasons, he later told me, that he quit her household. After her death Jephson wrote an extremely revealing book that described his devotion but also his frustrations in working for the princess. I did the first interview with him, but it hardly made up for never interviewing Diana.

Once her interview with Bashir had aired in Great Britain, ABC bought it for broadcast here. I was assigned to introduce it. I wrote to Princess Diana and said how deeply moved I was by the interview and that I wished I had been able to do it myself. She wrote back a thank-you note and said she hoped one day we still might do our interview. It never happened. The next time I reported on Princess Diana was at her funeral.

NOW A GROUP OF PEOPLE I could talk with again and again, each of whom I have interviewed at least twice. This list could actually be much longer, but to balance that small list of the impossible-to-get, I will keep it relatively short.

Cher. She always has something new to say that is amusing, candid, and sometimes wonderfully outrageous. Over the years, in the course of several interviews, she has talked with me openly about her early struggle with reading and writing when she didn't know she was dyslexic; about her difficult marriage with Sonny Bono, who wanted to control her life; about her love affairs; why she likes men much younger than herself; her feelings about aging (she's against it); and almost any subject I wanted to bring up. She lives by her own standards and lets others live by theirs. Cher may change her costumes, her hair color, and even her attitude, but she is always the same delight to talk to. I think this goes for her onstage performances, as well. (My daughter, by the way, will travel many miles to see Cher perform.)

Bette Midler. I could say practically the same thing about Bette as I said about Cher. And I will travel many miles to see Bette perform. She can be hilariously funny and seriously touching. She is such a talent that when she sings "Wind Beneath My Wings," it brings tears to my eyes. Watching her as Delores Delago, the bawdy mermaid in a wheelchair, I also get tears, but this time from laughing. Bette, in her stage act, sometimes tells dirty jokes, imitating the risqué singer of the past, Sophie Tucker. Bette even named her only child Sophie. The whole performance has special meaning to me because, as I have said, Sophie Tucker appeared at the Latin Quarter as its star attraction year after year. I knew her well and to this day can sing her theme song, "Some of These Days." Bette has much more talent than Sophie Tucker, but she has the same delivery and love of a great joke, no matter how offensive. I also adore her humor about herself. I once asked her in an interview, on a scale of one to ten, how she would describe her looks. "On a scale of one to ten?" she said. "Oh, I think I'm about a fifty-five. I think I'm a happening girl." She sure is.

I have a special feeling about Michael Douglas and his beautiful wife, Catherine Zeta-Jones. It is not just that we three share the same birthday, it's more of a family thing. I've known Michael's father, Kirk, and his wife, Anne, for many years. Kirk is now in his nineties, and when he was in his seventies he wrote a very honest memoir about his early life as a poor Jewish boy, called *The Ragman's Son*. I did the first interview with Kirk when the book came out. I particularly remember it because it was during the time my mother's health was beginning to fail and I was traveling back and forth from Los Angeles to New York. At the same time as I was interviewing Kirk, I was also talking on camera with Michael about his own hugely successful career. (He was on one of my Academy Award *Specials*.) I have probably done at least four interviews with Michael. There was never a time when he wasn't thoughtful and candid. I interviewed him during a troubled period when his first marriage was ending. Then I rejoiced when he married Catherine, and I interviewed them both. I consider them friends. Last summer I attended a preview of Michael's latest movie, *The King of California*. He plays an aging man with a long beard. It is an extraordinary performance. I congratulated him, and he whispered in my ear, "When I look at myself in this movie, I see my father." "Yes," I said, "but you are a much better actor." (Forgive me, Kirk, but he is.)

Tom Hanks. He is the same off camera as on. He is intelligent, unpretentious, and, of course, a great talent. It is amazing to think that in our first interview back in 1989, he said he had fears of not making it. Tom had a difficult childhood; his father and mother divorced when he was five, and Tom went with his father as he moved around the West Coast from job to job and from wife to wife. Yet he described his childhood as being as nice and "normal" as possible. "It was almost like being a celebrity because when I was ten and in yet another school, it was like, 'Who is this kid?' Frances, my dad's then wife, was Chinese. That was something that we really never thought about. It was a fact. But other people reacted amazed. But then when you add up that she's also my third mother, and this is the tenth house that we've lived in, and I've been to eight different schools, people would just sort of look at us and just shake their heads, because they didn't know what made us tick."

With that heritage Tom should be one of the most neurotic actors around, but instead he is a family man who has been married to the actress Rita Wilson since 1988. About his career, he said, "Hey, this is what I do and it's not a big deal. I'm not a rocket scientist and I don't have state secrets that I have to keep from everybody. I think they expect demons, some terrible thing, some drive, some bad side, otherwise how would I get to be in this position that I'm in now? Obviously, they think, something very, very deep and some psychological thing makes him go off and do this as a job in the first place and that's not really it."

"So what is it?" I asked.

"It's because it's fun," Tom answered, "and I think I'm pretty good at it. I deliver the goods, which is what a bricklayer does when he's hired to lay bricks or take a mattress off the truck. He's paid to take the mattress off the truck. I take the mattress off the truck and this is, 'Wow, look how that guy takes those mattresses off the truck!' "

I asked, "What's the best thing that success this past year has given you?"

"Probably a certain amount of confidence," he replied. "I feel as though I finished my master's now. I have that bachelor's and now I guess it's time to go for the Ph.D."

Two Academy Awards later Tom not only has his Ph.D., he could teach the course. But he doesn't. He remains a hardworking, happily married, funny, and very nice man.

George Clooney. I don't have to tell you why I like George. He is open and very funny to talk with but also thoughtful and committed to the values in which he believes. His movies show both sides. The first time I interviewed George was in 1995. After years of struggling for success in a series of television flops, he had landed his big break in the medical series *ER*. Unlike many stars of television, George successfully made the transition to films. His first big hit was *From Dusk Till Dawn*, and our conversation took place just before its release. Two things I remember most from that interview. One: he had a pet pig—not a piglet—a big fat pig named Max. Max was inside, not outside, the house when George introduced us. (Max has since died.) The other thing is his answer when, knowing he was divorced and a bachelor, I asked if he wanted to remarry. Most of the time, when I ask this rather prosaic question, the answer is, "Yes, when I find the right person." This is usually followed by a poignant expression of a desire to have children. Not George, who said he would never marry again. When I asked why, he said simply that he was not good at it. Nor did he want children.

The last time I interviewed George was in 2006. I asked then if the women he took out ever expected or hoped he would marry them and if so what did he tell them. "You know what's funny?" he said. "It is because of you that I don't have to. It's already out there. So you've done all the work for me, and I thank you for that."

You're welcome, George.

Tom Cruise is someone I have interviewed many times and probably will interview again. Yet, while Tom wants to be open and candid, he has learned over the years to deflect with a laugh any question that makes him uncomfortable. He doesn't dodge tough questions about Scientology or his love for his wife, Katie, but anything that may make him explore himself is handled with a big grin and that forced laugh. But let me say this about Tom. Raised by a single mother and three sisters, he could not be more considerate toward women. His Scientology beliefs, however controversial, have inspired him to live his life trying, as he has often said, "to do good. I try to help people any chance I get, wherever I have the opportunity to give back to the life that I have."

He is, in short, one of the nicest people I know, even though I usually walk away from one of our interviews wondering what, if anything, I got.

Angelina Jolie. It's not just that I applaud her work with the United Nations High Commissioner for Refugees and her personal commitment to raising what are now six young children. I really like her.

I first interviewed Angelina in July 2003. She was plugging *Lara Croft Tomb Raider: The Cradle of Life*, a sequel to her highly successful adventure film, *Lara Croft: Tomb Raider*. (Hardly a milestone in one's career, unlike *Girl, Interrupted*, for which she'd won an Academy Award three years before.) Her bizarre three-year marriage to actor Billy Bob Thornton (during which she'd worn a vial with drops of his blood around her neck and added his name to the many tattoos on her body) was officially over. She had adopted a little boy from Cambodia, whom she named Maddox.

I thought Angelina was gorgeous. I also thought she was unusually open. In one of the more startling interviews I've ever done, she told me of her recurring thoughts of death as she was growing up (at fifteen she took home courses in embalming) and of cutting herself with knives because it made her feel better. "I was self-destructive, always," she said. "I didn't feel close enough to another person. I didn't feel alive enough. Early on in my first sexual relationship, I brought knives out and had a night where we attacked each other. It was so stupid because I still have a mark next to my jugular vein. But it was a release of some kind. It felt so primitive, and it felt so honest. And then I had to deal with not telling my mother, and hiding the gauze bandage that I wore to high school."

But all that faded, she said, when she adopted Maddox. "It's an amazing thing to take care of a child and have a child trust you and love you. It makes me feel like I somehow have a purpose. If he's okay, if he's healthy, nothing else matters to me," she said. "And that's just such a clarity I never knew."

At the time, her relationship with Maddox was the only relationship she wanted. I asked if she could imagine herself getting married again and she answered no. "I think that having a child, as I do now, would mean that this person would become a father to my son, and that means it would have to be permanent. I haven't had a good experience with my own father or with the men in my life, so I don't want to have a temporary relationship for my son."

As for adopting more children, she said she hoped to adopt "many," but she didn't want to give birth to her own child. "I think it's so wonderful when a couple loves each other and they have a child. But now, as an adoptive parent, I have this weird feeling that there would be that kid that I would have adopted if I hadn't had my own."

That was in 2003. All this changed, of course, when she met Brad Pitt. Still no marriage, but six children, three adopted and three their biological children. At this writing Angelina seems to have the purpose she so long ago yearned for.

Then there's a man who some say would make a great president. However, there is one small impediment: he wasn't born in this country. I am talking about Arnold Schwarzenegger, the current governor of

California. Schwarzenegger has a remarkable story to tell. When he came to this country from Austria as a champion bodybuilder, no one took him seriously. He had a funny name he refused to change, a muscle-bound body some thought strange, and a strong accent. But he also had contagious warmth, a brilliant mind, and a vision. He, of course, became one of the strongest box office figures in the business. He also married one terrific lady, a member of Kennedy royalty, Maria Shriver. I could interview Schwarzenegger again and again. He always has something interesting to say. This is from an interview done for my Academy Award night *Special* of 1990:

"What makes one guy a champion and the other one not?" I asked.

Schwarzenegger: "It's drive. It's the will. There are certain people that grow up with a tremendous hunger and it's usually kids that have struggled when they were young. When you grow up comfortable and in peace and happiness, all those things will produce a very balanced person and a good person, but it will not create the will and determination and hunger that you need to be the best in the world."

In case you are wondering if Schwarzenegger was talking about himself, here was his answer to my next question.

"Do you have a philosophy by which you live?"

Schwarzenegger: "Staying hungry. That's it."

Clint Eastwood. Another Hollywood legend whose talent and creativity have not diminished with age. If anyone has seen my *Specials*, especially when we rerun certain of my interviews, they will be familiar with the following story. In 1982 I interviewed Clint for the second time. This one was done in a sunny field, with wildflowers, in Carmel, California, about forty minutes by plane from Hollywood. He was then fifty-two and unmarried. As I reported in the introduction to my piece: "Eastwood stands tall, shoots straight, and pulls in higher grosses than anyone else. He keeps a low profile, keeps his private life private, and seldom gives interviews. Everything about him is sparse, including the dialogue." Here's a portion of how it went.

ME: You hear people say that you are aloof, mysterious, and similar to the characters you play on camera. Are you afraid of showing emotions?

EASTWOOD: I don't think so. I think the image of the character I play comes out reserved because that is probably something that is very easy for me. I don't feel compelled to tell every thought that is in my mind. I know a lot of people get a catharsis, they get release from that, and that's why psychiatrists make so much money. But to me I don't particularly want to unload on anybody.

ME: Never went to a psychiatrist?

EASTWOOD: I never felt the urge. I always felt I could go out and walk through this field and look at these flowers and trees and just unload myself.

ME: Do you ever tell a woman you are close to?

EASTWOOD: Oh, we talk about certain things, but there's never a 100 percent. Let me put it this way, if you break it down from 100 percent, you might talk 60 percent. Would you want to know 100 percent of what there is to know?

ME: I think it's nice to know. You would drive me nuts, and I would drive you crazy because I would be asking more and more.

Eastwood then looked deep into my eyes and, with a mischievous smile, said, "Well, we could try and see if it worked out."

At which point, for the first and last time in an interview, I lost it. I got all flustered and goofy and told the cameraman to stop tape. What's worse, after the interview, Eastwood asked if I wanted to stay and have dinner with him. God knows why, but I said I had to fly back to Los Angeles with my crew. So actually, it isn't that I want to do the interview over. It's that I want to do the dinner. Who knows what might have happened? Oh, well, as I said, he is married to a lovely woman named Dina, and they seem very happy. Wonder if she gets through 100 percent?

Did I tell you that I could interview Oprah Winfrey over and over? In my opinion every accolade she receives she deserves. The woman has overcome so much and accomplished so much and changed so many lives for the better. My relationship with Oprah goes back many years. Perhaps the most revealing interview I did with her was in April 1988. At that time her program had been on national television for only a year and a half but was already the highest-rated syndicated talk show in the country. No wonder. Talk about revealing yourself. She kept very little of her own life back, and, in so doing, millions of people could relate to her and know that she had suffered as many of them had. In this regard the toughest part of our conversation was when Oprah talked about being raped when she was nine years old and not even realizing it.

"I remember being at a relative's house and I had been left with a nineteen-year-old cousin and he raped me. And I knew it was bad, and I knew it was wrong mainly because it hurt so bad. He took me to get ice cream and to the zoo afterward and told me that if I ever told we would both get into trouble. So, I never did. I went into the fifth grade that fall and I remember Maria Gonzales on the playground telling me how babies came into the world. So I went through the entire fifth grade every day thinking, 'I'm going to have a baby.' "

It happened again, Oprah said, with a boyfriend of another relative who lived in her mother's house. "What happens to you after a while, you start to think you are marked. What it did for me was it made me a sexually promiscuous teenager. If no one has shown you any kind of affection or attention, you confuse that with love and so you go searching for it in other places." Oprah said she used to bring boys home when her mother wasn't there until, at fourteen, she was sent to live with her father. He was very strict with her, she said, "because he knew what he had to deal with."

Listening to this, I said, "Oprah, I hear you and wonder, 'Where did this lady come from? How did you get to be this?' "

Oprah answered beginning with this sentence: "Somewhere," she said, "I have always known that I was born for greatness." She went on, "I have always felt it. I don't regret being born illegitimately. I don't regret all of that past confusion. I don't regret it at all. It has made me exactly who I am. I probably would not, without my past, sexual abuse included, be able to handle what is happening to me now."

Years later in another interview Oprah said that she had been criticized by some and called arrogant for saying that she knew all along she had been born for greatness. She explained that she didn't mean that she herself was great, but that, as she put it, "Every soul has its calling. So I believe that I was born at the right time, born to do great things. That's what I meant by being born to greatness."

Let me tell you why else I remember this 1988 interview with Oprah. Oprah told me of entering a contest, "Miss Fire Prevention," of all things. She was just sixteen and the only black contestant. She never expected to win, but she did.

"And I said I wanted to be a journalist, like Barbara Walters. And you know why I said that? I had not a clue what I really wanted to do with my life but I had seen you on the *Today* show that morning and for me, you were a mentor. You were the only woman I knew who was doing anything. And so I thought, 'Yeah, that's a good thing. That's what I'll do. That's what I'll say.' I really had no intention of going into the business but it sounded like a good answer and I ended up doing it. It was a self-fulfilling prophecy for me."

Oprah told me she copied how I sat, with her hand under her chin as I often did, and when she finally auditioned, she looked down at her questions, as I did, even though she had no real questions. Then she would look up and talk. "I had Barbara Walters in my head," she said. "And for the longest time, I'd watch you every morning and I'd go on the air and I would imitate you."

"I take full responsibility for you," I told this great accomplished woman.

"As well you should," said Oprah.

So who cares if some of my interviews are a bust? I can claim, rightly or wrongly, that I mentored Oprah Winfrey.

Celebrities Who Affected My Life

*I*F AN INTERVIEW is informative, touching, intellectually or emotionally affecting, I learn something. Even doing the homework teaches me something. But after having conducted hundreds of interviews, few stick to my bones, as it were. There are some, however, which because of my own inner needs, have stayed with me, affected my life, and perhaps even changed me.

When I talked to Bette Davis in 1987, she was seventy-eight and physically diminished by a severe stroke that had left her face twisted and her speech badly impaired. Yet she had the same feisty spirit that had marked all of her more than ninety films and won her two Academy Awards. But what stuck with me from that interview were her views on marriage. I was always interested in what made a marriage work since I seemed not to be very good at it. Here now Bette Davis's prescription for a good marriage.

"Separate bathrooms," she laughed. "That gives you a chance."

Davis had her share of chances, having been married four times. (She must have thought of her bathroom solution too late.) She had walked that tightrope between being an independent, successful woman and one who also wanted a man to dote on her. Her favorite song, she told me, was "Someone to Watch Over Me." Davis had never found that someone. "Nobody ever thought I needed it," she said. "I was always competent, earned my own way, and nobody would have thought I needed someone to watch over me." That certainly resonated with me.

The other topic I have continuously chewed over is the difficulty women have balancing a career with a family. As I have pointed out, while I had been torn for years making choices between Jackie and my work (Barbara Bush would have told me, "No choice, children first"),

Jackie and I never stopped loving each other even during the toughest of times. Bette Davis, on the other hand, had a daughter she professed to have adored but who published a vicious and hurtful memoir about her mother. Davis was distraught about this and, after the memoir was published, never spoke to her daughter again. She didn't feel she had done anything to deserve the humiliation, she said, and blamed the estrangement on her ambition, and lifelong "dedication" to get to the top.

At the end of the interview I asked Bette Davis to describe herself, which she did in her halting speech, in just five words, "I—am—just—too—much."

Maybe her daughter felt that way, too.

If Bette Davis was just too much, so, in spades, was Katharine Hepburn. I've never had a mentor but if I could have, I would have chosen Hepburn. She was such an independent woman, opinionated and positive about things, that when she said something it was as if it were written in stone and you had to pay attention to it. In one of my interviews with her—I did four—she said, "I know what's right and wrong and I see things in black and white. Don't you?" I had recently returned from the Middle East and said, "There are times, Miss Hepburn, when I see things not in black and white but in shades of gray." Katharine Hepburn drew herself up and said, "Well, I pity you." So much for the diplomatic middle road.

She loved to terrify people, and if ever the expression "Her bark was worse than her bite" applied to anyone, it applied to Hepburn. For years she had refused my requests for an interview. When she finally agreed she said she wanted to meet me first. Early evening. Five p.m. At her brownstone in the East Forties in New York. Something like five minutes after five, I showed up all smiles and eager to please. When the door was opened, there was Hepburn at the top of her stairs, looking just as Hepburn should look—pants, turtleneck sweater, another sweater tied around her neck, hair piled up. "You are late," she barked. "Have you brought me chocolates?" (I hadn't, but from then on I never showed up without them. She always sent me a thank-you note in her almost-illegible spidery handwriting. She had inherited what she called "the shakes" from her grandfather, and she had tremors in her hands.) We got on quite well that day, and I visited her many times after that, often accompanied by the gregarious and good-natured gossip columnist Liz Smith, and by Cynthia McFadden, Hepburn's young friend who was living with her at that time. We spent many evenings sitting in Hepburn's small but cozy living room on the second floor of her town house.

A fire was usually lit, and we were served dinner on a tray, big ample portions of meat and potatoes, ice cream for dessert. Hepburn, then seventy-one, would give us her opinions. Careers and marriage did not mix. Children and careers were out of the question.

Suffice it to say Hepburn's opinions on the balancing act of marriage, career, and children stayed with me. She was so certain in private and in our interviews, I can repeat them almost verbatim to this day.

"It's impossible," she told me. "If I were a man, I would not marry a woman with a career and I'd torture myself as a mother. Supposing little Johnny or little Katie had the mumps, and I had an opening night. I really would want to strangle the children. I'd be thinking to myself, 'God, I've got to get in the mood and what's the matter with them—get out of my way.' "

She made a gesture of pushing the kids away, and in her distinctive, wobbly voice, also a result of "the shakes," went on to give her solution to the confusing gender roles that had befallen men and the growing number of working women. "I put on pants fifty years ago and declared a sort of middle road. I have not lived as a woman. I have lived as a man." "How?" I asked her. "Well, I've just done what I damn well wanted to," she replied. "I've made enough money to support myself, and I ain't afraid of being alone."

For a woman who wasn't afraid of being alone, she had an awful lot of men in her life. She had even been married once, very briefly, when she was young, and had affairs with her agent, Leland Hayward, and the billionaire eccentric Howard Hughes before settling down to a twenty-seven-year love affair with Spencer Tracy. They never married. They couldn't. Tracy, her costar in nine films, was already married, a Catholic, and the father of two children, one of whom was deaf. But, she said, "We were as good as married."

Tracy died of heart failure in 1967, just two weeks after completing his last film with Hepburn, *Guess Who's Coming to Dinner*. She found him lying on her kitchen floor and immediately called his wife, Louise. It was the first time the two women had talked, and when Mrs. Tracy and her children arrived to make the funeral arrangements, the first time they met. Hepburn didn't attend the funeral out of respect for Tracy's family. "I was not his wife," she told me in a quiet voice. Instead, she said, she drove by the funeral to watch the crowds gathering to honor him. She never watched *Guess Who's Coming to Dinner*. "The memories," she said, "were too painful."

For all her tough talk about the impossibility of marriage, family, and career, there were photographs of Spencer Tracy all over her house, along with a portrait of him and some paintings he had done himself. Theirs was a true love story, with or without children and the legal trappings of marriage. When she died in 2003 at the age of ninety-six, the lights of Broadway were dimmed in tribute. In my case I treasure every memory of our interviews and the small, private dinners we shared. "Thank you for the champagne and the chocolates," she wrote me after one such dinner. "I certainly needed my fix."

Hepburn left me an odd inheritance. In one of our interviews—I did the last when she was eighty-four—I asked why she thought she had become so much of a legend, and she said that she had become a "sort of thing." "What sort of thing?" I asked, to which she replied, "I'm like a tree." She said this very quickly but I picked up on it and asked, "What kind of tree are you?" She replied, "I hope I'm not an elm, with Dutch Elm diseases or a weeping willow dropping all its leaves." Instead, she chose to be an oak tree. "I saw one recently in the woods, a white oak, strong and great like that," and she stretched out her arms in imitation. A terrific moment. Except, to this day, I am ridiculed for asking her what kind of tree she wanted to be. Doesn't matter that she introduced the whole thing; I am stuck with it. Johnny Carson was just one of the people who wouldn't let the tree issue go, so when he heckled me about it during an interview some years later, I finally broke down and asked him what kind of tree *he'd* like to be. "A tumbleweed," he replied.

Audrey Hepburn also affected my life, even though she was totally different from the great Kate. Unlike the older, no-nonsense Hepburn, Audrey was fragile and vulnerable. She was so enchanting and beautiful playing a princess in her first American film, *Roman Holiday*, in 1953, for which she won the Academy Award. Thin as a rail, she dressed in Givenchy, not pants, and became every young woman's idol, including mine. I cut my hair like hers, short with bangs, wore little sleeveless black dresses copied from Givenchy originals, and used gobs of eyeliner to try to make my eyes as wide and dramatic as hers. Few people tried to imitate Katharine Hepburn's angular, high-cheekbone look, but for a while we were a nation of Audrey Hepburn wannabes. I daresay, in the 1950s and 1960s, every man—and every woman—was a little bit in love with Audrey Hepburn.

She was about to turn sixty when I interviewed her in Mexico in 1989. By then she'd been married twice, first to actor Mel Ferrer, then to an Italian psychiatrist, Andrea Dotti, and for the last nine years she'd been living happily with Robert Wolders, a Dutch actor and the widower of a much older actress, Merle Oberon. Hepburn had two grown sons, one from each marriage, and was still lovely, still enchanting. She was also unflappable. During the interview a bird flying overhead relieved itself, splattering on her perfectly pristine white dress, and she couldn't have cared less.

Audrey Hepburn had her own answer to the dilemma of combining work, a husband, and children. Her solution? "I quit movies to stay with my children," she said. "I couldn't take the stress of being away from my sons. I missed them too much. I became emotionally unhappy."

It was a difficult decision for the actress, who made twenty movies and earned four more Academy Award nominations after that Oscar for *Roman Holiday.* "I was miserable both ways," she said. "I have the greatest admiration for women who have a career, who can take care of the husband and take care of their children. But I couldn't." Hepburn felt she could do three jobs at once: make a movie, shop, and cook. And that was it. "I cannot deal with too many emotions," she said.

I asked her if looking back, she regretted giving up her career. "Oh, Lord, no," she said. "Had I done it the other way around, I'd be miserable today. If I just had movies to look back on and not have known my boys."

For years Audrey had been a special ambassador for UNICEF. She was tireless in her efforts to make life better for impoverished children. She had just returned from tours of Honduras, El Salvador, and Guatemala when we met for our interview. "I have this extraordinary thing that's happened to me," she said. "To be able to express my need to help children and to take care of them in some way."

Audrey Hepburn died much too young, at the age of sixty-three, in 1993, at her home in Switzerland. The cause was cancer. But she lives on in her films—forever radiant and the fantasy of every young woman watching a rerun of *Breakfast at Tiffany's, Charade,* or *Funny Face.*

So here were these three very smart women also with very different approaches to the balance of family life and career.

Where did this leave me? I used to say you could have a great marriage and a great career (notice I use the word "career," not "job") or a great marriage and great children or a great career and great children, but you couldn't have all three at the same time. I have changed my mind. Today there are many husbands who care deeply about having a strong relationship with their children and will help with their care. They'll even help with the housekeeping. And there are companies like ABC that let women work part-time or do job sharing. On *The View* some of our working mothers bring their children in, breast-feed when they need to, and do their jobs well. Do women need more help? Day-care centers at work, more flexible hours? Sure. But things have improved so much that I do think these days you can have marriage, career, and children. But make no mistake about it, it is not easy. I was never able to do it.

The ability to take a tragic situation and turn it into optimism and purpose is rare. There's no better example than a man you've probably never heard of. (I include him even though he is not a celebrity.) Over the years people have often asked me who, among the countless interviews I've done, is the most memorable. If I'm thinking historically, I say Anwar Sadat. But if I'm thinking on a human level, the answer is Robert Smithdas, whom I first interviewed more than thirty years ago on the *Today* show and again, in 1998, for *20/20*.

Robert Smithdas is a teacher and a poet. He is also totally blind and profoundly deaf. I remember his putting his thumb on my lips and his fingers on my vocal cords during our first interview. Lord knows how, but he was able to understand what I was saying. I was absolutely flabbergasted.

Smithdas had graduated from college at the top of his class, the first deaf and blind person to do so since Helen Keller. He then earned a master's degree from New York University, the first graduate degree ever, anywhere, for a deaf and blind student. In the years since I first interviewed him, he had married and was teaching other blind and deaf people at the Helen Keller National Center on Long Island. At his side, also teaching, was his wife, Michelle. She, too, was blind and deaf.

If ever a person gets beset by frustration or poor-me self-pity, one day, even one hour, with Robert and Michelle Smithdas will cure all. In the course of our profile with the couple for *20/20*, we first went with them to church. Michelle had just had electrodes implanted in her inner ear and was thrilled to finally have some limited hearing; Bob felt the vibration of the choir simply by touching the pew. Later I went to their apartment, where Bob made us chicken cacciatore, even slicing the onions. He cooked on a gas stove, gauging the heat of the flame as expertly as any chef. He and Michelle could see nothing and hear little, but how rich their lives were and how independently they lived!

They communicated by "finger-spelling" into the palms of each other's hands. Michelle, who also holds a master's degree (Columbia University's Teachers College), could tell if her husband was angry or upset if "he finger-spells too fast." An interpreter from the Helen Keller Center finger-spelled my questions to the couple, and they answered me in their own voices. At home they each wore vibrating pagers to signal that the doorbell was ringing or to "find" each other in their apartment. They had some help from sighted friends, especially from one truly special woman named Linda Stillman. Mrs. Stillman had spent five years with Michelle while she was attending Columbia, finger-spelling the graduate school lectures for her and translating the necessary textbooks into braille. Can you imagine the task this was for both women? The patience each must have had? The enormous reward for both when Michelle received her master's degree?

Michelle and Bob were both avid readers, especially Bob, who read about twenty braille magazines a month, ranging from *The Economist* to *Popular Mechanics* to *Martha Stewart Living*. And neither one complained about their disabilities. Michelle had had some sight and hearing as a child, but an illness and then an accident robbed her of both. Still, she told me, "I am rather happy with what I am able to do and for what I have. Especially for my husband." Throughout our day together she was smiling and upbeat.

Bob, who had lost his sight and hearing at the age of four, admitted that he missed the ability to see his friends and especially to hear them. "Blindness takes you away from scenes, but deafness takes you away from people," he said. "But at this stage in life, I am very used to being deaf-blind."

When I left their house, I was humbled at what an open and optimistic mind can achieve, and brimming with admiration for them. I determined to remember, every day, how blessed I am. To anticipate your question, I don't remember each day, but I should, and I try.

No one has lied to me more or touched me more than the late Richard Pryor. At our first interview in 1979, Richard said, "Are we going to end up liking each other?" I answered truthfully, "I don't know." Richard then said, "Oh good. I'm glad it's still out there."

If Robert and Michelle Smithdas are examples of people who have risen above the difficult circumstances of their lives, the brilliant actor and comedian Richard Pryor is my example of a man who took the enormous talent he was born with and destroyed it. He couldn't help it, and his struggles affected me from the first time we met.

I did end up liking him. How could I not? He told me of his horrific childhood. He, a young boy, living in a house with his mother, who was a prostitute, listening to the moans and grunts of the lineup of men who came up to her room. He, trying to ignore the men rapping on the door to get in. He, a little older, sleeping with a girlfriend he liked, only to be told by his father that he had slept with the girl, too. So how could he possibly trust anyone, male or female?

At the time of this first interview, Richard was a huge star. He was appearing in the film *The Wiz* with Diana Ross and Michael Jackson. Almost every young comedian, black or white, wanted to be like him and follow his cutting-edge humor. I, too, was also taken by his brilliance and felt I could ask him anything. He wasn't offended. He welcomed it.

ME: Are you totally off drugs?

RICHARD: No. I love drugs. I really do. But I can't do them a lot because it messes my life up and every time I get in trouble it's because I end up drinking too much or snorting too much. But I like drugs. I like some cocaine every now and then.

Richard had a beautiful white girlfriend named Jennifer Lee living with him, and he spoke of their relationship as being "magic time." I stupidly thought he was talking of his love for her. He was actually talking of their doing drugs together. Still, I liked Jennifer and she seemed to be genuinely devoted to him and to trust him. So did I.

That is why, when in 1980, Pryor set himself ablaze and then ran screaming through the streets of his Los Angeles neighborhood with more than half his body burned, I believed everything he told me. He had been rushed to the hospital and after a month or so of treatment, he sat down once more with me. He looked god-awful, emaciated and shaking, and although his face had not been burned, he could barely sit because his scarred body was still so painful.

"Richard, how did it happen?" I asked as gently as I could.

"It was stupid," he replied, laughing. "Me and my partner had been drinking this Jamaican rum and it spilled and he went to get a towel out of the bathroom to wipe it up and I lit a cigarette and the next thing I knew, I was on fire."

"Were you on drugs?" I asked.

"No," said Richard, almost offended that I had asked.

Six years later we talked again. There had been enough rumors so that I knew that the last time I had talked to him, Pryor had looked me right in the eyes and lied.

"I asked you about the accident and you carried on and said, 'Oh, it had nothing to do with freebasing, it had nothing to do with drugs.' In short, you lied to me."

"That's true," Pryor said sheepishly. "One reason that I like to lay it on is this. My lawyer at the time had made a statement to the press about how it happened. He didn't really know what happened, and he was trying to cover my ass. By saying it wasn't freebasing, I was trying to cover his ass. Inside I'd be screaming. I wanted to tell you the truth."

ME: It was no accident.

PRYOR: Yes. To tell the truth, I got crazy one night and went mad and tried to kill myself.

ME: You really did it deliberately, didn't you?

PRYOR: Yes. I was crazy. I had gone over the top. So I don't really even know how I did it. I remember pouring rum all over my clothes and lighting a cigarette lighter.

ME: Knowing that you wanted to die. No accident. Why did you want to kill yourself?

PRYOR: I was ashamed.

ME: Of what?

PRYOR: I was ashamed of myself. I had come to this. God had given me all this. And what did I do with it? I could only end up in a room alone, smoking a base pipe. All day long, I couldn't stop. I put the pipe down. It jumped back into my hand. I couldn't stop five minutes. Do you understand that? Five minutes. I said to myself, all right, five minutes. I won't smoke anymore. It wasn't a minute that would go by. I had to pick that pipe back up. I couldn't tell you. I couldn't tell anyone.

Pryor tried to put the pieces together again. But it was never the same. Jennifer had left him after the fire. Nothing in his life seemed to be working out. Then he got multiple sclerosis. From time to time I called him and we talked about this and that, but we never did another interview. He didn't want to. I didn't want to push. Jennifer, who had always loved him, came back. They finally married and she took care of him until his death. Jennifer knew how fond I was of Richard, and she called me herself in 2005 to tell me that he'd died. He was sixty-five. Even though he had lied to me, I still think he may have been the most painfully honest man I have ever interviewed.

Now I am going to take a huge leap from a man who destroyed his own life to a man who has tried to uplift the lives of others. I speak of the Dalai Lama, whose words have affected not only me but millions around the world. I met and interviewed the Dalai Lama in 2005 for an unusual two-hour *Special* we called *Heaven: Where Is It? And How Do We Get There?* (By the way, we were originally going to call it *Heaven: Does It Exist?* but we were told we shouldn't because some evangelical Christians have no doubt that heaven exists and might boycott the program. Not that we were threatened, but why offend if we didn't have to? After all, we wanted the evangelicals to watch the program, too.)

I had briefly met the Dalai Lama some years before in the most improbable place—the boardwalk at Venice Beach, California. I was married to Merv. We'd decided we weren't getting enough exercise so off we went at 6:30 a.m. to bicycle. The only person we saw was a man walking his dog until a car drew up and six monks in saffron robes emerged to look at the ocean. One of them was the Dalai Lama. I went up to him, said something inconsequential like, "Good morning, Your Holiness," to which he responded in kind (well, without the "Your Holiness" part). Then the monks got back in their car, and Merv and I went off on our bikes, leaving behind the man and his dog. I can only imagine what his wife thought of his mental stability when he went home for breakfast and said, "Guess what, honey? I just saw Barbara Walters and the Dalai Lama on the boardwalk."

It was harder getting to the Dalai Lama this time. Physically. I flew to New Delhi with my producer, Rob Wallace, and a camera crew, then on to a small airport an hour or so outside Dharamsala, the little mountain sanctuary given to the Dalai Lama for his government-in-exile in 1960 by Indian prime minister Jawaharlal Nehru. This followed the Dalai Lama's expulsion from Tibet by the occupying Chinese. We timed our visit to coincide with his annual two weeks of teachings to his monks and pilgrims. We should have looked at the weather report.

The air got colder and colder as we drove up into the mountains, where monkeys looked down at us with surprise from the trees and we looked up at them with our own surprise. Rain added to the cold when we finally reached the narrow, cobblestoned streets of Dharamsala. Our hotel had no heat or hot water, and I slept fully dressed under a lot of blankets. Still, the chill went right through you.

The Dalai Lama didn't seem chilled at all as he sat outside in the rain, wearing his one-shoulder red robe, chanting for hours to his young monks. There were a few headphones for translations into different languages, but they were hard to come by. Evidently he occasionally said something funny because his students would laugh and he would giggle. It really was a giggle, not a laugh, and quite infectious.

We did our interview after he was through with his teachings. It was still damp and cold, but everything about the Dalai Lama was warm. Including his hands. When I extended my hand to shake his, he took it in both his hands and just held it. His eyes were warm, too, and merry.

Our subject was heaven, remember, and Buddhists have a unique concept of what heaven is. "Ten directions," the Dalai Lama told me. "East, south, west, and north, and above and below." Buddhists don't believe in heaven as a final destination, but as a place to further develop spirituality. "For Buddhists, the final goal is not reach there, but become Buddha, one's self," he said in his accented, imperfect English. Buddhists believe in reincarnation. The better you have lived your life, the happier your life will be when you're reborn. Conversely, the Dalai Lama said, "If someone do very bad thing, kill or steal, he could be born even with an animal body." (Gives a new meaning to "bad dog.")

The Buddhist religion is far more complex than my brief explanation, but the Dalai Lama, who told me that he considers himself a teacher rather than a god as some feel he is, was deliberately trying to make his belief accessible. In fact, to some degree, reincarnation makes sense to me. I'm certainly not a Buddhist, but part of me believes that someone like my sister, Jackie, or others who had very difficult lives, could come back to something better. They may have done something in a former life that reduced them to a not-so-happy existence but they have paid that price and earned a chance at happiness. On some spiritual level that reaches me.

What touched me the most about the Dalai Lama was his definition of the purpose of life. It was, he said, "to be happy." How does one accomplish that? I asked. "I think warmheartedness and compassion," he replied. "Compassion gives you inner strength, more self-confidence. That can really change your attitude."

It was that simple. I compared his definition with those of some of the other great religious leaders I had interviewed for the *Special*. The brilliant Catholic archbishop I'd talked with, Theodore Cardinal McCarrick, archbishop of Washington, had said the primary purpose of life for Catholics was to go to heaven. Muslims shared a similar goal, said Imam Feisal Abdul Rauf, the spiritual leader of the Masjid al-Farah Mosque in New York. We also talked with a noted evangelical leader, Pastor Ted Haggard of the New Life Church in Colorado Springs. The purpose of life, he told me, was to be born again and to accept Jesus into your life. Otherwise, he said, you (and also, I) would probably not get to heaven. Pastor Haggard was smiling and pleasant. Unfortunately he was later defrocked by his own congregation due partly to revelations of homosexual offenses. To me this didn't diminish his beliefs. It only accentuated the hypocrisy of his character.

Members of the Jewish faith had a different goal than going to heaven. According to Rabbi Neil Gillman, a professor of philosophy at New York's Jewish Theological Seminary, Jews put more emphasis on living a "decent" life on earth for its own sake, not for any reward.

And here was the Dalai Lama saying that the purpose of life was simply to be happy. And achieving it was as easy as being warmhearted and compassionate. I was so affected by that simplicity and by the sweetness of his personality that when the interview ended, I asked the Dalai Lama if I could kiss him on the cheek. He smiled and suggested we kiss as they do in New Zealand. And so we rubbed noses like the Eskimos. He then put a white scarf around my neck and the necks of my camera crew and my producer, giggled, and walked away.

But his message lingered. As I told you before, after the visit concluded, as a special treat, I took my small staff on a whirlwind tour of several cities in India, including the dazzling pink city of Jaipur and Agra, where we saw the Taj Mahal at dusk and again in the early hours of sunrise. Magnificent. For that week I was the most adorable person. I never got angry, I never raised my voice, and nothing bothered me. I was devoid of jealousy and ambition. I was also slightly boring. But then came the plane trip home and our return to the Western world. Little by little the old emotions seeped back in. Still, I continue to remember his simple formula for the purpose of life and I try to practice what he preached. Compassion. Warmheartedness.

Finally Christopher Reeve, a mountain of a man who took his once-strong life, diminished by a tragic accident, and found a new strength that inspired the world. It was not just that I admired Chris's dignity and courage, I got to care about him as a person for his spirit, his humor, his determination. He had suffered an affliction that would have made most people withdraw from life. Instead he confronted it and changed the way people looked at quadriplegics.

Most everyone is aware of Christopher Reeve's story. The handsome actor, best known for his role as Superman, was paralyzed from the neck down after a freak horse-riding accident. The fall occurred on May 27, 1995, during a cross-country competition when Reeve's horse stopped suddenly at a jump. Reeve, an experienced equestrian, pitched forward, caught his hands in the horse's bridle, and was catapulted headfirst onto the ground. The fall crushed his spinal cord. He was barely alive.

In a way I became Christopher's television chronicler. He talked for the first time about his condition on *20/20* in September 1995. We did our last of many interviews in November 2003, eleven months before he died. But we regularly saw each other as friends off camera. It turned out we shared the same birthday, September 25.

I had met Reeve only once, very casually, before his accident. There were journalists he knew far better than he knew me, but he had watched a good deal of television and seen many of my interviews during his hospitalization and the long months later at the Kessler Institute for Rehabilitation in New Jersey. I seemed not to interrupt my subjects, he eventually told me. This was important to him. He could only talk for minutes at a time, because a tube in his throat was connected to a respirator that sent air into his lungs and also released air over his vocal cords. He could speak as long as the breath held. Then he had to wait for the respirator to generate another breath before he could speak again. It was a slow process, and the interviewer had to be patient. Because I seemed to listen, Reeve chose me to be the person to whom he would tell his story.

We met at the rehab center four months after he'd been paralyzed. I had no idea what to expect. I had discussed the interview with David Sloan, my executive producer on *20/20*. We decided that a proper amount of airtime would be about fifteen to twenty minutes. We thought the interview would be too painful for viewers to listen to much longer than that. We were also concerned with what Reeve might look like. Would he be disfigured, difficult to look at? Would he be like someone from an Edgar Allan Poe horror story? Yes, I know that sounds crass, but I had to think in television terms.

When we came face-to-face, however, there he was, sitting straight up in a wheelchair, handsome, with a big smile on his face. His paralyzed arms and hands were strapped to the arms of the chair so they wouldn't flop, and his head rested between two black pads to keep it straight. He wore slacks and a sweater. The collar of his sweater had an ascot tucked in. The ascot covered the air hose, which, in turn, was attached to his respirator. If the respirator got turned off or the air hose was disconnected even for a minute, Reeve would die.

Sitting next to him, lovely and calm and also wearing a big smile, was Dana, his wife and the mother of their three-year-old son, Will. And so began Reeve's recollection of his first days in the hospital.

"In my dreams, I'd be whole, riding my horse, playing with my family, and we'd have a beautiful boat that Dana and I had worked on together. We'd be making love," Reeve said. "Then suddenly I wake up and it's two in the morning, and I'm lying in bed and I'm on a ventilator and I can't move."

His story was not just about him; it was also a love story. His relationship with Dana had grown and flourished after the accident in spite of the fact that Chris had very little physical sensation. He could feel her kisses and touches to his face. There was some sensation at a little spot by his left rib and at the sole of his left foot, but nothing more. He felt neither hugs nor, mercifully, pain.

"When I first was coming out of unconsciousness," Chris told me, "I thought, 'Maybe it's not worth everybody's trouble. Maybe I should have them pull the plug.' " At that point Dana touched her husband's face and said to me, "I know it went through the minds of every member of the family: 'How can someone like him live like this?' But once he was in the ICU and I could just be near him and next to him and look at him and touch him, I felt, 'Well, I haven't lost him. He's here.' "

Still, she said, the decision whether to live or die was up to him.

"Do you know when he made the decision not to have someone pull the plug?" I asked.

"When the children walked into the room," Dana answered. They were their little boy, Will, and Alexandra and Matthew, Chris's teenage daughter and son from an earlier relationship. "The minute they all came in," Chris added, "I could feel the love and knew that we were still a family and how lucky we all were that my brain was on straight, and the thought vanished and has never come back again."

The challenges were enormous. "You have lung problems, skin problems, bowel problems, bladder problems, all caused by the spinal cord," he said. "The brain can't get messages through to control these things." He had to have his lungs cleared at least every half hour because he couldn't cough. He couldn't even perspire. "It's summer and I can't go outside," he said. "I'd overheat and I could black out."

Chris was so candid, so compelling, his story so tragic and yet so uplifting, that we aired it on 20/20, not for the originally planned twenty minutes but for a full hour. We repeated the interview twice more, each time to huge ratings.

There was something else that Reeve told me privately, off camera, and it made me grin. While he was lying in the hospital, just becoming conscious with tubes connected to all parts of his body, a doctor in a white coat came in and with a Russian accent, commanded: "Turn over!"

Are you nuts? Reeve thought.

"I said: 'Turn over!' " the doctor repeated.

As Reeve was about to try to answer "the imbecile," he realized there was something familiar about the man in the white coat. He wasn't a doctor at all. He was Reeve's old buddy from acting school at Juilliard, Robin Williams. Reeve waited for a breath and almost choked with laughter. He realized, he told me, "If I can laugh, I can live."

Over the years I probably did a half a dozen reports on Reeve's intense, in some cases unheard-of, efforts at rehabilitation. I visited Chris and Dana in their home outside New York City. It had been completely renovated to allow for wheel chair accessibility. We showed Chris's progress and his setbacks. We talked about the bodily functions he could no longer do himself and his terror that the respirator could turn off in the middle of the night.

We did reports on Chris's acting. He appeared as a quadriplegic in a remake of the Alfred Hitchcock suspense film *Rear Window*, and we showed him as a film director, as a motivational speaker, and as a fierce advocate, like Michael J. Fox, for stem cell research. He also founded the Christopher Reeve Foundation, which searches for cures to paralyzing spinal cord injuries and in the meantime seeks to improve the quality of life of those afflicted like him.

The Reeves and I spent almost every September 25 together, along with our friends Michael Douglas and Catherine Zeta-Jones. It was not just Chris's and my birthday, but, as I've said, Michael's and Catherine's as well. I remember the effort it was one year when we decided to celebrate the occasion in my apartment, bringing all of Chris's special equipment up in the narrow elevator—the oxygen, the respirator, the automated wheelchair with Chris in it. Dana fed Chris birthday cake. We laughed a lot, and Dana sang.

By the time of our last interview, Chris had made remarkable progress. Due to years of all kinds of exercises, including special water therapy and pushing himself to an extraordinary degree, he could finally breathe for half an hour or so without his respirator. This meant that for the first time, he could smell things. I gave him a rose to sniff and he beamed with pleasure. We drank coffee together, and he could finally enjoy the aroma. Best of all, he was beginning to have feeling in one of his fingers and in his chest. I could now give him a real hug.

Maybe, I thought, his dream of recovering will come true.

Over the years Chris had occasionally developed life-threatening infections from which he miraculously recovered. Then, in the fall of 2004, he got another serious infection. This time he didn't make it. He died on October 10, the day after he'd managed to go to one of Will's hockey games. Chris was fifty-two.

Dana and I stayed in touch. She was due to sing on *The View* in the summer of 2005. She had a lovely voice and we were all looking forward to her appearance. Then, suddenly, for no apparent reason, she canceled. I was perplexed and a little annoyed. Later I heard the reason. She had never smoked but she'd gotten lung cancer.

Dana died on March 6, 2006, at the young age of forty-four. All of us who knew her were heartbroken.

There are many portions of my interviews with Chris that I could include here, but I've chosen one in particular from our very first conversation.

CHRIS: You also gradually discover that your body is not you, and the mind and the spirit must take over, and you move from obsessing about "Why me?" and "It's not fair" into "Well, what is the potential?" I've received more than 100,000 letters from all over the world, and it makes you wonder, why do we need disasters to really feel and appreciate each other? I'm overwhelmed by people's support of me and if I can help people understand this can happen to anybody, that's worth it right there. So I really sense being on a journey.

ME: Do you think you will walk again?

CHRIS: I think it is very possible I will walk again.

ME: And if you don't?

CHRIS: Then I won't walk again.

ME: As simple as that?

CHRIS: Either you do or you don't. It's like a game of cards, and if you think the game is worthwhile, then you just play the hand you're dealt. Sometimes you get a lot of face cards, sometimes you don't. But I think the game is worthwhile. I really do.

Whenever I feel even a little bit of despair, I think of Chris and I tell myself once more how lucky I am and that the game is worthwhile.

So here they are, some of the people I've interviewed whose character and philosophy have stayed with me. I think of each of them from time to time and consider myself fortunate to have known them. I may have briefly touched their lives, but they touch mine to this day.

ℳonica

*I*T WAS AND REMAINS THE most-watched news *Special* in television history. It was also the biggest "get" of my career. Her name was Monica Lewinsky. She was a White House intern. Every print and television journalist, talk-show host, and magazine vied for the first interview with the young woman who almost brought down the president of the United States. When the two-hour interview aired on March 3, 1999, almost fifty million people tuned in. There were reports that the water level in some cities dropped during the commercial breaks as large numbers of people were flushing at the same time.

Unless you are very young, you probably remember a lot about the Monica Lewinsky and Bill Clinton saga. As it unfolded in the late 1990s, the words "blow job" became part of our public vocabulary, and when the president, in his testimony before a grand jury, questioned the meaning of the verb "is," we all scratched our heads and realized we ourselves didn't actually know. Most of all we had our opinion of Monica Lewinsky, disgraced, reviled by the press, a promiscuous, silly young woman. When I finally interviewed her I felt otherwise. But first here is how I got the "get."

On January 21, 1998, when the Clinton-Lewinsky story broke, I was in Seattle for an interview with Microsoft founder Bill Gates. As I finalized my questions for the world's wealthiest man, a sex scandal was the last thing on my mind. But it became the first thing on my mind that morning when the world found out that an independent counsel named Kenneth W. Starr was investigating whether President Clinton encouraged a former White House intern named Monica Lewinsky to lie about their alleged affair. The story had been broken by the Drudge Report on the Internet and the *Washington Post*. The ABC news desk called me in Seattle to make sure I had a heads-up so we could see if an interview with Lewinsky would ever be possible. I was not the only one the news desk called. It was the policy then at ABC for big interviews to be assigned to a correspondent, usually Diane Sawyer or me. Connie Chung, who was at ABC at this time, was also in the mix. This three-way competition was often frustrating and difficult for all of us. In this case, however, the "get" was so important (and ABC knew that every network was after it) that we were each told to do our best to land the prize interview.

Some background: Monica Lewinsky was a twenty-two-year-old intern in the White House when she first met President Clinton in the summer of 1995. When she saw the president, she later told me, "my breath was taken away" and whenever she encountered him after that they shared "intense eye contact." There is a now-famous photograph of Monica wearing a beret, gazing adoringly at Clinton when he was out shaking hands with the crowd. Still, the relationship between them might have developed into nothing more had there not been a government shutdown that fall. Due to a budget impasse, most paid staffers were forced to stay home, and young volunteers like Monica took on added responsibilities. On November 15, the second day of the government shutdown, Monica found herself alone with Bill Clinton in the office of his chief of staff. It was then, she later testified, that she showed the president her thong panties and, later that evening, performed oral sex on him while he took a phone call. Their sexual liaison continued two days later when Monica brought pizza to the president and, again, they had oral sex. Starting with pizza and panties, this became one of the most famous and scrutinized affairs in history.

Monica, by all accounts an energetic and hard worker, obtained a permanent White House job before her internship ended. This allowed her relationship with the president to continue with sporadic and furtive assignations in the hall, pantry, or bathroom outside the Oval Office. She also received, she later told me, at least fifty late-night telephone calls from the president. By the spring of 1996 some senior White House staffers began to take notice of the time Monica was spending in and around the Oval Office and, in April, arranged to have her transferred to a higher-paying job in the Pentagon. Monica was devastated by her removal from the White House, but the president promised she could return after the November presidential elections.

It was at the Pentagon that Monica began to confide in an older colleague named Linda Tripp, who had herself once worked in the White

House. Frustrated that the president was not keeping his promise to bring her back to the White House, Monica grew increasingly upset and eventually told Linda Tripp about the ongoing relationship. She loved the president, she told Tripp, and thought he loved her. Monica was not the first young woman to have fantasies about a powerful older man, and Tripp probably knew it. But Tripp, it turned out, had her own agenda. She hated Bill Clinton and was collecting material for a book, so she began secretly tape-recording her conversations with Monica on the phone and in person, as proof of the illicit romance.

Tripp then betrayed her young friend by contacting the office of the independent counsel, which was already investigating various other alleged improprieties involving the Clintons. Would Starr's team like to listen to her taped conversations with Monica? They would.

Monica had no idea how much trouble she was in until she kept a date to meet Tripp in January 1998 at the Pentagon City Mall. She thought they were going to discuss her sworn affidavit in a civil lawsuit brought against Clinton by a woman named Paula Jones, stemming from his tenure as governor of Arkansas. Jones, then a state employee, claimed that Clinton had pressured her for sex and she was suing him for sexual harassment. Monica had been subpoenaed and drawn into the case by Jones's lawyers because it would help their case if they could show a pattern of predatory behavior by Clinton. But Monica lied. No, she'd sworn in the affidavit, she had not had a sexual relationship with the president. What she hadn't reckoned on were the contradictory tapes Tripp had supplied to the independent counsel's office. And so began the high-stakes game Monica had stumbled into.

Tripp was not alone when Monica met her at the mall. She was accompanied by two armed FBI agents who led her to room 1012 in the adjoining Ritz Carlton hotel, where six members of Ken Starr's staff were waiting for her. It was, Monica told me later, the most frightening day of her life. For hours on end they threw questions at her and threatened her with twenty-seven years in prison for perjury, witness tampering, and obstruction of justice. Even worse, she said, the prosecutors also threatened her mother with criminal charges of obstruction of justice because of statements Monica had supposedly made in the Tripp tapes about her mother's knowledge of the affair. The prosecutors promised Lewinsky immunity, then and there, if she told them everything about her relationship with Clinton and agreed to wear a wire to record conversations with the president's friend Vernon Jordan (he'd offered to help her find a job in New York), the president's secretary,

Betty Currie, and possibly even the president himself. To her credit, which has rarely been acknowledged, Monica refused. When Monica said she wanted to call her lawyer, the prosecutors all but forbade it. After twelve hours of resisting their demands, Monica was able to phone her mother, who came down to Washington from New York City and joined Monica that night. Monica's mother and father were divorced, but she and her mother telephoned her father in Los Angeles. Terrified, her father, a doctor, hired an attorney he knew, and Monica went home with her mother to New York. Monica was so distraught, her mother later told me, that she made her daughter shower with the bathroom door open so that she could be sure that Monica did not harm herself.

Most of us still remember just how big this story of an intern's relationship with the president became. Countless news stories dissected every bit of leaked information—and misinformation—about the nature of this relationship. In a short time Monica Lewinsky became one of the most recognizable names in the world, with regular reports on the scandal in everything from *The Times* of London to the *Borneo Bulletin*. In 1998 her name was mentioned in the U.S. press alone more than 100,000 times.

So here was my problem: how to meet this young woman and persuade her to talk to me.

The key, as I saw it, was William Ginsburg, the lawyer Monica's father had called in panic and despair. Ginsburg was a successful trial lawyer in Los Angeles whose specialty was medical malpractice. His field of work had led him to become a close friend of Monica's father, a radiation oncologist. With his bow ties and a trial attorney's gift for gab, Ginsburg took immediately to the press and was soon spending much of his time on camera helping to feed the media's insatiable appetite for this story. He spent so much time in TV studios that the only way we were able initially to get to him was when my imaginative and aggressive producer, Katie Thomson, saw him speaking live on NBC and persuaded a security guard there to put Ginsburg on the phone as he was exiting the building. While everyone was trying to get to Ginsburg, Katie did. (Almost every correspondent has a booker-producer like Katie. They were, and still are, indispensable in tracking down and helping to line up big interviews.) We were then able to arrange one of the more unusual meetings of my career.

That Saturday, Katie and I flew to Washington, D.C., to meet Ginsburg confidentially at a private place called the Cosmos Club. When we sat down at the bar, Ginsburg immediately confirmed that there was a relationship between Monica and the president. He explained the legal jeopardy that Monica was in, the independent counsel's office having told Monica that she might serve more than twenty years in prison. He was horrified that Monica, a nice kid, he said, whom he had known since she was a baby, was in this position.

Ginsburg then said he would like to speak to me more frankly than he felt comfortable doing in front of my producer. It turned out that he was a bit of a fan and said he enjoyed watching me on 20/20. It helped that ABC's much-loved film critic, the late Joel Siegel, was a high school buddy of Ginsburg. Joel and I were friends and when asked, he had told Ginsburg that he could trust me. In any event he was prepared to talk to me candidly and totally off the record. No wonder. He said that Monica's relationship with the president had "never been consummated," that it wasn't intercourse, and that I should draw my own conclusions.

What he was telling me, he said, nobody knew. I pushed further, but that was all he would reveal. But it was more than just sexual. Clinton also gave her little gifts, like a hat pin, a marble figurine of a bear, and a special edition of Walt Whitman's *Leaves of Grass*. Among her gifts to him was a pottery frog. "What about the rumors of a stained dress?" I asked. He said he didn't know of any such dress.

"You cannot disclose anything I've told you," Ginsburg warned me after our meeting and, as I had many other times in my career, I kept quiet. I would, of course, have loved to report what he had confided in me, but I had agreed to speak with him off the record and I had to keep my word. Though his revelations would have made headlines, I couldn't afford to lose his trust. What I wanted was for him to lead me to Monica.

So I kept Ginsburg's confidence, despite all kinds of wild speculation in the press about the Lewinsky-Clinton relationship. Media reports began to appear, some quoting White House officials, questioning Monica's character and credibility. She was, they said, a stalker, a liar, a desperate attention seeker. (Hillary Clinton, much later on, said she herself had believed those accusations.) Armchair psychologists said her parents' divorce when she was fourteen and her problems with her weight made her an emotionally disturbed young woman.

White House accusations or not, I believed Ginsburg—indeed, it would be hard to make up a story like that. When I was later able to share some of what he told me with my colleagues, our senior political correspondent, George Stephanopoulos, one of Bill Clinton's former top aides, didn't find it surprising that the president had talked to Monica at length at odd hours of the night. He said that Clinton had done the same with him, and as a night owl the president was happy to find people with whom he could hold forth into the wee hours. But George was stunned when I told him about Monica's gift to him of a ceramic frog. He said that very few people knew of the president's "thing for frogs," and that made him very inclined to believe Monica did indeed have a close relationship with the president.

While Monica and her family were still in hiding from the press, her lawyer was on TV more than I was. There was a Sunday when he appeared on the talk shows of all the networks, one right after the other. (I think it was a world record.) Countless articles and reports were appearing about Monica and her family, most of them unflattering. Ginsburg was trying to shoot them down. He was also trying, so far unsuccessfully, to get Monica immunity. Finally, in February, her father felt it was time to speak out. Thanks to Ginsburg, he decided to speak to me. It would be the first big "get" of the story. He didn't want to do the interview at his home in Los Angeles, so we rented a suite in a relatively quiet hotel and managed to keep the interview under wraps until it was done.

Bernard Lewinsky had been characterized as a fabulously wealthy Beverly Hills doctor but in fact was a hardworking cancer specialist whose practice wasn't even in Beverly Hills. He was also a private man who was devastated by the prurient press coverage of his daughter. Like Monica he was outraged that the independent counsel had forced his ex-wife, Marcia Lewis, to testify to a grand jury, where she might possibly incriminate her daughter. Monica had been staying with her father in Los Angeles, and together, on February 11, they watched as cameras showed Monica's mother being helped out of the courthouse after she collapsed under the stress of the questioning. In his interview with me, Dr. Lewinsky said, "What Ken Starr has brought upon her is unconscionable in my mind. To pit a mother against her daughter, to coerce her to talk, is reminiscent to me of the McCarthy era, of the inquisition, and you could even stretch it and say the Hitler era."

The interview aired on *20/20* on February 20, 1998, and Dr. Lewinsky's comparison of the Starr inquiry with Hitler's tactics attracted a lot of attention and some criticism. But many felt the interview finally put a human face to the name Lewinsky and helped people understand more about the pressure the family was under. It also gave me a leg up in trying to eventually get the interview with Monica. Her father was satisfied with our interview and now trusted me to be fair and accurate.

Meanwhile Monica remained a shut-in, unable to talk with her friends or venture outside without fear of being descended on by hordes of media. When she did go out, she was often the subject of unflattering photos and cruel nicknames, based on her weight, such as "Tubby Temptress" and "Portly Pepperpot." Anytime she stopped at a deli or ate at a restaurant, reports appeared of everything she supposedly consumed.

As William Ginsburg was the only direct point of contact to Monica, journalists went all out to court him. I seemed to be ahead of the game, but I also played every card I could. *Time* magazine was about to throw a huge gala celebrating its seventy-fifth anniversary. It was going to be attended by everyone from President Clinton to Tom Cruise. I was invited (along with every major journalist), and as I was allowed to bring a guest, I asked Ginsburg. He was delighted, but because Clinton was there, I found that my table was at the rear of the room while the dignitaries, stars, and well-known journalists, including most of my colleagues, were seated ringside. So I had a lousy time but I thought, "Oh well, it may pay off later."

But don't think I was the only one romancing Ginsburg. The competition was getting more and more fierce. Once when I called Ginsburg he was having dinner with Mike Wallace of *60 Minutes*. Ginsburg told me of one of my colleagues who offered to introduce Monica's father, a photography enthusiast, to famed photographer Richard Avedon. Ginsburg himself was receiving countless dinner invitations in addition to tickets to the theater and special events. He recognized what it was all about, and though he took it all with a grain of salt, he was flattered by the attention.

In spite of my not enjoying the *Time* party, all was going well for me with Ginsburg. We were by now developing a quite friendly relationship. In April '98 I found myself in the enviable position of being the first and only reporter to have a private meeting with Monica. If I had reason to be in California, Ginsburg told me, he might arrange for me to "drop by" Dr. Lewinsky's house. That was reason enough for me to go to California. Ginsburg brought me to the Lewinsky home in the Brentwood section of Los Angeles, ironically just blocks away from the site where Nicole Brown Simpson and Ron Goldman had been murdered four years before. It was a fairly modest home in which Dr. Lewinsky lived with his second wife, Barbara, the walls decorated mainly with photographs he had taken.

When Monica entered the room, you would have thought she had nothing pressing on her mind. She was smiling and cheerful. My first thought was that she was prettier than she appeared in photographs. She had beautiful skin, shiny black hair, and although she was somewhat heavy, she was far from obese. She was what my grandmother would have described as zaftig, which sort of means plump in a good way. Monica had been shopping and had bought some new hats. She happily tried them on for me, and they were very becoming. I was reminded of the beret photograph. Monica told me that her stepmother had taught her how to knit, and that had helped her pass the time while her legal fate was still in jeopardy. Before the knitting she had spent most of the time watching television and surfing the Internet for information about her case. This was the only time on my visit that we discussed the case. I didn't want to say anything at this first meeting she might take offense at. I was impressed that she wasn't whining or crying over what had happened to her. I remarked that I knew how difficult all this must be for her. She said that she had never been involved in any scandal before. "I was basically a good kid growing up," she told me. "I didn't smoke or take drugs. I had good grades and never shoplifted." I told her: "Next time, shoplift." She laughed, and I felt we had the beginning of a relationship. (Monica later told me that my offhand remark meant a great deal to her. She said it showed I had a sense of humor. "It is humor," she said, "that got me through a lot of the pain. It is how I connect with people.")

But she was still a long way from being able to give an interview. As the independent counsel continued his investigation, she lived in constant fear of being arrested. Her father shared her fears. After six months with no immunity deal, and irritated by all the time Ginsburg was spending talking to the press, Dr. Lewinsky and Monica fired him. On June 2 they replaced him with two Washington insiders, Plato Cacheris and Jacob Stein.

I liked Ginsberg personally, but that was that for my Monica-Ginsburg relationship. Onward.

As it happened, I knew both of the new lawyers from two controversial and newsworthy interviews I had done with former clients—Cacheris had represented Fawn Hall, Lt. Col. Oliver North's beautiful blond secretary who had smuggled potentially incriminating documents in the Iran-Contra case out of the office in her underwear, and Stein had worked for Senator Bob Packwood, who had faced accusations by twenty-nine women, all former employees or acquaintances, of sexual misconduct. Both clients had told me they were pleased with my interviews, considering them very fair. This, I hoped, would help.

We called and wrote the new legal team, but by that time the Lewinskys had hired an experienced and respected spokeswoman, Judy Smith, to handle media inquiries. (This is the same Judy Smith I've already mentioned whose PR firm handled Saudi Arabia. We were together there for weeks, and she was very good at what she did.) I arranged a meeting with her to discuss Monica, but Judy was noncommittal and I began to worry about my prospects.

Finally, that summer, Monica's new lawyers were able to work out a deal for her to get "transactional" immunity, which meant that she would not be prosecuted for anything related to the case in exchange for cooperating fully with the independent counsel and testifying truthfully.

By the end of July, Monica turned over the infamous stained blue Gap dress, which testing revealed did contain the president's DNA. That August, with her immunity intact, she testified to a grand jury that she did have a sexual relationship with the president, even though she had denied it in her affidavit in the Paula Jones lawsuit. She was forced to disclose in detail every meeting and conversation with the president. Eleven days later, on August 17, Bill Clinton became the first sitting American president to testify to a federal grand jury about his own conduct. The testimony was given over closed-circuit television from the White House, but of course it leaked out. After months of denials he admitted to "inappropriate intimate contact" and "inappropriate sexual banter" with Monica Lewinsky. He denied, however, that he and Monica had sexual relations since, he said, they never had sexual intercourse. To Clinton, and later, it seemed, to Monica, only actual intercourse constituted "sexual relations." The president also denied committing perjury, tampering with evidence, or asking others to lie under oath.

In a four-minute address to the nation that night, he confessed, "I misled people, including even my wife. I regret that." But, and this was important, he didn't apologize to Monica or her family. Monica later told me in our interview that Clinton's speech that night had made her feel "like a piece of trash," someone who had just serviced him. After that address, cameras captured Clinton, his wife, daughter, and dog, Buddy, boarding the presidential helicopter to fly off for a vacation on Martha's Vineyard. The uncomfortable image was of Chelsea Clinton, walking in-between her parents, holding their hands.

The president's admission didn't help Monica. By now she was the butt of every comedian's joke.

Finally, on September 9, armed guards delivered independent counsel Kenneth Starr's report and its eighteen boxes of accompanying material to the House of Representatives. Two days later Starr's report was released to the public. For almost five hundred pages it described in virtually pornographic fashion every encounter Monica Lewinsky had with President Clinton. Could anything have been more mortifying to either of them? *The Starr Report* became a best seller, and, still hoping I might be doing an interview with Monica, I was one of the people who read every page of it. I thought it was horrendous and unnecessarily graphic. It didn't need five hundred pages to make its point. I felt very sorry for Monica and even for the president, who was obviously suffering while still trying to run the country.

The morning the report came out, President Clinton, at a Washington, D.C., prayer breakfast, for the first time publicly apologized to Monica Lewinsky and her family, including them in a list of people he acknowledged hurting.

Monica never wanted to testify about her relationship with the president, but after being forced to do so in such detail, she now thought she was free of the independent counsel, the grand jury, and the FBI. Ready to move on with her life, she began to think seriously about giving an interview. She wanted to tell her own story in her own words. But she had another consideration: huge legal bills. By the end a whole team of attorneys was working on the case. Monica said that at some point her legal fees were $15,000 a day and, as a result, she owed more than a million dollars. Her mother and four of her friends who had testified before the grand jury had also accrued legal bills. Monica wanted to pay it all back. Her family also realized that she would need money for her own living expenses. She had become so notorious that finding a regular job would be difficult if not impossible.

Monica now faced a very difficult decision. It is the policy of network news divisions in the United States not to pay for interviews. That is not the case in many foreign countries, like the UK. There were also U.S. talk and interview shows not under news departments that would pay plenty for her first interview, as would many magazines. What would she do?

I hadn't seen or talked to Monica since our meeting at her father's house almost five months earlier. I heard that she and Judy Smith were meeting with many different journalists. I never knew who they were. For obvious reasons everyone kept the meetings private. Meanwhile Monica's family had enlisted the help of a friend, Richard Carlson, a former television journalist and director of the Voice of America. Carlson worked quietly behind the scenes with Monica, going through bags of mail requesting interviews, appearances, and even endorsements. One food company wanted Monica to do a commercial for their coffee creamer, wearing a navy blue Gap dress and complaining, "Oh no, not again" when the product spilled on her.

I began to hear about huge deals being offered. It was reported that Rupert Murdoch was dangling some five million dollars for a package that included two television interviews for his Fox network—one to be shown here on the Fox channel, another with a British broadcaster to be seen internationally. In addition he was offering a book deal with a publishing company he owned and lord knows what else. This was never confirmed, but there was no doubt that Monica could sell her first exclusive interview for all kinds of money.

This was not the first time, or the last, that someone in the headlines has had to make that kind of a decision. I will digress for a moment to talk of Paris Hilton. In June 2007 the young woman was serving time in jail for, among other things, driving with a suspended license. At that time I had a great many conversations with Paris's mother and with Paris herself, who called me from jail. I assumed that I would be doing the first interview with her. But as it turned out Paris's father, Rick Hilton, was asking for money. Both NBC and ABC found ways of paying the family by purchasing personal photographs and videos of Paris. This was not uncommon practice. However, ABC offered much less money than NBC. The network felt the amount it was offering was legitimate, but the six-figure amount that Rick Hilton was asking for was not. Rick Hilton then told me that NBC had offered so much money that ABC was, in his words, "not in the galaxy," and therefore the interview with Paris would be done by that network. When I said I thought Paris's credibility might be a factor, he answered that it was too much money to turn down. Eventually, when news of the NBC offer leaked out, it made extremely unpleasant headlines and the network withdrew from the deal. The family then offered the interview to me for no money, but by then the whole thing seemed shoddy to me, and I turned it down. My network stood by my decision. Paris finally did an interview with Larry King, which was fine if bland, but her tarnished reputation was not helped by her family's push for money.

Of course the Paris Hilton negotiations were long after my discussions with Monica, but the situation was similar—money versus credibility.

With this predicament, I turned to David Westin, the president of ABC News. David, himself a highly regarded attorney, had first come to ABC as its legal counsel. We discussed Monica's need for money and the fact that her family, specifically her mother, Marcia Lewis, felt that her daughter should accept one of the big deals being offered so that Monica could free herself from debt. David suggested that we meet with Mrs. Lewis, and we arranged to get together in the office of a new attorney for Monica, an entertainment lawyer named Richard Hofstetter. As it turned out, I also knew him well from past negotiations.

I had also previously been in touch with Marcia Lewis. We had talked several times on the phone. I liked her, and she was not at all the way she was being described by the press. She had been much maligned as a flashy, spoiled Beverly Hills socialite and castigated for supposedly not stopping her daughter's relationship with the president. By some accounts she had actually encouraged it. Mrs. Lewis had recently married a man I knew, R. Peter Straus, who owned a string of newspapers and radio stations in New York. Peter, a widower, was a distinguished man. I could not imagine that he would have married a woman of Marcia Lewis's description. I telephoned Peter, and it was he who had put me in touch with his wife. On the phone she was soft-spoken and polite. The last thing she seemed to want was exposure. Although she could certainly have sold her own story to help offset both her own and her daughter's legal bills, she was turning down all requests for interviews, including mine. Indeed, she never sold her story to anyone. In my conversations with Marcia she seemed concerned only with her daughter's welfare.

When David Westin and I met with her, Marcia called Monica, who was in California, and the three of us talked by speaker phone. David and I said together that Monica could indeed make a lot of money right now. We did not underestimate that. But over and above the money was the matter of her damaged reputation and her future credibility. For the rest of her life, we said, her credibility should be her major concern. Somehow she would find the money to pay her legal bills.

I fully believed what we were saying. Of course I wanted to do the interview, but I was not so ambitious that I didn't have a conscience.

It was at this meeting that David came up with a most important compromise. He reiterated that ABC could not pay Monica any money for the interview but that the network would agree to air it just once and only in the United States and Canada. If Monica then wanted to do an interview for money for the international market, she could do it right after ours. If she was paid for that interview, it would be none of our business. No one in Europe would have seen our interview, and this meant the interest overseas would be huge. No decision was made in Hofstetter's office, but David and I left hopeful.

Monica and I continued to talk on the phone. (By this time Monica was no longer being represented by Judy Smith.) In one conversation Monica told me that her mother had tried repeatedly to get her away from President Clinton, but that from an early age she had been hard to control. As she said later in our interview, "I'm stubborn. . . . From the time I was two years old, one of my first phrases was, with hands on my hips, 'You are not the boss of me.' I've been that way ever since." Monica still had that same determination. Despite all the people who had advised her, she was pretty much going to make her own decision.

That fall Monica accepted an invitation to come to my apartment for dinner. She had evidently met with the other journalists, and it seemed that I was the front-runner, but the question of credibility and no payment versus selling her story for big money still loomed ahead. The decision had not been made. Monica arrived wearing a long black skirt and dark glasses and brought me a very nice scarf she had knitted. When I had seen her knitting at her father's house, she reminded me of Madame Defarge from Dickens's *A Tale of Two Cities*, who stitched the names of the people she thought should be executed during the French Revolution. "Are you knitting the names of people you want to destroy?" I asked her, but I don't think she knew what I was talking about.

Monica was warm and funny, the kind of girl who gives you hugs. I introduced her to Icodel, and Monica hugged her, too. Whenever I talked with her after that, she always asked me about Icodel. At dinner I brought up the money issue in the most forceful way. "Look," I said. "You are going to have to do a major interview. It will have to be truthful and probably painful to do, but you can come out as a woman who cares about the truth and has tried to be honest or you can be seen as the person many people want to believe you are—an opportunist greedy for fame and money. That is essentially your choice. I can give you the forum and the opportunity to present yourself with the greatest dignity." That was it. I couldn't make the case anymore. Whatever would happen would happen.

I didn't hear from Monica for over a month. Then, in November, she called to say she would like to meet the people who might be working on her interview. I asked her to lunch at my apartment.

With me were Phyllis McGrady, the ABC News vice president of special projects, and producers Martin Clancy and Katie Thomson. Monica brought some of her knitting to show us. Each item had a cute label that said, "Made especially for you by Monica." We joked that the label made her knitting worth a lot of money. I also admired an upholstery tote bag that she used to carry her yarn and needles, and she told us that she had made the bag herself, finding the vintage fabric and sewing it together. (Later she launched a small and ultimately unsuccessful business selling similar upholstery bags.)

I don't like to spend too much time with subjects before an interview, as answers don't seem fresh if the person has already told them to me. So at our meeting, whenever Monica began to discuss something that could be a part of our hoped-for interview, I tried to cut her off. But she was so anxious to speak freely that it was difficult to stop her. Besides, we were fascinated. She told us details about the infamous blue dress; up until then it had been hard for us to understand why she would keep a soiled dress. She said that she had lots of clothes, because of her fluctuating weight. After she gained some weight she didn't like the way the Gap dress looked on her. To save money she usually didn't pay to dry-clean her clothes until just before she was going to wear them. When she finally decided to wear the dress again, she showed it to Linda Tripp. Then she noticed the stain and told Linda (and I will never forget these words) she figured it was either from Bill Clinton or it was spinach dip. Spinach dip, for heaven's sake! Had it been spinach dip, Clinton would never have been impeached. (If I were writing a different kind of book, this would be the place to put in a good recipe for spinach dip.)

I did ask Monica why she had to give so much detail of every sexual encounter in her testimony. She said people didn't realize she had told not just Linda Tripp about the president but ten other people, including her mother and her aunt. The independent counsel had questioned all of them. If her testimony differed from theirs, she could be accused of lying, lose her immunity, and be prosecuted.

During lunch we discussed the kind of promotion we would do—we would not show Monica's answers, only her face and our questions, and in our ads and promotion we would keep a sense of decorum.

When the lunch was over Monica finally, finally, at last said that she would do her first interview with ABC. That meant no money. To take the high road and turn down millions of dollars in order to prove her credibility was a great act of courage. I don't think Monica ever got full credit for that. There were still hurdles, but now, almost a year after the story broke, after months of my cultivating contacts, consulting with representatives, meeting with members of her family, and slowly gaining her trust, Monica agreed to break her silence with me. I believed in my heart that I could do the best possible interview for her.

After the lunch I asked Martin Clancy to walk Monica home, and although they only strolled together a few blocks down Madison Avenue, Martin found himself described as Monica's "mystery man." The supermarket tabloid the *Star* had a large photo identifying him as "Monica's Santa," and exclaimed that they "went on a Manhattan shopping spree—and everything was bought on his credit card!" The article went on to say, "It seemed like a lovely romantic day out on the town together."

We laughed at this, of course, but it meant we had to take every means to keep our future interview a secret until absolutely every issue was resolved.

Strangely enough Monica had been having trouble reaching an agreement with an American publisher for a book deal. A lot of publishers felt her story had already been told in *The Starr Report*. But on November 16, 1998, it was announced that Monica Lewinsky would be telling her story to Andrew Morton, the British author who in 1992 had collaborated with Princess Diana on a best-selling book about her unhappy marriage. The book deal was worth more than a million dollars to Monica, easing her financial burden.

Then I got a call from Freddie DeMann, an entertainment executive who had previously managed the careers of Madonna and Michael Jackson. He was the father of one of Monica's best friends from Beverly Hills. He asked if Monica did the interview with me, could the book come out in conjunction with the interview?

David Westin agreed that the book could come out right after my interview. We would help to promote it, and indeed, as it turned out, there were passages from it that I had to read during my interview. We had promised to help Monica where we could, and we did. We couldn't pay her, but we wouldn't stand in the way of her making money as long as it didn't affect my interview.

The next month Monica agreed to do a paid interview for England's Channel 4. She earned something like $600,000 for an interview with British broadcaster Jon Snow, which was then sold to stations around the world. Monica also was paid another half million dollars for a photo spread in *Hello!* magazine, a popular European publication. Not a bad payday, but millions less than she would have made had she sold her first television interview.

As soon as we had Monica's agreement, we began work on the interview. I read the hundreds of pages of transcripts of those Linda Tripp tapes, but that was just the beginning. I also reread *The Starr Report* and skimmed through the supplemental evidence that had been released.

Plus I read the grand jury testimony of the key players in the case and various speeches President Clinton had made. The volume of material seemed endless. I read practically all day and all night for weeks. Fortunately I had help from some of our best producers, not just Martin and Katie but Chris Vlasto, who helped break the Lewinsky story. We didn't want the questions to sound too tawdry, and yet this was a story about sex, so we worked hard to maintain some kind of balance. Katie opened up one meeting by musing, "I've been in the White House many times and I don't understand how someone could flash her underpants to the president." The very first question we wrote was this: "You lifted the back of your jacket, and showed the president of the United States your thong underwear. Where did you get the nerve? I mean, who does that?"

An early pass contained more than two hundred questions. My hard-working assistant Monica Caulfield put each of them on my usual index cards. (Throughout the Lewinsky affair we had to refer to her as "the original Monica" to avoid confusion with our interview subject.) I then cut the questions down to the ones I felt were vital to ask. We were chugging right along when we hit a snag. More than a snag, we hit an iceberg. It turned out that our interview was not going to happen anytime soon. Unbeknownst to us Monica still had to gain permission from the independent counsel to speak to us, something that proved far more difficult than we had anticipated. Monica's immunity agreement said that *"pending a final resolution of this matter,"* Monica could not speak to *"representatives of the news media"* without first obtaining the approval of the office of the independent counsel. She was free to collaborate on a book and accept all kinds of money from a nonnews show, no matter how sleazy—but she could not speak to ABC News without permission.

To do an interview with me could violate Monica's immunity agreement, which meant that the independent counsel could still prosecute her. ABC then began to reach out to anyone they could in Ken Starr's office. (By the way, Monica had never then or ever since met Ken Starr.) Weeks dragged on without approval. The independent counsel felt that a "final resolution" of the matter had not occurred since Congress had not yet decided the president's fate.

David Westin was tremendously helpful in this matter and in all our negotiations. He considered enlisting the aid of famed First Amendment lawyer Floyd Abrams to file a lawsuit to overturn the ban on Monica giving the interview. The independent counsel knew we meant business.

In December 1998 the House voted to impeach President Clinton on two articles: that he perjured himself before the grand jury and that he obstructed the administration of justice. He vowed not to resign. We had now written and rewritten our questions more than a dozen times, but the year ended with no Monica Lewinsky interview.

In January 1999 the Senate impeachment trial began, along with the promise from the independent counsel's office that once that trial was over, they would no longer stand in the way of Monica doing an interview. Our new concern was that Monica had been subpoenaed to give testimony, which would be shown to the public. Though her physical image was very familiar, it was the first time the public heard her voice. Her answers were brief and we hoped they wouldn't quell our audience's appetite for our interview. They didn't.

On February 12, in only the second impeachment vote in its history, the U.S. Senate acquitted Clinton of both articles of impeachment. Four days later the independent counsel sent Monica's lawyers a letter granting her permission to give me an interview. They imposed three restrictions, only one of which affected us: Monica was forbidden to say anything about the conduct of the prosecutors or their investigation, including the terrible day she was detained in a hotel room and interrogated after she met Linda Tripp at the mall. But there was no such restriction placed on me. As I had already received a copy of Monica's about-to-be-published book, I decided in my broadcast just to read the book's description of that night.

We wanted to get the interview done quickly so it could air within the crucial "sweeps" period, when network ratings set advertising rates. ABC set the date, Wednesday, March 3. We made another decision. There were so many questions to ask and so much interest that we wanted two hours. The network, mindful of its second place in the ratings, happily handed over the airtime. All we had to do now was the interview.

On the morning of February 20, with great secrecy and security, we took Monica through the building garage and into *20/20*'s studio. She was twenty-two when she first met Bill Clinton; she was now twenty-five. She was nervous but looked very pretty. Her heavy dark hair was pulled off her face. Her lips glistened. She wore a simple black suit, and because she was afraid of looking heavy, we sat her in a chair with arms to cover part of her body. The interview lasted just over four and a half hours, and the resulting transcript ran to 150 pages. Here are some of the highlights.

On our opening question about how she had the nerve to show the president her thong, she said it was "a flirtation, a dance. One person does something and then you meet that person and raise the stakes."

She described the president as "a very sensuous man who has a lot of sensuous feelings. He also has a very strong religious upbringing and struggles with his sensuality. He tries to hold himself back and then can't anymore."

She proclaimed that her relationship with Bill Clinton was not just about sex. "Everyone will probably find it hard to believe, but when I asked him did he want to get to know me as a person, he started to tear up and told me that he never wanted me to think that he didn't. And that's not what this relationship was about."

When I asked her why she thought the president was attracted to her, she said, "He thought that I had a lot of energy and that I lit up a room and that he thought I was smart."

She said that after the relationship progressed she told Clinton that she was in love with him. He responded, "That means a lot to me." But when she asked if he loved her, he said no.

She had wanted to have intercourse with him but when she asked him to, he said, "When you get to be my age, you'll understand that there are consequences for those kinds of things." She then told me, "I got really upset because to me that completes a relationship, and now I would never know what it was like to be that intimate with him."

Later when she was officially banned from the White House, weeks, sometimes months, would go by without her seeing him. The almost nightly telephone calls stopped coming. Clinton tried to break up with her, but she refused to walk away and continued to try to see him.

"Where was your self-respect?" I asked. "Where was your self-esteem?"

Her answer was very sad. "I don't have feelings of self-worth that a woman should have," she said. "And I think that's been the center of a lot of my mistakes and a lot of my pain."

She showed the most emotion when talking about the toll the investigation and all the media attention had taken on her family. She said that not only was she suicidal at certain points, her parents had also felt great despair. With tears filling her eyes, she lamented, "People have no idea what this has done . . . that behind the name 'Monica Lewinsky,' there's a person, and there is a family, and there has been so much pain that has been caused by all this. . . . It was so destructive."

As for the notorious dress, she said she put it in a closet at her mother's apartment and her mother didn't even know it was there. Then she said that even though Ken Starr's people didn't actually know she had the dress, she nevertheless turned it over to them. I asked why.

"Because I had to. Getting and keeping my immunity became very important to me. I had to tell the truth about absolutely everything, including the dress, for if they found it, I might be brought up on charges of perjury.

"This dress," she continued, "is one of the most humiliating things that has ever happened to me. Every man that I have met since this thing has happened eventually says to me, 'So what is the real story with the dress?' I wish I had never had it."

My final question to her was, "What will you tell your children when you have them?" She replied simply, "Mommy made a big mistake."

On the evening of March 3, I had the producers of the show and a few friends to my apartment to watch the program. It was an inflammatory evening in more ways than one. I had made a fire, but the flue wasn't open. The room began to fill with smoke and the fire department came. (I was very sad to learn three years later that two of those firemen died in the 9/11 attacks.)

As the show began I couldn't help but wonder how many people around the country were watching. So many had said, "Oh, I'm not going to watch Monica Lewinsky, that's beneath me." I thought that a lot of them would be true to their word, but at one point I went over to the window and looked down at the street below. There wasn't a car on the avenue. Nothing was moving.

Strangely, the biggest question we got after the interview aired was about the shiny lipstick Monica was wearing. ABC received hundreds of phone calls and e-mails from viewers asking its name. Turned out it was a color called Glaze from a new makeup line by the clothing store Club Monaco. The lipstick quickly sold out around the country.

It is now ten years since the Monica Lewinsky story broke. After her book and interviews, since she couldn't escape it, Monica tried to capitalize on her fame and took some TV jobs. She became a spokesperson for the Jenny Craig diet and then hosted a reality dating program called *Mr. Personality* on Fox. Nobody wanted to give her a real job. She eventually decided to try to become a private person again and went back to school. In December 2006 she earned a graduate degree from the highly respected London School of Economics. Her thesis was titled "In Search of the Impartial Juror: An Exploration of the Third Person Effect and Pre-Trial Publicity."

After Monica's graduation, the *Washington Post* columnist Richard Cohen wrote this about her:

It does not take a Freudian to appreciate why Lewinsky chose the topic she did. She is the victim of publicity and her life has been a trial—enough to floor almost anyone. She is a branded woman. Yet she did what so many women that age would do. She seduced, or so she thought, an older man. Here was her crime. She was a girl besotted. But now she is a woman with a master's degree from a prestigious school. She is going to be 34. Where is the guy brave enough, strong enough, admirable enough to take her as his wife, to say to the world that he loves this woman even if she will always be an asterisk in American history? I hope there is such a guy out there. It would be nice. It would be fair.

The last time I spoke to Monica, I told her that I would be writing about her in this book. She was still trying very hard to get a job. Most of all she wants, as she has always wanted, to have a husband and a family. I agree with Richard Cohen. It would be nice. It would be fair.

The View

*I*N 1997 *THE VIEW* sneaked up on me. The last thing I was thinking about was daytime television. I knew that Oprah Winfrey and Phil Donahue, who were on the air during the day, were each very popular. I had even appeared on their programs, but I had little interest in television until early evening when the news came on. I was fully occupied doing *20/20* along with the *Barbara Walters Specials*. By this time I had been doing four *Specials* a year for twenty years with great success, and for most of those years, with my producer, Bill Geddie. My plate was full. I had no room for gravy.

Enter gravy. The 11:00 a.m. period on ABC, which was controlled by the network and not by syndicators, was floundering. A lot of pleasant people had attempted to do a show during that time period, but no program lasted for more than a year or two. Unlike the earlier-morning and late-afternoon programs, it was considered a very tough time slot. By 11:00 a.m., it was thought, most nonworking women had sent the kids off to school and had finished their housework. It was time to go out and do the marketing, the errands, and maybe pick up the little ones from nursery school. So, sort of in desperation, the daytime network executives, who had nothing to do with the news department executives for whom I worked, came to me and Bill Geddie and said, "Got any ideas for a daytime program?"

Well, now that they mentioned it, I *did* have a concept that occasionally drifted through my head, and when the program finally made it to air, here is what I actually said: "I've always wanted to do a show with women of different generations, backgrounds, and views." These women, I imagined, could chat away on all sorts of subjects. Then we could add a celebrity interview or two, perhaps followed by an informative segment on health, fashion, or whatever we deemed of interest to women. It was a relatively simple concept. I had two inspirations. The first came from watching the ABC Sunday-morning news program *This Week with David Brinkley*. Near the end of each hour-long broadcast, Brinkley moderated a roundtable with three or four other journalists who commented on the latest events in the news. It was informative, free-flowing, and often very amusing. I thought it was the best part of the program.

My other inspiration came from a woman named Virginia Graham, who at one time had a modestly successful daytime program called *Girl Talk*, on which I occasionally appeared, sometimes along with another guest or two. Again the conversation was unrehearsed, and when it spun off in different directions, it could be a lot of fun. So I wondered, if we took a small and varied group of women and made them a permanent cast, would that work for an informative and entertaining hour? I thought it might.

The network was not overly impressed but said they would consider it enough to have us make a pilot. Furthermore, they insisted that I would have to be one of the women on the panel. Otherwise they didn't think they could sell the program to advertisers. I told them that if I could appear on the show just two or three times a week and not have to be the daily moderator, I would give it a try.

The key, of course, was to choose the right women with the right chemistry. Just a simple thing: find four smart women of different ages and different personalities who could disagree without killing one another and, better still, might actually like each other.

First step: we rented a large hotel suite, outfitted it with comfortable sofas and chairs, brought in cameras, put a mini control center in an adjacent room, where, on a television monitor, we could then watch the various applicants talk and see how they related to one another. We would give them a list of subjects from the newspapers that day and let them just go at it.

We had talked to dozens of talent agents, and the word got around that we were planning a gabfest with a bunch of women. The result of this was that we were deluged with résumés, phone calls, and tapes. Everybody and her aunt knew the perfect person. All you have to do is talk, the various applicants thought. So why not me?

The very first group of four looked promising but who knew? As a possible moderator, we were considering an attractive woman named Meredith Vieira. Meredith had, at one time, been a correspondent on

60 Minutes on CBS, but because at the time she had one young child and was pregnant with a second, she didn't want to travel. Don Hewitt, the program's executive producer, felt that all his reporters had to travel to do stories and he couldn't, in all fairness, make an exception for Meredith, so they came to a rather unhappy parting of the ways. More recently I knew Meredith from ABC, where she was working on a newsmagazine the network was trying out, called *Turning Point.* Unfortunately the program didn't make it. Meredith's contract at ABC was not renewed, and she was at loose ends. I checked and heard from her producers that she was not just smart but, almost more important to me, possessed a wicked sense of humor.

At first Meredith wasn't really interested in appearing on a daytime program. Her whole professional life had been on news broadcasts. Why should she take the risk of going on an untried daytime talk show? But her husband, Richard Cohen, who had himself been a news producer at CBS, persuaded her to consider it. "It could be fun," he said, "and you won't have to travel." She could also be back from the studio before the kids got home from school. What did she have to lose?

Score one for our possible moderator.

Sitting on the couch next to Meredith was Star Jones, an African American woman who had been a prosecuting attorney in Brooklyn and distinguished herself first reporting for Court TV and, later, covering the O. J. Simpson trial for *Inside Edition.* Star was large in every way, from her résumé to her weight to her personality. She was funny and knowledgeable, especially on subjects relating to the law. Her favorite word was "allegedly." She was single, in her thirties, and looking for a husband. The reports that Bill and I got were that she was sometimes difficult to work with, but we thought, as part of an ensemble, she would be okay.

Then there was the woman we agreed might provide real humor. Her name was Joy Behar. A comedian, she had worked small clubs around town but was almost unknown to the wider public, including me. One night I went to a benefit honoring Milton Berle, an old family friend whom I have mentioned before. I was sitting next to Regis Philbin when the entertainment began and onstage came a good-looking redhead who told a joke about the author Salman Rushdie. Rushdie had written a book which some Muslims found blasphemous, and a directive had been issued that he should be killed. As a result Rushdie was in deep hiding, protected by Scotland Yard. "I'll tell you the difference between men and women," said Behar. "Rushdie has been in solitary confinement for five years with no visitors at all allowed . . . and in that time he's been married twice." Well, it loses something when I tell it, but I thought, "This woman is perfect for us."

Finally we auditioned a lively young girl in her twenties who told us that she was appearing occasionally on MTV. Her name was Debbie Matenopoulos. She was kind of ditsy and likable, and we thought she might be just right for the youngest member of the panel.

Here is what was so amazing. This group of four was the first panel we tried out in two full days of auditions. We thought they were great but we didn't think we should just go with the first group, so we tried out something like fifty women and mixed them up in different groups of four. Finally, toward the end of the second day, Bill and I looked at each other and said, "You know, the first group was the best. Let's go with Meredith as the moderator and Star, Joy, and Debbie on the panel." I would join the group twice a week on the days I could fit it in among my other assignments.

As for the name, we liked *The View from Here*, but we were told that name was being used by a program in Canada so we shortened it to *The View*, and that was that.

Bill and I were co–executive producers. Together we worked out a format based on my original idea. The basis of the program would be the unrehearsed and spontaneous chat sessions among the women. We would call this segment, "hot topics." Essentially the program still follows that early format.

Bill was and is indispensable. He hired a director and a bunch of bright young producers, gave them marching orders, and whipped the show into shape. The producers, most of whom are still with us, start with Alexandra "Dusty" Cohen, who, as supervising producer, is Bill's right arm. Then there are two coordinating producers, Matthew Strauss and Patrick Ignozzi; Donald Berman and Sue Solomon are responsible for booking the guests. We also have had, from day one, the talented and creative director, Mark Gentile, and a wondrous young woman, Fran Taylor, who has managed, no matter what their size or shape, to dress all the cast members. Linda Finson supervises production and the budget of the show. These are just some of the staff who, then and now, helped to make *The View* a success. We have had very little turnover throughout the years.

In the beginning my job was to do the outside work, which was primarily to deal with the network, the advertisers, the publicity people, and the press. In short I had to keep us afloat.

The View was launched on August 11, 1997. We deliberately put it on when the viewing audiences were at their summer low. This, we felt, would give us a chance to work out the kinks and get used to one another. We felt fresh and new. The set, however, was neither fresh nor new. The network didn't have enough faith in our budding program to invest in a new set. What we inherited was left over from an unsuccessful ABC soap opera called *The City*. It was located on West Sixty-sixth Street, next to the Hudson River. A few more steps to your right and you'd be in the river.

One more thing: we were a network program, not syndicated. In syndication the programs are sold to individual stations all over the country. They can appear on any network or station at any time. For example, Oprah airs at 9:00 a.m. in Chicago but at 4:00 p.m. in New York. Because we are a network program, we are on the air every day during the same time period, 11:00 a.m. in the East and 10:00 a.m. everywhere else. When we made our debut, all of the ABC-owned and -operated stations were obliged to carry us. (There are ten of them.) But at that time of day, stations not owned by ABC but affiliated with the network had the choice of carrying the show or not. What we did not know was that more than 20 percent of the country would not be carrying the show in the morning time period. Sometimes, the affiliates would run it in overnight hours. This included quite a few big cities like Boston, Philadelphia, and Washington, D.C., as well as many smaller markets. Other cities, like Miami, Pittsburgh, and Milwaukee, didn't carry the show at all. Week after week, part of my job was to phone the heads of these various stations (many of whom I knew personally) or their station managers, to try to persuade them to carry *The View*.

It was like the riddle of the chicken and the egg. If we wanted to get big guests to come on the program, we needed ratings to entice them. Therefore we had to have as many stations carrying us as possible. On the other hand, if we didn't have those big-name guests and the big ratings, the affiliates wouldn't carry us. They would instead stick to their own programs, which they felt would do better than *The View*. But little by little the viewers got a taste of our program and liked the taste. Over time our ratings began to rise, and gradually the stations climbed aboard. Today we have almost 100 percent coverage.

My being involved with the program had other ramifications. I could help book the big-name celebrities. For example, I had interviewed Tom Selleck for one of our *Specials*. He, like the very nice man he is, agreed to be our first celebrity guest. In the first week we had Michael J. Fox and Sylvester Stallone visiting us, both good pals doing me a favor. In the beginning the big-name guests only wanted to come on the show when I was on. This occasionally still happens, and I try to be on the program if it is someone I know really well, like Tom Cruise or Michael Douglas. But as the program became more popular, it became easier to book guests whether I was on or not.

Our panel knew none of our early concerns. What they knew was that *The View* was a great opportunity for them. Our first few weeks went surprisingly well. We five women would then, and still do, arrive in the large makeup room at 9:00 a.m., a full two hours before the program goes on the air live. We then receive a sheaf of papers from a researcher, with the news stories of the day. Talking and laughing, we decide which subjects we want to tackle. If it starts a discussion or better still, an argument, we know we are onto something, but we are careful not to leave the argument in the dressing room. We save it for the broadcast so we can let the chips fall where they may. Then as now we loved stories that concerned sex. Surefire winners. I often cringed because I thought they went too far, but Meredith and Joy both had raunchy senses of humor, so vaginas and penises became part of our almost daily vocabulary. I sometimes said, "Enough with the penises," but the conversations were lively and just shocking enough. Besides, I rather liked my position as the panel prude.

Star often had the most to say, and her views were almost always interesting and provocative. She soon became the audience's favorite member of the panel. She was also the one viewers remembered the most, being the only African American of the group. An extra plus was that, as a lawyer, her habit of saying "allegedly" kept us out of trouble.

Joy was truly funny. She was also opinionated and very smart. We had made the right choice.

Meredith made a terrific moderator. While her hair and makeup were being done, she sat with an assistant, and together they wrote all the introductions to whatever the hot topics would be. Her introductions were on the teleprompter. The rest of the hot topics were ad-libbed.

However, as charming and funny as Meredith could be, it took the audience a while to identify with her. At first, she came across as just another pretty lady. In time, though, the audiences came to realize that she was probably the most outrageous of all of us. One day she would tell us that she didn't wear underwear, the next day she would tease about her three children and tell stories about her cat who peed all over the house.

Meredith could get away with almost anything, but she also had her serious side. Her husband, Richard, has multiple sclerosis and had colon cancer. Meredith talked of this from time to time, although never in a maudlin way. We all talked about personal aspects of our lives. We were a kind of family sharing our good times and bad.

Joy, the viewers learned, was divorced, had a daughter, Eve, and had been living with Steve, a former teacher, for almost twenty years. He was often the butt of her good-natured jokes.

Star's dream, she told us, was to marry an African American Christian man with a good job. She was not, she told us, about to support any man. In the meantime she discussed her dates. Most of them didn't seem to last, and we secretly prayed that she would meet some real nice guy real soon.

We also, as time went on, worried about her increasing weight gain. But none of us had the courage to say anything to her. Star didn't take to criticism easily and could tell us to mind our business—especially because, on the air, she constantly talked about how much she liked her body. The audience could relate to her, but in retrospect, we should have pushed the matter as she was becoming dangerously obese. I regret that I didn't confront her, although later Star told me she wouldn't have listened anyway.

In the early months of the program, of all the women, I shared the least about my life. I was afraid to let go too much on *The View* because I was known as a serious interviewer on *20/20*. As a result I came across as rather reserved, and sometimes I inhibited the others. I worked on this and knew that I was making progress when, one day, having made a joking remark, my daughter said, "At last, Mom, people know you have a sense of humor."

Part of my reticence to talk about myself was that Roone Arledge, still the president of ABC News and my boss, had been against my doing the program at all. He didn't forbid it, though he could have. Instead he said that he thought my involvement might take away from my authoritative position in news. (This was many years before television journalists were expected to have personalities as well as deliver the news.) I thought about it for a while and decided it was a challenge I wanted to take, but Roone's admonition stayed in my mind. Fortunately, as it turned out, the viewers knew me so well from all those years on the air that they were able to accept the fact that I wore two hats. Indeed, I think, as my daughter expressed, the fact that I could have fun and laugh made me more likable to the viewer. So everything seemed to be working.

What wasn't working, which is why I left discussing her for last, was Debbie Matenopoulos. At first she was sweetly lovable, but it quickly became apparent that her life was more about going out to parties than reading a book or a newspaper. As a result, instead of coming across as young and "with it," she came across as young and not very well informed.

Saturday Night Live began to do skits about Debbie, and although that was a sort of compliment and let a lot of people know that *The View* even existed, it also led a lot of people to feel that we had a scatterbrain on the program. That is how Debbie came across, and it was amusing only up to a point. Our research showed that she was turning off viewers and affecting the ratings of the program. Finally, in the fall of 1998, a little more than a year after the show went on the air, the network told Debbie that they could not renew her contract. We were personally fond of her and allowed her to say that she was leaving *The View* to study acting, and we gave her a big going-away party. Debbie officially left on January 6, 1999.

(In 2006, during our ninth year of *The View*, Debbie came back as a guest host. She had grown up to be a most charming woman. She was married and a cohost of *The Daily 10* on E! *The View* had, after all, helped to launch her career, and that made me happy.)

After Debbie left the show, we were again deluged with tapes, phone calls, letters, people stopping us on the street, all of whom wanted to fill Debbie's position. Every time I got a phone call from someone I hadn't seen in years, I knew it was about the job on *The View*. Even Michael Eisner, then chairman and CEO of the Walt Disney Company, which owns ABC, had a candidate for us. "Please send a tape," we told him. (And we didn't hire the young woman.)

We thought it would be good if we could find a young Hispanic woman, as we didn't have such a person represented on the program. But we didn't limit ourselves to Hispanics. For four months we tried out new faces on the panel. Finally, after narrowing the list down to three young women, we chose not a Hispanic, not an African American, not another Caucasian, but an American-born Chinese girl named Lisa Ling. She was lovely to look at, very bright, and, most important, the chemistry seemed right with the rest of the women. We all felt comfortable with her.

Lisa joined *The View* in May 1999, but almost from her first days, she told me she really wanted to work on a news program. Her opportunity came after she had been with us for three years or so, when *National*

Geographic offered her an exciting and demanding position as their roving television correspondent. She was so good that Oprah later hired her as a regular on her program. So alas, in December 2002, Lisa left us.

"Here we go again," we said. Contest. Tapes. E-mails. Almost a year after Lisa left we finally made our choice, and what a great choice it was. We hired twenty-six-year-old Elisabeth Hasselbeck, a survivor of the hit television show *Survivor*. If Elisabeth could eat worms and stand up to all of the challenges of that show, she could certainly survive us. Elisabeth was married. (Her husband is a football player, Tim Hasselbeck.) And what's more, to our joy, a year after she joined us, Elisabeth got pregnant, and when her little girl, Grace, was two, she got pregnant again. In November 2007, her son Taylor Thomas was born. We told Elisabeth that all this was great for our ratings and thanked her for obliging us with babies.

Elisabeth also had something else that Bill and I felt was very important to the program. Meredith, and most certainly Star and Joy, were outspoken liberals, especially where politics were concerned. It made the program, in many discussions, lopsided. Elisabeth, perhaps surprising in a young woman just in her twenties, was very conservative and a supporter of George W. Bush, which helped to promote good and lively discussions. In the beginning Elisabeth had trouble speaking up, but as time went on, she more than held her own, especially when it came to defending Bush's actions in Iraq.

So we made it through the first nine years of the program, and who ever thought the program would last nine years? Certainly not me.

If imitation is considered the sincerest form of flattery, then we certainly should have been flattered. The more successful *The View* became, the more the program was copied. In the fall of 1999 NBC News put on a program immediately following the *Today* show which featured three women, the best-known being Florence Henderson, chitchatting about the news of the day, followed by interviews. Called *Later Today*, the program never caught on and lasted only a year. Then, in 2001, Dick Clark Productions introduced *The Other Half*, with Clark himself at the helm, I guess more or less assuming my role. The show had different men, again chitchatting away, followed by interviews. It was aimed at women and for a while, given the male point of view, it was mildly amusing. In some cities the program went on opposite *The View*, but it did us no harm. *The Other Half* sputtered along for two years and then it, too, folded. What the producers didn't realize was how vitally important the right chemistry between the cohosts was. We were either very smart with our choice of cast, or very lucky. In addition our program was well produced. We worked for years to get the right balance of talk and guests.

Since we were a bunch of women, our approach, our questions, our whole attitude toward celebrities was different. We were looser and more fun, and the guests, male or female, along with plugging their books or movies, enjoyed weighing in on the hot topics they had just heard us discussing. We also made certain that at least one of us had read the book or seen the movie or TV show, and our guests appreciated that. We got the biggest stars to come on. (Just plop yourself on our couch and discuss your film and your sex life.)

It wasn't just show business celebrities who joined us. Over the years we've had many major political figures sit down on the couch. Here are some: Hillary Clinton, Barack Obama, John Edwards, John McCain, Joe Biden, Chris Dodd, Ron Paul, Al Sharpton, and Nancy Pelosi. General Colin Powell was with us in 2008 on Martin Luther King Jr.'s birthday, and soon after her election, Chile's first female president, Dr. Michelle Bachelet, came on the program. In 2003 I even "married" New York's mayor, Michael Bloomberg. Well, not exactly. Just for the fun of it, one day, each of us had to pick our dream husband. I chose the mayor, saying he was rich, brilliant, and, besides, I thought he was cute. We had a cardboard cutout of him when suddenly, to my surprise, he walked onstage, threw aside the cutout, and we were a couple. The marriage, however, has never been consummated.

We had a scare or two. In the spring of 2002, CBS News came after Meredith offering her a lot more money to join a new early-morning lineup that was planning yet another *View*-like panel. Meredith was tempted. But she didn't really want to chance her future on a brand-new show, and she was very happy on *The View*. In the end we found a solution. The quiz show *Who Wants to Be a Millionaire* was starting a syndicated daytime version. I talked to ABC about having Meredith host the program, and they thought it was a great idea. Meredith then got additional income and began another aspect of her career as the host of a quiz show. We breathed a sigh of relief when she turned down the CBS offer.

Things began to change in the summer of 2003, however. Star, whose weight was becoming more and more of an issue, decided to take drastic measures. She had reached the point where her heavy breathing was noticeable on the air, and she could barely walk. After consulting her doctors she decided to have gastric bypass surgery that would shrink her stomach and make overeating uncomfortable if not dangerous.

Star was quite sick for several weeks after the procedure and missed some time on the program. We expected her, when she felt well, to talk about the procedure on the air as it was such an important aspect of her life and could hardly be kept secret—or so we thought. Star had even told me that she would discuss the whole operation and its aftermath with me on 20/20. But after the operation Star said she didn't want to become what she called a "poster child" for the procedure and have to answer a lot of questions. I understood that, but it put us all in a terrible position. It meant we virtually had to lie for Star, especially when she said again and again on the air that her weight loss was due primarily to portion control and Pilates. But she was also our colleague, and we felt we couldn't "out" her. It became more and more difficult to keep up the charade, especially since the program consistently featured segments on diet and weight loss. Joy, in particular, resented having to go along with a lie that implied that all one needed to do was sit-ups and ingest one cookie instead of two.

Star, however, had other news that did make us happy. In November, four months after her procedure, she was introduced to an attractive, single, African American bachelor named Al Scales Reynolds. Just what she was looking for. We rejoiced for her, and when we met Al at *The View*'s annual Christmas party, we liked him very much. Before long, Star told us that she and Al were to be married the following autumn. Al proposed in front of cameras by getting down on one knee at an all-star NBA basketball game. He gave her a large diamond ring. All the tabloid television programs aired the proposal, and almost every day someone in our studio audience would shout for Star to show off the ring. These were happy times.

Then a shadow fell. Star came to Bill and me and said that she wanted a very big wedding. It was the one time in her life, she said, that she wanted to feel like a princess. Being royal, however, costs a lot of money, and Star's solution was to try to get what she could for free, like possibly the invitations and flowers and her wedding cake and brides-maids' dresses, in return for promoting these items on the air. She hoped to do that on *The View*, but if that was not possible, she said, she would find other programs that would agree. We then did a few seg-ments on her wedding, focusing on the invitations and the wedding gowns, thinking the audience would like it. And they did.

But I think we made a great mistake. We should have told her that these free "gifts" in return for promotion were unacceptable, and that she could not barter them away. We soon stopped the promotions on *The View*, but we couldn't prevent Star from doing them on other pro-grams as her contract allowed her to make limited appearances on shows other than *The View*. But she was beginning to attract bad publicity. As she made more requests or demands, suppliers, or some who were not asked to supply, leaked to the tabloids what she was doing. The *New York Post* began to call her "Bridezilla." It was not a compliment, and it became a national story. We were very distressed about this. Such publicity was not helping our show, and it sure wasn't helping Star. Instead of being the lovable, romantic bride, she was now being seen as the greedy bride.

The lavish wedding took place in November 2004, a year after she and Al had met. The over-the-top celebration became even more fodder for the tabloids. Star, who had begun by being the most popular member of our panel, was now rapidly becoming the least popular. Viewers were saying they didn't recognize her anymore. She was beginning to appear false, and Star's popularity had been built on the audience being able to relate to her.

At this time the ABC daytime executives once more conducted focus groups and found that Star was losing us viewers. They warned her agents that they were thinking of not renewing her contract, which would be up in August 2006. They then evidently firmed up their position, because just before Christmas of 2005, they came to Bill and me and told us that they had decided to replace Star on the program. They also wanted us to tell her right away. We hesitated. Not only was it just before Christmas, but Star had written a book called *Shine!*, which was about to be published. In the book she told readers how she had achieved "physical, emotional and spiritual happiness." She was a changed person, she said. (She did not mention the gastric bypass.) Star told us that she was going on a multicity tour for the book. Bill and I felt then that we could not possibly give her bad news at the start of what she hoped would make her book a best seller. Beyond this, we were genuinely fond of Star. She had been so terrific for so many years on the program, and we were fervently hoping she would turn her image around. Though my opinion mattered, it was the network that did the actual hiring and firing of the talent. We asked the network to hold off on their decision.

Finally, in April, ABC told Star's agents that her contract would definitely not be renewed. Bill and I told Star we would protect her career and not let anyone know that she was being fired. She could say she was writing another book, that she wanted to start a new chapter in her life, whatever she wanted to say. We felt we owed her this, and she agreed that this was what should be done.

To add to our difficulties, we had an even bigger departure to contemplate. After nine years as the moderator on *The View*, Meredith had decided to accept a dazzling offer of much more money from NBC to replace Katie Couric on the *Today* show. I talked with Meredith about the offer. *The View* had brought her fame and we were proud of that, but we could not match NBC's salary. I was and am very fond of Meredith, and this, I agreed, was an opportunity she couldn't possibly turn down. With tears and cheers, we said good-bye to Meredith in June 2006. Now we would not only be losing Star but Meredith as well. We needed a big, new, bold attraction.

That's when Rosie O'Donnell entered the picture. I had been an admirer of Rosie for years. I had often appeared on her own very popular television show and had even substituted for her when she was ill. Rosie had left that show in 2002, she said, to spend more time with her life partner, Kelli, and their growing family, which, by 2006, numbered four children. I was fond of both Rosie and Kelli.

Rosie and Kelli had made a beautiful and touching documentary of a cruise for gay families that they had arranged and been on. On March 28, 2006, I went to see the premiere screening of the documentary. It made me laugh and cry. I knew that Rosie had spent most of the past four years since she had left her own program painting pictures. I even own one of the paintings. But now, with this documentary, it seemed that Rosie might be returning to public life. Could it be, I wondered that night, that Rosie might agree to become our new moderator? So I asked her and then and there she said yes. The next day I told Bill. He, too, thought it was a great idea. I called Rosie to make sure she hadn't changed her mind. She hadn't.

The ABC executives were a bit hesitant initially. Since Rosie had left television, she had been in a nasty legal dispute with the publishers of a magazine that bore her name, had produced a Broadway show starring Boy George that was a flop and didn't exactly add to her reputation, and, most important, had revealed to all that she was a lesbian, something she had not publicly discussed during her own show. The network, at first, was afraid that Rosie might be too volatile a personality and too controversial. But I vouched for her and told them that I thought she had mellowed with the years. Also, I thought, times had changed and gays and lesbians were pretty much accepted all over the country. After we put Rosie in touch with the heads of the network, they, too, agreed that it would be a great coup to have her on *The View*. Rosie would start on the show in the fall, agreeing to sign for only one year. I had nothing to do with the contractual arrangements, which turned out later on to be a blessing.

Of course we told Star, who, I point out again, already knew that her contract was not going to be renewed. The trouble was that there was very bad blood between Star and Rosie. Rosie had from time to time been a guest on *The View*, and she and Star had tangled on a variety of issues both on and off the air. When Rosie was interviewed on other programs, before she began on *The View*, she had accused Star of being dishonest about her weight loss. As a guest on *The View*, Rosie had said to her face, "It's like Twinkle Twinkle Shrinking Star." Had Star continued to be on the program, we probably would not have reached out to Rosie. But because Star was not going to remain on *The View*, our decision about Rosie was not going to affect Star's departure one way or another.

We reassured Star once more that we would never say that the network had dismissed her. I reiterated that she could give any reason she wanted for leaving and could also choose the date to depart the program. We would dedicate a full-hour retrospective tribute to her and give her a farewell party on the air. Again Star agreed to this.

Star told us she wanted to leave after Meredith, and chose Thursday, June 29, to make her own announcement. But on Tuesday, June 27, while we were live on the air, Star suddenly grasped my hand and Joy's and said that after much "prayer and counsel," she had decided to leave the program. Her announcement took us totally by surprise. Thinking she had just decided to move up her announcement date, I asked the audience to rise and give her a standing ovation. But, as it turned out to our astonishment, Star had, over the previous weekend, given an interview to *People* magazine. In the magazine, which was about to hit the newsstands, she announced that she had been fired. It was not the drop in her popularity among viewers that had caused her dismissal, Star insisted, but the "new direction" the show wanted to take—that is, Rosie. She said that unlike the rest of us—that is, Bill and especially me—she was going to tell the truth. Here Bill and I were risking our own reputations for honesty to protect her. Instead she was damaging *our* credibility. We were very hurt.

The network immediately held a crisis meeting with us to decide what to do. I felt that Star should continue until the day she was due to leave. I hate confrontation and thought that if she continued it might make matters less explosive. Bill felt strongly that Star now could not be trusted. The network agreed. Star was asked not to return.

That was almost three years ago. Star seemed to have had a difficult time finding another job. I still feel it might have been easier for her to find a new position if she had left the program in the graceful way we had suggested. But in August 2007 she debuted on Court TV, hosting her own program. Star has said that she had a long time to think. Before the new program began she admitted that she had indeed undergone a gastric bypass. I give her great credit. She looks very different now than she did on *The View* (among other changes, she wears glasses), but the intelligence and the charm are still there. Unfortunately, Star's program only lasted six months, but I realized how much I missed her. Not just on the air, where she had made a huge contribution to the success of *The View*, but off. I wrote a note to her in the fall of 2007 and asked if we could meet. We did, for breakfast, and made our peace.

We did not attempt to replace Star on *The View*. We thought one new member of the cast was enough for the season. But also, there was no one we could think of who had the qualities Star had originally brought to the program. Instead, Bill arranged for a variety of guest "cohosts," many of them African Americans.

Rosie O'Donnell began cohosting *The View* on September 5, 2006. She introduced a whole new and challenging chapter of the program. How to describe it? It was like a roller-coaster ride or a bumpy trip on a fast-moving bus. Rosie had originally said she wanted to ride the bus, not drive it. But this backseat role was simply not in her nature. Rosie is a big talent, funny, smart, opinionated, passionate—and controlling.

Almost from her first weeks Rosie had difficulty accepting Bill as the producer in charge of the program. She challenged his decisions. She didn't want features on beauty or fashion or medical subjects, all of which had been popular on the show. In the months that followed they had almost no relationship. At one point Bill confided in me that he was not sure he wanted to continue on the program. Rosie also had difficulty with Mark Gentile and with some of the crew—the floor managers, the stagehands, and the audio engineers. There was so much bad feeling that when *The View* had its annual Christmas party, many of the staff refused to attend until they learned that Rosie wouldn't be able to come. These situations troubled me, but I hoped that in time they would clear up. Still, Rosie was a professional. She gave her heart to the program, and sometimes it was difficult for her. I understood that.

From the beginning Rosie openly discussed her emotional problems. She was on medication, she told us. She suffered from depression and often felt rage. Her mother had died when Rosie was four days away from her eleventh birthday. The loss was always with her. She repeatedly said she missed the love and approval of a mother. Sometimes, she said, she saw me in that role. That was fine with me. I often felt maternal toward Rosie.

We did a special hour on depression, with Rosie discussing her own problems. At one point she hung upside down in a kind of harness to show what she did at home to relieve her depression. This was an important television program. It not only provided information to our viewers, but her candor helped us understand Rosie's emotional swings. In the early weeks of the program, we were all rather anxious about what kind of a mood Rosie would be in when she entered the dressing room. One day she would be upbeat and smiling, the next day dark and subdued. Gradually we learned to go with the flow, as they say, and not take too seriously or personally her morning disposition.

The View had been a great success for years, including the season before Rosie joined the program, but she took it to new heights with her great humor and energy. She was wonderful with children and treated us to charming stories about her own kids. She also loved Broadway, and we booked as many Broadway stars as we could. On her birthday Rosie asked to have a whole program of musical numbers performed by the casts of the Broadway shows she liked the most. We did so, in tribute to her. Rosie has probably sold more tickets to Broadway shows than any advertisements could have.

The premise of *The View* is that of a team working together, but for Rosie it was more like Diana Ross and the Supremes, as little by little she took over. Still, she was such a talent that we lived with it. All was pretty steady until the Donald Trump feud took place over the Christmas holidays. *The View* was about to go on a holiday hiatus. I left the program a week before the vacation began to join my friend the columnist Cindy Adams, on Judge Judy's yacht. While I was gone, Rosie attacked Trump on the air, calling him a "snake oil salesman," making fun of his hairstyle, and saying, among other things, that he had declared bankruptcy. I knew that was incorrect because in the past I had interviewed Trump on the subject. Trump threatened to sue ABC, *The View*, Rosie, and me. From my boat in the Caribbean, I joined Bill in a conference call to Trump. He was furious. Bill and I told him we would clear up the issue of the bankruptcy. That was all we said, and we assumed that would be the end of it. But it wasn't. Within a half hour Trump was talking to everyone. There wasn't a radio or TV show that he did not go on, hurling the most personal insults against Rosie. Trump had been my friend for many years. He often appeared on *The View*, and I had attended his wedding to the beautiful Melania. So I tried to make peace. ABC insisted that we make clear that he had not declared bankruptcy. I returned to *The View* a week before Rosie finished her vacation, and with the assistance of ABC's legal department, Rosie's own lawyer, and her brother, who advises her, we drafted a statement. I went on the air and said very clearly that Trump had not been bankrupt. End of possible lawsuit. I then criticized Trump for his insulting remarks about Rosie and did what I thought was a very strong defense of her. I said how valuable she was to the program and how much the viewers and the critics loved her. Trump then attacked me. Things got worse.

When Rosie finally returned to *The View*, to my amazement she angrily berated me in the dressing room for not defending her enough. She said I had told Donald Trump during the conference call from the yacht that I didn't want her on the program. Bill and I insisted that I never said any such thing. She refused to believe us. The funny thing is that even though her accusations were totally wrong and extremely upsetting, I could somehow understand her turmoil. Perhaps she thought of me as the mother who had once more abandoned her.

How did I get caught in the middle of a mess I'd originally had no part in? Yet, though it was a mess to me, the viewers loved the feud and the ratings soared.

Things got calmer. Rosie and I returned to our earlier friendly state. And the viewers, who now never knew what to expect from the outspoken Rosie, tuned in each day to see what she would do or say. ABC's executives were happy with Rosie. So, along with the network, I said to myself, "It is a new *View*. What is good for *The View* is good for me."

But if the result of the Trump feud was higher ratings, it also meant that now Rosie seemed to be enjoying feuds. She had a little feud with Kelly Ripa, another with Paula Abdul and her show, *American Idol*, and a bigger one with Bill O'Reilly, who began to call on his own program for her to be fired. She also, almost daily, attacked President Bush and condemned the invasion of Iraq. Elisabeth Hasselbeck, who supported Bush, reacted strongly and she and Rosie faced off time and again on the air. But it never became personal. However, as the weeks rolled on, the program became more and more political, and Rosie became more and more controversial. We were the talk of the industry. Like her or hate her, you could not stop watching Rosie. The network, though, was beginning to be uncomfortable. Even so, in the spring of 2007, they began to negotiate with Rosie for the next season. I deliberately had nothing to do with the negotiations. I didn't want another Star Jones experience, where the network made the decision and I took the blame.

By now I understood Rosie better and hoped she would come back. However, ABC Daytime and Rosie's representatives came to an impasse, and in April 2007, Rosie announced that she would not be returning to *The View*. I was disappointed, but unlike Star's departure, this announcement was all very amicable. Rosie said she would stay on the program until the end of June. We went on with business as usual.

Then came Wednesday, May 23. Joy said on the air that she thought George Bush should be impeached. Elisabeth defended Bush, and the beginning arguments were relatively civil—until Rosie jumped in. For several weeks Rosie had been expressing the thought that by invading Iraq, we Americans could also be considered terrorists. Some people, especially Bush supporters, took this to mean that she had said our troops were terrorists. Rosie never meant that. But as various viewers and critics began accusing her of that, she demanded that day that Elisabeth, who she felt represented the conservative point of view, defend her against these accusations. (It was similar to her demanding that I defend her against the remarks she had made about Donald Trump.)

Elisabeth responded by saying Rosie should defend her own remarks. Tempers became inflamed. There was name-calling and shouting. The accusations back and forth grew stronger. It was horrendous to watch. I know. I was not on the program that day, but I was at home watching. I called the control room and told them to go to commercial. It didn't happen. The shouting match went on. Bill Geddie later said if he had gone to commercial while Rosie was still talking, she might very well have walked off the set and that would have been worse.

Finally, thank heaven, we did go to commercial, and when we came back there was a guest, Alicia Silverstone, to be interviewed and the program went back to normal. But great harm had been done. That night every news program carried the screaming match, as did all the morning news programs. Everyone loved this catfight of all catfights. Elisabeth was in despair. She never expected such a confrontation. Rosie, I am sure, must also have been miserable.

The afternoon of the outburst, Rosie announced that since the next day, Thursday, was Kelli's fortieth birthday (it really was), she would be taking the day off. I moderated the Thursday show and opened the program by saying, "Auntie Barbara is back. There is peace in the kingdom." But as luck or irony would have it, President Bush gave a press conference on immigration at 11:00 a.m., and our program was not seen in most of the country. My attempt at peace and humor went unnoticed.

We were about to go off on the long Memorial Day weekend and had pretaped our Friday and Monday shows. (If I write another book, remembering that the Trump business also happened during a Christmas week holiday, I may title it *My Holiday Misadventures*.) Holiday or not, the network and I waited anxiously to hear whether Rosie was coming back to the program to finish her last three weeks.

Finally the word came. Rosie e-mailed me that she would not be coming back to *The View*. She gave no reason for leaving the program. What a way to end her year with us. ABC put out a brief statement on its Web site. Brian Frons, the president of ABC Daytime, thanked her "for her tremendous contribution to *The View*." I wrote in part that "I had brought Rosie to the show and she contributed to one of our most exciting and successful years." Rosie's press representative issued a statement from Rosie that said she was "extremely grateful" and added, "It has been an amazing year and I love all three women."

So there it was. I felt exhausted and sad. I e-mailed Rosie and said so. "I am very sorry that you decided not to come back but you must have felt it best for you and your family. I want you to know that my admiration and affection for you will remain unchanged." I meant it.

In the fall of 2007, however, I almost changed my mind when Rosie published a book called *Celebrity Detox*. She sent me an advance copy with a handwritten note proclaiming: "Here's my book. I hope you like it. Remember Barbara Walters, I love you for real." When I read the note I smiled, but when I read her book I wanted to cry. Rosie once more called me a liar who betrayed her when it came to the Donald Trump feud. (Will she ever get over him?) Other harsh and insulting accusations, some logical, some off the wall, filled page after page. Mixed up in the criticisms were protestations of love. It was such a seesaw of emotions that I didn't know how to answer her.

I am not a Pollyanna, but I truly believe that Rosie did not intend to hurt me. She herself must have come to regret what she'd written, because she canceled most of her television interviews promoting the book.

Rosie is a remarkable and loving woman. She has admirable personal values, and if she sometimes overreacts, it is out of her misplaced rage, hurt, and passionate convictions.

However, I admit that along with the sadness I felt when Rosie left *The View*, I also acknowledge some relief. The roller-coaster ride was over. We would take a deep breath and start a new chapter of *The View*.

But now came the question of where we would possibly find another high-profile, smart, funny, and savvy TV person. Brainstorm. Whoopi

Goldberg. Whoopi had appeared on *The View* something like twenty times over the years. Whenever we needed a special guest, we called on Whoopi. Now she was living in New York and doing an early-morning radio show. Could she, would she, also do *The View*?

She could. She would.

Our eleventh season began on September 4, 2007, the day after Labor Day. The audience went wild when Whoopi walked onstage. She sat down next to Joy and became a joy all to herself. Whoopi has such wisdom along with her humor. She is mellow and at the same time contributes to the edginess the program needs. We had made the perfect choice.

The following week, we announced that we were adding another permanent member to the cast. There would be no more different cohosts each day. Sherri Shepherd, a stand-up comedian, was becoming a favorite on our program. Like Whoopi, she had appeared on *The View* many times. She is divorced with a little boy, good-natured, down-to-earth, and naturally funny. With the two new additions to our panel, once more our ratings have soared. Joy, who has been on *The View* since day one, continues to add her own special brand of intelligence and humor. And Elisabeth is not only a lovely person off camera and on, but she more than holds her own, even when the whole panel might disagree with her. Believe me, it ain't easy. But it works. Indeed, almost thirteen years since *The View* made its debut, the program is more successful than ever.

Bill and I wanted *The View* to return to its roots as the program you could sit back and watch while sipping your second cup of coffee, and hear different opinions, on different subjects, from different women. Most of all we wanted everyone to just have a really good time. We are.

Exit

THE VIEW WAS A big part of my life, but not the biggest. What I was really known for was my work on 20/20, ABC's newsmagazine. But I was about to change all that.

On Monday, January 26, 2004, after twenty-five years on 20/20, I made the announcement that I was leaving the program. My contract still had two and a half years to go, and it was assumed that when it ended I would renew it for another five years. I left totally voluntarily. I had told no one of my decision except David Westin, president of ABC News, and Bill Carter, the leading television reporter of the *New York Times*. As planned, Bill Carter broke the story in his paper. This is how he put it:

> After conducting some of the most memorable television interviews of the last quarter-century for the ABC newsmagazine 20/20, Barbara Walters has decided to leave as co-anchor of the program.
>
> Ms. Walters has informed the president of ABC News, David Westin, that she will step down from 20/20 in September, and plans to scale back her workload to five or six news specials each year, including her highly rated Oscar night interviews, in addition to her regular appearances on *The View*, the ABC show she created. ABC News is expected to announce her departure from 20/20 today.

It was a big story in the television industry. Almost no one expected it. How to explain? Well, shortly after, for the same paper, the reporter

Virginia Heffernan wrote what she called my "Exit Interview." Here is part of that article:

> HEFFERNAN: You've been at *20/20* for twenty-five years. Why are you leaving now?
>
> WALTERS: I wanted to leave at the top. I had a sensational year including the second interview with Martha Stewart. Newsmagazines in general are somewhat in jeopardy. I didn't want anyone to say, "She was forced out. She had to leave."
>
> HEFFERNAN: But have you gotten tired of television news?
>
> WALTERS: It's changing. For example: we're going to hear that a woman had a love affair with a frog. The producers are going to come to me and say, "Barbara, this woman had a love affair with a frog. Diane Sawyer already has the woman lined up. Do you want to do the frog?" And I will say, "O.K., but only if I can get the frog and his mother." And they'll say: "But the frog wants an hour. And before you do the frog, the frog is going to do Oprah, O.K.?"

That about summed it up.

But it wasn't only about the competition from Diane or Oprah or any one person. It was more about the changing nature of the newsmagazines. The hard-news stories we used to report on were few and far between except on CBS's stalwart *60 Minutes*. But that newsmagazine catered to an older audience. *20/20* was after the young—the eighteen-to forty-nine-year-olds. That was the age group advertisers sought out, so increasingly we were after more celebrities, especially those with problems: more murderers and more frogs.

And it seemed that every celebrity, every murderer, every frog had a lawyer or a press agent all interviewing the interviewer to determine where they could get the most airings for their clients, what kind of questions would be asked, and how much promotion and advertising would be guaranteed. The interviewer had to *audition* to land the interview. The press agents for the celebrities were the worst, with endless demands and restrictions. ("You can't ask this." "You can't talk about that.") It wasn't much fun anymore for me, and it certainly wasn't prestigious.

I was plenty busy. Between 2002 and 2004 I interviewed around a hundred people for *20/20*, from Mariah Carey to Al Gore, and, after a twenty-five-year wait, a new interview with Fidel Castro. But interviews with heads of state, even someone as hard to land as Castro, were becoming less appealing to newsmagazines. Celebrities with problems were becoming less appealing to me.

It wasn't just that. Everybody in my business works hard. Well, almost everybody. But at that point I was swamped. I was not only fully involved with 20/20 and *The View*, which by then, seven years since its debut, was running full steam, I was also doing a minimum of three one-hour prime-time *Specials* a year.

On an average day I would get into my 20/20 office at 12:30, having just finished appearing on *The View* in a different building. I would go to the ABC cafeteria to pick up a salad and eat at my desk. When I came back to my office, there was a lineup of producers waiting to discuss whatever story they were doing with me. There was also my superconscientious booker, Katie Thomson, standing with a list of future guests. Then there was David Sloan, the executive producer of 20/20, with another list. If I was doing a *Special* Bill Geddie would be on the phone, anxious to discuss which interviews we should try to get that would not conflict with 20/20.

All this I could handle, and would have continued to, were it not for the big "get" and the pressure to be the first to secure an interview with whoever was making news, whoever was involved in a scandal, whoever was appearing in the newest film, whoever was accused of murdering his or her parents or wife or lover. In my last two years on 20/20 getting the "gets" had gotten out of control. I was not only competing with the newsmagazines on the other networks—*Dateline, 48 Hours, 60 Minutes*, and its spinoff, *60 Minutes II*—but with the new crop of nightly entertainment interview programs like *Entertainment Tonight* and *Access Hollywood* and the like. And finally, I was competing right inside my own network.

A little history.

ABC was the only network to have two competing women on two nighttime newsmagazines, Diane Sawyer and me. Roone Arledge had orchestrated that. If there was a big star on another network, Roone could not rest until he secured that star for ABC. It was the reason ABC had such a strong news lineup. For example, Roone had offered Dan Rather an anchor job at ABC while Walter Cronkite was still doing the evening news at CBS. It was CBS's determination to keep Dan that made that network take Walter off the program in 1981, before, he later said, he truly wanted to leave. Walter had many good years left as an effective anchor, but CBS more or less said "bye-bye," and Dan took over the news program. So Roone not only made waves at ABC, he also created choppy waters at other networks.

In 1989 Roone had lured Diane away from CBS, where she had been appearing very successfully on *60 Minutes*. He convinced her that, whereas on *60 Minutes* she was one of an ensemble, at ABC she would have her own magazine program and could choose to do any stories she wanted. Roone then created a new magazine program on Thursday nights at 10:00 p.m., called *Prime Time Live*. Diane's partner was the brash former White House correspondent Sam Donaldson. They were described as a sort of beauty-and-the-beast pairing—the cool, lovely Diane and the boisterous and irreverent Sam. But it was a pairing that didn't click. Still, ABC now had an hour newsmagazine at 10:00 p.m. on Thursday nights and another, *20/20*, on Friday nights, also at 10:00 p.m. Eventually, Charlie Gibson replaced Sam as Diane's partner. By this time, *Prime Time* was successful and after a certain point we at *20/20* felt we were competing as much with *Prime Time* as we were with newsmagazines on other networks.

Then, in 1999, Diane, a terrific reporter and so hardworking, took on another formidable assignment as the coanchor with Charlie Gibson of ABC's morning program, *Good Morning America*. That program was locked in a ferocious battle with its NBC counterpart, my old stomping ground the *Today* show. The morning shows were huge moneymakers, much more than the newsmagazines, because they had much more commercial time to sell, being on five days a week. It was therefore all the more important that Diane snag the big "get." We at *20/20* were suddenly competing not just with *Prime Time* but with *GMA* as well and we hated the whole idea.

Diane and I struggled to figure out what to do, especially when we were competing for the same newsmaker or celebrity for our respective newsmagazines. We each had a booker to help pave the way with a potential guest's lawyers, press agents, and other handlers. Then we would come in for the last round of phone calls or meetings. Our bookers were notoriously competitive. Diane and I were more polite. We would say something like this to the press agents: "I hope you will do the interview with me. If not, I hope you will do it with my colleague [Barbara or Diane]," whatever the case might be. We were out for the kill ourselves, but if we didn't get the interview, we didn't want one of the other networks to get it.

We were both so successful on our newsmagazines that, although most people don't remember this, in September 1998, the year before Diane started to appear on *GMA*, ABC put us on as cohosts on a Sunday-night edition of *20/20*. The network figured if one of us was good, two would be better. But although we enjoyed working together instead of competing, our hearts weren't in it. We were keeping our best stories for our own programs. The Sunday program died within a year. It was also decided that instead of *Prime Time* and *20/20* being two separate newsmagazines, they would merge into two nights of the more successful *20/20*. The staffs would also merge, but Diane and I would each still anchor on our own night. It was an awful time. The producers couldn't figure out which pieces should go on which nights, and in spite of having the same name, the programs were still competing. We hadn't taken lemons and made lemonade. We'd taken lemonade and made lemons.

The dual *20/20*s lasted just two years. When David Westin took over from Roone as president of the News Division we went back to two separate shows, *Prime Time* and *20/20*. By that time Hugh Downs had retired from *20/20* to live in Arizona. When Hugh left, I had a new partner, John Miller. John was ABC's crack investigative reporter. He also, among all of us, was the only person to have interviewed Osama bin Laden. I adored John. He was so smart and funny, but our partnership was short-lived. John gave up the fame and money of broadcasting to move to Los Angeles and join the L.A.P.D.'s chief, William Bratton, as bureau chief for the Counter-Terrorism and Criminal Intelligence Bureau. Currently John is assistant director of public affairs for the FBI in Washington. After John left, I was fortunate to have another John, John Stossel, as my new partner. John and I had worked together for so many years on *20/20* that it was an easy transition. But usually neither John nor Charlie, Diane's partner on both *Prime Time* and *GMA*, went after the "gets." Those were left more often to Diane and me.

There was one more wrinkle. Roone, in his ever-expanding desire to hire all the best talent, had persuaded Connie Chung to leave CBS, where she had been paired with Dan Rather on the evening news. Their duet in 1993 was as big a failure as the combination of Harry Reasoner and me years before. Roone promised Connie an anchor job, which put her in the position of competing with not one but two other female anchors, Diane and me.

I was and am very fond of Connie, and it couldn't have been easy for her. Whenever she wanted to go after a "get," she was told that Diane or I had first dibs. Connie's big coup was the first interview with Gary Condit, the congressman alleged to have been involved in the disappearance and presumed murder of Chandra Levy, an intern in Washington. But she had to struggle to get any other important interviews and she was understandably unhappy. Soon after her Condit piece, CNN offered her a job. David Westin, with great relief, I think, released her from her ABC contract.

So Connie left, but that didn't really help the situation between *GMA*, *Prime Time*, and *20/20*. Finally, in desperation, Westin assigned a conscientious arbitrator named Kerry Smith to make the choice as to who should go after which interview. It was a thankless job for her, and a particularly difficult setup for me. Kerry Smith's theory was that whoever seemed to have been working on the story earlier should be the one to whom it would be assigned. Diane not only had her bookers on *Prime Time* but another whole set of bookers on *Good Morning America*. They booked both short-term and long-term. I also knew that in the early-morning competition, it was more important for the daily *GMA* to score a big "get" than for the weekly *20/20*. I was running as fast as I could, but it seemed to me it was an uneven playing field.

Moreover, Diane could offer a guest a package of two or three appearances on *GMA* as well as a more lengthy appearance on *Prime Time*. I didn't have that option. To make it even more difficult, the *Today* show was doing the same thing. The competition between the two programs was fierce. And my lighthearted daytime program, *The View*, was just not in the league of *GMA*, *Today*, or the other newsmagazines.

Today, when Diane and I no longer compete, we have a relationship of good humor and affection. I mean that sincerely. Diane is a wonderful reporter, the best. Back then, however, we often found ourselves in that hated competition, and as much as we wanted, there seemed to be nothing we could do about it. We never criticized each other in public or in print, but the conflict was well known inside ABC.

So that was more or less how things stood in 2003. I complained to Jackie about the show almost every time I talked with her. "Why don't you leave, Mom?" she would say. "You've been doing that program for twenty-five years. What else do you have to prove? Leave now while you still feel good about it." Maybe she was right, I thought. I also sought the advice of Monica Caulfield, my trusted assistant. She, perhaps more than anyone, knew what my schedule was like. I remember her saying, "It's a great big world out there and it will set you free." Still, I wasn't sure. That summer I walked the beach with two wise and close couples, Elizabeth and Felix Rohatyn and Louise and Henry Grunwald, and discussed over and over again my feelings about wanting to give up

20/20. Felix had been the U.S. ambassador to France. Henry had been, for years, the editor in chief of Time Inc. Both men knew what it was like to leave extremely important and influential positions. Their wives were also very informed and understanding. I could fully explore my conflicted feelings with the four of them.

The View, then, was like dessert, fun and not hard to do. The *Specials* took time but were in general also fun. Working on 20/20, on the other hand, seemed debilitating and exhausting. But would I miss it? Would I miss the rare interview with the president or a head of state? Would I, now that I was not on a major news program, miss being seated at some black-tie dinner next to a visiting prime minister? To that I said no. It is usually much more fun *not* to be seated next to a prime minister, especially when he or she speaks no English. But I might not even be invited to the party. As an agent I knew said of one of his clients who had retired, "I love you—and I will miss you." Moreover, and more important, I realized that I was ending the major part of my career and might have trouble filling my days. Oh, well, I told myself, I can finally learn Spanish, go to museums, travel, and stay in a foreign country for more than one day. I kept walking the beach until I was sure.

Then, in the fall of 2003, David Westin called and asked if he could come to my office and talk. He wanted to tell me of a new plan to make the booking competition between Diane and me less difficult. He was as unhappy with the situation as I was. But by then I had made up my mind. Before he could describe his plan, I stopped him. "No need to tell me," I said. "Don't be upset. But I'm leaving 20/20." He was stunned, and I realize now that I never did hear what his plan was. But I did tell him *my* plan and my reasons. I asked him to please keep my decision a secret from everyone until I had decided how and when to announce it. I asked him not to tell even Michael Eisner. This was a big thing to ask, but David understood. I think the world of David Westin. He is a man of his word, and his word was all I needed. Then he said, "Whatever you want to do, I just can't afford to lose you. You are an icon. [Nice to hear, I thought, but there are a lot of icons these days.] You will stay in News. We will work something out."

And we did. As I had no agent, I asked a brilliant entertainment lawyer, Allen Grubman, to represent me and meet with David to discuss my future at ABC News. True to his word, Westin offered me a new long-term contract and asked if I would agree to do four to five prime-time *Specials* a year. These would include the two very popular hours I had been doing for so many years, *10 Most Fascinating People* and the

Academy Award *Special*. The others would be mutually agreed to. As it has turned out, in the years since I left 20/20, I have also done three extremely highly rated and controversial noncelebrity *Specials*—one on transgender children who consider themselves born into the wrong bodies, and two others, one on the question of the existence of heaven, and the other on the new science of longevity, leading to the search to live to beyond a hundred. (I am planning to do that myself. Where are my vitamins?) David also asked me to continue to contribute commentary when a president, head of state, or important celebrity whom I'd interviewed, died. From time to time, he said, I might also be asked to do an interview for a *Special* if it was deemed very important. (This would be the case for my interviews in France with the doctor of the woman who had the first face transplant after her dog mauled her, and the hour with Terri Irwin in Australia.) I also contributed to the coverage of the funerals of Presidents Ronald Reagan and Gerald Ford.

I agreed to continue to do this kind of reporting and signed the contract. Forget the language lessons, forget the museums. I would still have a full plate but, on the other hand, I would be out of the daily competition. What a great relief that has turned out to be.

We decided that although I would make the announcement of my leaving 20/20 a few months later in January 2004, I would continue on the program until September so that I could launch the person who would take my place. David Westin chose Elizabeth Vargas, a fine reporter.

When January came I called Bill Carter and said I wanted to speak to him confidentially. Bill had done quite a few stories on me in the past, including a 1992 *New York Times Magazine* cover story. I wanted to release my statement in the most dignified way, so I gave my news to him as an exclusive. The day before the article was to appear, David Westin told Michael Eisner and Jeffrey Schneider, the ABC News vice president who oversees communication.

The next morning, Carter's column appeared on the front page of the *New York Times* Business Section. When I finally saw my words in print I felt both scared and relieved. My twenty-five years on 20/20, the mainstay of my career, were over. I had done the deed, and I was on to a new and uncharted course of my life.

I thought my colleagues would not be surprised. They knew how heavy a workload I had and how I struggled over the "gets." Certainly, I thought, my executive producer, David Sloan, knew. I would really miss working with David. He was my friend as well as extremely talented at his job. But, as it turned out, neither he nor anyone on the staff had any idea. As soon as I arrived in my office, I hastily called the staff together. Some were in tears (perhaps because they were also concerned about losing their jobs; David Sloan and I assured them this would not happen). Most just hugged me and asked that I do my last story or any future stories with them. I loved my producers. We had worked very closely together, preparing and editing. I was very hands-on. Some of them had worked only with me all these years on the program. I promised to keep my hand in and do stories for *20/20* now and then. It was an extremely emotional meeting.

That fall ABC News presented a two-hour retrospective *Special* of my work called *25 on 20/20*. It was painstakingly produced by Martin Clancy, who had worked with me on so many interviews and reports for so many years. Martin chose highlights from each of the twenty-five years and each category of interview. There were the heads of state, the politicians, the human interest stories, the murderers, alleged or convicted, the celebrities, the famous and the infamous. It was a list, culled from hundreds of interviews, that even surprised me. I was very proud of the program, which aired September 17, 2004.

After I left *20/20*, the show underwent somewhat of a change. My departure made it even more difficult for the program to attract the big "gets." The format often turned instead to theme programs, with one subject being investigated or analyzed for an hour. John Stossel did a whole series of programs looking at myths about things we fear but shouldn't. There were also hours on subjects like hate, lust, happiness, and greed. The program still ran important interviews but less often with big stars or world leaders. Those super "gets" more and more went to Oprah or to Diane for *Good Morning America*. Even so *20/20* still continues and is an important and valuable program.

Once I announced that I was leaving, I was deluged with requests for interviews and invitations to be honored by this or that organization. It was like reading my own obituary. I hadn't retired from television, but it looked as if I had. I turned down all the so-called honors and most of the interviews. I thought the "exit" interview I had done for the *New York Times* said it all. The interviews I did do were with Oprah, one for her magazine *O* and one for her television program. As I have written, Oprah is one of the people I could interview again and again. Now the tables were turned and she wanted to interview me.

Not only did I feel I owed her these interviews because of our long-term relationship, I also felt, as I haven't told you before, that I owed her my life. Well, not exactly. This is what happened. In 1995 I was at a luncheon honoring top women in communications. The lunch was supposed to be over by 2:00 so we could all get back to work, but the event went long, and Oprah was forced to go overtime in her presentation to author Toni Morrison. It was close to 3:00 when I got back to my office, where I was startled to be greeted by my terrified assistants in tears, by the then president and COO of ABC, Robert Iger, and by the police. Seems that while I was listening to Oprah, a freak windstorm had blown a beam off a construction site across the street from my office and sent it crashing through my windows. My desk, which was glass, was shattered by the beam, and my whole office was covered in shards. I don't want to think what would have happened if I'd been at my desk at the time.

For my television interview with Oprah, her producers asked if my daughter would appear. Jackie, who almost always chose to stay out of the limelight, said yes. She actually has stage fright, so this appearance was an act of love. I laughed when Oprah asked Jackie how she felt about my leaving *20/20*. Jackie responded that she had wanted me to leave so I could have more time for myself. "But the bad thing is," she said, "she's going to call me all the time now."

I especially wanted to do the interview for Oprah's magazine. I subscribe to *O* and always find many articles I want to read. Oprah flew to New York in August and came to my apartment to do the interview. Everyone in my home loved her—Cha Cha, Icodel, and wonderful George. (George Pineda, who had worked for Merv, became my treasured chief of staff a few years after my divorce. He handles many of my business affairs as well as taking care of almost every aspect of my life.) Oprah was so warm and gracious. We all had our photographs taken with her, and later she signed them individually, placed them in silver frames, and sent them to us. We are true fans.

She and I talked about a variety of things for the magazine, but what affected me the most is the last question and answer. I reprint it here:

OPRAH: What does being "Barbara Walters" mean?

ME: I'm not sure. I realize how blessed I have been but sometimes I still feel inadequate. I don't cook. I can't drive. Most of the time, when I look back on what I've done, I think: *Did I do that? Why didn't I enjoy it more? Was I working too hard to see?*

As I said this, I looked up at Oprah and saw that she had tears in her eyes. I had touched a chord. Without any more words, we both knew what we had achieved and perhaps what we had given up. Most hard-working women would understand what we felt.

One of those hardworking women is Connie Chung, who gave a lovely luncheon for me soon after I left 20/20. Connie invited almost every female television journalist from New York and Washington. Most I knew. There was also a whole new and younger group. During the toasts I heard over and over how I had "paved the way," "opened the doors," and "fought the wars" for them. I felt proud and happy . . . and a hundred years old.

Then ABC gave an official party for me on September 22, two days before I was to leave 20/20. I thought it would be a smallish affair with publicists and publishers invited because, after all, I was going to con-tinue to do *Specials* and would need to keep up my contacts. I decided, therefore, not to invite any of my own friends who were not in the busi-ness. I figured it would be a routine party with a lot of industry people and would bore them. I also told Jackie, who was living in Maine, not to come in for it. "It's no big deal," I told her.

The party was held from 6:00 to 8:00 p.m. in one of the cavernous floors of ABC's Times Square studio, where *GMA* originated every weekday morning. I didn't want to be the first to arrive, so I came shortly before 6:30 to find the entrance lined with dozens of paparazzi. Were they all there for me? Was anybody else coming? I entered to find the room jammed. People laughing, talking, greeting one another. There were people from every network, and many, it appeared, hadn't seen each other in years. David Westin, who had been so sensitive to my needs those last months, was at the door, greeting everyone.

All of my colleagues (producers, editors, writers, on and on) were there—must have been a hundred of them—as well as all the ABC cor-respondents: Peter Jennings, now very warm and gracious, along with Diane Sawyer, Charlie Gibson, Robin Roberts, Elizabeth Vargas, and John Stossel, and all my colleagues from ABC News. Ted Koppel and Sam Donaldson, my old buddies from my earliest days at ABC, flew in from Washington and then flew back the same night. The then secretary-general of the United Nations, Kofi Annan, was there, as were New York's Mayor Michael Bloomberg, Donald and Melania Trump (in happier days for the Trumps and me), and, most touching to me, Christopher Reeve, who came in his specialized wheelchair with his wife, Dana. And there was the mix of Geraldo Rivera, Bill O'Reilly, Roger Ailes (head of the Fox News Channel), Paula Zahn, Connie Chung, Maury Povich, Judge Judy, Bryant Gumbel, Katie Couric, and, of course, all the ladies of *The View*. Henry Kissinger, one of the rare guests not in the business, arrived to join the mix.

Peter Jennings took the microphone and talked about some of the stories we had covered together over the years, starting with Sadat's historic trip to Jerusalem in 1977. Peter had been at ABC when I arrived there thirty years earlier. He now saw working with me in a happier light, and with his lovely wife, Kayce, was in great form that night. Who could ever have imagined that the following year Peter would die of lung cancer? His death devastated all of us.

Michael Eisner sent sentimental greetings via tape. Anne Sweeney, the very smart president of ABC, told of being a page at the company years earlier and how she had been told not to approach the "talent," which was me. Fortunately I had evidently been very friendly to her. Hey, you never know when the page will one day turn up as the president.

Then some surprises. Dan Rather, who had just days before been excoriated by the White House and much of the press for a controversial and, it turned out, inaccurate news report on George W. Bush, braved the waiting line of paparazzi shouting questions at him. So did Martha Stewart, who had been convicted and would soon start her prison sentence. The fact that both Dan and Martha came meant a great deal to me.

Everybody kissed me and toasted me. Do I sound like an awful jerk? Should this have meant so much? I'm not sure, but it did. I felt rather like Sally Field, who famously said upon accepting an Academy Award, "You like me . . . you really like me."

When the reception broke up at about 9:00 p.m.—late, as no one seemed to want to leave—I once again walked past the long line of paparazzi. Cameras snapped. Flashbulbs flashed. I laughed and posed. With me were David and Sherrie Westin, Phyllis McGrady, and David Sloan. I invited all of them to the famous restaurant Le Cirque for a two-martini dinner. Finally, thoroughly sloshed, I went home with memories that warm me to this day.

If I had second thoughts about leaving *20/20*, and sometimes in the wee small hours of the night I did, by morning they were gone. Most of what I felt was relief. No more phone calls, letters, arguments, pleas for the next "get." No more hours and hours of homework each week, except for *The View* and my *Specials*. And then, as the song goes, "The days dwindled down to a precious few," and it was time to go.

I was hoping that the last interview I would do on *20/20* would be with President Bush. In September, after he had won the Republican nomination for reelection, I had put in a request to interview him. I was told he would consider it. Earlier in the summer, however, I had received a whispered phone call from a woman named Mary Kay Letourneau. She had recently been released from a seven-year term in prison for her sexual relationship with an underage student named Vili Fualaau. (Later they married.) I had talked with Mary Kay years earlier before she was sent to prison, and she told me then that I had seemed sympathetic. She now said, over the phone, that she was considering telling all about her experience before and after her prison sentence and would I be interested in doing the very first interview since her release? I said yes and hoped I could do it in August or early September. But Mary Kay couldn't make up her mind if she really did want to talk. Finally she did, just a week before my last day on the air. I would have to go to Seattle, Washington, to do the interview, as she was not allowed to leave the state. The way the timetable worked out, it meant that her interview would air Friday, September 24, 2004, my announced last day on 20/20.

While I was weighing this, a call came from President Bush's office. He had agreed to do the interview with me. Were we ready to commit for next week?

The president of the United States or a convicted child molester? The president? The child molester? The president? The child molester? The powers that be chose Mary Kay Letourneau.

I rest my case.

To Be Continued . . .

*J*UST FOR THE FUN OF IT I sat down to write this final chapter on New Year's Day, January 1, 2007. A lot of things came together for me that weekend that, as it has turned out, still hold true. Let me turn back the page.

I had just finished a telephone call with Jackie, who was bringing me up-to-date on New Horizons, her camp in Maine for troubled adolescent girls. The program has been very successful, and I believe that she has saved many a young girl's life. I am so proud of what she has accomplished. I undoubtedly did some things wrong when she was growing up, but I tell myself that I also must have done some things right to have helped produce this very special woman. I love her dearly and admire her enormously.

By chance I had lunch yesterday with some friends, including a nice man I went out with a long time ago, John Heimann. We used to see each other when Jackie was in her terrible teens. He reminded me of how worried I was about her and about myself back then. If I could have only looked ahead and seen her as she is today. The road has long since smoothed out.

I took a vacation over the holidays and part of it was spent with my close friends Annette and Oscar de la Renta. Oscar is, of course, the famed dress designer, but he also owns a great resort in Punta Cana in the Dominican Republic. Annette and Oscar are the kindest hosts. I have gone to their home every Christmas for many years now.

At night the de la Rentas often invite friends from all over the area. One evening a couple brought their son who was severely mentally and physically impaired. I was used to avoiding films and plays about such children. Although this boy was far more disabled than my sister, I was afraid it might stir up old sad memories. But the point of this story is that I was not upset. My strongest emotion was the compassion I felt for the young man and his parents. I was no longer second-guessing what I might have done or not done about my sister. That road has finally smoothed out, too.

Because I have so small a family, my friends have become my family. That's why I spend holidays with some of them and, throughout the year, try to see each of them as often as possible. I think a lot of people consider friends to be even closer than relatives. I would list all of my friends' names, but I am bound to leave some out and that would do more harm than good. I am writing about certain of those friends now because they were the ones I happened to see over the holidays.

After I returned to New York I had a busy weekend. On December 31, I had lunch with my friend Lola Finkelstein, who, you may remember, was with me in Israel twenty-five years ago for Moshe Dayan's funeral. She now has four married children, eleven grandchildren, and two sets of twin great-grandchildren. She is a very well read and highly intelligent woman. Her great passion these days is playing bridge. Our lives are so different that you may think we would have little in common, but we have so many memories to share and we know each other so well. I tell her how rich she is with such a large, loving family. She tells me how rich my life is with such a fascinating career. We are both right. We also know that nobody has everything. We hug each other and say so.

Earlier this week I also had a New Year's lunch date with my oldest pal in terms of years of friendship, Joyce Ashley. She is a fine psychoanalyst. We have known each other since childhood and gone through marriages, divorces, and all kinds of experiences together. We tell each other, as we often do, how extremely fortunate we are to have the other in our life.

Looking back, which is often what one does during the time of the New Year, I realize how many people have been a close part of my life and for so long. My assistant Monica Caulfield had been with me for twenty-seven years. She was my right arm. I watched her grow and blossom and marry Billy Dahlinger, such a perfect match. Monica was simply wonderful. In April of 2008, Monica retired and moved out of New York City. I will never forget our wonderful years together and wish her great happiness.

I have another assistant, named Monique Medina. Monique has only been with me for five years but she is as lovely and calm and efficient as

Monica. The fact that one of my assistants was named Monica and the other Monique drives people crazy. Someone would call up and say, "Is this Monica?" and the answer was, "No, this is Monique." So the next time they called, they would ask, "Is this Monique?" Answer, "No, it's Monica." No wonder they sometimes hung up.

While I am talking about the people I live with professionally practically day in and day out, I must mention once more that beautiful brunette, Lori Klein, who has been doing my makeup now for fifteen years. My on-camera face is pretty much like my off-camera face, only for the past few years, when I am on the air, Lori has given me false eyelashes. They look great, but I can't put them on by myself, so if Lori glues them on in the evening before I go out, I try to sleep with them in place so I'll look good the next day. This usually doesn't work out. I wake up looking cockeyed, with one eyelash on and one off. Anyway, the point of all this is not to discuss eyelashes but to tell you how special Lori is. She is always peaceful, always supportive. Many chapters ago, I wrote about Bobbie Armstrong, my makeup artist during my days on the *Today* show and when I first went to ABC. She was a comfort in those difficult years, just as Lori is today.

Then there is Bryant Renfroe, whom I have also written about. Bryant has been styling, cutting, and coloring my hair now for twenty-four years (sorry that you had to find out I am not a natural blond). When I travel I am contractually permitted to take with me one person, supposedly an assistant, but more often than not, I take Bryant. He is not just a great traveling companion, but the producers welcome him because Bryant is also a whiz at dealing with airline reservations and is a superwhiz when it comes to computers. In flight he often calls up on his computer many of the videos I need to see, and I am able to watch a lot of material I might otherwise have missed. For example, in September 2006, on our endless trip to Australia, where, as I've said, I interviewed Terri Irwin, Bryant had on his computer the whole memorial service for her husband that I had not had time to view and needed to see before doing the interview. Bryant also gives me the latest news which he reads on his BlackBerry. He jokingly says, "I am strong like bull," so let me tell you that he also helps me put my carry-on into the overhead compartment. All that and he cuts my bangs.

Monica, Monique, Lori, Bryant—invaluable as coworkers and friends.

Then at home sweet home, which wouldn't be sweet without my

beloved Icodel Tomlinson, thirty-five years of running our home with the loveliest smile you have ever seen. Icodel is an angel on earth and my trusted confidante. I would, however, be remiss if I didn't remind you of another resident in our home. Well, actually Icodel says she is really one-half dog and one-half person. I am talking about Cha Cha, my honey-colored Havanese. My home is a place of serenity except for the rare occasions when Cha Cha feels she must bark.

After all these digressions I returned to New York in time for New Year's and spent a glamorous but cozy New Year's Eve at the home of Sir Howard Stringer, now the chairman and CEO of Sony Corporation, and his wife, Dr. Jennifer Patterson. Sir Howard (before he was knighted by the Queen), you may remember, was the man at CBS who offered me the big contract to leave ABC. Even though I turned him down, we liked each other so much that we became good friends. His wife, Jennifer, is a delight, very smart and very funny. This was the second New Year's I spent with them and other mutual friends, including two wonderful writers, Nora Ephron and her husband, Nick Pileggi. We drank champagne, toasted one another, and watched the fireworks from their terrace. This year they had a new guest, Queen Noor of Jordan, the widow of King Hussein. Queen or not, she had no other plans for New Year's Eve. She arrived looking gorgeous in a slinky white evening gown, hardly the picture of the grandmother she had recently become. I had done the very first interview with the young American-born queen and her husband when they married back in 1978. I had also done the first television interview with her after the death of her distinguished and long-reigning husband. More firsts to think about. More memories. My long-ago reporting on peace between Israel and Egypt seems like something that happened in another century. Come to think of it, it was.

At midnight Howard and Jennifer turned on the television so we could all watch the ball drop in Times Square. Times Square is on Forty-second Street and Broadway. Just six blocks away is the street sign that reads "Lou Walters Way." People who pass the sign may be puzzled as to who Lou Walters was and why there would be a street named after him. When I see that sign, as I often do, pictures flash through my mind. All those opening nights watching my father's productions . . . sitting at his table near the entrance of the club . . . my father with his "squawk box" on the table so he can give directions backstage . . . my mother all dressed up, and my sister, so eager to go backstage, where she feels most at home. The columnists come up to the table and clasp my father's hand. "Great show, Lou," they say. And I am there, serious, shy.

On New Year's Eve, as on Thanksgiving, birthdays, any celebration—there we all are. I still dream about my family. Sometimes sweet dreams, sometimes sad. But we were indeed a family and what I am is what they helped me to become. I look up at that sign when I chance to pass it and smile.

I "RETIRED" FROM 20/20, but I did not, as many thought, retire from television. I am still working every day, what with *The View* and the *Specials*. Moreover, I have a new venture: radio. I now do a weekly live program on Sirius satellite radio with Bill Geddie. We take phone calls from listeners, discuss hot topics, argue, agree, and just have a swell time. It is fun to work with Bill, whose opinions are just different enough from mine to make for lively discussions. I don't need to put on makeup or get my hair done for Sirius, and I expect to be doing radio until my dotage. Sirius also is airing almost all the interviews I did for my *Specials* over the past thirty years. Listeners seem to enjoy hearing them as much as they used to enjoy viewing them.

I particularly liked doing the *Special* last year that I told you about, called *Live to Be 150*. It was cutting-edge science, including the latest in stem-cell research and a drug that now fights aging in mice and may in the future work on humans. Mind-boggling! As part of the *Special* I interviewed half a dozen on-the-ball men and women who were each 100 years old or older. My favorite was 101-year-old Dorothy, who came with her 94-year-old boyfriend. Dorothy told me that she is happier now than she has ever been. She had been married, she said, for forty-six years before her husband died, but it was a bad marriage and finally she had found true love. So there you are. It really is never too late.

I also enjoyed for the same *Special*—well, "enjoyed" isn't exactly the right word—speeding at 150 miles an hour with Paul Newman at the wheel of his race car. I held on for dear life as we careened around two laps of the track. Later in the day, Paul came in first in his race, beating guys half his age. Sadly, this turned out to be his last television interview. He died in 2008 at age 83. He was a superb actor and a generous, caring man. Most of all, as I wrote to her, he cared about his extremely talented and living wife, Joanne Woodward.

So now there is the question of when to truly retire. Let me tell you a final story.

Last New Year's, before I went out to celebrate, I watched my very dear friend Beverly Sills host a program on public television called *Great*

Performances. Few people have delivered greater performances than Beverly, who was one of the world's most acclaimed operatic sopranos. She was a relatively new friend; I had only known her for about thirty years. After Beverly made the decision to end her operatic career, she went on to become the general director of the New York City Opera, then chair of Lincoln Center, and still later chair of the Metropolitan Opera. When she left the New York City Opera, her husband, Peter, gave her a gold ring with an engraved inscription. When I decided to leave 20/20, Beverly gave me the ring. She said I should pay attention to what was inscribed. The ring says, "I did that already."

Sadly my darling Beverly died of cancer in July 2007. In September, I spoke at the memorial service the Metropolitan Opera held for her. Thousands of people filled the opera house, up to the highest tier. To me the most important person there was Beverly's daughter, Muffy. Muffy was born totally deaf and has never heard her mother sing. But Muffy is an amazing woman, smart and sensitive, with Beverly's sense of humor. She is truly her mother's daughter. We stay in close touch and share our love of her remarkable mother. I miss Beverly every day.

Memories. Memories. Mine are mostly good. The ghosts have receded, but occasionally they come to the fore. I recently gave a dinner party, and, as is sometimes my custom, at the end of the meal I introduced a question for each guest to answer in turn. The question I posed was, "Looking back at your life, what do you regret the most?" When Sarah Simms Rosenthal, whose husband, Dr. Mitchell Rosenthal, had been so helpful with Jackie, answered, "I regret not having been with my mother when she died," tears stung my eyes. I, too, still regret not having been with my mother at the end. But no one can undo the past.

This is the most important thing: I am probably happier and more at peace than I have ever been. I know I had a fantastic career. I know I traveled everywhere and met almost every important person there was to meet. I achieved more than I could ever have imagined.

My colleague Don Hewitt repeatedly tells me that he and I lived through the golden age of television news. Perhaps he is right. But I don't want to spend my days looking back. I do know this, however: In this time of instant Internet news, cell phones that take videos, and a profusion of blogs where everyone is a reporter, there will be little chance for any single person to have the kind of career that I've had. If I was, perhaps, atop of the game, I also had the advantage of being ahead of the game. How lucky I was. How lucky!

Perhaps I have made it a little easier for some of the women who followed in my footsteps—maybe even for some in other careers. Television is no longer a man's world. Perhaps, too, I helped to change that. If so, I am very grateful. I am blessed seven times over. And there are even some days when I think I deserve it. But I also think it may be time for me to finally say, "I did that already."

It is time to stop auditioning.

Except for this book.

Afterword to the Vintage Books Edition

S O WHAT HAS HAPPENED since last we met? *Audition* was published May 6, 2008. Before that date, almost no one had read the book because the publisher had embargoed it. There were no advance copies released, not even to book reviewers, because we didn't want any portions of it to dribble out in gossip column items. The publishers were very serious about keeping everything secret.

You can imagine my shock and dismay, therefore, when, a week before the pub date, the news broke that I'd written about a secret romance I'd had thirty years before with Senator Edward Brooke, the married black senator from Massachusetts. You must have seen the salacious, scandalous "leak" because it was everywhere—the gossip columns, entertainment programs, the tabloids, and practically every talk show. And who was responsible? Oprah.

Here's how it happened. Oprah did the first interview with me about the memoir. We taped the hour-long program in Chicago on April 24, 12 days before the publication date, with the agreement that it would not air until May 6. I knew the one and only Oprah would be the perfect person to launch *Audition*, and indeed, her questions were penetrating and far-ranging. We talked about my sister, Jackie, and my father. We talked about *The View* and about my long-ago forbidden relationship with Senator Brooke. I told her that I'd written to tell him about his inclusion in the memoir, and he had graciously responded. I was happy with Oprah's interview and didn't give it much thought after I returned to New York. Until the sensational story suddenly hit the airwaves.

It turned out that Oprah's people were using the Senator Brooke material as her on-air promotions for our interview and the press had picked it up. I probably would have done the same thing had I been her.

But the result was that until my memoir was published, all anyone knew was that I had had an affair with a married black man. At first I was appalled. That reminiscence took up fewer than six pages out of the book's six hundred, and I worried that people would think my candid and hopefully dignified memoir about my personal and public life was just about that ancient affair. As you have read, I had written about it because I was trying to point out how different our mores were three decades ago. Today, with a black man as our president, these differences seem even more apparent.

The night of May 6, Michael Bloomberg, New York's mayor and an old friend, threw a book party for me at his home. It was a great success. There were people there from my past, pals from my present, my adored daughter, Jackie, my beloved Icodel and George, colleagues from my television world, and, of course, the ladies from *The View*. The story about my affair with Senator Brooke was still making headlines, and in my remarks I jokingly disclosed that *View* cohost Sherri Shepherd, an African American, was actually my daughter. That got a big laugh, but I didn't know what to expect from the public when I set out on the book's publicity tour. The first book store I went into had a big sign in front of the stacks of *Audition*: "Read the scandalous book everyone is talking about." Gulp. But you know, in the early days of publication, the so-called "scandal" helped catapult my memoir instantly to the top of the bestseller lists, where it remained for months. And when people did read the book with its glorious silver and gold cover, they realized, thank goodness, that there was a good deal more to it than Senator Brooke. So thank you, dear Oprah. Once more, you did me a very good turn.

The book tour was both exhilarating and exhausting. The publisher had booked me into sixteen cities on both coasts and seemingly every state in between—plus Canada. Some pre-dawn travel mornings, I felt I was back on the *Today* show. But it was always uplifting. People waited in line, sometimes for hours, in all kinds of weather. (So many people crowded into a theater in Portsmouth, New Hampshire, that the balcony started to buckle and the fire department evacuated the building.) Many people who came to the signings had already bought the book and were coming to buy another and have me sign it. Almost all of them had their own stories to tell—someone in their family similar to my sister, or a child who had experienced a turbulent adolescence, like my daughter. Many women told me about the discrimination they'd faced while climbing the ladder to accomplishment, and said they felt a kinship with me and my own struggles. The tour was gratifying on so many levels, not the least of which was the acknowledgment of how many people still bought and read books.

I finished the better part of my tour in late June, but took a break on June 18 to welcome Michelle Obama to *The View* as a cohost, sitting at the table with the rest of us. She was charming and lovely in a black and white dress she told us had cost her $148. I mention this because it came up in Damascus, where I spent the Fourth of July week and had a private off-the-record, off-camera meeting with Syria's President Bashar al-Assad and his Syrian-born, English-educated wife, Asma Assad. You can imagine my amazement when President Assad asked if it was true that Michelle Obama's dress had cost only $148. It turned out that President Assad was as up to date on American fashions as he was on American politics. I had, rather boldly, brought a copy of *Audition* for Mrs. Assad, whom I had met once before. For the president, I brought a copy of Barack Obama's *Dreams from My Father.* During our meeting, I also mentioned a controversial book that had just been published in America—*What Happened: Inside the Bush White House and Washington's Culture of Deception.* Written by President Bush's former press secretary, Scott McClellan, it is a damning account of McClellan's unhappy experience in the White House. I had decided not to bring it to President Assad as I saw no reason, when abroad, to put down my own president. To my surprise, President Assad told me he already had a copy of the book. I found both President and Mrs. Assad well informed and, Syria having been designated a terrorist country, anxious to have a better relationship with America.

Damascus surprised me. I had been there briefly once before but I hadn't remembered it as so modern, with beautiful restaurants and shops selling name-brand European merchandise. Yet, five minutes away from the up-to-date section of the city was the ancient bazaar with its mosques and churches rising out of narrow winding streets where one could purchase anything from spices to precious jewels. Fortunately or unfortunately, I didn't have time for shopping. I had to hurry home to leave almost right away for a quick trip to Paris.

Carla Bruni, the glamorous new wife of France's President, Nicolas Sarkozy, had recently produced an album of breathy romantic music. The album was about to be introduced in America and, as she knew my name, she had decided that I would be the one to do an interview with her for the States. I found France's first lady enchanting. We were doing the interview in the grand salon of the famed Ritz Hotel. Mme. Sarkozy arrived exactly on time with a tote bag full of T-shirts. She asked our opinion of which one to wear. We chose the pale blue. She then changed in the ladies' room. During the course of the interview, she played the guitar, sang a song from her new album, and answered some rather personal questions. I had read of her publicized affairs with various married men, like Eric Clapton and Mick Jagger. Didn't that make her an adulteress, I asked? I admired her reply. Because she had been single at the time, it was not she who was being adulterous but rather the married men who were the adulterers. Touché, Mme. Sarkozy.

I had a brief summer vacation when I returned from France and suddenly it was fall. For much of the autumn, it seemed to me that I was either giving talks or presenting awards, most as a result of my book. In one ten-day period, I made a speech for a *New York Times* forum, another for a *Newsweek* magazine forum, and still one more for a motivational conference in Toronto. I received an award from The City College of New York, gave an award to Condoleezza Rice, moderated a debate for the Aspen Institute which featured former Secretary of State, Madeleine Albright, and gave out honors to recipients at the Spanish Institute dinner. *!Hola!*

It was a relief to get back to my day job, my *Specials* for ABC News and appearing at least twice a week on ABC's daytime pride and joy, *The View*. This little late-morning talk show I created with the inspired contribution of Bill Geddie almost thirteen years ago shot up this year in a blaze of political controversy, with Whoopi Goldberg, Joy Behar, and Sherri Shepherd holding forth on the more or less liberal Democratic point of view and Elisabeth Hasselbeck bravely fighting for the conservative Republicans. Sparks flew. Often the sparks were more like firecrackers. Every morning during the long primary season brought more heat, more humor, and yes, even some light to the show. Trying to keep on my ABC News hat of objectivity, I steered somewhere in the middle. My aim was to keep the peace without hindering the pace.

Many new viewers began to turn into the program to get the news of the day. There was hardly a morning when we didn't make the papers, hardly a week without our spirited political opinions being mentioned on the cable talk shows or the news magazines. We were America's kitchen table in the long and riveting campaign for the presidency. Barack Obama had been on the program several years earlier, before he was a candidate for the presidency, and as I told you, Michelle Obama had been a cohost in June. Cindy McCain had also appeared as a cohost and had described her appearance as a happy occasion. But in September 2008 when Senator John McCain, the Republican nominee, agreed to be on with us, along with a second appearance by Mrs. McCain, we really created a splash. That is, I thought it was a splash. Others, including the McCains, seemed to feel it was more of a tidal wave.

With all five of us women sitting on the couch, I began the interview by pressing the senator to tell us how he was going to be able to reform Washington as he had been proclaiming for weeks, when he himself had been in Washington for twenty-six years. He sputtered, and then Joy, who is not known for being cautious, asked the senator how he could have approved the negative Obama ads his campaign was running when, she said, they were lies. Wow. Even Elisabeth couldn't save McCain. We asked him other questions as well, about Roe vs. Wade, separation of church and state, and his choice of Sarah Palin as a running mate. And when Cindy McCain joined us, I certainly didn't feel we were tough on her, although I remember how she bristled and didn't answer when I asked how many houses she and her husband actually owned. (Later, Mrs. McCain complained that we picked their "bones clean.") The senator left our studio to make another appearance on a kinder, gentler cooking show. But I don't think he had expected to have had the kind of heat we generated on our show without an oven.

This interview, however, earned us the reputation of being perhaps the most candid and straightforward show on television, certainly on daytime television. Our ratings soared. Surrounding the election of Barack Obama, we had the highest ratings we'd had in all the twelve years of the program and we were daytime's number-one program, after Oprah. After the election, a columnist asked what on Earth we (along with many other talk programs) were going to be discussing? I said that there was always our old standby: sex.

Not to worry, we are still going strong. No wonder, with those four opinionated, smart and savvy women. And yes, off camera we are indeed fond of each other. That is the other thing. We can argue and bitch on camera, but no one holds a grudge when the camera lights go off. That is no small lesson to be learned.

So that's how things were for us when I got the best surprise of all. On Monday, November 24, 2008, I was in my dressing room at *The View* when I got a phone call from ABC News (my other hat) saying Barack and Michelle Obama would like to do an interview with me the next day and could I do it? Could I? As then President-Elect Obama said in his acceptance speech, "Yes we can." I had a very hectic day that Monday: the regular version of *The View* and then an extra taping of the program to be aired over the Thanksgiving holiday, my hour radio show in the afternoon, and finally at about 6:00 p.m., a meeting with my producers to draft questions for the Obama interview. We wrote one set for President-Elect Obama and another for Mrs. Obama, who was to come out partway through the show and join her husband. We particularly scrutinized the questions about the dismal economy. We finished drafting the questions about 10:00 p.m. and then revised them three times more before the program began. We took an early morning plane to Chicago, and by 5:00 p.m. I was sitting in the hotel room where we would be conducting the interview. As I have written, I have interviewed every president and first lady since Richard Nixon. But never have I been more impressed than I was with this couple. Mr. Obama addressed our questions on the economy, foreign policy, his cabinet, and other matters in the news, directly saying he was no miracle worker but that he was ready to address the mound of problems piling up on his plate. Then Mrs. Obama joined for what turned out to a warm and spontaneous conversation. At one point, the president-elect asked me to stop the interview while he told his wife she had lipstick on her teeth. She wiped it off and then asked her husband, "Is it gone now?" It couldn't have been more natural and I told them laughingly that I was going to leave that part in the interview. To my amazement, no zealous press secretary asked me to remove that part in the editing. In deference to the president-elect, I probably would have, but it is typical of this couple that no one asked me to do it. Not that there weren't also serious questions for Mrs. Obama. We discussed the responsibility she was assuming of being the first black first lady and I asked how the couple was going to raise their two young daughters in the glare of the White House. There would have to be boundaries, they said. The girls were going to have to make their own beds and clean up their rooms.

We had an hour with the Obamas and then raced to the airport. We stayed up all night and, working with six tape editors and three producers, presented a full hour *Special* twenty-four hours later. I also promoted the program live on *Good Morning America*, *The View*, four radio shows, five entertainment programs, the local ABC news program, and the network's *World News Tonight* and *Nightline*. By 10:00 p.m., when the interview aired, we were all exhausted but very proud of the program. That same week, the *New York Times* chose *Audition* as one of the year's books "that tower above the rest."

If that wasn't enough, at the end of 2008 I also had my annual year-end *Special*, *The 10 Most Fascinating People*, which has been on ABC for sixteen years. I think we had our best group. It included, among others, actors Tom Cruise, Will Smith, and Frank Langella, athlete Michael Phelps (who won eight gold medals at the Beijing Olympics), and Rush Limbaugh (it was fun arguing with him, especially when he described himself as "a harmless, loveable little fuzzball").

As it turned out, 2008's *10 Most Fascinating People* had the highest ratings for the *Special* in four years and easily won its time period. Moreover, both Will Smith and Tom Cruise telephoned me personally to say how happy they were with their interviews. Cruise called on my cell phone. Great to pick up the phone and hear someone say, "Hi Barbara, it's Tom." Smith and Cruise are friends with each other and I can see why. Both are particularly nice men. Not just because they call me.

The same week that *10 Most Fascinating People* aired, I flew to California to interview Patrick Swayze at his ranch an hour outside of Los Angeles. Patrick had been diagnosed with incurable pancreatic cancer a year ago and this was the first time he had spoken out about his deadly disease. Patrick and I go back a long way. I had talked with him way back in 1988 and we enjoyed and respected each other. Not only that, we had danced together. Rather, Patrick danced and I just held on until the final dip. Now, talking with him and his wife of thirty-three years, Lisa, it was a different atmosphere. A very thin Patrick had just finished performing in a new action-filled television series. He had managed, in spite of a great deal of pain, to complete the thirteen-week series. Now it was time to take stock. I was touched that he had chosen me to do the interview. He spoke with anger, anguish, and some humor about the disease that was slowly taking his life. He was fighting it, he said, with all his might, hoping for a cure but realizing there was none. Not at this time. When the interview was over and I hugged him a final good-bye, he once more took me in his arms and dipped me to the floor. It was all I could do not to sob in his arms.

Needless to say 2008 was quite a year. But yes, I am still planning to slow way down. Believe me, I am, I am.

New York
February 2009

Partial List of Interviewees

King Abdullah of Jordan
King Abdullah of Saudi Arabia
Leslie Abramson
Andre Agassi
Judith Agnew
Vice President Spiro Agnew
Prince Albert of Monaco
Marv Albert
Madeleine Albright
Alan Alda
Muhammad Ali
Ted Allen
Tim Allen
Kirstie Alley
Tom Anderson
Julie Andrews
Maya Angelou
U.N. Secretary General Kofi Annan
Yasir Arafat
Lance Armstrong
David Arquette
Arthur Ashe
Jeanne Ashe
Fred Astaire
Brooke Astor
Robert Atkins
President Ayub Khan of Pakistan
Lauren Bacall
President Michelle Bachelet of Chile

Joan Baez
Oksana Baiul
Daniel Baker
Jim Bakker
Lucille Ball
Roseanne Barr
Mayor Marion Barry
Drew Barrymore
Mikhail Baryshnikov
Kim Basinger
Warren Beatty
David Beckham
Victoria Beckham
David Begelman
Prime Minister Menachem Begin
    of Israel
Annette Bening
Candice Bergen
Ingrid Bergman
Halle Berry
Sue Billig
Wafa bin Laden
Molly Bingham
Delinah Blake
Robert Blake
Bill Blass
Mayor Michael Bloomberg
Richard Blow
Andrea Bocelli

Seema Boesky
Debbie Boggs
Wade Boggs
Jon Bon Jovi
Boy George
Joan Braden
Sarah Bradford
James Brady
Sarah Brady
Christie Brinkley
Senator Edward Brooke
Garth Brooks
Helen Gurley Brown
Kobe Bryant
Lloyd Bucher
Claus von Bülow
Delta Burke
Carol Burnett
George Burns
Paul Burrell
Barbara Bush
President George H. W. Bush
President George W. Bush
Laura Bush
Brett Butler
Robert Butler
Nicolas Cage
Maria Callas
James Cameron
Naomi Campbell
Truman Capote
Mariah Carey
Princess Caroline of Monaco
Liz Carpenter
Jim Carrey
Diahann Carroll
Johnny Carson
President Jimmy Carter
Rosalynn Carter
Barbara Cartland
Johnny Cash
Fidel Castro
Mark David Chapman

Charles, Prince of Wales
Chevy Chase
President Hugo Chávez of Venezuela
Don Cheadle
Cher
Connie Chung
Marcia Clark
Kathleen Neal Cleaver
President Bill Clinton
Senator Hillary Clinton
George Clooney
Glenn Close
Janet Langhart Cohen
Richard Cohen
William Cohen
Joan Collins
Carlton Conley
Sean Connery
Howard Cosell
Courteney Cox
Michael Crichton
Walter Cronkite
Hume Cronyn
Bing Crosby
Kathryn Crosby
Tom Cruise
Billy Crystal
Macaulay Culkin
Mary Cunningham
Miley Cyrus
the Dalai Lama
Tyne Daly
Matt Damon
Ted Danson
Christopher Darden
Bette Davis
Moshe Dayan
Michael Deaver
Ellen DeGeneres
Cristina DeLorean
John DeLorean
Patrick Dempsey
Bo Derek

John Derek
Prime Minister Morarji Desai of India
William DeVries
Chris DeWolfe
Neil Diamond
Leonardo DiCaprio
Barry Diller
Celine Dion
Waris Dirie
Senator Elizabeth Dole
Senator Robert Dole
Phil Donahue
Kirk Douglas
Kyan Douglas
Michael Douglas
Hugh Downs
Dave Dravecky
Richard Dreyfuss
Minnie Driver
David Duchovny
Patrick Duffy
Kitty Dukakis
Governor Michael Dukakis
President Jean-Claude Duvalier of Haiti
Michèle Duvalier
Clint Eastwood
Abba Eban
John Ehrlichman
President Dwight D. Eisenhower
Julie Eisenhower
Mamie Eisenhower
Jenna Elfman
Julius "Dr. J" Erving
Linda Evans
Rupert Everett
Jerry Falwell
Dakota Fanning
Empress Farah of Iran
Louis Farrakhan
Mia Farrow
Donna Fasano

Richard Fasano
Farrah Fawcett
Christy Ferer
Geraldine Ferraro
Will Ferrell
Tina Fey
Sally Field
Harvey Fierstein
Siegfried Fischbacher
Michael Flatley
Kelly Flinn
Calista Flockhart
Henry Fonda
Jane Fonda
Betty Ford
President Gerald Ford
Harrison Ford
Henry Ford II
Michael J. Fox
Jamie Foxx
Redd Foxx
Tommy Franks
James Freed
Tom Furth
Priscilla Galey
Prime Minister Indira Gandhi of India
Janeane Garofalo
Andy Garcia
Judy Garland
James Garner
Bill Gates
David Geffen
Richard Gere
Brigitte Gerney
Gordon Getty
Manucher Ghorbanifar
Mel Gibson
Frank Gifford
Kathie Lee Gifford
Newt Gingrich
Haim Ginott
Judith Giuliani

Mayor Rudolph Giuliani
Robin Givens
Senator John Glenn
Bernhard Goetz
Whoopi Goldberg
Fred Goldman
the Goldman family
John Goodman
Berry Gordy
Vice President Al Gore
Princess Grace of Monaco
Katharine Graham
Kelsey Grammer
Linda Gray
Amy Grossberg
the Grossberg family
Bryant Gumbel
Secretary of State Alexander Haig
H. R. Haldeman
Fawn Hall
Geri Halliwell
Armand Hammer
Tom Hanks
Woody Harrelson
Pamela Harriman
Jean Harris
Rex Harrison
Mariette Hartley
Teri Hatcher
Anne Hathaway
President Václav Havel of
    Czechoslovakia
Goldie Hawn
Tom Hayden
Patricia Hearst
Anne Heche
Katherine Heigl
Marg Helgenberger
Leona Helmsley
Sonja Henie
Prince Henrik of Denmark
Audrey Hepburn
Katharine Hepburn

Jerry Herman
Don Hewitt
Faith Hill
Paris Hilton
John Hinckley Sr.
Jo Ann Hinckley
Abbie Hoffman
Paul Hogan
Bob Hope
Anthony Hopkins
Whitney Houston
Jennifer Hudson
Kate Hudson
Karen Hughes
Sarah Hughes
Muriel Humphrey
Elizabeth Hurley
King Hussein of Jordan
Saddam Hussein
Anjelica Huston
John Huston
Julio Iglesias
Don Imus
Jeremy Irons
Terri Irwin
Hugh Jackman
Jackie Jackson
Jermaine Jackson
Jesse Jackson
Michael Jackson
Reggie Jackson
Byron Janis
General Wojciech Jaruzelski of
    Poland
Jay-Z
Patrick Jephson
President Jiang Zemin of China
Elton John
Don Johnson
Lady Bird Johnson
Luci Baines Johnson
Paula Johnson
Scott Johnson

Angelina Jolie
The Jonas Brothers
Jerry Jones
Star Jones
Barbara Jordan
Naomi Judd
Wynonna Judd
Brian "Kato" Kaelin
Robert Kardashian
Diane Keaton
Caroline Kennedy
Senator Edward Kennedy
Ethel Kennedy
John Kennedy Jr.
Robert Kennedy
Rose Kennedy
Teresa Heinz Kerry
Jack Kevorkian
Adnan Khashoggi
Mohammed al-Khilewi
Margot Kidder
Nicole Kidman
Billie Jean King
Kristin Kinkel
Henry Kissinger
Calvin Klein
Beyoncé Knowles
Mayor Ed Koch
Helen Kornbleuth
Ken Kornbleuth
Robert Kramer
Carson Kressley
Cheryl Ladd
Ann Landers
Michael Landon
K. D. Lang
Frank Langella
Angela Lansbury
Robert Lanza
Jude Law
Mary Wells Lawrence
Matt LeBlanc
Jack Lemmon

Jay Leno
Mary Kay Letourneau
David Letterman
Bernard Lewinsky
Monica Lewinsky
Rush Limbaugh
Mary Lindsay
Heather Locklear
Shelley Long
Sophia Loren
Frank Lorenzo
Greg Louganis
Courtney Love
Susan Lucci
Clare Booth Luce
Shannon Lucid
Joan Lunden
Loretta Lynn
Shirley MacLaine
Gail Magruder
Jeb Magruder
Tobey Maguire
Margaret Mahler
Barbara Mandrell
Ila Manner
Dolores Manzie
Nick Manzie
President Ferdinand Marcos of
    the Philippines
Imelda Marcos
Queen Margrethe of Denmark
Penny Marshall
Steve Martin
Ricky Martin
Carol Saroyan Matthau
Walter Matthau
Kimberly Mays
Abigail McCarthy
Denise McCluggage
Matthew McConaughey
Steven McDonald
Cynthia McFadden
Robert McFarlane

Senator George McGovern
Phil McGraw
Phyllis McGuire
Mark McGwire
Terry McMillan
Ann Meara
Edwin Meese
Prime Minister Golda Meir of Israel
Erik Menendez
Lyle Menendez
Tammi Menendez
Melina Mercouri
Catherine Meyer
Princess Michael of Kent
Bette Midler
Michael Milken
John Miller
Heather Mills
Anthony Minghella
Liza Minnelli
Helen Mirren
Martha Mitchell
Robert Mitchum
Vice President Walter Mondale
Demi Moore
Jean Moore
Julianne Moore
Mary Tyler Moore
Michael Moore
Charles A. Moose
Gary Morton
Mr. T
President Hosni Mubarak of Egypt
Rupert Murdoch
Eddie Murphy
Mike Myers
Martina Navratilova
Patricia Neal
Liam Neeson
Rick Nelson
Willie Nelson
Prime Minister Benjamin Netanyahu
   of Israel

Fred Neulander
Paul Newman
Mike Nichols
Patricia Nixon
President Richard Nixon
Tricia Nixon
Queen Noor of Jordan
Carroll O'Connor
Chris O'Donnell
Kelli Carpenter O'Donnell
Rosie O'Donnell
Shaquille O'Neal
Tatum O'Neal
President Barack Obama
Michelle Obama
Laurence Olivier
Jack Osbourne
Ozzy Osbourne
Sharon Osbourne
Donny Osmond
Marie Osmond
Joel Osteen
Al Pacino
Senator Robert Packwood
Sarah Jessica Parker
Ed Parsons
Dolly Parton
Jane Pauley
Nancy Pelosi
Teddy Pendergrass
Ross Perot
Jacqueline Peterson
Lee Peterson
Milton Petrie
Michelle Pfeiffer
Michael Phelps
Prince Philip of England
Pisner Quintuplets
Brad Pitt
Maury Povich
Colin Powell
Katherine Ann Power
Priscilla Presley

Jason Priestley
Victoria Principal
Richard Pryor
President Vladimir Putin of Russia
Col. Mu'ammar Qaddafi of Libya
Vice President Dan Quayle
Marilyn Quayle
Queen Latifah
Anthony Quinn
Leah Rabin
Prime Minister Yitzhak Rabin
    of Israel
Lee Radziwill
John Ramsey
Patsy Ramsey
Cathy Randa
Maureen Reagan
Nancy Reagan
President Ronald Reagan
Harry Reasoner
Sumner Redstone
Christopher Reeve
Dana Reeve
Donald Regan
Christian Reichardt
Rob Reiner
Burt Reynolds
Shah Reza Pahlavi of Iran
Donna Rice
Denise Rich
Lionel Richie
LeAnn Rimes
Kelly Ripa
John Ritter
Joan Rivers
Jason Robards
Julia Roberts
Chris Rock
David Rockefeller
Vice President Nelson Rockefeller
Richard Rodgers
Dennis Rodman
Jai Rodriguez

Ginger Rogers
Kenny Rogers
Betty Rollin
Pete Rose
Diana Ross
Mickey Rourke
Dean Rusk
Margaret Rutherford
Meg Ryan
President Anwar el-Sadat of Egypt
Jehan el-Sadat
Sarah, Duchess of York
Susan Sarandon
Prince Saud al-Faisal
Diane Sawyer
Lawrence Schiller
Curt Schilling
Chancellor Helmut Schmidt of
    Germany
Arnold Schwarzenegger
General Norman Schwarzkopf
Arthur Seale
Jerry Seinfeld
Monica Seles
Tom Selleck
Robert Shapiro
Cybill Shepherd
Shi Pei Pu
Brooke Shields
Teri Shields
Dinah Shore
Carole Simpson
David Sinclair
David Smith
Will Smith
Michelle Smithdas
Robert Smithdas
Lord Snowdon
Suzanne Somers
David Spade
Larry Speakes
Steven Spielberg
Jerry Springer

Sylvester Stallone
Ringo Starr
Danielle Steel
George Steinbrenner
Gloria Steinem
Alexandra Stevenson
James Stewart
Martha Stewart
Ben Stiller
Jerry Stiller
David Stockman
Leopold Stokowski
Sharon Stone
Barbra Streisand
Jeremy Strohmeyer
Kerri Strug
Roland Summit
Gloria Swanson
Patrick Swayze
Jessica Tandy
Lionel Tate
Elizabeth Taylor
Prime Minister Margaret Thatcher
    of England
Marquerite Simpson Thomas
Marlo Thomas
Justin Timberlake
Joe Torre
General Omar Torrijos of Panama
Daniel J. Travanti
John Travolta
Donald Trump
Ivana Trump
Kathleen Turner
Ted Turner
Beth Holloway Twitty
Kenneth Tynan
Mike Tyson
Usher
Peter Ustinov
Governor Jesse Ventura
Meredith Vieira

Janet Viertel
Sol Wachtler
Terry Waite
President Lech Walesa of Poland
Barbara Walker
Bree Walker
Cornelia Wallace
Joyce Wallace
Mike Wallace
Jay Warburton
Kim Warburton
Senator John Warner
Denzel Washington
Desiree Washington
Sherron Watkins
Faye Wattleton
John Wayne
Andrew Lloyd Webber
Raquel Welch
Ed Werner
Valerie Werner
Kanye West
Charles Westphal
Betty White
Heather Whitestone
Harold Willens
Esther Williams
Jayson Williams
Robin Williams
Tanya Williams
Oprah Winfrey
Debra Winger
Henry Winkler
Stan Winston
Anna Wintour
Stevie Wonder
Tiger Woods
James Wright
Andrew Wyeth
President Boris Yeltsin of Russia
Renée Zellweger
Catherine Zeta-Jones

Acknowledgments

FIRST AND FOREMOST there is Linda Bird Francke. This book would not have been written without her. Much of the historical material, which I had forgotten, is Linda's. But that is not all. We worked so well together that we began to refer to ourselves as "the other." The only reason I regret this book being finished is because I miss Linda.

Morton Janklow is not just my brilliant agent but he and his wife, Linda, have been dear friends for so many years. He guided me through negotiations and has been there for me from day one.

Betsy Shuller is the best researcher and fact-checker one could have. She is organized and efficient and an adorable person.

Peter Gethers is a wise, clear-eyed editor whose advice was to change little and encourage a great deal. Both were appreciated.

I must thank Sonny Mehta, the editor in chief and president of Alfred A. Knopf, for publishing my book.

Then there is George Pineda. There are no proper words to describe what George Pineda means in my life. He runs so many aspects of my day-to-day world in the most unassuming way. He will probably hate my even crediting him now as he is so discreet in his ways. But it is George who coordinated everything, including the computer, which would have driven me mad, mad, mad without his help. The sentence in my life which everyone knows is, "When in doubt, ask George."

Vartan Gregorian has been telling me for so many years to write a book. Now I have, and Vartan read every page, giving me solid and valuable advice. Thank you, Vartan.

My daughter, Jacqueline Danforth, read and bravely okayed the important and very personal chapter about her.

The following people generously gave me their time and insight: David Westin, Phyllis McGrady, Bill Safire, Sam Donaldson, Lou Weiss, Richard Wald, Herb Schlosser, and my wonderful producers at ABC, chief among them Bill Geddie, Martin Clancy, Katie Thomson, David Sloan, Alan Goldberg, Karen Burnes, and Brad LaRosa. Thanks also to Sheelagh McNeill at the ABC News Research Center.

And deep gratitude to my friends who have heard me talking endlessly about this book and never shut me up.

Finally, and most important, thanks to all those viewers who have been with me at one time or another, over the years. It is your loyalty for which I am most grateful.

Index

Maternal grandparents: from the personal collection of Barbara Walters

Latin Quarter: from the personal collection of Barbara Walters

Mother, father, and the Duchess of Windsor: from the personal collection of Barbara Walters

Mother, father, and sister Jackie: from the personal collection of Barbara Walters

Sister Jackie: from the personal collection of Barbara Walters

Cousin Shirley and husband: from the personal collection of Barbara Walters

Sister, father, BW, Lee Guber, and mother: from the personal collection of Barbara Walters

Lee Guber, BW, and daughter: from the personal collection of Barbara Walters

BW and daughter: from the personal collection of Barbara Walters

BW and Merv Adelson: from the personal collection of Barbara Walters

BW and "Zelle" in 1990s: from the personal collection of Barbara Walters

BW and Icodel: from the personal collection of Barbara Walters

BW and daughter, present: Virginia Sherwood/American Broadcasting Companies, Inc.

BW and Richard Nixon: NBCU Photo Bank

Dancing with President Ford: from the personal collection of Barbara Walters

BW and President and Mrs. Carter: American Broadcasting Companies, Inc.

BW and Ronald Reagan: American Broadcasting Companies, Inc.

BW and President and Mrs. Reagan: American Broadcasting Companies, Inc.

BW and President and Mrs. George H. W. Bush: American Broadcasting Companies, Inc.

BW and President Clinton: Official White House Photograph

BW and President George W. Bush:

Virginia Sherwood/American Broadcasting Companies, Inc.

BW and Golda Meir: NBCU Photo Bank

Raquel and Moshe Dyan: American Broadcasting Companies, Inc.

BW and Anwar Sadat and Menachem Begin: Shlomo Arad/American Broadcasting Companies, Inc.

BW and Shah of Iran, 1977: American Broadcasting Companies, Inc.

BW and King Hussein and Queen Noor: Ann Limongello/American Broadcasting Companies, Inc.

BW and Yasir Arafat: American Broadcasting Companies, Inc.

BW and Mu'ammar Qaddafi: Kimberly Butler/American Broadcasting Companies, Inc.

BW and Fidel Castro: American Broadcasting Companies, Inc.

Note from Fidel Castro: from the personal collection of Barbara Walters

BW and Margaret Thatcher: American Broadcasting Companies, Inc.

BW and Jiang Zemin: American Broadcasting Companies, Inc.

BW and Hugo Chávez: Donna Svennevik/American Broadcasting Companies, Inc.

BW and Henry Kissinger: American Broadcasting Companies, Inc.

BW and Gen. Norman Schwarzkopf: Steve Fenn/American Broadcasting Companies, Inc.

Note from President George H. W. Bush: from the personal collection of Barbara Walters

Note from Princess Diana: from the personal collection of Barbara Walters

BW and Dalai Lama: Rob Wallace/American Broadcasting Companies, Inc.

BW and Truman Capote: NBCU Photo Bank

BW, her mother, and Bing Crosby: American Broadcasting Companies, Inc.

BW and John Warner and Elizabeth Taylor: American Broadcasting Companies, Inc.

BW and John Wayne: American Broadcasting Companies, Inc.

BW and George Burns: American Broadcasting Companies, Inc.

BW and Katharine Hepburn: Ken Bank/ American Broadcasting Companies, Inc.

Note from Katharine Hepburn: from the personal collection of Barbara Walters

BW and Jimmy Stewart: Bob D'Amico/ American Broadcasting Companies, Inc.

BW and Sylvester Stallone: Bob D'Amico/American Broadcasting Companies, Inc.

BW and Audrey Hepburn: Craig Sjodin/American Broadcasting Companies, Inc.

BW and Arnold Schwarzenegger: Craig Sjodin/American Broadcasting Companies, Inc.

BW and Clint Eastwood: Steve Fenn/ American Broadcasting Companies, Inc.

BW and Christopher Reeve: Ken Regan/American Broadcasting Companies, Inc.

BW and Bob and Michelle Smithdas: Virginia Sherwood/American Broadcasting Companies, Inc.

BW and Will Smith: Craig Sjodin/ American Broadcasting Companies, Inc.

Note from Monica Lewinksy: from the personal collection of Barbara Walters

Interview questions for Monica Lewinsky: from the personal collection of Barbara Walters

BW and Oprah Winfrey and Cha Cha: 2004 Harpo Print, LLC/All Rights Reserved. Photographer: George Holz

BW and Mark David Chapman: Steve Fenn/American Broadcasting Companies, Inc.

BW and Jean Harris: Kimberly Butler/ American Broadcasting Companies, Inc.

BW and Robert Blake: Virginia Sherwood/American Broadcasting Companies, Inc.

BW as a swimsuit model for CBS: from the personal collection of Barbara Walters

BW in Citgo Gas ad: NBCU Photo Bank

Today show: NBCU Photo Bank

Today show: NBCU Photo Bank

BW and Harry Reasoner: American Broadcasting Companies, Inc.

BW and Roone Arledge, Don Hewitt, and Joan Ganz Cooney: American Broadcasting Companies, Inc.

BW and Hugh Downs: Steve Fenn/ American Broadcasting Companies, Inc.

BW and John Stossel: Virginia Sherwood/American Broadcasting Companies, Inc.

BW and Diane Sawyer: American Broadcasting Companies, Inc.

BW and Meredith Vieira, Star Jones, Joy Behar, and Debbie Matenopoulos: Lorenzo Bevilaqua/American Broadcasting Companies, Inc.

BW and Elisabeth Hasselbeck, Rosie O'Donnell, and Joy Behar Yolanda Perez/American Broadcasting Companies, Inc.

BW and Elisabeth Hasselbeck, Whoopi Goldberg, Sherri Shepard, and Joy Behar: Donna Svennevik/American Broadcasting Companies, Inc.

Young BW with her dog: from the personal collection of Barbara Walters

BW modeling in Paris: from the personal collection of Barbara Walters

BW at racetrack: NBCU Photo Bank

BW laughing: courtesy of the Norman Parkinson Archive

BW in front of painting: from the personal collection of Barbara Walters

Cha Cha in glasses: from the personal collection of Barbara Walters